CliffsAP™
European History

by

By Michael J. Romano

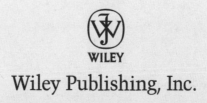

WILEY

Wiley Publishing, Inc.

About the Author

Michael J. Romano has a Ph.D. in History and is an adjunct professor at various local N.Y. colleges. He has been an educator and Supervisor of Social Studies in the New York State System. Dr. Romano is also a presenter at local, regional, and national Social Studies Councils.

Author's Acknowledgments

This book was a family project. I would not have been able to complete the book without the cooperation of my daughters, Mary, Joann, Linda, and Susan, as well as my future son-in-law, Raymond. I appreciate the support and help given by my wife, Lucy, who provided me with the encouragement to write the book. Finally, a lasting thanks to my parents, Giuseppe and Concetta, for instilling in me a love of education and of history.

Publisher's Acknowledgments

Editorial

Project Editor: Suzanne Snyder

Acquisitions Editor: Greg Tubach

Copy Editor: Donna Frederick

Technical Editor: Marcus Stadelmann

Composition

Proofreader: Vicki Broyles

Wiley Publishing Indianapolis Composition Services

CliffsAP™ European History

Published by:
Wiley Publishing, Inc.
111 River Street
Hoboken, NJ 07030
www.wiley.com

Copyright © 2003 Wiley Publishing, Inc. New York, New York

Published by Wiley Publishing, Inc., New York, NY
Published simultaneously in Canada

Library of Congress Cataloging-in-Publication Data available from publisher.

ISBN: 0-7645-8687-4

Printed in the United States of America

10 9 8 7

1B/RV/QY/QU/IN

Ⓦ Wiley Publishing, Inc.   is a trademark of Wiley Publishing, Inc.

Table of Contents

PART III: AP EUROPEAN HISTORY PRACTICE TESTS

Study Guide Checklist

❑ 1. Become familiar with the format of the exam, particularly the weight given to each subject area in the multiple-choice section.

❑ 2. Review the "Types of Multiple-Choice Questions" section, making sure you understand the different types of multiple-choice questions you may encounter.

❑ 3. Review "The Free-Response Section," paying attention to the suggestions on reading and analyzing the questions. Read the sample essays. Would you have handled the questions differently?

❑ 4. Read over the FAQs about the exam.

❑ 5. Use the survey sections in Part II to prepare for taking the practice exams.

❑ 6. Strictly observing the time allotments, take Practice Test I, section by section (take Section I, check your answers; take Section II, check your answers).

❑ 7. Review the answers and explanations in Section I and the sample essays and comments in Section II.

❑ 8. Analyze your strengths and weaknesses. Did you miss a specific type of multiple-choice question or were you weak on a particular area—the courts or public policy, for example? Use the analysis for further preparation.

❑ 9. Strictly observing the time allotments, take Practice Test II, section by section (take Section I, check your answers; take Section II, check your answers).

❑ 10. Analyze your strengths and weaknesses. Did you miss a specific type of multiple-choice question or were you weak on a particular area—the courts or public policy, for example? Use the analysis for further preparation.

❑ 11. Strictly observing the time allotments, take Practice Test III, section by section (take Section I, check your answers; take Section II, check your answers).

❑ 12. Analyze your strengths and weaknesses. Did you miss a specific type of multiple-choice question or were you weak on a particular area—the courts or public policy, for example? Use the analysis for further preparation.

PART I

INTRODUCTION

Introducing the AP European History Examination

What Is the Advanced Placement Program?

The Advanced Placement Program has been established by the College Board, a nonprofit organization, which oversees college admission examinations. The Advanced Placement Program allows highly motivated secondary-school students to take college level courses in 32 subjects in which AP examinations are available. Students who take these high school AP courses, such as European History, and receive a satisfactory grade on the AP examination (usually a 3 or higher) receive college credit. It is estimated that over three thousand universities and colleges worldwide grant credit to students who are successful on these examinations. Some institutions even grant sophomore status to students who have taken a number of these AP examinations and receive a grade of 3 or better.

In May 2000, about 1.3 million AP examinations were administered and close to 13,000 students throughout the world participated. Three high school and three college history teachers design the AP European History course and other AP courses. The committee outlines the content of the courses and what should be on the examinations. They also meet to update the curriculum, to reflect the latest changes and events in the world, as well as to make changes in the format of the test. In 1998, the committee altered the nature of the Document-Based Questions (DBQs) from 14 to approximately 10 or 12 questions.

AP examinations are offered every May at participating schools. Below is a suggested time line for registration for the AP examinations:

- **JANUARY:** Consult your AP teachers, guidance counselor, and AP coordinator for specific dates and fees for the examinations. If any special test modifications are needed, you should notify the AP coordinator at this time.
- **MARCH/APRIL:** Check with your counselor/AP coordinator to determine if the special modifications have been established or if you need to take the test at another school.
- **MAY:** The AP European History Examination and other AP examinations are administered.
- **JUNE:** Examinations are graded.
- **JULY 1:** Students can receive their exam grades via telephone. The College Board mails the test results to the individual schools.

Students can get additional information about the AP European History examination and programs on-line at **www.collegeboard.org**. Students can also ask their teachers for a copy of the Advanced Placement Course Description: European History, which is also available at the College Board Web site.

Themes of the AP European History Course

The College Board designed AP programs in European History for students to develop an understanding of the important themes in European History from 1450 to the present and how these themes helped shape the world in which we live. The themes revolve around the following:

- Intellectual and cultural history
- Political and diplomatic history
- Social and economic history

Intellectual and Cultural History

The intellectual history theme focuses on the changes in attitudes toward religious institutions that began in Europe in the fifteenth century. Such changes led to a secularization of learning as well as changes in attitude toward education, literature, arts, politics, and social values. These intellectual developments are responsible for the scientific and technological advances within European society.

The cultural history theme provides an analysis of how these new intellectual concepts influenced different social groups and impacted areas of popular culture such as attitudes, family, religion, and work. Cultural history also examines the influence of global expansion on European culture.

Political and Diplomatic History

The political history theme explores the rise of the nation state, and nationalism, as well as the rise of political elites in different countries and their ideologies. Political history also examines the forms of political protests, reform, revolution, and the extension and limitations of political and civil liberties in Europe.

The diplomatic history theme includes not only a study of foreign policy but also how domestic and political events influence relations with other countries. The roles of international law, balance of power, and collective security are examined to determine how the failure of diplomacy can lead to conflict. The importance and consequences of technology are evaluated in relation to these conflicts. The rise of colonialism (and subsequent decolonization), imperialism, and global interdependence are also analyzed as part of diplomacy.

Social and Economic History

The social history theme includes an analysis of the shift in social classes from a hierarchical order to one of social mobility. Changes in gender roles, attitudes towards race, ethnicity, and influence of sanitation, urbanization, diet, and changes in food are examined within the scope of social history.

The economic history theme entails an examination of changes in agricultural production and organization and the development of commercial practices such as mass production and consumption. Economic history also includes the study of the consequences of industrialization, competition, the role of the state in economic activity, and the importance of global interdependence in our world.

The examination questions are broken down as follows:

Themes of the AP European History Examination		
Intellectual and cultural themes	20–30%	16–24 questions
Political and diplomatic themes	30–40%	24–32 questions
Social and economic themes	30–40%	24–32 questions

In the multiple-choice questions, 50% of them are from 1450–1815 (see chapters titled "The Renaissance (c1350–c1550)" through "The Age of Revolution: The French Revolution and Napoleonic Era") and 50% are from 1815–Present (see chapters titled "Mercantilism and the Agricultural and Industrial Revolutions" through "Contemporary Europe").

Although the AP European History Examination tests specific themes, there will always be questions that are cross-topical and require you to draw on a bank of knowledge that may be pre-1450 but impact post-1450 events. For example, the Black Death occurred during the Medieval Period but impacted society during the fifteenth century. However, there will not be questions in any of the sections that will specifically ask about events that took place before 1450.

The AP European History Exam Format

The AP examination is three hours and 55 minutes in length. The examination is divided as follows:

- **Section I:** 80 Multiple-Choice Questions — 55 minutes. These questions test your knowledge of the three major themes. It is anticipated that the students will not be familiar with all the material covered.

- **Section II:** Free-Response portion of the test — 130 minutes.

  - **Part A:** A mandatory 15-minute reading of the Document-Based Question (DBQ). Students then have 45 minutes to answer the DBQ.

  - **Part B:** Students have 70 minutes to answer two thematic essays. It is recommended, but not mandatory, that students spend 5 minutes planning for each essay and 30 minutes writing each of the essays.

    The thematic essays cover a variety of historical periods and change every year to ensure that different time periods are addressed. The groupings are not necessarily chronological.

The AP European History Exam's Scoring Procedure

The critique for grading the AP European History exam is as follows:

Section I

Multiple Choice: This section is worth 50% of the total grade. The raw score of the multiple-choice is obtained by adding up the number of right questions minus the number you answered incorrectly and multiplying by 0.25. Thus, you can answer 60 questions, leave 20 blank and still be on track to get a score of 3. Usually, if you get a raw score of 48 out of 50 for multiple-choice and do well on the essays, you can earn a 3.

Section II (Free-Response Section)

- **Part A:** DBQ—worth 45% of the grade.
- **Part B:** Thematic Essays—worth 55% of the grade.

AP Grades

The total raw scores are converted to a 5-point scale.

	Scoring
5	Extremely Well Qualified
4	Well Qualified
3	Qualified
2	Possibly Qualified
1	No Recommendation

Students who achieve a score of 3 or better receive college course credits for their AP scores. However, some colleges require that students achieve a score of 4 or 5 to receive credit. Students should contact their college directly for their AP policies and should also go on-line for a college search (**www.collegeboard.com**) to try to get information about a particular school's AP policies.

How to Use this Book

This book has various features that will enable you to score well on the AP test and get the most out of your review.

- **Review the format of the AP examination as outlined in the Introduction.**

- **Read the section on "Preparing for the Examination."**

- **Study the review chapters.** Focus on those sections that you think are your weak areas. Complete the sample questions at the end of each chapter.

- **Take the three Sample Practice Tests.** Once again, check your answers with the correct responses in the book.

- **Check all your answers for the Multiple-Choice Questions.** Carefully read all explanations for the correct and incorrect answers as well as for the ones you were unable to answer.

- **Read your essay answers for the DBQ and Thematic Essays.** Compare your responses with the models outlined in the book.

Preparing for the Examination

Helpful Hints for Studying for the AP European History Examination

There is no set way to study for the AP European History exam. However, the following procedures can help you:

Keep the big picture in mind: The writers of this examination design questions to determine if you have mastered the main ideas or generalizations about a particular period or event in history. What are the main events associated with this question? Who are the key personalities? What are the important results? An example of this type of question is as follows:

---

1. Which was one of the factors that contributed to Adolf Hitler's rise to power?

  A. The Communist party supported the Weimar Republic.

  B. The Nationalist Socialist Party (NSDAP) won a majority of votes in the Reichstag.

  C. Hitler used military power to seize direct control of the government.

  D. An alliance with the Nationalists gave Hitler a parliamentary majority.

  E. France and England supported the Nazi Party.

The correct answer is **D**. The Nationalist Party supported Hitler's Nazi Party because they were anti-communists and Hitler had promised to restore the greatness of Germany.

This question requires students to understand the economic, political, and social conditions within Germany during the 1920s, the anger of the German people towards the Versailles Treaty, as well as Germany's relations with its former enemies from World War I (France and England). This illustrates the "big picture of events" in that the student must frame his/her response within this broad context.

Avoid studying trivial information: This test assesses how well you know information in the context of the broad political, social, and economic trends of the historical era. There are no rote-memory questions on the test that require little historical analysis. There will never be a question such as the following:

---

1. Who was the Russian Czar in 1917?

    A. Nicholas I

    B. Nicholas II

    C. Alexander I

    D. Alexander II

    E. Alexander III

The correct answer is **B**.

Avoid studying straight military history: Military battles are only important as they relate to political, economic, and social events or as an introduction of technology.

Look for chronology and order of difficulty: Test questions are organized in chronological order in the multiple-choice questions. Each group of questions will be more difficult than the preceding group of questions. The first group of questions is usually on the Renaissance and the Reformation, the Enlightenment, French Revolution, and so on. You will notice a break when you go from one group to another. The first 20–25 questions are usually the easiest, and the most difficult are given at the end of the test. Usually the questions from 30–60 are in the middle range of difficulty.

Focus on the connections in history: History should not be studied as incidents in isolation but as a series of strands that are connected by cause and effect and interconnecting events. For example, students should try to understand how the importance of individuals as well as reasons in society contributed to the Renaissance and also to the Scientific Revolution and the Enlightenment. The belief in reason led to the idea that not only kings, but individuals could rule government, which led to the growth of democracy. In analyzing the causes of World War I, one should assess this event in the context of the growth of nationalism, imperialism, and industrialization in the world of the nineteenth century. This approach to history helps the student understand how the events are connected in history and to comprehend the big picture in history.

Types of Multiple-Choice Questions

There are several types of European History multiple-choice questions on the examination. They include the following:

- Identification questions
- Analysis questions
- Reading/quotation questions

- Skill-based questions, including maps, graphs, and charts
- Illustration-type questions, including political cartoons, posters, photographs, works of art, and sculpture
- "Except"-type questions

Identification Questions

The majority of the questions are of this variety: Identify a person and connect it to an historical event or idea, a group of people, an invention, or a development. You need to have a basic knowledge of the topic, and the questions are very direct and straightforward. There is little historical analysis required to answer this type of question. Approximately 45% of the questions are of this type.

---

1. Which was an immediate result of the Protestant Reformation?

   A. breaking of the religious unity of Europe

   B. strengthening the political power of the pope

   C. increasing the influence of the Roman Catholic Church

   D. restoration of political unity to Western Europe

   E. the growth of mercantilism

The correct answer is **A**. You need to know what the Protestant Reformation was and how it influenced Europe. If you had known that the Protestants were against strong Papal authority and religious wars were fought during the sixteenth century, it would help you eliminate choices **B**, **C**, **D**, and **E**.

---

2. The main purpose of the Congress of Vienna was to

   A. establish strategies to rebuild the Russian economy

   B. turn back the clock in Europe to conditions that existed in Europe prior to the French Revolution

   C. create a European Court of Justice

   D. promote the ideals of the French Revolution

   E. establish collective security systems to insure peace

The correct answer is **B**. You must know that the Congress of Vienna was convened to help end the chaos in Europe after the upheavals of the French Revolution and Napoleon's domination of Europe. You can also answer this question correctly by knowing that the Congress of Vienna was a conservative reaction to the democratic ideals of the French and Napoleonic Revolutions.

These questions are very direct and you must have specific information about these events.

Analysis Questions

This type of question requires less specific information but tests your ability to draw conclusions by considering cause and effect. In this type of question, you need less specific information but must have a broader understanding of the historic period, trend, or relationship. Knowing the time frame of the events and the chronology of the period will help you determine how one event influenced another and can help you select the correct answer. Approximately 25–30% are analysis-type questions.

---

3. Which of the following resulted from the revocation of the Edict of Nantes?

    A. France succeeded in breaking up the Triple Alliance.

    B. Huguenots were granted the right of freedom of worship in France.

    C. The French aristocrats suffered a decline in power.

    D. The Catholic Church in France was freed from the domination of Louis XIV.

    E. Many French Protestants emigrated to England and Holland.

The correct answer is **E**. This is an analysis question of the cause and effect variety. This question requires you to evaluate/assess each choice to determine its validity. If you recall that the Edict of Nantes granted religious freedom to the Protestants and that Louis XIV's revocation in 1685 was part of his effort to assume absolute control, you would know that **D** is incorrect because Louis XIV wanted absolute power to extend over all aspects of society. Choice **C** is incorrect because French Huguenots were forced to flee France and went to the northern Protestant countries of England and Holland.

---

4. The Thermidorian Reaction refers to

    A. the Metternich System

    B. the restoration of Charles II of England

    C. the fall of Robespierre

    D. Napoleon's Hundred Days

    E. the *Declaration of the Rights of Man and Citizen*

The correct answer is **C**. You can answer this question if you are able to connect the Thermidorian Reaction to the time period of the French Revolution of 1789 and how it affected the country. By putting the event in order, you can eliminate other choices. The Metternich System refers to efforts by Prince Metternich of Austria after the Congress of Vienna (1814/1815) to stop the spread of the revolutionary ideas of the French. You can also eliminate choices **B**, **D**, and **E** because the timeframe for the restoration of Charles II took place in the seventeenth century, Napoleon's Hundred Days in 1815, and the Declaration of the Rights of Man and Citizen in 1789. This elimination process leaves choice **C**. The Thermidorian Reaction of 1794 was the successful effort of the French moderates/conservatives to depose Robespierre because of the excesses of the Reign of Terror.

Reading/Quotation Questions

This type of question requires you to read a quote or a passage from pieces of literature and identify the author or the philosophy of that school of thought. These types of questions do not require specific information and are not too difficult to answer. You should look for key words or ideas to help you understand the passage. Approximately 10% of the questions are of this type.

---

5. **Statement:** A prince being thus obliged to know well how to act as a beast must imitate the fox and the lion . . . one must therefore be a fox to recognize traps, and a lion to frighten wolves.

   This quotation is from:

   A. writings of Machiavelli

   B. writings of Rousseau

   C. writings of Locke

   D. writings of Darwin

   E. writings of Adam Smith

The correct answer is **A**. The theme of the passage is how a ruler should rule. You should be able to associate this idea with Machiavelli to help you select Choice **A**. If you do not recognize the passage, you can use the process of elimination. Rousseau/Locke are associated with the social contract and natural rights. Darwin's theme is survival of the fittest, and Smith supported capitalism. By eliminating all of the other choices you are left with **A**.

Skill-Based Questions (Maps, Graphs, Charts)

This type of question requires map skills and limited information to answer the question. When answering these questions, be sure to note the title, legend, or key before answering. Maps usually present information about social, economic, and political issues. Approximately 10% are this type of question.

Graph and chart questions are usually easy to answer because they contain all the data necessary to arrive at the correct answers. Graphs and charts are useful in determining patterns of change over a period of time. Approximately 10% are this kind of question.

There will be examples of these types of questions on the three sample tests at the end of the book.

Illustration-Type Questions (Political Cartoons, Posters, Photographs, Works of Art, and Sculpture)

Political cartoons are distorted to emphasize a point of view. This type of question is relatively easy if you avoid reading too much into the question. Read the captions and titles carefully.

Like political cartoons, poster questions are very straightforward and easy to answer. Once again you must read the document carefully and try to place it in the context of the time period. Photographs/works of art/sculpture questions ask you to identify what is taking place or to put the work of art in historical perspective.

There will be examples of these types of questions in the three sample tests at the end of the book.

"Except"-Type Questions

This type of question can be confusing because you are being asked which of the five choices does not belong. When you see the question, immediately circle the word EXCEPT. Cross out the choices that would be correct if you leave out EXCEPT. Then you are left with the correct choice. Approximately 10% of the questions on the exam are this type of question.

---

6. All of the following were totalitarian states in the 1930s EXCEPT

   A. Germany

   B. Italy

   C. Spain

   D. France

   E. Russia

The correct answer is **D**. Germany under Hitler, Italy under Mussolini, Spain under Franco, and Russia under Stalin represented forms of totalitarianism. France was unlike the totalitarian regimes of Germany, Italy, Spain, and Russia. France's traditional policy of political pluralism and democracy avoided totalitarianism. The key to this question is to circle EXCEPT and then cross out all the examples of totalitarian government. This will leave you with choice **D**.

Hints/Strategies for Mastering the Multiple-Choice Questions

- **Read the questions carefully and underline the key words in each question.** This helps you to avoid careless mistakes. Focus on the main idea of the question and what is being asked.

- **Answer the easy questions first.** This strategy will instill confidence and enable you to budget your time more efficiently.

- **Read all choices carefully before making a selection.** Sometimes the initial choice may seem correct but only by being patient can you choose the best answer.

- **Go with your first instincts.** Most of the time your first choice is the best. Don't change any answers unless you are absolutely certain.

- **Use the process of elimination.** Cross out the incorrect answers so that you can narrow down the possible correct choices. This technique will increase the possibility of getting the right answer.

- **Make educated guesses.** If you can eliminate two or three choices, your odds of getting the correct answer improve. If you have no idea about the question, leave it blank. However, don't guess blindly. You are penalized one-fourth of a grade for incorrect answers and no points if you leave a question blank.

- **Budget your time.** Don't get stuck on one question. Circle the questions you can't answer and return to them after you finish the 80 questions. Sometimes, you might find clues or hints in other questions. Remember, you are not penalized for unanswered questions.

The Free-Response Section

Students have two hours and ten minutes to write three essays in this section of the test.

- **Part A:** Document-Based Question—Comprises 45% of the free-response section. There is a 15-minute mandatory reading of the documents provided in the test, and 45 minutes is allowed for writing the essay.

- **Part B:** Thematic Essay—Comprises 55% of the free-response section. You will have 70 minutes to write two thematic essays.

In order to write the DBQ or thematic essays, it is important that you understand the meaning of the key words and what is being asked. Below is a list of frequently used terms on the AP essay questions:

- **Analyze:** To explain or give reasons for the cause of an event; to show relationships between events. *Example:* Analyze the way in which society was changed as a result of the ideas contained in the *Communist Manifesto*.

- **Assess/Evaluate:** To judge the validity of a statement; to determine the advantages and disadvantages of a generalization. *Example:* Democracy developed in England through evolution, while in France democracy developed through revolution. Include facts in your evaluation to support your argument.

- **Compare/Contrast:** To identify similarities and differences between two or more things. *Example:* Compare and contrast the totalitarian regime of Adolf Hitler in Germany with that of Joseph Stalin in Russia.

- **Describe:** To tell about or to draw a picture about a particular event. *Example:* Describe the political, economical, and social consequences of the Protestant Reformation.

- **Discuss:** To examine various points of view or present different sides of the subject. Write about a topic. *Example:* Discuss the extent to which the Versailles Treaty influenced the use of nationalism and totalitarianism in Italy and Germany.

- **Explain:** To make clear or plain; to give greater detail or to tell the meaning of something. *Example:* Explain how political, economic, and social factors contributed to the French Revolution of 1789.

Strategies for Writing the Essays

Part A: Document-Based Question (DBQ)

The Document-Based Question is an exercise that tests your ability to analyze and synthesize different historical viewpoints. The primary purpose of the DBQ is to evaluate how students can answer a question from the documentary evidence. It is not a test of a student's prior knowledge. In writing the DBQ, a student acts like an historian who must arrive at a conclusion from the available writings. There is no single correct answer. By using a variety of documents, you can defend or refute a particular viewpoint. There are approximately 10 to 12 documents on the examination.

The following is a helpful set of steps for writing the DBQ:

1. Read the questions/historical background carefully. Determine your task. Underline the keywords in the question (Analyze, Discuss). Write down any information that you can connect to the question or to the historical background.

2. Read all the documents. Circle key phrases or words in the documents that are related to the main theme.

3. Take note of the source of the document, and the author's point of view or bias. Make a chart of the key ideas of each document. Separate them to reflect both sides of the question.

4. Decide on your thesis statement. Outline the essay. Include an introductory statement that leads up to your thesis.

5. DO NOT summarize or give a laundry list of documents. Remember to include relevant outside historical facts as long as they are accurate.

6. Weave or incorporate the documents together.

7. Write a conclusion to show that you have proven the thesis.

Scoring the DBQ

The DBQ is graded on a 1–9 scale. Since 2000, the College Board has introduced a core-scoring method to grade the DBQ. Core-scoring means that you may earn a total of six Basic Core points if you demonstrate basic competence, such as having an acceptable thesis statement or using a majority of documents. You may earn an additional three points in Expanded Core points only if you successfully earn all six Basic Core points. The following chart specifically identifies the two cores of points. You should use this scoring guide or rubric when you are writing your practice DBQ essay contained in this book. Compare your essay to the rubric to make sure you have provided all the required information.

Generic Core-Scoring Guide for AP European History Document-Based Question (Score Scale 0–9)			
Basic Core	**Points**	**Expanded Core**	**Points**
1. Has acceptable thesis	1	Expands beyond basic core of 1–6 points. A student must earn points in the basic core area before earning points in the expanded core area.	0–3
2. Uses a majority of documents	1		
3. Supports thesis with appropriate evidence from documents	1	Examples:	
4. Understands the basic meaning of documents cited in the essay	1	Thesis is clear, analytical, and comprehensive	
5. Provides an analysis of bias or point of view in at least two or three documents	1	Uses all or almost all documents	
6. Demonstrates an analysis of the documents by grouping them according to a particular viewpoint	1	Insightful analysis of the documents	
		Evaluates bias or point of view in at least four documents cited in the essay	
		Analyzes the documents by creating additional groupings or other forms of analysis	
		Incorporates relevant "outside" historical content	
Subtotal	6	Subtotal	3
		Total	9

A Practice DBQ

Directions: The following question is based on the accompanying Documents 1–10.

1. Analyze the responsibility of the European powers towards the outbreak of World War I.

Historical Background: From 1815 to 1914, Europe enjoyed a period of peace and prosperity. However, the arms race, the alliance system, and the issue of nationalism in the Balkans created tension. The assassination of Archduke Ferdinand of Austria-Hungary in June 1914 in Sarajevo by a Bosnian youth was the spark that led to World War I.

Document 1

Per Capita Expenditures of the Great Powers on Armaments						
	1870	1880	1890	1900	1910	1914
Great Britain	$3.54	$3.46	$3.84	$12.60*	$7.29	$8.23
France	2.92	4.02	4.66	5.21	6.47	7.07
Russia	1.28	1.50	1.26	1.44	2.32	3.44
Germany	1.28	2.16	2.80	4.06	4.06	8.19
Austria-Hungary	1.08	1.70	1.50	1.46	1.68	3.10
Italy	1.38	1.74	2.52	2.34	3.36	3.16
*Boer War Costs						

Source: *From Europe, 1815-1914,* by Gordon A. Craig, 1966.

Document 2

Heir to Austria's Throne Is Slain with His Wife by a Bosnia Youth to Avenge Seizure of His Country

Sarajevo, Bosnia, June 28 . . . Archduke Francis Ferdinand, heir to the throne of Austria-Hungary, and his wife, the Duchess of Hohenberg, were shot and killed by a Bosnian student here today. The fatal shooting was the second attempt upon the lives of the couple during the day, and is believed to have been the result of a political conspiracy.

Later details show that the assassin darted forth from his hiding place behind a house and actually got on the motor car in which the Archduke and his wife were sitting. He took close aim first at the Archduke, and then at the Duchess. The fact that no one stopped him, and that he was allowed to perpetrate the dastardly act indicate that the conspiracy was carefully planned and that the Archduke fell a victim to a political plot. The aspiration of the Serbian population in Bosnia to join with Serbia and form a great Serbian kingdom is well known. No doubt today's assassination was regarded as a means of forwarding the plan. . . .

Source: *New York Times,* June 29, 1914. 1. c. 1914 by The New York Times Company.

Document 3

Gavrilo Princip, arrested and tried, gives his reasons for the assassination:

No, I am not sorry. I have cleared an evil out of the way. He (Francis Ferdinand) is a German and an enemy of the South Slavs. He treated them badly . . . Every day a high treason trial. Every day it went worse with our people. They are impoverished . . . I killed him and I am not sorry. . . . I regarded him as an energetic man who as ruler would have carried through definite ideas and reforms which stood in our way . . . For union (of the South Slavs) one must sacrifice many lives, and it was for this reason that Franz Ferdinand fell. Nevertheless, the main motive, which guided me in my deed was: the avenging of the Serbian people . . .

Source: *Current History,* August 1927, pp. 703–706.

Document 4

German Chancellor Bethmann-Hollweg Notifies the German Ambassador of the Kaiser's Position:

Finally, concerning Serbia, His Majesty naturally can not take any stand in the questions between Austria and Serbia, for they are beyond his competence, but (Austrian Emperor) Francis Joseph may be sure that His Majesty, in accordance with his treaty obligations and old friendship, will stand true by Austria's side.

Source: *Kautsky Documents,* published in December, 1919, by Weimar Republic.

Document 5

. . . the Royal Serbian Government has done nothing to repress these movements. It has permitted the criminal machinations of various societies and associations directed against the Monarchy, and has tolerated unrestrained language on the part of the press, the glorification of the perpetrators of outrages and the participation of officers and functionaries in subversive agitation. . . .

. . . (The) Royal Governments see themselves compelled to demand from the Royal Serbian Government a formal assurance that they condemn this dangerous propaganda against the Monarchy. . . .

. . . To accept the collaboration in Serbia of representatives of the Austro-Hungarian Government for the suppression of the subversive movement . . . the Austrian Hungarian Government expects the reply of the Royal Government no later than 6 o'clock on Saturday morning.

Source: This is an excerpt from the Austro-Hungarian Red Book No. 7, sent to Serbia on July 23, 1914.

Document 6

Sir George Buchanan, British Ambassador to Russia notes:

I had a telephone message this morning from [Russian Foreign Minister] Sazonof . . . [who] said that Austria's conduct was both provocative and immoral; she would never have taken such action unless Germany had first been consulted; some of her demands were quite impossible of acceptance. He hoped that His Majesty's Government would not fail to proclaim their solidarity with Russia and France.

The French Ambassador gave me to understand that France would fulfill all the obligations entailed by her alliance with Russia, if necessity arose, besides supporting Russia strongly in any diplomatic negotiations.

Source: British Blue Book, No. 6, *Official Diplomatic Documents,* 87.

Document 7

Emperor William II's telegram to Czar Nicholas II on July 29, 1 a.m., a day after Austria-Hungary declared war on Serbia (July 28):

It is with the gravest concern that I hear of the impression, which the action of Austria against Serbia is creating in your country. The unscrupulous agitation that has been going on in Serbia for years has resulted in the outrageous crime, to which archduke Franz Ferdinand fell a victim. The spirit that led Serbians to murder their own king and his wife [in 1903] still dominates the country. You will doubtless agree with me that we both . . . have a common interest as well as all Sovereigns to insist that all the persons morally responsible . . . should receive their deserved punishment. In this case politics play no part at all. . . .

I am exerting my utmost influence to induce the Austrians to deal straightly to arrive at a satisfactory understanding with you. I confidently hope you will help me in my efforts to smooth over difficulties that may still arise.

Source: *Schilling Diary,* "How the War Began in 1914: Diary of a Russian," Foreign Document Office, p. 45.

Document 8

Nicholas II replies to William II's telegram:

. . . In this most serious moment, I appeal to you to help me. An ignoble war has been declared to a weak country. The indignation in Russia shared fully by me is enormous. I foresee that very soon I shall be overwhelmed by the pressure brought upon me and be forced to take extreme measures which will lead to war. To try and avoid such a calamity as a European war I beg you in the name of our old friendship to do what you can to stop your allies from going too far.

Source: *Schilling Diary,* p. 46.

Document 9

The Allied and Associated Governments affirm and Germany accepts the responsibility of Germany and her allies for causing all the loss and damage to which the Allied and Associated Governments and their nationals have been subjected as a consequence of the war imposed upon them by the aggression of Germany and her allies.

Source: Article 231 of the *Treaty of Versailles*

Document 10

In this excerpt from May 7, 1919, Count Brockdorff-Rantzau, leader of the German delegation to the Versailles Peace Conference, protested:

It is demanded of us that we shall confess ourselves to be alone guilty of the war. Such a confession from my lips would be a lie. We are far from declining all responsibility for the fact that this great World War took place or that it was fought in the way that it was. . . . But we energetically deny that Germany and its people, who were convinced that they fought a war of defense, were alone guilty. No one would want to assert that the disaster began only at that disastrous moment when the successor of Austria-Hungary fell a victim to murderous hands. In the last fifty years, the imperialism of all European states has chronically poisoned international relations. Policies of retaliation, polices of expansion, and disregard for the right of peoples to determine their own destiny, have contributed to the European malady, which came to a crisis in the World War. The mobilization of Russia deprived statesmen of the opportunity of curing the disease, and places the issue in the hands of the military powers. . . .

Source: *German White Book,* pp. 3–4

Analysis of the DBQ Question and Documents

Analysis of the Question

This question presents you with the task of determining who was responsible for World War I. You must decide if the Versailles Treaty, Article 231, placing the blame solely on Germany, is accurate. To determine the validity of Article 231, you have to assess whether England, France, Austria-Hungary, and Russia bear responsibility and how conditions prior to World War I contributed to its outbreak. You should include relevant outside information to help support and reinforce your thesis statement.

Analysis of the Documents

- **Document 1:** This chart shows that Germany and Great Britain spent the most per person on armaments. The chart could be used to show that the countries were preparing for war and that this arms race led to fear among neighboring countries.

- **Document 2:** The headline clearly shows that the Archduke Ferdinand was killed by a political conspiracy. It is important to note that this is an American viewpoint; the U.S. declared its neutrality in 1914.

- **Document 3:** Princip's statement that he killed Archduke Ferdinand for national reasons might be relevant in assessing responsibility.

- **Document 4:** Bethmann-Hollweg's statement affirms his decision to support Austria. This document could be used to show Germany's responsibility towards the war.

- **Document 5:** This Austrian-Hungarian excerpt contains specific demands on Serbia. This document may be used to show how Austria's ultimatum was either reasonable or unreasonable.

- **Document 6:** This document states how Great Britain had decided to stand firm with Russia and France.

- **Document 7:** Emperor William II's telegram demonstrates his efforts to prevent Russian action against Austria. This document can be used to contrast Germany's attitude with her position in Document 4.

- **Document 8:** Nicholas II's reply shows how he was appealing to William II to help him stop Austria. This document can be useful to show how Russia was trying to contain the force of the war.

- **Document 9:** According to the Versailles Treaty, Germany accepted the sole responsibility for the war. This statement should be evaluated in light of other documents.

- **Document 10:** This excerpt shows that Germany rejected that it alone was responsible for the war. The Count's claim that the imperialism of all European nations caused the war can be used to show how all the nations were responsible.

First Student DBQ Essay

The origin of the outbreak of World War I has been a source of controversy. The question of who was responsible was raised during the war and answered specifically in the Versailles Treaty. In Article 231 of the Versailles Treaty, Germany and her allies accepted the responsibility for causing all the losses and damages associated with World War I (Doc. 9). Rather than Germany being blamed as the sole cause of the war, the responsibility for World War I was the result of conditions in Europe at the beginning of the twentieth century as well as the failure of European diplomacy to effectively deal with the crisis that developed after the assassination of Archduke Ferdinand in 1914 (Doc. 10).

In the period between 1871 and 1914, a number of developments took place that created tension between the major powers. In 1871, the Unification of Germany upset the balance of power, and the decision of Emperor William II in 1890 to build up a navy comparable to that of Great Britain created an arms race that haunted Europe (Doc. 1). From 1890 to 1914, England, France, and Germany substantially increased their per capita expenditures on armaments (Doc. 1). Germany's decision to add an expensive fleet of gun battleships to its expanding navy heightened tensions with England. German nationalists, like Admiral Alfred von Tirpitz, saw a large navy as a source of pride and patriotic unity. However, the British saw it as a military challenge.

By 1914, Europe had developed an alliance system of England, France, and Russia (Triple Entente) and the Triple Alliance (Austria-Hungary, Germany, and Italy). These alliances divided Europe into rival camps. Thus, the alliances and armaments pursued for defense proved to be a means of creating tension. The alliance systems also guaranteed that the crisis would be Europe-wide. The immediate crisis that threatened the peace of Europe occurred on June 28, 1914, when Gavrilo Princip, a Serbian nationalist, assassinated the heir to the Austrian-Hungarian throne, Archduke Ferdinand, while they were visiting Sarajevo, the capital of the Austrian province of Bosnia (Doc. 2). Princip, who later was proven to be a member of the Black Hand, a radical Serbian nationalist group, assassinated the Archduke because he wanted an independent state free of Austrian-Hungarian control. Austria-Hungary resisted this movement in order to preserve their empire. Since Princip was loosely connected with the Serbian government, Austria-Hungary wanted to punish Serbia. Austria sought Germany's help and Chancellor Bethmann-Hollweg offered Austria a blank check of support (Doc. 4).

Subsequently, Austria issued an ultimatum requiring Serbia to cease all subversion in Austria and all anti-Austrian propaganda in Serbia. They also wanted a joint commission to investigate all aspects of the assassination at Sarajevo (Doc. 5). These demands amounted to Austrian control of the Serbian state. Serbia turned to its big Slavic brother, Russia, for assistance. The British Ambassador to Russia began to inform the government in England that the Russians wanted their support and that France was going to support Russia.

It was apparent that the diplomatic situation was out of control. Military plans and timetables began to dictate policy. When Austria-Hungary declared war on Serbia on July 28, William II tried to prevent Russian mobilization against Austria (Doc. 7). However, Nicholas II, Czar of Russia, realized that once Austria had mobilized its troops, Russia would be forced to take action that would lead to war (Doc. 8). Count Brockdorff-Rantzau, leader of the German delegation at the Versailles Treaty, believed that the mobilization of Russian troops had made political efforts secondary to military considerations (Doc. 10).

The march toward war could not be stopped. On August 1, Germany declared war on Russia; on August 3, France declared war on Germany; on August 4, England declared war on Germany after she violated Belgium neutrality in her attempt to invade France. Sidney Bradshaw Fay in his book *The Origins of the World War* claims that none of the great powers wanted war and all of them must bear responsibility for the conflict. Serbia wanted Austro-Hungarian territories and subject nationalities in the Austria-Hungary empire wanted their independence. Russia and Germany were rivals in the Balkans and each wanted to dominate the area. Britain and Germany were competing for world dominance and saw each other as threats to their security. Finally, in August of 1914, each country believed that they had been wronged and they rallied to defend it. The majority of the population enthusiastically embraced the outbreak of war.

Reader's Comments on the First Student DBQ Essay

- The student makes effective use of the documents and adds relevant outside information, such as the Alliance System.

- The various points of view of each of the documents are clearly addressed.

- The student identifies the documents with the proper number assigned to them.

- Sentence structure flows smoothly.

- The thesis is clearly stated within the first paragraph and put into historical context.

- The student makes a strong argument to show that the responsibility for World War I was shared by all the European powers.

Possible student score: 8–9

Second Student DBQ Essay

I agree that Germany was solely responsible for World War I. Document 9 Article 231 of the Versailles Treaty states that Germany accepts the responsibility for causing all the "loss and damage to which the Allied government . . . and their nationals have been subjected."

In Document 1, the increased spending on armaments by Germany would indicate that she was preparing for war. In 1910, Germany was spending $8.19 per capital expenditures which was only four cents less than Great Britain's amount of $8.23.

When Archduke Ferdinand was assassinated, Germany promised, as stated in Document 4, "that His Majesty, in accordance with his treaty obligations and old friendship, will stand true by Austria's side." With this blank check from Germany, Austria-Hungary issued an ultimatum that demanded that the Serbian Government "condemn this dangerous propaganda against the Monarchy . . . (Doc. 5). The ultimatum also demanded that Serbia accept the "collaboration in Serbia of representatives of the Austro-Hungarian Government for the suppression of the subversive movement . . ."

In Document 6, the British Ambassador to Russia notifies his government in London that Austria's stand was provocative and that she would never have taken this stand unless Germany had been consulted.

Based on the documents presented, I believe that Germany was solely responsible for World War I. The large arms buildup, the alliance system, and the blank check to Austria encouraged Austria to take a hard line. If Germany had not been so forceful, World War I would not have happened.

Reader's Comments on the Second Student DBQ Essay

- The student discussed the documents superficially and merely lists the documents.

- The student strings the documents together to create an essay but there is no analysis of the documents.

- The student's thesis fails to analyze the responsibility of other European countries and merely focuses on Germany.

- There is no outside information.

Possible student score: 1–3

Part B: The Thematic Essay

The Thematic Essay part of the free-response section requires students to answer two essays from a set of three questions from Group I and three questions from Group II. You must select one question from each group. The first group of questions covers the period from the Renaissance to the Napoleonic era and the second group covers the period from the Napoleonic era to the present. Students have 70 minutes to answer both questions. It is usually suggested that they use 5 minutes as planning time for each question and 30 minutes for writing time. Most thematic essays are descriptive because you are asked to analyze, assess/evaluate, and compare/contrast the causes and effects of an historical subject. The Thematic Essay, unlike the DBQ, requires you to incorporate all relevant outside information and to represent it in an organized and coherent fashion.

Topics of Thematic Essays

The three themes of intellectual/cultural, political/diplomatic, and social/economic have all been equally represented in this section of the examination in recent years. The common topics have been the Renaissance, Reformation, Enlightenment, French Revolution, Napoleon, art interpretation, economic/political issues of the nineteenth century, Marxism, Imperialism, Nationalism, Communism, Cold War, and post–World War II economic changes in Europe.

The following is a list of strategies for writing the thematic essays:

1. Read the questions in each group. Jot down key facts that you know about each question. Select the question for which you have the most information. Focus on those questions which you may have previewed or which you may have discussed in class.

2. Underline the key directive words such as assess, evaluate, explain, compare, and contrast.

3. Make your choice and begin to organize your information.

4. Develop your thesis statement (your position) and outline the facts you want to include in your essays.

5. Check the facts in your outline to be sure you are correct. DO NOT include any incorrect or unsure information.

6. Begin to write. Include an introductory paragraph, a supporting paragraph, and a summary/conclusion of your position. Be sure to use concrete historical examples to support your ideas.

7. Proofread your essays. Check to see if they are organized; look for factual inconsistencies, poor sentence structure, or anything that may weaken the support of your thesis statement.

A Practice Thematic Essay

Assess the validity of the following statement: The Bolshevik Revolution of 1917 directly influenced the Russian people and other nations.

Before writing this essay, check the above strategies for writing the thematic essay and follow these three steps:

1. Jot down what you know about the topic: causes, personalities, effects of the Russian Revolution on people and countries of the world.

2. Underline the key word, **assess**, which means to determine if the statement is accurate.

3. Frame certain questions in your mind such as: Did the Russian Revolution really change the lives of the people and the government? Did the Russian Revolution influence other nations?

First Student Thematic Essay

The Russian or Bolshevik Revolution of 1917 had a major impact on the people of Russia and other nations. An underlying cause of the Russian Revolution was that compared to Western Europe, the country was an undeveloped nation. The Romanov czars who had ruled Russia for close to 300 years were absolute rulers. Through the secret police, the czars vigorously suppressed demands for reform and punished reforms by imprisonment, execution, or exile to Siberia. Economically, Russia had not been industrialized. Serfs or farmers made up more than 75% of the population. They were still bound to the lands like the serfs of the Middle Ages.

In the late nineteenth century, Alexander II and his son Nicholas II began the process of industrializing Russia. The landless peasants provided the cheap labor and French investors provided the resources. The Russians constructed iron and steel mills, textile factories, and railroads. Russia's Industrial Revolution created two new economic classes: workers and capitalists. The workers and the middle class business owners began to demand more rights. Both groups desired a voice in the government and opposed Czarist absolutism.

The immediate cause of the Russian Revolution was Russia's involvement in World War I. The country was unprepared for war. Russian industries were not developed enough to meet the demands for war supplies. The transportation system could not supply the armies at the front. At one time, only one out of three soldiers had a rifle. Poorly equipped troops suffered enormous losses. Especially in the cities, people faced shortages of food and other goods because of the war. Czar Nicholas II ignored demands to withdraw from the war and did nothing to improve these conditions. In March, 1917, riots and strikes erupted in Petrograd; crowds protested the war and shortage of food. When Czar Nicholas II's troops refused to fire on the striking city workers and some joined the protest, the Russian Revolution had officially begun. Nicholas II abdicated and a new provisional government of Alexander Kerensky was established. This new government guaranteed civil liberties but refused to withdraw from the war. When the Kerensky government was unable to solve the food crisis and refused to support the land seizures by the peasants, the Bolsheviks under the leadership of Lenin began to gain supporters using the slogan of Peace, Land, and Bread. The Bolsheviks gained followers because they promised to end the war, provide food for the people, and obtain land for the peasants. On November 6/7, 1917, armed Bolsheviks seized power and set up a communist government.

Immediately upon seizing power, the Bolsheviks (who later became known as the Communists) sought to transfer Russia's economic system from capitalism to communism. Under a program called War Communism, the government nationalized mines, factories, railroads, and land and prohibited most private ownership. War Communism proved a failure. Factory workers failed to maintain production schedules and farmers curtailed their production because the state seized their surplus crops without payment. In 1921, Lenin was forced to crush riots by peasants and workers and an open rebellion by previously pro-Bolshevik soldiers at Kronstadt. Lenin put to death 15,000 soldiers. In March, 1921, Lenin introduced the New Economic Policy which re-established limited economic freedom in an attempt to rebuild agriculture and industry. Peasants and small retail traders were allowed to sell their products in free markets for profit. However, heavy industry, railroads, and banks were wholly nationalized. By 1928, the NEP had revived Russia's economy, and agriculture and industrial output had reached pre-World War I levels.

The transformation of Soviet society had a profound impact on the lives of women. The Russian Revolution immediately proclaimed complete equality for women. In the 1920s, divorce was made easily available and women were urged to work outside the home and liberate themselves sexually.

The Revolution turned Russia into a communist country which affected Europe as well as the rest of the world. In 1922, the communists reorganized Russia into four republics and renamed the country the Union of Soviet Socialist Republics (USSR) or the Soviet Union.

The Russian Revolution also created fear that communism would spread to other countries. According to Karl Marx, the Father of Communism, communism could only be successful if there was a worldwide revolution to spread their ideas. In Italy, the Fascist dictator Benito Mussolini and in Germany, the Nazi dictator Adolf Hitler claimed that only their form of totalitarianism could save their nations from the evils of communism. By battling the communist movement, the Nazis, like the Fascists in Italy, gained the support of property holders, bankers, and industrialists.

The Communist Revolution also affected Russia's relationship with the United States. The United States did not recognize the USSR until 1933. Although the United States and Russia were allies in World War II against Germany, they reverted back to their pre-war hostilities at the end of the war in 1945. The United States and Russia entered a Cold War which lasted from 1947 to 1989. The Cold War, which has often been described as a war of words between the forces of democracy and communism, led to tension in Europe, Asia, Latin America, and Africa. The ideas of communism also led to the rise of Mao-Tse-Tung in China and Fidel Castro in Cuba. Both of these leaders were successful in establishing communist governments in their countries. The fear of communism also led to the development of nuclear arsenals that threatened the safety of the world.

Although the Soviet Union collapsed in 1991, communism still exists in Cuba and China. The fall of communism in Russia has left the country with unresolved economic, social, and political issues. Poverty is still a problem in Russia and the quality of life continues to decline.

Evaluating the Sample Thematic Essay

- Did the essay show a thorough understanding of the theme of the question?

- Did the essay include relevant facts, examples, and details to support the theme?

- Were the facts, references, and examples accurate?

- Was the essay well developed and did it demonstrate a logical and clear plan of organization?

- Did the essay contain an introductory and concluding statement that support the theme or refute the question?

- Did the essay show an ability to analyze and evaluate events?

Reader's Comments on the First Student Thematic Essay

- The thesis statement is clear.

- The essay provides specific background on the causes of the Russian Revolution and how War Communism and the NEP changed the economic life in Russia.

- The reference to the Kronstadt Rebellion demonstrated the ruthlessness of communism.

- The changing role of women in the Soviet Union also provided concrete facts about how communism influenced Russia.

- The essay uses historical facts such as a reference to how communism influenced events in the United States, Italy, Germany, China, and Cuba.

- The essay structure is logical and well developed.

- A weakness of the essay was the failure to include how Stalin affected Soviet life through the Five Year Plans and collectivization policies.

Possible student score: 8–9

Second Student Thematic Essay

The Russian or Bolshevik Revolution took place on November 6/7, 1917. Lenin, the leader of the Bolshevik (Communist Party), gained the support of the people by promising land, peace, and bread.

When he was in office, Lenin began to change the economy. He introduced the New Economic Policy, which allowed Russians some economic freedom but heavy industry was still nationalized. The Russian Revolution also created fear in other countries. Benito Mussolini in Italy and Adolf Hitler in Germany rose to power because they claimed that they would save the country from communism.

The Communist Revolution also led to a Cold War with the United States and led to the rise of communism in China and Cuba. The fear of communism also contributed to the nuclear arms race, resulting in the fear of nuclear warfare.

Reader's Comments on the Second Student Thematic Essay

- The thesis is absent or never really stated.

- The student neglects to discuss or evaluate any specific information.

- The student really does not have the factual information to write and develop the answer.

- There is no logical development of ideas.

Possible score: 2–3

Some Frequently Asked Questions about the AP European History Exam

Q. What should I do on the day of the test?

A. Relax. Have a good breakfast but not a huge one. You need energy for the test but avoid eating too much because it could make you sleepy. Don't drink too much coffee, tea, or soda, which might lead to frequent use of the rest room during the examination. Bring a healthy snack for the break. The additional food will give you extra energy.

Bring two sharpened No. 2 pencils for the multiple choice section of the examination. Bring an eraser or be sure that your pencils have good erasers. If you change a response on the multiple choice questions, you must erase the answers thoroughly in order to ensure that there are no stray marks. For safety's sake, bring additional pencils. Be sure to have two pens with dark blue or black ink. All the essays must be written in pen.

Bring a watch so that you can monitor your own time. Normally, the proctor will keep you informed of the time.

Bring your high school code with you. Your guidance counselor will have this information.

Relax and be positive. Don't cram information a few minutes before the examintion.

Q. How long is the test?

A. The test is three hours and five minutes.

Section I: 80 multiple-choice questions — 55 minutes

Section II: Free-response questions — 130 minutes

Part A – Mandatory reading of the Document Based Question (DBQ) – 15 minutes; Suggested writing time — 45 minutes

Part B – Students will have to answer two thematic essays — 70 minutes

The total examination takes about 3-1/2 hours, which includes the reading of the instructions, collecting the papers, and the 5–10 minute break.

Q. Will guessing hurt my score?

A. Make an educated guess. If you are able, narrow down the choices to two or three, then go for it. The odds of getting the correct answer will improve. If you are unable to eliminate any choices, or don't have a clue about the question, skip it and go on to the next question. Don't guess blindly! Remember you will be penalized 1/4 of a point (0.25) for every wrong answer.

Q. Is there a specific length for the free-response questions?

A. The readers grade your responses on content, not length. It is important that your essay is organized and hits the essential points of the questions. The reader is looking for specific information and it is important that you avoid information that is not relevant to the topic. Budget your time so that you can devote sufficient time to answer the questions. Remember there are six free-response questions for Part B. The proctor will suggest that you move on to the next section, but you will not be mandated to go on to the next part. Remember that the readers are looking for how well you organize and synthesize your information. Do not just present a collection of facts.

Q. Is is necessary to use all the documents for the DBQ question?

A. You should use as many documents as necessary to answer the questions. Obviously, you should use more than half of the documents in order to fully support your thesis or the focus of the essay. It is also important that you analyze and evaluate the documents rather than merely list them. The reader is looking to see how well you use the documents to analyze the information to support your historical thesis.

Q. Do penmanship, spelling, and neatness count?

A. The readers will not penalize you for poor handwriting, lack of neatness, and misspelled words. The readers are looking at your essay holistically and understand that you are pressed for time and have to write quickly. However, if your penmanship is poor and your essay is illegible, it becomes harder to get the best score when the readers are not exactly sure of what you are stating. If you have poor handwriting, spend a few extra minutes in writing the essay. The graders are marking thousands of essays and cannot devote too much time to trying to decipher each paper. You should also avoid last-minute revisions inserted in different places because it can confuse the readers and gives the impression that you are not organized. Usually, your first draft contains the essential information. Do not doubt yourself.

Q. Where can I outline my ideas for the essay questions?

A. Most students use the green booklet that contains the DBQ and the Thematic Essays. All your writing is done in the pink booklet. You should underline key phrases or terms for each of the questions, such as discuss, analyze, and compare, and any key facts that you associate with the questions. This simple technique will help you to focus on the main idea of the question. Use the green booklet only to outline the key ideas. If the proctor provides you with additional scrap paper, do not write an entire question and then rewrite it in the pink booklet. Remember, you are only graded for the information in the pink booklet.

Q. How much should I prepare for the examination?

A. Preparing for the examination is something that you will be doing with your class and teacher during the entire year. Take good notes on all your readings and make sure that your assignments are done thoroughly and completely. Make a list of authors or historians and their viewpoints on the different topics which you have discussed during the year. This summary can be used to briefly review the highlights about each time period.

Q. How much should I review?

A. Start studying for the test at least a month in advance. Start slowly, perhaps 1/2 hour once or twice a week. Become familiar with the format of the test. Organize a study group with your class to discuss practice essays and how to rate them. Use the guide in this book as your model.

Don't cram. Get a good night's sleep and relax on the day of the test.

Q. When are the scores reported and who receives them?

A. The examination is graded in June and the scores are sent to the high school and colleges students have designated by the middle of July. If you want to get your scores earlier (July 1) by phone, you can call toll free (888) 308-0013. There is a fee for this service which is payable by credit card. You will also need your AP number as well as your Social Security number.

Q. Can I withhold or cancel my scores?

A. Yes. If you want to withhold or cancel a score, you must contact the College Board by June 15 of the year that you take the examination. There is a $5 fee for withholding the score but not for cancelling the score. Be sure that you have your AP number, the name of your high school, city, and state. Before you consider either withholding or cancelling a score, consider that college officers are looking for students who are willing to challenge themselves rather than just at the results.

How to Make Effective Use of this Book

1. The purpose of this book is to give you an overview of the AP European History Examination. The book will provide you with the structure and format of the examination.

2. This book is not a textbook but a tool to help you prepare for the examination by providing you with the essential information that you need to prepare for the test.

3. Throughout the year you should use the review chapters in this book to help you study for unit tests and quizzes. You should also analyze the questions at the end of each chapter to help reinforce the material that you are studying. Always read the reasons for the correct as well as the incorrect choices to help you better understand why a particular response is right.

4. Refer to the strategies for answering the Multiple Choice, DBQ, and Thematic Essay through the year.

5. Do the practice examinations in the book so that you become familiar with the format of the test.

6. Follow the specific directions (time allotments, and so on) for each part. This will give you a good barometer on how to budget your time for the examination.

PART II

SUBJECT AREA REVIEWS WITH SAMPLE QUESTIONS AND ANSWERS

The Renaissance (c1350–c1550)

The word **Renaissance** means *rebirth* in French. The Renaissance was a period of artistic and cultural achievement in Europe from the fourteenth to the sixteenth century. It was characterized by a number of distinctive ideas about life, specifically secularism, individualism, humanism, and materialism. The spirit of the Renaissance influenced European society for generations, making the Renaissance truly a golden age in European history.

If the Renaissance was a rebirth of culture, you might think that the period before the Renaissance was one of gloom and darkness. Actually, historians have shown that the Medieval Era, or Middle Ages, did produce art, architecture, literature, and other ideas in law, languages, and economics that influenced Europe in the fourteenth century and provided the foundation for the Renaissance. However, during the Middle Ages, writers and philosophers viewed society as a preparation for the afterlife. Renaissance writers were interested in the present or secular world.

The table below explains some of the important differences between the Middle Ages and the Renaissance:

Differences between the Middle Ages and the Renaissance		
	Middle Ages	*Renaissance*
Purpose of art	Glorify God	Glorify the individual
Politics	Local/feudal lords ruled	Kings in England, France, and Spain centralized power
Society	Church as center of activity	Secular/material world becomes a vital part of life
Religion	Focus of one's life	Important but not most dominant
Education	Church promoted it to prepare students for religious life	Stressed teaching of history, arts, ethics, and public speaking

Italian Renaissance

The Renaissance began in Florence, Italy, and subsequently spread to the rest of Italy and then to Northern Europe. Unlike other areas of Europe, Italian cities had survived the economic crises of the late Middle Ages. Italian towns had remained important centers of Mediterranean trade and boosted their production of textiles and luxury goods. Furthermore, Italy was the center of ancient Roman history. Architectural remains, statues, and amphitheatres were visible reminders to Italians of the "Glory of Rome."

The Italian City-States

At the time of Renaissance, Italy was made up of numerous **city-states** that were geographically situated to benefit from the revival of trade that had developed as a result of the Crusades. The northern city-states of Florence, Venice, and Genoa acted as middlemen in the lucrative trade with the East. These Northern independent city-states marketed goods such as wool, silk, and other products to countries in Europe and Asia. They became prosperous centers of banking, trade, and manufacturing.

The cities of Northern Italy also benefited from being able to absorb stimulating new ideas from their advanced Byzantine and Muslim neighbors on the Mediterranean Sea. By 1350, the city-states of Florence, Venice, and Genoa were urban regions with a population of about 100,000, a large figure by medieval standards. The conditions were right for these cities to undergo a cultural explosion.

At the height of the Renaissance, several city-states, including the Republic of Genoa, the Republic of Florence, the Duchy of Milan, the Venetian Republic, the Papal States, and the Kingdom of Naples, were important. Within these city-states, merchants used their wealth as stepping-stones to economic and political leadership. Bankers made loans to kings and supported other commercial ventures that contributed to economic growth across Europe. Men like Francesco Sforza in Milan and Cosimo de'Medici in Florence, who gained power because of their own merit and not based on birth, became sponsors of the arts. They began to realize that their wealth enabled them to enjoy the material pleasures of life as well as fine fashion, arts, and architecture.

Florence: The Symbol of the Renaissance

Florence, the most dominant of the Italian cities, became known as the symbol of the Renaissance. Like ancient Athens, Florence attracted people of talents from other Italian city-states. The **Quattrocento**, a common historical term for the Golden Age of the Renaissance, began in the 1400s when the Medici family of Florence exerted power over that city. The Medici family was a merchant family who amassed a fortune in the wool trade and expanded into banking. It provided Florence with political and artistic leadership.

Through marriages, the Medici family became affiliated with the major houses of Europe. Besides acquiring the "Grand Dukes of Tuscany" title, the Medici family produced three popes (Leo X, Clement VII, and Leo XI), two queens of France (Catherine de Medici and Marie de Medici), and several cardinals of the Roman Catholic Church. The rise of the Medicis in Florence coincided with the triumph of the capitalist class over the guild merchants and artisans. The Medicis also exerted control over the government without holding any permanent official position, ruling Florence as part of the Grand Duchy of Tuscany until the 1700s. However, the Medicis were driven from power and expelled from Florence three times: in 1433 to 1434, from 1494 to 1512, and from 1527 to 1530. The attempts (such as the Pazzi conspiracy of 1478) of the Florentine republicans to restore the former liberties ultimately failed because of the Medicis' wealth and connections.

In 1434, **Cosimo de'Medici** (1389–1464) took control of the government of Florence. He was a shrewd political leader who was also the wealthiest man of his time but chose to rule Florence by staying behind the scenes. He controlled local politics by insuring that all eight members of the city council were loyal to him. He ruled for thirty years as a dictator and won the support of the people by championing popular causes.

Lorenzo de'Medici (1449–1492), Cosimo's grandson, also known as Lorenzo the Magnificent, was a clever politician who never held any public office but ruled with absolute control behind the scenes. Lorenzo represented the Renaissance ideal. He was a generous patron of the arts who saw the beauty of present life as complete fulfillment. Poets and philosophers visited the Medici palace. Lorenzo, who wrote poetry, supported artists such as Michelangelo (1475–1564) and Botticelli (1445–1510) and encouraged them to visit Florence.

Lorenzo's son, **Giovanni de'Medici** (1475–1521), who became Pope Leo X from 1513–1521, was also an important patron of the arts. He is remembered more for his interest in art than as a pope. He was a patron of the genius Raphael (1483–1520), who was one of the Renaissance's greatest Italian painters. Raphael painted a number of Madonnas, mostly during his time in Florence. Giovanni also promoted the rebuilding of St. Peter's Church in Rome.

Humanism and Society

The defining concept of the Renaissance was **humanism**, a literary movement that began in Italy during the fourteenth century. Humanism was a distinct movement because it broke from the medieval tradition of having pious religious motivation for creating art or works of literature. Humanist writers were concerned with worldly or secular subjects rather than strictly religious themes. Such emphasis on secularism was the result of a more materialistic view of the world. Unlike the Medieval Era, Renaissance people were concerned with money and the enjoyment of life and all its worldly pleasures. Humanist writers glorified the individual and believed that man was the measure of all things and had unlimited potential.

Humanism had far-reaching effects throughout Italy and Europe. The advent of humanism ended the church dominance of written history. Humanist writers secularized the view of history by writing from a nonreligious viewpoint.

The Humanists also had a great effect on education. They believed that education stimulated the creative powers of the individual. They supported studying grammar, poetry, and history, as well as mathematics, astronomy, and music. Humanists promoted the concept of the well-rounded, or Renaissance man, who was proficient in both intellectual and physical endeavors.

Humanist writers sought to understand human nature through a study of classical writers such as Plato and Aristotle. They believed that the classical writers of Ancient Greece and Rome could teach important ideas about life, love, and beauty. The revival of interest in the classical models of Greece and Rome was centered primarily among the educated people of the Italian city-states and focused on literature and writing.

During the Middle Ages in Western Europe, Latin was the language of the Church and the educated people. The Humanist writers began to use the *vernacular,* the national languages of a country, in addition to Latin.

Some important Italian Humanists are:

- **Giovanni Pico della Mirandola** (1463–1494) was an Italian who lived in Florence and expressed in his writings the belief that there were no limits to what man could accomplish.

- **Francesco Petrarca,** known as **Petrarch** (1304–1374) was the Father of Humanism, a Florentine who spent his youth in Tuscany and lived in Milan and Venice. He was a collector of old manuscripts and through his efforts the speeches of Cicero and the poems of Homer and Virgil became known to Western Europe. Petrarch's works also led to the rise of people known as *Civic Humanists,* or those individuals who were civic-minded and looked to the governments of the ancient worlds for inspiration. Petrarch also wrote sonnets in Italian. Many of these sonnets expressed his love for the beautiful Laura. His sonnets greatly influenced other writers of the time.

- **Leonardo Bruni** (1369–1444), who wrote a biography of Cicero, encouraged people to become active in the political as well as the cultural life of their cities. was a historian who today is most famous for *The History of the Florentine Peoples,* a 12-volume work. He was also the Chancellor of Florence from 1427 until 1444.

- **Giovanni Boccaccio** (1313–1375) wrote *The Decameron.* These hundred short stories were related by a group of young men and women who fled to a villa outside Florence to escape the Black Death. Boccaccio's work is considered to be the best prose of the Renaissance.

- **Baldassare Castiglione** (1478–1529) wrote one of the most widely-read books, *The Courtier,* which set forth the criteria on how to be the ideal Renaissance man. Castiglione's ideal courtier was a well-educated, mannered aristocrat who was a master in many fields from poetry to music to sports.

Humanism and Women

Humanism represented some advances for women. During the Middle Ages, few women could read or write outside of the convents. In the cities of the Renaissance, upper-class girls received an education similar to boys. Young ladies studied the writings of ancient Greek and Rome. Some women could also speak one or two modern languages such as French or Spanish and a small minority achieved some fame. In the latter sixteenth century, at least 25 women published books in Italy. **Laura Cereta** (1469–1499) reflected the success and failure of humanist women. Educated in a convent, she learned languages, philosophy, theology, and mathematics. However, by 15, like other educated women, she had to choose between marriage and full participation in social life or to study and withdraw from the world. Although Cereta chose marriage, she was widowed after only eighteen months of marriage and spent the remaining twelve years studying and withdrawing from society.

Although some Renaissance women were better educated than their medieval counterparts, their education prepared them for the social function of domestic or home life. They were expected to use their education to run a household. Educated men, however, were supposed to know how to rule and to participate in public affairs. The ideal was different for men and women. The ideal woman offered balance to man. She was vibrant but not too reserved. She also had to be beautiful because that was a sign of goodness.

Spreading Humanism

Two inventions helped spread the ideas produced by the Humanists across Italy and the rest of Europe. About 1450, **Johannes Gutenberg** (c1390–1468), a German printer, invented printing from a movable metal type press. The first European book printed by machine was the **Gutenberg Bible** (1456). With the Gutenberg Bible, the European age of printing had begun. As compared to the medieval practices of hand copying or block printing books at a tediously slow pace, the movable type press tremendously increased output and decreased costs. As books became more readily available, more people learned to read and write. The increased circulation of books by Italian writers helped to spread more of the ideas of the Renaissance to other parts of Europe.

Northern Renaissance

In the last quarter of the fifteenth century, the ideas of the Italian Renaissance spread to Northern Europe. Northern writers interpreted Italian ideas and attitudes towards the classical antiquity in terms of their own traditions. These writers in Holland, England, Germany, and France were more Christian, or at least more pious, than those of Italy. The secular and pagan themes of Greece and Rome received more attention from the Italians. In Northern Europe, the Renaissance had a distinct religious character and stressed biblical and early Christian themes along with the original works of the classical world. These writers tried to create a more perfect world by combining the best elements of the ancient world with Christian culture. Unlike the Italian Humanists, who stressed secularism and individualism, the Northern Humanists focused on broad programs of social reform based on Christian ideals.

Some of the most important writers of the Northern Renaissance include:

- **Sir Thomas More** (1478–1535) of England wrote his *Utopia* (which means "nowhere") in 1516 to describe a fictional ideal society somewhere off the main land of the New World. In More's *Utopia,* all children received an education in the Greco-Roman classics. There also was social equality since all profits from business and property were held in common. *Utopia* asserts that man, through his own efforts, can construct a perfect world. More's ideas were original in that he contradicted the long-standing view that evil existed in society because man was basically corrupt. Instead, More maintained that the acquisition of private property promoted vice and corruption. If a society could reform or change the institution that molded an individual, society could improve. More played a major role in introducing humanism into England. He was decapitated in 1535 by Henry VIII for not supporting Henry's break with the Catholic Church. In 1935 the Catholic Church made him a saint.

- **Desiderius Erasmus** (c1466–1536) of Holland, known as "The Prince of Humanists," dominated the intellectual thought of the northern Renaissance. His *In Praise of Folly* satirized ignorance, superstition, and many Church practices. He criticized the religious abuses of the Church and called for men to lead lives exemplifying simple Christian piety. He also published a Greek edition of the New Testament.

- **William Shakespeare** (1564–1616) of England is often considered the greatest poet and playwright of all time. Shakespeare's best known plays include the histories, *Henry IV* and *Henry V*, and the tragedies, *Romeo and Juliet, Hamlet, Julius Caesar* and *Macbeth*. Shakespeare helped set the standards for the English language.

- **François Rabelais** (1483–1553) of France, a friar and classicist, wrote the romances *Gargantua* and *Pantagruel*. With tongue-in-cheek humor, he portrayed a comic world of giants whose adventures satirized education, politics, and philosophy.

- **Michel Eyquem de Montaigne** (1533–1592) of France introduced the essay as a literary form to Europe. He expressed skepticism towards accepted beliefs and urged people to reject superstition and intolerance.

- **Geoffrey Chaucer** (c1342–1400) of England wrote the *Canterbury Tales*, a collection of witty short stories. This is one of the early classics of English literature.

Politics of the Renaissance

Italy

During the Middle Ages, the test of a good government was whether it provided justice, law, and order. Politically, the Renaissance produced a different approach to power. During the Renaissance, the test of a good government was whether it was effective as well as able to increase the power of the ruler. The Florentine **Niccolo Machiavelli** (1469–1527) put this new approach into practice. Machiavelli served the Florentine Republic as secretary and diplomat but was dismissed from office when the Medici family came back to power in 1512. In an attempt to regain the favor of the government, Machiavelli wrote *The Prince* (1513), a virtual instruction manual for a prince or ruler on the manner in which he should rule. This major work, which focuses on ethics and government, describes how rulers maintain power by methods that ignore right or wrong. Rulers need to accept the philosophy that "the end justifies the means." Machiavelli believed that politicians should manipulate people and use any means to gain power. He did not advocate amoral behavior but thought that a politician's actions should not be governed by moral consideration. A prince had to combine the cunning of a fox and power of a lion to achieve his goals.

The most able practitioners of Machiavelli's approach to politics were the fifteenth- and sixteenth-century monarchs: Louis XI of France, Henry VII and Henry VIII of England, and Ferdinand and Isabella of Spain. These leaders acted according to the principles discussed in *The Prince*. They invested in their government a strong sense of authority and leadership. In the sixteenth century, **Jean Bodin's** (1530–1596) work, *The Six Books on the State,* outlined the first systematic and clear conception that absolute sovereignty resided in the nation regardless of the forms of government. The "state" was an absolute sovereign that tolerated no rival legal authority above it except God. Bodin's ideas would contribute to the rise of absolutism in Europe.

France

Although France won the **Hundred Years' War** (1337–1453), a series of wars fought between France and England, the French country was left devastated. Farmland was destroyed and many French nobles lost their lives. Yet, the French monarchy became stronger since the war had weakened the power of the nobles. A revival of commerce, leading to the rise of the bourgeoisie (middle class), further strengthened the power of the king. Throughout the late fifteenth and early sixteenth centuries, the French kings consolidated their powers. Louis XI, who ruled from 1461 to 1483, was the most successful of these monarchs. He curbed feudal anarchy, set up an efficient government, and is considered to be the architect of French absolutism.

England

After the Hundred Years' War, England struggled to rebuild its economy. Unfortunately, the end of this war led to a civil war, known as the **War of the Roses**, between the House of York (symbolized by a white rose) and the House of Lancaster (symbolized by a red rose). After a 30-year struggle (1455–1485) a Lancasterian, Henry Tudor, gained control of England and his line ruled England until the seventeenth century. Henry Tudor (**Henry VII**) re-established the monarch's authority over the nobles and promoted trade and prosperity. His most famous accomplishment was the establishment of the **Star Chamber**, a court to check aristocratic power. There was no jury, and torture was a common remedy for all problems.

Spain

Spain, unlike France and England, was divided into many separate kingdoms. The various groups who lived on the peninsula lacked a common tradition. Muslims (Moors) and Jews had significantly influenced Spanish society. Until the 1100s, the Moors had controlled most of the country and many Jews had achieved high positions in finance, government, and medicine. The **Reconquista** represented a centuries-long attempt to unite Spain and expel Arabs and Jews. In 1469, **Ferdinand V of Aragon** (1452–1516) was married to **Isabella of Castile** (1451–1504), thus uniting the Christian kingdom of Spain. In 1492 (the same year that Columbus landed in America) the combined armies of these kingdoms drove the Moors from Granada and from Europe. Under their reign, Spain remained a loose confederation of separate states. Ferdinand and Isabella worked together to consolidate royal authority and to strengthen the Spanish kingdom. They used the *hermandades,* a local police force, to strengthen royal justice. The Church was also used as a vehicle of state authority. Ferdinand and Isabella revived the **Inquisition** in 1478, a religious court controlled by the monarchy. They monitored and persecuted persons suspected of heresy, especially converted Jews, known as the *marranos* or *conversos*. The Inquisition ultimately led to the expulsion of all Jews. Despite this sanctioned intolerance, by the end of their reign, Ferdinand and Isabella had established a strong central government, which enabled Spain to become a leader in the exploration of Asia and the discovery of the New World in the Americas.

Artistic Achievements of the Renaissance

Renaissance art has the following characteristics:

- It imitates the classical work of Greece/Rome and rejects the medieval forms of art.

- It is very realistic. Artists studied human anatomy in detail and worked from live models. They also created the technique of three-dimensional perspective.

- It portrays secular themes and glorifies the achievements of the individual.

Some Renaissance artists include the following:

- **Giotto** (1267–1337) was born in Florence and helped to make it the first great center of the Renaissance. He is famous for his frescoes (paintings on walls), such as *St. Francis Preaching to the Birds*. His realistic paintings replaced the artificial two-dimensional art represented in the the Middle Ages. He also designed a bell tower, usually called Giotto's Tower, for the Cathedral of Florence.

- **Lorenzo Ghiberti** (1378–1455) was a Florentine sculptor. He is famous for the bronze doors of the Baptistery, a great cathedral in Florence. The ten panels on the door took 21 years to complete and depict realistic scenes from the Bible.

- **Donatello** (1386–1466) was the most influential Florentine artist before Michelangelo. He revived the classical figure of the nude body with its balance and self-awareness. His work, *David,* was the first nude statue of the Renaissance.

- **Leonardo da Vinci** (1452–1519) is known as a "Renaissance man," a person expert in many fields who has a wide range of interests. He was a painter, sculptor, inventor, architect, musician, engineer, and scientist. He dissected human corpses to see how muscles and bones worked. His sketchbooks include plans for a flying machine and underwater boats. His paintings also include *The Last Supper,* which was painted with oil on a plaster wall. His most famous painting is the *Mona Lisa.*

- **Michelangelo** (1475–1564), like da Vinci, was skilled in many areas. He was a sculptor, engineer, poet, painter, and architect. His murals of biblical figures and scenes on the ceiling of the Sistine Chapel are his most famous work. His sculptured masterpiece of the fourteen-foot statue of *David* in the city of Florence is considered a propaganda tool to inspire the citizens in their struggle against Milan. Michelangelo also carved the *Pieta,* showing Mary grieving over the dead Jesus, and designed the dome of St. Peter's Church in Rome.

- **Raphael** (1438–1520) worked in Florence and Rome. He is considered to be the greatest painter of the Renaissance. Although he is famous for his beautiful Madonnas, especially *Sister Madonna,* his fresco, *The School of Athens,* is considered to be the greatest masterpiece of the Renaissance Art. Raphael's realistic portrayal of Aristotle and Plato, combined with God, the Father, holding the globe and St. Augustine dictating the City of God, exemplify the realistic religious themes of the Renaissance. His use of proportion and perspective add to the quality of the fresco.

Raphael's fresco, *The School of Athens*.
© Ted Spiegel/CORBIS

- **Frans Hals** (c1580–1666) painted portraits of everyday life that captured the spirit of the Dutch people. His well-known work, *The Laughing Cavalier,* is probably one of the most reproduced paintings in art.

- **Rembrandt** (1606–1669) is considered the greatest Dutch painter. He is famous for his realism and dramatic use of light and shade. His paintings include religious subjects and scenes from everyday life. His most famous works include the *Night Watch* and *Aristotle Contemplating the Bust of Homer.*

- **El Greco (The Greek)** (1541–1614) was a Spanish artist. He painted religious scenes, such as *The Assumption of the Virgin,* and landscapes, such as *View of Toledo.*

- **Albrecht Dürer** (1471–1528) was a German artist who is famous for his metal and wood engravings. His most noteworthy work is *Praying Hands.*

Chronology of the Renaissance

· 1337–1453	Hundred Years' War between England and France. The war leaves both nations crippled.
c.1353	Boccaccio's *Decameron* becomes the first great prose work of the Renaissance.
c.1390	Geoffrey Chaucer's *Canterbury Tales* becomes one of the first works written in the vernacular, or language of the people, of the author's homeland. England's Chaucer had become familiar with the works of Dante and Boccaccio while traveling in Italy.
1434	Cosimo de Medici establishes his family's dominance in Florence.
c.1450	German Johannes Gutenberg revolutionizes the world of the written word with the introduction of the movable type printing press.
1453	Ottoman Turks capture Constantinople; end of the Byzantine Empire.
1455–1485	The English House of York and House of Lancaster fight each other for political control in the War of the Roses.
1469	Marriage of Isabella of Castile and Ferdinand of Aragon.
1478	The Inquisition is introduced into Spain to control the activity of the *marranos* (Jews who had converted to Christianity).
1485	The Tudor dynasty is established in England with the end of the War of the Roses.
1492	Completion of the Reconquista; expulsion of the Jews from Spain.
1503–1506	Leonardo da Vinci labors on his signature piece, the *Mona Lisa*.
1508–1512	Michelangelo paints the Sistine Chapel ceiling.
1509	Erasmus publishes *In Praise of Folly*.
1513	Niccolo Machiavelli writes *The Prince*.
1516–1519	Desiderius Erasmus produces his Greek and Latin translations of the *New Testament*.
1527	The Sack of Rome by Holy Roman Emperor, Charles V.

Sample Multiple-Choice Questions

1. Which situation contributed most to the beginning of the Renaissance?

   A. Strong rulers censored new ideas.

   B. Europe became increasingly isolated from other regions.

   C. The emphasis on religious uniformity increased.

   D. A wealthy class that supported the arts emerged.

   E. Europe began to discover the writings of St. Thomas Aquinas.

2. An important characteristic of Renaissance Humanists was their emphasis on

   A. accepting ideas based on Confucian thought

   B. the teachings of the Roman Catholic Church

   C. magic and alchemy

   D. the idea that the glorification of the individual was sinful

   E. classical Roman and Greek writings

3. Which of these books describes Renaissance court life and behavior?

   A. Castiglione's *The Courtier*

   B. Machiavelli's *The Prince*

   C. Augustine's *City of God*

   D. Boccaccio's *Decameron*

   E. More's *Utopia*

4. The intellectual and cultural center of the Renaissance was

   A. Florence

   B. Rome

   C. Naples

   D. Venice

   E. Genoa

5. The northern Humanists were different than the southern Humanists because they emphasized

   A. economic gain and materialism

   B. social reform based on Christian ideals

   C. pagan virtues

   D. scholastic dogma over reason

   E. emphasis on democracy as a political system

6. "The question arises about whether it is better to be loved more than feared or feared more than loved. The reply is that one ought to be both feared and loved, but it is much safer to be feared than loved."

   Who would have supported the ideas contained in the above passage?

   A. John Locke

   B. Niccolo Machiavelli

   C. Sir Thomas More

   D. St. Augustine

   E. Castiglione

7. Which is the best description of the War of the Roses?

   A. Civil wars between the English houses of York and Lancaster

   B. A war between England and France

   C. Civil wars between the English king, Henry VI, and the aristocracy

   D. Minor disputes among English gentry

   E. Struggles for democratic rights

8. A common theme running through Erasmus' works was

   A. paganism

   B. Christian education for moral and intellectual improvement

   C. a monastic life of contemplation and divorce from the material world

   D. emphasis on formalism in religion

   E. disloyalty to the church

9. Renaissance men's view of educated women was that they should

   A. be encouraged and given an equal place in society

   B. have a voice in the affairs of the city

   C. not be encouraged in any manner

   D. be allowed to add a social touch to the household, but otherwise remain subservient to men

   E. be treated as equals in all activities

10. A basic idea contained in Sir Thomas More's *Utopia* was:

   A. Evil exists because men and women are basically corrupt.

   B. Political leaders must learn how to manipulate their subjects.

   C. Social order is only an unattainable ideal.

   D. Corruption and war are due to acquisitiveness and private property.

   E. Government derives power from a social contract with the people.

Answers to Multiple-Choice Questions and Explanations

1. **D.** In the fifteenth century a wealthy class of merchants and bankers, such as the Medici family who had amassed large fortunes in Florence, became the major sponsors of Renaissance artists. Art was used as a way to glorify the success of the sponsors and their families. Strong Renaissance rulers were more concerned with developing countries into nations than with censoring new ideas. The Catholic Church, however, was more concerned with censorship, such as in the case of Galileo and Copernicus. Religious uniformity declined in the Renaissance. Writers such as Erasmus criticized some of the abuses of the Church. These criticisms gave rise to the Protestant Reformation, which destroyed the religious unity of Europe. Humanism rejected the Scholastic philosophy of St. Thomas Aquinas and focused on the writings of the Greeks and Romans. Europe became less isolated as it increased trade with Asia and explored new lands in the Americas.

2. **E.** Renaissance Humanists and writers emphasized classical Roman and Greek writings, examining the worldly subjects that the Romans and Greeks had studied. These Humanist writers hoped to use these ancient writings to increase their knowledge about their own times. Petrarch, a Humanist writer, saw the fourteenth century as a rebirth of ancient Roman culture. Humanism was not concerned with the ideas of Confucius nor with magic and alchemy. A basic tenet of Humanism was the importance of the individual as a unique personality capable of fulfilling all of his potential.

3. **A.** Castiglione's *The Courtier* greatly influenced court behavior and was widely read by European gentlemen to learn the social mores and patterns of conduct for elite groups. Machiavelli's *The Prince,* on the other hand, describes the politics of Renaissance Italy. St. Augustine's *City of God* is an expression of Christian historical and religious thought in the third and fourth centuries C.E., which is by far the wrong time period. *The Decameron* is a collection of tales describing sensual and worldly society.

4. **A.** The first literary and artistic manifestation of the Renaissance appeared in Florence, which was an enormously wealthy city. Rome, Naples, Venice, and Genoa never dominated the cultural life of the Italian Renaissance like Florence and the Medici family who ruled during the city's Golden Age.

5. **B.** The northern Humanists promoted social reform based on Christian ideals as a way to develop an ethical way of life combining the best elements of classical and Christian cultures. The Dutch writer Erasmus ridiculed upper class privileges in the hope of getting people to think about reforms in society. He stressed reason over scholastic dogma. Sir Thomas More of England wrote about an ideal country (Utopia) that was free from war, injustices, and poverty. His works did not consider democracy a viable form of government. The northern Humanists based their program on Christian ideals, not economic gain and materialism. They stressed biblical and Christian themes and not the pagan themes characterized by the Italian Renaissance.

6. **B.** Niccolo Machiavelli wrote *The Prince* describing the competitive politics of the Italian city-states. Machiavelli believed that a ruler had to use whatever means necessary to achieve success. For Machiavelli, power was achieved through fear, not by being well-loved. John Locke was an English philosopher who wrote *Two Treatises on Government* in 1690 to justify the Glorious Revolution, which ended absolutism in England. Sir Thomas More wrote *Utopia* about an ideal society. St. Augustine wrote *The City of God* describing how Christianity could lead to a world of peace and perfection.

7. **A.** The Wars of the Roses, the civil war between the houses of York (symbolized by the white rose) and Lancaster (the red rose) disrupted trade, agriculture, and domestic industry. The Wars of the Roses were a struggle between different feudal factions and not between the English king, Henry VI, and the aristocracy or among the English gentry. This civil war was not fought to promote democracy.

8. **B.** One of the fundamental themes in all of Erasmus' scholarly work was the importance of Christian education for moral and intellectual development. The Dutch Humanist Erasmus advocated the "philosophy of Christ, not paganism." Erasmus had been forced to enter a monastery as a young orphan and intensely disliked the monastic life. He did not advocate the formalism, ceremony, or laws of the Church. Even though Erasmus was extremely critical of the Church, he still remained loyal to it.

9. **D.** During the Renaissance, women did receive a better education, but this education was intended to adorn the home of the husband, not to challenge men intellectually. Renaissance men believed that educated women violated nature and thus ceased to be women. They felt they were a threat to male dominance and did not want them to have an equal place in society, a voice in the affairs of the city, or to be encouraged in any manner.

10. **D.** Sir Thomas More promoted the concept that corruption and war were due to society's flawed institutions, such as ownership of private property. His approach was extremely radical in that he contended that society, not the inherently corrupt nature of humanity, was responsible for corruption. Machiavelli, not More, promoted that political leaders should learn how to manipulate their subjects. Exemplified by his *Utopia,* More believed that society could be perfected through the reform of the social institutions that mold the individual. John Locke and Jean Jacques Rousseau, not Sir Thomas More, promoted the belief that government was a contract between government and the people.

The Reformation (1517–1640)

The Protestant Reformation, led by such figures as Martin Luther, Ulrich Zwingli, and John Calvin, was a turning point in the history of Western Europe. Followers of the Protestant Reformation were known as **Protestants** because they protested abuses within the Roman Catholic Church. The protest of these abuses led to a revolution that destroyed the religious unity of Europe and established various Protestant denominations or sects, a large concentration of which were located in Northern Europe.

Protestantism also led to a series of religious wars in Western Europe and to the dominance of religious leaders by political rulers. The underlying tone of the Reformation was one of national pride. Kings questioned whether they had to follow the leadership of a distant pope who lived in Italy. In Germany, local rulers supported Martin Luther's attacks on the church because they saw it as an opportunity to increase their power. Outside of Germany, the Protestant reformer, John Calvin who was influenced by Ulrich Zwingli, had a great impact on the rest of Europe. Calvin's ideas spread from Geneva, Switzerland, to Northern Europe, England, and Scotland. The invention of the printing press after 1450 led to the further spread of the Protestant Reformation. Since books could be reproduced inexpensively and in large quantities, they could be easily obtained throughout Europe, shortly after reformers such as Luther completed them.

The Catholic Reformation, or Counter Reformation — officially launched by the Council of Trent — was an attempt to stop the spread of Protestantism and to end the abuses within the Church. The church re-established its authority and renewed the Inquisition, a secret order of church officials, to rid the church of heretics, Jews, and Moslems. The efforts of the Jesuits under the leadership of Ignatius Loyola led to warfare between Catholics and Protestants throughout the first half of the seventeenth century and created a religious split between the Protestant countries of Northern Europe and the Catholic countries of Southern Europe. Protestantism allowed for greater religious freedom for some individuals but ultimately led to spiritual disunity and political disorganization for Europe.

Background of the Protestant Reformation

The causes of the Protestant Reformation were religious, political, economic, and intellectual.

- **Religious:** Many people were critical of certain church abuses or practices, such as the following:
  - **Simony:** Catholic Church officials sold positions to the highest bidders who used these positions for their own personal gains. Many church leaders also held multiple positions that made it difficult for them to take care of their parishioners.
  - **Immorality:** Many church leaders violated the law of celibacy and neglected their religious duties for more worldly activities.

- **Nepotism:** Catholic Church officials appointed relatives to high offices regardless of their abilities.

- **Sales of indulgences:** The selling of indulgences was a practice that originated in the time of the Crusades. Church leaders sold indulgences as pardons, supposedly to reduce the punishment in the hereafter for certain sins. The sale of indulgences was often used as a way to raise money to fund certain church activities.

- **Clerical ignorance:** The Black Death in Europe in the fourteenth century had destroyed one-third of the population of Europe including many members of the clergy. The Catholic Church was forced to recruit many priests who could barely read or write and knew little or no Latin. Many of these peasant priests were unable to intelligently deal with Luther's challenge.

- **Decline of Church prestige:** People lost respect for the Church because of the **Babylonian Captivity** (1309–1377). During the early 1300s, the papacy came under the influence of the French monarch. In 1305, Philip IV of France persuaded the College of Cardinals to choose a new French bishop as the new pope. Clement V, who wanted to escape the civil wars that were disrupting Italy and was critically ill with cancer, was convinced to settle in Avignon, a small city in southern France. For the next sixty years, the popes lived in Avignon under the control of the French king and never entered the city of Rome. This long period of exile is known as the Babylonian Captivity, after the period of exile of the Jews in Babylon in the 500s B.C.E. The seven popes at Avignon concentrated on monetary and bureaucratic matters to the exclusion of spiritual concerns. Furthermore, the general atmosphere at Avignon of luxury and extravagance also hurt the prestige of the pope.

- **The Great Schism (1377–1417):** There were two different popes who claimed to be pope and the embarrassment of two popes excommunicating each other did little to help the Church. In 1377, Pope Gregory XI ended the Babylonian Captivity when he returned to Rome. However, he died shortly after he returned. After his death, the Roman mobs forced the College of Cardinals to elect an Italian as Pope (Urban VI, who ruled from 1378–1389). Some Cardinals, however, declared that the election was invalid because they had voted under duress. In addition, Urban VI had alienated some members of the Church hierarchy with his proposals to reform the Church. The Cardinals then selected a new pope (Clement VII, who ruled from 1378–1394) who settled in Avignon. The powers of Europe aligned themselves with either Urban or Clement, along political lines. England and Germany recognized Pope Urban VI; Scotland, France, Aragon, Castile, and Portugal recognized Pope Clement VII; the Italian city-states at first recognized Urban and then after being alienated by his reform policies, opted for Clement. In the 1400s, western European leaders were committed to the idea that the Church was ruled not by the pope but by a General Council representing bishops, cardinals, theologians, and lay people. In 1409, the Council of Pisa met to unite the Church behind one pope. It resulted in the election of a third pope, since neither the pope at Rome or in Avignon wanted to resign. In 1414, the **Council of Constance** met in Germany and forced all three Popes to resign. The Council chose Martin V, ending the Great Schism. This period of disunity weakened the political influence of the Church as many Europeans began to feel a greater sense of loyalty to their monarchs rather than to the pope.

- **Failure of Reform Leaders: John Wycliffe** (1328–1384) in England and **Jan Hus** (1369–1418) in Bohemia (today the Czech Republic) were forerunners to Luther. Wycliffe denied the pope's supreme religious authority, translated the Bible into English, and encouraged people to read the Bible themselves. Wycliffe was condemned as a heretic (one who denies the basic teachings of the Church) in 1380 and again in 1384. He was persuaded to moderate his views and received only a mild punishment. He died peacefully in 1384 in retirement. Hus, who advocated ideas similar to Wycliffe, was burned at the stake for his beliefs. Hus's execution led to a rebellion against the church that took years to resolve.

- **Political:** By the sixteenth century, many secular leaders resented the interference of clergy in state affairs and wanted to reduce the Church's influence. These leaders were also jealous of the wealth and power of the Church. National-minded rulers considered the pope to be a foreign ruler.

- **Economic:** Members of the rising middle class, peasants, and rulers disliked Church taxes such as Peter's Pence (a yearly tax on all Christians) and the fact that a good portion was being sent to Rome. Many of the kings also wanted to take control of the vast landholdings of the Church throughout Europe.

- **Intellectual:** The Renaissance, which had weakened a respect for authority, encouraged some people to question the Church's teachings in science, history, and religious dogma. Humanists, especially in Northern Europe, attacked the abuses of the Church. Dutch humanist **Desiderius Erasmus** (1466–1536), who wanted an orderly change, argued for the revival of simple piety based on a renewed study of the Bible. These movements convinced many people that it was time for changes.

Protestant Leaders

Martin Luther

Martin Luther (1483–1546) was a German Augustinian friar and a theologian at the University of Wittenberg. Luther, who had studied for a law degree, underwent a religious conversion in 1505. Caught in a terrible thunderstorm, he promised St. Ann that he would enter the seminary if he survived. He kept his promise and by 1512, received a doctorate in theology. Although a popular teacher at the university, Luther was still troubled by the question of his own salvation and felt that he was not worthy of it. He also believed that salvation was earned by faith, not by good works such as prayers, sacraments, or fasting. Furthermore, Luther had traveled to Rome in 1510 and was shocked by the immoral behavior of the Catholic clergy.

The issue that initiated the Protestant Reformation concerned the sale of indulgences, mentioned earlier in this chapter. Indulgences had often been used as a means of raising money for Church activities. In 1517, **Pope Leo X**, who was eager to construct St. Peter's Basilica in Rome, was hard-pressed for funds. Furthermore, Albrecht, Archbishop of Mainz, had borrowed money from the Fuggers, a wealthy banking family, to pay for a papal dispensation that allowed him to hold several Church positions. Pope Leo X authorized **Johann Tetzel** (1465–1519), a Dominican friar, the right to preach and sell indulgences, the proceeds of which were to go to build the new cathedral at St. Peter's Church and to repay the loan to the Fuggers. One of the popular beliefs of the time, which became Tetzel's slogan, was "As soon as gold in the basin rings, the souls in purgatory spring." This slogan created much business and horrified persons such as Luther, who condemned the sale of indulgences and were critical of the pope getting wealthy from the money collected in Germany. On October 31, 1517, Luther nailed his **95 Theses** (statements) to the door of the castle church at Wittenberg, a medieval way of indicating that an issue should be debated. Pope Leo X initially ignored Luther's pleas for reform and refused to get involved, considering Luther's action a local issue.

From 1517 to1520, Luther wrote a series of works, such as *On Christian Liberty* (1519), *Babylonian Captivity of the Church* (1520), and *Freedom of Christian Man* (1520), which outlined his basic beliefs. These beliefs were:

- **Salvation through faith alone.** Influenced by the words of St. Paul in Romans 1:17, Luther rejected the Church's position that a combination of good works and faith was necessary for salvation.

- **Religious authority rested with the Bible not the pope.** Luther considered the Bible the final authority because each individual could read it and thus determine church doctrine and practices. There was no need for a pope or any higher authority.

- **The church consisted of the entire community of Christian believers.** The Catholic Church identified the church only with the clergy.

- **All work is sacred and each person should serve God in his or her own individual calling.** The monastic or religious life is not better than the secular life.

- **Marriage of clergy should be permitted.** Luther married a former nun and had seven children.

- **Baptism, Communion, and Penance were the only sacraments instead of the seven Roman Catholic Church sacraments (Baptism, Communion, Confirmation, Penance, Matrimony, Holy Orders, and Extreme Unction).** Luther also disagreed with the Church's doctrine of **Transubstantiation** (the idea that the bread and wine of the Eucharist are transformed into the actual body and blood of Christ). Luther supported **Consubstantiation**, the belief that the bread and wine undergo a spiritual change whereby Christ is really present but the elements themselves are not transformed.

- **Secular rulers were the supreme authority in all matters except theological ones.** Political leaders supported Luther's belief because it gave them an opportunity to gain control of the vast church lands and wealth and limited the power of the pope.

In 1520, Pope Leo X issued a **Papal Bull** (or official statement by the pope) demanding that Luther recant his ideas or be burned at the stake as a heretic. In an act of defiance, Luther publicly burned the Bull and claimed that he no longer recognized papal authority. The pope excommunicated him in 1521 and ordered him to appear before the **Diet of Worms**, a meeting of German nobility and the **Holy Roman Emperor Charles V** in Worms, a city along the Rhine. Luther had not been arrested because he was under the protection of **Frederick the Wise of Saxony** who was sympathetic to many of Luther's ideas. At the Diet, Emperor Charles V ordered Luther to recant his beliefs. In dramatic fashion, Luther proclaimed that he would not recant, stating, "to go against conscience is neither right nor safe." Declared a heretic and banned from the Empire, Luther was hidden by his protector Frederick of Saxony and did not leave Germany. In Saxony, he translated the Bible into German, which influenced the spread of his religion. He also organized a new religion, known as Lutheranism, based on his ideas. At the **Diet of Speyer** in 1529, Charles V again ordered that his rulings against Luther and his followers be enforced. Lutheran princes issued a defiant protest (again contributing to the origins of the term "Protestant").

During the 1520s, Lutheranism spread throughout northern Germany, Denmark, Norway, and Sweden, where rulers seized church property and closed down monasteries. The German princes of the North protected Luther from the pope and the Holy Roman Emperor while gaining political power by assuming many of the privileges once reserved for the Church. In southern Germany, Catholicism prevailed in the Rhine Valley in the direct possession of the Hapsburg dynasty, which reached as far north as the Netherlands.

Many peasants in Germany followed Lutheranism because they were suffering economic hardship. The peasants looked to Luther for support, mistakenly believing that Luther's idea of the priesthood of all believers was a call for social justice. Christian liberty for them meant the end of harsh manorial burdens. In 1524, German peasants, excited by the prospects of freedom, demanded an end to serfdom. Bands of angry peasants went about the countryside pillaging and burning and ransacking monasteries. However, Luther was terrified by the **Peasant Revolts** (beginning in 1524) against the feudal system and attacked the extremists in his tract entitled, "Against the Murdering Thieving Hordes of Peasants." He exhorted the nobility to put down the rebellion, which resulted in the death of 70,000–100,000 peasants. Feeling betrayed by Luther, many peasants rejected his religious leadership.

Luther rejected the ideas of a number of other religious sects (which together comprise what is called the **Radical Reformation**) that developed out of his challenge to religious authority. One such sect was the **Anabaptist**, which denied the validity of child baptism and believed that children had to be rebaptized when they became adults. Anabaptists also proposed the radical idea of separation of church and state. Another sect, known as the **Anti Trinitarians**, denied the validity of the Holy Trinity. They rejected the idea that the Holy Spirit could be considered one of three persons in God, saying it had no scriptural validity. Luther was a conservative and supported efforts by the Catholics and Lutherans to persecute those who held these beliefs.

Ulrich Zwingli

Luther's incredible skill with languages and the printing press made his ideas well known outside of Germany. **Ulrich Zwingli** (1484–1531) introduced religious reform ideas in Switzerland, campaigning against church abuses and preaching against all practices that were not found specifically in the Scriptures. Like Luther, Zwingli rejected celibacy, the worship of saints, fasting, and confession, and regarded the Bible — not the pope — as the final authority. However, he disagreed with Luther by denying all the sacraments and insisting that the Eucharist, which he called the Last Supper or Communion, was only a symbol and that Christ was not actually present.

Zwingli set up a theocracy (a government that is led by religious leaders or ruled by someone who is said to have divine authority) from 1523 until 1525. He required church attendance by all citizens and regulated many aspects of their personal lives. Zwingli's brand of Protestantism spread from Zurich to all but five of Switzerland's thirteen cantons. Civil war broke out between Protestants and Catholics. In 1531, Zwingli died in battle fighting a religious war against the Swiss Catholic cantons. In 1531, a peace treaty was signed that allowed each canton to determine its own religion. This agreement served as a model for the other European countries fighting religious wars.

John Calvin

John Calvin (1509–1564) was another influential reformer in Switzerland. Trained as a lawyer, he fled from Catholic France to safety in Geneva because he feared persecution for being a Protestant. In 1536, he published *The Institutes of Christian Religion*. Although he was a generation younger than Luther, he was influenced by Luther's writings, which first appeared in France in 1518. Like Luther, he believed that the Bible was the final authority and salvation was possible by faith alone. However, Calvin had his own views on the power of God and the nature of human beings as well as the role of the state:

- **Predestination:** Calvin viewed man as sinful and corrupt and believed that God had already determined from the beginning who was going to be saved (the Elect) and who was going to be damned. Since God was all-powerful and predetermined our fate, there was no room for free will. Those predestined for salvation could be identified by the virtue of their moral life. In time, the Elect would also be identified by their material and economic success. The belief that poverty was a sign of damnation contributed to the idea known as **the Protestant work ethic** and served as a justification for capitalism. The Calvinist doctrine permitting the charging of interest on loans also helped to support the ideals of capitalism.

- **Unity of church and state:** Unlike Luther, Calvin did not believe that the church should be ruled by the state. He insisted that it should be a moral force in the secular government. Under his theocratic state, Calvinism became the official religion of Geneva. He imposed laws that controlled the religious and secular life of the people. He closed down all the taverns, outlawed card playing or any other forms of amusement, and was intolerant of anyone who did not follow these rules.

During the 1540s and 1550s, Calvinism spread throughout Europe under different names. In Scotland, where John Knox helped to make it a state religion, it was called Presbyterianism. In England, the Calvinists were called Puritans who later brought it to America. In France, Calvin's followers were known as the Huguenots. Many were attracted to Calvinism by its simplicity and strict moral life.

The English Reformation (1517–1640)

In England, political and emotional considerations, rather than religious reasons, were the causes for the reform movement. **King Henry VIII** (who reigned from 1509–1547) led the

English Reformation. In 1509, Henry married **Catherine of Aragon** — the aunt of the powerful Emperor Charles V, King of Spain and the Holy Roman Empire. After twenty years of marriage, Catherine failed to produce a male heir to the throne; all of her sons died in infancy (one daughter, Mary, survived). Henry, meanwhile, had fallen in love with **Anne Boleyn**, a young woman at the Court, that he wanted to marry. As a Catholic, however, he was unable to obtain a divorce. In 1527, Henry appealed to the pope for an annulment, thinking that the pope would grant it because of Henry's past service and the fact that he had written a pamphlet against Luther and had even received the title, "Defender of the Faith."

When **Pope Clement VII** (who reigned from 1523–1534), who was under the control of the Holy Roman Emperor Charles V, refused to grant the annulment, Henry took matters into his own hands. Between 1529 and 1533, Henry used Parliament to dissolve ties with the Church in Rome. Parliament cut off all revenue to Rome and no longer recognized the pope's supreme authority in religious matters in England. In April 1533, Henry appointed Thomas Cranmer as Archbishop of Canterbury, who declared Henry's marriage to Catherine null and void. Henry had already secretly married Anne who was three months pregnant. In September, Anne gave birth to a baby girl (Elizabeth) who later ruled England from 1558–1603 as **Elizabeth I**. Still seeking a male heir, Henry married a total of six more times. His third wife, **Jane Seymour**, finally produced his male heir, Edward, who ruled from 1547–1553 as **Edward VI**.

In 1534, Parliament passed the **Act of Supremacy,** which made the king of England instead of the pope the head of the Church of England. As the leader of the Church of England (known as the Anglican Church), Henry did not change any of the doctrines or rituals except the one regarding the authority of the pope. However, he seized the monasteries, which were Catholic and represented 25% of the country's wealth. He also distributed the Catholic Church's land to the nobles who supported him, while persecuting Protestants as heretics. In 1539, Parliament passed the **The Acts of Six Articles** that made Catholic beliefs obligatory in England. After Henry's death in 1547, there were some doctrinal changes. His son, **Edward VI** (who reigned from 1547–1553), introduced Calvinism. During this time (in 1549), Archbishop Thomas Cranmer prepared the *Book of Common Prayer*. This book, a version of which is still used today, includes the order for all services of the Church of England.

Mary (who reigned from 1553–1558), Edward's half sister and daughter of Catherine of Aragon, tried to restore the links with the papacy but was unsuccessful. Mary had many Protestants killed. She earned the nickname "Bloody Mary" from her opponents. Finally, under Elizabeth, a religious settlement (the Elizabethan Settlement) was worked out in which the Church of England followed a moderate course that provided for a Church of England (or Anglican Church) that was Protestant with Catholic features and made concessions to both Protestants and Catholics:

- Protestant concession: Priests in the Church of England were allowed to marry.

- Catholic concession: The Church of England kept some of the symbols of Catholicism, such as the golden crucifix and rich robes.

The Book of Common Prayer also was revised to be somewhat more acceptable to Catholics. While Elizabeth restored religious peace, she was threatened from Catholic Spain. In 1588, Philip II assembled the **Spanish Armada**, a fleet of 130 ships and 19,000 sailors, who were ready to invade England. When they reached the southwest coast of England in July, the bad weather and the strength of the English fleet defeated the Armada.

The Catholic Reformation

The Catholic Reformation or **Counter Reformation** is the term used to describe the efforts taken by the Roman Catholic Church to combat Protestantism during the sixteenth and seventeenth centuries. The reform of the Church began under the leadership of Pope Paul III (who reigned from 1534–1549). He supported the creation of the **Index of Prohibited Books** in Catholic countries that listed heretical works that Catholics were forbidden to read, including the writings of Desiderius, Erasmus, and Galileo. The Church, under Pope Paul III, also revived the medieval Inquisition (church courts), which put heretics on trial for their religious beliefs and killed many of them.

The centerpiece of the Counter Reformation was the **Council of Trent** (1545–1563), which was convened by Pope Paul III and reaffirmed the dogma of the Church. Its main resolutions were the following:

- The rejection of the Protestant belief that salvation was obtained solely by faith. Salvation, instead, was obtained by a combination of good works and faith.

- The statement that the Bible, Church tradition, and Church law were sources of religious authority and faith. To that end, the individual needs the guidance of the Church in understanding the Bible.

- The reaffirmation of seven sacraments, celibacy, and the monastic life.

- The condemnation of abuses, such as nepotism and simony, within the Church.

- The mandatory seminary education of the clergy in each diocese.

- The call for more religious art. (Some believe that these efforts played a role in the development of the Baroque style of art.)

The **Jesuits (Society of Jesus)** became the spiritual soldiers of the Counter Reformation to combat Protestantism. **Saint Ignatius Loyola** (1491–1556), a former Spanish soldier and nobleman, founded the Jesuits in 1534. They were committed to pious living and Loyola demanded absolute obedience and absolute faith. They were a tight-knit organization and received rigorous training in education and philosophy. The Jesuits played a significant role in upholding the Church's dogma for the following reasons:

- They won political influence as advisors to kings.

- They educated the youth in schools and universities.

- They carried the Christian message to Latin America, Asia, and Africa and preserved Catholicism in southern Germany and much of Eastern Europe.

- They used the Inquisition, especially in Italy and Spain, to suppress heresy, to control Protestantism, and to reassure the dominance of Catholicism.

Although the Council of Trent had re-established the power and influence of the papacy, the Protestant Reformation had dealt the Church a serious blow in the following ways:

- The religious unity of Europe was destroyed.

- Northern Europe (England, Scotland, Wales, Holland, northern Germany, Switzerland, Denmark, Norway, and Sweden) was Protestant and Southern Europe (Southern Germany, Italy, Spain, Portugal, Austria, Hungary, and southern Poland) was predominantly Catholic.

- Civil authority gained control over church authority. The idea that the state was superior to the church in all matters except spiritual led to the rise of nationalism.

- The importance of the individual reading the Bible encouraged the growth of education and the rise of capitalism. Max Weber, a nineteenth-century German sociologist, claims that the Calvinistic stress on hard work and material success as a symbol of salvation contributed to the growth of capitalism in many Protestant countries.

- In the sixteenth and seventeenth centuries, wars of religion erupted in Europe between Protestants and Catholics.

Religious Wars and Revolts

The Reformation resulted in a series of wars between Protestants and Catholics in Germany, the Netherlands, France, and Central Europe.

War in Germany

In 1531, Protestant rulers formed the **League of Schmalkaden** to defend themselves against the efforts of **Charles V**, the Holy Roman Emperor, to establish Catholicism in Germany. Charles V was the most powerful of the Hapsburg rulers and controlled land in Spain, the Netherlands, Austria, and Central Europe. He appealed to the pope for help in trying to regain control of these German provinces, but the pope refused because he resented the Hapsburg's power and still blamed Charles V for the sack of Rome in 1527. After two decades of warfare, Charles was forced to accept the **Peace of Augsburg** (1555), establishing the permanent division of Germany into Lutheran and Catholic areas. In a compromise statement, the ruler accepted the statement "Cius regio, eius religio" ("whose region his religion") that meant the political ruler would determine the religion of the area.

Dutch Revolt Against Spain

In 1556, Charles V retired to a monastery and divided his empire between his brother Ferdinand (who became the new Holy Roman Emperor and received Austria, Hungary, and Bohemia) and his son Philip who received Spain, Milan, Naples, the colonies in the Americas, and the Netherlands. **Philip II** (who reigned from 1556 to1598) was a deeply religious ruler who worked very hard and whose goal was to make Europe Catholic. Philip wanted to impose

55

a more centralized government on the Netherlands as well as strengthen Catholicism in response to the growing strength of Calvinism. He sent the **Duke of Alva** (1508–1583) with 20,000 soldiers to deal with the threat. Alva established the **Council of Troubles** (called the Council of Blood by its opponents) and executed 18,000 people as heretics. He also revived the Inquisition.

At first, the Calvinist and Catholic provinces of the Netherlands united in 1576. They ultimately separated into two sections: the Calvinist Union of Utrecht (modern-day Netherlands) and the Catholic Union of Arras (modern-day Belgium). Led by William of Orange (1533–1584), the Dutch declared their political and religious independence in 1581. After 1584, the English began to support the Dutch rebels with money because they resented Philip's effort to restore Catholicism in England. Spain was driven out of northern Netherlands in the 1590s and the war ended in 1609. In 1648, Spain officially recognized the independence of the northern provinces (Netherlands) but still retained control of the southern provinces (Belgium).

Civil War in France

Francis I (who ruled France from 1515 to 1547) gained control of the French Church when he signed the **Concordat of Bologna** (1516) in which he recognized the supremacy of the papacy in return for the right to appoint French bishops. The settlement established Catholicism as the state religion in France. However, John Calvin's ideas spread in France, especially among the nobles who used Calvinism to support their opposition to the monarchs as a way to gain power. Some also were attracted to the piety of the Calvinist religion in contrast to the corruption and wealth of the Catholic Church. These French Calvinists, known as the **Huguenots**, sought to regain power over a series of weak monarchs. From 1562–1589, a total of nine civil wars occurred for reasons of power among the upper classes and for reasons of religious concerns among the lower classes. On August 24, 1572, the **St. Bartholomew's Day Massacre** resulted in the death of over 20,000 Huguenots and led to civil strife between Protestants and Catholics.

In 1589, **Henry IV of Navarre**, a Calvinist and member of the Bourbon family, became king when Henry III, a Catholic, was assassinated. Henry IV tried to unite France but was unable to convince Paris (a stronghold of Catholicism) to support him. Henry was more interested in political unity than religious unity and converted to Catholicism in 1593. He was allowed to enter Paris and is claimed to have said, "Paris is worth a Mass." In 1598, he issued the **Edict of Nantes,** which granted religious and civil freedom to the Protestant minority. This was the first significant recognition by a major country that there could be more than one legalized religion in a state. The Edict led to a truce in the religious wars in France.

Thirty Years War (1618–1648)

The most important and bloodiest of the religious wars was the **Thirty Years War**. An uneasy truce had existed in Germany since the Peace of Augsburg in 1555. This agreement allowed Lutheran and Catholic rulers to determine the religion of their subjects but it did not make any provisions for the inroads of Calvinism. Catholics were alarmed that the Lutherans were gaining conversions and territory in violation of the settlement. Lutherans feared that the Peace of Augsburg would be undermined by Calvinist and Catholic gains. In the early seventeenth century, Germany was divided into the Protestant Union, which was supported by the English, French, and the Dutch, while Spain and the Hapsburg Empire supported the Catholic League. The Thirty Years War was the first continental war in which all the major European nations were involved. It was a struggle between emperors and the states of Germany; the French and the Hapsburgs; the Spanish and the Dutch; as well as efforts by Denmark and Sweden to extend control over the Baltics. Historians have divided the Thirty Years War into four phases.

Thirty Years War			
Phases	*Causes*	*Highlights*	*Results*
Bohemian (1618–1625) Took place in the modern-day Czech Republic and the Slovak Republic	Calvinists demanded more freedom from Catholic Hapsburg ruler	Defenestration of Prague: Two of the Emperor's officials thrown out of window in Prague during negotiations; Rebels defeated at Battle of White Mountain (1620)	Bohemia becomes Catholic by 1635
Danish (1625–1629)	King Christian IV, Protestant leader of Denmark, intervenes to defend fellow Protestant in Northern Germany	Albert of Wallenstein, leader of the Holy Emperor's (Ferdinand's) forces, scores major victories and defeats the Danes	Edict of Restitution (1629): Calvinism outlawed and Lutherans required to return all Catholic property seized since 1552
Swedish (1629–1635)	Gustavus Adolphus, King of Sweden and Protestant leader, intervenes to support fellow Protestants	Adolphus military genius; dies in Battle of Luetzen (1632); Ends Swede's effectiveness; Swedes supported by French.	Edict of Restitution revoked; Southern Germany remains Catholic; War continues; Cardinal Richelieu of France, provides aid to Sweden as a way to destroy Hapsburg power.
Swedish/French (1635–1648)	French want to destroy Hapsburg power. Religious issues became secondary to political. Cardinal Richelieu wants to keep the Hapsburgs from becoming too powerful.	Coalition of Catholic France and Protestant countries (Holland, Switzerland) fight Catholic Hapsburg; Most destructive phase	Peace of Westphalia ends the Thirty Years War.

The **Peace of Westphalia** (1648) marked an end to the Thirty Years War with the following results:

- The Peace of Augsburg was renewed and Calvinism was recognized.

- The Edict of Restitution was revoked.

- German princes were granted sovereignty and the right to raise armies and conclude alliances with foreign powers. With the power in the hands of 300 princes and no central government, the power of the Holy Roman Empire was ineffective and unification of Germany was delayed until the nineteenth century.

- France and Sweden obtained some territory from the Holy Roman Empire.

- Switzerland and Holland were guaranteed independence free from Hapsburg domination.

- The papacy was denied the right to participate in German religious affairs, a restriction symbolizing the reduced role of the Church in European politics.

As a result of the Thirty Years War, over 8 million of Europe's inhabitants were killed. The entire area of Germany was destroyed and much of its culture was lost. Agricultural areas suffered catastrophically. The Hapsburg and Holy Roman Empire were greatly weakened. The age of religious wars ended permanently and Protestantism was established in Europe. Finally, the concept of the balance of power emerged as a force in international diplomacy, whereby nations went to war with one another, not for religion but to ensure that one power did not dominate the continent.

Chronology of the Reformation

1517	Luther's 95 theses are posted on the door of the Wittenberg Castle.
1519	Luther debates John Ecks, a theologian, on the authority of the pope. Ulrich Zwingli begins his teaching of Protestantism in Switzerland.
1521	Pope Leo I excommunicates Luther. Luther declared an outlaw by Emperor Charles V at the Diet of Worms.
1524	Peasants' rebellion in Germany partly stirred by Luther's writing. Luther condemns their actions.
1527	Henry VIII of England petitions Pope Clement II for a divorce from Catherine of Aragon.
1529	German Lutheran princes meet at the Diet of Speyer to protest imperial decrees against their faith (origin of the term Protestant).

1533	Archbishop of Canterbury Thomas Crammer annuls the marriage of Henry VIII and Catherine of Aragon.
1531	Ulrich Zwingli killed.
1534	The Act of Supremacy recognizes Henry VIII as the head of the Church of England. The English Reformation is complete.
1536	John Calvin publishes *The Institutes of Christian Religion* in Geneva.
1539	Six Articles are passed by the British Parliament reaffirming many sacraments of the Catholic Church.
1540	The Jesuits founded by Ignatius Loyola (1534) are recognized and encouraged by Rome to fight the spread of Protestantism.
1543	John Knox begins the Calvinist Movement in Scotland.
1545	Pope Paul III calls the Council of Trent, which reaffirms traditional Catholic doctrines on seven sacraments and authority of the pope.
1547	Parliament repeals the Six Articles.
1549	The British Parliament adopts the Anglican mass and *Book of Common Prayer* as the models for the new state religion.
1555	Peace of Augsburg allows German princes the right to choose the religion of their subjects. There is no mention of Calvinism.
1558	Elizabeth I of England ascends to the throne and reigns for 45 years.
1568	William of Orange leads a rebellion against Spanish powers.
1584	William of Orange is assassinated.
1588	Spanish Armada is defeated by the English.
1589	Reign of Henry of Navarre (Henry IV of France) begins; he converts to Catholicism in 1593.
1598	Edict of Nantes is passed, granting religious toleration to the French Protestants (the Huguenots).
1618	The Thirty Years War begins.
1620	Holy Roman Emperor Ferdinand II defeats the Bohemians at the Battle of White Mountain.
1632	Gustavus Adolphus, Swedish Protestant King, wins a military victory at Luetzen, though he is fatally wounded.
1648	Peace of Westphalia is signed; Thirty Years War ends.

Multiple-Choice Questions

Pope is no judge of matters pertaining to God's word and faith; the true Christian must examine and judge for himself."

Which of the following was the most likely author of this statement?

A. Martin Luther

B. John Calvin

C. Ulrich Zwingli

D. John Knox

E. Henry VIII

2. Luther believed in all of the following *except:*

A. salvation through faith alone

B. the Bible was the final authority of God's word

C. sale of indulgences to remove punishment for sins

D. priesthood of all believers

E. baptism and communion were the main sacraments

3. A main tenet of Calvinism was:

A. toleration of other religions

B. encouragement of Latin in prayer service

C. concept of a forgiving God

D. concept of predestination

E. only the clergy could interpret the Scriptures

4. The goal of the Peace of Augsburg (1555) was to:

A. resolve the issue of Calvinism

B. end the Thirty Years War

C. restore Catholicism in Germany

D. end the civil war between Lutherans and Catholics in the German states

E. unite the German states

5. The Council of Trent (1545–1563) sought to:

A. Reaffirm basic Catholic doctrines and reform Church abuses.

B. Establish a rapport with Protestant leaders in Northern Europe.

C. Review Catholic dogma to align with changes instituted by Protestants.

D. Allow secular rulers a greater voice in Church affairs.

E. Replace Latin with vernacular in Church services.

6. Luther disagreed with the church's doctrine of Transubstantiation, which means:

A. The belief that the bread and wine undergo a spiritual change whereby Christ is present but the elements themselves are not changed.

B. Salvation is earned by passing through a good-works phase, coupled with ongoing faith.

C. Man has certain basic rights that exist independently of all man-made laws.

D. The idea that the bread and wine of the Eucharist are transformed into the actual body and blood of Christ.

E. Clergy members can and should be encouraged to marry and produce offspring.

7. The Edict of Nantes allows for:

A. recognizing the importance of the military in state affairs

B. granting religious toleration to the French Huguenots

C. providing for religious services for Jews

D. limiting the power of the king in religious matters

E. establishing control of the Estates General over the king

8. "Paris is well worth a Mass" is attributed to:

A. Henry Navarre

B. King Christian IV

C. Gustavos Adolphus

D. Pope Martin V

E. Philip II

9. A major result of the Thirty Years War was:

A. Power of Holy Roman Emperor was weakened.

B. German Catholicism flourished in northern Germany.

C. Different states within the Holy Roman Empire were united.

D. Local German economies became developed.

E. England emerged as a dominant power in Europe.

10. The religious organization that was organized in the sixteenth century to combat the spread of Protestantism was:

A. Society of Jesus

B. Order of St. Francis

C. Order of St. Ursula

D. Order of St. Vincent

E. Order of St. Dominic

Answers to Multiple-Choice Questions and Explanations

1. A. Martin Luther in his 95 Theses denied the Pope's supremacy and claimed that the Bible was the final authority. He asserted that every individual should read and interpret the Bible. Christianity is the priesthood of all believers. Calvin, Zwingli, and Knox all denied the authority of the pope. However, Martin Luther influenced all of these men with his 95 Theses. Henry VIII broke with the pope because of the Church's refusal to grant him a divorce.

2. C. In his 95 Theses, Luther condemned the sale of indulgences. He believed that only through faith could there be salvation. Thus, he rejected the authority of the pope and accepted the Bible as the final authority. Luther also rejected the seven sacraments of the Catholic Church and accepted only baptism and communion. Luther maintained that the clergy was not better than the laity and supported the priesthood of all believers.

3. D. Calvin emphasized the doctrine of predestination. He believed that God had predetermined who was to be saved (the Elect) and who was to be damned and they had no choice in the matter. Calvin believed in an all-powerful, but non-forgiving God. Calvin was not tolerant of other religions and rejected Latin because it was identified with the Catholic Church. He also did not believe that the clergy had any special right to interpret the Scriptures. Only the Elect could interpret the Scriptures.

4. D. The Peace of Augsburg was signed in 1555 after two decades of civil war between Lutherans and Catholics in Germany. This agreement provided a compromise permitting German rulers to choose the religion of their subjects, either Catholicism or Lutheranism. It did not mention Calvinism, did not unite Germany, and did not restore Catholicism. The Peace of Westphalia (1648) ended the Thirty Years War.

5. A. The Council of Trent (1545–1563) reaffirmed basic Catholic doctrines such as papal supremacy and the exclusive right of the Church to interpret the Bible. It also prohibited abuses such as the sale of indulgences and simony (selling of Church appointments). The Council of Trent rejected all compromises with Protestant leaders and sought to increase the power of the papacy and limited the influence of secular rulers in church affairs. The Council of Trent rejected the vernacular and would only accept the Latin version of the Bible, the Vulgate translated by St. Jerome.

6. D. Transubstantiation refers to the idea that the bread and wine of the Eucharist are transformed into the actual body and blood of Christ. Luther instead believed in Consubstantiation, which is the belief that the bread and wine undergo a spiritual change whereby Christ is present but the elements themselves are not changed.

7. B. In 1598, Henry IV issued the Edict of Nantes, which granted religious toleration to the minority French Protestants, the Huguenots. The Edict of Nantes helped to end the civil war between Catholics and Protestants that had engulfed France for 27 years. The Edict did not address issues such as the importance of the military, religious toleration for Jews, nor did it provide any control for of the Estates General over the king. The Edict of Nantes helped Henry IV lay the foundation for French absolutism.

8. **A.** Henry of Navarre was a Calvinist and member of the Bourbon family. In 1593, he converted to Catholicism in order to end the civil war between Catholics and Protestants. Henry was willing to sacrifice his religious principles for political necessity. He was a politique, more interested in political unity than religious unity. King Christian IV (who ruled from 1625–1629) was the Protestant leader of Denmark during the Thirty Years War. Gustavos Adolphus (who ruled from1629–1635) was King of Sweden during the Thirty Years War. Pope Martin V was chosen pope in 1417 in order to end the Great Schism. Philip II (who ruled from 1556–1598) was ruler of Spain.

9. **A.** The Thirty Years War weakened the power of the Holy Roman Empire. Individual German states, numbering over 300, obtained complete independence from the Holy Roman Empire. The treaty also ensured that the emperor would remain an ineffectual force within German politics and that Germany would remain divided for the next 200 years. In Spain, the Hapsburgs became a second-rate power. The Thirty Years War also destroyed the economy of Germany and ensured that Protestants would flourish in northern Germany and Catholicism would flourish in southern Germany. The war also established a balance of power in Europe so that neither France nor England would dominate the continent.

10. **A.** The Society of Jesus was founded in 1534 by Ignatius Loyola. Known as the Jesuits, they became the leading spiritual soldiers fighting Protestantism. The Jesuits controlled the Spanish and Italian Inquisitions that helped to stop the spread of Protestantism. The Order of St. Francis and the Dominicans were founded in the Middle Ages. The Ursuline Order, the first woman's religious group, was founded in 1535.

The Age of Discovery and the Rise of Absolutism and Constitutionalism (1400–1700)

The Renaissance spirit of inquiry not only led to changes in religion, but also led Europeans to explore the outside world. Beginning in the fifteenth century, European nations undertook expeditions to find a direct water route to India, believing that control of the trade route with East Asia would bring vast wealth. Asian traders and Italian merchants from the city-states of Venice and Genoa held a monopoly on the existing trade routes and prices were very high. Many Europeans wanted to bypass the Mediterranean and trade directly with the East as a way to increase profits. Others sought fame and fortune and the titles that went with the exploration of new lands. Finally, some saw these expeditions as an opportunity to spread the glory of God.

Technological development during the fourteenth and fifteenth centuries also contributed to this age of increased exploration. Notable improvements in map making and shipbuilding, which gave rise to the Caravel, a ship with both square and triangular sails that enabled it to sail more effectively against the wind than the square-rigged ships, enabled Europeans to sail farther than ever before. The Caravel also had an improved rudder that enabled it to achieve easier turns than earlier ships, plus a larger cargo area which enabled the Caravel to carry the amount of supplies needed for longer voyages. Navigational improvements, moreover, such as the mariner's compass, the sextant, and the astrolabe, made ocean voyages less dangerous.

The financial capital that was needed to promote these explorations supported the need for strong leadership with the ability to centralize and consolidate power. This consolidation of power contributed to the rise of the absolute rulers who controlled every aspect of their respective governments. In France, the reign of Louis XI (1643–1715) symbolized absolutism at its height. There would be absolute rulers in Eastern Europe like Peter the Great of Russia but none would surpass the power of the French monarch. While France represented the classic model of absolutism, England provided the example of a constitutional parliamentary government, which defined the limits of the king. Spain, similar to France, developed a strong absolutist government, but had a short period of greatness, which ended at the close of the sixteenth century.

The Age of Discovery

Historians have called the period from 1415–1650, the **Age of Discovery**. This term refers to the era's phenomenal advances in geographical knowledge and technology. Portugal, situated on the extreme southwestern edge of the European continent, got a head start in overseas exploration before the rest of Europe. Prince Henry (1394–1460), the son of the Portuguese king, was called the Navigator because of the annual expeditions that he sent down the western coast of Africa. He established a school of navigation along the southwestern coast of Portugal. Prince Henry gathered mapmakers, ship builders, and trained captains at the school to help them perfect their trade. In 1415, he encouraged Portugal to search for a direct water route to India around the coast of Africa. Some important **Portuguese explorers** were the following:

- **Bartholomew Diaz (1450–1500):** In 1488, Diaz was the first man to sail around the Cape of Good Hope in Africa.

- **Vasco Da Gama (1469–1524):** In 1498, Da Gama discovered an all-water route to India by sailing around the tip of Africa, and was the first European to reach India by water. By doing so, he showed it was possible for Europeans to obtain Asian goods without having to use an overland route. In 1502, on a second voyage, Da Gama returned home with Asian spices that were worth more than $1 million in gold and 60 times the cost of the actual voyage. This voyage generated a great deal of excitement in Western Europe.

Portugal gained control of the rich spice trade of the Indian Ocean by overpowering Muslim forts and deploying squadrons of naval ships to defeat the Arab fleets that patrolled the Indian Ocean. A scholar once commented that Christianity came to India on cannon balls. The Portuguese successfully mounted cannons on ships, using them in 1509 to blast open Goa, a port city on India's west coast, and in 1511, Malacca, near modern Singapore. These battles ended Arab domination of the South Asian trade and established a Portuguese foundation for a trading empire for most of the 1500s. In capturing the port city of Malacca, the Portuguese seized the waterway that gave them control of the Spice Island, just west of New Guinea. Portugal's control of these areas broke the old trade route from the East. In 1504, spices could be bought in Lisbon for only one-fifth of what it cost when they had been purchased from the Arabs and Italians.

The success of Portugal inspired Spain to gain a share of the rich trade with the East. However, the Spanish decided to try the westward route rather than down around the Cape of Good Hope to reach the treasures of the East. The Spanish were hoping to beat the Portuguese to the East, which Da Gama had not yet reached, and they also wanted to break the Muslim-Italian monopoly of the spice trade. Some important **Spanish explorers** were the following:

- **Christopher Columbus (1451–1506):** Convinced that he could reach Asia by sailing west, Columbus managed to persuade Ferdinand and Isabella of Spain to provide three ships for a journey. In October 1492, after a 33-day voyage from the Canary Islands, Columbus landed in the Bahamas instead of the East Indies. Undeterred, he named the territory the "Indies." In three subsequent voyages, Columbus explored the entire Caribbean islands.

- **Ferdinand Magellan (1480–1521):** In 1519, Magellan led several ships from Spain, rounded the southern tip of South America, and crossed the Pacific. However, Magellan became involved in a local war between two rival tribes and was killed in the Philippine Islands. By 1522, one of Magellan's ships managed to return to Spain, thereby completing the first circumnavigation of the globe. Magellan's voyage proved that the territory where Columbus landed was not part of the Far East but an entirely new continent. This new island group gave Spain a base from which to trade with China and spread Catholicism in Asia.

The Spanish also sent out **conquistadors** (or conquerors) who sought fame, wealth, and power in the unexplored lands in the New World. These included the following:

- **Hernando Cortés (1485–1547):** Cortés landed in Mexico in 1519. By 1521, he had formed an alliance with the enemies of the Aztec and defeated the mighty Aztec Empire. The Aztecs controlled their vast empire of 38 provinces of central Mexico through terror. Their state religion, the Cult of Huitzilopochtli, which required human sacrifice, led to constant warfare against their neighbors in order to obtain sacrifices for these religious practices. When Cortés arrived in 1519, the provinces were in revolt against the Aztecs who were demanding higher tribute. Thus many of these subjugated people joined the Spanish against the Aztecs.

- **Francisco Pizarro (1476–1541):** Between 1531 and 1533, Pizarro conquered the Inca Empire of Peru and established Spanish control in western Latin America.

Spain's conquests were successful for the following reasons:

- **Superior technology:** The Spanish used armor, horses, and muskets — all of which the Indians had never seen.

- **Introduction of disease:** The Spanish carried diseases, such as measles, mumps, and smallpox, to which the natives had never been exposed and had no natural immunity, thus killing millions.

- **Support:** Spain found allies among the natives, such as the Tlaxcaltec in Mexico, who disliked the Aztecs.

The results of Spain's conquests in the Americas were the following:

- There was an influx of gold and silver from the New World, which contributed to Spain's growth as a major power in the sixteenth century.

- New foods, such as potatoes and tomatoes, were introduced to Europe.

- Europeans began transporting slaves from Africa to the Americas to serve in the mines and farms in the New World. Over ten million slaves were involved in the trans-Atlantic slave trade from 1451 to 1870.

- Diseases destroyed about 25 million, or 80 percent, of the Native Americans. Syphilis appeared in Europe for the first time in 1493 because sailors and settlers returned to their homelands infected with this disease.

The Rise of Absolutism in France

The foundation of French absolutism was established in the seventeenth and eighteenth centuries. The following people helped achieve the foundation of French absolutism:

- **Henry IV (b. 1553, ruled 1589–1610):** The **Duke of Sully** (Maximilian de Bethune, 1560–1641), Henry IV's chief minister, established economic growth and financial stability for France, reducing the crushing debt that had accumulated during the religious wars between Catholics and the Calvinists (Huguenots) by reforming the tax system and tax collection. The Duke also instituted a program of economic improvement by constructing new roads and bridges that improved transportation and promoted economic prosperity. Henry IV strengthened the power of the monarch by limiting the power of the nobles over the regional parliaments. In 1610, Henry IV was assassinated by a fanatic who thought that Henry was a menace to the Catholic Church.

- **Louis XIII (b. 1601, ruled 1610–1643):** Louis was only nine years old when he became king. His mother, Marie de Medici, replaced the Duke of Sully and ran the government inefficiently until her son was 23, spending money lavishly on court expenditures as well as pensions to discontent nobles. In 1617, Louis XIII forced his mother into retirement because she had excluded him from running the government even though he had been declared of age in 1614. They were reconciled in 1624 and she was able to secure the appointment of her protégé, Cardinal Richelieu. (At this time, religious leaders held official positions in the government in many Catholic countries.) By 1630, she became jealous of Richelieu's influence and urged Louis to dismiss him. Instead, the king sent his mother into exile and she never returned to France. Afterwards, the king gave full support to Richelieu, who was appointed prime minister.

- **Cardinal Richelieu (1624–1642):** Richelieu's goal was to establish the supremacy of the king and French domination of the European continent. He achieved these objectives by destroying the fortified castles of the French nobles, which had long been a symbol of their independence. He also crushed the political power of the Huguenots. When the Huguenots revolted in 1625, Richelieu personally supervised the siege of their walled city, La Rochelle, and forced it to surrender. By the Peace of Alais in 1629, the Huguenots were allowed to keep their religion but they lost their fortified cities, military, and territorial rights. Richelieu did not want the Huguenots to ever again be able to defy the king and then withdraw behind a strong defense. Through his spy system, he efficiently destroyed any conspiracy that threatened royal power. By the use of the **intendant system**, he transferred local government functions from the nobles to royal officials, further weakening the power of the nobles. The intendants were royal officials who collected taxes, recruited soldiers, and carried out government policies in the provinces. All of these officials regularly communicated to Richelieu. He also levied taxes without the consent of the Estates General, the French parliament. All these steps served to strengthen the power of the king. In foreign affairs, Richelieu involved France in the Thirty Years War, supporting the Protestants in order to weaken the domination of the Hapsburgs and establish French control on the continent.

- **Louis XIV (b. 1638, ruled 1643–1715):** Louis was only four when his father died and his mother Queen Anne selected **Cardinal Mazarin** as Prime Minister. Mazarin, resented by the people because he was Italian, continued Richelieu's strategies for centralizing power; however, he lacked Richelieu's shrewdness. Mazarin's attempts to increase the royal revenue led to civil wars, called the **Fronde**, that lasted intermittently from 1649 to 1652. The term *fronde* means a slingshot and *frondeurs* were originally mischievous street children who threw mud or shot rocks at passing carriages of the rich. The term came to symbolize anyone who opposed the policies of the government. In 1649, a bitter civil war ensued between the monarch and the **Frondeurs** (the nobility and the middle class). Riots wrecked Paris and violence continued intermittently for a number of years, resulting in Louis XIV and Cardinal Mazarin fleeing the city. However, internal differences between the nobles and the middle class and the overall chaos in the country contributed to Louis XIV's eventual return. The Frondeurs had no systematic program other than the overthrow of Mazarin.

The rebellions had a traumatic effect on Louis XIV, who became convinced that the sole alternative to anarchy and the power of the nobles was to establish an absolute monarchy. After the death of Mazarin in 1661, Louis became his own prime minister and adopted the ideal of the **Divine Right of Kings.** This concept had been developing in France since the sixteenth century. According to Bishop Jacques Bossuet, one of Louis' advisers, the king was chosen by God to rule, and only God had authority over the king, not a parliamentary body or any group of nobles. This Divine Right Theory of rule provided the justification for the absolute sovereignty of Louis and his monarchy. Louis' statement, "L'Etat c'est moi" (I am the state) represents his belief that there was no higher authority that could ever control him.

During Louis XIV's 72-year reign, France became a dominant power in Europe. European countries envied France's success in industry and agriculture. **Jean Baptiste Colbert** (1619–1683), Louis' able finance minister, helped revive trade and the economy. While he did not invent the system of mercantilism, discussed later in the chapter on "Mercantilism and the Agricultural/Industrial Revolution," he rigorously applied it to France. To advance prosperity, Colbert promoted good farming methods, internal improvements (roads and canals), support of both old and new industries, and the creation of a strong merchant marine, which enabled France to establish trading posts in North America as well as Asia. Colbert's goal was to make France self sufficient by centralizing the economy through government control of trade and industry.

Louis XIV also sought to control religion, believing that more than one religion could not exist and that religious unity was essential for absolute control. In 1685, he revoked the **Edict of Nantes**. He destroyed Huguenot schools and churches and took away their civil rights. The Huguenots escaped France and settled in Holland, England, and America. Many of those who fled were craftsmen and business people and their loss hurt the French economy.

Louis kept France at war for much of the time that he ruled. He pursued an aggressive foreign policy, wanting France to achieve its natural boundaries along the Rhine River. To this end, Louis created a personal army that was employed by the state instead of the nobles. The French armies were able to gain some territory in Germany and its surrounding areas. France was engaged in the following wars: the War of Devolution or the First Dutch War (1667–1668); the Second Dutch War (1672–1678); and the War of the League of Augsburg (1681–1697). By the end of the Fourth War, the **War of the Spanish Succession** (1702–1714), fought because of Louis' efforts to lay claim to the Spanish throne for his grandson, the European countries of Holland, Great Britain, and Austria were able to contain Louis' territorial ambitions. In 1713, France signed the **Peace of Utrecht**, which forbade the union of France and Spain, stating that the two countries could not be ruled by the same monarch. The treaty also made Louis XIV's grandson, Philip IV, the new king of Spain. The treaty ended French expansionism and left France on the brink of bankruptcy.

The reign of Louis XIV is considered the Golden Age of France. French became the language of polite society and replaced Latin as the language of diplomacy and scholarship. Louis, who was referred to as the Grand Monarch or the Sun King because like the sun he was the center of all power, was a strong patron of the arts. He loved the stage and encouraged writers like Molière, Racine, and Louis De Rouvroy Saint-Simon to pursue their crafts. The French style of classicism and fashion were the models for all of Europe.

Louis XIV's palace at Versailles influenced the architectural style of Europe. It was built 12 miles outside of Paris, at a cost of over $100 million, and filled with 1400 fountains — this palace served as a fundamental tool of state policy under Louis. He was able to control the nobles who were forced to live at Versailles and also used the elaborate architecture to impress his subjects and foreign visitors. Versailles became a reflection of French genius. Peter the Great of Russia and Frederick the Great of Prussia would try to model their palaces on the one in Versailles. By the time of Louis' death in 1715, France was the leading nation on the European continent. However, his extravagant life style at Versailles burdened the peasants with taxes, the long war emptied the treasury, drained the manpower of the country, and held back economic development of the country.

The Rise of Constitutionalism in England

While France witnessed the rise of Absolutism in the 1600s, England would develop a parliamentary system of government limiting the power of the king. The foundation for the development of constitutionalism in England was established in the Middle Ages. The **Magna Carta** (1215) limited royal power by stating that the king could not tax without the consent of the Grand Council (consisting of the nobility and the high clergy). The Grand Council later evolved into the Parliament, which alone levied taxes. By the 1300s, the Parliament or the Grand Council included middle-class representation. Because the enlarged council served as a model for England's future legislature, it is often called the **Model Parliament**. By the fourteenth century, Parliament had compelled English monarchs to accept guidelines on the question of taxes as well as other issues. In the fifteenth century, after the War of Roses (1455–1485), **Henry Tudor** established the Tudor Dynasty following the defeat of Richard III of the House of York in 1485, becoming **Henry VII** (b. 1457, ruled 1485–1509) after he married Elizabeth of York and was crowned King.

The Tudors

After the death of Henry VII, **Henry VIII** (b. 1491, ruled 1509–1547) and **Elizabeth** (b. 1533, ruled 1558–1603) strengthened the power of the Tudor monarchy by governing intelligently and following a popular foreign policy. The Tudors were successful because they skillfully mastered Parliament by outwardly consulting it, but actually dominating the legislature. They also aided the middle class by providing law and order and encouraging trade. In 1603, the Tudor dynasty ended when Elizabeth died childless. Her cousin King James Stuart of Scotland (James VI) ascended to the throne.

The Stuart Monarchs

James I (b. 1556, ruled 1603–1625) created resentment and hostility by telling Parliament at their first session that his power could not be challenged. Although the king had the power to summon and dismiss the Parliament, he needed its support to raise money for additional revenue that was beyond his ordinary expenses. Parliament refused to grant him additional revenue. James I squandered his revenue on an extravagant lifestyle at the court and was unable to live within the fixed and customary level of the crown. From 1610–1611, James I and Parliament were involved in continuous debates on how to finance the government.

In religious matters, the **Puritans** (a Calvinist sect) viewed James I as the enemy. They wanted to purify the Anglican church of all traces of Catholicism. In 1604, when they petitioned James I to reform the Church of England, James refused to make any changes. James I presided at the **Hampton Court Conference** (1604). The goal of the conference was to examine the different versions of the English Bible, which had been translated from the original Hebrew and Greek. From this conference, originated the movement from which came the authorized **King James Version** of the Bible, the first edition of which appeared in 1611. James I also followed an unpopular foreign policy of friendship with Catholic Spain.

Like his father James I, **Charles I** (b. 1600, ruled 1625–1649) wanted to rule by the Divine Right. Yet Charles was more politically inept than his father, running into friction with Parliament when they refused to grant him a lifetime of custom duties, instead granting him a one-year period. Charles used his wife's dowry to fight a war against Spain, which was a failure. However, when he needed additional money for his military expedition against Spain, he requested a forced loan from his wealthier subjects. Several members of the gentry refused to vote for the loans and Charles threw them into jail. In 1628, Parliament again declined to give Charles additional resources unless he signed the **Petition of Rights,** which forbade the king to do the following:

- Levy taxes without the Parliament's consent

- Proclaim martial law in peacetime

- Imprison anyone without a specific charge

- Quarter troops in the home of private citizens without their permission

Charles ended up signing the petition in order to get his funds. Charles ruled without the Parliament for eleven years (1629–1640).

In 1637, Charles tried to impose Anglican practices on Calvinist Scotland. They revolted and Charles was forced to call upon Parliament, referred to as the **Short Parliament** because it lasted only three weeks, to raise money for the war against the Scots. They turned down his request unless Charles addressed their grievances. The Scots defeated Charles' army and invaded northern England. The Scots demanded money in order to leave Scotland. Thus, in 1640, Charles again appealed to the Parliament for money. This Parliament, known as the **Long Parliament** because it lasted 20 years, managed to pass laws limiting the power of the king. The king was compelled to summon Parliament every three years and could not dissolve Parliament without its consent. Parliament also impeached Charles' chief advisors, supporting what was known as the **Grand Remonstrance**, a list of 204 Parliamentary grievances from the past decades. In 1642, Charles I charged five Parliament members with high treason and tried to arrest them. When Parliament refused to hand the members over, the king decided to personally arrest them. The five members fled, having received information in advance. Parliament then demanded sole command of the military forces. Charles refused and in August he fled London to Nottingham to recruit and gather his army, declaring war against Parliament. The English Civil War had begun.

Highlights of the English Civil War (1642–1649)

The English Civil War concerned religious differences and also centered on whether authority or sovereignty rested in England with the monarchy or the Parliament. It had two phases: Phase I (1642–1646) and Phase II (1646–1649).

The participants in the English Civil War were:

- **Cavaliers** or **Royalists:** These were supporters of the king. This group consisted of the wealthy landowners, the Anglican clergy, and the Catholics.

- **Roundheads:** These were supporters of the Parliament. This faction was generally made up of the middle class, merchants, small nobility, Puritans, and the Presbyterian Scots who had opposed Charles' efforts to impose his religion on them.

Phase I (1642–1646)

At first, the Cavaliers gained victory until Scotland intervened on the side of Parliament and **Oliver Cromwell** (1599–1658), a Puritan leader in Parliament, emerged as a leader. Cromwell organized the **New Model Army** composed of well-paid and disciplined soldiers. In 1644, Cromwell's Model Army defeated Charles and the Royalists at Marston Moor. In 1646, Charles gave himself up to the Scots, who turned him over to Parliament, which was led by Cromwell.

Phase II (1646–1649)

The victors then quarreled among themselves. The Presbyterian wing of the Puritan movement, supported by the Scots, decided to set up a constitutional monarchy, with Charles at the head and Presbyterianism as the established church. They were opposed by the army — which was more radical than Parliament and wanted a republic — some of whose members, like Cromwell, were Independents who favored some religious toleration for all groups except Catholics and were opposed to Presbyterianism as the established church. To add to the confusion, Parliament refused to pay the troops. Charles took advantage of this situation between Parliament and the army and fled London. In 1647, the Scots allied with Charles, who promised that he would support Presbyterianism in England. In August, 1648, the Scots invaded England but the army, led by Cromwell, defeated them at the Battle of Preston. Charles was captured. The second civil war had made Cromwell the undisputed leader. In 1648, the **Rump Parliament** was established which removed all Presbyterian members and was under the control of Cromwell. After a formal trial, Charles I was accused of treason and condemned to death. Charles I was beheaded on January 30, 1649. The Civil War was over.

From 1649–1653, the Rump Parliament claimed to have supreme power. The monarchy was abolished and a **Commonwealth**, a Republican form of government, was established. In 1653, Cromwell expelled the Rump Parliament because the Parliament was lax in paying the troops, had been accused of accepting bribes, and filled vacancies in Parliament by nominations and not by elections. In 1653, Cromwell took the title of Lord Protectorate and established a military dictatorship. He suppressed rebellions in Ireland and Scotland, advanced English trade, and greatly increased English power. However, Cromwell's rule did not gain popular support as people resented the severe moral code of the Puritans. The Anglicans, who were more numerous than the Puritans, also opposed Cromwell's policy of intolerance. When Cromwell died in 1658, people were tired of his stern military rule and deposed his son Richard in 1660. Charles II, son of Charles I, was invited to return from exile and accept the throne.

The Stuart Restoration (1660–1688)

Mindful of his father's fate, **Charles II** (b. 1630, ruled 1660–1685) pledged to work with Parliament. He accepted the Parliament's right to levy taxes and agreed to call Parliament into regular sessions. During his reign, the Cavalier Parliament restored the Church of England as the official church. In 1670, Charles signed a secret treaty with Catholic France in which he received subsidy in return for some vague promise that England may become Catholic. In 1673, Parliament passed the **Test Act**, which excluded all Catholics from public office. It also tried to pass a law excluding James, Charles' Catholic brother, from inheriting the throne; it failed. At this time, Parliament was divided into two groups: the **Whigs**, who wanted a constitutional monarchy under a Protestant king; and the **Tories**, who supported the king, but feared the restoration of Catholicism. The Whigs, fearful of Charles II's pro-Catholic tendencies, did what they could to limit his power. In 1679, under the control of the Whigs, the Parliament passed the **Habeas Corpus Act**. This act prohibited imprisonment without due cause and guaranteed a fair trial.

Upon the death of Charles II in 1685, **James II** (who reigned from 1685–1688), assumed the throne. As a converted Catholic, James antagonized the Parliament by appointing pro-Catholic ministers to important posts, which angered the Whigs who supported the Church of England. James' efforts to set up a standing army created fears among the Tories. When the wife of James gave birth to a son, Parliament was fearful that Catholicism would be re-established in England.

The Glorious Revolution

In 1688, Parliament secretly offered the English crown to **William**, the Protestant ruler of Holland, and his wife **Mary**, the Protestant daughter of James II. They accepted. When William arrived in England, James II fled to France. In 1689, Parliament proclaimed William and Mary the new king and queen of England, under the conditions that they accept the **Declaration of Rights**, which later was enacted into law as the **Bill of Rights**. This bloodless overthrow of the previous monarch in 1688 is called the **Glorious Revolution** because there was such little violence.

The Glorious Revolution had the following effect upon English government:

- It ended the Divine Right Theory in England.

- It re-established the principle of supremacy of the Parliament over the monarch.

- Parliament passed the **Bill of Rights** (1689), a series of laws stating that the king could not levy taxes, make laws, or maintain an army without the consent of the Parliament. People were guaranteed basic civil liberties such as freedom of speech, right to petition, protection against excessive bail or unusual punishment.

- English rulers had to be Anglican.

- It laid the foundation for the constitutional monarchy. Over the centuries, the British monarchy would be permitted to reign, but not to rule completely.

The Golden Age of Spain and Its Decline

In the sixteenth century, Spain became a rich and powerful country as a result of its vast empire in the new world. **Charles V** (b. 1500, ruled 1519–1556), Charles of Hapsburg, was the grandson of King Ferdinand and Queen Isabella. As king of a united Spain and the Holy Roman Empire, he was the most powerful ruler of Europe during the first half of the sixteenth century. He controlled lands in Spain and its colonial empire as well as the Netherlands, Southern Italy, Austria, and other lands in central Europe.

Charles V abdicated the Spanish throne to his son, **Philip II** (b. 1527, ruled 1556–1598). Throughout his reign, Philip, who considered himself the champion of Catholicism, was involved in religious wars resulting from the Protestant Reformation. The country's wealth was drained as Philip tried to halt the Reformation. He was unable to put down the Dutch revolt because they wanted to practice their own religion. In 1588, the defeat of the seemingly invincible **Spanish Armada** prevented an invasion of England and ended all efforts to restore Catholicism, as well as Spain's dominance of the sea. Spain lost large portions of their empire to England and Holland. Royal expenditures increased but income from the Americas suffered. Spanish kings seem to lack the will to reform. By the middle of the seventeenth century, Spain was no longer considered a great power.

During the sixteenth century, Spain did produce one of the world's greatest literary masterpieces. **Miguel de Cervantes** (1547–1616) wrote **Don Quixote**, a book that describes the fabric of Spanish society in the sixteenth century. The main character, Don Quixote, a knight, lives in a world of dreams traveling around the countryside seeking military glory. Cervantes is considered the greatest of all Spanish authors. In English, the term *Quixote* means idealistic, but impractical. This term describes Spain in the seventeenth century.

Chronology of the Age of Discovery and the Rise of Absolutism and Constitutionalism

1415	Prince Henry the Navigator establishes his school of navigation.
1445	Portuguese conquer Cape Verdi, Africa.
1488	Bartholomew Diaz reaches the Cape of Good Hope.
1492	Christopher Columbus sails for India.
1493	Pope Alexander VI establishes the Line of Demarcation. Spain receives everything west of the line between Azores and Cape Verdi. Portugal receives everything east of the line between Azores and Cape Verdi.
1494	Treaty of Tordesillas moves the Papal Demarcation Line of 1493 west to give Brazil to Portugal.
1497	Giovanni Cabazo (John Cabot) explores Nova Scotia, Newfoundland, and New England.
1500	Pedro Cabra reaches Brazil.
1513	Vasco Nunez de Balboa reaches the Pacific.
1519–1522	Ferdinand Magellan becomes the first man to circumnavigate the globe.
1519	Hernando Cortés conquers the Aztecs of Mexico.
1531–1533	Francisco Piazza conquers the Incas of Peru.
1534–1541	Jacques Cartier explores the St. Lawrence River in Canada.
1542–1543	The Portuguese land in Japan.
1558	Elizabeth I of England ascends to the throne as the last Tudor monarch.
1588	Spanish Armada, under Philip II is defeated by the English Navy.
1589	Henry of Navarre becomes King Henry IV and begins the Bourbon Dynasty.
1603	James VI of Scotland, cousin of Elizabeth I, becomes James I of England, the first Stuart king.
1610	Louis XIII and Cardinal Richelieu reign.
1618	Thirty Years War begins.
1625	Charles I becomes king.
1629	Charles accepts the Petition of Rights prohibiting taxation without parliamentary approval.
1637	Charles I forces a new prayer book upon Scotland's Presbyterians.
1643	Louis XIV becomes king of France.
1648	Peace of Westphalia ends Thirty Years War.

1649	Charles I is beheaded on charge of treason.
1653	Oliver Cromwell establishes Commonwealth of England.
1658	Oliver Cromwell dies.
1660	Restoration: Charles II becomes king.
1685	Louis XIV revokes the Edict of Nantes.
1688–1689	Parliament disposes James II and replaces him with Protestant leader William of Orange and wife, Mary; bloodless overthrow is known as the Glorious Revolution.
1689	Peter the Great becomes Czar of Russia.
1715	Louis XIV dies.

Sample Multiple-Choice Questions

1. Which of these events during the Age of Exploration was a cause of the others?

   A. Europeans brought food, animals, and ideas from one continent to another.

   B. European diseases had an adverse effect on the native populations of new territories.

   C. Warfare increased as European nations competed for land and power.

   D. Advances in learning and technology made long ocean voyages possible.

   E. Christianity was brought to the Native Americans.

2. Which of these explorers was the first to reach India by sailing around the Cape of Good Hope to India?

   A. Prince Henry the Navigator

   B. Bartholomew Diaz

   C. Vasco Da Gama

   D. Christopher Columbus

   E. Ferdinand Magellan

3. "The person of the king is sacred, and to attack him in any way is an attack on religion itself. Kings represent the Divine Majesty and have been appointed by Him to carry out His purposes. Serving God and respecting kings are bound together." –Bishop Jacques Bossuet

   The author of this statement would most likely believe in

   A. natural rights

   B. the Divine Right of Kings

   C. theocracy

   D. democracy

   E. constitutional monarchy

4. Which person would most agree with the above statement?

   A. Henry IV of France

   B. Oliver Cromwell of England

   C. Elizabeth I of England

   D. Louis XIV of France

   E. Henry VIII of England

5. Louis XIV was able to control the nobility by

A. working closely through the Estates General

B. appointing them to higher positions within the government

C. gaining their support for his foreign policy

D. requiring them to live at the Versailles for at least part of the year

E. gaining the support of the Huguenots

6. Cardinal Richelieu was able to establish absolute control for Louis XIII of France by all of the following except

A. destroying the castles of the nobles

B. levying taxes without the consent of the Estates General

C. disbanding the Intendant System

D. eliminating the nobility from any government position

E. crushing any group of nobles who threatened royal power

7. James I of England strongly believed in

A. the supremacy of Parliament

B. religious freedom

C. the Divine Right of Kings

D. majority rule

E. constitutional monarchy

8. Which is the best way to describe Oliver Cromwell's Protectorate?

A. constitutional monarchy

B. democracy

C. Puritan military dictatorship

D. absolute monarchy

E. parliamentary democracy

9. Historians refer to the English Revolution of 1688–1689 as Glorious because:

A. It was a bloodless and successful revolution.

B. It allowed the Stuarts to stay in power.

C. It restored the Puritans to office.

D. It established democracy.

E. The king gained power at the expense of the nobility.

10. Therefore, the Parliament declares:

"That the (king's) pretended power of suspending laws . . . without consent of Parliament is illegal. That levying money (taxes) for or to the use of the crown (king) . . . without grant (consent) of Parliament . . . is illegal."

This seventeenth-century excerpt can be found in the

A. English Bill of Rights (1689)

B. Declaration of the Rights of Man and the Citizen

C. Napoleonic Code

D. Magna Carta

E. Locke's Two Treatises of Government

Answers to Multiple-Choice Questions and Explanations

1. **D.** The Renaissance spirit of inquiry and the development of navigational devices such as the compass and astrolabe made better navigation possible for Europeans. Advances in geographic knowledge due to the improvement in the field of cartography also encouraged explorers to venture farther away from home. Finally, new and improved ships such as the Caravel provided the vessels that Europeans needed to launch their voyages. The Age of Exploration led to the Columbian exchange in which Europe brought horses, cattle, and sheep to the Americas and returned with corn, potatoes, peanuts, and tobacco. Europeans also brought diseases to the Americas such as smallpox. These advances also contributed to the Europeans engaging in a series of wars from the sixteenth to the eighteenth centuries. They were caused partly by colonial rivalry. The English defeated the Spanish Armada in 1588 and England and France fought in four major wars. Missionaries also saw exploration as a struggle to convert Native Americans to Christianity.

2. **C.** Vasco Da Gama rounded the Cape of Good Hope and sailed on to India. He established trading posts at Goa and Calicut. In 1487, Bartholomew Diaz rounded the Cape of Good Hope at the southern tip but storms and a threatened mutiny forced him back. Prince Henry the Navigator set up a school for sailing that inspired Portugal to search for all water routes around Africa to the East. Christopher Columbus sailed west and landed in the Bahamas while Ferdinand Magellan circumnavigated the globe in 1522.

3. **B.** Bishop Bossuet believed in the Divine Rights Theory. This theory was used to justify unlimited royal power. Bishop Jacques Bossuet summed up the theory in his book, *Discourse on Universal History* (1681). Bossuet claimed that the king was an agent of God and his authority to rule came directly from God. The king was entitled to unquestioning obedience. The Divine Rights Theory rejects the Natural Rights Theory, which supports the idea that we are given basic rights from God, not the king. In a democracy and in a constitutional monarchy, power is derived from either the people or a constitution (set of laws) which outline the limits of the government. Theocracy is a government ruled by religious leaders, not the king.

4. **D.** Louis XIV would most agree with this statement. Louis XIV ruled France from 1643 to 1715, and believed in the Divine Right of Kings. He said, "I am the State" and took the sun as his symbol of power. He ruled out the Estates General, which is the French Parliament, and crushed opposition to his government. During his 72-year reign, France became the center of culture and Louis also built the Versailles Palace, which became the perfect symbol of the Sun King's wealth and power. John Locke was a seventeenth century English philosopher who proposed the social contract theory. According to this theory, a king ruled with the consent of the people and his power was not unlimited. If a king violated the rights of his people, they had a right to overthrow him. Henry IV of France founded the Bourbon Dynasty. He strengthened the monarchy but did not base it on divine right. Oliver Cromwell was a Puritan leader who ruled through his army and not divine right. Henry VIII and Elizabeth I believed in absolute rule but worked with Parliament.

5. D. Louis XIV required all the great nobility of France to live at the Versailles Palace, at great cost to the Royal Court. The nobles were free from paying any taxes. Left at their own estates, the nobles could be a threat to the power of the monarch. By luring the nobles to Versailles, he turned them into courtiers, battling for privilege rather than power. Louis never called a meeting of the Estates General and appointed members of the upper middle class, not the nobles, to high positions of power within the government. Louis also never needed the support of the nobles for the war. In 1685, he revoked the Edict of Nantes, which had granted the French Huguenots religious toleration. Louis XIV exiled many of the Huguenots, and others fled to Holland and the Americas. He wanted their support only if they converted.

6. C. Cardinal Richelieu did not eliminate the Intendant System. He introduced the institution of the intendants, state-appointed officials. These officials held a wide range of powers over the local area that they administered. The intendants were used to enforce royal orders in the provinces and to weaken the power and influence of regional nobility. Richelieu destroyed the fortified castles, which had long been a symbol of noble independence. Although a few nobles held important offices, a majority of state officials were members of the middle class. Richelieu crushed aristocratic conspiracies ruthlessly.

7. C. James I (1603–1625) of England believed in the Divine Right Theory. According to James, the monarch had a divine responsibility only to God. Rebellion is the worst form of political crime. He rejected the supremacy of the Parliament, rule by the majority or a constitutional monarchy. James believed that there were no privileges and immunities that could stand against a divinely appointed God. James I rejected religious toleration and the demands of the Puritans to change the Church of England. He wanted them to conform or he claimed he would chase them out of England.

8. C. Oliver Cromwell was designated as a Lord Protectorate in 1652 to restore law and order. He ruled as a military dictator through his army. Cromwell levied heavy taxes, divided England into twelve military districts, and proclaimed quasi-martial law. He ruled until his death in 1658. Cromwell's government was not a parliamentary democracy since all power in his government resided in him.

9. A. The Glorious Revolution was a bloodless and successful revolution. In 1689, Parliament secretly offered the English crown to William, the Protestant ruler of Holland and his wife Mary (Protestant), daughter of James II. Parliament was fearful that James II would re-establish Catholic rule in England. When William and Mary accepted and arrived in England, James II fled the country. Parliament proclaimed William and Mary the new king and queen. This relatively bloodless revolution ended divine-right rule in England and established the supremacy of Parliament. The Glorious Revolution ended the Stuart's power, did not restore the Puritans to office, or establish democracy. The Glorious Revolution provided for a constitutional monarchy in which the king's power was limited and not increased at the expense of the nobles. The wealthy landowners through Parliament were the dominant force in the government.

10. A. This seventeenth-century excerpt is found in the English Bill of Rights. This excerpt rejected the idea that the king is an absolute ruler. In 1689, James II of England was forced to abdicate his throne because of his Catholicism and his wish to become an absolute ruler. The British Parliament invited William and Mary to rule provided that they agreed to sign a series of acts that became known as the Bill of Rights. This bill limited the power of the king to repeal any law, levy taxes, or maintain an army without the consent of Parliament. The monarch also agreed not to interfere with parliamentary election and debates. The people were also guaranteed basic civil rights. The Bill of Rights guaranteed the superiority of Parliament over the king. The National Assembly of France in 1789 issued the Declaration of the Rights of Man and the Citizen. It proclaimed that the government rested on the consent of the people not on the divine rights of the king. This declaration ended the absolutism of Louis XVI and turned France into a constitutional monarchy. The Napoleonic Code was laws that consolidated the achievements of the French Revolution such as social equality, religious toleration, and trial by jury. The Magna Carta (1215) was signed by King John and was passed to protect the feudal nobles against the tyranny of the king. John Locke's *Two Treatises on Government* was written to justify the Glorious Revolution and that government was organized to protect the life and liberty of all.

The Scientific Revolution and the Enlightenment (1500–1780)

The Scientific Revolution of the sixteenth and seventeenth centuries changed the way educated people looked at the world. It evolved from the Renaissance's stress on the importance of individuals to understand the world around them, and was the key factor that moved Europe from a worldview that was primarily religious to one that was primarily secular. Although a more secular society was likely not their goal, Luther's and Calvin's attacks against the authority of the pope provided a powerful example of how to challenge traditional authority. Their questioning attitudes produced an environment that encouraged the inquiry necessary for science to flourish.

Science in the Middle Ages was designed to help a person reach a better understanding of God and not the world. A medieval scientist would have found it inconceivable to examine the universe outside the realm of religion. During the Renaissance from the 1300s up until the early 1500s, science was still considered a branch of religion, and scientific thought held that the earth was a stationary object at the center of the universe. Beginning with Copernicus, however, who taught that the earth revolved around the sun, Europeans began to reject the Aristotelian-medieval scientific thought. Copernicus, Galileo, and Newton developed a new concept of a universe based on natural laws, not a mysterious God.

The new scientific approach promoted critical thinking. Nothing was to be accepted on faith. Belief in miracles and superstition was replaced by reliance on reason and the idea that rational thinking would uncover a plan governing the universe. This critical analysis of everything in society from religion to politics and the optimism that the human mind could find the solution to everything was known as the **Enlightenment**. Sixteenth- and seventeenth-century intellectuals, writers, and philosophers were optimistic that they could change society for the better. Writers, such as David Hume and Emil Kant, were primarily interested in teaching people how to think critically about everything, while philosophers, such as Voltaire, Montesquier, Rousseau, Smith, and Diderot, were not revolutionaries but reformers who criticized the existing social, political, and economic structure in order to improve them. They found their hope in **Enlightened Despots**, or monarchs, the most important of which were Frederick the Great of Prussia, Joseph II of Austria, and Catherine the Great of Russia, who would improve the life of their subjects and increase knowledge. However, the reforms of society were not accomplished by these despots, but came instead by the revolutionary forces instrumental in the French Revolution at the end of the eighteenth century.

The Scientific Revolution

To understand how the Scientific Revolution dramatically altered how society viewed the world and the role of man in society, you must realize that the medieval worldview was ruled by the ideas of the third-century B.C.E. Greek philosopher, Aristotle, the second-century B.C.E. Egyptian philosopher, Ptolemy, and theologians. Their ideas had been recovered during the

Middle Ages as Western Europe began to trade with the East. Medieval theologians, such as St. Thomas Aquinas, brought these writings into harmony with Christian doctrines. The Aristotelian view of the world supported the Ptolemaic view of a motionless earth at the center of the universe, and this world was made up of four elements: earth, air, fire, and water. This view offered a common-sense approach for the Christians, who put human beings at the center of the universe. Although widely accepted during the Renaissance, the traditional view of science began to be questioned by various rulers, such as Florence's Medici family, who supported the investigations of Galileo.

The views of Aristotle and Ptolemy were shattered by **Nicholas Copernicus** (1473–1543). In his book *On the Revolutions of the Heavenly Spheres* (not published until after his death in 1543 because he feared the ridicule of fellow astronomers), Copernicus suggested that the sun was the center of the universe and that the earth and planets revolved in circular orbits. This **Heliocentric Theory** that the sun — and not the earth — was the center of the universe contradicted contemporary scientific thought and challenged the traditional teachings of hundreds of years. Copernicus' book had enormous scientific and religious consequences. By characterizing the earth as just another planet, he destroyed the impression that the earthly world was different from the heavenly world. Religious leaders understood the significance of Copernicus's findings all too well; of him, Luther is reported to have said, "The fool wants to turn the world of astronomy upside down." Calvin, like Luther, also condemned Copernicus. The Catholic Church, however, reacted slowly and did not declare Copernicus' theory false until 1616, continuing to hold to the view that the earth was the center of the universe. The slow reaction of the Church reflected the slow acceptance of Copernicus' theory. Other events created doubts about traditional astronomic ideas as well, such as the discovery of a new star in 1572 and the appearance of a comet in 1577. These events began to dramatically alter the acceptance of the earth as a motionless object.

Copernicus' ideas influenced others in the field of science. A Danish astronomer, **Tycho Brahe** (1546–1601), set the stage for the study of modern astronomy by building an observatory and collecting data for over twenty years on the location of the stars and planets. His greatest contribution was this collection of data, yet his limited knowledge of mathematics prevented Brahe from making much sense out of the data.

Johannes Kepler (1571–1630), a German astronomer and assistant to Brahe, used his data to support Brahe's data and Copernicus' idea that the planets move around the sun in elliptical, not circular, orbits. Kepler's three laws of planetary motion were based on mathematical relationships and accurately predicted the movements of planets in a sun-centered universe. His work demolished the old systems of Aristotle and Ptolemy.

While Kepler was examining planetary motion, **Galileo Galilei**, a Florentinian (1564–1642), continued the attack on traditional views of science. Using observation rather than speculation to help him formulate ideas — such as his laws on the motion of falling bodies — Galileo established **experimentation**, the cornerstone of modern science. He applied experimental methods to astronomy by using the newly invented telescope. Using this instrument he discovered the four moons of Jupiter, and that the moon had a mountainous surface, much like the earth. His discovery destroyed an earlier notion that planets were crystal spheres (the earth was the center of the universe and around it moved separate transparent crystal spheres: the moon, the sun, five planets, and fixed stars), and challenged the traditional belief in the unique relationship between the earth and the moon. Galileo's evidence reinforced and confirmed the theory of Copernicus. Following the publication of his book, *Dialogue on the Two Chief Systems* (1632), which openly criticized the works of Aristotle and Ptolemy, Galileo was arrested, imprisoned, and tried for heresy by the Papal Inquisition and was forced to publicly recant his views. In modern times, Galileo's trial has come to symbolize the conflict between religious beliefs and scientific knowledge.

The greatest figure of the Scientific Revolution was **Sir Isaac Newton** (1642–1727), an Englishman. He integrated the ideas of Copernicus, Kepler, and Galileo into one system of mathematical laws to explain the orderly manner in which the planets revolved around the sun. The key feature of his thesis was the **law of universal gravitation**. According to this law, every body in the universe attracts every other body in precise mathematical relationships. Newton's law mathematically proved that the sun, moon, earth, planets, and all other bodies moved in accordance with the same basic force of gravitation. Such proof showed that the universe operated by rules that could be explained through mathematics and that a religious interpretation was not the sole means of comprehending the forces of nature.

The Scientific Revolution also led to a better way of obtaining knowledge. Two important philosophers were **Francis Bacon** (1561–1626), and **Rene Descartes** (1596–1650). Both were responsible for key aspects in the improvement of scientific methodology. Francis Bacon was an English politician and writer, who advocated that new knowledge had to be acquired through an **inductive** reasoning process (using specific examples to prove or draw conclusion from a general point) called **empiricism**. Bacon rejected the medieval view of knowledge based on tradition, and believed instead that it was necessary to collect data, observe, and draw conclusions. This approach is the foundation of the scientific method.

Rene Descartes was a French mathematician and philosopher who stressed inductive reasoning. He believed that it was necessary to doubt everything that could be doubted. His famous quote — "Cogito ergo sum"; "I think therefore I am" — proved his belief in his own existence and nothing else. He believed that, as in geometry, it is necessary to use inductive reasoning and logic to determine scientific laws governing things. Descartes' view of the world (called today **Cartesian Dualism**) reduced natural law into matter and the mind, or the physical and the spiritual. Bacon's inductive experimentalism and Descartes' inductive, mathematical, and logical thinking combined into the scientific method, which began taking hold of society in the late seventeenth century.

Some consequences of the Scientific Revolution include the following:

- A scientific community emerged whose primary goal was the expansion of knowledge. Learned societies like the French Academy of Science and the Royal Society of London were founded to promote the growth of scientific ideas among different countries.

- A modern scientific method arose that was both theoretical and experimental and its practitioners refused to base their conclusions on traditional and established sources or ancient texts. The belief that human reason was the vehicle that would unlock the secrets of the universe ended the dominance of religion on society. The Age of Reason in the eighteenth century, with its faith in the rational and skeptical mind, would provide the background for the Enlightenment.

There was little linkage, however, between science and technology. The Scientific Revolution had little effect on daily life before the nineteenth century. The revolution in science in the sixteenth and seventeenth centuries was primarily an intellectual one.

The Enlightenment

The Scientific Revolution was the single most important event that fostered the creation of a new intellectual movement in the late seventeenth and early eighteenth centuries called the **Enlightenment**, or, sometimes, the **Age of Reason** — a time period defining the generation that came of age between the publication of Newton's ideas in 1687, and the death of Louis XIV in 1715. The Enlightenment's core of thought was that natural law could be used to examine and understand all aspects of society.

The Enlightenment's leaders believed that by using scientific method they could explain the laws of society and human nature. It was an optimistic creed — armed with the proper methods of discovering the laws of human nature, Enlightened thinkers were convinced they could solve all problems. They believed it was possible to create a better society and people and that progress was inevitable. They were free from the restraints of religion and focused instead on improving economic and social conditions. Consequently, the movement was profoundly secular.

Some important Enlightened thinkers include the following:

- **Thomas Hobbes (1588–1679):** An English writer, Hobbes was influenced by the experimental attitude toward nature and decided to apply it to politics. Writing at the time of the English Civil War, Hobbes was forced to flee London to Paris in 1648 because he feared for his life. In 1651 he wrote *Leviathan,* a title he chose after the sea monster from the biblical book of Job. Hobbes believed that humans in their original state of nature were unhappy. In the state of nature, Hobbes asserted that man was quarrelsome, turbulent, and forever locked in a war against all. He supported an absolute monarch (although he did not support the Divine Right Theory of government) because he thought that man needed protection from destroying himself and an all-powerful ruler was the best source of such protection. Thus, man enters a social contract to surrender his freedom to an absolute ruler, in order to maintain law and order. The subject could never rebel and the monarchs had the right to put down any rebellion by any means possible.

  Hobbes's ideas never won great popularity. In England, Royal Absolutism, a cause he supported, never gained acceptance. He was overshadowed by his contemporary John Locke.

- **John Locke (1632–1704):** Like Hobbes, Locke was interested in the world of science. His book, *Two Treatises on Government* (1690) was written as a philosophical justification for the Glorious Revolution, which refers to the bloodless overthrow of James II in 1689 and the end of absolutism in England. This work translated his belief in natural law into a theory of government that became known as **The Social Contract**. Locke argued that man is born basically good and has certain natural rights of life, liberty, and property. To protect these natural rights, people enter into a social contract to create a government with limited powers. Locke believed that if a government did not protect these rights or exceeded its authority, the people have a right to revolt, if necessary. Locke's ideas of **consent of the governed**, social contract, and the right of revolution influenced the writing of the United States *Declaration of Independence* and the U.S. Constitution. Locke's ideas also laid the foundation for the criticisms of absolute government in France.

It was in France that the Enlightenment reached its highest development. Some of the reasons for this were the following:

- French was the international language of the educated class.

- In addition to being the wealthiest and most populous country, France was the cultural center of Europe.

- Although critical books were often banned by the French censors and their authors jailed or exiled, the writers were not tortured or executed for their statements. Thus, the French intellectuals battled powerful forces but did not face the overwhelming difficulties of writers in Eastern or Central Europe.

The French used the term **philosopher (Philosophes)** to describe the thinkers of the age. The philosophers were committed to bringing new thought to all of Europe. They wanted to educate the economic and social elite but not necessarily the masses. Philosophers who were not allowed to criticize either the church or state openly, circulated their work in the form of books, plays, novels, dictionaries, and encyclopedias, using satire and double meaning to spread their messages and thus prevented their writings from being burned or banned. **Salons**, gatherings organized by wealthy women held in large drawing rooms in their homes, were also used to help philosophers avoid trouble with authorities. At these meetings, philosophers would gather to discuss politics, philosophy, and current issues. These discussions allowed the writers greater freedom to spread their words. Enlightened thinkers considered themselves part of an intellectual community. They shared their ideas through books, personal letters, and visits back and forth amongst themselves.

Some of the important French philosophers were the following:

- **Baron de Montesquieu (1689–1755):** A French aristocrat who wanted to limit royal absolutism. In his book, *The Spirit of Laws* (1748), he urged that power be separated among three branches of government: executive, legislative, and judicial. Each branch would check the other branches, thus preventing despotism and preserving freedom. Montesquieu admired the British system of government and was critical of the absolutism of the French monarchy because all power was concentrated on one person. His theory of the separation of powers greatly influenced the framers of the United States Constitution.

- **Voltaire (1694–1778):** Born François-Marie Arouet, Voltaire is considered to be the greatest of all the Enlightened philosophers. Educated by Jesuits, he challenged the authority of the Catholic Church. Although he believed in God, his God was a distant deistic God—a clockmaker who built an orderly universe and then let it operate under the laws of science. Voltaire hated religious intolerance, urged religious freedom, and thought that religion crushed the human spirit. In his book, *Candide,* he wrote against the evils of organized religion, and in his *Treatise on Toleration,* he argued for religious tolerance. Voltaire denounced organized religion because it exploited people's ignorance and superstitions.

Deism was intended to construct a more natural religion based on reason and natural law. His most famous anti-religious statement was "Ecrasez l'infame," "Crush the horrible thing."

In 1717, he was imprisoned in the Bastille for eleven months, after which he was forced to live in exile for three years in Great Britain, a period of time that greatly influenced the rest of his life. Like Montesquieu, Voltaire came to admire Britain's system of government. He praised their limited monarchy, respect for civil liberties, and freedom of thought. He promoted freedom of thought and respect for all. Typical of his outlook is the statement attributed to him: "I disapprove of what you say, but I will defend to the death your right to say it." Voltaire became a European celebrity who in 1743 lived in the court of Frederick the Great of Prussia, and became a supporter of Enlightened Despotism.

- **Jean Jacques Rousseau (1712–1778):** Like other Enlightened writers, Rousseau was committed to individual freedom. However, he attacked rationalism and civilization, considering them to be destroying rather than liberating man. Instead, spontaneous feeling was to replace and complement the coldness of intellectualism. According to Rousseau, man was basically born good and needed protecting from the corrupting influences of civilization. These ideas would later greatly influence the Romantic Movement of the nineteenth century, which rebelled against the culture of the Enlightenment.

Rousseau's book, *The Social Contract,* published in 1762, begins with the famous line, "All men are born free but everywhere they are in chains." He believed that as social inequalities develop, people enter into a social contract agreeing to surrender their individual rights to the community and the general will, or the will of the majority, in order to be free — thus creating a government as a necessary evil to carry out the general will. If the government fails, people have the right to replace it. Although Rousseau's concept of the General Will appealed to democrats and nationalists after the French Revolution of 1789, it has also been used by dictators like Adolf Hitler to justify totalitarian rule by claiming that a dictator or one-party ruler speaks for the General Will to which all citizens owe obedience.

In 1762, Rousseau also published *Emile,* a book that stirred controversy because of its attacks on civilization and its new theory of education. He criticized education that focused on the development of reason and logical thinking and advocated greater love, tenderness, and understanding towards children. Rousseau argued for more humane treatment of children and for children to develop naturally and spontaneously. Children had to explore nature as a way to raise their emotional awareness. *Emile* helped to change the educational and child rearing practices in eighteenth-century Europe.

- **Denis Diderot (1713–1784):** Diderot published his writings and the ideas of many Enlightened philosophers in his *Encyclopedia* (1751). This 25-volume collection of political and social critiques, which included writers such as Voltaire and Montesquieu, attacked abuses of the French government, including religious intolerance and unjust taxation. The *Encyclopedia* was an example of the eighteenth-century belief that all knowledge could be organized in a systematic and scientific fashion. Diderot hoped that this information would help people to think and act rationally and critically.

The **Physiocrats** were economic thinkers in eighteenth-century France who developed the first complete system of economics. Like the Philosophes, the Physiocrats looked for natural laws to define a rational economic system. However, the Physiocrats, unlike the Philosophes, were close to the government as advisors. Some famous Physiocrats include the following:

- **François Quesnay (1694–1774):** Quesnay was the French leader of the Physiocrats and a physician to Louis XV. He supported a hands-off, or laissez-faire approach to the government's involvement in the economy.

- **Adam Smith (1727–1790):** He was a Scottish economist. While not an actual Physiocrat member, Smith had met with the Physiocrats on the continent and adopted and refined many of their ideas. In his *Wealth of Nations,* published in 1776, the same year as the U.S. *Declaration of Independence,* Smith argues against strict government control of mercantilism. He outlined the nucleus of the economic system that came to be known as **capitalism**. Smith believed in a hands-off, or **laissez-faire** approach to business. He argued that individuals should be left to pursue their own economic gain. The role of the state is to act as a policeman who intervenes only when necessary. Smith thought that the invisible hand of supply, demand, and competition would ensure that people would act in the best interest of everyone.

Enlightened Despotism

Many philosophers believed that Enlightened reform would come by way of Enlightened monarchs. **Enlightened Despots** were rulers who tried to justify their absolute rule by claiming to rule in the people's interest by making good laws, promoting human happiness, and improving society. Encouraged and instructed by philosophers like Voltaire who did not trust the masses and believed that change had to come from above and not from the people, the monarchs of Prussia, Russia, and Austria were able to mesh their need for a more effective state with the need for economic, educational, and social reform. The most notable Enlightened Despots of these countries were the following:

- **Frederick the Great (b. 1712, ruled 1740–1786) of Prussia:** As King of Prussia, Frederick invited Voltaire to his court and sought his advice on how to be an Enlightened ruler. He did away with the torture of accused criminals, improved the educational system, allowed his subjects to believe as they wish in religion, and promoted industry, agriculture, and commerce. He was an efficient statesman and made Prussia into the best-ruled nation in Europe. Emmanuel Kant (1724–1804) of Germany, the greatest German philosopher of his age, suggested that Frederick was an Enlightened ruler because he allowed freedom of the press and gave Catholics and Jews permission to settle in Prussia.

- **Peter the Great (b. 1672, ruled 1682–1725) of Russia:** He was a contemporary of Louis XIV of France. Technically, he might not be considered an Enlightened Despot because he never tried to justify his absolutism by claiming to rule in the people's interest. Nevertheless, he was responsible for trying to make Russia a part of Europe after centuries of domination by the Mongols. Peter's efforts to Westernize Russia included introducing his country to Western ideas in science, education, military training, and industry. He ordered his male subjects to shave their traditional long beards and discard their oriental garments. He also extended control over the Russian Byzantine Church. Western artisans were invited to the country and, with their workers, helped to build a new seaport on the Gulf of Finland called St. Petersburg, "his window to the West." This seaport provided a trade route with Western Europe.

- **Catherine the Great (b. 1729, ruled 1762–1796) of Russia:** The German wife of the Russian czar, Peter III, Catherine deposed her husband and ruled as an autocrat. She read the works of Montesquieu and Voltaire and imported Western culture to Russia. She also revised and codified Russian law, patronized the arts, created hospitals, and undertook other public welfare projects. The Pugachev serf uprising of 1773 led her to reverse her trend toward reform of serfdom and return to nobles the absolute control of their serfs.

- **Maria Theresa (b. 1717, ruled 1740–1780) of Austria:** She realized upon inheriting the throne that Austria was weak and began a series of reforms. She established a national army, limited the power of the Catholic Church, revised the tax system and the bureaucracy, and reduced the power of the lord over the serfs. She also improved the educational system.

- **Joseph II (b. 1741, ruled 1780–1790) of Austria:** Joseph II furthered the reforms of his mother, Maria Theresa. He abolished serfdom and introduced a single tax for everyone, a Physiocratic idea. He granted religious tolerance to Calvinists and Lutherans, and eliminated many of the restrictions on Jews. Joseph abolished capital punishment, reformed the educational and judicial system, and established hospitals. After his death, his brother **Leopold II** (b. 1740, ruled 1790–1792) was forced to back away from these reforms as a way to quell a series of peasant and aristocratic revolts.

Chronology of the Scientific Revolution and the Enlightenment

1543	Posthumous publication of *On the Revolution of the Heavenly Spheres* by Copernicus.
1590	The first microscope is made by Zacharias.
1605	Publication of *The Advancement of Learning* by Sir Francis Bacon.
1608	Telescope is invented.
1609	Publication of *On the Motion of Mars* by Johannes Kepler.
1616	The Catholic Church bans Copernicus' ideas.
1628	Publication of William Harvey's theory of blood circulation.
1632	Publication of *Dialogues on the Two Chief Systems of the World* by Galileo.
1633	Galileo imprisoned for heresy.
1637	Publication of Rene Descartes' *Discourse on Method*.
1642–1646	Civil War in England.
1642	Birth of Isaac Newton.
1651	Thomas Hobbes' *Leviathan* is published.
1655	Evangelist Torricelli constructs the first mercury barometer.
1682	Edmund Halley observes a "new" comet.

1687	Publication of Isaac Newton's *Principia*.
1690	John Locke publishes *An Essay* concerning human understanding.
1694	François Arouet (Voltaire) is born.
1712	Jean Jacques Rousseau is born.
1734	Voltaire publishes *Letters on the English*.
1739–40	David Hume publishes *The Treatise of Human Nature*.
1743	Antoine Lavoisier, "father of modern chemistry" is born.
1740	Baron de Montesquieu publishes *The Spirit of Laws*.
1751	Denis Diderot publishes first volume of the *Encyclopedia*.
1756	Wolfgang Amadeus Mozart is born in Austria.
1759	Voltaire publishes *Candide*.
1762	Catherine the Great begins her rule in Russia.
1768–1771	*Encyclopedia Britannica* is published.
1776	America's Declaration of Independence; Adam Smith publishes *The Wealth of Nations*.

Sample Multiple-Choice Questions

1. During the Scientific Revolution and the Enlightenment, the works of many scientists and philosophers were similar in that they

   A. relied heavily on the idea of medieval thinkers

   B. favored an absolute monarchy as a way of improving economic conditions

   C. received support from the Catholic Church

   D. supported the Divine Right Theory of government

   E. examined natural laws governing the universe

2. Which statement was a belief of many writers of the Enlightenment?

   A. The wealthy class should govern society.

   B. Democracy was the best form of government.

   C. Kings are responsible only to God.

   D. Ideas can be proven by reason.

   E. Traditional values were important.

3. Which of the following European rulers cannot be considered an Enlightened monarch or despot?

   A. Catherine the Great

   B. Maria Theresa of Austria

   C. Joseph II

   D. Frederick the Great

   E. Elizabeth I

4. John Locke and Jean Jacques Rousseau would be most likely to support

    A. a return to feudalism in Europe

    B. a government ruled by a divine right monarchy

    C. a society ruled by the Church

    D. the right of citizens to decide the best form of government

    E. a government ruled by Enlightened Despots

5. The Heliocentric Theory of the universe was proposed by

    A. Aristotle

    B. Descartes

    C. Copernicus

    D. Kepler

    E. Ptolemy

6. "In every government, there are three sorts of power . . . when the legislative and executive are united in the same person or in the same body of magistrates, there can be no liberty because . . . the same monarch or senate . . . (may) enact tyrannical laws." The author of this passage was:

    A. Montesquieu

    B. Bossuet

    C. Voltaire

    D. Hobbes

    E. Louis XIV

7. Voltaire's statement "Ecrasez l'infame" (crush the horrible things) refers to:

    A. the government of Louis XIV

    B. the Catholic Church

    C. the military

    D. the middle class

    E. the poor

8. Which of the following writers is correctly paired with one of his major works?

    A. Adam Smith — *Leviathan*

    B. Voltaire — *Emile*

    C. Jean Jacques Rousseau — *Essays on Human Understanding*

    D. Baron Montesquieu — *Social Contract*

    E. Denis Diderot — *Encyclopedia*

9. "Every individual generally neither intends to promote the public interest, nor knows how much he is promoting it. . . . . He is . . . led by an invisible hand to promote an end, which was no part of his intention." This passage reflects the ideas of

    A. Adam Smith

    B. Thomas Hobbes

    C. Baron Montesquieu

    D. John Locke

    E. Jean Jacques Rousseau

10. The phrase "Cogito ergo sum" (I think therefore I am) has been attributed to:

    A. Galileo Galilei

    B. William Harvey

    C. Rene Descartes

    D. Johannes Kepler

    E. Sir Francis Bacon

Answers to Multiple-Choice Questions and Explanations

1. **E.** Scientists of the sixteenth and seventeenth centuries believed that by using reason and observation one could determine the natural laws that governed the universe. The English scientist Isaac Newton, for instance, calculated the natural law of gravity to help explain the operation of the forces of nature. The philosophers of the eighteenth-century Enlightenment believed that science and reason could explain the laws of society, and in their writings tied together the ideas of the Scientific Revolution. Both scientists and philosophers of this period rejected the ideas of the Middle Ages, which they believed were based on superstition and not reason. They also challenged the authority of the Catholic Church, which had rejected the ideas of Copernicus and Galileo, and were critical of the Divine Right Theory. These scientists and philosophers instead supported absolute monarchs who promoted economic and social progress for the people.

2. **D.** A belief of the Enlightenment was that ideas can be proven by reason. In the eighteenth century, French philosophers believed that one could use reason to understand the universe and rejected traditional ideas based on authority. They also believed that government existed not for the wealthy but was a social contract between the people and the government. Most of the *Philosophes* opposed democracy. According to Voltaire, the best form of government was a monarchy or Enlightened Despot. They also rejected the notion that the king was responsible only to God. These writers criticized traditional values that were based on superstition and blind obedience to the past.

3. **E.** Elizabeth I (1558–1603), Queen of England, was born before the era of the Enlightened Despot. She preserved Protestantism in England and achieved world power for England. Catherine the Great of Russia, Maria Theresa of Austria, Joseph II of Austria, and Frederick the Great of Prussia were Enlightened Despots. They justified their absolutism by claiming to govern in the people's interest, and sought to advance society by promoting social justice. Catherine the Great encouraged legal reforms; Maria Theresa created a system of compulsory education in every community; Joseph II wanted to make all persons equal before the law; and Frederick the Great promoted religious freedom.

4. **D.** John Locke and Jean Jacques Rousseau would be most likely to support the citizens' right to decide the best form of government. Locke and Rousseau believed that people entered into social contracts to protect their basic rights and create a government; hence Enlightened Despotism was anathemic to their way of thinking. According to Locke, if the government fails to live up to its obligations, people have a right to change it. Rousseau asserted that people make the laws and the rule of the majority is supreme. Both philosophers were widely influential: Locke's ideas influenced the framers of the U.S. Constitution, while Rousseau has been hailed as a champion of democracy for advocating that political authority lies with the people. Neither of these writers supported a society governed by the Catholic Church; instead, they rejected feudalism and challenged the Church's authority.

5. **C.** Copernicus proposed the Heliocentric Theory of the universe, which stated that the earth revolved around the sun and that the sun was the center of the universe. Aristotle was a

Greek philosopher who believed that a motionless earth was fixed at the center of the universe. Descartes was a French scientist and mathematician who today is considered the founder of analytic geometry. Kepler, a German astronomer and mathematician, determined that planets follow an elliptical not a circular path about the sun. Ptolemy was an Egyptian astronomer who placed the earth as a stationery object with the sun revolving around it.

6. **A.** The author of this passage is Montesquieu, who argued in his work *The Spirit of Laws* that governmental power had to be separated among three branches: executive, legislative, and judicial, each checking the other, instead of permitting power to be concentrated in one person, the king. This type of government would prevent despotism. Bossuet and Louis XIV believed in a Divine Right Theory in which all power was bestowed on the king by God. Voltaire believed in Enlightened Despotism and was a member of the Court of Frederick the Great. Hobbes claimed that only an absolute ruler with unlimited power could restore order to society.

7. **B.** Voltaire's statement refers to the Catholic Church. Although educated by Jesuits, Voltaire was critical of the perceived bigotry and narrow-mindedness that he felt was at the core of all religious tradition. He was a deist who believed that God created the universe and then allowed it to act according to scientific law. Concerning answer choices **A, C, D,** and **E,** Voltaire wrote *The Age of Louis XV* in 1745 and portrayed him as a dignified ruler. Voltaire did not write about the military but did praise the poor for their simple piety.

8. **E.** Denis Diderot is correctly associated with the *Encyclopedia* which was a collection of political and social articles written by various Enlightened writers (Voltaire, Montesquieu, and Rousseau). These articles attacked the abuses that existed in France prior to the French Revolution. The other answer choices are incorrect for the following reasons: Adam Smith wrote *The Wealth of Nations,* Voltaire wrote *Candide,* John Locke wrote *Essay on Human Understanding,* and Rousseau wrote *Social Contract.*

9. **A.** This passage reflects the ideas of Adam Smith in *The Wealth of Nations* (1776). Smith's ideas embodied a policy called laissez faire, which enabled the bourgeoisie to further its own economic interests but also increased the national wealth. Smith argued that the "invisible hand" of free competition for one and for all disciplined the greed of selfish individuals and provided the most effective means of increasing the wealth of both rich and poor. Hobbes believed in absolute government. Montesquieu proposed that separation of powers provided the best form of government. Locke and Rousseau promoted the Social Contract theory of government in which the government was formed to protect the rights of the people.

10. **C.** Rene Descartes was the French scientist and mathematician who wrote *Discourse on Mathematics,* in which he claimed that all experience is validated by observation of natural phenomena. Descartes stripped away his belief in everything except his own existence. The other answers choices are wrong for the following reasons: Galileo Galilei's observation of the heavens confirmed Copernicus' theory; William Harvey was an English physician who demonstrated that blood circulated through the body; Johannes Kepler was a German astronomer whose observations showed that the planets followed an elliptical orbit around the sun; and Sir Francis Bacon popularized the scientific method of observation.

The Age of Revolution: The French Revolution and Napoleonic Era

In 1789, France was widely considered a nation to be envied. It was the center of the intellectual movement of the Enlightenment. French scientists, such as François Lavoiser (1743–1794), the Father of Modern Chemistry, and Jean Baptiste Lamarck (1744–1829), who did initial work on how forms of life adjust to the environment, led the world, French books were read everywhere, and French was the international language spoken among the educated and aristocratic circles of many countries. With a population of about 25.5 million, France was the most populous nation in Europe and Paris, and although smaller than London, was the cultural center of Europe. French exports to Europe were greater than those of Great Britain. Nearly half of the gold pieces circulating in Europe, at the time, were French.

Despite its power and appearance of wealth, France had deep-rooted problems. The French government had become corrupt and ineffective, clinging to an outdated social structure that carried over from the Middle Ages. Under this old order or *Ancien Regime* (**Old Regime**), there were three estates, or orders, in society. The structure of this old order no longer corresponded to the real distribution of power or the influence among the French. The government was also heavily in debt and unable to balance its budget or deal with the crisis of doing so.

Efforts to reform the country led to a series of events that ultimately ended in the bloody French Revolution that destroyed the Old Regime. As the French Revolution progressed from its moderate stage to its more radical phase known as the "Reign of Terror," other European nations became concerned because the Revolution's slogan of "Liberty, Equality, and Fraternity" threatened the established social order of the nineteenth century. The monarchs of England, Austria, Russia, and Prussia, therefore, formed the Grand Alliance to stop the spread of the Revolution. The forming of this Alliance led to war with France.

The French Revolution also led to the rise of the legendary leader, Napoleon. In 1799, Napoleon, who called himself a "son of the Revolution," seized control of France. From 1800–1815, Napoleon dominated the European continent. He was a military genius who established a French empire that controlled every European country except England. He was an efficient administrator who instituted a number of Enlightenment reforms that captured the support of the people. He spread the idea of the French Revolution throughout Europe, but his ambition and repression of liberty contributed to his downfall. After losing many troops in the disastrous Russian campaign of 1812, Napoleon was defeated at the Battle of Nations in 1813 by a coalition of European forces.

In 1814, the European nations met at the Congress of Vienna in an effort to undo the effects of the French Revolution and to turn back the clock to the way the world was prior to 1789. The representatives also sought to establish a policy of a balance of power to ensure that one person or country such as Napoleon or France would never dominate the European continent. This balance of power led to a hundred years of peace and prosperity in Europe. During this time, Europe became a powerful force in the world and extended its control over the areas of Asia and Africa.

The French Revolution

In 1789, the structure of French society, which fostered great inequalities among the people, led to a revolt against Louis XVI. The French Revolution led to a period of reform, chaos, and conservative reaction. Historians, such as Crane Brinton, acknowledge that democratic revolutions, such as the English Puritan Revolution of 1689, the American Revolution of 1776, and the French Revolution, may have a set of individual characteristics that are different from each other but follow a sequel of events that are similar to all democratic revolutions.

France under the Old Regime

The political, economic, and social conditions of eighteenth-century France was called the Old Regime. The class structure of France was divided along the following lines:

- **The First Estate:** The clergy of the Catholic Church represented about 1% of the population but owned about 10–15% of the land. They paid no direct taxes to the government except for a voluntary tax every five years. The Roman Catholic clergy of the First Estates included bishops and abbots, but not the parish priests who were often as poor as their parishioners.

- **The Second Estate:** Nobles and landowners in France consisted of less than 2% of the population and owned about 20% of the land. They also were exempt from taxes. Like the First Estate, the Second Estate was a privileged class. It collected feudal dues from the peasants, and its members held the best government jobs and army positions.

- **The Third Estate:** The middle class (bourgeoisie), urban lower classes, and peasant farmers, who comprised 98% of France's total population and owned about 40% of the land. Although the middle class had grown in France, the majority of the Third Estate was the peasants who lived on the lands. The bulk of the taxes fell on the Third Estate. The most burdensome taxes were the *taille* (a tax on agricultural goods such as produce), capitation (poll tax), a tithe (a church tax of about 10%), a *gabelle* (a salt tax), a *vingtieme* (an income tax), and dues to the local lord for the use of his mill (wine press, and so on). The bourgeoisie, the rising commercial and professional classes, paid less taxes than the peasants but felt unjustly treated. They were denied good jobs and wanted to reform a system that was outdated and did not give them the political and social rights on par with their economic conditions.

The absolutism of the king denied the people both a voice in the government and a way for them to make their grievances known. By using **lettres de cachet** (letters bearing the royal seal), the king was able to put his opponents into jail indefinitely without charges, bail, or trial.

The immediate cause of the French Revolution was financial. In 1789, France was sinking under a mound of debts. The French debt stood at four billion livres and it could not be carried because revenue fell short of expenditures. France was not poor, but tax exemptions and tax evasions by the wealthy, as described in the Estates list earlier, had led the country to a serious financial crisis. The extravagant cost of maintaining the Versailles Court and the debts incurred from the wars of Louis XIV as well as the money raised to support the War of American

Independence against France's rival, Britain, added to the problem. By 1789, half of the income tax went just to pay off the interest on this enormous debt. The French debt was being held by aristocrats, merchants, manufacturers, and financiers. However, the financial crisis was not due to national poverty.

However, France was not bankrupt. **Louis XVI** (b. 1754, ruled 1774–1792) was a weak and indecisive ruler whose unpopular wife, **Marie Antoinette**, was considered a foreigner (she was a Hapsburg from Austria) and a vain, frivolous person who refused to cut expenses. Louis appointed a number of advisers, such as Swiss financier Jacques Necker who proposed to abolish tax privileges, but they were forced to resign after they proposed taxing the First and Second Estates. The king was fearful that taxing the First and Second Estates would weaken his royal power because these Estates wanted to exert greater political influence in the government. By 1786, the depressed economy and the lack of public confidence made it increasingly difficult for the government to obtain new loans. Louis XVI had no other option but to raise taxes. His adviser, Calonne, convened an "Assembly of Notables" (composed of high-ranking nobles and clergy), hoping to gain endorsement for a general tax on all landowners. The nobles insisted that they wanted to share in the control of the government. A deadlock ensued and Louis dismissed his adviser. He tried to push the same program through the Paris Parlement (comprised of 13 regional royal courts). When the Paris Parlement refused to grant Louis XVI the power to raise taxes unless a meeting of the Estates General was called, the king had run out of options. He was forced to reconvene the Estates General (described in the next section), a legislative body that included the representatives from all three estates.

The Meeting of the Estates General and Creation of the National Assembly

On May 5, 1789, the **Estates General** met at Versailles. The Estates General was first summoned in 1302 at Paris by Philip IV in order to obtain national approval for his anti-clerical program. The power of the Estates General was never clearly defined, nor did that body ever obtain the financial control which made the English Parliament a powerful institution. The Estates General did not meet as a single body but convened separately as regional units, and its power varied inversely with the power of the king. Thus, as royal absolutism gained greater control in France, the Estates General became less significant. The Estates General had not met since 1614 and people looked to the meeting with enthusiasm because conditions in the country were bad. Peasants were starving and there were riots in Paris. People looked to the Estates General to save the country. The Estates General was made up of the First (clergy), Second (nobles), and Third (middle class, workers, and peasants) Estate. Each Estate had drawn up a list of grievances called *cahiers de doleances*. As part of the electoral process of 1789, the *cahiers* were intended to inform and instruct the deputies of local views and authorize reform. There was general consensus among the three Estates that the royal power had to be limited, that the Estates General had to meet regularly, and that the individual liberties had to be guaranteed by law. However, the middle class, especially the lawyers who primarily made up the Third Estate, placed a greater emphasis on protecting the citizens' rights than the needs of the peasants. An immediate issue arose over the voting procedure.

The Estates General voted by unit and not by individual members. Each Estate had one vote. Therefore, the privileged classes — the First and Second Estates combined — could outvote the Third Estate. On **June 17, 1789**, after six weeks of deadlock over voting procedures, the Third Estate declared itself the **National Assembly** and was joined by much of the low-ranking clergy and some of the nobles. The renaming was effectively a claim that this new body was now sovereign.

Louis XVI locked the National Assembly's members out of the meeting hall. In retaliation, they met at an indoor tennis court at Versailles and took the **Tennis Court Oath** (June 20, 1789) not to disband until they had written a constitution for France.

The Tennis Court Oath officially began the French Revolution because power was coming from the National Assembly and not the king. On June 27, 1789, the king rejected violence and ordered the delegates to meet with the National Assembly. The National Assembly had become the legal form of government without resorting to violence. This body was to function as the legislative branch of government until the end of September 1791 and charged itself with writing a constitution. To reflect this mission, it called itself the **National Constitutent Assembly** where the voting would be per capita and not by unit.

The Moderate Stage (1789–1792)

In the summer of 1789, food shortages, rising bread prices, and rumors that the king had sent troops to Versailles to dissolve the National Assembly incited people to action. On July 14, Paris mobs, looking for weapons, stormed the **Bastille**, a fortress symbolic of the Old Regime. The crowd cut off the head of the commander and marched around Paris with his decapitated head. This was a foreshadowing of the future. Disorder spread throughout France and set off what became known as **The Great Fear**. Peasants rose up against the nobles, burned castles, and destroyed records of feudal dues.

On August 4, 1789, at a stormy all-night session, the National Assembly took two preliminary legal steps to end the abuses of the Old Regime:

- **Abolished Feudalism:** Abolition of feudal dues and tithes owed by the peasants; nobles were forced to give up special status and their exemption from taxes; all male citizens could hold government, army, or church office.

- *Declaration of the Rights of Man and Citizens:* Issued by the Assembly on August 26, 1789, this document shows the influence of Enlightenment thinkers such as Locke. It was modeled in part on the American *Declaration of Independence*, and contains the following decrees:

  - Men are born free and equal before the law.

  - Men are guaranteed freedom of speech, religion, and due process before the law.

  - Taxes had to be paid according to the ability to pay.

  - The right to rule rested not only on the king but also on the general will of the people.

The principles of the Declaration were captured in the slogan of "Liberty, Equality, and Fraternity." It became the symbol of the French Revolution.

In October, about 7,000 women marched to Versailles demanding bread. After protesting in front of an audience and the king, they eventually forced the royal family to return to the **Tuileries**, their palace in Paris. The royals were virtually prisoners there until their execution in 1793.

The National Assembly, fearful of the mob, returned to Paris. The Assembly now had a two-fold function: solve the financial crisis and draw up a new constitution for France. The members, who were largely made up of the bourgeoisie class, addressed the following issues:

- **Financial Measures:** To pay off the huge debt, they seized church property and sold the land to aid the government.

- **Religious Matters:** The National Assembly abolished church titles. They seized the land of the church and religious freedom was granted to all groups. In 1790, the **Civil Constitution of the Clergy** was approved which subjected the Catholic Church to state control. The Civil Constitution declared the Church was independent from the pope and that the Catholic clergy was to be paid by the government and elected by the people. The Civil Constitution ended papal authority over the Church in France and dissolved monasteries and convents.

  Pope Pius VI and a majority of the French clergy denounced the Civil Constitution, as well as the Declaration of Rights. This attack on the Catholic Church turned many people against the Revolution and made the Church the Revolution's bitter enemy.

- **Legislative Matters:** In 1791, the National Assembly (also called the Constituent for its work on the new constitution) completed its task by producing a constitution. The Constitution of 1791 provided for a constitutional monarchy, limited the powers of the monarch, and created a legislative assembly. The elected legislative assembly passed the nation's laws, collected taxes, and decided on issues of war and peace. Members of the assembly had to be property owners and were elected by taxpaying citizens. The National Assembly also divided France into 83 departments ruled by local assemblies, thus eliminating the provincial system. The assembly also extended rights to Protestants and Jews, and abolished slavery in France.

Meanwhile, Louis XVI's brother, who was a leader of the émigré nobles and had fled the country in order to actively restore the Old Regime, convinced the king to flee France. On June 20, 1791, the royal family was captured near the French border town of Varennes and was escorted back to Paris by a taunting mob.

News of the Revolution created excitement and fear in Europe. European liberals and radicals hoped that the Revolution would lead to a reordering of society everywhere. However, conservatives such as **Edmund Burke** of Great Britain, in *Reflections on the Revolution in France* (1790), predicted that it would lead to chaos and tyranny. **Mary Wollstonecraft** (1759–1797) challenged Burke's ideas in *A Vindication of the Rights of Woman* (1792). Wollstonecraft argued that it was time for women to demand equal rights, and her ideas were similar to those of the Frenchwoman **Olympe de Gouges** (1745–1793). De Gouges was disappointed with the *Declaration of the Rights of Man and Citizens* because it did not grant equal rights for women.

In her *Declaration of the Rights of Women*, she asserted that "woman is born free and her rights are the same as those of man." De Gouges was guillotined in 1793 in part because of her royalist policies and her criticism of Robespierre, the leader of the Reign of Terror. The works of Wollstonecraft and de Gouges marked the birth of the modern women's movement for equal rights.

Some European monarchs were fearful that these revolutionary ideas would spread and endanger their countries. In August 1791, the king of Prussia and the emperor of Austria, the brother of Marie Antoinette, issued the **Declaration of Pillnitz**. They threatened to intervene if necessary to protect the French monarchy. In retaliation, France declared war on Austria in 1792. The Revolution entered a new stage.

The Radical Stage (1792–1795)

The war went badly for the poorly equipped French soldiers. Prussia joined immediately with Austria, and by the summer of 1792, the two powers were on the verge of invading Paris. On July 25, Austria and Prussia issued the **Brunswick Manifesto** promising to destroy Paris if any harm came to the French king. The legislative assembly declared the country in danger. In Paris, the *sans-culottes* (which literally means "without breeches," indicating their support of the trousers worn by the lower class), were committed to the working-class people and determined to push the Revolution in a more radical action. Many believed that the king was conspiring with the invading army and was responsible for the battle disasters of the French army. On August 10, 1792, the Paris mob stormed the Tuileries and slaughtered the king's guard. In September, the *sans-culottes,* under the leadership of **Georges Danton**, who was the Minister of Justice and had organized the defense of Paris against the Prussians, carried out the September massacres. The mob attacked the prisons and killed over 1,000 people, including nobles and clergy who they believed were traitors to the cause of the Revolution. Danton subsequently was killed during the Reign of Terror.

The Radicals took control of the National Assembly and called for the election of a new legislative assembly—the **National Convention**—based on universal suffrage. Meeting for the first time in September 1792, the National Convention abolished the monarchy and proclaimed France a republic. All members of the National Convention were Jacobins and Republicans. However, there was a split in the convention between two competitive groups: the **Girondists**, named after a department in southwestern France, and the **Mountains**, so named because its members usually sat high in the hall. The Girondists favored a decentralization of power and were fearful of the powers of the *sans-culottes*. They supported voting rights based on property ownership.

The Mountains were led by **Maximilien Robespierre**, a middle-class lawyer who represented the *sans-culottes,* the working class of Paris. Robespierre favored a strong central government with the power to help the poor and control the economy. Known as "Mr. Incorruptible," he wanted to create a "Republic of virtue" and accused the Girondists of sympathy towards the king.

In 1793, the National Convention put Louis XVI on trial. The trial split the convention. The Girondists wanted to imprison the royal family and exile him after the European powers had been defeated. The Mountains wanted to execute him. On January 21, 1793, Louis XVI was beheaded on the fast-falling blade of a brand-new **guillotine** (Dr. Joseph Guillotin, a member of the legislature, had introduced the device as a more humane method of beheading rather than the uncertainty of the axe) and later that same year Marie Antoinette was beheaded. The execution of Louis XVI sent shock waves throughout Europe. England, Spain, the Netherlands, Austria, and Prussia united in the first coalition to stop the spread of these revolutionary ideas. This became known as the **First Coalition**.

The Reign of Terror (1793–1794)

By 1793, France faced even greater problems. Not only was the country at war with countries in opposition to the Revolution, but rising prices, unemployment, and in Vendee (the western part of France) a rebellion led by royalists and priests threatened the government. In the face of these problems, the *sans-culottes* joined with the Mountains to oust the Girondists from the National Convention in May 1793.

These Radical Jacobins centralized all control in a 12-man **Committee of Public Safety**, which had dictatorial powers. The goal of the Committee was to save the Revolution from foreign and domestic enemies. The Committee subjected the entire nation to compulsory military service, and the war against the Coalition became a national mission. Between August 1793 and September 1794, France raised an army of over 1.1 million men, the largest Europe had ever seen. Troops from the port city of Marseilles set the theme with the call for people to rally around the fatherland. The song sung by these troops would become "La Marseillaise," the national anthem of the French nation.

The French were victorious over the European Coalition because they had the ability to draw on the power of patriotic dedication to the nationalist state and a national mission. This was the foundation of modern nationalism, as citizens, reinforced by the ideas of democracy, were stirred by the danger of a common enemy. The Committee had turned the concept of a gentlemanly eighteenth-century game of war into a struggle between good and evil.

To protect the Revolution against domestic enemies, the Committee of Public Safety instituted a **Reign of Terror**, which lasted from late summer of 1793 to August 1794. The Committee arrested all persons suspected of treason and sentenced them to death. It is estimated that about 40,000 people lost their lives to the guillotine, to gunfire, or were drowned on barges set out to sea. The Reign of Terror had no respect for class origin. About 8% were nobles, 14% were bourgeoisie, mainly of the rebellious southern cities, 6% were clergy, and no less than 70% were of the peasant and working class.

The Committee of Public Safety also instituted price and wage controls, food rationing, monetary controls to stop inflation, the metric system, and censorship of all written material. In late 1793, Robespierre, who had become the chief architect of the Reign of Terror, proclaimed a **Republic of Virtue**. This was his bold scheme to de-Christianize France and to promote revolutionary values. He removed Christian symbols from public buildings, turned the Cathedral of Notre Dame into a Temple of Reason, and created a new non-Christian calendar. His actions alienated many people, especially the Catholic majority.

The Reactionary Stage (1795–1799)

By 1794, the Reign of Terror had spiraled out of control and its horrors turned the French people against their actions. In March 1794, Robespierre executed Danton, one of the Jacobin Committee leaders, for arguing that it was time to end the Reign of Terror. Fearful that it may be next, the Convention decided to arrest Robespierre and he was guillotined on 8 Thermidor (July 28, 1794), one of the months of the new non-Christian calendar. The death of Robespierre began the **Thermidorian Reaction**. Tired of violence and virtue, the moderates regained control of the National Convention. A new constitution was written in 1795, which set up a republican form of government. The middle class was in control since only men of property could vote and hold office (women were not allowed to vote). The **New National Convention** set up two branches of the legislature: The **Council of 500** (the lower house) and the **Council of Elders** (an upper house of 250 members over the age of 40). The Convention removed all economic controls, closed the Jacobin clubs, allowed Catholic services to be held again, and granted amnesty to those who were considered enemies during the Reign of Terror.

In 1795, the National Convention chose a five-member executive group that became known as the **Directory**. Attacked by the aristocracy and the *sans-culottes,* who were critical of the government economic policies, the Directory began to lose power. Unable to deal with the worsening inflation problem and fearful of a royalist uprising, it turned to the military for support. On October 5, 1795, a rebellion broke out in Paris and the Directory ordered a young general, Napoleon Bonaparte, to crush it. He saved the Republic, but the savior would ultimately be the destroyer of the government. Napoleon was rewarded for his loyalty with the command of the French army fighting the Austrians in Italy.

The Napoleonic Era (1799–1815)

Napoleon Bonaparte (1769–1821) was born on the Mediterranean island of Corsica, which had been owned by the Italians until annexed by the French, and was the son of a poor village lawyer. When the French Revolution began, he was a low-level military officer, but he quickly rose in rank and won important victories against the British and Austria. He was a popular military general who appealed to the people who looked to a strong military leader to end the disorder and corruption that existed under the Directory.

In November 1799, he overthrew the Directory by a *coup d'etat* (a swift overthrow of government by force) and formed a new government, the **Consulate**. The Consulate was made up of three Consuls, but all the power was vested in Napoleon as the First Consul. In 1802, the constitution made him Consul for life and in 1804, he was crowned Emperor. For each of these constitutional changes, Napoleon held a national **plebiscite** (a yes or no vote). The French people, hoping for stability, supported him at each step in his rise. Napoleon's popularity was due to his effective domestic policies, as described in the following list. His reforms provided efficient government and furthered the revolutionary principle of equality.

- **Concordat of 1801:** Made peace with the Catholic Church. Pope Pius VII renounced claims to Church property confiscated during the Revolution. The government could nominate bishops but the pope confirmed them and could remove them. Napoleon acknowledged that Catholicism was the religion of the majority of the French people but affirmed religious toleration for all. By this agreement, Napoleon protected the peasant owners of former church land and pleased the overwhelmingly Catholic French population.

- **Napoleonic Code (1804):** Established a uniform legal system to replace an outdated and inequitable medieval system. Emphasizing the revolutionary principles of equality, the Code created equal treatment before the law, providing religious toleration for Protestants and Jews, and abolishing serfdom and feudalism. However, the Code undid some reforms of the French Revolution. Women lost most of their rights under the Code. Male heads of households regained complete authority over their wives and children.

- **Free Public Education:** Was expanded by Napoleon. He established a government-supervised public school system of uniform educational standards. The University of France, a government agency and not an educational institute of higher learning, controlled all levels of education.

- **"Legion of Honor":** Was a society created by Napoleon for public recognition for those who had rendered distinguished military and civilian service to France. Membership was based on merit, not social status, which was in accord with the principle of equality. Nevertheless, he practiced nepotism, placing his relatives on the thrones of countries that he conquered. Napoleon centralized government and directly placed local government under national authority.

- **The Bank of France:** Founded in 1800, introduced a sound currency and balanced budget. Everyone was expected to pay taxes and there were no tax exemptions because of birthright. By collecting taxes fairly and paying off the debt, Napoleon restored the government to financial health. These measures pleased the bourgeoisie. Napoleon also encouraged business enterprises.

Napoleon Dominates Europe

When Napoleon assumed power in 1799, Russia, Austria, Prussia, and Great Britain formed the **Second Coalition**. Napoleon took command of the French forces, which were at war with the Second Coalition. He was able to win significant victories and by 1802 ended the war favorably for France. Napoleon was a military genius who was able to take advantage of the changes brought about by the French Revolution. He effectively used the *levee en masse* (the call to use all able-bodied men to rally around the country) to help spread the ideals of Liberty, Equality, and Fraternity, with the emphasis on fighting for the fatherland. The troops called him the "little Corporal" because he defeated four armies larger than his own. They trusted him because he allowed them independence on the battlefield and combined the forces of light artillery, infantry, and cavalry to develop an effective fighting tool.

In 1805, France resumed war with the **Third Coalition** (Austria, Sweden, Russia, and Great Britain), and between 1805 and 1807 France had defeated all these countries except England. In 1805, Napoleon defeated the Austrian and Russian army at Austerlitz. He then abolished the **Holy Roman Empire** and created the **Confederation of the Rhine**, reducing the number of German states from 300 to fewer than 100, an act for which he has sometimes been called the

"Grandfather of German Unity." In October 1806, Napoleon defeated the Prussian forces at the **Battle of Jena** and the Russians at **Friedland** in June 1807. Shortly after, Tsar Alexander I and Napoleon met privately on a raft in the middle of the Niemen River, not far from Tilsit, a border area between Prussia and Russia. The result of this meeting was the signing of the **Treaty of Tilsit** in July 1807, by which the French and Russian empires became allies against Great Britain. Alexander accepted Napoleon as the Emperor of the West and Napoleon continued to occupy Berlin with his troops, taking away about one-half of Prussian territory. In return, Russia received a free hand in its design on Switzerland, then a Swedish possession. King Frederick William II of Prussia, who was originally restricted to pacing nervously along the banks of the Niemen River, was eventually drawn into the negotiations as a mere formality. He had been defeated at Jena and had little military resources to resist any agreement.

By 1807, Napoleon's Grand Empire dominated continental Europe from the Atlantic coast to the Russian plains. His empire included Spain, northern Italy, Naples, and parts of Germany and the newly independent Confederation of the Rhine. As Napoleon took control of each area, he instituted reforms. He stripped away the power of the nobles and their privileges in order to destroy the last vestiges of the Old Regime. In 1805, the British forces destroyed the French navy at the **Battle of Trafalgar**. This battle gave England command of the seas and put an end to Napoleon's plan to invade the British Isles. Unable to defeat the British navy, Napoleon decided to wage economic warfare through the **Continental System** instead. He forbade the European nations to import British goods. Napoleon considered England "a nation of shopkeepers" and believed that the Continental System would ruin the British economy. In the end, the Continental System was a failure. European nations needed British goods, and the French navy was not strong enough to prevent widespread smuggling. French commerce lost much of its business, and unemployment spread while the British found new markets in North America.

Resentment against the Continental System was one of the causes of nationalistic revival, which eventually ended Napoleon's dream of complete European domination. Some other reasons for Napoleon's decline included:

- **The Peninsular War (1808–1814):** Napoleon's decision to put his brother Joseph on the throne of Spain's Bourbon King Charles V angered the Spanish people and they revolted, waging a guerrilla war that tied down the French soldiers for a number of years. Eventually British and Spanish forces under the **Duke of Wellington** drove the French out of Spain.

- **The Invasion of Russia:** When Alexander I of Russia withdrew from the Continental System in 1812, Napoleon invaded, leading an army of about 600,000 men into Russia. The Russian army retreated and adopted a scorched earth policy of burning crops and villages as they went along. Napoleon captured Moscow in September but found the city in ashes. Napoleon ordered the Grand Army to retreat because there was not enough food to supply his army during the winter. The 1,000-mile retreat from Moscow was a disaster in which Napoleon lost three-fourths of his army. In 1813, the combined forces of Russia, Prussia, and Austria defeated Napoleon at the **Battle of the Nations**.

On April 11, 1814, Napoleon abdicated his throne and was exiled to **Elba**, a small island off the Italian coast. The Bourbons were restored to power and Louis XVIII, brother of Louis XVI, was crowned the new king of France. The king accepted the Napoleonic Code and honored the land settlements made during the Revolution. However, in 1815, Napoleon escaped from Elba and marched to France. The king fled and Napoleon was welcomed back as a hero. His return lasted only 100 days, however. On June 18, the Allied army of Russia, Austria, Prussia, and Great Britain defeated Napoléon at the **Battle of Waterloo**. Louis XVIII returned and Napoleon was exiled to the remote island of **St. Helena** where he died in 1821.

The Congress of Vienna (1814–1815)

After Napoleon's defeat, the four great powers (England, Russia, Prussia, and Austria) and France met in Vienna in September 1814 (the **Congress of Vienna**) to draw up a peace settlement. Their goal was to redraw the map of Europe as it existed pre-1789 in order to ensure order and stability.

Congress of Vienna		
Diplomat	**Country**	**Objectives**
Prince Klemens von Metternich	Austria	To restore Europe to the way it was before the French Revolution. Metternich dominated the Congress and rejected the ideas of the French Revolution. He was a conservative who despised democracy and nationalism; his ideas influenced Europe between 1815 and 1848 and his anti-democratic policies were followed by leaders in Western Europe.
Lord Castlereagh	England	To ensure that France would not become a powerful nation again.
Tsar Alexander I	Russia	To organize an alliance system (Holy Alliance) of Christian monarchs to fight revolutions throughout the world; also to become king of Poland.
Perigord Talleyrand	France	To ensure that France would retain the rank of a major power. Talleyrand proves to be the great mediator among the four.
Karl von Hardenberg	Prussia	To recover Prussian territory lost to Napoleon in 1807 and gain additional territory in northern Germany (Saxony).

Despite their different goals, the leaders of the Congress of Vienna agreed to establish a balance of power in Europe to ensure that one nation, like France, would never become politically and militarily strong enough to dominate the continent. The diplomats encircled France through the following:

- Adding Belgium and Holland to create the kingdom of the Netherlands, a much larger state north of France

- Giving Prussia lands along the Rhine River

- Enhancing Austrian influence over the Germans by creating the **German Confederation** of 39 states with Austria designated as the president of the Confederation

- Allowing Austria to again take control of lands in Italy

They also wanted to restore the power to monarchs based on the **Principle of Legitimacy**. This meant returning to power the ruling families deposed by more than two decades of revolutionary movement. Bourbon rulers were restored in France, Spain, and Naples. Dynasties were restored in Holland, and the Papal States were returned to the pope.

The Congress also provided for compensation, rewarding those states that had made considerable sacrifice to defeat Napoleon: Austria was given Lombardy and Venetia; Russia was given most of Poland and Finland; and Prussia was awarded the Rhineland and part of Poland. To enforce this settlement, Metternich organized the **Quadruple Alliance** of Austria, Prussia, Russia, and Britain. The purpose of the Alliance was to maintain the balance of power and stop and suppress any revolutionary ideas of nationalism and democracy, which threatened to upset the Vienna settlement. The cooperation among the major nations of Europe is often referred to as the **Concert of Europe**. Alexander I organized the **Holy Alliance** consisting of most European monarchs who pledged to rule by Christian principles. The Holy Alliance was ineffective, idealistic, and existed only on paper.

Even though the Congress of Vienna denied the principles of nationalism and democracy, the settlement lasted for 100 years. Europe would not see another war on the Napoleonic scale until World War I in 1914. During this hundred years' period, Europe was able to direct its resources towards an Industrial Revolution that would directly affect the political, economic, and social fabric of the continent. The statesmen of Vienna, however, underestimated how this new Industrial Revolution would lead to the creation of a new alignment of social classes and the development of new needs and issues.

Chronology of the French Revolution

May 5, 1789	The Estates General meets for the first time in 175 years.
June 17, 1789	The Estates General becomes the National Assembly.
June 20, 1789	The Tennis Court Oath. Members of the Third Estate meet on tennis courts at Versailles and promise not to disband before they write a new constitution.
June 27, 1789	Louis XVI recognizes the National Assembly.
July 14, 1789	Storming of the Bastille (celebrated as French Independence Day today).
July–August, 1789	The Great Fear sweeps the countryside.
August 4, 1789	National Assembly ends feudalism in France.

August 27, 1789	*Declaration of the Rights of Man and Citizens* is published.
October 5 and 6, 1789	Women march on Versailles; royal family is forced to return to Paris.
November 1789	National Assembly confiscates church property.
July 12, 1790	Civil Constitution of the Clergy adapted.
June 20 to 25, 1791	Royal family caught and arrested at French border in failed effort to escape.
August 27, 1791	Declaration of Pillnitz. Austria, Prussia, and other European monarchies express willingness to intervene in France.
1791–1792	Legislative Assembly convenes, and it abolishes slavery and grants religious tolerance to Protestants and Jews.
April 20, 1792	France declares war on Austria.
August 10, 1792	*Sans-culottes* storm the Tuileries.
September 2–7, 1792	The September Massacre.
September 21, 1792	The National Convention meets. It abolishes the monarchy and creates a new Government/Constitution.
January 21, 1793	Execution of Louis XVI of France.
October 16, 1793	Execution of Marie Antoinette.
1793–1794	Reign of Terror.
July 28, 1794	Maximilien Robespierre arrested and executed.
1795–1799	Directory rules France ineffectively and inefficiently.
November 9, 1799	Napoleon overthrows the Directory and seizes control of the government.
July 15, 1801	Napoleon signs Concordat with Pope Pius VII giving the French government control over the Church in France.
March 27, 1802	Treaty of Amiens with Great Britain.
May 18, 1804	Napoleon crowns himself Emperor.
October 21, 1805	Nelson defeats Napoleon at the Battle of Trafalgar.
1806	Battle of Jena—Prussia defeated.
1807	Battle of Friedland—Russia defeated; Treaty of Tilsit between France and Russia.
March 1810	Napoleon marries Marie Louise.
June 24, 1812	France invades Russia.
October 1813	Grand Alliance defeats France at the Battle of Nations.
April 11, 1814	Napoleon is exiled to Elba; Louis XVIII crowned king of France.
September 1814	Congress of Vienna meets.
1815	Napoleon escapes Elba and begins his rule of 100 days.
June 1815	Wellington defeats Napoleon at the Battle of Waterloo.

Sample Multiple-Choice Questions

1. Which of the following was the basic cause of the French Revolution?

   A. A majority of the French people wanted to replace the monarchy with the republic.

   B. France was a weak country and in economic decline in 1789.

   C. The past abuses of the Old Regime.

   D. The support of nobles for the absolute government of Louis XVI.

   E. The invasion of France by foreign countries.

2. The French bourgeoisie supported the French Revolution mainly because:

   A. they believed in the Theory of Divine Right of Kings

   B. they were not allowed to own property under the Old Regime

   C. they resented their lack of political power under the Old Regime

   D. they wanted a democratic form of government

   E. the government set up a voting system based on universal male suffrage

3. The *Declaration of the Rights of Man and Citizens* adapted by the National Assembly in the French Revolution was

   A. a declaration of war against Austria and Prussia

   B. a statement of the main principles of the French Revolution

   C. a constitution establishing a republican form of government

   D. laws that confiscated Church property

   E. an announcement of the French military victory over the enemies of the Revolution

4. Which of the following represents the correct chronological order of events during the French Revolution?

   (1) Reign of Terror

   (2) Execution of Louis XVI

   (3) Meeting of the Estates General

   (4) Tennis Court Oath

   (5) The Directory

   A. 3, 2, 4, 1, 5

   B. 1, 3, 4, 2, 4

   C. 3, 4, 2, 1, 5

   D. 5, 3, 1, 2, 4

   E. 2, 3, 5, 4, 1

5. Which social group had the greatest number of victims during the Reign of Terror (1793–1794)?

   A. bourgeoisie

   B. clergy

   C. nobility

   D. foreigners

   E. peasants

6. The goal of Napoleon's continental system was to

A. increase exports to the continent

B. defeat the British through economic warfare

C. increase imports to the continent

D. unite the Italian states

E. create a unified Germany

7. All of the following are true about the Code of Napoleon EXCEPT:

A. provided equal treatment before the law

B. guaranteed religious toleration and trial by jury

C. abolished what remained of serfdom and feudalism

D. is the basis of law in Latin America and is still used in France

E. improved the rights of women

8. In Goya's painting *The Third of May 1808*, the painter depicts the shooting of Spanish civilians by:

A. Napoleon's troops

B. those involved in the Decembrist Revolution

C. Bismarck's troops trying to eliminate Austria's influence over Germany

D. Garibaldi's Red Shirts trying to unify Sicily

E. the Estates General

9. What was a major goal of the Congress of Vienna?

A. To establish democratic governments in all European nations

B. To maintain a balance of power in Europe

C. To preserve the reforms of the French Revolution

D. To encourage nationalism

E. To re-establish the Holy Roman Empire

10. The most influential figure at the Congress of Vienna was

A. Talleyrand

B. Metternich

C. Napoleon Bonaparte

D. Nicholas II

E. Otto Von Bismarck

Answers to Multiple-Choice Questions and Explanations

1. **C.** The Old Regime, which described the political, economic, and social conditions in Europe before 1789, was marked by absolutism in government, inequality among classes, and unequal and burdensome taxation. In 1789, France was divided into Three Estates. The First Estate was made up of the clergy and the Second Estate was composed of the nobles. They made up about 2% of the population, but owned about 40% of the land and paid no taxes. The Third Estate was made up of the middle class (bourgeoisie), city workers, and the peasants who were 98% of the population, and controlled 60% of the land and paid a variety of different taxes, such as the tithe to the clergy and feudal dues to the nobles. A majority of the French people supported the monarch until 1791. In 1789, France was one of the wealthiest countries in Europe and not in economic decline. The nobles supported Louis XVI but wanted more influence in the decision-making process. The foreign powers invaded France in 1791, two years after the French Revolution had begun.

2. **C.** The French bourgeoisie supported the French Revolution mainly because they resented their lack of political power under the Old Regime. The bourgeoisie (middle class) included prosperous bankers, merchants, and manufacturers who propped up the French economy. It also included the officials who staffed the royal bureaucracy. The estates system allowed the clergy and the nobles to monopolize all the benefits while the majority received very little. The French bourgeoisie did not support the belief in the Divine Right Theory. They still were loyal to the monarchy but one with less absolute power. They did not support democracy. The middle class owned about 20% of the land but had little or no political influence.

3. **B.** *The Declaration of the Rights of Man and Citizens* was a statement of the main principle of the French Revolution. The declaration guaranteed basic civil rights and that all political sovereignty rested in the hands of the people, not the king. It also proclaimed that all male citizens were equal before the law. Its principles captured the slogan of the French Revolution, "Liberty, Equality, and Fraternity." The declaration established a constitutional monarchy, not a republican form of government. The Civil Constitution of the clergy led to the confiscation of church land. The declaration was a statement of political principles and not an announcement of any military victories.

4. **C.** The correct chronological order is the meeting of the Estates General (May 1789), the Tennis Court Oath (June 20, 1790), the execution of Louis XVI (January 21, 1793), the Reign of Terror (July 1793–1794), and the Directory (1795–1799).

5. **E.** Of the 40,000 who died during the Reign of Terror, about 70% were from the peasant class. About 15% were bourgeoisie and the remaining 15% were clergy and nobility. There were no major executions of foreigners.

6. **B.** The Continental System was designed by Napoleon to defeat the British through economic warfare. Unable to invade the British Isles, Napoleon ordered the European continent closed to British trade. Russia, his ally, at first agreed to the boycott of British goods. Britain responded with its own blockade of European ports. Napoleon's Continental System failed to bring Britain to its knees. Although British exports declined,

its powerful navy kept open vital trade routes to the Americas and Indies. The Continental System did not increase exports, nor did it increase imports to the continent. Restriction on trade hurt Europe and created a scarcity of goods and sent prices soaring. Throughout Europe, people blamed Napoleon for a decline in trade and an increase in business failure. Napoleon's Continental System was an economic policy and did not have an influence on uniting Italy nor in creating a unified Germany. Italy and Germany would be unified during the reign of Napoleon's nephew Napoleon III in the 1860s and 1870s.

7. **E.** The Napoleonic Code did not improve the rights of women. The Code had several weaknesses in regard to women. Women could not vote. A wife owed obedience to her husband, who had total control over property. An unmarried woman could not be a legal guardian. The Code recognized civil marriages and divorces; however, it was easier for a man to sue for a divorce than a woman. Male heads of households regained complete authority over their wives and children. The Napoleonic Code embodied the Enlightenment principle of equality of all citizens before the law and religious toleration and trial by jury. The Code also abolished the remnants of serfdom and feudalism. It is still the basis of law in Latin America and France.

8. **A.** The painting *The Third of May 1808* shows the execution of Spaniards by Napoleon's troops. In 1808, Napoleon replaced the king of Spain with Napoleon's brother, Joseph, who introduced liberal reforms that sought to undermine the Spanish Catholic Church. The Spanish remained loyal and conducted a campaign of hit and run raids. These attacks kept Napoleon bogged down when troops were needed elsewhere. The painting does not depict events associated with the Decembrist Revolution, Bismarck, programs of Nicholas I, or the Estates General.

9. **B.** A major goal of the Congress of Vienna was to maintain a balance of power in Europe. Following Napoleon's defeat, diplomats of the victorious nations and France met in Vienna from 1814 until 1815. This was a peace conference to reconstruct war-torn Europe. Although the leaders of the Congress had different objectives, they were determined to turn back the clock of Europe to the time before the French Revolution. They wanted to establish a balance of power, or a distribution of military and economic power, to prevent any one nation from becoming too strong. To ensure this balance of power, Prince Metternich of Austria created the Concert of Europe. The Concert included all the major European states and pledged to maintain the balance of power and to suppress any uprising inspired by the ideas of the French Revolution. The representatives of the Congress of Vienna did not support establishing democratic governments in all European nations. They opposed the French revolutionary ideas of equality and democratic governments. Napoleon brought about the end of the Holy Roman Empire. The leaders of the Congress of Vienna were interested in stopping the spread of democracy and nationalism and not interested in re-establishing the Holy Roman Empire, which Napoleon had destroyed.

10. **B.** Metternich was the most influential figure at the Congress of Vienna. This is because Prince Metternich of Austria set a pattern of anti-democratic policies that was followed by most of the rulers of Europe. For 50 years, he was the most influential diplomat in Europe. **A** is incorrect because Talleyrand of France played a secondary role to Metternich. Napoleon Bonaparte was exiled at St. Helena and did not attend the meeting in Vienna. Nicholas II of Russia and Otto Von Bismarck of Germany were leaders of their respective countries in the middle of the late nineteenth or early twentieth centuries.

Mercantilism and the Agricultural and Industrial Revolutions

The Age of Exploration — besides leading to the discovery and conquest of new lands such as the Americas, and overseas expansion and new trade routes such as with Asia — brought about national economic changes. The fierce competition for trade and empire among European monarchs led to the widespread adoption of **mercantilism**, an economic policy under which nations sought to increase their wealth and power by obtaining large amounts of gold and silver and by exporting more goods than they imported. The increased gold and silver flowing into Europe from the Spanish colonies contributed to a price revolution known as **inflation**, which encouraged trade and businesses of all types. As prices of goods went up, businessmen were willing to take risks to invest money in the hope of making more money. This new attitude spurred the growth of early European capitalism. As trade routes shifted in the sixteenth century from the Mediterranean and the Baltic to the Atlantic, Venice and Genoa soon declined and Portugal and Spain became the dominant powers. In the seventeenth century, cities like London, Paris, and Amsterdam became the centers of commercial activity. These changes were part of the Commercial Revolution that influenced Europe.

The Agricultural and Industrial Revolutions, like the Commercial Revolution, also impacted European society. The discovery of new machinery and science in farming had far-reaching effects. The use of new crops, techniques, and the introduction of better methods of soil rotation enabled Europe to grow more food. This helped to raise the standard of living. The Agricultural Revolution provided the food for the expanding city population and directly led to a population explosion in Europe. The Industrial Revolution, which occurred in Great Britain, had a greater effect on society than the French Revolution. The transformation from an agrarian to an industrial society influenced the political, economic, and social structure of European society. The landed aristocracy, which had begun to lose influence with the rise of the middle class, would be completely overshadowed by the birth of a newly capitalist class of businessmen. The shift from the rural to an urban society created new problems on how to deal with the conditions created by the factory system. New philosophies and economic ideas such as Romanticism, Socialism, Nationalism, and Communism arose to meet the problems created by industrialization. The Agricultural and Industrial Revolutions transformed not only Europe in the nineteenth century but also had a major impact on the world in the twentieth century.

Mercantilism and Capitalism

From the sixteenth through the seventeenth centuries, European monarchs adopted a policy of mercantilism aimed at strengthening their national economy. Mercantilists supported several basic ideas:

- **A nation's wealth is measured by the gold and silver (bullion) it possesses.**

- **A nation must export more goods than it imports.** In other words, there must be a favorable balance of trade in order for a nation to build up its supply of gold and silver.

- **Colonies exist for the benefit of the mother country.** Colonies supply raw materials not available in Europe for manufacture and trade, and also serve as a market for the mother country's manufactured goods.

- **Strict laws must regulate trade with the colonies.** The regulation of trade strengthened the nation's economy because, in addition to providing gold and silver, the colonies could not set up industries to manufacture goods nor buy goods from foreign countries. This strict regulation ensured that all revenue went to the government.

- **The government must promote and protect local industries by taxing imported goods.**

- **Governments can increase revenue by imposing a single national currency and selling monopolies to large producers in certain industries as well as big overseas trading companies.**

- **Self-sufficiency must be promoted.** A country had to use everything it needed within its own borders and not depend on other countries for goods.

The establishment of European colonies in the Americas, the direct trade with Asia and Africa, and the continued expansion of the Commercial Revolution led to some major changes in Europe:

- Large quantities of gold and silver from the New World during the 1500s affected the economy of Western Europe. Since consumers had more money to spend, it drove up prices and this led to **inflation**, which led to a decline in the value of money as the prices of goods and services increased. The purchasing power of the people declined.

- The traditional divisions of classes of society were affected. Because the growing demand for goods led to increased production, Western Europe's guild system was impacted. The guild system originated in medieval times; it was an association of people who all worked at the same occupation, and the guild controlled membership, wages, and prices. The institution of the guild had to change to meet the growing production needs of a nation-centered economic system. A middle class of merchants, bankers, and capitalists thus emerged who were devoted to the goal of making profits. This new social class grew in number and power and began to resent the fact that it lacked social status and power. This discontent led to conditions that gave rise to the French Revolution, as was discussed in the previous chapter.

Although farmers benefited from the changing market because they were able to sell surplus crops, they lacked political power. The nobility whose income still depended on a fixed asset suffered a decline in economic power; as a class, however, the nobility still ranked high on the social scale.

- The economic changes of the sixteenth and seventeenth centuries led to the rise of **capitalism**, or using money to make a profit or more money. The Dutch, who controlled the major trade routes in the seventeenth century, were the first people to practice capitalism. The merchants of Amsterdam bought surplus grain and sold it at the highest prices when they heard about poor harvests in other parts of Europe. Since they controlled the trading routes, they were able to enforce a monopoly and control all the shipments to other parts of Europe. In the mid-1630s, the Dutch replaced the Italians as the bankers of Europe.

Expanded trade and the push for building overseas empires promoted capitalism's growth. Entrepreneurs or merchants organized, managed, and assumed the risk of doing business by hiring craftsmen, supplying them with raw materials, and selling the finished goods. It was the beginning of the **domestic system**, which was a system in which weavers and crafters produced goods at home. When entrepreneurs were unable to raise money for a project or thought it was too risky, capitalists developed new ways to create wealth by forming **joint stock (also known as trading) companies** that allowed people to pool large amounts of capital needed for overseas ventures. The Dutch, British, and French founded trading companies, such as the Dutch East India Company and the British East India Company, in the 1600s. Capitalists also reduced the risk of liability from dangerous investments during the seventeenth century by creating insurance companies such as Lloyds' of London.

In the ways mentioned above, the European expansion of money and goods revolutionized Europe's economy and transformed its society. These changes in trade, manufacturing, and investments laid the foundation for the Agricultural and Industrial revolutions.

The Agricultural Revolution

Up until the middle of the eighteenth century, farming remained very much as it had been under the manorial system of the Middle Ages. Although farmers labored hard and long, they produced scanty crops. Before the Agricultural Revolution, farmers did the following:

- Worked to raise food for themselves and their landlords instead of making a profit by selling produce on the markets
- Relied upon a few ancient tools such as the wooden plow, the hoe, the rake, and the shovel
- Continued the three-field system, which kept one-third of the land idle at any one time
- Knew very little about fertilizers, crop rotation, and animal breeding

The Dutch led the way in the Agricultural Revolution. In the 1600s, they built dikes or dams to reclaim land by draining it and thus making it useable. They also used fertilizers from livestock to renew the soil and combined fields into larger ones to make better use of the land.

During the eighteenth to nineteenth centuries, British and Americans improved on the Dutch experiment by inventing new tools and processes that led to the mechanization of agriculture. The following is a table that lists some of the improvements in agriculture:

Inventor	Invention
Jethro Tull (English) 1674–1741	Seed drill (1701) This device planted seeds in rows replacing planting the seed by hand. This method also permitted cultivation between rows, increasing the amount of food produced per acre.
Charles "Turnip" Townshend (English) 1675–1738	Crop rotation (1750) Helped to conserve soil fertility and made more land available for production. Alternated grain with soil enriching plants such as turnips and clover.
Robert Bakewell (English) 1725–1795	Scientific breeding of animals
Charles Newbold (American) 1764–1835	Cast-iron plow (1797) Turned soil deeper and more easily than the wooden plow.
John Deere (American) 1804–1886	Self-cleaning steel plow (1837) Improved upon the cast iron plow.

The **Enclosure Movement** contributed to large-scale farming. Between 1760 and 1830, the English Parliament — the majority of which were large landowners — passed a series of laws called the **Enclosure Acts**, in which they took over and fenced off land formerly shared by peasant farmers. In the 1500s, enclosed lands gained pasture for sheep and increased work output. By the 1700s, the land-owning aristocracy began to fence in the common lands of villages and replace the strip farms of medieval times with **larger fields** that could be cultivated more efficiently. The large landowners employed new farming techniques that led to increased production, but at a price. Machines displaced many farm laborers. Small farmers were forced off the land because they could not compete with the larger, more efficient farmers. They migrated to the towns and cities in large numbers to seek factory jobs.

The Agricultural Revolution contributed to a rapid growth of population in Europe. In Great Britain alone, the population soared from 8.6 million in 1700 to almost 15 million in 1800. Similarly, the population in Europe rose from 120 million to about 190 million by the beginning of the 1800s. Reasons for this population explosion included the following:

- The risk of famine was reduced because of the vast quantities of food being produced by the new agricultural methods.

- People ate a more balanced diet, contributing to overall better health.

- A better diet for women made them able to have stronger babies.

- Vaccines were developed against diseases such as smallpox. Improved medical care further slowed deaths from diseases.

The Industrial Revolution

The Agricultural Revolution helped to trigger the **Industrial Revolution**. The Industrial Revolution can be viewed in two ways:

1. A slow, gradual process began during the Stone Age and continues to evolve to the present with changes in technology.

2. A shift took place between 1750 and 1830 in the production of goods from handmade items to items made by more expensive and complicated machines. These changes also resulted in the transfer of work from home (the domestic system) to the factory system.

Although both views are valid, for this book's purposes I will adopt the second view. The Industrial Revolution began in England in the second half of the eighteenth century for the following reasons:

- England was rich in raw materials secured from the colonies and worldwide trade. It was also rich in natural resources such as coal, which was used to power steam engines and iron ore, which was used to build the machines.

- Wealthy men had the capital to invest in machinery and factories.

- The Agricultural Revolution provided a large pool of displaced workers needed to run the mines, build factories, and run machines.

- A stable government encouraged science, inventions, and the application of new methods of industry. The Royal Society of London (1660), the world's oldest scientific society, spurred scientific research.

- As an island, England was cut off from the wars of continental Europe. The country was unharmed and free to develop its new industries.

The Industrial Revolution in England began with a series of technological developments in the textile industry, improvements in the sources of power (steam), and revolutions in transportation. Below are lists of important inventions that improved production, provided sources of power, and instituted changes in transportation:

Textile Industry	Inventions	Impact
John Kay (English) 1704–1764	Flying shuttle (1733)	Sped up weaving and increased producing power.
James Hargreaves (English) 1720–1778	Spinning jenny (1764)	Made it possible to spin several threads at once. Mechanized the spinning wheel.
Sir Richard Arkwright (English) 1732–1792	Water frame (1771)	Water-powered spinning machine increased the rapidity of spinning.
Samuel Crompton (English) 1753–1827	Spinning mule (1779)	Combination of spinning jenny and water frame. Produced strong fine thread. Spurred the invention of better weaving machines.

continued

Textile Industry	Inventions	Impact
Edmund Cartwright (English) 1743–1823	Power loom (1785)	Water-powered, provided rapid and automatic weaving.
Eli Whitney (American) 1765–1825	Cotton gin (1793)	Quick method of separating the seed from the cotton fiber. Increased supply of cotton for factories.

The improvement of production in the textile industry opened up new markets, and the adoption of Watt's steam engine meant that factories could now be built in any convenient location, not just near bodies of water. The development of the steam locomotive paved the way in England (1830–1850), which meant lower transportation costs, larger markets, and cheaper goods. Building railroads also took workers from their rural life and made them more inclined to become urban dwellers.

Steam Power	Inventions	Impact
Thomas Newcomen (English) 1663–1729	Steam engine (1765)	Served chiefly to operate a pump to drain water from coal mines.
James Watt (English) 1736–1819	Improved Newcomen's work (1769)	Opened up the age of steam. Watt's engine adapted for textile-mill use and for transportation.
Robert Fulton (American) 1765–1815	Steamship (1807)	Sped up shipping and lowered costs.
George Stephenson (English) 1781–1848	Steam locomotive (1814)	Paved way for the railroad era.

Industrialization swept across Europe from west to east, from England in the eighteenth century to Holland, Belgium, France, and the United States by 1830. By the 1850s, Germany, Italy, and Austria became industrialized and by the end of the nineteenth century, industrialization had spread to Eastern Europe and Russia. In the twentieth century, it spread to Asia, Africa, and Latin America.

Results of the Industrial Revolution

The Industrial Revolution brought about many economic and social changes, of which the most dramatic were increased production and availability of goods. Goods mass produced were cheaper than those in pre-industrial Europe and therefore more people were able to purchase them. The increased purchase of goods brought great riches to the entrepreneurs and also led to the growth of more jobs. Families migrated to the cities as the demand for workers increased, and entrepreneurs built factories around small market towns. In 1750, the population of Manchester was 17,000 people and by 1800 there were over 70,000 inhabitants. By the middle of the nineteenth century, England had more people living in cities or urban areas than in the countryside.

Unfortunately, the rapid and unplanned growth of the cities contributed to deplorable living conditions. The working class, or poor, lived in crowded and unhealthy conditions with no running water, no sewage or sanitation system, and garbage rotting in the streets. Cholera and other diseases spread rapidly. Although life in rural areas had always been difficult for the poor, the new concentration of so many people in one spot made it even worse. The lack of transportation within the cities and the slowness of the government to address the need for new sanitary codes contributed to the problems.

Industrialization also affected the family structure. Before, entire families had worked together as a unit under the domestic system. Under the factory system, family members held different jobs and did not work together; moreover, women and children frequently worked under horrible conditions — often 12–14 hours per day. In 1821, Michael Sadler, a British legislator, began Parliamentary investigations into the textile industry. The **Sadler Committee** discovered that children were regularly beaten and abused by factory owners. These investigations led to the passage of legislation regulating the employment of children in factories as well as in mines. Unfortunately, many parents did not support these laws because they needed the earnings of their children since their own wages were so low.

Many individuals saw industrialization as a threat to their way of life. Hand-loom weavers, for instance, lost their jobs and were replaced by machines. A group of anti-industrialists known as the **Luddites** opposed the new technology. They smashed machines to preserve their jobs and burned factories. These rioters were known as Luddites, named after a mythical figure, Ned Lud, who destroyed machines in the 1780s. Luddites were treated harshly and were hanged or sent to penal colonies in Australia.

Another group that opposed industrialization was known as the **Romantics**. The Romantics were composed of artists, writers, and composers who rebelled against the Enlightenment's emphasis on reason and stressed emotion. Some important Romantic writers were Samuel Coleridge, Sir Walter Scott, and Victor Hugo. Romantic composers included Frederic Chopin, Franz Liszt, and Hector Berlioz; Romantic artists included J. M. Turner and Eugene Delacroix. By emphasizing feelings, the Romantics helped create humanitarian movements to fight poverty and industrial evils. Poets such as William Blake (1757–1827) and William Wordsworth (1770–1850) wrote about the horrors of the Industrial Revolution. They viewed modern industry as ugly and as a brutal attack on nature and humanity.

The hardships and changes brought about by the Industrial Revolution gave rise to various solutions that led to new theories of economics. One of them was the **Classical School of Economics,** which rejected the government restriction of mercantilism in favor of free trade. Classical economics appealed to the new middle class since they looked upon tariffs and other government restrictions as obstacles to progress. Some important leaders in this movement are listed in the following table:

Leaders	Writings	Main Ideas
Adam Smith (Scottish) 1723–1790	*Wealth of Nations* (1776)	Laissez Faire: The government should not get involved with national economy. It should act as an agency to ensure that everyone is following the laws of the society. The "invisible hand" of supply and demand will promote the best interest of society. Smith's ideas became the basis of the economic system of capitalism during the Industrial Revolution.
Thomas Malthus (English) 1776–1834	*Essay On the Principle of Population* (1798)	Poverty and misery were unavoidable because population growth was increasing faster than food supply. War, disease, and famine were checks on population growth. Smaller families could stop the population growth.
David Ricardo (English) 1772–1823	*The Principles of Political Economy and Taxation*	Iron Law of Wages: Human wages must be sufficient enough to buy food. When wages are high, families have more children, but that increases the supply of labor, which leads to lower wages and higher unemployment. Like Malthus, Ricardo believed in limiting size of the family and opposed governmental help for the poor for fear it would lead to greater suffering.
Jeremy Bentham (English) 1748–1832	*Principles of Morals and Legislation*	Utilitarianism: The goal of society should be the greatest happiness for the greatest number. What is good for the individual is what gives him the most pleasure. However, if the individual harms the common good, government can intervene. This was a retreat from laissez faire.
John Stuart Mill (English) 1806–1873	*On Liberty* (1859)	A follower of Benthem who supported freedom for the individual but feared pursuit of one's own interest might harm others. Wanted government to pass laws to remove the evils of society. Advocated the rights of workers to organize, equal rights for women, and universal suffrage.

Many nineteenth-century thinkers condemned the evils of industrialization and capitalism and offered socialism as a means to end the poverty and injustices in society. **Socialism** can be defined as state (rather than private) ownership of the means of production (farms, factories, and railroads) and other large businesses that produce and distribute goods. The goal of the socialists was a society that operated for the welfare of all the people, and they felt that state ownership was a means to that end.

Socialism began in France and England in the early 1800s. The early socialists were called **Utopian Socialists** because they offered no practical plan for achieving their ideal society. They thought that industrialists would support socialism as soon as they realized how effective it could be. The most outstanding Utopian Socialists were the following:

- **Henri Comte de Saint Simon (1760–1825):** A French socialist who advocated the end of private property. He believed that a cadre of skilled businessmen and scientists should run the state for the betterment of the lower class.

- **Robert Owen (1771–1858):** A successful English industrialist who created a model industrial community in Scotland at New Lanark, the site of cotton mills. Contrary to the prevailing practices, he paid high wages, reduced working hours, ended child labor, built decent homes, provided education for the workers, and permitted the workers to share in management and profits. His New Lanark community prospered, but he was disappointed that others did not follow his example.

- **Louis Blanc (1811–1882):** He believed that every person had a right to a job and that the state should provide work for the unemployed in government-sponsored or national workshops. His ideas were successful for a short time in France during the Revolution of 1848.

- **Karl Marx (1818–1883):** In the 1840s this German writer and economist advocated a more militant form of socialism called **Communism**. He used this term to distinguish his views from those of the Utopian Socialists whom he condemned as unrealistic dreamers. His basic ideas are contained in *The Communist Manifesto*, a pamphlet he wrote in collaboration with **Friedrich Engels** (1820–1895) in which he called for a worldwide revolution to end the abuses of capitalism. *Das Kapital*, published from 1867 until 1895 is a three-volume work, the first published in 1867, the second in 1885, and the third in 1895.

The basic theories of Marxism are the following:

- **Economic View of History:** Marx argues that economics determines the course of history. Economic conditions shape the institutions of society such as religion and government.

- **Class Struggle:** History is a continuous class struggle between the "haves" and the "have nots." In ancient times it was between the patricians and the plebs; in the Middle Ages between the lords and the serfs; in industrial society between the capitalists and the workers (**proletariat**). Capitalists exploit the workers by paying them just enough wages to keep them alive. Marx predicted that the future would bring a violent revolution by the workers to overthrow the capitalists.

- **Inevitability of Revolution:** Marx predicted that the hostility between the classes would be aggravated as the rich get richer and the poor get poorer. As conditions worsen, especially during depression or war, the working class will inevitably revolt and establish a "dictatorship of the proletariat." This dictatorship will create a collective classless society. Marx also believed that the revolution would first come to industrial nations such as the United States and England, not an agricultural country such as Russia.

- **Surplus Value:** Capitalists take advantage of workers by not paying them the true value of their labor. The workers receive only a small portion of their just price or just enough to keep them alive. The difference between the worker's wage and the price of the good produced is the surplus value. This surplus value is the profits for the capitalist and contributes to the class struggle that inevitably leads to revolution.

- **Communist Society:** Once the proletariats establish a classless society, the "state will wither away" as it will no longer be needed as a result of the elimination of all other classes besides the proletariat. Private property will be abolished and the production of goods and availability of services would make the Marx principle "from each according to his ability to each according to his needs" a reality.

Marx brought a revolutionary zeal to the class struggle because he wanted to unite the workers of the world by organizing socialist parties. In 1864, a socialist organization was founded in London, which became known as the First International. However, internal struggles led to its dissolution in 1876. In 1889, socialist parties of many countries organized the Second International, and these parties became powerful across Europe.

Chronology of the Agricultural and Industrial Revolutions

1705	Thomas Newcomen builds the steam engine to pump water out of coal mines.
1733	James Kay invents flying shuttle.
1764	James Hargreaves invents spinning jenny.
1768	Richard Arkwright invents the water frame.
1769	James Watt patents steam engine allowing for the first time in history a steady and unlimited source of power.
1771	Robert Owen, one of the early Utopian Socialists, is born.
1776	Adam Smith publishes *Wealth of Nations*, which develops the theory of laissez-faire capitalism
1779	Samuel Crompton combines the concept of spinning jenny and water frame in the mills.
1785	Edmund Cartwright invents the power loom for machines.
1793	Eli Whitney invents the cotton gin.
1798	Thomas Malthus writes *Essay On the Principle of Population*.
1803	The first steam wagon appears on the streets of London.
1807	Robert Fulton drives the steamboat *Clermont* up the Hudson from New York to Albany.
1832	Great Reform bill passed by British Parliament; rotten boroughs eliminated; greater voting for middle class.
1833	The Factory Act passed in England prohibiting the employment of children.
1837	The telegraph is developed; the Chartist Movement is born.
1848	*The Communist Manifesto* by Karl Marx and Friedrich Engels is published.

1849	The last of the Navigation Acts are repealed.
1851	England connected to the European continent by wire.
1867	The Reform Bill of 1867 is passed in England and the franchise is increased by 124%.
1872	Secret Ballot becomes a law in England.
1891	Pope Leo XII issues *Rerum Novarum,* which addresses the struggle between capitalists and workers.

Sample Multiple-Choice Questions

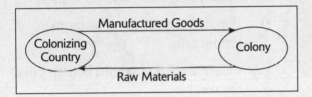

1. Which economic system is shown in this diagram?

   A. Socialism

   B. Command economy

   C. Laissez-faire capitalism

   D. Mercantilism

   E. Traditionalism

2. The Industrial Revolution began in England for all of the following reasons EXCEPT:

   A. England had an adequate supply of raw materials.

   B. Considerable money was available for investments.

   C. There was a large supply of available workers.

   D. The government was stable.

   E. Prices were high due to an inadequate food supply.

3. A direct result of the eighteenth century Enclosure Act in Great Britain was:

   A. an increase in agricultural efficiency

   B. an increase in rural population

   C. exports of food and fiber to the continent

   D. an increase in small farms

   E. a de-emphasis of scientific farming

4. Most of the technological advances of the early Industrial Revolution occurred in the following area:

   A. textiles

   B. chemicals

   C. railways

   D. ships

   E. heavy machinery

5. The Luddites of the nineteenth century were

   A. political liberals

   B. apprentices

   C. workers who smashed the machinery which eliminated their jobs

   D. communists

   E. union laborers

6. One of the most important Utopian Socialists was

   A. Louis Blanc

   B. Robert Owen

   C. Karl Marx

   D. Thomas Malthus

   E. David Ricardo

7. One result of the Industrial Revolution in nineteenth-century England was

   A. an increase in the number of guilds

   B. less need for capital

   C. a decline in the need for colonies

   D. an increase in the rural population

   E. an increase in urbanization

8. Which of the following is *not* associated with his contribution to the Agricultural Revolution?

   A. Jethro Tull — Reaper

   B. Charles Turnip Townshend — crop rotation

   C. Robert Bakewell — scientific breeding of animals

   D. Charles Newbold — cast-iron plow

   E. John Deere — self-cleaning plow

9. Adam Smith would most likely have supported the belief that:

   A. The government should regulate all businesses.

   B. The free market would benefit all members of society.

   C. Monopolies are good for a state.

   D. Population will grow faster than production.

   E. The free market would benefit only the wealthy.

10. "The story of history is the story of class struggles. Revolution is necessary to overthrow the ruling class and eventually create a classless society in which no one will be exploited."

    Which of the following people expresses the above viewpoint?

    A. Karl Marx

    B. John Locke

    C. Jean Jacques Rousseau

    D. Robert Owen

    E. Adam Smith

Answers to Multiple-Choice Questions and Explanations

1. D. Mercantilism is the economic system shown in the diagram. European monarchs adopted this economic policy from the sixteenth to the eighteenth centuries in their quest for colonies and trade. Under mercantilism, colonies existed for the benefit of the mother country. Colonies provided raw materials for the mother country, and in return the colonists were expected to serve as a market for manufactured goods. Mercantilism also required that a country achieve a favorable balance of trade by exporting more than it imported. European countries passed strict navigation laws to ensure that the colonies traded with the mother country.

Socialism is an economic system in which the government controls production and distribution of goods and wealth in a country. Command Economy is one in which the government makes all the economic decisions. Laissez-faire capitalism is an economic system that promotes private ownership and individual control of goods and services of a country. Laissez-faire also promotes the belief that government should not interfere in the operation of private businesses. A traditional economy is one in which hunting, gathering, farming, and herding cattle is the basis of society.

2. E. High prices due to inadequate food supply was not one of the contributing factors that gave rise to the Industrial Revolution in England. The Agricultural Revolution in the first half of the eighteenth century had provided England with a surplus labor supply and the means to feed them, as well as surplus capital. These agricultural changes prepared England for what Professor W. W. Rostow in his study, *The Stages of Economic Growth,* has termed "the industrial takeoff."

3. A. Enclosure, or fencing in of land, was a widespread practice in Great Britain after 1760. The Enclosure Acts allowed powerful landlords to use open fields, strips, and village commons, and evicted tenant farmers from leased lands. As millions of acres were enclosed, farm output increased. Profits also rose because large fields needed few people to work them. The improvement of agricultural efficiency had a human cost, however. Villages shrank as small farmers, who were forced off their land because they could not compete with large landholders, left in search of work. England did not export food to the continent, but instead used its improved food production to supply its growing population. The Enclosure Act contributed to the growth of scientific farming as the British continued to improve farm production. Charles Townshend's use of crop rotation and Robert Bakewell's experiments in scientific breeding highlighted the importance of science in agriculture.

4. A. The Industrial Revolution first took off in the textile industry. In the 1700s, as the demand for cotton goods grew, inventors came up with a string of devices that revolutionized the British textile industry. In 1733, John Kay's flying shuttle sped up weaving by the loom and created a demand for more thread. One invention led to another, such as the spinning jenny, the water frame, the power loom, and the cotton gin. The innovations in the textile industry improved productivity. Improvements in chemicals, railways, ships, and heavy machinery would occur in the nineteenth century as the need for markets led to the development of different sectors of the economy.

5. **C.** The Luddites were skilled artisans who resisted the new labor-saving machines that were costing them their jobs. They were conservatives and not political liberals. These men were reacting to industrialization by using violent methods and did not turn to Communism or unions as a way to meet their demands.

6. **B.** Robert Owen was an important Utopian Socialist. Utopian Socialists were convinced that if there were no difference between the rich and poor, fighting among people would disappear. These people were called Utopian Socialists after Thomas More's ideal community. The name implied that they were impractical reformers. Robert Owen, a wealthy British manufacturer, created a model industrial community in Scotland at New Lanark. He established a model community in which wages were high, working conditions and hours were good, and workers shared in management and profits. Owen's New Lanark community prospered, but other manufacturers did not follow his example. Louis Blanc was a French socialist who believed that the state should provide national workshops for the unemployed. Karl Marx was a communist. Thomas Malthus and David Ricardo were economists who described how population growth adversely affected the life and wages of workers.

7. **E.** One result of the Industrial Revolution was an increase in urbanization. The Industrial Revolution brought a rapid movement of people from rural areas to the cities or urban areas. Small towns around coal or iron mines grew up around factories. The town of Manchester jumped from 17,000 people in the 1750s to 40,000 by 1780 and 70,000 by1801. The people living in the cities of 20,000 or more in England jumped from 1.5 million in 1801 to 6.3 million in 1851. The Industrial Revolution destroyed the guild system but led to the rise of unions. Industrialization created the need for more capital to invest in the new machinery and the need for colonies as a source of markets and raw materials. The increase in urban population contributed to the decline, not the increase, in rural population.

8. **A.** Jethro Tull (1674–1741) invented the seed drill (1701). Tull's seed drill planted seeds in straight lines rather than by hand. The drill distributed seeds in an even manner and at the proper depth. This method also permitted cultivation between rows, increasing the amount of food produced per acre. Cyrus McCormack invented the reaper in 1834.

9. **B.** Adam Smith believed that the free market would benefit all members of society. In 1776, Adam Smith wrote *The Wealth of Nations*. Smith argued that the free market, the natural laws of supply and demand, should be allowed to operate and regulate all businesses. He tried to show how manufacturing, trade, wages, profits, and economic growth were all linked to the forces of supply and demand. The free market would produce more goods at lower prices making them affordable to everyone. A growing economy would also encourage capitalists to reinvest and spur continued economic growth. Smith believed in laissez faire (leave business alone) and that the market place was better off without any government regulation. Smith rejected monopolies and encouraged competition. Thomas Malthus discussed the relationship between population growth and production. Smith believed that a growing economy would not benefit only the wealthy.

10. **A.** In 1848, Karl Marx outlined his ideas of history in *The Communist Manifesto*. He proposed a scientific theory of history in which economic conditions determine history. He wrote that history is a struggle between the "haves" and "have-nots." In ancient times, the struggle was between plebeians and patricians. During the Middle Ages, the struggle

was between lords and bourgeoisie. In industrial societies, the final struggle is between the factory owners, who are the "haves," and the workers, who are the "have-nots." Marx predicted that there will be a worldwide revolution in which the workers will rise up against the owners and form a classless society. He felt that the conflict was inevitable because workers worldwide are being oppressed by capitalist owners. John Locke was a seventeenth-century English philosopher who wrote *Two Treatises of Government* to justify the Glorious Revolution. Jean Jacques Rousseau was an eighteenth-century French philosopher who wrote *The Social Contract*. His ideas influenced the French Revolution. Robert Owen was a nineteenth-century industrialist who is associated with Utopian Socialists. Adam Smith was the founder of modern economics and believed in laissez faire, which laid the foundation for the economic system of capitalism.

The Struggle for Democracy in Nineteenth-Century Europe (1815–1914)

The years from the end of the Congress of Vienna, 1815 to 1848, are often referred to as the **Age of Reaction**, or the **Age of Metternich**. Prince Klemens von Metternich of Austria set in motion a 30-year pattern of anti-democratic policies followed by conservatives—monarchs, nobles, landowners, and church elders—who dominated the continent of Europe. Metternich firmly believed that the American and French Revolution had been responsible for a generation of war, which caused bloodshed and suffering in Europe. As a conservative, he had a passionate hatred of liberalism because it had generally became associated with national aspirations. The idea that each national group had a right to establish its own independent government threatened the very existence of the nobility as well as the Austrian Empire. The conservatives, like Metternich, wanted to return the kings of Europe to power and restore the historic social class structure in society. Many peasants supported the conservatives because they wanted to preserve their traditional ways that were being threatened by industrialization.

In spite of the careful plans of the Congress of Vienna, there were a series of revolts inspired by nationalism or liberalism in countries such as Italy, Spain, Greece, and Portugal. These revolts began to spread to Austria, the German states, and France. Borrowing their ideas from the Enlightenment, the liberal thinkers of the 1820s and 1830s, many of whom represented the middle class, wanted a government based on a written constitution that guaranteed the natural rights of the people. The struggle between liberalism and conservatism erupted in full-scale revolts in 1848. The tidal wave of revolution ended the Age of Metternich and for many opponents of the old order it was the springtime of the people. The revolutions of 1848, beginning in Paris, affected all the countries on the European continent except Great Britain and Russia.

In the German states, following the 1848 uprisings, Prussia's failure at democratic changes contributed to the growth of militarism within the country. Austria, meanwhile, struggled against the forces of democracy, and nationalism threatened the foundation of its polyglot, multinational empire. In France, the revolutions of 1848 continued France's uneven march toward democracy as the country grappled with the forces of liberalism and conservatism.

In Russia, which was unaffected by the 1848 revolutions, efforts to modernize and reform the economy came into conflict with the goals of the Russian czar to retain absolute control. In Britain, however, different democratic reforms had evolved throughout the nineteenth century that helped to broaden the franchise and voter participation. By the end of the nineteenth century, both Britain and France had created the foundation for a liberal democratic government.

The Age of Metternich (1815–1848)

Prince Klemens von Metternich (1773–1859) of the Austrian Empire took stern measures to combat the spread of democracy and nationalism. He began his diplomatic career in 1801 as

Ambassador to Saxony, later to Prussia in 1803. In 1806, the Austrian Emperor appointed him Ambassador to Napoleon's court and by 1809, he was Foreign Minister, an office he held until 1848. In 1810, Metternich was successful in arranging the marriage of Maria Louise, the 18-year-old daughter of the emperor, to Napoleon, who had divorced his wife, Josephine. He also secured a temporary alliance with France. In 1813, Metternich joined the War of Coalition against Napoleon, when the French invaded Russia. Metternich reached the height of his power at the Congress of Vienna (see "The Age of Revolution: The French Revolution and Napoleonic Era"). After 1815, Metternich devoted his energies to upholding the settlements of the Congress of Vienna and maintaining the power of the Hapsburg Dynasty in Europe.

The **Metternich System** employed censorship of speech and the press, espionage, and the suppression of revolutionary and national movements. He also used secret police and spies to establish control. The **German Confederation**, as states under Metternich's control were called, were forced to adopt the **Carlsbad Decrees** (1819), which banned freedom of speech and the press. Other countries in Europe adopted similarly restrictive policies. In Britain, the **Six Acts** (1819) were designed to control radical leaders, and in France the **Four** or **July Ordinances** (1830) forbade freedom of the press and reduced the number of eligible voters. Britain, Austria, Russia, and Prussia also formed a **Quadruple Alliance** and were later joined by France in 1818 (**Quintuple Alliance**) to keep peace and maintain order of the existing status quo. This cooperation among the major powers became known as the "Concert of Europe."

Despite repression, reformers continued to demand democracy and independent governments. Frequent uprisings throughout the 1820s and 1830s weakened the Metternich System.

The Revolutions of the 1820s

From 1820–1823, revolutions broke out in Spain, Sardinia, Portugal, and Greece. The revolts in Spain and Sardinia were easily crushed by the members of the Quintuple Alliance. A constitutional monarchy was established in Portugal in 1822. In their rebellion against the Ottoman Empire, the Greek revolutionaries won worldwide support. Many Europeans wanted to support their cause because Christian Europe saw it as a struggle against the Muslims as well as a way to gain territory and weaken the Ottoman Empire. In 1824, the work of the Romantic painter **Eugene Delacroix** (1798–1863) entitled *The Massacre of Chios* glorified the struggle of Greek freedom fighters against the Ottomans and won the support of nationalists. In 1829, Greece won its independence.

The Revolutions of the 1830s

A series of revolutions broke out in the 1830s, which first took place in France and then spread to Belgium, Poland, Italy, and Germany. After the fall of Napoleon, **Louis XVIII**, brother of Louis XVI, was returned to the throne. Although undemocratic, Louis protected the people against the return of absolutism and aristocratic privilege. When Louis died in 1824, his brother **Charles X** (who reigned from 1824–1830) inherited the throne and decided to re-establish the old order, believing in absolute rule. In 1830, he suspended the legislature, limited the right to vote, and restricted the press. This sparked the **July Revolution** (July 26–29, 1830). Angry students, workers, and intellectuals rioted in Paris for three days. Charles abdicated and fled to Britain. The workers and the intellectuals wanted a republic, but the upper middle class, who retained control, wanted a constitutional monarchy. Through the efforts of Talleyrand and the Marquis De Lafayette, the lower house of the Chamber of Deputies agreed upon **Louis Philippe** as king, a cousin of Charles X and who in his youth had supported the revolution of 1789.

The French called Louis Philippe the **citizen king**; he was plain spoken, dressed in a frock coat and top hat, carried an umbrella, and owed his throne to the people. Like the people, he adopted the dress of the common man. He replaced the Bourbon flag with the Tricolor of the Revolution and increased the electorate to include the upper middle class. The vast majority of the people, however, could still not vote and Louis' policy favored the middle class at the expense of the workers.

The news of the successful July Revolution in France served as a spark to revolutions throughout Europe, leading Metternich to say, "When France sneezes, Europe catches a cold." In 1830, Belgium revolted against Dutch rule, protesting against being governed by people who had a different language and religion. The Belgians received support from Louis Philippe in France and from England, and in 1831 they became an independent state. In 1839, all the great powers recognized Belgium as a neutral state. Nationalist uprisings also took place in Italy, Germany, and Poland; these revolts were easily crushed by Austria and Russia, however. The successful revolutions in France and Belgium showed that even in Western Europe, the Metternich System could not contain the forces of democracy and nationalism.

The Revolutions of 1848 and Their Aftermath

The specter of revolutions, which according to Karl Marx haunted Europe in 1848, were similar to those that had previously haunted Europe in 1789 and 1830. In 1848, however—a time of social and economic change—the revolutionary demands were widespread and irrepressible. Agricultural disasters, such as the Irish potato famine, widespread unemployment, and tension between the urban workers and the new class of capitalists created by the Industrial Revolution added to the discontent. The power of nationalism in the German and Italian states, moreover, added fuel to an already smoldering fire.

France

As usual, France started the revolutionary tide by revolting early in February of 1848. King Louis Philippe aroused the opposition of both the liberal and the radical **Republicans**. The liberal Republicans were moderate and middle class who supported the expansion of the suffrage for all male voters. The radical Republicans wanted to promote social and economic changes to help the lives of the workers. They both opposed a monarchy and the liberal Republicans, who had formerly supported Louis Philippe, denounced the rampant corruption of his government, and voting restrictions. Unemployed workers, who had no vote, were also unhappy with Louis Philippe's government. In February, when the government prohibited a scheduled political meeting held by Republicans to honor George Washington, angry crowds took to the streets of Paris.

During the **February Days** (February 22–23) workers, students, and radicals rioted, and demonstrators clashed with troops. On February 24, as the turmoil spread and the workers took control of Paris, Louis Philippe abdicated and fled to England. A provisional government was created composed of Political Republicans (middle class liberals) and Social Republicans (the working class group), who set national elections for April. Differences divided the government, however: The middle class liberals in control of the government were led by **Alphonse Lamartine** (1790–1869), who favored moderate reforms and had little sympathy for the working poor, although they gave some concessions to the workers. **Louis Blanc** (1811–1882), a Social Republican, was allowed to establish national workshops to provide jobs for the unemployed. In June of 1848, the upper and middle class who had won a majority of the votes in the April election (based on universal male suffrage), shut down the workshops claiming that they were a waste of money. Angry crowds stormed the streets again. This time, however, the bourgeoisie and peasants, fearing that the Socialists might take their land, turned against the workers. The **June Riots** (June 23–26) were unlike previous uprisings in France in that they constituted full-scale class warfare involving half of Paris. After three terrible days and the death or injury of 10,000 people, the government with the support of the army and the peasants crushed the rebellion.

Seeking to restore order, the National Assembly issued a constitution for a **Second French Republic** (the first lasted from 1792–1804 when Napoleon became emperor). The new constitution of this government created a strong president with a one-house legislature, elected by universal male suffrage. In November, **Louis Napoleon**, nephew of Napoleon Bonaparte, was elected. He was installed as president of the Second French Republic on December 20, 1848.

After his election, Louis Napoleon created a conservative government. He cooperated with the National Assembly, but when it refused to change the constitution so he could run for another term, he initiated a coup d'etat in 1851 and assumed dictatorial powers. Napoleon was fearful that the radicals would win the 1852 election. He replaced the Second Republic with the **Second Empire** (the first was that of Napoleon I) and crowned himself **Emperor Napoleon III** in 1852. Like his uncle, his actions were approved by a **plebiscite** (an expression of the popular will) of the voters. Until 1860, Napoleon III's government retained the outward appearance of a democracy but it was a dictatorship. He exercised control through his secret police and enforced censorship of the press and state-controlled elections. After 1860, Napoleon III believed that economic progress would reduce political and social tensions, and by rebuilding much of Paris he would enhance the glory of the empire. He carried out a vast public-works policy, which included rebuilding roads, canals, and railroads. Working with **Georges Hausmann** (1809–1891), Napoleon III supported the transformation of Paris into a modern city, clearing slums and creating wide boulevards. Sanitary conditions improved and a sewage system was developed to remove waste. Napoleon III also gained the support of city workers by legalizing unions and granting them the right to strike.

The Second Empire fell when Napoleon became involved in the ill-fated Franco-Prussian War (1870–1871) in which he was captured and exiled to Britain for his last years. The **National Assembly** (1871–1875) was established and met to decide on a new government. In March 1871, a radical government (the **Paris Communes**) took control of Paris. The **Communards**, as the rebels were called, included workers, socialists, and bourgeoisie republicans. As patriots, they rejected the peace with Germany that the National Assembly had negotiated and refused to recognize the authority of the National Assembly. In May, the loyal troops of the National Assembly crushed the revolt, in which it is estimated that over 20,000 people were killed, and the city of Paris was burned. By 1875, the National Assembly had agreed to establish a new government called the **Third Republic**, which consisted of a two-house legislature, a **Chamber of Deputies** elected by universal male suffrage, and a senate chosen by an indirect election. Since many parties were represented in the Chamber of Deputies, no one party could dominate the government. This led to instability as governments rose and fell depending upon their ability to gain the support of the different political parties. The Third Republic was also threatened by domestic difficulties such as the Boulanger and Dreyfus affairs.

The Boulanger Affair (1887–1889)

In 1887, **General Georges Boulanger** (1837–1891), Minister of War who had won the support of the army by improving its military life and a believer in a monarchial form of government, was encouraged by his supporters to overthrow the government. He waited too long and republicans had enough time to expel him from the country. Boulanger fled to Belgium, where he later committed suicide. The successful handling of this affair improved the prestige of the government.

The Dreyfus Affair (1894–1906)

Alfred Dreyfus (1859–1935), a Jewish Republican Army captain, was court-martialed by royalist officers and declared guilty of selling secret military documents to the Germans. Many suspected an anti-Semitic conspiracy. The country was divided between his supporters and those who believed the charges were legitimate. He was acquitted in 1906 and awarded the Legion of Honor. The Dreyfus affair strengthened the Third Republic because it showed the monarchists as being the faction guilty of anti-government activities.

The Third Republic was also successful in separation of Church and State and provided free education. Despite a bumpy road, France established a stable government providing many social benefits by the end of the nineteenth century. The Third Republic lasted for 65 years.

The Austrian Empire

The Austrian Empire consisted of many different national groups: Germans, Hungarians, Czechs, Rumanians, Poles, Slavs, and Italians. Although the revolutions in the 1820s and 1830s had little effect on the empire as whole, the Hapsburg Empire, headed by **Emperor Ferdinand I** (1793–1875, emperor 1835–1848), was vulnerable to revolutionary changes. With its collection of different nationalities, the spectre of nationalism haunted the empire. Its government was reactionary and the social system provided little hope for the people. As news of the February Days in France spread across Europe, people within the Austrian Empire began to revolt. Many demanded more democracy and students, supported by the workers, demonstrated in the streets of Vienna, manning the barricades and invading the Imperial Palace. In March, the revolution spread to Budapest. The Hungarian nationalist leader **Lajos Kossuth** (1802–1894) demanded independence. He also called for an end to serfdom and a written constitution to protect basic rights in Hungary. The Czechs made similar demands.

Fearing for his life, Metternich resigned and fled to England in disguise. Ferdinand I agreed to the reforms and abdicated. Conflicts among the different nationalities (Hungarians against Croats; Serbs against Romanians; Czechs against Germans) weakened the revolution, however. The alliance of the working class and the middle class soon collapsed and the Austrian army regained control of Vienna. In October of 1848, the Hungarians invaded Austria and by April 1849 a Hungarian Republic with Kossuth in charge was created. In June of 1849, with the aid of the Russians, Austria defeated the Hungarians. Kossuth fled into exile while thirteen of his guards were executed. In Northern Italy, the two provinces of Milan and Venice revolted in favor of a united Italy. These revolutions were also crushed. The revolutions in the Austrian Empire had failed. However, the Austrian Empire still had to confront the problems associated with the rise of national aspirations within the different ethnic groups in its empire, as well as the issue of nationalism. By the end of the nineteenth century, these problems would have serious ramifications for the Austro-Hungarian Empire.

Prussia

After Austria, Prussia was the largest and most influential German kingdom. Prussia included the Rhineland, the central region around Berlin, West Prussia, and East Prussia. In the 1830s, Prussia had provided leadership in creating an economic union called the **Zolverein**. Prior to 1848, the goal of middle-class Prussian liberals was to transform absolutist Prussia into a liberal constitutional government. Then Prussia would take the lead in uniting all of Germany into a liberal unified government.

The events in France in 1848 had repercussions in Prussia, where Emperor **Frederich Wilhelm IV** (b. 1795, ruled 1840–1861) had promised reforms but always hesitated. When riots broke out in Berlin on March 10th, the king promised to grant Prussia a liberal constitution written by an elected assembly and merge it with a new national German state that was being created. Although the demands of the workers, which included a ten-hour workday and minimum wages, differed from those of the Prussian aristocracy who wanted to assert their power over the king, the king allowed the election of a constituent assembly to draw up a constitution. In December of 1848, the king drew up his own constitution that was very similar to what the assembly had planned, allowing for freedom of the press and a two-house legislature with universal male suffrage for the lower house. However, power still remained in the hands of the upper class because weighted votes were given to those who paid more taxes.

Meanwhile, delegates from many German states met in Frankfurt from May of 1848 until May of 1849 as part of the **Frankfurt Assembly** to discuss their vision of how a united Germany would be established. This meeting, which was not sanctioned by Frederich Wilhelm was hampered by conflicting aims and divisions. Although all agreed on a united Germany, delegates disagreed over whether it should be a republic or a monarchy. Moreover, a major dispute arose over what areas would be included in the new Germany. Those who supported the **Grossdeutsche** ("large Germany") view wanted to include the German-speaking province of Austria under German rule. The **Kleindeutsche** ("small Germany") wanted to exclude Austria and include only Prussia with the small German states. When the Austrians opposed any division of their territory, the delegates decided on a united Germany excluding Austria. They completed drawing up a liberal constitution and offered the Imperial Crown of a united Germany to

Frederich Wilhelm. He contemptuously refused to accept the "crown from the gutter" and re-established his authority by dissolving the assembly under threat from the Prussian military. The failure of the Frankfurt Assembly destroyed the hope of a united Germany under a liberal parliamentary government and laid the foundation for the rise of Prussian militarism that created a united Germany in 1871.

Russia

The European revolutions of the 1820s and 1830s had very little effect on Russia. The Russian czar had ruled for centuries with absolute power and the ideals of thc Enlightenment and French Revolution had never taken hold in that country. **Alexander I** (b. 1777, ruled 1801–1825) initially was receptive to libcral ideas such as promoting education, ending censorship, and granting greater freedom for Jews, but he became very conservative after Napoleon's invasion in 1812. At the Congress of Vienna, he sided with the conservatives and opposed all efforts at liberal reform. He imposed strict censorship and insisted that all his subjects follow the Russian Orthodox Church.

When Alexander I died in 1825, his young brother **Nicholas I** (b. 1796, ruled 1825–1855), ascended to the throne. At the time of the succession, a group of young officers, known as the **Decembrists**, led a revolt in December. They supported **Constantine**, Nicholas' brother, who they believed would promote a more liberal government, a constitution, and the modernization of Russia. Nicholas I crushed the rcvolt, executed some of the Decembrists, and cracked down on all dissenters. Nicholas created the **Third Section**, the dreaded secret police, who hunted down all those critical of the govcrnment and strictly enforced the czar's decree that books from Western Europe be banned in the country. To bolster his regime, Nicholas I enthusiastically supported the ideals of Russian absolutism:

- **Orthodoxy:** the strong connection between the Russian Orthodox Church, of which the czar was the official head, and thc government

- **Autocracy:** the absolute powcr of the czar

- **Nationalism:** respect for Russian tradition and suppression of non-Russians within the empire

The autocratic regime of Nicholas I was not threatened by the revolutionary movements that dominated Europe in 1848. From 1848 to 1849, Russian troops put down a revolt by Polish nationalists and suppressed all democratic institutions. Nicholas also followed a policy of Russification, which forced Poles and other racial groups to use the Russian language and follow the approved Russian Orthodox religion. Many unsuccessful peasant revolts occurred during Nicholas' reign.

Alexander II (b. 1818, ruled 1855–1881) came to the throne during the **Crimean War** (1853–1856), which had developed at the end of the reign of Nicholas I, when Russia tried to seize Ottoman lands along the Danube River. Because neither France nor England wanted to see Russia expand into the Mediterranean, France joined England in supporting the **Ottoman Empire**, known as "the sick man of Europe," by sending fleets into the Black Sea. The term

"the sick man of Europe" was used because after the loss of Hungary in 1699, the Ottoman Empire had entered a long period of territorial disintegration. In 1856, Russia's defeat in the Crimean War revealed how far Russia lagged behind the Western countries economically, technologically, and culturally. Alexander realized that he had to introduce reform and modernization.

In 1861, Alexander issued the **Emancipation Edict**, abolishing serfdom, an institution that had long disappeared from Western Europe. Although the serfs became free citizens and were no longer the personal possessions of the lords, freedom brought problems. Peasants now had to buy the land that they had worked on for so long, but were too poor to purchase it. Furthermore, the land allotted to the peasants was either too small to be efficient or not able to support a family. Peasant communities, not individual peasants, received approximately one-half of the land and each peasant community was jointly responsible for payment of all the families in the village. The government had hoped that collective responsibility would prevent the development of a class of landless peasants. In reality, the serfs, while legally free, were still bound to the land since they could not leave until the village paid off the debt. Thus, discontent still festered within the peasant class. In 1917, the Bolshevik leader, Lenin, would build on this resentment to help him gain power (see "Europe in Crisis (1917–1939)").

Alexander II also realized that in order to compete with Western Europe he had to make some efforts to modernize and industrialize the economy. In 1860, the country had only about 1,250 miles of railroads, but by 1880 it had about 15,550 miles. Industrial suburbs developed around Moscow and St. Petersburg. Despite these changes, Russian intellectuals began to question the future of Russia. Some, known as **Westerners,** thought that Russia should model itself after Western Europe. Others, such as the **Slavophiles**, thought that Russia should retain its own spirit and tradition and avoid westernization. As the number of dissenters grew, terrorism became common. In 1881, Alexander II was assassinated and the era of reform came to an abrupt end.

Alexander III (b. 1845, ruled 1881–1894) was a reactionary, determined to avenge his father's death to ensure his autocratic rule by reinforcing the pillars of Russian absolutism through the secret police and censorship. Although Russian efforts at political reforms were frozen, Russia continued to industrialize because the czar realized that the country needed to develop its economy to remain a great power. The gigantic **Trans-Siberian Railway** connecting Moscow with Vladivostok on the Pacific Ocean, 5,000 miles away, was a source of pride for Russia. The success of the railroad encouraged foreigners to use their capital to build factories in Russia. Foreign capitalists began to build and develop the steel and coal industry in Russia. By 1900, only Germany and the United States were producing more steel than the Russians, and Russia was producing and refining half the world's steel output. While Russia was establishing itself as an industrial country, however, Alexander III failed to realize the problems created by industrialization, such as the need for political, constitutional, and economic reforms. These issues led to major changes in Russia at the beginning of the twentieth century.

Britain: Democracy through Evolution

Although England had established the framework for democracy during the seventeenth century, it still maintained many undemocratic features. Although there was a Constitutional

Monarch and a Parliament with two political parties, the government was not representative of the people. Less than five percent of the population could vote and the British Parliament represented the interest of the wealthy. Parliament was made up of the **House of Lords**, which consisted of hereditary nobles and high ranking clergy of the Anglican Church. The House of Lords had the power to veto any law passed by the **House of Commons**. During the nineteenth century, however, England embarked on a series of evolutionary changes that gradually made the country more democratic. One such series of changes came at the conclusion of the Napoleonic War in 1815, when England suffered a temporary depression that sparked food riots in many cities. In 1819, the government met force with force, which led to the **Peterloo Massacre** in Manchester. In the 1820s, however, reformers began to make some changes. Religious toleration was granted to Catholics, membership was allowed in unions, and the justice system was restructured allowing for a revised penal code.

In the 1830s, a greater series of political reforms were enacted that had a lasting influence on the country. The **Whigs** (representing the middle class and concerned about business interests) and the **Tories** (representatives of the nobles and landowners) fought over a reform bill about representation, as the House of Commons had not been reapportioned since the seventeenth century. The Industrial Revolution had led to the growth of cities at the expense of the rural areas. Although the population of urban areas had increased dramatically, the rural areas were still sending the same number of representatives to the House of Commons even though fewer voters or sometimes no voters lived there. These areas became known as the so-called "**rotten boroughs**" because they were underpopulated and did not represent the people. The **Great Reform Bill of 1832** abolished the rotten boroughs. Adequate representation was given to the industrial areas and, by reducing property qualifications, there was an increase in the number of voters from 500,000 to 800,000. The Reform Bill of 1832 was the first step towards democracy. These changes began to put power in the hands of the industrial towns.

Because the Reform Bill did not enfranchise city workers, they organized the **Chartist movement**, a reform movement representing the working class and some lower middle-class workers. In the **People's Charter of 1837**, from which the movement derived its name, the Chartists petitioned the government for the following:

- Universal male suffrage
- Secret ballots
- Equal election districts
- Elimination of property qualifications for members of Parliament
- Annual elections
- Salaries for members of Parliament

In 1848, as revolution swept across Europe, Chartists marched on Parliament and presented their petition. Parliament, as it had done in 1837, rejected the Chartists' petition. The Chartists failed in the short run, but by the beginning of the twentieth century all of the Chartists' demands, with the exception of annual parliamentary elections, came to pass.

The efforts to expand the franchise continued throughout the later half of the nineteenth century. In 1867, Prime Minister **Benjamin Disraeli** (1804–1881), who dominated the

135

Conservative Party (formerly the Tories), was able to convince Parliament to approve a Reform Bill that doubled the number of voters by reducing property qualifications. The Reform Bill extended votes to men who either owned a house or paid rent. Disraeli had hoped that the newly enfranchised city voters would join together with the wealthy land owners and outvote the merchants and factory owners — the **Liberals** (formerly Whigs). However, Disraeli failed to change the voting behaviors of the city workers, and they continued to support the Liberals to achieve more democratic reforms. In 1884, the Liberals, under Prime Minister **William Gladstone** (1809–1898), enacted the **Reform Bill of 1884**, which extended the right to vote to agricultural workers. From the mid-1850s to the first two decades of the 1900s, the Liberals or the Tories were in control of the government. Disraeli, in the 1880s, sponsored laws to improve public health and housing for workers in the cities. Gladstone supported free public education for all children; government jobs based on merit, and not on birth or wealth; and the legalization of unions, as well as the adaption of the secret ballot.

In the 1900s, unions and socialist members formed their own **Labour Party** that began to push for social legislation that protected the rights of workers. The Labour Party grew in strength and by 1924, gained a parliamentary majority with the support of the liberal party. The efforts of the labor party laid the foundation for such social legislation as unemployment insurance, old-age pensions, and disability insurance, which was eventually enacted after World War II.

Chronology of the Struggle for Democracy in Nineteenth-Century Europe (1815–1914)

1819	Metternich imposes the Carlsbad Decree upon the German Confederation.
1820–24	Revolutions in Spain, Sardinia, Portugal, and (in 1821–1824) Greece.
1824	Charles X becomes king of France; Eugene Delacroix's painting *Massacre at Chios* celebrates the Greek struggle for freedom and independence.
1825	Decembrist Revolt in Russia.
1830	Greeks gain independence; Revolution begins in France; Charles X flees to England; Louis Philippe becomes the citizen king.
1832	The Reform Bill nearly doubles the electorate in England and abolishes rotten boroughs.
1832	The Factory Act in Britain restricting child labor is established.
1837	Chartist Petition passes.
1845–47	Potato famine occurs in Ireland.

1848	The *Communist Manifesto* is first published; Revolutions break out in Italy, France, Hungary, Austria, and Prussia — all fail; Metternich resigns and flees to England.
1849	Frankfurt Assembly selects Frederich Wilhelm as emperor of the new German Empire, but he refuses the crown.
1852	Louis Napoleon becomes Emperor Napoleon III.
1861	Czar Alexander II of Russia issues the Emancipation Edict that abolishes serfdom.
1867	The Reform Bill in Britain reduces property qualifications for voters.
1870–1871	Franco-Prussian War takes place. France is defeated and Napoleon is exiled; The Second French Empire ends.
1884	A Reform Bill extends the right to vote to agricultural workers in Britain.
1894	The Dreyfus Affair divides France.

Sample Multiple-Choice Questions

1. Which of the following countries gained its independence in 1830?

  A. Italy

  B. Germany

  C. Ireland

  D. Poland

  E. Greece

2. The July Revolution of 1830 resulted in

  A. the rise of Louis Napoleon to power

  B. the selection of Charles X as the new king

  C. the appointment of Louis Philippe as king by the Chamber of Deputies

  D. conflict with England

  E. the granting of universal suffrage to all men who owned property

3. Which of the following statements is *least* accurate about the June Days in Paris in 1848?

  A. The peasants supported the workers.

  B. Class warfare broke out between the workers and bourgeoisie.

  C. The government, with the support of the army, crushed the rebellion.

  D. The government did not fully support the national workshops.

  E. The June Days led to the creation of the Second Republic.

4. Louis Napoleon (Napoleon III) gained popularity for all of the following EXCEPT

   A. granting workers the right to strike

   B. sponsoring a public works program

   C. modernizing Paris

   D. having successful foreign policy victories

   E. encouraging massive railroad building

5. Which of the following was *not* a demand of the Chartists?

   A. universal suffrage for men and women

   B. secret ballots

   C. elimination of property qualifications

   D. annual election of Parliament

   E. equal election districts

6. The Reform Act of 1832 in Britain

   A. granted universal manhood suffrage

   B. introduced the secret ballot

   C. ended the rotten boroughs

   D. limited the power of the House of Lords

   E. increased the power of the monarchy

7. The Frankfurt Assembly was

   A. a middle class body that wanted to write a constitution for a liberal, united Germany

   B. united behind a republican form of government

   C. supported by Austria

   D. called by Bismarck to enhance Prussia's prestige

   E. concerned primarily with economic issues

8. All of the following countries experienced a revolution in 1848 EXCEPT

   A. France

   B. Italy

   C. Germany

   D. Austria

   E. Britain

9. The Decembrist Revolt of 1825 occurred in

   A. Russia

   B. France

   C. Germany

   D. Austria

   E. Italy

Year	Suffrage granted
1815	to less than 5% of the male Anglican population
1820s	to wealthy male Roman Catholics and wealthy non-Anglican Protestants
1832	to men with a certain amount of property
1860s	to a large category of working-class men
1880s	to farm workers and most other men

10. Which conclusion can be drawn from the above table? Base your answer to this question on data from the following table and your knowledge of British history.

   A. Anglicans gained the right to vote after the Catholics.

   B. Revolutions gained the right to vote for men.

   C. The right to vote was gradually extended over a period of time.

   D. By 1860, all men had the right to vote.

   E. All Roman Catholics could vote by 1830.

Answers to Multiple-Choice Questions and Explanations

1. **E.** The Greeks, with the assistance of the European powers (England, France, and Russia), successfully revolted against the Ottoman Empire, setting the stage for nationalists throughout Europe. The Europeans supported the Greek's struggle for independence because Christian Europe saw it as a struggle against the Muslims as well as a way to weaken the Ottoman Empire. Ottoman atrocities towards the rebels also fanned the fires of Europe's outrage. In 1830, England, France, and Russia declared Greek independence. Italy and Germany became independent united nations during the late 1860s and early1870s. Ireland and Poland did not become independent nations until the twentieth century.

2. **C.** The July Revolution of 1830 resulted in the Chamber of Deputies appointing Louis Philippe as king. Charles X, the successor to Louis XVIII, tried to re-establish the old order and repudiate the constitutional charter, which protected against a return to royal absolutism in 1830. Angry students, city workers, and intellectuals rioted for three days in Paris. When Charles X fled to England, the Chamber of Deputies enthroned Louis Philippe as a united monarch. Louis Philippe, known as the citizen king, replaced the Bourbon flag with the tri-color flag of the French Revolution. He enacted a liberal constitution and reduced the property qualifications to vote in order to enfranchise more members of the middle class. Louis Napoleon rose to power as a result of the revolution of 1848. Charles X was forced to abdicate and flee to England in 1830. After the Congress of

Vienna, France and England were at peace with each other for the rest of the century. In 1848, not 1830, universal male suffrage was enacted in France. The provisional republic established in 1848 granted universal male suffrage.

3. A. The peasants did not support the workers. The peasants, like the middle and upper class, were frightened by the socialist outlook of the workers. Peasants who owned lands hated the radicals of Paris. Fearing the socialists might take their land, they attacked the workers and opposed the national workshops. In June 1848, the upper and middle class won control of the government and shut down the national workshops because they considered them to be a waste of money. When the city workers took to the streets, the bourgeoisie turned against the protesters. After three terrible days, the government put down the revolts. Over 10,000 people were either killed or injured. The government of moderate Republicans at first supported national workshops as a compromise solution for the socialists. However, as the workshops grew and became more radical, the government dissolved them on June 21. In 1848, the revolutionaries proclaimed the Second French Republic, and guaranteed universal male suffrage. The French people elected Louis Napoleon, the nephew of Napoleon Bonaparte, as president. The republic lasted until 1851.

4. D. Louis Napoleon (Napoleon III) was never successful in his foreign policies ventures. Nationalists were disappointed with Napoleon III's humiliating failure in Mexico (1862–1866). To revive his popularity, Napoleon III tried to check Prussian power, and opposed German unification. In the Franco-Prussian War (1870–1871), the French army was defeated and Napoleon III was taken prisoner and exiled. The defeat of Napoleon III led to the end of the Second French Empire and the Second Republic. After 1860, Napoleon III gained popularity by granting workers the right to form unions and the right to strike, both of which had been denied by the earlier government. Napoleon III tried to avoid social and economic tensions by promoting the welfare of all his subjects through government reforms. He believed that by modernizing Paris through a public works program, he could improve living conditions. Rebuilding Paris provided a model for urban planning. Napoleon III also promoted mass railroad building as a way to help promote economic growth.

5. A. The Chartists did not support universal suffrage for men and women. The Chartist movement was formed in 1838 to secure the vote for the working and lower middle class as part of their larger demand for universal manhood suffrage. Although the Chartists did not call for women's rights, women in the Chartist movement organized the first British association to work for women suffrage. The Chartist movement lasted about ten years. In subsequent years, the Chartist demands, such as secret ballots, elimination of property qualifications, and payment of regular salaries for members of Parliament, were eventually enacted. The annual election of Parliament was the only demand that never became a law.

6. C. The Reform Act of 1832 ended the rotten boroughs. The Reform Bill redistributed the seats in the House of Commons, giving representation to large towns and eliminating rotten boroughs — rural towns who lost so many people that there were few or no voters. These rotten boroughs were still sending members to Parliament. Universal male suffrage and secret ballots were part of the demands of the Chartists in 1848. The Parliament Act of 1911 limited the power of the House of Lords. There was never any discussion to increase the power of the monarchy. The Glorious Revolution of 1689 had established a limited monarchy which has continued to serve as a symbol of unity for the people of England until the present.

7. **A.** The Frankfurt Assembly was supported by the middle class, who wanted a constitution for a liberal united Germany. After the revolution broke out in France, the National Assembly, which met in Frankfurt and became known as the Frankfurt Assembly, met to write a constitution for a united Germany. Frederich Wilhelm IV refused to accept the crown from the Assembly and efforts to unite Germany failed. The Frankfurt Assembly did not support a republican form of government but wanted a liberal monarchial form of government modeled on England. Austria did not support the work of the Frankfurt Assembly and opposed any unification efforts that eliminated her influence in the German states. Bismarck was not in power during the history of the Frankfurt Assembly. The primary interest of the delegates was political not economic unification.

8. **E.** In 1848, England was not affected by the revolutions that swept the European continent. Throughout the 1820s and 1830s, England had enacted several liberal reforms that allowed great voter participation. In 1848, the Chartists marched on Parliament to demand the franchise for city workers. Although Parliament refused, there was no outbreak of violence or rioting. By 1848, England was becoming increasingly more dominated by the middle class and the ability of the British to enact meaningful reforms allowed the working class to achieve its goals without social upheaval. In 1848, France, Italy, Germany, and Austria were all affected by revolutions.

9. **A.** The Decembrist Revolt of 1825 occurred in Russia. The Decembrists were young army officers who staged a revolt for a more liberal, constitutional government to replace the autocracy of the Russian czar. The Decembrists were the first upper-class opponents of the Nicholas I's absolute rule; having little use for liberal reformers, he crushed their revolt. France, Germany, Austria, and Italy did not experience any revolutions in 1825.

10. **C.** The table supports the conclusion that the right to vote was gradually extended over a period of time. In the 1800s, political power remained with the landed aristocracy (male Anglican population), while the middle and working classes had no voting rights. The Reform Act of 1832 lowered the voting qualifications and gave more middle class people the right to vote. The proportion of voters increased from 1 in 100 to 1 in 32 men. City workers, however, were still deprived of their right to vote. In 1848, the Chartists, a reform group of the working class, petitioned the government for universal manhood suffrage, as well as removal of property qualifications for members of Parliament. The Chartist movement failed, but their reforms were eventually implemented. In 1867, property qualifications were reduced so that more city workers could vote. In 1884, Prime Minister William Gladstone supported a reform bill that extended the right to vote to all farm workers and other men. This bill increased the number of voters by one million men. By 1830, only wealthy male Catholics could vote.

The Age of Nationalism in Europe

Between 1850 and 1914, strong nation states developed in Germany and Italy. The nation states were built upon the principle of **nationalism**: the bonding of a people by a common language, history, traditions, beliefs, and goals. Nationalism originated with the French Revolution and with Napoleon, who helped to spread it throughout Europe. As it took hold in the emerging urban societies of the late nineteenth century, people began to transfer their allegiance from a monarch to a country and to put national interests above all considerations. Nationalism provided people with a sense of belonging and power, as well as a connection to the state, which had been disrupted by the Industrial Revolution. The Industrial Revolution had altered the relationship between the worker and the employer, and the allegiance that had once been directed to the employer, was now refocused towards a unified state. The national states became a way of coping with the challenges of rapid economic and political changes. Strong leaders were able to direct this energy towards industrialization and modernization.

The revolutions of 1848 had not satisfied the demands of the nationalists in Italy and Germany. Camillo Cavour, the moderate nationalist prime minister of Piedmont-Sardinia, realized that the independent kingdom of Italy could be united into a single political state only by combining force with diplomacy. In Germany, Otto Von Bismarck, chief minister of Prussia, skillfully fought three wars to unify Germany into one single nation under Prussian leadership. These men were the driving forces behind unification and were masters of the art of power politics or **realpolitik**.

The spread of nationalism had negative as well as positive consequences, however. The emergence of a unified Germany threatened to upset the balance of power that had existed since the Congress of Vienna in 1815 and endangered the dominant role of Great Britain on the continent. In the multinational Austrian and Ottoman empires, nationalism had a divisive rather than a unifying effect. Competing nationalist factions in these empires promoted fragmentation, which sparked conflicts and bloodshed that dramatically affected Europe in the twentieth century.

Unification of Italy

Italy was not a united nation before 1861. Napoleon sparked dreams of national unity, but at the **Congress of Vienna** (see Chapter 5), Prince Clemens von Metternich insisted that Italy be a geographic expression and not a united nation. The Congress divided the country into the following separate states:

- Rich northern industrialized provinces of Lombardy and Venetia were ruled by Austria.
- Duchies of Parma, Tuscany, and Modena were under local rulers but controlled by Austria.
- Papal States in the middle were under Church control.

- The kingdom of Two Sicilies, also called Naples, in the southern half of the boot and the poorest section of the country, were under local rulers dominated by Austria.

- The kingdom of Piedmont-Sardinia consisted of the northwestern provinces of Nice, Savoy, and Piedmont. It was the only independent state in Italy. (It borders France and Switzerland and is referred to as Sardinia throughout the chapter.)

Between 1815 and 1848, the goal of a united Italy began to appeal to Italians. The **Carbonari** (chimney sweepers) was a secret society organized during the time of Napoleon I and was committed to establishing a united Italian republic. The Carbonari fermented uprisings in 1820, 1821, and 1831, but these revolts were crushed by Austria. After the failure of these revolutions, Italians began to lose faith in the Carbonari. By 1831, most of the Carbonari members had joined the **Young Italy Society**, which was instrumental in provoking the uprisings of 1848 throughout Italy.

Stages of Italian unification.

Map courtesy of Frommer's Travel Guides.

The revolution of 1848 in Italy also led to hostility with the pope. Prior to the revolution of 1848, **Pope Pius IX** (b. 1792, ruled 1846–1878) was considered a liberal pope who had expressed support for Italian unification. However, his initial support gave way to fear and hostility when someone assassinated his minister. The pope was forced to temporarily flee from Rome when a Republic was proclaimed. Pope Pius IX was restored to power when French military forces were sent to protect him; these troops remained there for the next twenty years. The pope would not only become an opponent of national unity, but also of modernization. In 1864, Pope Pius IX issued *The Syllabus of Errors,* in which he denounced rationalism, liberalism, and modern civilization. He insisted that Catholics should not be aligned with current ideas or progress.

Only in **Sardinia** did the revolutionists gain any ground when **King Victor Emmanuel II** granted a liberal constitution to the people in March 1848, complete with elections and parliamentary control of taxes. Thus, to many Italians, Sardinia appeared to be the logical state to achieve the goal of Italian unity.

Italian Nationalists

Desiring to free Italy from Austrian control, the following men were instrumental in promoting Italian unification:

- **Giuseppe Mazzini** (1805–1872) was a writer, an orator, a former member of the Carbonari, and the founder of the Young Italy Society in 1831, a non-secret society dedicated to the liberation of Italy. Mazzini is considered the soul of Italian unification. His speeches and pamphlets stirred up the passions of the people for a united Italy with a democratic republic in Italy. In his most widely read book, *The Duties of Man,* he placed a pure duty to the nation between duty to family and duty to God. His failure in the revolutions in 1848 forced him to flee from Italy. He continued his fight for freedom from abroad.

- **Giuseppe Garibaldi** (1807–1882) was a friend of Mazzini and also supported a democratic republic. Garibaldi was a military leader who personified the romantic, revolutionary nationalism of Mazzini and had fought in the jungles of Uruguay in that country's struggle for independence. Initially, he organized a guerrilla band of 1,000 **Red Shirts** that conquered Sicily in May 1860. The name "Red Shirts" came about because red was the symbol of revolution. Like Mazzini, Garibaldi supported a democratic republic for a united Italy. He is considered the military leader of Italian unification.

- **Camillo Cavour** (1810–1861) became prime minister of Piedmont-Sardinia in 1852. He strengthened the country by encouraging industrial development, building railroads, fostering education, and freeing the peasants. He sought to make Sardinia the model of a liberal progressive constitutional government as a way to gain support. He understood that his goal of a united Italy could only be achieved by using force to get Austria out of northern Italy. However, Cavour realized that Sardinia under Victor Emmanuel II could never do it by itself. Cavour sought the support of the international community, especially Napoleon III of France who believed in the principle of nationality as well as the expansion of France. From 1852 until his death in 1861, Cavour used power politics of war and diplomacy to achieve his goal of unifying Italy.

Steps to Italian Unity

In 1855, Sardinia, led by Cavour, allied with France and Great Britain in the Crimean War against Russia. Although Sardinia gained no territory from the war, Cavour established a rapport with France.

In 1858, Cavour negotiated a secret diplomatic alliance with Napoleon III to aid Sardinia in case Austria attacked it. In July 1859, Cavour goaded Austria into declaring war against Sardinia. With the assistance of Napoleon III, who had been promised Nice and Savoy, Austria was defeated. Napoleon III, however, did an about-face and pulled out of the war because of criticisms at home from French Catholics for supporting a war against Catholic Austria, as well as threats from the Prussians, who had mobilized and expressed sympathy for Austria. Furthermore, a detachment of French troops was still in Rome defending the pope, while the army fought Austria in the North. In July 1859, Napoleon III, without consulting Cavour, signed the Franco-Austria agreement that gave Lombardy to Piedmont but excluded Venetia. Cavour resigned but revolutions continued to spread across Italy. Tuscany, Modena, Parma, and Romagna drove out Austria. Cavour returned in early 1860 and after a plebiscite, he arranged for the annexation of these areas with Sardinia. The northern states, except Venezia, met at Turin, the Piedmontese capital, in 1860. Napoleon III recognized the expanded kingdom of Piedmont in return for Sardinia's transferring Nice and Savoy to France, where a plebiscite by the people supported annexation to France.

In May 1860, Garibaldi, with his band of 1,000 Red Shirts, landed on the shores of Sicily. Garibaldi's guerrilla band captured the imagination of the Sicilian peasantry and with popular support was able to outwit the 20,000-man royal army. Within months, he had liberated the Kingdom of the Two Sicilies and Naples. He was prepared to attack Rome and the pope.

While Garibaldi conquered the Kingdom of the Two Sicilies, Cavour shrewdly sent Sardinian troops into the Papal States (but not Rome). Rome was protected by French troops and Cavour did not want to antagonize Napoleon III. Fearing Garibaldi's popular appeal, Cavour organized a plebiscite in the conquered territories; however, Garibaldi put aside his republican sentiments and did not oppose Cavour. The people of the Kingdom of the Two Sicilies voted to join Sardinia. In March 1861, **Victor Emmanuel II** was proclaimed the king of Italy — Cavour had succeeded.

The new Kingdom of Italy did not include Venetia or Rome. Venetia was ceded to Italy in 1866 and Rome was annexed in 1870 and designated as the capital of Italy in 1871. From 1870 to 1929, the pope adopted a policy of self imprisonment on the Vatican grounds. In the **Lateran Treaty** of 1929, Italy recognized the existence of Vatican City, about a square mile in area, as an independent state and the pope as its sovereign leader. Italy was a parliamentary democracy but only a small minority of Italian males had the right to vote. Relations between the new government and the Church were strained. The Pope had forbidden Catholics to participate in the new government, a ban that was not lifted until 1912.

Regional divisions still existed in Italy, despite unification. The industrial North had little in common with the agrarian South whose population was booming, and whose illiterate peasants were still dominated by large landowners. Living standards were low in the South and the government encouraged Italians to migrate to Canada, South America, and the United States.

Italians entered the twentieth century in the hopes of trying to play the role of a great world power, but its dire economic position would not allow it to realize its dreams. This frustration would dominate Italian society for many years.

Unification of Germany

Nationalism in the German states developed gradually in the 1800s. Napoleon had unintentionally aided its growth by abolishing the Holy Roman Empire and reducing the more than 300 German states to about 100. The Congress of Vienna in 1815 reduced the number of German states even further to 39 and organized them into the **German Confederation**, a weak body dominated by Austria. The failure of the Confederation to provide effective leadership stirred German nationalists to seek unity by other means. German unification was also helped by the following:

- The formation of the **Zollverein** in 1834, a German customs union under the leadership of Prussia. All of the German states except Austria were joined into a single economic union, similar to the European Common Market, which promoted free trade among the member states and maintained high tariffs against non-member states.

- The **Prussian Aristocracy**, or **Junkers** (meaning "young master" of a noble family), began to support the efforts of the **Hohenzollerns**, the ruling dynasty of Prussia, in their efforts to lead the struggle for German unification.

There were obstacles to German unification, however:

- **Prussia,** with its booming industrial economy and militaristic Junker class, aroused the opposition of Austria and other German states in the South. These southern German states were agricultural and Catholic, unlike the northern states, which were predominately Protestant and led by Prussia.

- **France** viewed a unified Germany as a potential threat to its leadership in Europe. France also believed that a divided Germany would make France more militarily secure.

German Nationalists

The unsuccessful revolts of 1848 and the rise of industrialism in Germany contributed to the vigorous growth of a nationalist movement that had the support of the growing middle class and city workers. The failure of the Frankfurt Assembly in 1848 also paved the way for unification under autocratic and anti-democratic leadership. The leaders of German unification were:

- **Otto Von Bismarck** (1815–1898), who became chief minister of Prussia in 1862. He was a Junker and a member of the conservative landowning class. Bismarck despised democracy and claimed that Germany could only be united "by blood and iron," not by speeches. Determined to avoid the blunders of 1848, Bismarck emphasized the importance of the military and was a master of power politics. He believed that the end justified the means, yet, he was flexible and very pragmatic.

- **Wilhelm I** (ruled 1861–1888) was the king of Prussia who became emperor in 1871. He fully supported Bismarck's policies that led to the formation of a unified German Empire.

- **Helmuth von Moltke** (1800–1891) was a Prussian general and chief of staff who built up a strong army and navy that enabled Bismarck to achieve success.

Steps to German Unification

The Rise of Prussian Military Power

In 1861, the Prussian parliament refused to grant the military budget that Bismarck and Wilhelm I requested. Many in Parliament were liberals who wanted Parliament to have control over government policies. These men did not like professional armies and they considered the Prussian Junkers, from whom the official corps were recruited, as their main rivals to the state government. Wilhelm I wanted to increase the efficiency of the army and make it the strongest in the world. Bismarck, also known as the **Iron Chancellor**, secured funds by ignoring the constitution and the legislature. He collected taxes and ruled illegally until 1866 when the Prussian parliament sanctioned his actions.

The Danish War (1864)

Denmark's attempt to annex Schleswig-Holstein, which was largely inhabited by Germans, led first to an alliance with Austria. Denmark was quickly defeated by Prussia, Holstein was given to Austria, and Schleswig was given to Prussia. Prussia and Austria disagreed over the administration of these provinces. This set the stage for the next step in Bismarck's plan.

Austro-Prussian War (1866)

Austria and Prussia quarreled over the administration of Schleswig and Holstein, such as who should keep internal order and who should have the right of passage. Bismarck was able to provoke Austria into declaring war on Prussia. The austro-Prussian War was also known as the **Seven Weeks War** because the efficient Prussian army, under General Helmuth von Moltke, quickly crushed the Austrian forces. Realizing that Prussia might need Austria for an inevitable conflict with France, Bismarck granted lenient peace terms. Austria had to pay a small indemnity and recognize Prussia's dominance of the German states.

In 1867, Bismarck dissolved the German Confederation. Prussia and 21 other German states formed the **North German Confederation**, ruled by the Prussian king and a bicameral legislature. The bicameral legislature was composed of the lower house (the **Reichstag**), which represented all the people elected by universal male suffrage, and the upper house (the **Bundesrat**), which represented the German states. Bismarck, being practical and wanting to avoid any desire for revenge on the part of Austria, allowed Austria and the four southern states to remain independent. However, these four states were tied to Prussia by the Zollverein and by a defensive military alliance.

Franco-Prussian War (1870–1871)

Realizing that only a war could get the southern states to join the Northern Confederation, Bismarck provoked a war with France. The immediate cause was a dispute over the Spanish throne. When Prince Leopold, a relative of the Prussian king, became a candidate for the throne, Napoleon III protested. The French minister went to Ems to talk to Wilhelm I who refused to settle the dispute. Wilhelm I sent a telegram to Bismarck informing him of his decision and Bismarck edited the telegraph so as to make it insulting to the French. Napoleon III declared war on Prussia in July 1870, and by September, the Emperor was captured and the French forces had been defeated. Unlike his treatment of Austria in the Austro-Prussian War, Bismarck treated France harshly, bringing Paris to submission by starving the city for over five months. By the **Treaty of Frankfurt** in May 1871, France ceded Alsace and Lorraine to Germany and agreed to pay a huge indemnity to Germany. The harshness of the treaty laid the foundation of hate and anger that would poison Franco-German relations for the next generation and planted the seeds for World War I.

German Empire

As Bismarck expected, the four southern Catholic states, delighted by the victory over France, joined the Prussian-dominated North German Confederation. The **German Empire** was officially announced at Versailles in January 1871 with Bismarck as Chancellor and Wilhelm I as Emperor or **Kaiser**.

The German Empire was a federation of monarchies, a union of 25 German states, in which Prussia dominated. Although the Reichstag was popularly elected, real power remained in the hands of the Kaiser and the **Chancellor**. The Kaiser was not a figurehead, but instead commanded the armed forces, conducted foreign affairs, and appointed his choices to major government positions. The Chancellor (prime minister) and other cabinet members were responsible to the Kaiser, not the legislature.

In the German Empire, autocracy, not democracy, was the real form of government. As Chancellor, Bismarck pursued a policy that was conservative and nationalistic. In 1872, Bismarck launched his **Kulturkampf**, "the battle for civilization." His goal was to make Catholics put loyalty to the state above the Church. Bismarck's move against the Catholic Church backfired, however. Catholics rallied behind the Church, and the **Catholic Center Party** gained strength. Being a realist, Bismarck made peace with the Church. Bismarck also saw a threat to the new Germany in the growing power of the Socialists. In 1878, Bismarck tried to suppress the Socialists by securing laws that forbade Socialist meetings and subjected their leaders to arrest. His efforts failed and made the Socialists even more popular. Again, Bismarck changed his course, and between 1883 and 1889 secured the passage of social insurance programs, such as workmen's compensation, old age insurance, and sickness benefits that set an example for other industrial countries.

In 1888, Wilhelm II (b. 1859, ruled 1888–1918) became Kaiser. He was a strong defender of Divine Rights and of autocracy in government. When he and Bismarck disagreed over policies in 1890, Bismarck was dismissed. Wilhelm II's rule was autocratic and his nationalist program helped lead to World War I.

Crisis in the Multinational Empires

The Austrian-Hungarian Empire

The rising spirit of nationalism in Europe directly affected the Austrian Empire, which was a multinational empire consisting of over 20 million people. Although less than one-third were German speaking (the Austrians), they were the dominant nationality and held leading positions in the government. The Hapsburgs, the empire's ruling family, were also Austrian. The other subjected nationalities in the empire included Hungarians (or Magyars), Czechs, Slovaks, Poles, Serbs, Croats, and Slovenes. Emperor **Francis Joseph I** (b. 1830, ruled 1848–1916), realized that the government had to make some reforms; throughout the 1850s, he tried hard to centralize the state and Germanize the language and culture of the different nationalities. Austria's efforts to repress its nationalities depleted its military strength, however. Her humiliating defeat against France and Sardinia in 1859 forced her to give up territory in Italy, and after her disastrous defeat in 1866 in the war with Prussia, brought renewed pressure for reforms.

To buttress the empire, Austria was forced to grant equal partnership with the Hungarians. The **Ausgleich**, or **Compromise of 1867**, established the **Dual Monarchy** under which Austria and Hungary were separate states, each having its own parliament and legislature. The two states were joined together under the leadership of Francis Joseph I who became the Emperor of Austria and King of Hungary. Each half of the empire agreed to deal with its own nationalities as it saw fit. The chief problem for the empire was the question of governing the many nationalities and the many different minorities. Croats and Romanians in the Hungarian domains were oppressed even more than before the Ausgleich. By 1900, nationalist discontent had left the government paralyzed, especially in the Balkan regions.

The Ottoman Empire

The Ottoman Empire also was multinational in scope, extending from Eastern Europe and the Balkans to North Africa and the Middle East. The empire included Arabs in the Middle East, southern Slavs, Albanians, Romanians, Bulgarians, and Greeks in the Balkans. In the Balkans, Serbs had won their autonomy in 1829 and the Greeks their independence in 1830.

Many Serbs and Greeks still lived in the Balkans under Ottoman control, however. Other nationalist groups, such as the Bulgarians and the Romanians, wanted their independence. These nationalist stirrings became tied up with the ambitions of European powers. European countries, such as Great Britain, France, and Russia, sought to benefit from the "sick man of Europe," a term used because since the loss of Hungary in 1699, the Ottoman Empire had entered on a long process of territorial disintegration. Russia wanted the Dardanelles, which would provide access to the Mediterranean. Britain opposed these ambitions, while France, after gaining Algiers, sought additional territory.

The crumbling Ottoman Empire forced many moderate Ottoman statesmen to reform the empire on the European model. During the 1830s, reform, known as the **Tanzimat** or Reorganization, was introduced which called for equality before the law for Jews, Muslims, and Christians, as well as modernizing the economy and the military. The Tanzimat reforms did not bring about revolutionary changes, however, nor did they halt the growth of nationalism. The adoption of western ideas, moreover, disturbed many conservative Muslims who saw them as a departure from Islamic tradition and holy laws. These Islamic conservatives became the supporters of **Sultan Abdulhamid** (b. 1842, ruled 1876–1909), who abandoned the European model and tried to rebuild the autocratic power of the earlier rulers. His repressive policies of intolerance towards minorities in the empire also led to the brutal genocide of the **Armenians**, a Christian people in the mountainous regions of the empire.

In 1878, when the Ottoman Empire was forced to grant independence to Serbia, Montenegro, Bulgaria, and Rumania, a group of reformers (mostly composed of army officers) known as the **Young Turks** insisted that the only way to save the empire was to change the government by establishing a constitutional monarchy and modernizing the military. In 1908, the Young Turks overthrew the Sultan and forced him to implement these reforms. Their efforts, however, were unable to stop the rising tide of nationalism in the Balkans that plunged Europe into war in 1914 and ultimately destroyed the remnants of the Ottoman Empire.

Chronology of the Age of Nationalism in Europe

1834	The Zollverein, a German Customs Union, is formed.
1831	Young Italy Society, a nationalist youth organization, is founded by Mazzini.
1848	The Frankfurt Assembly meets in order to create a unified constitutional German state; Revolutions break out across Italy.
1848	Pope Pius IX flees Rome after one of his ministers is assassinated.
1852	Count Camillo de Cavour becomes prime minister of the Kingdom of Sardinia.
1859	Cavour tricks Austria into declaring war upon Sardinia.
1860	Giuseppe Garibaldi and his Red Shirts invade Sicily.
1861	Italy becomes unified under Victor Emmanuel II, excluding Rome and Venetia.
1862	Otto von Bismarck becomes chief minister of Prussia.
1864	During the Danish War, Prussia allies with Austria to prevent Denmark from annexing Schleswig-Holstein.
1864	Pope Pius IX issues the Syllabus of Errors warning all Catholics against the dangers of liberalism.
1866	Bismarck provokes Austria into fighting the Austro-Prussian War; Prussian troops easily win the Seven Weeks War; Venetia is added to kingdom of Italy.

continued

1867	The Ausgleich, a compromise establishing a dual monarchy in Austro-Hungarian monarchy, is created.
1870–1871	Franco-Prussian War begins and ends.
	The German Empire is established after the conclusion of peace treaty with France.
1872	Bismarck launches the Kulturkampf, an attack against Catholics.
1878	The Congress of Berlin sets ground rules for imperialism and grants independence to Serbia, Montenegro, and Romania, weakening the Ottoman Empire.
1890	Bismarck is dismissed as chancellor.
1890	Young Turks organize to modernize the Ottoman Empire.

Sample Multiple-Choice Questions

1. Which of the Italian states was independent in 1850?

   A. Kingdom of the Two Sicilies

   B. Piedmont-Sardinia

   C. Venetia

   D. Parma

   E. Papal States

2. Who is considered the diplomatic force behind Italian Unification?

   A. Cavour

   B. Mazzini

   C. Garibaldi

   D. Victor Emmanuel II

   E. Gioberti

3. On which of the following did Mazzini and Garibaldi agree upon?

   A. United Italy should be a constitutional monarchy.

   B. United Italy should be a democratic republic.

   C. United Italy should be ruled by a dictatorship.

   D. The pope should be the leader of a united Italy.

   E. Foreign assistance was necessary to drive Austria from Italy.

4. The Zollverein (1819) was designed to do which of the following?

   A. Promote the interests of the Junkers.

   B. Create a uniform currency.

   C. Establish a large standing army.

   D. Set up a customs union to promote free trade.

   E. Set up an "all German Parliament."

5. Which is the correct chronological order of events that led to the unification of Germany?

   A. Franco-Prussian War, Danish War, Ems Dispatch, Austro-Prussian War (Seven Weeks War)

   B. Austro-Prussian War (Seven Weeks War), Danish War, Ems Dispatch, Franco-Prussian War

   C. Danish War, Austro-Prussian War (Seven Weeks War), Ems Dispatch, Franco-Prussian War

   D. Danish War, Ems Dispatch, Austro-Prussian War (Seven Weeks War), Franco-Prussian War

   E. Ems Dispatch, Danish War, Franco-Prussian War, Austro-Prussian War (Seven Weeks War)

6. Bismarck's Kulturkampf in Germany was directed against

   A. liberals

   B. middle class

   C. Catholic Church

   D. Socialists

   E. Prussian landowners

7. The Ausgleich was established by the Austrian government in 1867 to grant equal partnership to which of the following groups?

   A. Serbs

   B. Croats

   C. Magyars (Hungarians)

   D. Germans

   E. Italians

8. The "sick man of Europe" in the nineteenth century referred to:

   A. Russian Empire

   B. Austrian Empire

   C. Second French Empire

   D. German Empire

   E. Ottoman Empire

9. Which of the following statements is most accurate about German unification in 1871?

   A. Austria was the chief architect

   B. France supported unification

   C. Russia was instrumental in providing military assistance

   D. German unification was accomplished by democratic and liberal methods

   E. Prussia used military methods and autocratic rule to unite Germany

10. After the revolutions of 1848, who became an obstacle to the unification of Italy?

    A. Bismarck of Prussia

    B. Napoleon III

    C. Pope Pius IX

    D. Giuseppe Garibaldi

    E. Victor Emmanuel II

Answers to Multiple-Choice Questions and Explanations

1. **B.** Piedmont-Sardinia was the only independent Italian state in 1850. Piedmont-Sardinia took the lead in the process of unification. At the Congress of Vienna, Metternich was determined to keep Italy united merely as "a geographic expression." The kingdoms of Parma and Two Sicilies were under local rulers controlled by Austria. Austria annexed Venetia and the Papal States were under Church control.

2. **A.** Cavour is considered the diplomatic force behind Italian unification. Cavour became prime minister of Piedmont-Sardinia in 1852. He realized that he could not unify northern Italy without the help of France. Through a series of diplomatic maneuvers, he secured the help of Napoleon III for the war against Austria and seized on the nationalist fever in central Italy to get Parma, Modena, and Tuscany to vote for annexation to Piedmont-Sardinia. Cavour was also shrewd in getting Garibaldi to offer his conquests to Victor Emmanuel, securing the unification of northern and southern Italy. Mazzini is considered the soul of Italian unification. Mazzini was forced to exile after the failure of the revolutions in Italy after 1848. Garibaldi was a military leader. Victor Emmanuel was the first king of a united Italy. Gioberti was a Catholic priest who wanted a federation of Italian states under the presidency of the pope.

3. **B.** Mazzini and Garibaldi believed that Italy should be united as a democratic republic. In 1831, Giuseppe Mazzini founded Young Italy. The goal of this society was to make Italy one, free, independent, democratic republican nation.

   From 1848–1849, Mazzini helped set up a republic in Rome but French forces crushed it. Garibaldi, a disciple of Mazzini, also wanted to create a republic. Garibaldi defended Mazzini's Roman Republic against the French in 1849. Neither Mazzini nor Garibaldi believed in a constitutional monarchy or a dictatorship. They were anti-clerical and wanted to seize control of the Papal State. Neither of them thought foreign assistance was necessary to help drive Austria from Italy.

4. **D.** The Zollverein was a customs union designed to promote free trade among member nations. Under Prussian leadership, it was found to stimulate trade and increase revenues of member states. The Zollverein excluded Austria. The Junkers were the landowning aristocracy of Prussia. The Zollverein dealt only with free trade, not the establishment of a uniform currency, a large standing army, or an all German Parliament.

5. **C.** The correct chronological order is the Danish War (1864), Austro-Prussian War (1866) or Seven Weeks War, Ems Dispatch (1870), and Franco-Prussian War (1870–71)

6. **C.** Kulturkampf was directed against the Catholic Church. Bismarck had laws passed that gave the state the right to supervise Catholics and approve the appointment of priests. Bismarck did not attack the liberals whom he had already won over by his unification of Germany. Neither did he attack the middle class nor the Prussian landowners who had supported him since he became prime minster. Bismarck did attack the Socialists but that was not known as Kulturkampf. Bismarck's social welfare measures were an attempt to win the support of the working class from the Socialist Party.

7. C. The Ausgleich in 1867 granted equal partnership to the Magyars (Hungarians). Austria and Hungary were joined together under the leadership of Francis Joseph. The Serbs, Croats, and Italians were different nationalities living in areas that were considered part of the Austrian-Hungarian Empire.

8. E. The "sick man of Europe" term was used to describe the feeble Ottoman Empire over the 100-year period from 1815 to 1914. In the 1800s, Europeans were eager to divide up the Ottoman lands. Russia wanted the Dardanelles, and Austria-Hungary took the provinces of Bosnia and Herzegovina, angering Serbia who wanted the area. However, England and France sought to preserve the empire because they feared a general European war if the empire collapsed. The Ottoman Empire became a pawn among the powerful European nations. The Russian and Austrian Empires had internal problems but each of them played an active role on the diplomatic scene in Europe during the nineteenth century. The Second French Empire of Napoleon III had a short life from 1852 to 1871. The German Empire began in 1871 and played an important role on the European continent from 1871 until 1918 when Germany was defeated in World War I.

9. E. In 1848, Otto von Bismarck, who was Prussia's chief minister and later Chancellor from 1862–1871, believed that Germany could only be united by "Blood and Iron," meaning military power. Bismarck did not believe in democracy. In a series of wars, he eliminated Austria as a factor in German unification and united North and South Germany by the Franco-Prussian War. Austria and France opposed unification of Germany. Austria feared a loss of influence and France wanted Germany as a weak, disunited neighbor. Russia played no major role in the unification of Germany. Bismarck skillfully used diplomacy to keep Russia friendly to Germany. Bismarck rejected democracy and liberal methods to unite Germany.

10. C. After 1848, Pope Pius IX was an obstacle to the unification of Italy. Pope Pius IX, who at first was known as "the liberal pope," rejected unification after he was temporarily driven from Rome during the upheavals of 1848. For many generations, the papacy would oppose national unification as well as modern trends. In 1864, Pope Pius IX, in the *Syllabus of Errors,* denounced liberalism and modern civilization. Bismarck and Cavour were allied in the Seven Weeks War against Austria. By the peace treaty, Austria ceded Venetia to Italy. Napoleon III joined forces with Cavour to help Piedmont defeat Austria. Garibaldi secured the Kingdom of the Two Sicilies that helped unite northern and southern Italy. Victor Emmanuel II was the first king of united Italy.

Although the Industrial Revolution and nationalism shaped European society in the nineteenth century, **imperialism** — the domination by one country or people over another group of people — dramatically changed the world during the latter half of that century.

Imperialism did not begin in the nineteenth century. From the sixteenth to the early nineteenth century, an era dominated by what is now termed **old imperialism**, European nations sought trade routes with the Far East, explored the New World, and established settlements in North and South America as well as in Southeast Asia. They set up trading posts and gained footholds on the coast of Africa and China, and worked closely with the local rulers to ensure the protection of European economic interests. Their influence, however, was limited. In the **Age of New Imperialism** that began in the 1870s, European states established vast empires mainly in Africa, but also in Asia and the Middle East. Unlike the sixteenth and seventeenth century method of establishing settlements, the new imperialists set up the administration of the native areas for the benefit of the colonial power. European nations pursued an aggressive expansion policy that was motivated by economic needs that were created by the Industrial Revolution. The expansion policy was also motivated by political needs which associated empire building with national greatness, and social and religious reasons that promoted the superiority of Western society over a backward society. Through the use of direct military force, economic spheres of influence, and annexation, European countries dominated the continents of Africa and Asia. By 1914, Great Britain controlled the largest number of colonies and the phrase "the sun never sets on the British Empire" described its vast holdings. Imperialism had consequences that affected the colonial nations, Europe, and the world. It also led to increased competition among nations and to conflicts that would disturb the peace of the world in 1914.

Old Imperialism

European Imperialism did not begin in the 1800s. In their efforts to find a direct trade route to Asia during the age of old imperialism, European nations established colonies in the Americas, India, South Africa, and the East Indies, and gained territory along the coast of Africa and China. Meanwhile, Europe's Commercial Revolution created new needs and desires for wealth and raw materials. Mercantilism maintained that colonies could serve as a source of wealth, while personal motives by rulers, statesmen, explorers, and missionaries supported the imperial belief in "Glory, God, and Gold." By 1800, Great Britain was the leading colonial power with colonies in India, South Africa, and Australia. Spain colonized Central and South America. France held Louisiana and French Guinea, and Holland built an empire in the East Indies.

In the first half of the nineteenth century colonialism became less popular. The Napoleonic Wars, the struggle for nationalism and democracy, and the cost of industrialization exhausted the energies of European nations. Many leaders also thought that the costs to their respective empires outweighed the benefits, especially the cost of supervising the colonies. However, in the mid-nineteenth century, Europe, especially Great Britain and France, began an economic revival. During the Victorian era, which lasted from 1837 to 1901, Great Britain became an industrial giant providing more than 25% of the world's output of industrial goods. In France, Napoleon's investment in industry and large-scale ventures, such as railroad building, helped to promote prosperity. Thus the Industrial Revolution stirred ambitions in many European countries and renewed confidence in themselves to embark on a path of aggressive expansion overseas.

New Imperialism

From the late 1800s through the early 1900s, Western Europe pursued a policy of imperialism that became known as the New Imperialism. This new imperialist age gained its impetus from economic, military, political, humanitarian, and religious reasons, as well as from the development and acceptance of a new theory — social Darwinism — and advances in technology.

Economic Reasons

By 1870, it became necessary for European industrialized nations to expand their markets globally in order to sell products that they could not sell domestically on the continent. Businessmen and bankers had excess capital to invest, and foreign investments offered the incentive of greater profits, despite the risks. The need for cheap labor and a steady supply of raw materials, such as oil, rubber, and manganese for steel, required that the industrial nations maintain firm control over these unexplored areas. Only by directly controlling these regions, which meant setting up colonies under their direct control, could the industrial economy work effectively — or so the imperialists thought. The economic gains of the new imperialism were limited, however, because the new colonies were too poor to spend money on European goods.

Military and Political Reasons

Leading European nations also felt that colonies were crucial to military power, national security, and nationalism. Military leaders claimed that a strong navy was necessary in order to become a great power. Thus, naval vessels needed military bases around the world to take on coal and supplies. Islands or harbors were seized to satisfy these needs. Colonies guaranteed the growing European navies safe harbors and coaling stations, which they needed in time of war. National security was important for Great Britain decision to occupy Egypt. Protecting the Suez Canal was vital for the British Empire. The Suez Canal, which was opened up in 1869, shortened the sea route from Europe to South Africa and East Asia. To Britain, the canal was a lifeline to India, the jewel of its empire. Many people were also convinced that the possession of colonies was an indication of a nation's greatness; colonies were status symbols. According to nineteenth-century German historian, Heinrich von Treitschke, all great nations should want to conquer barbarian nations.

Humanitarian and Religious Goals

Many Westerners believed that Europe should civilize their little brothers beyond the seas. According to this view, non-whites would received the blessings of Western civilization, including medicine, law, and Christianity. **Rudyard Kipling** (1865–1936) expressed this mission in the 1890s when he prodded Europeans to take up "The White Man's Burden" to civilize the uncivilized. Missionaries supported colonization, believing that European control would help them spread Christianity, the true religion, in Asia and Africa.

Social Darwinism

Many Europeans embraced the idea of **Charles Darwin's** "survival of the fittest" and applied it to human societies and nations. Social Darwinism fostered imperialistic expansion by proposing that some people were more fit (advanced) than others. The Europeans believed that they, as the white race, were dominant and that it was only natural for them to conquer the inferior people as nature's way of improving mankind. Thus, the conquest of inferior people was just, and the destruction of the weaker races nature's natural law.

Western Technology

Superior technology and improved medical knowledge helped to foster imperialism. Quinine enabled Europeans to survive tropical diseases and venture into the mosquito-infected interior of Africa and Asia. The combination of the steamboat and the telegraph enabled the Western powers to increase their mobility and to quickly respond to any situations that threatened their dominance. The rapid fire machine gun also gave them a military advantage and was helpful in convincing Africans and Asians to accept Western control. The following table summarizes the causes of the new imperialism:

Causes of New Imperialism			
Economic	*Military/Political*	*Humanitarian/Religious*	*Technology*
Need for markets	Need for military bases	White man's burden	New medicine
Raw materials	National security	Spread of Christianity	New weapons
Source of investments	Source of pride-nationalism	Social Darwinism (superiority of Western society)	Transportation

Imperialism in Africa

Africa was known as the Dark Continent and remained unknown to the outside world until the late nineteenth century because its interior — desert, mountains, plateaus, and jungles — discouraged exploration. Britain's occupation of Egypt and Belgium's penetration of the Congo started the race for colonial possession in Africa.

Suez Canal

In 1875, Britain purchased a controlling interest in the **Suez Canal** from the bankrupt ruler of Egypt who was unable to repay loans that he had contracted for the canal and modernization. The French, who organized the building of the Suez Canal under Ferdinand de Lesseps in 1859, owned the other shares. The Suez Canal was important because it shortened the route from Europe to South and East Asia. The canal also provided the lifeline to India, which Britain had made part of the British Empire in 1858. In 1882, Britain established a protectorate over Egypt, which meant that the government leaders were officials of the Ottoman Empire, but were really controlled by Great Britain. The British occupation of Egypt, the richest and most developed land in Africa, set off "African fever" in Europe. To ensure its domination and stability in the area, Great Britain extended its control over the Sudan as well.

Exploration of the Congo

In 1879, **Leopold II of Belgium** (b. 1835, ruled 1865–1909) sent **Henry Stanley**, the Anglo-American newspaperman, to explore the Congo and establish trade agreements with leaders in the Congo River Basin. Stanley, who had found the great explorer **David Livingston** in 1871, sold his services to Leopold II. Leopold formed a financial syndicate entitled The International Association for the Exploration and Civilization of the Congo. Leopold II was a strong-willed monarch and his intrusion into the Congo area raised questions about the political fate of Africa south of the Sahara. Other European nations were fearful that he wanted to extend control over the entire area.

The Scramble for Africa

Otto von Bismarck (1815–1898), Chancellor of Germany, and **Jules Ferry** (1832–1893), Premier of France who was considered the builder of the modern French Empire, arranged for an international conference in Berlin to lay down the basic rules for colonizing Africa. The **Congress of Berlin** (1884–1885) established the principle that European occupation of African territory had to be based on effective occupation that was recognized by other states, and that no single European power could claim Africa. The Berlin Conference led to the "Scramble for Africa." Between 1878 and 1914, European powers divided up the entire African continent except for the independent countries of Ethiopia and Liberia. Liberia was settled by free slaves from the United States and became an independent republic in 1847. Ethiopia gained its independence by routing an Italian invasion in 1896. European countries divided Africa as follows:

France

The French had the largest colonial empire in Africa, over 3½ million square miles, half of which contained the Sahara Desert. In 1830, France had conquered Algieria in North Africa. Between 1881 and 1912, France acquired Tunisia, Morocco, West Africa, and Equatorial Africa. At its height, the French Empire in Africa was as large as the continental United States.

Great Britain

Britain's holdings in Africa were not as large as France's but it controlled the more populated regions, particularly of southern Africa, which contained valuable mineral resources such as diamonds and gold. In 1806, the British displaced Holland in South Africa and ruled the Cape Colony. However, the British soon came into conflict with the **Boers** (farmers), the original Dutch settlers who resented British rule. In the 1830s, the Boers left British territory and migrated north and founded two republics, the Orange Free State and Transvall. The Boers soon came into conflict with the powerful **Zulus**, a native African group, for control of the land. When the Zulus and the Boers were unable to win a decisive victory, the British became involved in 1859 and eventually destroyed the Zulu empire. In 1890, **Cecil Rhodes**, who was born in Great Britain and had become a diamond mine millionaire, became prime minister of the Cape Colony. He wanted to extend the British African Empire from Cape Town to Cairo and decided to annex the Boer Republic. In the **Boer War** (1899–1902), the British, with great difficulty, defeated the Boers and annexed the two republics. In 1910, the British combined its South African colonies into the Union of South Africa. Whites ran the government, and the Boers, who outnumbered the British, assumed control. This system laid the foundation for racial segregation that would last until the 1990s.

Germany

Late unification delayed Germany's imperialistic ventures, but it also wanted its place in the sun. Germany took land in eastern and southwestern Africa.

Italy

Italy was another late entry into the imperialistic venture. Italy took control of Libya, Italian Somaliland, and Eritrea, which is the north-most province of Ethiopia near the Red Sea. Italy's efforts to gain control of Ethiopia ended in bitter defeat.

Portugal

Portugal carved out large colonies in Angola and Mozambique.

Imperialism in Asia

India

The British took control of India in 1763, after defeating the French in the **Seven Years War** (1756–1763). The British controlled India through the **British East India Company**, which ruled with an iron hand. In 1857, an Indian revolt, led by native soldiers called *sepoys,* led to an uprising known as the **Sepoy Mutiny.** After suppressing the rebellion, the British government made India part of the empire in 1858, as mentioned previously. The British introduced social reforms, advocated education, and promoted technology. Britain profited greatly from India, called the "Brightest Jewel of the British Empire." The Indian masses, however, continued to live close to starvation and the British had little respect for the native Indian culture.

The Dutch held the Dutch East Indies and extended their control over Indonesia, while the French took over Indo China (Cambodia, Laos, and Vietnam). The Russians also got involved and extended their control over the area of Persia (Iran).

China

Since the seventeenth century, China had isolated itself from the rest of the world and refused to adopt Western ways. The Chinese permitted trade but only at the Port of Canton, where the rights of European merchants were at the whim of the emperor. Imperialism in China began with the **Opium War** (1839–1842), when the Chinese government tried to halt the British from importing opium. This resulted in a war in which Britain's superior military and industrial might easily destroyed the Chinese. The **Treaty of Nanking** (1842) opened up five ports to the British, gave Britain the island of Hong Kong, and forced China to pay a large indemnity. In 1858, China was forced to open up eleven more treaty ports that granted special privileges, such as the right to trade with the interior of China and the right to supervise the Chinese custom offices. Foreigners also received the right of extraterritoriality, which meant that Western nations maintained their own courts in China and Westerners were tried in their own courts.

Between 1870 and 1914, the Western nations carved China into spheres of influence, areas in which outside powers claimed exclusive trading rights. France acquired territory in Southwestern China, Germany gained the Shandong Peninsula in northern China, Russia obtained control of Manchuria and a leasehold over Port Arthur, and the British took control of the Yangzi Valley. The United States, which had not taken part in carving up China because it feared that spheres of influence might hurt U.S. commerce, promoted the **Open Door Policy** in

1899. **John Hay**, the American Secretary of State, proposed that equal trading rights to China be allowed for all nations and that the territorial integrity of China be respected. The imperial nations accepted the Open Door in principle but not always in practice. For the United States, however, the Open Door Policy became the cornerstone of its Chinese policy at the beginning of the twentieth century.

By the 1900s, China was in turmoil. There was rising sentiment against foreigners because China had been forced to give up so many political and economic rights. This anti-foreign sentiment exploded into the **Boxer Rebellion** or Uprising (1899–1901). The Boxers were a secret Chinese nationalist society supported by the Manchu government and their goal was to drive out all foreigners and restore China to isolation. In June 1900, the Boxers launched a series of attacks against foreigners and Chinese Christians. They also attacked the foreign embassies in Beijing. The imperialistic powers sent an international force of 25,000 troops to crush the rebellion, which ended within two weeks.

The Boxer Rebellion failed, but it convinced the Chinese that reforms were necessary. In 1911, revolutions broke out across the country and the Manchu emperor was overthrown. **Dr. Sun Yat Sen**, the father of modern China, proclaimed a republic and was named the new president. He advocated a three-point program of nationalism (freeing China from imperial control); democracy (elected government officials); and livelihood (adapting Western industrial and agricultural methods). The Chinese republic faced many problems and for the next thirty-seven years, China would continue to be at war with itself and with foreign invaders.

Japan

Japan was the only Asian country that did not become a victim of imperialism. In the seventeenth and eighteenth centuries, the Japanese expelled Europeans from Japan and closed Japanese ports to trade with the outside world, allowing only the Dutch to trade at Nagasaki. In 1853, **Commodore Matthew Perry**, an American naval officer, led an expedition to Japan. He convinced the *shogun*, a medieval type ruler, to open up ports for trade with the United States. Fearful of domination by foreign countries, Japan, unlike China, reversed its policy of isolation and began to modernize by borrowing from the West. **The Meji Restoration**, which began in 1867, sought to replace the feudal rulers of the shogun and increase the power of the emperor. The goal was to make Japan strong enough to compete with the West. The new leaders strengthened the military and transformed Japan into an industrial society. The Japanese adapted a constitution based on the Prussian model with the emperor as the head. The government was not intended to promote democracy but to unite Japan and make it equal to the West. The leaders built up a modern army based on a draft and constructed a fleet of steam iron ships. The Japanese were so successful that they became an imperial power by defeating China in 1895, seizing Korea in 1910, and shocking the world by defeating Russia in the **Russo-Japanese War** of 1904–1905. Japan's victory was the first time that an Asian country had defeated a European power in over 200 years.

Imperialism in the Middle East

The importance of the Middle East to the new imperialists was its strategic location (the crossroads of three continents: Europe, Asia, and Africa), vital waterways (canals and the Dardanelles), and valuable oil resources. The Europeans divided up the Middle East in the following manner:

- **Great Britain:** Britain's control of the Suez Canal forced her to take an active role in Egypt as well as acquire the militarily valuable island of Cyprus to secure oil resources for industrial and military needs. The British also secured concessions in Iran, Iraq, Kuwait, Qatar, and Bahrain. Pipelines were built to the Mediterranean Sea and the Persian Gulf.

- **Russia:** Traditionally, Russia sought to gain control of the Dardanelles as an outlet to the Mediterranean and an area of expansion. Russia helped to dismember the Ottoman Empire and gain independence for several Balkan states.

- **Germany:** In 1899, German bankers obtained the Ottoman Empire's consent to complete the Berlin-Baghdad Railroad.

Consequences of Imperialism

The new imperialism changed Western society and its colonies. Through it, Western countries established the beginning of a global economy in which the transfer of goods, money, and technology needed to be regulated in an orderly way in order to ensure that there was a continuous flow of natural resources and cheap labor for the industrialized world.

Imperialism adversely affected the colonies. Under foreign rule, native culture and industry were destroyed. Imported goods wiped out local craft industries. By using colonies as sources of raw materials and markets for manufactured goods, colonial powers held back the colonies from developing industries. One reason why the standard of living was so poor in many of these countries was that the natural wealth of these regions had been funneled to the mother countries.

Imperialism also brought confrontation between the cultures. By 1900, Western nations had control over most of the globe. Europeans were convinced that they had superior cultures and forced the people to accept modern or Western ways. The pressures to westernize forced the colonial people to re-evaluate their traditions and to work at discouraging such customs as foot binding in China and *sati* in India. *Sati* was the custom in which virtuous women (*sati*) threw themselves onto their husband's funeral fire in the hope that the sacrificial act would wipe away the sins of her husband and herself. Western cultures also introduced medicine stressing the use of vaccines and modern methods of hygiene that helped to save lives. The practice of modern medicine would increase life expectancy but eventually lead to a population explosion in Africa.

Imperialism created many political problems. European nations disrupted many traditional political units and united rival peoples under a single government that was trying to impose stability and order where local conflicts had existed for years, such as in Nigeria and Rwanda. Ethnic conflicts in many of these areas, which developed in the latter half of the twentieth century, can be traced to these imperial policies. Imperialism also contributed to tension among the Western powers. The imperial rivalries between France and Great Britain over the Sudan, efforts to contain the rivalry in Africa, the dispute between France and Germany over Morocco, and the continued controversy over the Ottoman Empire intensified the rivalries. These hostilities contributed to the conditions that led to World War I in 1914.

Chronology of the Age of Imperialism

1763	End of Seven Years War; Great Britain gains control of India
1830	France occupies Algeria
1839	The Opium War begins
1842	Opium War ends with Treaty of Nanking
1850	The Taiping Rebellion in China; Chinese revolts against the Manchu rulers, millions killed
1853	Commodore Perry opens up trade with Japan
1857	The Sepoy Mutiny against British rule in India takes place
1858	India comes under direct rule by Great Britain
1869	Suez Canal completed
1870	Cecil Rhodes arrives in Cape Town, South Africa
1875	Great Britain gains control of the Suez Canal and begins to establish a protectorate over Egypt (in 1882)
1884–1885	International Conference on Berlin meets to establish guidelines for European Imperialism in Africa
1882	British land troops In Egypt
1885	Germany controls German East Africa
1886	British take over Burma
1899–1901	The Boxer Rebellion in China against Westerners takes place
1899	Open Door Policy is proposed by United States for China
1899–1902	Boer War; British crush rebellion by Dutch farmers in South Africa
1904–1905	Russo-Japanese War; Japan takes Korea and Port Arthur from Russia
1910	Union of South Africa is formed
1911–1912	Manchu Dynasty overthrown; Dr. Sun Yat-Sen named President of Chinese Republic

Sample Multiple-Choice Questions

1. Which of the following is *least* associated with the "new imperialism"?

   A. Social Darwinism

   B. Economic control

   C. Political control

   D. Racial equality

   E. Military control

2. Which statement *best* expresses the motive for nineteenth century European imperialism?

   A. Living space was needed for the excess population in Western Europe.

   B. European leaders believed imperialism was an effective method of reducing the number of wars.

   C. European nations would benefit from some aspects of the conquered nation's culture.

   D. Imperialism would benefit the economies of the colonial Powers.

   E. European nations wanted democratic governments throughout the world.

3. Bismarck called the Berlin Conference in 1884–85 to

   A. establish rules for dividing up Africa among the European countries

   B. limit Russian expansion on the continent

   C. work with the Africans on seeking trade agreements

   D. prevent Belgium from taking over the Congo

   E. stop the spread of United States influence in Africa

4. Which European country had the *largest* amount of land in Africa?

   A. Great Britain

   B. Belgium

   C. France

   D. Italy

   E. Austria-Hungary

5. The nineteenth-century term "White Man's Burden" reflects the idea that

   A. Asians and Africans were equal to Europeans

   B. Asians and Africans would be grateful for European help

   C. imperialism was opposed by most Europeans

   D. Europeans had a responsibility to improve the lives of their colonial peoples

   E. democracy was the best form of government for Asia and Africa

6. "It has impoverished the dumb millions by a system of progressive exploitation. . . . It has reduced us politically to serfdom. It has sapped the foundation of our culture . . . and degraded us spiritually."

    –Mohandas K. Gandhi, 1930

    In the statement, the "It" referred to by Gandhi is

    A. British imperialism in India

    B. India's involvement in World War II

    C. the industrialization of India

    D. India's failure to support a guerilla movement for independence

    E. Britain's role in promoting independence for India

7. Which of the following was a result of the Sepoy Mutiny or mutiny in 1857?

    A. The British East India Company raised taxes.

    B. India declared its independence.

    C. India adapted Christianity.

    D. The British East India Company took direct control of India.

    E. The British government ended the rule of the East India Co.

8. Which statement best describes an effect of the Opium War on China?

    A. The British expelled all Chinese from Hong Kong.

    B. The British victory led to spheres of influence in China.

    C. The British ended the importing of opium into China.

    D. The British established a parliamentary democracy in China.

    E. Chinese isolation increased.

9. The Boxer Rebellion of the early twentieth century was an attempt to

    A. eliminate poverty among the Chinese peasants

    B. bring Western-style democracy to China

    C. restore trade between China and European nations

    D. introduce Communism

    E. remove foreign influences from China

10. A major goal of the Meiji Restoration was to focus on

    A. isolating Japan from the influence of foreign ideas

    B. existing peacefully with their Asian neighbors

    C. increasing the emperor's power by returning Japan to a feudal political system

    D. modernizing Japan's economy to compete with Western nations

    E. encouraging European powers to open up trading rights in China

Answers to Multiple-Choice Questions and Explanations

1. **D.** Racial equality is least associated with the new imperialism. In the 1890s, the imperialist nations believed that Western society was superior to the cultures of Africa and Asia. Social Darwinism, which applied Darwin's ideas about the survival of the fittest, was based on the sense of racial superiority not racial equality. The new imperialism of the 1890s, which was a result of the Industrial Revolution, led to direct economic and political control of the colonies. The imperialistic countries used military force to ensure their dominance.

2. **D.** The statement that best expressed the motive for nineteenth-century European imperialism is that imperialism would benefit the economies of the colonial powers. During the Age of Imperialism, a global economy developed. From the industrialized European nations' mass-produced goods, investment capital was directed to the colonial areas. In return, the people of Asia and Africa provided natural resources and cheap labor. Rubber, copper, and gold came from Africa, cotton and tin from southwest Asia. These raw materials spurred the growth of European industries and financial markets. The colonies also provided new markets for the finished products of the Industrial Revolution. Tools, weapons, and clothing flowed out of the factories and back to the colonies, whose raw materials had made them possible. Although imperialists argued that living space was needed for the excess population of Europe, no European country after 1870 acquired any colony to which European families in large numbers wished to move. The millions who left in the late nineteenth century persisted in heading for the Americas, where there were no European colonies.

   Imperialism was not an effective method of reducing the number of wars. In 1896, Ethiopia defeated Italy in its attempt to conquer the area. In 1898, Great Britain and France almost went to war over the Sudan in Africa. In 1905, Germany and France clashed over Morocco. European countries believed that Western civilizations were superior to the civilizations of colonial people. Colonial officials rejected the cultures of the conquered peoples and tried to impose Western customs and traditions on the colonies. European countries did not establish democratic governments in Asia and Africa, but instead ruled directly or indirectly through local rulers without the consent of the people.

3. **A.** The Congress of Berlin established ground rules for dividing up Africa among the European nations. In 1884–1885, European leaders met in Berlin to avoid conflicts among themselves. They agreed that European powers could not claim any part of Africa unless it set up a government office there. Europeans were also forced to send officials who exerted their power over local rulers. Leopold, king of Belgium, called the Berlin Conference to recognize control of the Congo Free State. Russia was not one of the European countries involved in the division of Africa. The Europeans did not invite any Africans to the Congress of Berlin. Africans were not given any role in how Europe divided up the continent. The United States was never interested in extending its influence in Africa. The United States area of imperial control was in Latin America and the Caribbean.

4. **C.** France had the largest amount of land in Africa. At its height, the French holding in Africa was as large as the continental United States. Great Britain's share of Africa was smaller but included more heavily populated regions. Belgium only controlled the regions of the Congo. Italy had holdings limited to Libya and two other areas. Austria-Hungary was never part of the partition of Africa.

5. **D.** The "White Man's Burden" reflects the idea that Europeans had a responsibility to improve the lives of their colonial people. In the 1890s, Rudyard Kipling's poem expressed the belief that Europeans had a sacred civilizing mission to bring the benefits of Western society to the impoverished people of the region. Kipling's poem encouraged Europeans to give unselfish service in distant lands. European civilization had reached unprecedented heights and they had unique benefits to bestow on all less advanced people. The "White Man's Burden" was based on the inferiority of Asians and Africans. The term never considered the gratitude of Asians and Africans for Europe's help. It was expected that these areas would openly embrace Western civilization. This attitude permeated imperialism and there was never the belief that democracy should be the form of government in Asia and Africa. Imperialism was based on one country conquering a weaker one.

6. **A.** Gandhi's statement refers to British imperialism in India. He studied law in Great Britain, but resented British colonial rule of India. During the 1920s and 1930s, he became leader of the Indian National Congress and led a nonviolent movement for self-government. He criticized British imperialists for their brute force, worship of money, and belief in the superiority of their culture. He claimed that the British policies had made the people of India poorer, turned them into serfs, and destroyed their spirit. Gandhi urged the people of India to revive their native industries and return to their traditional crafts to spur economic improvement and restore national pride. He urged Indians to boycott British goods and promoted nonviolent demonstrations to end economic exploitations by the British. World War II started in 1939, nine years after this statement was made. Gandhi did not support the industrialization of India. He opposed guerilla movements because these movements violated his principle of non-violent civil disobedience. The British were not supportive of independence for India.

7. **E.** The Sepoy Mutiny or rebellion resulted in the British government ruling India directly as a colony. The British controlled India through The British East India Company until 1857. The British, who crushed the Sepoy Native Indian Troops, changed their policy after 1857. The government ended the rule of the East India Company in 1858 and assumed control of the colony, ruling British India as a colony and ruling the native states indirectly as protectorates through British advisors. The British East India Company did not raise taxes since it did not control India after 1858. India did not achieve independence until after World War II. Hindu, not Christianity, is the major religion of India.

8. **B.** British victory in the Opium War led to spheres of influence in China. In 1839, when the Chinese tried to outlaw opium trade, the British refused, and continued to import the drug. This led to the Opium War. The Chinese were easily defeated and signed the Treaty of Nanking (1842). The British annexed Hong Kong and secured the right to trade at four Chinese ports in addition to Canton. These trading ports became spheres of influence in

which European nations secured exclusive trading privileges. After 1870, France, Germany, and Russia gained spheres of influence in China. These spheres of influence opened up China to trade rather than isolating it. The British remained in control of Hong Kong until the end of the twentieth century and did not establish democracy in China.

9. **E.** The Boxer Rebellion of the early twentieth century was an attempt to remove foreign influences from China. In the 1890s, anti-foreign feelings were high in China because many Chinese resented the growing influence of foreigners such as Great Britain, France, and Germany. In 1899, the Chinese formed a secret society called the Boxers (or Society of Righteous and Harmonious Fists), whose goal was to remove the foreigners who were destroying their lands with new technology such as telegraphs and machinery. The Boxers did not want any program to deal with poverty nor to promote democracy in China. They wanted to end trade with European nations. The Boxers were not Communists.

10. **D.** During the Meiji Restoration beginning in 1867, Japan's leaders focused on modernizing Japan's economy to compete with Western nations. Japan reversed its policy of isolation, ended feudalism, and began to modernize by borrowing from the Western powers. The goal of the Meiji leader, or enlightened ruler, was to make Japan a strong military and industrial power. Japanese leaders sent students abroad to Western countries to learn about their form of government, economies, technology, and customs. The government also brought foreign experts to Japan to improve industry. The Japanese adopted a constitution based on the model of Prussia with the emperor as the head. The new government was not intended to bring democracy, but to unite Japan and make it equal to Western powers. The Meiji Restoration did not isolate Japan from the influence of foreign ideas. The Japanese leaders borrowed Western ideas and adapted them to fit the needs of Japanese society. The Japanese introduced Western business methods but encouraged cooperation rather than competition among companies. Japan's modernization contributed to its rise as an imperial country. In 1895, the Japanese attacked and defeated China in the Sino-Japanese War. In 1904–1905, Japan clashed with Russia and defeated the Russians. In 1910, Japan annexed Korea.

World War I (1914–1918)

At the beginning of the twentieth century, the future of Europe was very bright. European culture and values dominated the known world. After 100 years of relative peace and rapid advances in science and technology, there was the belief that unlimited progress and growth would also lead to a permanent end to all wars. Beneath the surface, however, there were forces that were threatening this optimistic view of the future: the alliance system, nationalism lurking in the Balkans, imperialism creating rivalries in Africa, and the arms race. In August 1914, these forces combined to start World War I, shattering the dreams of a new future and marking the beginning of Europe's decline in the twentieth century. World War I destroyed the Austrian-Hungarian Empire, the German Empire, the Ottoman Empire, and the Russian Empire. World War I, also known as the Great War, contributed to the decline of France and Great Britain as their economy and population were decimated by the horrors of this war. The soldiers who fought in the trenches in France and Germany became part of a lost generation who had little hope for the future.

World War I was a different type of war because it was fought on the European home front as well as on the battlefield. The civilian population was forced to make sacrifices, such as meatless Monday, and women entered the work force to replace men who had gone to the battlefield. Industrialization and technology also changed the methods of warfare. Nations developed more destructive weapons, such as mounted machine guns and poison gas, that resulted in the death of millions.

World War I also was a turning point in history. By 1919, the world of 1914 lay in ruins and the map of Europe had changed to reflect the rise of national states in Czechoslovakia and Yugoslavia. World War I ended the Russian Empire and led to the rise of Communism. Fascism in Italy and Nazism in Germany developed in opposition to Communism as well as dissatisfaction with the Versailles Peace Treaty. The discontent of Germany and Italy, Russia's exclusion from the peace talks, and the resentment over the establishment of a Polish nation, as well as Japan's protesting the refusal of Western nations to recognize their claim over China all led to anger and bitterness for the next twenty years. These feelings contributed to World War II in 1939.

The Underlying Causes of World War I

The Alliance System

The Franco-Prussian War and the establishment of the German Empire opened up a new era of international relations. Bismarck, in a short period from 1861–1871, had turned Germany into one of the most powerful nations in Europe. After France's humiliating defeat in the Franco-Prussian War and the loss of Alsace-Lorraine, Bismarck wanted to keep France from regaining these lost provinces or from exercising *revanche* (revenge) on victorious Germany. He also

171

wanted to diplomatically isolate France and keep the Austrian-Hungarian Empire and Russia on friendly terms with Germany in order to avoid being dragged into a great war between the two rival empires. To achieve these goals, Bismarck created a system of alliances. As a result, Europe was divided into two rival blocs. The Alliance System was as follows:

- **Three Emperor's League (Dreikaiserbund):** This included Germany, Russia, and Austria-Hungary. The League established the principle of cooperation among the three powers in any further division of the Ottoman Empire. The League was also designed to neutralize the tension between Austria-Hungary and Russia. The alliance only lasted from 1881–1887. In 1887, Russia declined to renew the alliance because of tensions with Austria-Hungary over the Balkans.

- **Dual Alliance:** This alliance of 1879 was between Germany and Austria-Hungary in order to isolate France.

- **Reinsurance Treaty:** This secret treaty of 1887 was between Germany and Russia. Russia and Austria-Hungary were rivals over the Balkans. Bismarck wanted to be allied with both at the same time, in case any incidents developed. In 1890, the treaty ended and Germany chose not to renew it.

- **Triple Alliance:** This alliance, of 1882, included Austria-Hungary, Germany, and Italy. Italy was angry with France for preventing Italy from seizing Tunisia. The biggest weakness of the Triple Alliance was Italy's past history of animosity towards Austria and Italy's desire for **Italia Irredenta** (unredeemed territories), where Italians lived that were still under Austrian control, such as Trieste and Fiume.

- **Dual Entente:** This alliance of 1894 was a result of Germany's termination of the Reinsurance Treaty. Russia needed capital for development and French investors were willing to lend capital. France was also eager to check Germany's power and Russia needed an ally for its ambitions in the Balkans.

- **Entente Cordial:** Fearful of Germany's growing industrial and military strength, and the building of a powerful navy, Great Britain negotiated an unwritten military understanding with France in 1904. The alignment of Great Britain and France, her former adversary, was regarded as a diplomatic revolution. Great Britain's decision to end its splendid isolation was due primarily to Germany's colonial activity and her large military buildup that created fear that Germany was becoming too dominant in Europe.

- **Triple Entente:** Great Britain, France, and Russia joined together to maintain the balance of power against the Triple Alliance in 1907. The alliance system divided Europe into two rival camps, which not only aggravated the rivalry among the nations but also made government nervous about the motives of these nations. These alliances were intended to keep the balance of power. However, they could set a chain reaction leading to a general war.

Nationalism

The excessive nationalism preceding World War I created jealously and hatred among the European nations. In France, national pride was hurt by the loss of Alsace Lorraine in the Franco-Prussian War and the French considered Germany their natural enemy. Other countries wanted to extend their territories to include people of their race or background. Serbia, for instance, wanted to annex Bosnia-Herzegovina. Subject nationalities of Czechs, Yugoslavs, and Poles sought independence. This sort of national feeling contributed to tension on the European continent. In Eastern Europe, Russia, as the largest Slavic country, defended the rights of people of similar backgrounds. This policy was known as **Pan-Slavism**. For example, by 1914, Russia was ready to support Serbia, its Slavic brother, against any threats.

Economics

Economic rivalries created competition between Great Britain and Germany. Great Britain felt threatened by Germany's economic growth. By 1900, German factories were out-producing British ones and Germany was challenging Great Britain in the world markets.

Imperialism

The European imperialist countries, such as Great Britain, France, and Germany, competed for territory, markets, and resources in Asia and Africa. This competition led to friction. Great Britain resented Germany for blocking her plan for a Cape-Cairo Railway. Germany and Great Britain, however, acted to defeat Russia's efforts to acquire the Dardanelles, and Germany wanted to prevent the French from gaining Morocco.

Militarism

To protect their national and imperialist interests, Great Britain and Germany expanded their arms. When Germany began to acquire colonies, Kaiser Wilhelm II began to build up its navy. Admiral Alfred von Tirpitz of Germany saw a large navy as the legitimate mark of a great power and as a source of pride and patriotism. The British, however, saw German naval buildup as a challenge and a threat to British security and began to increase its military spending. The cycle of paranoia led to an arms race.

International Crises

The European powers before World War I confronted each other in a series of diplomatic clashes that could have resulted in war:

- **Moroccan Crisis of 1905:** On a visit to Morocco, a territory considered by the French to be a private sphere of influence, Kaiser Wilhelm II protested the French domination. Testing the strength of the Entente Cordial of 1904 between the French and the British, Wilhelm II advocated Moroccan independence and sent a warship to the country. He then demanded a conference on Morocco, which took place at Algeciras in Spain in 1906. The conference recognized the special interest of France in Morocco, but reaffirmed Moroccan independence. France was supported by Great Britain, Italy, and the United States, who under President Theodore Roosevelt had organized the conference.

- **Balkans Crisis of 1908:** Both Serbia and the Austrian-Hungarian Empire wanted to expand in the Balkans. When Austria annexed Bosnia-Herzegovina in 1908, Serbia protested and Russia sided with Serbia. The crisis was checked when Germany joined Austria's cause and balanced the Russian threat.

- **Second Moroccan Crisis of 1911:** Germany sent a gunboat, the Panther, to Agadir to protest the French occupation of the region. Germany compromised when it realized that Great Britain was supporting France. France was allowed to establish a protectorate in Morocco and, in return, Germany received some land area along Equatorial Africa, namely parts of the French Congo.

  The Moroccan Crises were setbacks for Germany but drew France and Great Britain into a closer alliance, as their national interests seemed to be the same — to limit German power.

- **Balkan Crises of 1912–1913:** As a result of the Balkan War of 1912 with the Ottoman Empire, four Balkan states — Serbia, Montenegro, Bulgaria, and Greece — seized territory from the Ottoman Empire. Serbia's dispute with Bulgaria over the spoils of war led to the Second Balkan War. Bulgaria was defeated and Serbia, backed by Russia, appeared to have won an outlet to the Adriatic Sea. Austria, with the backing of Germany and Italy, intervened and forced the creation of Albania out of the former Ottoman lands, thereby blocking Serbia's ambitions. The Balkan Crises of 1912–13 brought Russia and Serbia closer together and intensified the animosity of Russia and Serbia for the Austrian-Hungarian Empire.

  These crises, combined with the underlying problems created by the alliance system, excessive nationalism, economic competition, imperialistic rivalries, and the arms race, created an international atmosphere that could erupt into war with a simple spark. The spark occurred in the Balkans.

The Immediate Cause of World War I

By 1914, the Balkans was a powder keg of nationalist hatred and imperialistic rivalries. On June 28, 1914, **Archduke Ferdinand**, the heir to the throne of Austria, along with his wife **Sophie**, were assassinated on their fourteenth wedding anniversary when they were visiting Sarajevo, the capital of Bosnia. The assassin was a Serbian patriot named **Gavrilo Princip** who was a member of a secret group known as the Black Hand. The goal of the group was to organize South Slav people into a new single nation. Austria believed that Serbian officials aided the plot and were angered when it became known that Serbian officials were aware of the plot but did not warn them about it. Austria was determined to punish Serbia. The assassination set off a chain reaction during the months of July and August that plunged Europe into a major war. The following list describes the chain of events:

- **July 23:** Fortified in its demands by the blank check of support given it by Kaiser Wilhelm II of Germany on July 6, 1914, Austria presented to Serbia a harsh 48-hour unconditional ultimatum demanding that Serbia stop anti-Austrian propaganda and punish any Serbian official involved in the murder plot. Austria also wanted to join Serbia in investigating the assassination. Slavic Russia, the big brother to Serbia, encouraged her to stand tough against Austrian demands. Russia turned to France who promised to support her against Germany and Austria. The alliance system, designed to preserve peace, had turned the assassination from what might have been a local war into a conflict that would engulf the Great Powers. On July 28, 1914, Austria went to war against Serbia. Russia prepared for war beginning July 30, 1914.

- **August 1, 1914:** Germany declares war on Russia after Russia refuses Germany's request to stop mobilization.

- **August 3, 1914:** Germany declares war on France. The German plan to attack France quickly could succeed only by crossing through Belgium. Germany asked Belgium for permission to cross through the country. Belgium refused. However, Germany invaded anyway violating the Treaty of 1839, which had guaranteed Belgium's neutrality by all the Great Powers, including Prussia.

- **August 4, 1914:** Great Britain joins France and declares war on Germany.

- **August 6, 1914:** Austria declares war on Russia.

World War I had begun, involving the entire European continent in war for the first time since the Napoleonic conflict of the nineteenth century. European nations entered the war with enthusiasm and the hope that it would be a quick war. The common cry was, "The boys will be home by Christmas." British Prime Minister Edmund Grey was less optimistic, noting that "lamps are going out all over Europe. We shall never see them lit again in our lifetime." Grey believed that the war would permanently end the relative years of peace and prosperity that had existed in Europe since the end of the Congress of Vienna.

Although the Treaty of Versailles was later to blame Germany for the war, historians agree that all the nations of Europe bore responsibility for the events of August. The underlying causes of World War I can be attributed to the alliance system, aggressive nationalism, imperialism, and economic competition.

The Course of the War

World War I divided Europe into two camps:

- **Central Powers:** Germany, the Austrian-Hungarian Empire, and the Ottoman Empire. Bulgaria in 1915 joined to secure revenge against Serbia.

- **Allies:** Great Britain, France, Russia, Serbia, Belgium, and more than 25 other nations comprised the Allies. Japan joined in 1914 to acquire land in the Pacific and Italy joined in 1915 with the promise of gaining territory from Austria, overseas territories from Germany, and the Ottoman Empire. Italy had remained neutral on the grounds that Germany had provoked the war and violated the defensive nature of the Triple Alliance. In 1917, the United States became a member of the Allies due to Germany's unrestricted submarine warfare.

German Strategy

Count Alfred von Schlieffen (1883–1913) was chief of the general German staff from 1901 to 1905. The **Schlieffen Plan**, developed in 1905, was designed to prevent Germany from needing to conduct a two-front war. The plan was to quickly sweep through northern France, through Belgium in the West, and then turn to Russia in the East. The plan was to knock out France within six weeks as in the Franco-Prussian War and then transport troops to the eastern front to help the Austrians against the Russians.

Western Front

By the first week of September, the Germans were within 30 miles of Paris forcing government leaders to flee the city. However, the spirited defense of the Belgians, the more rapid mobilization of the Russians, and some unexpected victories in eastern Prussia by the Russian forces, forced Germany to revise its plan and send troops to the eastern front after all. At the Battle of the Marne River on September 5–9, the French fought heroically under the leadership of General Jacques Joffre and were reinforced by over 100,000 British troops. The French even recruited Paris taxies to bring reserve troops to the front. Germany fell back and Paris was saved.

Europe's hope for a quick war deteriorated into trench warfare as both sides dug in for the winter. At first, the trenches were built for a short amount of time, but as the stalemate continued, the Allies and Central Powers created a vast system of trenches that stretched from the Swiss frontier to the English Channel. Life in the trenches was not glamorous as soldiers roasted in the summer and froze in the winter. Sanitary conditions were horrible as soldiers shared their food with rats and their beds with lice. Between the two trenches, there was a "no man's land" and troops occasionally were sent over the top to attack the enemy trenches. The casualties were staggering. The British lost 60,000 per day and a total of 400,000 men at the Battle of Somme in 1916. At Verdun, both sides lost over 700,000 men and in 1917, at Passchendaele, the British lost 250,000 men for 5.0 square miles of Belgian Flanders. Erich Remarque's great novel *All Quiet on the Western Front* (1929) described the horrors of war on the western front.

Eastern Front

The eastern front did not get bogged down in trenches as in the West and the war was more mobile because battle lines covered much larger areas. In the beginning, the Russians fought well and pushed into East Germany, but General Paul Von Hindenburg and Erich Lundendorff defeated the Russians at the **Battle of Tannenberg**. The Russians lost over 30,000 men and 225,000 were captured in the fall of 1914, and by 1915, over 2.5 million Russian soldiers were either killed, wounded, or taken prisoner. These losses, combined with poor leadership of the government and the lack of food for soldiers and civilians, caused internal problems that led to the overthrow of Czar Nicholas in March 1917, and later the Communist Revolution in November 1917. The Communists, who had attracted support by promising an end to the war, withdrew from the war in 1918. The Communists signed the Treaty of Brest-Litovsk, which gave away large territorial concessions to Germany. (The Communist Revolution is discussed in the following chapter.)

Southern Front

In southeastern Europe, the British attacked the Ottoman Empire. In 1915, Winston Churchill, the first Lord of the Admiralty, organized the **Gallipoli Campaign**, which was designed to strike at the Germans and Austrians through the Dardanelles and the Balkans. Churchill wanted to provide Russian troops with supplies via the Black Sea. The campaign was a failure and Churchill resigned (during World War II, Churchill would also advocate this plan). In 1918, an Allied force won back much of the Balkans and an Italian offensive compelled the surrender of The Austrian-Hungarian Empire.

War in the Colonies and at Sea

Warfare in the colonial possessions went well for the Allies, seizing German possessions in Africa. Japan seized German outposts in China and the Pacific. It also tried to impose a protectorate over China. With Arab help, the British defeated the Ottoman Empire. The British success in Palestine was followed by the **Balfour Declaration** of 1917, which called for the creation of a Jewish state. In May 1915, German submarines sank the **Lusitania**, a British liner, claiming that it was carrying munitions. This act of agression killed 1,201 people, of which 139 were Americans. In 1915, President Woodrow Wilson's threat to break off diplomatic relations with Germany forced Germany to promise to stop sinking neutral ships without warning.

The British naval strength was supreme and they effectively blockaded Germany and kept control of the Atlantic sea-lanes. On May 31 to June 1, 1916, Germany tried to break the blockade at the **Battle of Jutland**. This battle fought between the British and German fleets involved over 250 ships and ended in a draw. It was the last great battle to be fought exclusively by surface ships. Afterwards, Germany concentrated on the use of the U-Boat. Germany's use of unrestricted submarine warfare inflicted great damages on the Allies but failed to break the blockade.

New Ways of Waging War

World War I is considered to be the first truly technological war. New weapons, such as the machine gun, larger artillery, armed tanks, poison gas, the airplane, and new systems of communication, added greatly to the destructiveness of the war. The machine gun, which had greatly been improved by World War I, provided a continuous stream of bullets that wiped out waves of attackers. This made it difficult for armed forces to advance and helped to create a stalemate. One light machine gun, the **Lewis Gun**, designed by Isaac Lewis, could fire approximately 500 bullets a minute and provided the fire power of 50 riflemen. Larger artillery could shell enemy lines for 15 miles away. In 1918, the Germans were shelling Paris from 70 miles away. One of the better improvements was a system called "sound ranging" for artillery, which could determine the exact enemy batteries and then accurately position guns for the areas before a battle.

Also part of the new warfare was the armored tank that moved on chained tracks, enabling it to cross many kinds of land. There is some doubt about the origin of the word "tank"; it is commonly accepted that it derived from the term "water carrier." The innocent name "tank" was initially given to divert any attention from the new war project. In September 1916, 49 tanks were introduced by the British at the Battle of Somme. The early tanks were slow and clumsy. However, they eventually improved and aided the Allies in their war efforts. Poison gas was introduced by the Germans at the Second Battle of Ypres in April 1915 and was eventually used by both sides. The eventual use of the gas mask mitigated the effects of this deadly weapon.

In December 1903, Orville and Wilbur Wright successfully flew a power airplane. The Wright brothers offered their design to the United States War Department as well as other governments and individuals in Europe. They were repeatedly turned down. By 1911, the United States and other European countries began to realize that there was money in the aviation business. With the outbreak of World War I, some believed that the plane could be an advantage. At first, airplanes were sent out over enemy positions to spot enemy formations and troop movements. The pilots independently armed themselves with pistols and sometimes rifles to shoot at an enemy plane. They also began to carry small bombs to drop over the side of their planes into enemy positions. Bombing raids were conducted at all times.

During the war, machine guns were mounted on planes so that planes fought each other in combat battles, which were known as "dog fights." World War I planes came in three varieties: single-wing (mono-planes), double-wing (bi-planes), and triple-wing (tri-planes). The more wings a plane had, the more mobility, stability it had, making it easier for the plane to evade gun fire or to better maneuver in a dog fight. The tri-plane was considered the favorite of the German flying ace, **Manfried von Richthofen**, better known as the Red Fox or the Red Baron. He is credited with shooting down 85 Allied planes. Planes were also used for moving supplies and for aerial photography during attacks to map positions.

Hot air balloons were still used during World War I. Many were placed on the western front as observers because they were cheaper than planes. The development of fighter planes made it more dangerous to use them; subsequently, the hot air balloons became less effective. Dirigible bombers, such as **Zeppelins**, were also used. They were extremely vulnerable to ground fire but could level buildings in seconds. Fast fighter planes and strong anti-artillery made it hard to bomb during day hours and still harder to bomb during night hours. It is estimated that there were over 9,000 casualties due to these bombings.

Communication systems significantly improved during World War I. Wireless radios enabled different groups on the battlefield to communicate quickly without requiring men as messengers. The radio system was used to transmit messages from relay stations to main headquarters during the war.

War on the Home Front

World War I was the first war in which the entire population of the country participated in the war effort. Once the hope for a quick war ended, government leaders realized that they had to mobilize all their resources. Total war meant economic planning, rationing, wage and price controls, and restricting the freedom of labor. The role of women changed greatly as many women started to work in factories. By 1917, women comprised 43% of the labor force in Russia. The number of women driving buses and streetcars increased tenfold in Great Britain.

Believing women would lower the wages, male-dominated professions were initially hostile towards their moving into their occupations. Government pressure and the principle of equal pay for equal work overcame these objections. As a result of the women's war efforts, Great Britain, Germany, and Austria granted women the right to vote immediately after the war. Children also participated through food drives and by collecting material that would help the war effort. The government also used wartime propaganda to maintain popular support of the war and control popular opinion. The government censored the news, controlled the arts, and created posters and movies to promote patriotism and arouse hatred towards the enemy.

Concluding the War

1917 was a pivotal year for the war. In early 1917, the British had intercepted and decoded a message from the German Foreign Minister to Arthur Zimmerman to his ambassador in Mexico. The telegram promised that in return for Mexico's support, Germany would help Mexico win back Texas, Arizona, and New Mexico (the territories lost in the 1840s to the United States). The British revealed the **Zimmerman Note** to the American government. On March 2, 1917, the note was published in American newspapers and intensified the anti-German feelings in the United States. In 1917, with Russia on the verge of defeat, Germany decided to resume its unrestricted submarine warfare.

On April 6, 1917, a month after the Russian Revolution, the United States entered the war. Germany gambled that they could gain quick victories before the impact of American troops could make a difference. The United States' entry made a difference, however. In 1918, the American Expeditionary Force of 2 million men led by General **John J. Pershing** helped to stem the tide at **Chateau Thierry** and the **Argonne Forest**. By autumn, Bulgaria and the Ottoman Empire sued for peace, and the Austrian-Hungarian government collapsed as subject nationalities revolted and splintered the empire into different national states. Revolutions also broke out across Germany. The military leaders informed the Kaiser that the war was lost and advised him to step down as the czar had done. Wilhelm II fled to Holland in early November, leading to the creation of a provisional republican government that agreed to negotiations based on U.S. President Woodrow Wilson's **Fourteen Points**. At 11 A.M., on the 11th day of November, 1918, Germany signed the armistice to end World War I.

The Treaty of Versailles

In January 1918, Woodrow Wilson, in a speech before Congress, outlined what he considered to be the war aims of the Allies. These Fourteen Points contained the ideals of "A Peace Without Victory." The most important of these Fourteen Points were the following:

- End of secret diplomacy
- Freedom of the seas
- Arms reductions

- Free trade

- National self determination

- The creation of an international peace organization called the League of Nations

In January 1919, representatives of the countries known as the "Big Four" met at Versailles and each had different objectives:

- **David Lloyd George** of Great Britain sought to preserve its empire and maintain its industrial and naval supremacy.

- **Georges Clemenceau** of France sought revenge for the lost provinces of Alsace and Lorraine and wanted to insure France against future German invasions.

- **Vittorio Orlano** of Italy wanted to gain *Italia Irredenta,* unredeemed territories from Austria, and colonies in Africa and the Middle East.

- **Woodrow Wilson**, President of the United States, sought a just peace based on creating a League of Nations.

Russia and the Central Powers, as well as Japan, were excluded from the conference. Italy walked out of the conference when the treaty did not meet its demands. The conflicting desires of the Allies led to a deadlock. France and Great Britain, who had suffered devastating economic losses and the loss of human life, thought that Wilson's approach was unrealistic. They were more interested in making sure that Germany never threatened the security of Europe again. Wilson, who was obsessed with the League of Nations, was willing to compromise on most issues to achieve this goal. The Versailles Treaty was far from the ideal originally requested by Wilson.

Provisions of the Versailles Treaty

- Article 231 — Germany accepted sole responsibility for the war (**War Guilt Clause**).

- Germany was also required to pay all the costs of the war, including civilian damages, pensions to widows, and others in Allied countries. The total cost was expected to be $132 billion over thirty years.

- Germany's overseas colonies were distributed among the Allies. Parts of her territory were ceded to other nations: Alsace Lorraine to France; Northern Schleswig to Denmark; West Prussia to Poland. France also gained control of the Saar coal mine as reparations. The Saar basis was to be occupied for 15 years by the major powers, after which the people if this area could vote on which country they wanted to join.

- The German army and navy were reduced to 100,000 men and it was forbidden from having an air force.

- The Rhineland, a 30-mile strip of land in Western Germany, had to be de-militarized and subjected to occupation by the Allies for fifteen years. Other treaties were signed in 1919 with Austria, Hungary, Bulgaria, and Turkey that redrew the boundaries of Europe in the following ways:

- Austria was obliged to recognize the independence of Czechoslovakia (combining the lands of the Czechs and Slovaks), including a significant number of Germans.

- Austria and Hungary became independent national states.

- Poland became independent for the first time in the century.

- Yugoslavia was created in the Balkans and dominated by the Serbs.

There were other treaties as well:

The Treaty of Trianon (June 1920). Hungary lost one-third of its territory to Romania, Yugoslavia, and Czechoslovakia by divesting it of all areas that were not Magyar.

The Treaty of Neuilly (November 1919). Bulgaria lost territory to Yugoslavia and Greece.

The Treaty of Sevres (August 1920), provided for the following:

- Liquidating the Ottoman Empire by abolishing Turkish control in the Middle East, Mesopotamia (Iraq), Palestine, including Trans Jordan, which became a British mandate, Lebanon, which became a French mandate.

- Turkey losing its non-Turkish territories and the Dardanelles, and the surrounding areas becoming internationalized and demilitarized.

These treaties, like the Versailles Treaty, were named after suburbs in Paris.

European leaders applied the principles of nationalism only to Europe. Despite the contributions of colonial soldiers who fought alongside European soldiers, the leaders at the Versailles Conference ignored Wilson's hope for self-determination for all people. France and Great Britain created systems of mandates over the former areas controlled by the Ottoman Empire. These mandates were to be held until these areas could stand alone. In actuality, they became European colonies. From Africa to the Middle East, colonized people believed that European leaders had betrayed them.

Impact of the War

The Versailles Treaty, which was the most important peace settlement that ended World War I, never really solved the problems that led to World War I. The United States rejected the treaty and did not join the League of Nations, which was established by 1920. France felt isolated when Great Britain backed out of a defensive alliance with her. Italy was angry because it did not get all the land that it was promised in its secret treaty with the allies. Japan was upset that the West refused to recognize its claims in China. Russia was angry because it had been excluded from the conference and Poland and the Baltic states were carved out of its Empire. Finally, Germany was angry because it thought that it was treated too harshly and was forced to sign the treaty. The cry that "Germany was stabbed in the back at Versailles" would provide the rallying cry for the Nazi's rise to power.

World War I exacted a further toll upon Europe:

- 10 million soldiers were dead and 20 million were wounded. It cost $332 billion for war costs and property damages.

- The Ottoman Empire was destroyed and the Hohenzollern Dynasty of Germany, the Hapsburg Dynasty of the Austrian-Hungarian Empire, and the Romanov Dynasty of Russia collapsed.

- Communism was established in Russia.

- The economies of Europe were weakened. Paying for the war brought heavy taxation and lower standards of living for the people of Europe. The United States emerged as a leading world power. America became a creditor nation from which the European nations borrowed in order to survive the devastation of the war.

- Psychologically, a generation was haunted by the horrors of the war and committed to never going to war again.

- World War I, which was called the war to end all wars, created the seeds that would plunge Europe into another major war within twenty years.

Chronology of World War I

1879	Bismarck forms an alliance between Germany and The Austrian-Hungarian Empire.
1882	Triple Alliance forms among Germany, The Austrian-Hungarian Empire, and Italy.
1891	Germany begins to modernize its navy.
1894	Franco-Russian Alliance is formed.
1901	Guglielmo Marconi transmits telegraphic radio messages from Cornwall to Newfoundland.
1902	Great Britain enters into a military alliance with Japan.
1903	Orville and Wilbur Wright successfully fly a powered airplane.
1904	Entente Cordiale is formed between Great Britain and France in response to the Triple Alliance.
1905	Revolution erupts in Russia; Albert Einstein formulates theory of relativity.
1906	Algeciras Conference — Great Britain and Italy support France's claim to Morocco against Germany's demand that Morocco be independent. This was a diplomatic defeat for Germany.
1907	Triple Entente is completed; Military alliance formed among Great Britain, Russia, and France.

1911	Second Moroccan Crisis — Germany challenges French control of Morocco. Germany is forced to compromise.
1912	S.S. Titanic sinks on its maiden voyage; Second Balkan War begins (1912–1913).
June 28, 1914	Assassination of Archduke Ferdinand, heir to the throne of the Austrian-Hungarian Empire.
July 28, 1914	The Austrian-Hungarian Empire declares war on Serbia.
Aug. 1, 1914	In response to Russian mobilization, Germany declares war on Russia.
Aug. 3, 1914	Germany declares war on France.
Aug. 4, 1914	Great Britain declares war on Germany after Germany violates Belgium's neutrality.
Aug. 8, 1914	Japan enters the war against Germany.
Sept. 5–9, 1914	German advance in West stopped at the Battle of Marne; Ottoman Empire and Bulgaria join forces with Germany.
Apr. 22, 1915	Germans employ poisonous gas for first time at the Second Battle of Ypres.
Apr. 25, 1915	British and French troops attack the Ottoman Empire at Gallipoli.
Apr. 26, 1915	Italy joins the Allies in the Secret Treaty of London and is promised colonies in Africa and the Middle East.
May 7, 1915	German submarine sinks the Lusitania, resulting in the loss of 139 American lives.
Feb.–Dec., 1916	Battle of Verdun over 700,000 men are lost
July–Nov., 1916	Battle of Somme fails to achieve major breakthrough for the Allies; The British use tanks for the first time.
1917	Sigmund Freud's *Introduction to Psychoanalysis* is published; Zimmerman Telegram brings the United States closer to war with Germany.
Mar., 1917	Russian Revolution leads to the abdication of Czar Nicholas II.
Apr. 6, 1917	United States declares war on Germany.
Nov. 6, 1917	Bolsheviks seize power in Petrograd.
Jan., 1918	President Woodrow Wilson issues his Fourteen Points, a framework for peace.
Mar. 3, 1918	Bolsheviks accept German peace terms at Brest-Litovsk.
Sept.-Oct., 1918	Allied offensive at Argonne breaks Germany's resistance.
Nov. 9, 1918	Kaiser William II abdicates German throne and flees to Holland.
Nov. 11, 1918	Armistice ends the fighting along the western front; Austrian Emperor Charles I steps down.
Jan., 1919	The Versailles Peace Conference.
June, 1919	Versailles Treaty signed, imposing harsh settlement on Germany.

Sample Multiple-Choice Questions

1. Bismarck's Alliance System was designed to

   A. promote relations with Great Britain

   B. provide an opportunity for Germany to expand its borders

   C. restrain Russia and the Austrian-Hungarian Empire and isolate France

   D. weaken the influence of the Ottoman Turks in the Balkans

   E. encourage relations with France

2. All of the following are usually considered the causes of World War I EXCEPT

   A. nationalism

   B. rivalry over colonies in Africa and Asia

   C. arms race between Germany and Great Britain

   D. rival alliances

   E. British appeasement of the Germans

3. The Schlieffen Plan was designed to

   A. prevent Great Britain from helping France

   B. rely on a slow defensive

   C. achieve a quick victory over France

   D. require Germany to defeat Russia quickly

   E. require the use of Austrian-Hungarian forces on the western front

4. The immediate cause that led Great Britain to declare war was

   A. the rivalry between Germany and the British in the Balkans

   B. violation of Belgium's neutrality

   C. Great Britain's treaty commitment to France

   D. Germany's use of submarine warfare

   E. German support of the Austrian-Hungarian Empire

5. Which of the following was characteristic of war on the western front?

   A. Airplanes allowed most of the fighting to be done in the sky.

   B. A number of inconclusive battles fought in trenches spread across the area.

   C. A propaganda war with little actual fighting took place.

   D. The terrain made it difficult to assemble large armies.

   E. A large-scale use of tanks occured.

6. Women in World War I

  A. contributed little to the war effort

  B. lost their economic position

  C. made economic gains but little political gains

  D. had very little change from their traditional roles during peace time

  E. maintained their nations' economies

7. Which of the following nations *did not* gain independence after World War I?

  A. Poland

  B. Czechoslovakia

  C. Hungary

  D. Yugoslavia

  E. Bulgaria

8. All of the following are part of Wilson's Fourteen Points EXCEPT

  A. freedom of the seas

  B. free trade

  C. end of secret treaties

  D. aid to rebuild Germany and the Austrian-Hungarian Empire

  E. reduction of the arms race

9. ". . . we shall fight for the things which have always been nearest our hearts, for democracy, for the right of those who submit to authority to have a voice in their own governments, for the rights and liberties of small nations, for a universal domination of rights by such a concert of free peoples as shall bring peace and safety to all nations and make the world itself at last free. . . ."

  –President Woodrow Wilson

This statement by President Wilson is directly advocating the idea of

  A. disarmament

  B. national self-determination

  C. territorial readjustments

  D. balance of power

  E. freedom of the seas

10. Article 231 of the Versailles Treaty

  A. contained the war guilt clause blaming Germany for World War I

  B. established the League of Nations

  C. ended the arms race

  D. divided Germany's colonies among the Allies

  E. returned Alsace-Lorraine to France

Answers to Multiple-Choice Questions and Explanations

1. **C.** Bismarck's Alliance System was designed to restrain Russia and isolate France. The rival aspirations of Austria and Russia in the Balkans were a major threat to peace. Bismarck was concerned that Germany would become involved if hostilities erupted. Bismarck also feared France's desire for revenge after her defeat in the Franco-Prussian War. These alliances were not formed for the purpose of promoting relations with Great Britain. In 1871, after Germany was united, Bismarck declared Germany to be satisfied. His alliances were not directly related to the weakening of the Ottoman Empire. Ottoman Empire eventually became an ally of Germany. Bismarck diplomacy was the isolation of a hostile France.

2. **E.** British appeasement of the Germans is not considered a cause of World War I. Nationalism in the Balkans, rivalry over colonial possessions in Africa and Asia, the arms race between Germany and Great Britain, and the system of alliances are considered underlying causes that led to World War I.

3. **C.** The Schlieffen Plan was developed for a quick victory over France. The Schlieffen Plan called for knocking out France first with a lightning attack through neutral Belgium before turning on Russia. The Germans thought that France could be defeated in six weeks. It was expected that Russia would take at least six weeks to fully mobilize before she could attack Germany. The Schlieffen Plan was directed at France and not at Great Britain. It relied on a quick offensive victory, not a slow defensive strategy. It was drawn up for a quick victory over France, not Russia, and did not include any Austrian-Hungarian troops for use on the western front.

4. **B.** The immediate cause that led Great Britain to declare war on Germany was the violation of Belgium's neutrality. On August 3, the Germans invaded Belgium. Great Britain and other European powers had guaranteed Belgium's neutrality in 1839. Outraged by the invasion of Belgium, Great Britain declared war on Germany. The rivalry between Germany and the British in the Balkans, and Great Britain's commitment to France were not immediate causes of the war with Germany. Germany's rival in the Balkans was Russia. The German use of submarine-warfare contributed to the United States' entry into the war. Germany's support of the Austrian-Hungarian Empire did not contribute to Great Britain's declaration of war. Germany's decision to support the Austrian-Hungarian Empire created problems for Russia.

5. **B.** A number of inconclusive battles fought in trenches across the area was characteristic of war on the western front. After the French stopped the German offensive at the Battle of the Marne in September 1914, the two opposing armies dug into the ground for trench warfare. The western front became deadlocked. Between the opposing trenches lay "No Man's Land," in which two armies fought over a few hundred yards and lost them without gaining a significant victory. In 1915, the British and French offensive never gained more than three miles of land from the enemy. At the Battle of Somme in 1916, close to one-half million men lost their lives for 125 square miles. Airplanes were used mainly for observations and later for small-scale bombing. The high casualty rate on the western front demonstrated that there were a number of costly battles. The government used

propaganda to convince the home front that their cause was just. The terrain did not stop the Allies and Central Powers from assembling large armies. Tanks were not used often because they were slow and clumsy.

6. **E.** Women kept their nations' economies going during World War I. In every country, a large number of women left their homes and domestic service to work in industry, transportation, and offices. Women worked in war industries and manufacturing. They also built tanks, plowed fields, paved streets, and ran hospitals. When a food shortage occurred, British women went to the fields to grow their own food.

7. **E.** Bulgaria was part of the Ottoman Empire until 1878. In 1878, Russia forced the Ottoman Empire to give Bulgaria its independence. After the war, Poland gained its independence after 100 years of foreign rule; Czechoslovakia and Hungary rose out of the old Austrian-Hungarian state; Yugoslavia was created in the Balkans with Serbian domination.

8. **D.** Wilson's Fourteen Points did not provide economic aid to rebuild Germany and the Austrian-Hungarian Empire. Wilson's Fourteen Points was a framework for peace that was directed at eliminating the causes of the war and not restructuring the defeated nations. Freedom of the seas, free trade, the end of secret treaties, and the reduction of the arms race were included in Wilson's Fourteen Points in the hope that "a just peace would be established to end all wars."

9. **B.** This statement by President Woodrow Wilson is directly advocating the idea of national self-determination. Self-determination means allowing people to decide for themselves under which government they wish to live. In January 1918, President Wilson of the United States issued the Fourteen Points, a plan for resolving World War I and future wars. Seven of these points were specific suggestions for changing borders and creating new nations. The guiding idea behind these points was self-determination regarding the right of any national group to set up an independent state. The principle of self-determination resulted in a band of new nations emerging where the German, Austrian, and Russian empires had once ruled. These nations included the Baltic states of Estonia, Lithuania, and Latvia. Poland regained independence after more than 100 years of foreign rule. Three new republics, Czechoslovakia, Austria, and Hungary, rose out of the old Hapsburg Empire. In the Balkans, the new Slav state of Yugoslavia became an independent nation, dominated by the Serbs. Disarmament means the reduction or limiting of national armies and navies. Territorial readjustments refer to the alignment of territories based on the interests of the nations who are strong enough to achieve their objectives. Balance of power is a policy designed to prevent any one nation from becoming too economically or militarily powerful. Freedom of the seas addresses the rights of neutral nations to trade with nations during wartime.

10. **A.** Article 231 of the Versailles Treaty contained the war guilt clause blaming Germany for World War I. The war-guilt clause also held Germany responsible for all damages that they caused to the Allied nations. Article 231 of the Versailles Treaty did not establish the League of Nations. The Versailles Treaty required only Germany to limit its army to 100,000 soldiers. Article 231, moreover, did not deal with the issue of German colonies nor the return of Alsace-Lorraine to France.

Europe in Crisis (1917–1939)

In Russia, World War I provided the spark that ignited conditions that had been simmering for decades. The Russian Czar Nicholas II, who had entered World War I in 1914 with the enthusiastic support of the people, would become the target of their anger and frustration. By 1915, Russia's staggering casualties, her inability to provide the basic necessities for her people, and Nicholas' lack of leadership sparked a revolution that ended the 300-year-old dynasty of the Romanov family and, like the French Revolution of 1789, had a major effect on the world.

Russia's March Revolution of 1917 started as an attempt by the middle class to gain a greater voice in the government by limiting the powers of the czar and providing for the guarantee of basic civil liberties. When this moderate provisional government failed to provide food for the people and insisted on participating in an unpopular war, the Bolshevik Party overthrew the government and set up a Communist dictatorship. The Communist Revolution turned out to be the cannonball of fire that would threaten all the other countries of Europe and influence world politics throughout the twentieth century. The disillusionment created by the dissatisfaction with the results of World War I and the economic problems caused by the Great Depression instilled doubts about the abilities of Western democracy to deal with these issues.

The fear of Communism also contributed to the rise of Fascism in Italy and National Socialism (commonly known as Nazism) in Germany. Communists in Russia, Fascists in Italy, and Nazis in Germany followed a totalitarian form of government which was unique in the history of the world: a state-established single party dictatorship that used technology and communication to control the political, social, intellectual, and cultural components of its subjects' lives. The rise of totalitarian dictatorships presented a serious challenge to Western democracy.

As the dictators in Italy and Germany and the militarists in Japan pursued aggressive actions in their quest for empires, European leaders, haunted by the memories of World War I, tried to avoid war through the policy of appeasement. Appeasement only heightened the demands of these aggressors, however, and led to World War II in 1939, which proved to be more horrendous than anyone could have imagined.

The Russian Revolution

Nicholas II (who reigned from 1894 to 1917) failed to understand the urgency of the problems created by industrialization, the rising influence of the middle class, and the anger of the exploited peasants and the proletariat, or working class. Because of these issues, political parties sprang up to meet the needs of various societal groups. The following groups were active at various times throughout the Russian Revolution:

Dates Founded	Party	Beliefs and Significance
1898	DS (Social Democrats) Also known as the Russian Social Democratic Labor Party	Workers who wanted to remove the czar by strikes and mass action. They preached the revolutionary doctrines of Karl Marx. In 1903, the party split at the Second National Congress into the Bolshevik and Menshevik Parties.
1903	Bolsheviks	Lenin was a Bolshevik leader who favored a small, disciplined party of professional revolutionaries. He believed that a radical revolution was necessary to destroy capitalism. However, Marx had predicted that a communist revolution was inevitable only in industrial societies, such as those in Western Europe and the United States. Lenin thought that Marxism could occur in an agrarian Russia, if it were led by an intellectual elite. The Bolshevik Party became the Communist Party in 1918.
1903	Mensheviks	Georgi Plekhanov (1857–1918) was the Menshevik leader who wanted a loosely-organized mass party membership and believed that a bourgeousie revolution must occur in Russia before it could move towards socialism. Plekhanov would support Russia's participation in World War I. In 1921, the Communist Party suppressed the Mensheviks.
1901–1922	SR (Social Revolutionaries)	Viktor Chernov (1876–1952) was the party leader. His program called for the socialization of land which was to be distributed among the peasants on the basis of need. In 1918, the party won a majority in the short-lived Constituent Assembly, which was disbanded by the Bolsheviks. The party was suppressed in 1922 by the Communists.
1905–1918	KD (Kadets), the Constitutional Democratic Party	Pavel Miliukov (1859–1943), a famous Russian historian, was the founder of the Constitutional Democratic Party. This party was a middle-class group that supported a program of liberal, constitutional monarchy with a liberal assembly. In 1906, the Kadets won a majority in the Duma. After 1907, the Kadets became fearful of the Social Revolutionaries and supported gradual constitutional change. Miliukov became foreign minister in the provisional government after the overthrow of the czar in March 1917. The Kadets were banned by the Bolsheviks in 1918.
1905	Octobrists	The Octobrists were led by Alexander Guchkov (1862–1936). The goal of the party was to help the government implement the October Manifesto. The Octobrists won the greatest number of seats during the Third Duma (1907–1912). In 1915, they joined the Constitutional Democratic Party, advocating a comprehensive program of reform. Guchkov became Minister of War in the provisional government.

Russo-Japanese War (1904–1905)

War broke out between Russia and Japan after the interest of the two nations conflicted over Korea and Manchuria. Nicholas entered the war with the hope that a call to fight for the Fatherland and faith in the czar would stem the unrest in his nation and lead to a short and quick victory. Despite its efforts, Russia suffered humiliating defeats and was forced to sign the **Treaty of Portsmouth** (1905). Russia ceded the southern half of the Sakhalin Islands to Japan, surrendered its rights to Manchuria, and acknowledged Japan's special interest in Korea.

Russian Revolution of 1905

As the disasters of the war spread to the home front, evidence of government corruption and inefficiencies became public. Workers stuck with demands for shorter hours. Liberals called for reforms in government and for a constitution.

On Sunday, January 22, 1905, **Father Gapon**, a Russian Orthodox priest, organized a march of 200,000 unarmed workers to present a petition to the czar at the winter palace in St. Petersburg. The workers wanted an eight-hour workday, a representative assembly, the right to strike, and other liberal reforms. When the procession of workers reached the Winter Palace, it was attacked by soldiers who fired on the crowd. Over 100 workers were killed and some 300 wounded. This incident, known as Bloody Sunday, led to a series of demonstrations and scattered uprisings across the nation. Universities closed down when student bodies staged a walkout about the lack of civil liberties. Lawyers, doctors, engineers, and other middle class workers established a Union of Unions and demanded a Constituent Assembly. Industrial workers all over Russia went on strike and in October 1905, the striking railroad workers paralyzed the nation. In St. Petersburg, the workers established *soviets* or revolutionary councils that had first begun as strike committees but developed into an elective body by the town workers. Over the next few months, the Soviets of Worker Deputies were established in over 50 different towns.

The Liberals in the **Zemstvos** (the provincial council elected by the landowners and peasants which had been established by Czar Alexander II in1864 as part of his land reforms) forced Nicholas II to make changes. In October 1905, the czar issued the **October Manifesto**, promising to pass a new constitution that guaranteed certain civil rights and liberties and created a lawmaking body, the **Duma**, elected by universal male suffrage. The Manifesto won over the moderates. However, many workers boycotted the election because they distrusted the czar and his supporters. Joined by the soldiers returning from the Russo-Japanese War, the workers denounced the Manifesto. In 1906, the first Duma met, but its powers were limited because it lacked control over finances and foreign affairs and was subject to dismissal by the czar. In 1906, at their first meeting, the members of the Duma put forth a series of demands including the release of political prisoners, trade union rights, and land reforms. Nicholas II rejected these proposals and dissolved the Duma.

Nicholas II appointed **Peter Stolypin**, a conservative minister who tried to restore order by arrests, **pogroms** (organized violence against the Jews), and executions. Alexander III had started these pogroms in 1881 as a way to established a uniform Russian culture. However, Stolypin realized that Russia needed reforms as well as repressive measures. He introduced land reforms, strengthened the Zemstvos, abolished all debts on the land, permitted peasants to abolish the **mirs** (land village communities), and transferred land titles to the peasants. This led to the rise of a wealthy class of peasants, the **Kulaks**. Stolypin tried to improve education but was assassinated in 1911 by conservatives who thought that his reforms were too radical. The Duma met several times during this time (1911–1917) but the restriction of suffrage to the upper class limited its power and it became like a debating society.

World War I

World War I, like the Crimean and Russo-Japanese war, quickly exhausted Russian resources. The transportation system was unable to provide soldiers with the food and supplies necessary to fight the war. As casualties mounted and reports circulated abut the poor leadership of the Russian generals, the public began to call for a new government led by the Duma and not the czar. Meanwhile, Nicholas II decided to personally join the army on the battle front to lead the war effort — a mistake because Nicholas II was not a military man. The fortunes of the military continued to decline as casualties rose and economic conditions worsened. In his absence, the czar put **Alexandra**, his wife, in charge of domestic affairs — another mistake as the Russians distrusted her because she was German-born and had little knowledge of how to run a government. Alexandra fell under the influence of a mystic monk **Gregori Rasputin**, who convinced her that he had the power to stop the bleeding of her son, Alexis, a hemophiliac. By 1916, Rasputin had used his influence over Alexandra to control who would and who would not be appointed to government. Rumors spread that Alexandra and Rasputin were lovers and stories about profiteering and corruption in government over supplies for the military hurt the government even more. In December 1916, Rasputin was assassinated by a group of palace nobles who wanted to restore prestige to the throne. Nevertheless, the czar continued to resist any efforts at reform.

The March and November Revolutions

Note: In Russia, the March and November Revolutions are known as the February and October Revolutions. At the time, Russia was still using the Julian Calendar which was thirteen days behind the Western or Gregorian Calendar used in Western Europe. In 1918, Russia adapted the Western Calendar. The following list contains the sequence of events using the dates on the Western Calendar:

- **March 8–12, 1917:** Food riots and strikes break out in Petrograd (St. Petersburg). Nicholas sends troops to suppress the revolt but the troops refuse to fire on the crowd.

- **March 12, 1917:** The Duma, after being dismissed by the czar, sets up a provisional government or temporary government headed by the moderate **Prince George Lvov**. The provisional government supports reforms such as freedom of speech, religion, the right to unionize, and other liberal programs.

- **March 15, 1917:** The czar abdicates.

- **March 17, 1917:** A republic is proclaimed. **Vladimir Lenin** (1870–1924), whose real name is Vladimir Ilyich Ulyanov, declares Russia the freest country in the world.

- **April 16, 1917:** Lenin is shipped back to Russia by the Germans in a sealed train from Switzerland. The Germans thought that Lenin would fight for peace immediately. After his arrival, Lenin began to attract support with the slogan "All land to the peasants; Stop the war; All power to the Soviets."

- **May 17, 1917:** A reorganized government is formed which includes the socialist, **Alexander Kerensky** (1881–1970). Kerensky tours the eastern front where he appeals to the soldiers to continue fighting. Encouraged by the Bolsheviks who opposed the war, there are demonstrations against Kerensky and Petrograd. The provisional government, however, not in tune with the desires of the Russian people, insists that the country's national duty is to continue involvement in World War I.

From the beginning, the provisional government's biggest problem was that it had to share power with the **Petrograd Soviets**, a council of workers or soldier deputies. The Soviets issued **Order No 1**, stripping officers of their authority and placing power in the hands of a committee of soldiers. Army discipline broke down and massive desertion and chaos spread over the country.

- **July, 1917:** Lenin fails in an attempt to overthrow the government and is forced to go into hiding. Things begin to turn in favor of the Soviets. Lvov retires and Kerensky replaces him on July 17, 1917. Then Kerensky appoints General Lavr Kornilov (1870–1918) as supreme commander of the Russian army. Kornilov and Kerensky disagree over military policy. Kornilov believes that Kerensky is weak and unable to restore order and stability to the country and to the military. Kornilov also wants to restore the death penalty for soldiers. Lenin returns from Finland and works closely with Leon Trotsky (1879–1940), a spellbinding orator whose real name is Lev Bronstein.

- **September/October 1917:** Kerensky dismisses Kornilov from office when they are unable to resolve their differences. In retaliation, Kornilov orders troops to seize control of the government in Petrograd. Kerensky appeals to the Soviets (the Council of Workers) for support. The Petrograd soldiers free the Bolsheviks from prison to help them prepare the city for attack. The Bolsheviks, led by Lenin and Trotsky, agree to support Kerensky in defense of the city. Within a few days, the Bolsheviks recruit over 25,000 men. When Kornilov's troops refuse to attack Petrograd, the coup fails. Kornilov is arrested but escapes. Later he becomes commander of the White Army during the Civil War in Russia. Kerensky now becomes the supreme commander and chief. As soon as the Petrograd soldiers are behind the Bolsheviks and Trotsky becomes head of the Petrograd Soviets, Russia is ripe for revolution. However, with Trotsky as the head of the Petrograd Soviet and with Lenin and the Bolsheviks able to control a militia of over 25,000 men, Kerensky is unable to reassert his authority.

- **November 6, 1917:** Bolshevik soldiers led by Trotsky storm the Winter Palace and other key centers in Petrograd. Kerensky escapes and lives briefly in Finland, London, Russia, and finally settles in the United States in 1939, where he would subsequently die of cancer in 1970. In Moscow and other vital areas, the Bolsheviks succeed in taking over and establishing control.

- **November 7, 1917:** The **Russian Soviet Federative Socialist Republic** is established with Lenin as the head of state. Trotsky is appointed foreign commissar and **Joseph Stalin** (1879–1953), whose real name was Josef Dzugashvili, the commissar for nationalities.

The Bolsheviks were successful in winning the revolution because Lenin and Trotsky were superior leaders who provided the answers to the anarchy that existed in Russia. Unlike the provisional government, they also appealed to the peasants, the industrial workers, and the soldiers exhausted by war, with their slogan of "Peace, Land, and Bread."

Soviet Russia from 1918 to 1928

Lenin's motto that promises — like the crust of a pie — were made to be broken, was used as his guide in organizing his government. An immediate problem for Lenin was the Constituent Assembly. The provisional government had finally scheduled elections for November 25, 1917, under universal manhood suffrage. Thirty-six million people voted and the results were a stunning blow to the Bolshevik Party, which received only one-fourth of the votes, the majority going instead to the Social Revolutionaries. Lenin had no intention of giving up power to the freely elected Constituent Assembly. The Assembly met in January, 1918, but after two days, Lenin ordered the soldiers to disburse the Assembly. This was Lenin's first step in the process of setting up a one-party dictatorship.

In March of 1918, Russia dropped out of World War I by signing the **Treaty of Brest-Litovsk** and ceding Latvia, Lithuania, Estonia, Russian Poland, and the Ukraine to Germany. Of course, much of this treaty was torn up after the Armistice. Russia had lost about one-third of its population in the war.

Civil War in Russia (1918–1921)

Opposition to Lenin's government began to develop. Officers of the old army joined by the Kulaks or well-to-do peasants (**Whites**) organized resistance to the Bolsheviks (**Reds**). The Whites wanted self-rule rather than a Bolshevik dictatorship. A small Allied mission was sent by the British, French, and Americans to help the Whites. In the spring of 1918, the Allies landed near Archangel in Northern Russia. Although they remained there until the end of 1919, their mission was unsuccessful as the anti-Bolsheviks (the Reds) could never really unite. To protect the revolution, the Reds acted ruthlessly, putting Czar Nicholas II and his family to death, defeating all threats, and thus winning the civil war. The Red Army was successful because Trotsky was a superb military organizer who reorganized the military into an efficient fighting force. The Reds also had a well-defined political program and under the guise of **war communism**. Lenin nationalized all major industries which contributed to a total war effort; he also used the **Cheka**, or the Commission for Combatting Counter-Revolution and Sabotage, as a secret police to control all dissent within Russia by the use of terror. Finally, the Reds appealed to Russian nationalism to counteract foreign aid to the Whites. By 1920, the Bolsheviks had firmly established control of Russia. In 1922, Russia became officially known as the **Union of the Soviet Socialist Republics (U.S.S.R.)**, containing four republics: Russia, Ukraine, Byelorussia, and the Transcaucasia, which combined the territories of Georgia, Azerbaijan, and Armenia.

Russia's New Economic Policy

The civil war in Russia had killed millions and the famine of 1921–1922 claimed additional millions. In March 1921, a major rebellion broke out in Kronstadt, a naval base near Petrograd that had been a stronghold of Bolshevism. The sailors were angry at the lack of political freedom and the failure of War Communism to provide enough food for the population. Lenin, with Trotsky's support, quickly crushed the rebellion. The Kronstadt rebellion was the first major internal uprising against Soviet rule in Russia since the end of the Civil War. Lenin realized that he needed to readjust his economic policies. In 1921, he introduced the **New Economic Policy (NEP)** to replace war communism. Under this system, the peasants were allowed to sell surplus crops on the open market and private owners were allowed to operate retail stores for profit. The major industries still remained in control of the government. The NEP, or the temporary retreat from Communism, revived the economy. By 1927, agricultural and industrial production had reached pre-World War I levels.

Trotsky, leader of the Left Opposition, was critical of the NEP because he believed that Communism had to become a worldwide revolution in order to survive and wanted to return to the state control of war communism. Nikolai Bukharin (1888–1938), leader of the Right Opposition, wanted to extend the NEP and restore even more private enterprise. He supported building Communism within the Soviet state. Neither of these men would pick up the mantel of leadership after Lenin's death.

The Rise of Stalin

Lenin suffered two strokes in 1922 and one more in March of 1923. He died in 1924 at the age of 54, leaving Trotsky and Stalin as the chief contenders for power. Stalin, a Georgian who had joined the Communist Party in 1902, was not interested in an ideological debate but wanted to gain power for himself. As Secretary of the Communist Party, he was able to establish power within the Soviet System. Trotsky was a brilliant theorist, who had engineered the success of the Red Army in the civil war but his theory of worldwide or permanent evolution did not appeal to the Soviet people. Stalin's theory of "Socialism in one country" (that Russia with its fast resources could build itself up as a Socialist country alone without support from the outside and with no need for a worldwide revolution) was more attractive to people when revolution seemed distant and the need to make the Soviet Union better was a more realistic demand. In 1925, Stalin expelled Trotsky from the party and sent him to Central Asia. Trotsky eventually fled to the West and was assassinated in Mexico on orders from Stalin. Stalin, who had used Bukharin to oust Trotsky from power, expelled him from the party in 1929 leaving Stalin in undisputed control of the Soviet Union.

In 1928, Stalin introduced his first Five Year Plan of centralized government, planning to increase industrial and agricultural production in order to transform the Soviet Union into an industrial giant. His emphasis was to increase the production of heavy industry such as coal and steel — a top priority in order to produce weapons that would strengthen the country militarily. Stalin appealed to the nationalism of the people by promising that his Five Year Plan would enable Russia to catch up with Western countries. Stalin financed this plan by means of the collectivization of the farmers, waging a preventive war against the Kulaks to bring them and their land under state control. The collectivization of the farms (forcible consolidation of individual farms into state-controlled enterprises) was an agricultural disaster and a human tragedy. Peasants were shot on sight if they refused to join the collective farms. Millions of peasants or Kulaks died because of Stalin's brutal policy. By 1935, 95 percent of Russian farms had become collective. There were different types of collective farms:

- **kolkhoz:** A collective farm that was owned and operated by its members who were forced to deliver large parts of their crop to the state at prices fixed by the state. Sometimes the prices were so low that the peasants earned little from their work. The only benefit was that each family was allowed to cultivate a small plot for their own use. On this plot, they could sell any surplus crops on the open market.

- **sovkhoz:** A larger farm than the kolkhoz, upon which the peasants were simply employees and paid a straight salary.

The government also set up hundreds of Machine Tractor Stations throughout the country. Collectivization helped to make it easier for the government to control the people. It was also a political victory for Stalin and the Communist Party as peasants were eliminated as a potential threat and the state was able to control and regulate farms, thus, taking what it needed for its industrial program.

From 1934 to 1938, Stalin also directed a series of **purge** trials, consisting of trumped-up or false accusations, mock trials, and then suicides or executions. Stalin's **Reign of Terror** resulted in the deaths of those who were important in the founding of the revolution or high military officers and anyone who was not loyal to him. Stalin intertwined terror within the state and it is estimated that he ordered the death of over 15 million people. By 1938, Stalin's cruel and brutal methods had enabled him to establish complete control over Russia and transformed the Soviet Union into an industrial giant. However, Stalin's cruelty had created fear and terror throughout the nation.

Western Democracies (1920–1929)

Great Britain, like other European countries, emerged from World War I with a set of unique problems. Its overseas trade was destroyed; the nation was deeply in debt; its factories were outdated. In 1920, over 2 million people were unemployed and unemployment averaged about 12% annually until the Great Depression in 1919.

The **Labour Party** surpassed the **Liberal Party** in strength. Labour leaders gained support by promising social legislation. The middle class backed the **Conservative Party**, which held power during most of the period. In 1923, the Labour Party reigned briefly under the leadership of **Ramsey MacDonald**, whose government failed because of his efforts to establish formal ties with the Soviet Union. From 1924–1929, **Stanley Baldwin** and the Conservative Party ruled as the fear of Communism and a general strike by miners contributed to a drift towards the right. The Conservative government introduced protective tariffs, with the result that other nations retaliated with protective tariffs against British goods. Agricultural production suffered competition from increased production abroad. The Great Depression of 1929 resulted in a series of coalition governments with leadership from all three parties, including Labour, led by Ramsey MacDonald who resigned in 1935 because of ill health, and was replaced by Conservatives Stanley Baldwin and later **Neville Chamberlain** in 1937, who ruled until the start of World War II.

Political Parties Active in Great Britain in the 1920s and 1930s		
Parties	*Leaders*	*Beliefs*
Conservative Party	Stanley Baldwin (1867–1947, in office 1922–24, 1924–29, 1935–37)	Conservatives called Tories before the 1832 suffrage bill.
	Neville Chamberlain (1869–1940, in office 1937–40)	Supported high tariffs and welfare payments as the number of unemployed began to rise in the 1930s.
		Drew support from the upper middle class, the industrialists, and prosperous farmers.
		Supported free enterprise.
Labour Party	Ramsey MacDonald (1866–1937, in office 1924–24, 1929–31, 1931–35)	Nationalization of major industries.
		Urged expanding the welfare program.
		Supporters came from the workers, small farmers, and shopkeepers.
Liberal Party	Lloyd George (1863–1945, in office 1916–22)	Formerly the Whig Party.
		Lost the upper class support to the conservatives and lower class support to the Labour Party.
		Become a minority party after 1922.

Empire Affairs

By the 1920s, the British empire covered one-fourth of the world. The British had colonies in Asia, Africa, North America (Canada), South America, the West Indies, and Australasia (Australia and New Zealand). Britain enacted the **Statute of Westminster** in 1931, which set up the **Commonwealth of Nations** that granted self rule to the colonies of Canada, Australia, New Zealand, and South Africa. These nations were linked together by economic and cultural ties but each member of the Commonwealth pursued its own course. They had supported Great Britain during World War I and were all part of the British Imperial War Cabinet that had helped set up war policy. By 1931, these nations had become vital trading partners with Great Britain. However, Great Britain was not willing to allow freedom for colonies in the other areas that they controlled because they, like other Western countries, did not believe that they were ready for self government.

The greatest opposition to colonial rule came from India, where Mohandas Gandhi (1869–1948) proposed a policy of non-violence of passive resistance to British rule and actions. Despite challenges from nationalist groups, the British Empire would still stretch around the world and be a source of wealth and pride.

The British still faced the Irish Question, which was the demand of the Irish for self- or home rule. Throughout the 1800s, the Irish demand for home rule intensified. The British refused to consider the question because of the concern for Ireland's Protestants. In the 1600s, English and Scottish Protestant settlers had colonized Ireland and took possession of the best lands primarily in the North, which became known as Ulster. Irish Protestants in the North were fearful that they would be a minority in an independent Catholic island. Finally, Parliament passed a home rule in 1914 but it was put on hold when World War I began. Irish militants refused to wait and launched the **Easter Rebellion** in 1916 but the British quickly crushed it. From 1919 until 1922, the **Irish Republican Army** waged savage guerrilla warfare until moderate leaders in Ireland and England worked out a compromise. Most of Ireland was free and became known as the **Irish Free State** or **Eire**. The six northern Protestant counties (Ulster) remained under British rule. The compromise ended the immediate violence but many nationalists and the IRA never accepted this division. The problems of Northern Ireland would be an unresolved issue throughout the twentieth century.

France (1919–1929)

Like Great Britain, France suffered enormous casualties in the war, including severe losses in its young population and in the destruction of nearly one quarter of its productive industries and agriculture. France had borrowed a great deal during the war and relied heavily on German reparations to help spur its economy. The inability of Germany to make these repayments created a financial crisis that led to the steady decline of the franc. In January 1923, **Raymond Poincare**, the French prime minister, sent troops into the Ruhr Valley to obtain payments when Germany defaulted on its loans. The French invasion led to a wave of patriotism in Germany and the government ordered the people of the Ruhr Valley to stop working and passively resist the French occupation. Poincare's action was attacked by the British and the United States. By the summer of 1923, a compromise was reached when a moderate German government, under Gustav Streseman (1878–1929), assumed leadership. The Germans called off the passive resistance and agreed to pay off the reparations in principal, but asked for a re-evaluation of Germany's ability to pay.

Throughout the 1920s, political divisions and financial problems plagued the French government, which was ruled by a coalition of parties from conservatives to Communists who competed for power. In foreign policy, France's chief concern was securing its borders against Germany. To prevent future invasion, France constructed the **Maginot Line**, a series of concrete fortifications along its western boundaries; it also sought security by building buffer states (making treaties with other countries) around Germany, including the USSR. In the **Locarno Pact** (1925), Germany promised to accept as permanent its western boundaries with Belgium and France as well as guaranteeing that the Rhineland remain demilitarized. In 1928, the **Kellogg-Briand Pact** was signed by France and later 64 other nations outlawing war as an instrument of foreign policy.

The Great Depression

The Great Depression did not begin with the **Wall Street Crash** of October 1929; its beginnings were much earlier. The popular image of the Roaring Twenties was not as glamorous as it appeared. Beneath the economic boom, there were serious problems. People were overextended on credit and speculators had invested heavily in the market with the hope of a good return to offset their borrowing. The United States led the world in industrial and agricultural output and the availability of their loans helped to finance the European recovery. In 1924, the United States developed the **Dawes Plan** that provided a solution for the reparation problem by lending money to Germany so it could pay France and Great Britain. In turn, France and Great Britain could pay back the United States loans taken out during WWI. In 1929, the **Young Plan** further reduced German reparation. The economies of the United States and Europe were so intertwined that when the market crashed in the United States in 1929, it had a worldwide effect.

As the U.S. economy faltered, American banks began to recall their loans, which had a dramatic effect on the European economies. The financial crisis led to a decline in production in the United States. Countries began to raise tariffs to protect their industries, which led to further decline. In 1931, the Credit-Anstalt, the most important bank in Austria, collapsed and banks throughout Germany and Eastern Europe began to collapse. By 1932, the economies of Europe were only producing at one-half of their 1929 level. In the United States, one-fourth of the population was unemployed. **Franklin D. Roosevelt** (1933–1945) proposed the **New Deal**, whose goal was to preserve capitalism through reform. He introduced social legislation including **Social Security** (a government program designed to provide basic income for those who have retired) and attacked the problem of mass unemployment by using federal government funds to support public works projects. Roosevelt supported the ideas of the English economist, **John Maynard Keynes** (1883–1946), who urged that the government prime the pump or spend during the depression in order to get the economy going again. Although the New Deal helped the United States, it failed to pull the United States out of the Depression until the war cloud rolled over Europe in 1939.

Great Britain

During the Great Depression, Great Britain did not follow Keynes' program. The national government (a coalition of Labourites and conservatives) followed orthodox economics by trying to balance the budget, going off the gold standard, and concentrating on the national markets. By 1937, production had grown by 27 percent, but Britain, like the United States, did not come out of the Depression until the coming of World War II.

France

Since France was less industrialized and more isolated from the world community, the Great Depression came late. Still, a steady economic downturn did occur through 1935 adding to an unstable political scene. In 1933, five coalition governments were formed and fell in rapid succession. In 1934, pro-Fascists rioted and threatened to overthrow the republic. In 1936, the

Communists, Socialists, and Radicals formed an alliance — the **Popular Front** — and united behind **Leon Blum** (1872–1950). Inspired by Franklin D. Roosevelt's New Deal, he encouraged social reform, complete with paid vacations and 40-hour work-weeks. The radical elements were not satisfied, however, and the wealthy began to sneak money out of the country. Blum was forced to resign in 1937 and was replaced by the conservative, **Edmund Daladier** (1884–1970), who overturned Blum's reforms.

The Rise of Totalitarianism

The democratic countries of Great Britain and France muddled through the depression. They survived, but neither of them had the strong leadership to meet the challenge. The void of democratic leadership on the European continent convinced many Europeans that dictatorships could provide the hope of the future, especially since the Soviet Union had been one of the countries least affected by the economic crisis.

The post–World War I period gave rise to Fascism in Italy and the National Socialist Party, commonly known as Nazism in Germany. The roots of Fascism and Nazism were found in racism, extreme nationalism, an emphasis on violence, and the glorification of war as the highest virtue in society. The economic, political, and social conditions of post–World War I contributed to the rise of each of these political movements, both of them forms of totalitarianism — a movement that stresses that the individual was less important than the state and the goals of the state were never subordinate to those of the individual. Fascism rose first in Italy in 1922 because of the dissatisfaction created by World War I. Nazism in Germany arose due to the problems created by World War I and the chaos caused by the Great Depression. Below is a chart highlighting the major characteristics of Mussolini's Fascist Italy and Hitler's Nazi Germany:

Leader	Benito Mussolini — "Il Duce" (Fascism)	Adolf Hitler — "Der Fuhrer" — National Socialist Party (Nazism)
Date	1922–1945	1933–1945
Country	Italy	Germany
Basic ideas	Attacked democracy and supported dictatorship.	Attacked democracy and supported dictatorship.
	Opposed goals of Marxism.	Opposed goals of Marxism.
	Advocated extreme nationalism.	Advocated extreme nationalism, uniting all German people. Belief in Aryan supremacy.
	Wanted to restore the greatness of the Roman Empire.	Was anti-Semitic — believed Germany was the Master Race and the Jewish people Germany's greatest enemy.
	Glorified violence in war.	
	Slogan: "Believe, Fight and Obey."	

Reasons for popular appeal	Economic distress — inflation drove up prices and widespread unemployment.	Economic distress — inflation spiraled out of control (loaf of bread 10,000 marks); government printed huge quantities of paper money to pay off its war debt; Great Depression caused havoc (6 million Germans out of work). The unemployment rate was at 43%.
	Fear of Communism where workers seize factories and peasants seize lands. Landowners and Industrialists supported Fascists who promised to fight Socialists and Communism.	Fear of Communism — by 1930, Communists polled over six million votes; Conservatives feared Communist takeover; Hitler promised to resolve economic crisis.
	Appealed to Nationalism — Nationalists and Militarists unhappy with Italy's failure to gain territories from Paris Peace Conference.	Appealed to Nationalism — Germans of all classes refused to accept Versailles Treaty; hated War Guilt clauses with heavy reparation payment; many accused Marxists and Jews for stabbing Germany in back; Nazis exploited nationalism.
	Weak government — no political party dominated the government, which was unable to maintain law and order and deal with threat of Fascism.	Weak government — in 1919, new German Republic in city of Weimar established; Weimar Republic parliamentary democracy but no single party dominance; unable to deal with country's pressing problems.
	Leadership of Mussolini — a Socialist, but became ultra-nationalist in World War I.	Leadership of Hitler — born in Austria; unsuccessful artist; wounded in World War I; shocked by Versailles Treaty; founded National Socialist Party in 1920; failed in Beer Hall Putsch (1923); jailed and wrote *Mein Kampf (My Struggle)*, outlining goals of Nazism.
	In 1919 organized veterans and discontented Italians into the Fascist party; fiery speaker who promised to end corruption and replace turmoil with order.	Charismatic orator who promised to restore greatness of Germany.

continued

Steps to power	Forms Fascio di Combattmento (it is the Union of Combat) who use violence to gain power.	Organizes Storm Troopers (SA, Brown Shirts), Hitler's personal army to fight Communists.
	Squadristi (Black Shirts) created to break up Socialist rallies and eliminate opponents.	Election of 1930 — Nazis gained 107 seats in parliamentary elections, step up from 12 in 1928.
	May 21 — Mussolini's Fascist Party gained 35 seats in General Election.	Hitler promises to deal with problems created by Great Depression.
	October 1922 — Fascists march on Rome, King Victor Emmanuel II appoints Mussolini as Premier.	January 20, 1933 — President Von Hindenburg, military hero of World War I, appoints Hitler as Chancellor.
		February 1933 — Reichstag Fire blamed on Communist Party.
		Hitler suspends all civil liberties.
		Nazis fail to gain majority in national elections; 44% of vote in elections.
		Hitler bans all parties.
		Reichstag passes Enabling Act, giving Hitler absolute power for four years.
		June 30, 1934 — Night of the Long Knives — Hitler's SSC (Black Shirts) arrested and put to death Ernst Rohm, leader of Brown Shirts, and 1,000 of his troops.
Features of government	Economic — Corporate State representing business, labor, and government; Fascist Party controls industry, agriculture and trade; workers forbidden to strike; private ownership permitted but strictly regulated; model for New Deal laws in U.S.	Heinrich Himmler (1900–1945), head of Gestapo or Secret Police — suppressed all opposition.
		Economic — brought business and labor under government control; state controls prices, production, and profits; workers not allowed to strike.
	Social policy — women encouraged to have large families; Women valued as The wives, not workers; Mussolini glorified as father figure.	Social Policy — Joseph Goebbel (1897–1945) used propaganda — Big Lie Technique — to glorify Hitler.
		Richard Wagner's music reinforces heroism of Nazism.

		Women offered bonuses for pure-bred Aryan children.
		Restriction of Catholic Churches.
		All Protestant Churches united into one single state religion; Jews blamed for all of Germany's problems; steps taken to drive Jews out of Germany.
Results	Reduced unemployment.	Public Works Program leads to economic recovery.
	Sponsored Public Works — the Pontine Marshes, south of Rome, were drained and restored to agricultural uses.	Renews Germany's power through the rebuilding of the armed forces.
	Settled dispute with Vatican: The Lateran Treaty (1929), recognizes the pope as the sovereign of Vatican City.	Berlin Olympics (1936) restore pride.
	Pope Pius XII recognizes Fascism as legitimate.	
	Olympic games (1932) raised pride of people	
Failings	Destroyed democracy.	Destroyed democracy.
	Living standards still low compared to Western Europe.	Super nationalism and militarism led to massive destructions of World War II.
	Efforts to restore Italian greatness lead to defeat in World War II.	Policy of anti-Semitism/genocide led to the death of millions of people.
	Many postwar problems.	

Failure of Appeasement

The challenge to world peace followed a set pattern during the 1930s. Dictators and militarists in Italy, Germany, and Japan took aggressive actions, which other European countries met with the policy of appeasement — capitulating to the aggressors's demands in order to keep out of war. France was demoralized from World War I and Great Britain believed that Hitler was justified in violating the Versailles Treaty because it was too harsh. Both countries also believed that Nazism was a better alternative than the specter of Communism spreading over Europe. Adopting an appeasement policy also was necessitated by the Great Depression, which had drained the strength of the Western democracies. The United States, which had rejected the Versailles Treaty in 1920, passed a series of neutrality acts in the 1930s that were intended to prevent U.S. involvement in a European conflict, but not to prevent a war. In Japan, the economic disasters of the Great Depression and the rise of militarists and ultranationalists led to the demand for expansion. Militarists argued that only by foreign conquests would Japan gain respect as a great nation as well as gain the necessary resources to help meet the nation's economic needs.

The actions of Japan, Germany, and Italy from 1931 to 1939 demonstrated the failure of the appeasement policy. The steps leading to the failure of appeasement are in the following list:

- **1931–32:** Japan invades Manchuria. The League of Nations fails to halt the aggressors and reveals its weaknesses.

- **1933:** Hitler pulls out of the League of Nations.

- **1935:** Hitler begins to remilitarize in violation of the Versailles Treaty. France and Great Britain do nothing to stop him.

- **1935:** Italy invades Ethiopia. The League of Nations puts an embargo on Italy. All goods are banned except for oil. Emperor Haile Selassie of Ethiopia protests to the League but nothing is done.

- **1936:** Hitler occupies the Rhineland in defiance of the Versailles Treaty. Hitler's generals warn him of Germany's military being unprepared in the event of a British military reaction. European nations continue to do nothing.

- **1936:** Hitler and Mussolini form the **Rome-Berlin Axis.**

- **1936: General Francisco Franco** (1892–1975) and his fascist supporters begin a revolt against the legally elected leftist government of Spain. This revolt touches off a bloody civil war. Conservatives supported Franco's forces, the Nationalists. The Loyalists include Communists, Socialists, and supporters of democracy. Great Britain, France, and the United States place an embargo on weapons so war cannot spread and remain neutral. Hitler and Mussolini aid Franco. The Soviet Union gets involved by supplying the republican government with weapons and military advisors. Nazis use Spain as a dress rehearsal to test their new weapons such as carpet bombing and blitzkrieg warfare.

- **April 1937:** German bombers attack the market square in the city of Guernica, Spain, killing over 1,600 people — an event later memorialized by Spanish artist Pablo Picasso, in his cubist masterpiece, *Guernica*, symbolizing the violent effect of war. (*Note:* Picasso willed this painting to Spain only when the nation was a republic. Franco, with the aid of the Nazis, took over in March 1939. After Franco's death in 1975, Spain received the painting.)

- **1936–1940:** Germany, Japan, and Italy sign the **Anti-Comintern Pact** in 1936 to oppose the spread of Communism. In 1940, Japan joined Italy and Germany in the **Rome-Berlin Tokyo Axis**. Japan launched a full-scale invasion of China. The Chinese, with the combined efforts of **Chiang Kai-Shek**, the Nationalist Leader, and **Mao Tse-tung**, the Communist leader, resist Japanese aggression. The United States and other European countries do very little.

- **1938:** Hitler invades Austria on the grounds that all German-speaking people belong together (**Anschluss**). Anschluss violates the World War I peace treaties. Western powers continue to do nothing.

- **September, 1938:** Hitler demands the Sudetenland, a German-speaking region of Czechoslovakia, bordering Germany. Hitler's Chief of the General Staff, Franz Halder (1884-1972) plots a coup against him to avoid a war, in the event Britain and France fight over the issue. The Soviet Union expresses a willingness to unite with France and Britain to defend the Czechs. At Mussolini's suggestion, a conference is held at Munich. Neville Chamberlain, who became prime minister of England in 1937, believed it was silly to get involved in quarrels with people "Whom we know nothing about." Chamberlain meets with Daladier, prime minister of France, Mussolini, and Hitler. President Eduard Benes (1884–1948) was not invited. The **Munich Conference** ceded the Sudetenland to Germany, which marks the apex of appeasement. Chamberlain returns to London and is met by a huge crowd proclaiming, "There will be peace in our time."

- **March 10–16, 1939:** Hitler takes all of Czechoslovakia. Mussolini invades Albania. Hitler demands the return of Danzig and the Polish Corridor, on the grounds that the areas were inhabited by German-speaking people.

- **August, 1939:** Hitler signs the Non-Aggression Pact with Stalin. They agree not to fight each other. This protects Germany against a two-front war, as in World War I. The pact also paves the way for Hitler's invasion of Poland. Stalin received Eastern Poland in the deal.

Chronology of Europe in Crisis

1894	Nicholas II becomes Tsar.
1895	Lenin arrested and sent to Siberia; he leaves for West in 1900, spending most of the next 17 years in Switzerland.
1904	Russo-Japanese War begins.
1905	Bloody Sunday Massacre in St. Petersburg; October Manifesto establishes a Constitutional Monarchy and institution of the Duma, a representation assembly.
1914	Outbreak of World War I.
1916	Rasputin assassinated.
March 15, 1917	Czar Nicholas abdicates.
March 17, 1917	Republic proclaimed.
April 16, 1917	Lenin arrives in Russia.
July 1917	Bolsheviks coup attempt fails; Lenin flees to Finland; Trotsky is arrested.

continued

November 6–7, 1917	Bolsheviks seize power.
March 1918	Treaty of Brest-Litovsk formally ends Russian involvement in World War I.
1919	Adolf Hitler joins the German Workers Party, later becomes the Nazi Party; Benito Mussolini organizes the Black Shirts.
1918–1921	Civil War takes place in Russia.
1919	Weimar Republic proclaimed in Germany.
1921	Lenin introduces New Economic Plan.
October 28, 1922	Mussolini's March on Rome.
January 1923	Massive inflation in Germany.
August 11, 1923	Unsuccessful Munich Beer Hall Putsch led by Hitler; Hitler jailed and spends eight months in jail where he writes *Mein Kampf*.
1924	Lenin dies; struggle for power between Trotsky and Stalin.
1928	Stalin begins Five Year Plan and collectivization of land among Kulaks.
1929	Mussolini signs the Lateran pact with the Vatican; Wall Street crashes and cessation of U.S. loans to Europe.
1930	Hitler and National Socialist Party win 107 seats in Reichstag elections.
1931	Japan invades Manchuria, part of China.
January 1933	President von Hindenburg accepts a cabinet with Hitler as chancellor.
February 1933	Reichstag fire blamed on Communists.
October 1933	Germany withdraws from the League of Nations.
1933–1938	Stalin's Purge Trials.
1934	Death of President Hindenburg; chancellor becomes president but retains title "Der Fuhrer."
1935	Hitler passes the Nuremberg Laws, depriving Jews of their citizenship; Germany begins to rearm; Mussolini attacks Ethiopia.
1936–1939	Spanish Civil War; Hitler and Mussolini support General Franco, a Fascist; Franco wins and stays in power until death in 1975.
1936	Formation of Rome-Berlin Axis.
1938	Munich Conference.
	Pablo Picasso paints *Guernica*.
1939	Nazi-Soviet Non-Aggression Pact is signed.
September 1939	Germany invades Poland.

Sample Multiple-Choice Questions

1. One characteristic of a totalitarian state is that

   A. minority groups are granted many civil liberties

   B. several political parties run the economic system

   C. citizens are encouraged to criticize the government

   D. the government controls and censors the media

   E. artists and musicians experience artistic freedom

2. Which statement best describes the relationship between World War I and the Russian Revolution?

   A. World War I postponed the Russian Revolution by restoring confidence in the czar.

   B. The Russian Revolution inspired the Russian people to win World War I.

   C. World War I gave the czar's army the needed experience to suppress the Russian Revolution.

   D. Opposition forces cooperated to fight the Germans.

   E. World War I created conditions within Russia that helped trigger a revolution.

3. ". . . The organization of the revolutionaries must consist first, foremost, and mainly of people who make revolutionary activity their profession. . . . Such an organization must of necessity be not too extensive and as secret as possible . . ."

This quotation expresses Lenin's idea to

   A. defeat Germany in World War I

   B. establish democracy in Russia

   C. maintain Communist power in Western Europe

   D. overthrow the Russian Government

   E. establish diplomatic relationships with the United States

4. Which slogan expresses the ideal of the Bolshevik Revolution of 1917?

   A. Liberty, Equality, and Fraternity

   B. Bread, Land, and Peace

   C. Lebensraum

   D. Nationalism, Democracy, and the People's Livelihood

   E. Russification

5. What was the major goal of Joseph Stalin's Five Year Plan in the Soviet Union?

   A. encouraging rapid industrialization

   B. supporting capitalism

   C. improving literacy rates

   D. including peasants in the decision-making process

   E. programs to westernize, educate, and enlighten the population

6. Which of the following did not contribute to Mussolini's rise to power?

A. peasant unrest in the countryside of Italy from 1919 until 1922

B. severe unemployment after the war

C. Nationalists demand that Italy should receive more territory from the Versailles Treaty

D. support of strong wealthy landowners and industrialists

E. close cooperation with the Communist Party

7. Mussolini's Corporate State provides

A. laissez-faire approach to business

B. the abolishment of private ownership of business

C. limits on profits but not on wages

D. prohibition of strikes by labor

E. encouragement for women to work in factories

8. Which of the following was a basic belief of the Nationalist Socialist Party?

A. Democratic government

B. need to cooperate with the League of Nations

C. rejection of excessive Nationalism

D. acceptance of Communism

E. superiority of the Aryan race

9. Which situation contributed to Adolf Hitler's rise to power in Germany after World War I?

A. support of Hitler's radical policies by the Social Democrats in the Reichstag

B. strong feelings of nationalism created by disappointment with the Versailles Treaty and the economic problems of the country

C. refusal by the League of Nations to admit Germany as a member

D. violence and terrorism promoted by Germany's former enemies

E. rapid growth of the economy leading to the rise of a middle class

10. A cartoon from the 1930s shows two "nursemaids" (one representing Neville Chamberlain of Britain, one representing Europe) tip-toeing past a cradle in which lies the "baby" (Hitler), sucking on a bottle upon which are the words "Munich Agreement" and clutching a cloth bundle upon which is written "added concessions." The caption states, "Shh-hh! He'll be quiet now — maybe!" Which policy did the "nursemaids" use to keep the "baby" quiet?

A. militarism

B. isolationism

C. imperialism

D. appeasement

E. collective security

Answers to Multiple-Choice Questions and Explanations

1. **D.** One characteristic of a totalitarian state is that the government controls and censors the media; it controls all aspects of a citizen's life through a one-party dictatorship. Dictators like Benito Mussolini of Italy, Adolf Hitler of Germany, and Lenin and Joseph Stalin of Russia suppressed rival parties and controlled the press. Critics were thrown in jail. Mussolini's Black Shirts assaulted and used terror against those who spoke against him. Hitler used the Gestapo, his secret police, to suppress all opposition; newspapers, radio, and films had to praise the virtues of Nazism. In Russia, Stalin controlled all artistic and cultural activities through the Communist Party. Totalitarian government suppresses civil liberties such as freedom of the press and speech and has little regard for minority groups. In a totalitarian state, the government bans all political parties. Dictators like Hitler and Mussolini allowed only the Nazi or Fascist Party to exist. Totalitarian leaders used their secret police to jail anyone who criticized the government. Stalin's secret policy, the Cheka, killed all enemies of the state. There is no tolerance for creative artists or musicians.

2. **E.** World War I created conditions in Russia that helped trigger the Bolshevik Revolution. Russia was not ready to fight a war. Russian soldiers lacked adequate supplies and weapons. By 1915, soldiers had no ammunition, rifles, or medical care. In 1915, Russian casualties were almost two million. In March 1917, workers led food riots all across Russia. In St. Petersburg, when soldiers refused to fire upon the striking workers, Nicholas II, czar of Russia, was forced to give up his throne and the leaders of the Duma, the Russian Parliament, set up a republic. The decision to continue the war, and the inability to provide food, resulted in the loss of support among the people. Lenin, who had been in exile when the March revolution broke out, was sneaked into the country by the Germans, who used him to undermine the support of the provisional government. In November 1917, the Bolsheviks seized control of the government. The decision of the czar to take personal charge of the war, proved to be a blunder because the army continued to fight poorly. Opposing forces did not cooperate to fight foreign invaders. The czar's army during World War I lost confidence in Russia's military leadership, and deserted. The Russian Revolution led to the withdrawal of Russia from the war. In March 1918, the Bolsheviks signed the Treaty of Brest-Litvosk with Germany. The harsh treaty ended Russia's participation in the war.

3. **D.** This quotation expresses Lenin's plan to overthrow the Russian government. Lenin believed that in order for Marxism to succeed in Russia, a revolutionary elite was needed. Marx claimed that revolution was only possible in an industrial country; however, Lenin believed that this elite or vanguard of the proletariat could start a revolution in an agrarian country and would exercise control until the state withered away. Lenin did not plan to defeat Germany but instead wanted peace to gain support for his government. He did not establish democracy or have any plan to spread Communism in Western Europe. Russia was the only Communist state in Europe in 1917. The United States would not recognize the Soviet Union until 1933, nine years after Lenin's death.

4. B. The slogan that expressed the ideal of the Bolshevik Revolution was "Bread, Land, and Peace." In 1917, Lenin gained the support of the people by promising bread or food to help feed the people, land for peasants through the confiscation of the nobles' estates, and peace to end World War I. The other answers are wrong for the following reasons: "Liberty, Equality, and Fraternity" was the slogan of the French Revolution; Lebensraum was Hitler's plan for territorial expansion in Europe; Dr. SunYat-Sen, father of modern China, endorsed a program which included Nationalism, Democracy, and the People's Livelihood; and Russification refers to a policy adopted by Tsar Alexander III in 1882 to unite the empire's many provinces.

5. A. The major goal of Joseph Stalin's Five Year Plans was to encourage rapid industrialization of the Soviet Union and turn it into an industrial giant. The Plans emphasized expanding heavy industries such as iron, steel, chemicals, electric power, and machinery in order to produce weapons and strengthen the country militarily. The Five Year Plans set up a command economy, which rejected private enterprise or capitalism.

6. E. Mussolini opposed the goals of a Socialist or Communist economy, condemning the Communist Marxist ideology that belittled nationalism and urged international working-class unity. Mussolini's view was that only fascism could save Italy from the evils of Communism. Backed by wealthy industrialists and landowners, Mussolini rose to power because peasants had begun to seize lands and factories, and fascism answered a need for order. Widespread unemployment among war veterans and frustrations among Nationalists that Italy had not received its just amount of territory also helped Mussolini.

7. D. Mussolini's Corporate State prohibited strikes by labor, but organized industry and labor into a small number of fascist-led associations that strictly controlled Italian workers, set wages, hours, and working conditions, and regulated profits. Although it rejected laissez faire, the Corporate State did not abolish private enterprise, allowing industries to remain under private ownership but watching them closely. Women were encouraged to be housewives and not workers.

8. E. The Nationalist Socialist Party (Nazi) endorsed a program which included a belief that the Germans belonged to the superior race of Aryans or light-skinned Europeans who were destined to rule the world. Nazi ideology rejected democracy and considered it a weak form of government; instead it glorified nationalism, had little use for the League of Nations, and opposed Communism.

9. B. The strong sense of nationalism created by the anger at the Versailles Treaty and the economic conditions at the end of World War I (widespread unemployment and inflation that destroyed the life savings of many people) led to Hitler's rise to power. Many Germans blamed the Treaty of Versailles for the country's troubles and condemned the Weimar Republic as a foreign system forced on the country by the victors. In their eyes, Germany's economic problems stemmed from the loss of its European territories, overseas colonies, and reparation payments of $132 billion. Germany's rampant inflation in the early 1920s, when 4 trillion marks were equivalent to one dollar, added to the unrest. Although the economy was revived in the mid-1920s, the Great Depression destroyed any hope of recovery. In the 1930s, Germany turned to Adolf Hitler and the Nazi Party because Hitler claimed that Germany had not lost the war, but had been stabbed in the back at Versailles. He promised to solve the economic chaos and restore Germany's greatness, convincing them that they were the master race.

10. **D.** Appeasement was the policy adopted by England and France in the 1930s, in which the two countries gave into the demands of Hitler and Mussolini in order to avoid war. Militarism is a policy that supports aggressive military preparedness. Isolationism is a policy that promotes non-involvement in foreign affairs. Imperialism or colonialism supports the extension of stronger nations over weaker ones. Collective security is a policy of international cooperation to promote peace.

World War II (1939–1945)

When World War II began in 1939, there was little enthusiasm, not even a noble slogan about the glory of war. Many saw the war as a continuation of the problems created in World War I. Dissatisfaction with the Versailles Treaty, the War Guilt Clause, the question of protection, problems created by new nationalist states, and the failure of collective security all contributed to the start of World War II. **The Axis Powers** (Germany, Italy, and Japan) pursued aggressive actions to redress perceived inequities that arose out of World War I. In 1936, the Italian leader Mussolini gave a speech in which he referred to a vertical line between Rome and Berlin as "an axis around which all European states" could collaborate. This treaty of friendship between Germany and Italy was later extended to Japan by the **Tripartite Treaty of 1940**. At first, democratic nations, such as the United States, England, and France chose to follow a policy of appeasement. But when that course of action failed to stop Germany from invading Poland, World War II began. Unlike World War I, which was fought primarily in Europe, World War II was truly a global war in that it was fought in all the major areas of the world, except for the Americas. Initially, the Axis powers were victorious, but the entry of the United States and the failure of the German invasion of the Soviet Union changed the tide in favor of the Allies — England, France, the United States, and the Soviet Union.

The war was one of the most devastating conflicts in history. New mechanized warfare and advanced technology made it even more damaging and destructive than World War I. Civilian populations also felt the war's full effects: Cities were bombed by saturation bombing, or fire bombing, such as used in Dresden and in Hamburg, Germany. The use of the atomic bomb over Hiroshima and Nagasaki in Japan (World War II ushered in the Atomic Age) demonstrated the horrors of nuclear war and modern technology. The aftereffects of the war were massive. There were enormous losses of lives and properties. Over 75 million people were killed worldwide and civilian deaths reached record numbers. Germany's defeat also exposed the horrors of the Nazi's policy of genocide that had led to the Holocaust and the deaths of millions of people.

World War II accelerated the decline of Britain and France as major powers, and the United States and Russia emerged as the two superpowers. Although the United States and Russia were Allies in the war, they were strange bedfellows. The fear of the spread of Communism eventually led to the ideological conflict of the Cold War that dominated international relations for the latter half of the twentieth century.

Outbreak of World War II (1939–1945)

Hitler's Empire

Poland

On September 1, 1939, Germany invaded Poland. On September 3, Britain and France finally decided to honor its agreement to defend Poland, and declared war on Germany. The Germans believed that they had a strategy to end the fighting in a short time. Their method was called **Blitzkrieg** — "lightning war." It involved tanks, airplanes, and trucks. By October of that year, Hitler's armies had crushed Poland. Germany soon annexed Western Poland. As agreed in the **Non-Aggression Pact of 1939**, Russia seized the eastern half as well as the Baltic countries. In November, Russia seized parts of Finland, which put up a valiant but unsuccessful resistance.

October 1939–March 1940

This was a time of **Sitzkrieg**, or "phony war." Hitler consolidated his gains in Poland and equipped his military in preparation for the coming attack against Europe. The French remained behind the **Maginot Line** and Britain sent troops there to wait for the expected attack. The Maginot Line was a series of concrete fortifications that extended 200 miles along the French border with Germany.

Conquest of Denmark and Norway

In April of 1940, lightning war struck again. Germany invaded Norway and Denmark in order to secure iron ore supplies. Both of these countries failed to overcome the Germans and fell within days.

Defeat of France 1940

In May, the German army invaded Northern France by going through neutral Holland and Belgium. Within weeks, Germany defeated these countries. The Germans had managed to bypass the Maginot Line (which did not extend into the Belgium frontier), split the Franco-British forces, and trap the entire British army on the beaches of Dunkirk. In a desperate gamble to triumph over the Germans, the British sent every available naval vessel, even pleasure ships, across the English Channel to rescue the troops. The **Miracle of Dunkirk** resulted in the ferrying of over 300,000 troops to safety.

Meanwhile, Mussolini, sensing an easy victory, declared war on France and proceeded to attack from the south in June.

On June 22, 1940, German forces captured Paris. The Germans soon occupied all of Northern France. In the south, a puppet state called the **Vichy Government** was established, headed by **Marshall Petain** (1856–1951). Not willing to accept defeat, French resistance forces, led by **Charles De Gaulle** (1890–1970), escaped to England where they worked to liberate their homeland; throughout the remainder of the war, the Vichy Government faced many battles with DeGaulle's resistance forces. The swiftness of the Nazi's victories caught the world by surprise. Most nations expected a conflict involving trench warfare, as was the case in World War I, where the war became stalemated and there were no quick victories. By 1940, Hitler ruled over all of continental Europe. Like Napoleon, he dominated the continent, with the exception of Britain. Italy was his ally, while the Soviet Union remained neutral.

Battle for Britain

Hitler hoped that Britain would recognize that it was standing alone and ask for peace. However, **Winston Churchill** (prime minister from 1940 to 1945 and 1951 to 1955), who succeeded Neville Chamberlain as prime minister in May 1940, refused to surrender. Churchill inspired the nation with his plea that he had nothing to offer but "blood, toil, tears, and sweat." When faced with this defiance, Hitler attacked.

On August 15, the German **Luftwaffe** (air force) began to bomb Britain in preparation for an invasion across the English Channel. Up to 1,000 planes attacked British airfields and key factories. The British Royal Air Force was able to defend itself and its country against these attacks with the help of radar that detected incoming planes. Losses were heavy on both sides. Following the advice of the leader of the Luftwaffe, **Hermann Goering** (1893–1946), Hitler ordered the bombing of British cities, in hopes of weakening British morale. From August 1940 until June 1941, London and other various cities were attacked through the night until dawn. Despite heavy losses for the British, this new plan turned out to be a mistake on the part of Germany. As a result of the increased bombing of civilian sites, Britain boosted its military production, and its anti-aircraft defense improved with the help of radar. By June 1941, Hitler abandoned his efforts to invade England in favor of a new campaign in Eastern Europe, specifically Russia.

Critical Turning Points in the War

Invasion of Russia

On June 22, 1941, Hitler launched a major attack against Russia called **Operation Barbarossa** after the German king who had participated in the First Crusade during the eleventh century. The goal of the Russian invasion was to gain control of the Ukraine's vast wheat fields and the Caucasus's oil fields. Hitler ordered a massive Blitzkrieg of three million men along a 2,0000-mile border, catching Stalin by surprise. By October 1941, German troops surrounded Leningrad in the North, which was within 25 miles of Moscow, and had conquered most of the Ukraine. Hitler's propaganda machine proclaimed the war to be over, but it was mistaken. Russia did not collapse; instead, history repeated itself. Like Napoleon's forces, the German invaders were not prepared for the cold Russian winter. Germans, in summer uniform, froze to death as the temperature plunged to –20° Fahrenheit. Their fuel and oil froze as trucks and weapons became useless. At the **Siege of Leningrad**, which lasted 900 days, the Russians fought valiantly. More than 1.5 million citizens died during this siege and some inhabitants even resorted to cannibalism to survive. Hitler's failure to conquer Russia drained Germany's resources and caused him to have to fight two fronts simultaneously, which ultimately contributed to Germany's defeat.

Entry of the United States

Although the United States had declared its neutrality in 1939, President Franklin D. Roosevelt realized that a Nazi victory would be a threat to the nation's interests. He worked closely with

Churchill to provide support during the Battle for Britain. In 1940, President Roosevelt traded 50 old destroyers to Britain in exchange for military bases in Newfoundland and the Caribbean.

In **March 1941**, Congress approved the **Lend Lease Act**, which allowed the president to lend or sell war materials to any country that he deemed vital to that country's defense. Roosevelt declared that the United States would become the "arsenal of democracy." The Lend Lease Act created a British-Soviet-U.S. economic alliance, providing the groundwork for the title of the **Big Three**, as these countries were later known. Hitler proclaimed the Lend Lease Act an economic declaration of war and began attacking American merchant ships.

In **August 1941**, Roosevelt and Churchill signed the **Atlantic Charter**, a broad set of peace principles, such as freedom from fear, want, and belief in national sovereignty, which was very similar to items contained in Wilson's Fourteen Points. The Atlantic Charter also called for a permanent system of general security, which laid the foundation for the United Nations. Meanwhile, the United States had taken economic steps to stop Japanese aggression in Asia. When Japan advanced into French Indo-China and the Dutch East Indies (present-day Indonesia), the United States banned the sale of oil to Japan. This move angered the Japanese. In retaliation, on **December 7, 1941**, the Japanese launched a surprise attack upon the United States military base at Peal Harbor, Hawaii. Close to 2,500 Americans were killed. On **December 8, 1941**, the United States and Britain declared war on Japan. Soon after, on **December 11, 1941**, Germany and Italy declared war on the United States. The conflict became a global war involving all the major powers. The American entry into the war was crucial because the U.S. aid to the Allies, along with the heroic support of the British and Soviet people and the assistance of the resistance groups in Europe, contributed eventually to an Allied victory.

The Road to Victory (1942–1945)

Churchill convinced Roosevelt that the focus of the war should be to defeat Germany first and then concentrate on Japan. Here are the highlights of the war following the entry of the United States:

- **May 1942:** In North Africa, the British, under the command of the British General **Bernard Montgomery** (1887–1976), defeated German and Italian forces led by the brilliant General **Erwin Rommel** (1891–1944), known as the Desert Fox, at El Alamein, only seventy miles from Alexandria, Egypt. In November 1942, American General **Dwight D. Eisenhower** (1890–1969) took command of joint Anglo-American forces in Morocco and Algiers. Combining with Montgomery's forces, they destroyed Rommel's army.

- **May–June 1942:** The United States defeated the Japanese at the **Battle of the Coral Sea** and later Midway. American victories stopped the Japanese advance in the Pacific and prevented another attack on Hawaii. The **Battle of Midway** established American naval superiority in the Pacific.

- **August 1942:** Under the command of the American General **Douglas MacArthur** (1880–1964), the American Marines launched their first offensive at **Guadalcanal** in the Solomon Islands. The attack was the beginning of an island-hopping strategy, the goal of which was to capture strategic Japanese-held islands and bypass others. These islands would serve as stepping-stones for a direct invasion of Japan.

- **August 1942–February 1943:** The **Battle of Stalingrad** began and—following a six-month struggle that involved house-to-house fighting—the Soviet forces defeated Germany. By January 1943, the Germans had lost over 300,000 men. The Battle of Stalingrad was the turning point in the war because the Russians had struck a deadly blow to Hitler's war machine and seized large quantities of German military equipment. The Russian forces took the offensive and slowly began to drive the Germans out of the Soviet Union.

- **January 1943:** Roosevelt and Churchill met at **Casablanca** and agreed to launch an invasion of Sicily and Italy and to fight until the Axis surrendered unconditionally. Roosevelt called this meeting the "Unconditional Surrender Conference." The reason for the announcement of unconditional surrender was to reassure Russia, who was fearful that the Allies might sign a separate treaty with Hitler. Russia was also suspicious about the failure of the Allies to establish a genuine second front through France. The Russians had suffered enormous losses on the Eastern Front and claimed that a second front would divert German forces from Russia.

- **July 1943–August 1944:** The Allies, under Generals Montgomery and **George Patton** (1885–1945), invaded Sicily and then mainland Italy. Mussolini resigned and Italy surrendered. In September, however, Nazi troops returned Mussolini to power. The Allies faced German resistance for the next 18 months until Germany was defeated.

- **November 28–December 1, 1943:** The leaders of the Big Three (Churchill, Stalin, and Roosevelt) met in **Teheran**, Iran, for the first time. They agreed on postwar occupation of Germany, demilitarization of Germany, and the creation of an international peace organization. Churchill and Roosevelt promised to open up a second front of warfare through France. This decision to invade Hitler via France meant that the American, British, and Russian troops would meet along a north-south line in Germany and that only Russia would liberate Eastern Europe—a strategy that had a profound impact upon post–World War II Europe.

- **Invasion of Normandy (D-Day), June 6, 1944:** Eisenhower directed the largest amphibious assault of the war on the beaches of Normandy in France. This established the second front; by August, Paris had been liberated, and by the end of 1944 all of France had been liberated. The next goal was Germany. Hitler was under attack on the Eastern and Western Fronts.

- **Battle of the Bulge, December 1944:** Germany launched a last-grasp counterattack in Belgium through the Argonne Forest. It slowed the Allied advance but the Allies continued to press forward toward Germany.

- **January 1945:** The Russian forces marched westward through Poland.

- **February 1945:** The Allied firebombing of Dresden killed over 135,000 people.

- The Big Three leaders met at Yalta in southern Russia on the Black Sea from **February 4 to February 11**. The **Yalta Conference** drew up the structure of postwar Europe. They agreed that Germany would be divided into four zones of occupation. Stalin agreed to hold free elections in Eastern Europe and declare war against Japan in return for land from Japan that had been lost in the Russo-Japanese War. The Big Three leaders also agreed to the veto system of voting in the Security Council of the United Nations. The Yalta Conference would be a source of controversy in the future because the concessions worked out over the status of the countries in Eastern Europe eventually broke down and became a source of friction between the United States and Russia.

- **March 1945:** The American firebombing of Tokyo killed more than 80,000 Japanese. The **Battle of Iwo Jima** ended after a vicious struggle, leaving 26,000 Americans dead.

- **April 1945:** Japan was defeated at the Battle of Okinawa. The Allies moved closer to Japan.

- Mussolini attempted to escape Italy but was caught and killed on April 28, and on April 30, Hitler and his associate committed suicide in a Berlin bunker.

- **May 8, 1945 (VE Day):** The war in Europe ended.

- **July/August 1945:** Churchill (after July 28, Attlee, the new British prime minister, took his place), Stalin, and Harry Truman (1884–1972) attended the **Potsdam Conference** in Germany. The conference addressed the issues of postwar Germany and free elections in Eastern Europe. Truman demanded that Stalin carry out free elections in the countries of Eastern Europe. Stalin refused and the sewn seeds of distrust would severely hamper the friendship between the United States and Russia as the war drew to an end.

- **August 6, 1945:** United States troops dropped the atomic bomb on Hiroshima and over 130,000 people were killed and 90% of the city was destroyed.

- **August 8, 1945:** The U.S. dropped an atomic bomb on Nagasaki, resulting in the death of 75,000 people. Russia declared war on Japan and invaded Manchuria.

- **September 2, 1945** (VJ Day): Japan surrendered.

The Holocaust

The effort of Hitler and the Nazis to destroy all the Jews of Europe is known as the **Holocaust**. In his policy of anti-Semitism, Hitler set out to drive Jews from Germany. In 1935, the **Nuremberg Laws** placed severe restrictions on the Jewish people. They were prohibited from marrying non-Jews, denied citizenship, forced to wear a yellow star of David, and prohibited from attending or teaching at German schools or universities.

On November 9, 1938, the **Kristallnacht** (Night of Broken Glass) riots took place. Nazi-led mobs attacked Jewish synagogues, businesses, and homes. The night of violence initiated a period of intense persecution for the Jews in which hundreds of people were killed and 30,000 people were sent to concentration camps.

In 1939, German Jews had lost all their civil rights, and after the fall of Warsaw, the Nazis began deporting them to Poland. Jews from all over Europe were moved into ghettos surrounded by barbed wire, forced to wear the Star of David, and turned into slave labor. By 1941, Hitler was carrying out the **Final Solution of the Jewish Question** — the murder of every single Jew. Jews, in all parts of Hitler's Empire, were systematically arrested and shipped like cattle to their death or to concentration camps. Victims were sent to "shower" rooms that were really gas chambers. Special camp workers stripped the victims' gold teeth or hair. Bodies were cremated while bones were crushed for fertilizer. The most infamous of these death camps was at Auschwitz in Poland, where 12,000 Jews were killed each day and close to 1 million in total. When the war finally came to an end, over 8 million Jews had been killed, as well as millions of homosexuals, gypsies, Communists, and Slavs. The ultimate monstrosity of the Nazi policy of genocide had contributed to the death of millions of people.

Impact of World War II

The human losses in World War II were staggering. The Soviet Union alone lost 28 million people. Throughout Europe and Asia, parts of cities were in ruins. Heavy bombings had destroyed major cities such as Hamburg and Dresden in Germany, and both European and Asian nations faced difficult problems of economic recovery.

Britain and France's colonial powers declined and they were forced to gradually relinquish their empires. Their colonies, now Asian and African nations, embraced nationalism and rejected the remnants of European imperialism.

Building on their foundation of the League of Nations, the Allies established a **United Nations** as an international organization to secure peace. In April 1945, representatives from 50 nations met in San Francisco to draft the charter for the United Nations. Unlike 1920 when the United States rejected the League of Nations, the United States became a member of the United Nations and the headquarters were set up in New York. The United States and Russia emerged as the two superpowers. The two countries had cooperated with each other to defeat Nazi Germany but by 1945, the alliance was slowly disintegrating. Conflicting ideology between democracy and Communism, and mutual distrust between the Allies and Russians eventually led to the rivalry known as the **Cold War**. The Cold War became the driving force that determined events for over 45 years.

Chronology of World War II

September 1, 1939	World War II begins; Germany invades Poland
1940	Germany conquers Norway, Denmark, Netherlands, Luxembourg, and France; Battle of Britain
1941	United States adopts Lend-Lease Act; Germany invades Russia; Soviet Union signs a Non-Aggression Pact with Japan; Japan bombs Pearl Harbor
1942	Battle of Midway; Battle of Stalingrad—German offensive stopped
1943	Casablanca Conference; Allied Forces take Sicily; Teheran Conference—First meeting of Big Three
1944	D-Day, June 6, at Normandy
1945	Yalta Conference; VE Day, May 8, Germany surrenders; Potsdam Conference—First meeting of Stalin and Truman; August 6—Atomic Bomb dropped on Hiroshima; September 2—VJ Day—Japanese surrender

Sample Multiple-Choice Questions

1. Which is the correct chronological order?

   A. Germany conquers Denmark, fall of France, Germany defeats Poland, Battle of Britain, Nazi invasion of USSR

   B. Germany defeats Poland, Germany conquers Denmark, fall of France, Battle of Britain, Nazi invasion of USSR

   C. fall of France, Battle of Britain, Germany conquers Denmark, Germany defeats Poland, Nazi invasion of USSR

   D. Germany defeats Poland, fall of France, Germany conquers Denmark, Battle of Britain, Nazi invasion of USSR

   E. Battle of Britain, fall of France, Germany defeats Poland, Nazi invasion of USSR, Germany conquers Denmark

2. The turning point of war in North Africa was the British defeat of the German forces at

   A. Coral Sea

   B. Midway

   C. Stalingrad

   D. El Alamein

   E. Leningrad

3. The Allied nations of World War II included all of the following except

   A. Britain

   B. United States

   C. Russia

   D. Austria

   E. France

4. The Sitzkrieg refers to

   A. a phony war from October 1939 to March 1940 where there was little fighting after the invasion of Poland

   B. the defeat of Poland

   C. a German counter-attack at Battle of the Bulge

   D. a German invasion of Russia

   E. the Battle of Britain

5. Prior to June 1944, what country carried the bulk of the land war against Germany?

   A. Britain

   B. United States

   C. Soviet Union

   D. France

   E. French Resistance Movement

6. All of the following were a result of the Teheran Conference EXCEPT

   A. second Front through France

   B. postwar occupation of Germany

   C. demilitarization of Germany

   D. first meeting of the Big Three

   E. demand for unconditional surrender of the Axis Powers

7. Which is considered the turning point of the war on the Eastern Front?

A. Battle of Leningrad

B. Battle of Stalingrad

C. Brest-Litvosk

D. Battle of El Alamein

E. Bombing of Dresden

8. Why did the wartime cooperation between the Soviet Union and the Western Powers break down at Potsdam?

A. The Western powers refused to acknowledge the division of Germany.

B. Stalin demanded more territory from Japan.

C. Stalin refused to carry out free elections in Eastern Europe.

D. Churchill insisted that Germany be blamed solely for the war.

E. The Soviet Union refused to join the United Nations.

9. At the Yalta Conference, the Soviet Union agreed to

A. the creation of the United Nations

B. free elections in Eastern Europe

C. share atomic secrets with each other

D. the joint invasion of Japan

E. no separate peace treaties with the Axis Powers

10. Which two nations became the major world powers after World War II?

A. United States and China

B. Soviet Union and China

C. United States and Soviet Union

D. United States and Great Britain

E. United States and France

Answers to Multiple-Choice Questions and Explanations

1. B. The correct chronological order is in September 1939, the German army defeated Poland; in April 1940, the Germans conquered Denmark; in June 1940, France fell; in August 1940, the Battle of Britain took place; and in June 1941, Germany invaded the USSR.

2. D. The British army defeated the German army at El Alamein, which is 70 miles from Alexandria, Egypt. This battle protected Britain's Suez Canal, the lifeline of the British Empire. The Coral Sea and Midway were naval battles fought by the United States Navy against Japan. Stalingrad and Leningrad were battle areas on the Russian front.

3. D. Austria was not an Allied nation during World War II. In 1938, Germany annexed Austria. The Big Three (United States, Great Britain, and Russia) as well as China and France comprised the Allied Nations.

4. A. Sitzkrieg refers to the phony war from October 1939 to March 1940 where there was little fighting after the German invasion of Poland. The defeat of Poland in four weeks demonstrated the effects of Blitzkrieg (Lightning War). In June 1941, the Germans invaded Russia with over 3 million men and expected that its Blitz attack would be over by the winter. German forces were repelled at the Battle of the Bulge. The Battle of Britain refers to the failure of German air power to defeat the British.

5. **C.** The Soviet Union carried the bulk of the land war against Germany. France was knocked out of the war in 1940 and Britain was never a land power. The Soviet Union bore the brunt of the war effort until the establishment of the second front in June 1944. The United States did not bear the brunt until D-Day. The French Resistance Movement had very little impact on the war effort against Germany and Russia.

6. **E.** The Teheran Conference did not demand the unconditional surrender of the Axis Powers. Churchill and Roosevelt had met in January 1943 at Casablanca and announced the policy of unconditional surrender. The Teheran Conference addressed the issue of the second front, demilitarization of Germany, and postwar occupation of Germany. It was also the first time Stalin, Churchill, and Roosevelt met.

7. **B.** The Battle of Stalingrad was the turning point of the war on the Eastern Front. The Battle of Stalingrad stopped the German advances in the south and turned the tide of the battle. Leningrad was besieged for 900 days. It is a heroic tale but not a turning point on the Eastern Front. Brest-Litovsk was the site of the peace negotiations between Germany and the Bolsheviks that ended Russia's participation in World War I. El Alamein was the turning point in North Africa. The bombing of Dresden in Germany dealt with Allied efforts in 1945 to defeat Germany. It was not a battle area on the Eastern Front.

8. **C.** Stalin's refusal to carry out free elections in Eastern Europe led to a breakdown of wartime cooperation between the Soviet Union and the Western Powers at Potsdam. President Truman, who had succeeded Franklin D. Roosevelt, insisted that Stalin carry out his pledge of free elections that he had agreed to at the Yalta Conference. Stalin's refusal laid the groundwork for the beginning of the Cold War. The Allied Powers had agreed to the postwar occupation of Germany. Stalin did not demand more territory from Japan nor did he refuse to join the United Nations. None of the Allied nations wanted to blame Germany solely for the war. They wanted to avoid the mistakes of the Versailles Treaty.

9. **B.** At Yalta, the Soviet Union agreed to "free elections" in Eastern Europe. Stalin was determined to create a buffer zone against Germany and wanted to decide the fate of Eastern Europe himself. Churchill and Roosevelt agreed to the compromise because they could not really stop Stalin and were unwilling to go to battle over Eastern Europe. The Allied nations had pledged to create a United Nations in 1941. The Soviet Union agreed to declare war on Japan but there was no discussion of a joint invasion. The allied nations did not share atomic secrets with each other. Stalin was never informed that the United States was developing the atomic bomb. The Casablanca Conference declared that there would be no separate treaties with the Axis Powers.

10. **C.** The United States and USSR became the two major world powers after World War II. The United States' industrial economy and military strength was unsurpassed and the Soviet Union's establishment of satellite nations in Eastern Europe had made her a dominant power. Chinese, British, and French economies were destroyed. China was wrecked by the Japanese invasion and civil war between the Communists and Nationalists. France's and Britain's military power were so weakened that they were unable to maintain their colonial empires.

The Cold War (1947–1980)

After the defeat of Germany, the Grand Alliance of the United States, Britain, and the Soviet Union failed to hold together. Once again, Europe became the battleground of a new war — the Cold War. The origins of the Cold War stemmed from the ideological differences between the United States and the Soviet Union, and disputes over Eastern Europe. By 1950, the Iron Curtain was in place and Western and Eastern Europe were going their separate ways. Despite efforts to coexist with the West after the death of Stalin in 1953, the Soviet Union maintained a firm grip on Eastern Europe and crushed any efforts at freedom by these satellite countries, establishing an empire in Eastern Europe that served as a buffer against any attacks. The split between the Soviet and Western Bloc influenced policies in other parts of the world, and the tensions of the Cold War led to the creation of a nuclear weapons system that cost billions of dollars and raised the fear of nuclear disaster.

Battered Europe recovered quickly and successfully with the aid of the Marshall Plan and economic cooperation among Western European nations regulating the coal, iron, and steel industries. The European economic miracle was also made possible because European nations coordinated the distribution of American aid so that barriers to European trade were quickly dropped. By the 1970s, a revitalized West Germany sought to bring about reconciliation between Eastern and Western Europe. These efforts achieved some success.

The devastating effects of World War II also contributed to the decline of European empires. England and France were too weak to hold on to their colonies in Asia, Africa, and the Middle East. The changes that affected Europe's growth and the decline of her imperial empire foreshadowed the winds of change that erupted in the 1980s and ultimately led to the end of the Cold War and Communism.

The Cold War and Communism After World War II

The United States and the Soviet Union had cooperated to win World War II. However, conflicting ideology and mutual distrust led to the **Cold War**, a continuing state of tension and hostility between the United States and the Soviet Union, the two superpowers.

The uneasy relationship between the United States and the Soviet Union was based on philosophical differences. The United States was a democratic capitalist country and the Soviet Union was a totalitarian Communist state. At first, the focus of the Cold War was on Eastern Europe whose territories the Soviet troops occupied. Stalin had forced a pro-Soviet Communistic government onto the Eastern European countries of Poland, Czechoslovakia, Hungary, Romania, and Bulgaria. The Red Army had overrun these countries on their march towards Berlin. Thus these countries became Soviet satellites and served as a defensive shield for the Soviet Union. Yugoslavia, however, did not fall under Soviet control. Although Josip Broz, known as **Marshal Tito** (1882–1980), was a Communist ruler, he defied Stalin and pursued nationalist policies. Tito was able to act independently because Soviet troops did not occupy Yugoslavia and the country did not border on the Soviet Union.

The Western powers feared the spread of Communism. In 1946, Winston Churchill, in a speech at Fulton, Missouri, proclaimed that an **Iron Curtain** had descended over Eastern Europe. Churchill's Iron Curtain speech became a symbol for the growing fear of Communism as well as the division of Europe into the Soviet-dominated countries of Eastern Europe and the Western Bloc of democratic states led by the United States. The Cold War rivalry divided Europe and led to crises around the world. Although the two superpowers never fought each other outright, they were involved in small-scale fighting by supporting opposite sides.

Greece and Turkey

In 1947, the government of Greece was in serious danger of being overthrown by the force of Greek Communists. If Greece fell, Turkey could also be in danger of becoming a Soviet puppet state. Britain informed the United States that it was unable to help Greece, and the United States accepted the challenge. In March 1947, President Truman asked Congress for $400 million in United States military aid for Greece and Turkey. The **Truman Doctrine** was the opening shot in the Cold War, asserting that the United States would support any country that rejected or resisted Communism. Truman proclaimed, "that the policy of the United States would be to support free people who were resisting attempted subjugation by armed minorities." The United States declared that its goal was to contain Communism or limit Communism to the areas already under Soviet control. United States aid helped to keep Greece and Turkey from falling under Communist control.

Berlin Blockade (1948–1949)

At the end of World War II, Germany was divided into four zones of occupation. Berlin was also divided into four zones: American, British, French, and Soviet. In 1948, the Soviet Union announced that the Allies could no longer use the land routes to Berlin that passed through the Soviet zone of occupation. The reason was because Stalin was angry that the West did not agree with him on a German unification plan and that the three Western Allies (Britain, France, and the United States) had decided to unite their zones of occupation. He was also upset about currency reform (the introduction of new currency for the Western zones) that foreshadowed the creation of a West Germany. To thwart the blockade, the Western Powers resorted to an airlift. The **Berlin Airlift** lasted for almost a year (321 days) as the United States flew in supplies of food and other necessities on a daily basis. In 1949, the Soviet Union lifted the blockade.

North Atlantic Treaty Organization (1949)

The threat of the Soviet Union and its bloc of Communist states to the security of Western Europe led to the formation of the **North Atlantic Treaty Organization (NATO)** in 1949. NATO was a military defensive alliance formed by the United States, Canada, and 10 Western European countries to help each other if any one of the nations were attacked. In 1952, Greece and Turkey were admitted, and in 1955, West Germany (Federal Republic of Germany) became a member. The Soviet Union responded in 1955 by forming its own military alliance, the **Warsaw Pact**, consisting of the USSR and seven satellites in Eastern Europe.

Birth of the Nuclear Race

In 1949, the same year that NATO was formed, the Soviet Union tested its first atomic bomb. The United States no longer had a nuclear monopoly. In 1952, the United States announced that it had developed a hydrogen, or H-bomb, a thousand times more destructive than the atomic bomb. In 1953, the Soviet Union announced that it, too, had tested an H-bomb. The nuclear race continued throughout the Cold War.

Victory in China

In 1949, after decades of civil war, the Communists under **Mao-Tse-tung** (1893–1976) defeated the Nationalist forces of **Chiang Kai-Shek** (1887–1945), despite the economic and military aid given the latter by the United States. The Communists were successful because of the support of the Soviet Union, Mao's promise of land to the peasants, and corruption within the Nationalist forces. In 1949, Chiang fled to Taiwan, an island off the Chinese coast. Throughout the 1950s and 60s, the United States recognized the Nationalist government as the legitimate government and refused to recognize Mao's Communist government.

Korean War (1950–1953)

At the end of World War II, Korea was divided at the **38th Parallel** between the United States, who occupied the South, and the Russian zone in the North. The Cold War intensified as Stalin backed the North Korean invasion of South Korea on June 25, 1950. The United Nations Security Council (which met in Lake Success, Long Island, and without Russia who was voluntarily absent) sponsored a resolution calling on North Korea to withdraw. When the request was ignored, the UN asked member nations to provide military aid and contribute troops. The majority of the military support came from the United States. In 1951, a cease-fire was discussed, but talks dragged on for the next two years. In 1953, an armistice was signed that left Korea still a divided country at the 38th Parallel.

Death of Stalin/De-Stalinization

In 1953, Stalin's death started a bitter struggle for power in the Soviet Union. Georgi Malenkov (1903–1988) served as Premier but party leaders exercised control behind the scenes. This so-called Troika consisted of Lavrenti Beria (1889–1953), head of the Secret Police, and Vyacheslav Moltov (1889–1986), Foreign Minister, who were determined that no one should dominate any regime like Stalin. However, Beria was soon arrested and executed. Malenkov was ousted after two years and replaced by Nikolai Bulganin (1895–1975), who was a mere figurehead. Moltov was demoted to a lesser position and disappeared from public life. **Nikita Khrushchev** (1894–1971) emerged as the new party leader. Khrushchev pursued a policy of de-Stalinization and in 1956, before the Twentieth Party Congress, attacked Stalin's abuses of power during his long years as the party leader. He attacked Stalin's cult of personality and claimed that Stalin had not followed the policies of Marxism and Leninism. Khrushchev initiated a "thaw in the Cold War" and called for peaceful coexistence. The Communist goals did not change, but Khrushchev began a policy of liberalization. The Soviet economic life improved and greater intellectual freedom was allowed. However, **Boris Pasternak**, a Soviet novelist, was not allowed to accept the Noble Prize for literature in 1958. Peaceful coexistence led to a relaxation of tension with the West. In 1958, Britain, France, and the United States met with Russia at the **Geneva Summit**. They discussed East-West relations in a friendly atmosphere but were unable to resolve their differences.

Uprisings in Poland and Hungary (1956)

Khrushchev's anti-Stalin campaign led to Nationalist revolts in Poland and Hungary. Workers in Poland went on strike for better working conditions and greater independence. **Wladyslaw Gomulka**, who had recently been released as a political prisoner, managed to win greater concessions for Poland while calming anti-Soviet feelings.

In Hungary, people revolted and demanded that the Soviet troops leave. **Imre Nagy**, a liberal Communist reformer, became president and declared Hungary's neutrality and withdrew from the Warsaw Pact. Khrushchev sent in a large army with tanks and crushed the rebellion. The Soviets deposed Nagy and installed a puppet regime under **Janos Kadar**.

U-2 Incident/Summit Meeting

In 1959, Khrushchev came to the United States, visited Disneyland, and appeared on American television. Cold War tension seemed to be diminishing. However, this hope ended quickly. In June 1960, prior to the Paris Summit Conference, the Soviet Union shot down an unarmed American U-2 reconnaissance plane, or spy plane, deep inside Russian territory. In Paris, Khrushchev demanded an apology from the U.S. for the plane's presence; but when Eisenhower refused to apologize, the summit ended. Subsequently, the crisis in Berlin and Cuba added to Cold War tensions.

Berlin Wall

In August of 1961, shortly after John F. Kennedy was elected president, Khrushchev ordered the construction of the Berlin Wall. The wall was made of concrete blocks and barbed wire and extended along the border between East and West Berlin, sealing off East Berlin, in violation of existing agreements.

Cuban Missile Crisis

In 1959, **Fidel Castro** (b. 1929) had overthrown the corrupt Cuban government of Fulgencio Batista, while promising to restore democracy. In 1961, he proclaimed Cuba to be a Communist state and began receiving support from Russia. In 1962, Khrushchev ordered missiles with nuclear warheads installed in Cuba, and President Kennedy announced a naval blockade of Cuba. During 13 tense days in October, the crisis was defused. The Soviets agreed to remove the missiles, and in return the United States promised not to invade Cuba. In October 1964, Khrushchev was forced into retirement and was replaced with **Leonid Brezhnev** (1906–1982). Party conservatives blamed Khrushchev for his de-Stalinization program, the split between China and the Soviet Union, the Cuban fiasco, and the failure to improve agricultural and industrial production.

The Brezhnev Era (1964–1982)

Next to Stalin, Leonid Brezhnev ruled the Soviet Union longer than any other leader. Brezhnev and his supporters stressed the ties with the Stalinist era by focusing on his good points and ignoring his crimes. Brezhnev strengthened the Russian bureaucracy and the KGB, and suppressed dissidents who spoke out against the government at home and in the satellite countries. The Soviets also invested in a large military buildup and were determined to never suffer again a humiliating defeat as in the Cuban missile crisis. Yet Brezhnev proceeded cautiously in the mid-1960s and sought to avoid confrontation with the West. He was determined, however, to protect Soviet interests.

Brezhnev Doctrine (1968)

In 1968, **Alexander Dubcek** (1921–1992) became head of the Czechoslovakia Communist Party and began a series of reforms known as the **Prague Spring** reforms. He lifted censorship, permitted non-Communists to form political groups, and wanted to trade with the West, but still remain loyal to Communism. In August 1968, Soviet leaders sent over 500,000 Russian and Eastern European troops to occupy Czechoslovakia. Brezhnev saw these reforms as a threat to the Communist system and claimed in what became known as the **Brezhnev Doctrine** that the "Soviet Union had the right to intervene militarily in any socialist country that it saw the need to do so."

The Brezhnev Doctrine was seriously tested in Poland. Throughout the 1970s, Poland had suffered economic hardship and Polish workers had rioted in 1970 and 1976 against increased food prices. In 1980, scattered strikes spread across Poland to protest the rise in meat prices. **Lech Walesa** (b. 1943), an electrician at the Gdansk shipyards, organized **Solidarity**, an independent trade union that called for political, industrial, and economic changes. Solidarity had the support of millions of workers, intellectuals, and the Catholic Church. In 1978, **Karol Wojtyla**, the former archbishop of Krakow, Poland, was elected **Pope John Paul II**, the first Polish pope. He supported the struggle for the rights of people across the world, but especially in his native country. Solidarity created concern in Russia, as well as in other Soviet Bloc nations. However, the Soviet Union, still facing criticism from its invasion of Afghanistan in 1979, played a waiting game. When Solidarity began to lose its cohesiveness, the Polish Communist leadership declared martial law and arrested Walesa and other leaders. Solidarity went underground and fought with great popular support, paving the way for greater changes in the Soviet Union and Eastern Europe during the latter half of the 1980s.

Détente

During the 1970s, the spirit of détente developed in the Cold War. **Détente** means a progressive relaxation of tension, and involved the following:

- **1972:** President Richard Nixon visited Moscow. The United States and Russia signed significant accords on space flights, health, and trading agreements. These accords included an agreement on joint space flight, cooperation in medical, science, and public health, and the end of the Trade Ban of 1949, which had prohibited the shipping of U.S. goods to the Soviet Union. They also signed the **SALT I Accord (Strategic Arms Limitation Talks)**, which was designed to limit the spread of nuclear weapons. Limits were set on both long-range missiles or intercontinental ballistics missiles, and defensive missiles.

- **1973:** Brezhnev visited the United States and spoke to the American people via television.

- **1975:** The United States, Canada, and 33 European nations met at Helsinki, Finland to sign the **Helsinki Pact**. The European countries formally agreed to recognize Soviet territorial gains in Europe, the division of Germany into two nations, and Soviet domination of Eastern Europe. The Soviet Union, the United States, and the other European nations also agreed to further the cause of human rights.

The spirit of détente came to an end with the Soviet invasion of Afghanistan in 1979. The Soviets invaded Afghanistan in order to keep Afghanistan's Communist government in power, justifying the invasion with the Brezhnev Doctrine. Many in the West were convinced that the Russians were violating the spirit of détente. The Afghanistan invasion drained the Soviet economy and morale at home.

By the time of Brezhnev's death in 1982, the Soviet Union faced many serious problems. The centralized economy was still inefficient and unable to produce enough food to feed the people, so the Soviet Union had to import grain from the capitalist nations. The Russian bureaucracy had little understanding of how the centralized economy had failed the people. Within the next few years, sweeping changes dramatically altered the future of Communism in Russia.

Political and Economic Recovery in Europe

World War II left Europe physically devastated and in weak economic condition. In 1947, United States Secretary of State John Marshall offered economic aid to all European countries. The **Marshall Plan**, officially known as the European Recovery Program, provided over $13 billion in aid for foodstuff, machinery, and raw materials. The goal of the program was to achieve recovery, not relief, and to lessen the dangers of Communism. Stalin forbade Eastern European countries to accept this aid and promised that the Soviet Union would help them instead.

As the Marshall Plan aid poured in, the battered economies of Western Europe began to improve. They rebuilt factories, farms, and transportation systems destroyed in the war. The close cooperation among European nations as required by the Marshall Plan also promoted economic growth. In 1950, French statesman Jean Monet and Foreign Minister Robert Schuman proposed an economic union of Western European nations to integrate all European coal and steel production. In 1951, France, West Germany, Belgium, Italy, the Netherlands, and Luxembourg accepted this idea. They set up the **European Coal and Steel Community**. By 1958, coal and steel moved freely among these six nations.

In 1957, these same six nations signed the **Treaty of Rome**, which set up the **European Common Market**. The goal of the organization was the reduction of all tariffs among the six and to include the free movement of capital and economic policies and institutions. By 1973, Britain, Denmark, and Ireland joined. The Common Market was a great success. In the 1980s, the Common Market expanded to include Greece in 1981 and Spain and Portugal in 1986; it then became known as the European Union. This union benefited Western Europe in several ways. By promoting economic cooperation among individual European nations, it reduced the threat of conflict to European prosperity. It also enabled Western Europe to compete for world markets with North America and East Asia.

West Germany

West Germany led the economic miracle. A free market economy with a social welfare network brought economic growth to West Germany. Politically, Germany evolved into a stable democracy. The United States worked closely with the Christian Democrats (heirs to the old Catholic Center Party, which had been organized in the 1870s to defend Catholic interests) to ensure that West Germany became an integral part of the Western alliance. From 1949 to 1963, **Konrad Adenauer** (1876–1967) provided strong leadership that helped to revive West Germany. At the age of 73, Adenauer ("die alte" — the old one) worked to rebuild the German economy by using the influx of refugees from Eastern Europe as a valuable labor resource in building up the country. Under his leadership, West Germany rebuilt their factories, cities, and trade. By the mid-1950s, industrial production surpassed prewar German levels, and by the 1960s, West Germany had become one of the leader countries in Western Europe. In April 1963, Ludwig Erhard, who had been Adenauer's economic minister, succeeded him. Under his leaderhip, the economy suffered a temporary recession. In 1969, **Willy Brandt**, leader of the **Social Democratic Party** and former Mayor of West Germany, became chancellor. Brandt was the first Socialist chancellor in 40 years and began his policy of "**Ostpolitik**," or Eastern Policy, seeking reconciliation between East and West Germany. He signed treaties with the Soviet Union, Poland, and Czechoslovakia, and entered into direct relations with East Germany. Brandt's long-term goal of unification of Germany was in the near future. In 1974, Brandt resigned because a close personal aide on his staff confessed that he was an East German spy. In that same year, the Socialist Democrats chose Helmut Schmidt as successor. Poor economic conditions plus attack by the Greens, a loose coalition of environmentalists, pulled strength away from the Socialists and ended their rule in 1982. **Helmut Kohle**, a conservative Christian democrat, became chancellor in that same year.

Great Britain

In Great Britain, World War II battered the economy. In 1945, the Labour Party under Clement Attlee (1883–1967) assumed power and began to transform Great Britain into a welfare state, nationalizing industries and expanding social programs to include social security and national health insurance. The national health insurance, called "Socialized Medicine," granted every citizen the right to free medical, dental, and hospital care, and nursing. The Labour government was succeeded by the conservatives, under Churchill, Anthony Eden (1955–1957), and Harold MacMillian (1957–1963). The conservatives gained leadership from 1951 to 1964 and restored some private enterprise to the iron and steel industries, introduced some fees for national health, and accepted the basic outline of the welfare state. Labour returned to power under Harold Wilson (1964–1970) from 1964 to 1970, restoring free medical service from birth to death, as well as state-funded universities and public housing programs.

Throughout the 1970s, power shifted between the Conservative and Labour Parties. Inflation, created by the Arab oil embargoes of 1973 and 1979 caused problems for England. Labor productivity was low. The pound was devalued in 1976 and frequent strikes hurt the economy. In 1979, **Margaret Thatcher** (b. 1925), a conservative, was elected prime minister and began to limit spending on social welfare programs. During her 11 years in office, she replaced government programs with a greater emphasis on private enterprise. She curbed the power of labor unions, cut the size of the government bureaucracy, and trimmed welfare service.

France

At the end of World War II, France was a weak country. The **Fourth French Republic** set up at the end of World War II suffered from the same weaknesses as the Third Republic — a weak presidency with a strong legislature with too many political parties that led to multiparty coalitions and frequent changes in government. In 1958, the threat of civil war in the North African colony of Algeria resulted in the downfall of the Fourth Republic. In 1958, **Charles De Gaulle** (1890–1970) was called out of retirement to head an emergency government. The National Assembly voted to give De Gaulle complete power for six months to draw up a new constitution for the country. In 1958, Charles De Gaulle set up the **Fifth French Republic**, which was accepted by an overwhelming majority. Its constitution provided for a much stronger president with the power to dissolve the legislature, submit popular issues to the people, and assume emergency power whenever necessary. De Gaulle became the first president of the Fifth Republic. Through De Gaulle's efforts, French prestige and power was restored and stability returned to the country. In July 1962, De Gaulle solved the Algerian issue by granting the colony its independence.

In his foreign policy, De Gaulle tried to make France an independent force in world affairs. His strongly nationalistic policies angered the United States and Great Britain. In 1963, he opposed British entry into the Common Market. In 1966, he decided to withdraw all French troops from NATO and demanded that all NATO bases and headquarters be removed from French soil. He even advocated the building of an independent French nuclear force. In 1965, De Gaulle was re-elected to a second term. However, by 1968, concern over inflation and housing as well as his expenditures on nuclear policies rather than on education, led to student revolts and strikes by 10 million workers. De Gaulle survived by promising educational reforms and wage increases. In April 1969, De Gaulle demanded a referendum to support a new constitution that would reduce the power of the Senate. His proposal for changes was rejected and he was forced to resign. De Gaulle's successors, Georges Pompidou (president from 1969–1974) and Valery Giscard D'Estaing (president from 1974–1981) continued to follow an independent foreign policy. However, France did agree to British entry into the Common Market. Like the rest of Europe, the economic recession of the 1970s and early 1980s hurt the country's prosperity. The French Socialist **Francois Mitterand** (president from 1981–1995) tried to revive the economy by nationalizing private companies and banks and increasing wages and other social benefits. However, the economic crisis deepened and Mitterand was forced to cut social programs and taxes. Mitterand was able to control inflation but unemployment increased. France continued to face economic problems during the 1980s.

Italy

At the end of World War II, Italy rejected and removed the monarchy, which had been associated with fascism, and set up a republic. Postwar Italy was economically divided into two regions — the prosperous and industrial North and the rural South, which was primarily agricultural. Politically, Italy had a multiparty system like France, and the Christian Democrats, who were allied with the Catholic Church, dominated the national scene. The leading figure in post-Fascist Italy was **Alcide de Gasperi** (1881–1954), who provided strength and stability for seven formative years. In the 1948 election, de Gasperi, supported by the United States and the Vatican, won a major victory over the Communists who were bidding for power. As in France, Italy's Communist Party was strong, but never won enough votes to be a majority. After 1948, the Christian Democrats would govern the country, but without the majority that they had won in 1948. Financial scandals and political corruption hurt the national parties. Yet, the alliance of the Catholic Church and the Christian Democrats supplied national unity to Italian politics by providing prime ministers with a coalition government.

Despite these problems, Italy developed economically, and by the 1970s had advanced into one of the 10 industrial powers. However, as in other European countries, the Arab oil embargo adversely affected the economy, which was more dependent on oil imports than other industrialized countries. By 1973, Italy's inflation rate was 25% and was still 16% in the early 1980s; her unemployment rate was high and the lire had dropped in value. Italy also suffered from terrorism, and the assassination of **Aldo Moro** in 1978, a respected Christian Democrat, by a radical group known as the **Red Brigade**, added to the difficulties of the Italian government.

The End of Colonialism

The post–World War II era marked the final collapse of European imperialism. Winston Churchill had hoped to maintain control of the vast holdings of the British Empire, but Britain was militarily too weak to defend its possessions. The Cold War also undermined British imperialism. The

United States supported the right of people for self-determination and so did the Soviet Union. The demise of the empire began in 1947, when India, "the jewel of the crown," declared its independence. This began a chain reaction. In 1948, the British withdrew from Palestine and left to the United Nations the task of determining the area's future. A Jewish state was created out of part of British-controlled Palestine.

The Arabs refused to accept (and have still not accepted) the state of Israel and immediately attacked it. The Israeli army defeated the Arabs but the issue of a Palestinian state was still not resolved. Wars broke out in 1956, 1967, and 1973. In Egypt, **Gamal Abdel Nasser** (1918–1970) nationalized the **Suez Canal** in 1956, ending British control. Britain, France, and Israel invaded, but the United States and Russia immediately condemned the attack. Working through the United Nations, they secured the withdrawal of the invading forces and stationed a United Nations Emergency Force on the Egyptian border. The negative response by the United States and Russia was a reminder to Britain that the "sun was setting on the British Empire." By 1957, Ghana declared its independence and the rest of the British African Empire declared its independence without any major upheavals.

The Dutch and French did not relinquish their control over the colonies as readily as Britain. During World War II, the Dutch colonies fell under Japanese control. After the war, Indonesian Nationalists set up a republic. The Dutch tried to restore control, but the United Nations Security Council secured a cease-fire and in 1949 and granted independence to Indonesia. France also struggled to maintain its empire in Indochina (Vietnam, Cambodia, and Laos). After World War II, the French promised partial independence, but their offer was rejected. Led by Nationalist **Ho Chi Minh** (1890–1969), the Vietnamese, who had fought against the Japanese in World War II, waged an eight-year struggle for freedom. In 1954, France lost Vietnam. The **Geneva Accords** recognized the independence of Cambodia and Laos and divided Vietnam into the North backed by the Communists and the South supported by the United States. By 1956, the French had ended their colonial rule over Morocco and Tunisia. The struggle over Algeria was different, as the French had controlled Algeria since 1830 and French settlers and the French military opposed Algeria's independence. Civil war threatened the country over this issue. In 1958, Charles De Gaulle took over the government and in 1962 made peace with Algeria and granted her independence. Within two decades of the conclusion of World War II, the colonial empires of the Western countries had been dismantled.

Chronology of the Cold War

1945	Potsdam Conference—Truman and Stalin disagree over the Yalta Accord on Eastern Europe.
1946	Churchill gives his Iron Curtain speech.
1947	India becomes independent. The Truman Doctrine is announced. The Marshall Plan is announced.

1948	The Berlin Blockade begins. The Berlin Airlift lasts for 314 days. Tito breaks with USSR.
1949	The Berlin Blockade ends. NATO is formed. Chinese Communists defeat the Nationalists. The German Federal Republic and German Democratic Republic are created. The Soviet atomic bomb is tested.
1950	The Korean War begins.
1952	Greece and Turkey join NATO. The United States tests the H-bomb.
1953	Stalin dies.
1954	Dr. Jonas Salk develops anti-polio serum. Ho Chi Minh defeats the French at Dien Bien Phu.
1955	The Warsaw Pact is formed.
1956	Khrushchev begins de-Stalinization. Uprisings occur in Poland and Hungary. Suez Canal Crisis takes place.
1957	Treaty of Rome creates the European Common Market. USSR launches Sputnik I and Sputnik II — the first earth satellites.
1960	Belgian Congo becomes free.
1961	The Berlin Wall is built.
1962	John Glenn orbits the earth. Cuban Missile Crisis occurs. Uganda becomes independent.
1963	Dr. Michael De Bakery — first use of an artificial heart.
1964	Leonid Brezhnev becomes leader of Russia.
1968	Tet Offensive takes place in Vietnam. Prague Spring begins in Czechoslovakia.
1969	Apollo 11 lands on the moon.
1970	Egyptian leader Gamal Abdel Nasser dies.
1972	President Nixon visits Moscow, signs SALT I, limiting anti-ballistic missile systems.
1978	Pope John Paul II elected as the first Polish pope.
1979	Margaret Thatcher leads Conservative Party to victory. The Soviets invade Afghanistan. The U.S. imposes a grain embargo on the Soviet Union.
1980	Solidarity is formed.

Sample Multiple-Choice Questions

1. Which of the following countries did *not* become a Russian satellite after World War II?

    A. Hungary

    B. Poland

    C. Czechoslovakia

    D. Yugoslavia

    E. Bulgaria

2. Which of the following were the two major alliances created after World War II in Europe?

    A. NATO and the Warsaw Pact

    B. Triple Entente and Triple Alliance

    C. Reinsurance Treaty and Triple Alliance

    D. Rome-Berlin Axis and Soviet Non-Aggression Pact

    E. Holy Alliance and Concert of Europe

3. The revolt in Hungary (1956), the demonstrations in Czechoslovakia (1968), and the formation of Solidarity in Poland (1980s) are similar in that they

    A. were movements to restore the power of the aristocracy

    B. were tolerated by the Communist leaders, who accepted the need for change

    C. represented a challenge to Communist leadership

    D. represented attempts to rid these countries of Western ideas and influence

    E. were attempts by the Communists to provide humanitarian aid

4. The leader of the Polish Solidarity movement was

    A. Lech Walesa

    B. Alexander Dubcek

    C. Leonid Brezhnev

    D. Wladyslaw Gomulka

    E. Irme Nagy

5. Which was one of the basic causes of the Cold War between the United States and USSR after World War II?

    A. struggle for colonies in Africa

    B. the Soviet Union support of Fidel Castro

    C. rivalry in Asia

    D. ideological differences

    E. the U.S. support of dissidents within the Soviet Union

6. Which is considered the most serious threat to world peace between the United States and USSR during the Cold War?

    A. Suez Canal Crisis

    B. Cuban Missile Crisis

    C. Vietnam War

    D. Afghanistan Conflict

    E. Algerian War for Independence

7. Nikita Khrushchev introduced the policy of

    A. peaceful coexistence

    B. détente

    C. perestroika

    D. glasnost

    E. spirit of Glassboro

8. The most significant occurrence in Africa since 1950 has been the

    A. decrease in the birth rate

    B. decline of European colonialism

    C. unification of East African nations

    D. establishment of Communist regime in most nations

    E. establishment of industrial economies

9. The Labour Party which controlled the English government after World War II introduced a

    A. democracy

    B. welfare state

    C. Communist state

    D. corporate state

    E. capitalist state

10. The primary purpose of the European Common Market (European Community) is to

    A. create a central location for the distribution of goods

    B. force Eastern European nations to change their trading partners

    C. establish a tariff-free flow of goods among member nations

    D. reduce European dependence on foreign oil reserves

    E. promote a one-product economy

Answers to Multiple-Choice Questions and Explanations

1. D. Yugoslavia did not become a Russian satellite after World War II. From 1945 to 1980, Marshal Tito, or Josip Broz, defied Stalin and pursued nationalist policies. Yugoslavia was not occupied by Soviet troops and did not border on the Soviet Union. Yugoslavia always remained free of Soviet domination. Hungary, Poland, Czechoslovakia, and Bulgaria were Russian satellites from 1947 to 1989.

2. A. NATO and the Warsaw Pact were major alliances created after World War II in Europe. The North Atlantic Treaty Organization (NATO) was formed in 1949 by the United States and 10 other nations as a defensive alliance against Communism. The Warsaw Pact was formed in 1955 consisting of the USSR and seven Soviet satellites in Eastern Europe. The Triple Entente, Triple Alliance, and Reinsurance Treaty were formed at the end of the nineteenth century or beginning of the twentieth century. The Rome-Berlin Axis and Soviet Non-Aggression Pact were signed in the 1930s before World War II began. The Holy Alliance and the Concert of Europe were an outgrowth of the Congress of Vienna in 1815.

3. C. The revolt in Hungary, the demonstrations in Czechoslovakia, and the formation of Solidarity in Poland are similar in that they represented a challenge to Communist leadership. In Hungary, Imre Nagy was a liberal Communist who wanted to withdraw from the Warsaw Pact. In Czechoslovakia, Alexander Dubcek wanted to liberalize his Communist regime and Solidarity was formed to promote political and social changes. In Hungary and Czechoslovakia the Soviet Union sent in troops. In Poland, the Communists declared martial law and arrested Solidarity leaders. These movements were designed to change Communism, not restore the power of the aristocracy. These movements were not tolerated by the Communists nor were they attempts to provide humanitarian aid. These movements were interested in promoting Western ideas of democracy and not an attempt to rid their countries of Western influence.

4. A. Lech Walesa was the leader of the Polish Solidarity movement. Lech Walesa was an electrician at the Gdansk shipyard who organized Solidarity, an independent trade union. In 1990 he was elected president of Poland after the fall of Communism. Alexander Dubcek was the leader of Czechoslovakia who tried to introduce reforms to change Communism. Leonid Brezhnev was the leader of the Soviet Union from 1964 to 1982. Wladyslaw Gomulka was part of the Polish uprising in 1956. Irme Nagy was the Hungarian leader who opposed the Soviet Union in 1956.

5. D. Ideological differences were one basic cause of the Cold War between the United States and USSR after World War II. The United States' political system is based on democracy, capitalism, and the importance of the individual. Both the United States and USSR supported self-determination in Africa to end Western imperialism. They disagreed on which form of government they would follow. Soviet support of Fidel Castro began in the 1950s. Rivalry in Asia was among the United States, Soviet Union, and China. The United States' support of dissidents within the Soviet Union was an ideological outgrowth of a difference between Communism and democracy.

6. B. The Cuban Missile Crisis is considered the most serious threat to world peace during the Cold War. In 1962, Nikita Khrushchev installed nuclear weapons in Cuba. The United States blockaded Cuba and would not allow Soviet ships to travel to Cuba. President John Kennedy convinced Russia to remove the missiles in return for a pledge not to invade Cuba and a promise to remove American missiles in Turkey. Khrushchev's decisions to remove the missiles from Cuba contributed to his forced retirement in 1964. Conservatives believed that he had "blinked" in the crisis and embarrassed the Soviet Union. The United States and the Soviet Union were not involved with each other during the Suez Canal Crisis, the Vietnam War, the Afghanistan Conflict, nor during the Algerian War for Independence.

7. A. Nikita Khrushchev introduced a policy of peaceful coexistence after the death of Joseph Stalin in 1953. Although Khrushchev believed that the Soviet Union would eventually bury the United States, he sought nonviolent ways to compete and coexist with non-Communist nations. He introduced a relaxation of tensions or a thaw with the United States. Yet by 1961, he built the Berlin War and brought the United States to the brink of war in the Cuban Missile Crisis. Détente is associated with the Brezhnev regime. Mikhail Gorbachev introduced perestroika and glasnost. The Spirit of Glassboro was a meeting between the United States and the Soviet Union held in New Jersey in 1967, which produced nothing of substance.

8. B. The decline of European colonialism is the most significant occurrence in Africa since 1950. At the end of World War II, most of Africa was under European rule. By 1959, only six nations were independent, Libya, Egypt, Ethiopia, Liberia, and the Union of South Africa. Since 1959, more than 40 nations have gained their independence. The population in Africa has been increasing despite the AIDS epidemic. There has been no unification of East African nations. Communism is no longer a threat to the African Continent. Despite its vast resources, a majority of Africa has not been industrialized.

9. B. The Labour Party introduced the welfare state after World War II. Clement Attlee, the Labour prime minister who succeeded Winston Churchill in 1945, transformed Britain into a welfare state. The Labour Party introduced social programs that provided for public housing, established old-age pensions, unemployment insurance, and the creation of a National Health Service or free medical care. The conservatives, under Margaret Thatcher in 1979, began to roll back the welfare state. England has had a parliamentary type democracy since 1689. It has never followed a Communist nor corporate state of government. The Labour Party nationalized the Bank of England but did not introduce Communism to England.

10. C. The primary purpose of the European Common Market was to establish a tariff-free flow of goods among member nations. In 1957, the European Common Market was formed by six industrialized Western nations to expand trade by ending tariffs and allowing capital and labor to move freely across the borders of these European nations. The Common Market was a trade agreement, not a distribution center for goods. It was only for Western industrialized countries. The Common Market did not reduce dependence on foreign oil reserves as the Arab Embargo of the 1970s demonstrated. The Common Market was for industrialized and diversified economies.

From 1945 until the 1980s, the problems created by the Cold War loomed over Europe. Under its shadow, however, Western Europe and the United States experienced remarkable economic growth. The Soviet Union and Communist Eastern Europe under the iron hand of Stalin also rebuilt. However, economic growth slowed and stagnated in the 1970s as the Soviet's economy was unable to meet the needs for military spending and consumer goods. In 1985, Mikhail Gorbachev became the leader of the Soviet Union and sought some reforms in Russia and the Communist Bloc. Gorbachev began to restructure Soviet economy and instituted political changes that would allow for greater openness in Soviet society. He also encouraged reforms in Eastern Europe. His policies contributed to the collapse of Communism in Eastern Europe and the breakup of the Soviet Union.

The year 1989, like 1789 (the French Revolution), was a remarkable year in European history. Freedom swept across Eastern Europe and Communist-led regimes collapsed peacefully in Poland, Hungary, Czechoslovakia, Bulgaria, and Albania. The collapse of the Berlin Wall in 1989 and the unification of Germany in 1990 symbolized the decline of the Soviet satellite system that dominated Europe for a half century. Gorbachev's policies also affected minorities within the multinational Soviet Empire. By 1991, the Baltic States had regained their independence. By the end of 1991, other Soviet republics declared their independence and Boris Yeltsin became president of the Russian Republic. After 74 years, Communism ceased to exist in Russia.

The collapse of Communism in Europe also unleashed ethnic tensions in Eastern Europe, which had been suppressed for many years. The Soviet domination of Eastern Europe had been based on absolute control without any regard for the different ethnic groups. In 1991, ethnic conflicts tore Yugoslavia apart in a long and tragic civil war. The conflict led to ethnic cleansing and tested the ability of Europe to deal with problems in post–Cold War Europe.

The latter half of the twentieth century witnessed changes in the European economy as well as social changes. Economic changes during the Cold War era in Western Europe affected European society. The family and the role of women underwent change as the divorce rate increased and the birth rate decreased. European society was also becoming more diverse as immigrants from foreign countries settled in Europe and provided low wages for the booming economy. During the economic recession of the 1970s, Europe began to resent the newcomers.

Throughout the 1980s and 1990s, Europe continued to promote economic unity to ensure its economic growth. The dream of a United States of Europe became a reality with the introduction of a new European currency (the Euro) at the beginning of the twenty-first century.

The Collapse of Communism in the Soviet Union and Eastern Europe

The 18-year rule of Leonid Brezhnev brought security for the Soviet bureaucracy. The government's central control continued to watch over all decisions. The system protected the elite but was apathetic toward the masses. The State could produce impressive results when it poured resources into major products such as weapons and the space race; however, Soviet consumer products, such as shoes, suits, and television sets, were far inferior to those in the West. People spent hours waiting in line to buy foods and goods. Economic efficiency and personal initiatives were discouraged.

The Soviet Union's war in Afghanistan drained the Soviet economy and provoked a moral crisis similar to the Vietnam War in the United States. The Soviet Union had invaded Afghanistan in 1979, when the Communist government of Babrak Kam was on the verge of collapse. The Soviet Union became bogged down in a no-win situation with determined Afghan fighters. In 1982, Brezhnev's successor, **Yuri Andropov** (1914–1984), Chief of the Secret Police (KGB), tried to introduce some moderate reforms in the Soviet Union. He sought to improve economic performance by providing factory managers with material incentives, and campaigned against worker absenteeism and high-level corruption. At 72, **Konstantin Chernenko** (1911–1985), who replaced Andropov after his sudden death in 1984, made no significant changes before dying in 1985. In 1985, the worsening economic conditions and the failure of old-line Soviet leadership led to the selection of **Mikhail Gorbachev** (b.1931) as the new leader of Russia. Gorbachev was an energetic individual who was determined to reform inefficiencies in the government and the economy. Gorbachev's reforms, however, unleashed waves of change that he was unable to control and resulted in the collapse of the Soviet Empire and Communism in Eastern Europe.

Gorbachev's reforms included **perestroika,** or economic restructuring. His program called for less government planning, and more power to local factory managers to make production decisions. The program also allowed some Soviet citizens to operate small retail businesses. Farmers were given permission to grow some food that could be sold on the free market. (Gorbachev's policy of perestroika was similar in some respects to Lenin's New Economic Policy of 1921. Lenin's program also allowed some capitalist ventures. While the State controlled the major industries, small businesses were allowed to open for private profits. Peasants were also allowed to hold on to small plots of land to sell their surplus crops.) The economy and the people were unprepared for these changes, however, and the economy stalled between central planning and the free market mechanism. Shortages grew worse and prices soared. By 1990, Gorbachev's economic initiatives had achieved very little success.

Gorbachev also introduced a policy of **glasnost** or openness in Soviet society. New election laws gave voters a choice among candidates even though the Communist Party remained the only legal party. Censorship ended and free speech was promoted. Attacks on the crimes of the Stalin era appeared often in Soviet plays and newspapers and the works of writers who had been banned for many years were made available. In 1988, a new constitution was adapted calling for elections of a new legislative body. In the past, voters had merely approved candidates who were hand-picked by the Communist Party. Now voters could choose from a list of candidates for each office. In 1989, the Soviet Union held its first elections with modified choices since 1917. In some areas where the Communist Party leaders ran unopposed, the people were so angry that they crossed off the ballots the names of party leaders and wrote in local candidates. By 1990, Gorbachev was forced to admit non-Communist parties into the political process.

In foreign affairs, Gorbachev withdrew troops from Afghanistan in 1989 and refused to accept the Brezhnev Doctrine, which claimed that the Soviet Union had the right to intervene in any Communist country under its control. In 1989, Gorbachev's reforms unleashed a wave of peaceful revolutions throughout Eastern Europe that overturned the existing Communist government in those countries and ended Soviet domination in Eastern Europe.

In Poland, the Communist government legalized **Solidarity**, an independent trade union, and held free democratic elections for the first time in over 50 years. On June 4, 1989, Solidarity candidates, who had outpolled Communist Party members, became the first freely elected opposition in a Communist country. In 1990, Lech Walesa was elected president of Poland.

Democracy spread to other Soviet satellite countries as well. In Czechoslovakia, Communism died in December of 1989. Massive street demonstrations led by students and intellectuals led to the ouster of the Communist leaders within 10 days. Vaclav Havel, a dissident playwright, was elected president in 1990. In Bulgaria, the Communist leadership stepped down without putting up any resistance. In Hungary, the Communist Party was broken up and free elections were held in 1990. The Hungarians also tore down the barbed wire "iron curtain" that separated Austria and Hungary and opened their borders to refugees from East Germany.

In East Germany, the Communist government was forced to open up its borders and in November of 1989, joyous Germans from both sides tore down the Berlin Wall, which had divided the nation for almost 30 years. During the first week alone, over 2 million Eastern Germans poured into West Germany, about one-half of the population. The Communist leaders were arrested and elections, which were won by the conservative pro-unification Christian Democrats, were held in March of 1990. By October 1990, Germany was united and Helmut Kohl, the leader of the Christian Democrats, became the first chancellor of a united Germany. Helmut Kohl was skillful in assuring the United States, other European countries, and the Soviet Union that they need not fear a reunified Germany. In July 1990, Kohl, in a historic agreement with the Soviet Union, affirmed its peaceful intentions, recognized the pre-1945 borders, and pledged that a united Germany would not own ABC weapons and promised never to use nuclear weapons. On October 3, 1990, East and West Germany formally became a single nation.

Communism died a bloody death in Romania. **Nicolae Ceausescu** (1918–1989), the Communist dictator, ordered his security forces to slaughter thousands of protesters, thereby sparking an armed uprising. After Ceausescu's forces were defeated, he and his wife were captured and put to death by a military tribunal. A provisional government emerged to govern the country. In May 1990, elections were won by the National Salvation Front, whose formerly Communist leaders called for a gradual and controlled transition to a free market economy.

In November of 1990, Gorbachev sought to end Soviet deficits through military cuts. Twenty-two members of NATO and the Warsaw Pact signed the Paris Accord (the treaty on conventional armed forces in Europe or the CFE), a general peace treaty that officially ended the Cold

War. They agreed to scale down their conventional armed forces. The CFE called for equal ceilings in NATO and the Warsaw Pact land-based forces from the Atlantic to the Urals. However, it excluded naval forces and U.S.–based ground and air forces earmarked for NATO. The Treaty expired in 1995. The United States, the Soviet Union, and the nations of Western Europe also signed the "Charter for a New Europe," declaring that relations in Europe would be founded on respect and cooperation. Meanwhile, Gorbachev continued to face problems at home. When the Baltic States declared their independence and Gorbachev refused to crush the revolt, his support was undermined. **Boris Yeltsin** (b.1931), first appointed chairman of the Communist Supreme Soviet of Russia in 1990 and then elected president of the Russian Federation in May 1991, declared Russia's independence from the Soviet Union. The rivalry between Gorbachev and Yeltsin added to the unstable conditions within the country. Meanwhile in a last-gasp effort, Soviet conservatives who were defeated at the Communist Party Congress in July 1990 kidnapped Gorbachev, who was on vacation, and tried to seize power in August of 1991. The coup failed in the face of popular opposition and Yeltsin's defiant stand. Gorbachev was returned to power as the head of the Soviet Union. In the conservatives' efforts to restore Communist Party power and to preserve the empire, they destroyed Communism. Anti-Communist revolutions swept across the nation as each republic declared its freedom and independence. Gorbachev resigned as president. On December 21, 1991, the Commonwealth of Independent Soviet States was formed. The formation of the CIS meant the death of the Soviet Union. On December 25, 1991, when Gorbachev resigned as president, the Soviet Union ceased to exist.

The Commonwealth of Independent States consisted of 11 of the 15 republics that formed the Old Soviet Union. This loose confederation dissolved into separate national economies, each with its own goals and policies. The collapse of the Soviet Union ended its role as a super power and led to economic hardships. After the breakup, Boris Yeltsin, the president of Russia, the largest republic, assumed leadership. His efforts to privatize the economy were disappointing, however. Prices skyrocketed, production fell 20%, and runaway inflation left a few rich and many poor. Public service suffered and the social safety net that Communism had provided was lost for people. Yeltsin's erratic behavior and illness, moreover, did not provide stable leadership. Despite economic aid from the West and the International Monetary Fund, Russia's economic conditions did not improve in the 1990s. In the presidential election of 2000, Vladimir Putin, a former KGB agent and Yeltsin's chosen successor, assumed the leadership of the country.

Ethnic Tensions in Eastern Europe

The Communist government had suppressed and controlled ethnic divisions in the multinational states of Eastern Europe; however, with the collapse of Communism, these tensions resurfaced. In the case of Czechoslovakia, these tensions were resolved peacefully. On January 1, 1993, the Czechoslovakian Federation was dissolved and two separate independent countries were established—the Czech Republic and the Slovak Republic. Ethnic divisions resulted in open warfare in other Eastern European areas, however. A civil war developed between the Armenians and Azerbaijanis in an area where many Armenians lived. Armenia eventually gained control of the area.

The greatest tragedy of ethnic conflicts was in the multinational state of Yugoslavia. Until Marshall Tito's death in 1980, Yugoslavia's many ethnic groups were kept in check; after his death, however, Yugoslavia fell into regional and ethnic chaos combined with economic decline. The revolutions of 1989 accelerated the breakup. Serbian President **Slobodan Milosevic** (b. 1941) wanted to grab land from other republics and create a greater Serbia. In 1991, Slovenia and Croatia declared their independence. Milosevic responded by attacking Slovenia. Slovenia was able to repulse the Serbian attack but Milosevic forces were able to take about 30% of Croatia. In 1992, the civil war spread to Bosnia-Herzegovina, when Bosnia declared its independence. The Bosnian Serbs, who represented about 30% of the population, refused to live under the more numerous Bosnian Muslims. With the support of Milosevic, the Serbs began a policy of ethnic cleansing — the forcible removal of non-Serbian groups from areas that they controlled. Ethnic cleansing recalled the horrors of the Nazi Holocaust as thousands of Bosnian Muslim villages were destroyed. Civilians were tortured and refugees were herded into United Nations refugee camps. The scenes of cruelty and horror shocked the Western world. When the Bosnian Serbs overran the Muslim city of Gorazde that the United Nations had declared a safe area and caused the death of several thousand civilians, the world had seen enough. Under the guise of NATO, Serbian military targets were bombed and the Croatian Army drove the Serbs from Croatia. In November of 1995, under a United States–sponsored peace meeting at Wright-Patterson Airbase in Dayton, Ohio, Bosnia was divided along religious and ethnic lines. Troops from NATO patrolled Bosnia to keep the peace.

Kosovo was another center of conflict in Yugoslavia. In 1990, Milosevic abolished self-rule in the Serbian province of Kosovo, where Albanian-speaking Muslims constituted the overwhelming majority and the Serbs were a small minority. Kosovo was significant for the Serbs because they considered it the birthplace of their liberty that evolved out of their defeat by the Ottoman Turks at the Battle of Kosovo in 1389. The Albanian Muslims, who lived in Kosovo and had hopes for self-rule from the Dayton Agreement, gained nothing. In 1998, militants formed the Kosovo Liberation Army (KLA) and began to fight for independence.

In the summer of 1998, Milosevic ordered an offensive against the KLA that displaced over 250,000 people within Kosovo. By January of 1999, the Western Powers led by the United States were threatening air attacks if Milosevic did not withdraw from Kosovo and accept self-government. When Milosevic refused, NATO began heavy bombing on March 24, 1999. The aerial bombing lasted for three and one-half months resulting in the withdrawal of Serbian troops from Kosovo. The aerial bombing of Kosovo was the first time that the NATO alliance was used to attack another sovereign nation. Milosevic's debacle in Kosovo eventually led to a loss of political power. In 2000, Milosevic was forced to call for new elections and lost to Vojislav Kostunica. Milosevic did not go quietly, only relinquishing power when massive street demonstrations demanded that he carry out the mandate of the people. In 2001, Milosevic was turned over to the War Crime Tribunal in The Hague, where he is being tried for crimes against humanity.

European Economic and Social Changes

The postwar recovery of Europe was a remarkable achievement but it had been a rocky road. By the 1960s, the European Common Market had revitalized Europe. The West German economy was booming and lagged behind only the United States and Japan. The European economy took a hit in the 1970s with the oil crisis and the high cost of energy. It also suffered from the worst economic decline since the 1930s as unemployment threatened to slow economic growth.

The postwar boom of Europe was fueled by cheap oil. In 1973, the Arab-led **Organization of Petroleum Exporting Countries (OPEC)** instituted an oil embargo against those countries that supported Israel in the Yom Kippur War with the Arabs. This embargo and the subsequent embargo in 1979 caused shock and led to massive increases in oil prices that plunged the world into the worst economic decline since the 1930s. The crisis hit Western Europe harder because 70% of its oil came from the Middle East. The optimism of Europe that was so prevalent in an earlier decade seemed to have faded away.

During the 1970s and 80s, the governments of Western Europe raised taxes, cut social services, and returned some nationalized industries to private ownership. Europe also tried to reduce its dependency on foreign oil. Western European countries turned toward alternative energy sources, including coal and nuclear power. In France, close to 50% of the electrical power became generated by nuclear reactors.

As the economy began to recover in the 1980s, the hope for European unity revived. In 1987, the Single European Act laid down a legal framework for establishing a free market of labor, capital, and service to the free flow of goods. In December 1991, 12 Western European nations committed to creating European political unity similar to a "United States of Europe" negotiated the **Treaty of Maastricht** (formerly the Treaty on European Unity), which was signed on February 7, 1992, at Maastricht in the Netherlands. One goal of the participating nations was to create economic and political integration by establishing a common currency, a single passport, and a common banking system. The treaty also established a structure that introduced cooperation in law enforcement, criminal justice, judicial matters, and asylum and immigration.

There has been some opposition towards European unity because many nationalists believed that unity would destroy their unique identity. Others were fearful that monetary unions required governments to meet stringent fiscal standards, which would drastically reduce their countries' social and health benefits. In January 2002, the European Union nations officially began circulating the European Dollar, known as the **Euro**, which has become the common currency of all the participating nations that have accepted it.

The economic changes within Europe during the second half of the twentieth century have dramatically affected European society. The standard of living rose throughout the 1950s, 60s, and 70s. In the mid-nineteenth century, food and drink cost roughly two-thirds of the average family income in Europe. By the mid-1960s, it took about one-third to two-fifths of the family income. This translated into more money available for consumer goods. The rising standard of living and the spread of standardized goods helped to level the gap between the rich and the poor in Western society; the result of which was European society became more democratic. Old class lines based on birth and wealth blurred as large numbers of people moved from the rural areas into the cities. The demands of the growing economy broke down rigid class divisions of the people as the need for jobs were based on skill not wealth. European governments also reduced class tension with social programs to help families meet their basic needs. Most European governments gave maternity grants and built public housing for low-income families and individuals. Educational opportunities increased the literacy rate. These steps provided a safety net to insure for the well-being of individuals.

These economic and social changes affected the lives of European citizens. A growing number of European women worked outside the home and as their incomes improved and standards of living rose, family life began to change. Many women began to realize that the interruption of their careers to care for small children led to lower wages. This attitude led to a decline in the birth rate. Family stability, moreover, declined as divorce rates rose.

Beginning in the 1970s, efforts were made to ensure legal and economic equality for European women. One influential writer was **Simone de Beauvior** (1908–1986), who in 1949 had argued that women could only become free by way of courageous actions and self-assertive creativity. The women's movement gained new rights for women. In Italy, prewar restrictions of divorce and abortion for women by Mussolini and the Catholic Church were removed.

As Europe enters the twenty-first century, the European Economic Union has become a powerful economic force. With less than 6% of the world's population, it controls over 35% of the world's trade. Europe has a promising future, but there are questions that need answered: What is the meaning of European Unity? Should the EU remain an exclusively Western union or should it be expanded to include the post-Communist nations of Eastern Europe? What role should the nations of the European Union play in the international diplomatic scene? How should the European nations deal with increased immigration and the continent's critical need for labor? How will the future of the continent be affected by the way Europe and the rest of the world approach and solve these concerns?

Chronology of Contemporary Europe

1982	Death of Brezhnev; Yuri Andropov becomes leader of Soviet Union; Helmut Kohl becomes West Germany's chancellor.
1983	Compact disc is introduced.
1984	Yuri Andropov dies; Apple Macintosh is launched.
1985	Mikhail Gorbachev succeeds Konstantin Chernenko as leader of Russia.
1986	United States President Ronald Reagan meets with Gorbachev.
1987	Single European Act — a legal framework establishing a free market of labor and capital.
1989	Soviet troops withdraw from Afghanistan. The first transatlantic optical fiber telephone cable links France, the United States, and United Kingdom.
1989	Revolutionary Movement throughout Eastern Europe leads to the end of Communism.

continued

March 1990	Pro-democratic groups achieve gains in Russia, Ukraine, and Byelorussia. Lithuania declares its independence followed by Latvia (May 4, 1990).
October 1990	Gorbachev wins the Nobel Peace Prize.
November 1990	German unification takes place.
August 1991	Gorbachev survives a coup by Soviet hard-liners.
December 1991	Soviet Union ceases to exist and the Commonwealth of Independent Sovereign States (CIS) replaces it. Treaty of Maastricht is signed promoting further economic integration within the European Community.
1992	Croatian and Serbian forces fight over division of Bosnia. Slobodan Milosevic introduces ethnic cleansing.
1993	Boris Yeltsin emerges as the dominant leader with the new Commonwealth in Russia.
1994	UN unsuccessfully tries to mediate the Bosnian controversy.
1998	Serbian forces begin an aggressive campaign against ethnic Albanians.
1999	NATO troops bomb Serbian forces in Kosovo and Milosevic is forced to withdraw.
2000	Vladimir Putin replaces Yeltsin as president of Russia. Vojislav Kostunica defeats Milosevic in Serbian election.

Sample Multiple-Choice Questions

1. All of the following were characteristics of life during the Brezhnev era <u>EXCEPT</u>

   A. poor economic production by Soviet industry

   B. lack of artistic freedom

   C. strict government control by the Soviet bureaucracy

   D. lack of consumer goods

   E. victory in the war against Afghanistan

2. Which of the following succeeded Brezhnev as leader of the Soviet Union?

   A. Konstantin Chernenko

   B. Yuri Andropov

   C. Mikhail Gorbachev

   D. Vladimir Putin

   E. Boris Yeltsin

3. Gorbachev's plan of *perestroika* was similar to

   A. Lenin's policy of War Communism

   B. Stalin's policy of Collectivization

   C. Lenin's New Economic Policy

   D. Stalin's Five Year Plan

   E. Khrushchev's policy of Improved Farm Production

4. *Glasnost* is based on the principle of

A. economic reform

B. revival of Stalin's ideas

C. religious reforms

D. expansion of Communism

E. political reform that promoted open speech and expression

5. Which of the following countries did <u>not</u> experience a peaceful exchange of power during the revolutions in Eastern Europe in 1989?

A. Poland

B. East Germany

C. Hungary

D. Czechoslovakia

E. Romania

6. Which of the following officially ended the Cold War?

A. unification of Germany in 1990

B. the demise of the Soviet Union in 1991

C. the revolutions in Eastern Europe during 1989 that ended Soviet domination in the area

D. the CFE Agreement of November 1990

E. destruction of the Berlin Wall

7. Recent events in the former nations of Czechoslovakia and Yugoslavia reflect a nationalist trend of

A. dividing nations along ethnic lines

B. encouraging multiethnic cooperation

C. uniting nations with similar interests

D. supporting the development of a command economy

E. re-establishing Communism

8. The main purpose of the Treaty of Maastricht was to

A. negotiate a reduction in tariff with the United States

B. open up the European Union to Russia

C. establish unified military forces to be used with NATO

D. create a common currency system and a central banking system for the European Union

E. adapt a common immigration policy among the European Union countries

9. Which of the following men was elected the first president of Poland in 1990?

A. Lech Walesa

B. Vaclav Havel

C. Nicole Ceausescu

D. Valdmir Putin

E. Vojislav Kostunica

10. One result of the collapse of the Soviet Union has been

A. reorganization of the Warsaw Pact

B. economic prosperity within the country

C. closer cooperation between the Soviet Union and China

D. spread of ethnic violence in some regions

E. Re-emergence of dictatorship with a command economy

Answers to Multiple-Choice Questions and Explanations

1. **E.** During Brezhnev's regime Russia was not able to gain victory in Afghanistan. Brezhnev ordered troops into Afghanistan in December 1979 to preserve Communist rule and airlifted special troops to Kabul, the capital. The Soviets occupied Afghanistan with 100,000 men. The war in Afghanistan dragged on until 1988 when Gorbachev withdrew the Russian troops. The Afghanistan War was not popular at home and Soviet losses destroyed the morale of the country. During Brezhnev's 18-year rule, the Russian economy lagged behind the West and consumer goods were not readily available. Brezhnev could not solve the basic needs of the people. People spent hours in line waiting to buy foods and other goods. Soviet goods were also inferior to the West. During the Brezhnev regime, the government controlled artistic expression and the Soviet bureaucracy controlled every aspect of the lives of the people.

2. **B.** Yuri Andropov succeeded Brezhnev as leader of the Soviet Union in 1982. He died in 1984 and was succeeded by Konstantin Chernenko, who ruled until 1985. Mikhail Gorbachev ruled from 1985 to 1991. Boris Yeltsin ruled from 1991 to 2000. Vladimir Putin was elected in 2000.

3. **C.** Gorbachev's policy of *perestroika* was similar to Lenin's New Economic Policy. *Perestroika* was designed to restructure the Soviet economy by permitting some private enterprise and allowing farmers to sell in the free market. Lenin introduced the New Economic Policy in 1921 to restore Russia's economic health. This plan allowed for some enterprises to be privately owned and also allowed farmers some economic freedom. Like perestroika, the NEP promoted foreign investments in the Soviet Union. Perestroika and the NEP were designed to promote the market economy under the umbrella of a command economy. Lenin's policy of War Communism, Stalin's policy of Collectivization and his Five Year Plan, and Khrushchev's policy of Improved Farm Production were designed to continue the command economy without the private enterprise system.

4. **E.** Glasnost is based on the principle of political reform that promoted open speech and expression. Under glasnost, Gorbachev ended censorship and encouraged people to freely discuss the country's problems. This openness in government went further than Gorbachev intended and led to free speech and free expression. Economic reform was called perestroika. Under glasnost, Gorbachev did not want to expand Communism, but wanted to cut military expenditures. Glasnost was intended for political, not religious reform, and was critical of Stalin's ideas of strict dictatorship.

5. **E.** Romania did not have a peaceful exchange of power during the revolutions in Eastern Europe in 1989 that swept across Eastern Europe. The Romanian iron-fisted dictator Nicola Ceausescu refused to support change and ordered security forces to smash the protests. His decision to slaughter thousands provoked a classic armed uprising. Ceausescu and his wife were captured and executed by a military court. In Poland, East Germany, Hungary, and Czechoslovakia, there was little or no violence during the transfer of power.

6. **D.** The CFE Treaty of November 1990 officially ended the Cold War. In this accord, the United States, Soviet Union, the 20 members of NATO, and the Warsaw Pact agreed to reduce the number of conventional forces in Europe and respect the existing postwar borders. This accord was a result of the revolution that ended Communist leadership in Eastern Europe. The destruction of the Berlin Wall and the unification of Germany contributed to the Paris Accord. The demise of the Soviet Union symbolized the failure of Communism, not the Cold War.

7. **A.** Recent events in the former nations of Czechoslovakia and Yugoslavia reflect a nationalist trend of dividing nations. In 1993, Czechoslovakia was separated into two independent countries — the Czech Republic and the Slovak Republic. In Yugoslavia ethnic tensions have engulfed the nations and split the countries. During the 1990s, Croatia and Slovenia declared their independence from the federation of Yugoslavia. Serbia wanted a greater Serbia. The emphasis to unite all nationalists living in Yugoslavia has led to civil war throughout the 1990s. Events in Czechoslovakia and Yugoslavia do not reflect a trend of encouraging multi-ethnic cooperation. In Yugoslavia, ethnic cleansing was used to unite all Serbs together while in Czechoslovakia, there was no effort to have Czechs and Slovaks work together before they were divided. Trends in Czechoslovakia and Yugoslavia indicate that the nations do not share similar interests. Since 2000, both countries support the private enterprise system. Neither of these countries supported a return to Communism. They rejected Stalin's dictatorial rule.

8. **D.** One of the purposes of the Treaty of Maastricht was to create a common currency system and central banking system for the European Community. In November 1991, 12 European nations met at the Maastricht, a Dutch town, and agreed to promote economic and political integration. In January of 2002, the European Union officially began circulating the Euro. The Treaty of Maastricht did not deal with tariff reduction with the United States nor was there any provision for unified military forces. The European Union has begun to try to deal with the influx of immigration (legal and illegal) from Eastern Europe and Third World countries.

9. **A.** Lech Walesa was elected president of Poland in 1990. Havel was elected president of Czechoslovakia in 1990. Ceausescu was the Communist leader of Romania whose government was overthrown in 1989 and was put to death. Putin is the present leader of the Soviet Union. Kostunica was elected president of Serbia in 2000.

10. **D.** One result of the collapse of the Soviet Union has been the spread of ethnic violence in some regions. Ethnic violence erupted in the former Soviet Republics of Armenia and Azerbaijan. In the Balkan Peninsula, ethnic conflicts destroyed the multinational state of Yugoslavia. After the fall of Communism, Croatia, Slovenia, Bosnia-Herzegovina, and Macedonia separated from Yugoslavia and became independent. The destruction of Yugoslavia was tragic because violence in Bosnia led to ethnic cleansing and resulted in the deaths of thousands in Bosnia, Kosovo, and other independent states in Yugoslavia. The Warsaw Pact officially ended in 1991 and has not been reorganized. The collapse of the Soviet Union has led to economic problems such as inflation and not economic prosperity. Russia has not established closer cooperation since its collapse, nor has there been a re-emergence of dictatorship with a command economy. Russian leaders have continued to support democracy and the private enterprise system.

PART III

AP EUROPEAN HISTORY PRACTICE TESTS

Answer Sheet for Sample Practice Test I

Remove this sheet and use it to mark your answers for the multiple-choice section of Sample Practice Test I.

1 Ⓐ Ⓑ Ⓒ Ⓓ Ⓔ	21 Ⓐ Ⓑ Ⓒ Ⓓ Ⓔ	41 Ⓐ Ⓑ Ⓒ Ⓓ Ⓔ	61 Ⓐ Ⓑ Ⓒ Ⓓ Ⓔ
2 Ⓐ Ⓑ Ⓒ Ⓓ Ⓔ	22 Ⓐ Ⓑ Ⓒ Ⓓ Ⓔ	42 Ⓐ Ⓑ Ⓒ Ⓓ Ⓔ	62 Ⓐ Ⓑ Ⓒ Ⓓ Ⓔ
3 Ⓐ Ⓑ Ⓒ Ⓓ Ⓔ	23 Ⓐ Ⓑ Ⓒ Ⓓ Ⓔ	43 Ⓐ Ⓑ Ⓒ Ⓓ Ⓔ	63 Ⓐ Ⓑ Ⓒ Ⓓ Ⓔ
4 Ⓐ Ⓑ Ⓒ Ⓓ Ⓔ	24 Ⓐ Ⓑ Ⓒ Ⓓ Ⓔ	44 Ⓐ Ⓑ Ⓒ Ⓓ Ⓔ	64 Ⓐ Ⓑ Ⓒ Ⓓ Ⓔ
5 Ⓐ Ⓑ Ⓒ Ⓓ Ⓔ	25 Ⓐ Ⓑ Ⓒ Ⓓ Ⓔ	45 Ⓐ Ⓑ Ⓒ Ⓓ Ⓔ	65 Ⓐ Ⓑ Ⓒ Ⓓ Ⓔ
6 Ⓐ Ⓑ Ⓒ Ⓓ Ⓔ	26 Ⓐ Ⓑ Ⓒ Ⓓ Ⓔ	46 Ⓐ Ⓑ Ⓒ Ⓓ Ⓔ	66 Ⓐ Ⓑ Ⓒ Ⓓ Ⓔ
7 Ⓐ Ⓑ Ⓒ Ⓓ Ⓔ	27 Ⓐ Ⓑ Ⓒ Ⓓ Ⓔ	47 Ⓐ Ⓑ Ⓒ Ⓓ Ⓔ	67 Ⓐ Ⓑ Ⓒ Ⓓ Ⓔ
8 Ⓐ Ⓑ Ⓒ Ⓓ Ⓔ	28 Ⓐ Ⓑ Ⓒ Ⓓ Ⓔ	48 Ⓐ Ⓑ Ⓒ Ⓓ Ⓔ	68 Ⓐ Ⓑ Ⓒ Ⓓ Ⓔ
9 Ⓐ Ⓑ Ⓒ Ⓓ Ⓔ	29 Ⓐ Ⓑ Ⓒ Ⓓ Ⓔ	49 Ⓐ Ⓑ Ⓒ Ⓓ Ⓔ	69 Ⓐ Ⓑ Ⓒ Ⓓ Ⓔ
10 Ⓐ Ⓑ Ⓒ Ⓓ Ⓔ	30 Ⓐ Ⓑ Ⓒ Ⓓ Ⓔ	50 Ⓐ Ⓑ Ⓒ Ⓓ Ⓔ	70 Ⓐ Ⓑ Ⓒ Ⓓ Ⓔ
11 Ⓐ Ⓑ Ⓒ Ⓓ Ⓔ	31 Ⓐ Ⓑ Ⓒ Ⓓ Ⓔ	51 Ⓐ Ⓑ Ⓒ Ⓓ Ⓔ	71 Ⓐ Ⓑ Ⓒ Ⓓ Ⓔ
12 Ⓐ Ⓑ Ⓒ Ⓓ Ⓔ	32 Ⓐ Ⓑ Ⓒ Ⓓ Ⓔ	52 Ⓐ Ⓑ Ⓒ Ⓓ Ⓔ	72 Ⓐ Ⓑ Ⓒ Ⓓ Ⓔ
13 Ⓐ Ⓑ Ⓒ Ⓓ Ⓔ	33 Ⓐ Ⓑ Ⓒ Ⓓ Ⓔ	53 Ⓐ Ⓑ Ⓒ Ⓓ Ⓔ	73 Ⓐ Ⓑ Ⓒ Ⓓ Ⓔ
14 Ⓐ Ⓑ Ⓒ Ⓓ Ⓔ	34 Ⓐ Ⓑ Ⓒ Ⓓ Ⓔ	54 Ⓐ Ⓑ Ⓒ Ⓓ Ⓔ	74 Ⓐ Ⓑ Ⓒ Ⓓ Ⓔ
15 Ⓐ Ⓑ Ⓒ Ⓓ Ⓔ	35 Ⓐ Ⓑ Ⓒ Ⓓ Ⓔ	55 Ⓐ Ⓑ Ⓒ Ⓓ Ⓔ	75 Ⓐ Ⓑ Ⓒ Ⓓ Ⓔ
16 Ⓐ Ⓑ Ⓒ Ⓓ Ⓔ	36 Ⓐ Ⓑ Ⓒ Ⓓ Ⓔ	56 Ⓐ Ⓑ Ⓒ Ⓓ Ⓔ	76 Ⓐ Ⓑ Ⓒ Ⓓ Ⓔ
17 Ⓐ Ⓑ Ⓒ Ⓓ Ⓔ	37 Ⓐ Ⓑ Ⓒ Ⓓ Ⓔ	57 Ⓐ Ⓑ Ⓒ Ⓓ Ⓔ	77 Ⓐ Ⓑ Ⓒ Ⓓ Ⓔ
18 Ⓐ Ⓑ Ⓒ Ⓓ Ⓔ	38 Ⓐ Ⓑ Ⓒ Ⓓ Ⓔ	58 Ⓐ Ⓑ Ⓒ Ⓓ Ⓔ	78 Ⓐ Ⓑ Ⓒ Ⓓ Ⓔ
19 Ⓐ Ⓑ Ⓒ Ⓓ Ⓔ	39 Ⓐ Ⓑ Ⓒ Ⓓ Ⓔ	59 Ⓐ Ⓑ Ⓒ Ⓓ Ⓔ	79 Ⓐ Ⓑ Ⓒ Ⓓ Ⓔ
20 Ⓐ Ⓑ Ⓒ Ⓓ Ⓔ	40 Ⓐ Ⓑ Ⓒ Ⓓ Ⓔ	60 Ⓐ Ⓑ Ⓒ Ⓓ Ⓔ	80 Ⓐ Ⓑ Ⓒ Ⓓ Ⓔ

Section I: Multiple-Choice Questions

Time: 55 minutes

80 Questions

Percent of total grade = 50%

Directions: Each of the questions or incomplete statements below is followed by five suggested answers or completions. Select the one that is best in each case and then fill in the corresponding oval on the answer sheet.

1. The following were all underlying causes of World War I EXCEPT

   A. various alliances between certain countries

   B. excessive nationalism in Europe

   C. the expansion of armies

   D. the desire of certain countries to spread democracy

   E. an increase of imperialistic competition among Great Britain, France, and Germany

2. Humanism focused on:

   A. the role of God in an individual's life

   B. the importance of the afterlife

   C. worldly and secular themes and the importance of the individual

   D. the use of Latin in education

   E. improving the status of women in society

3. "O my brothers, love your country. There is no true country without a uniform law. . . . And, . . . it is necessary that all should contribute to the making of them. Do not accept any other formula. . . . So long as a single [one?] of your brothers is not represented by his own vote, you have not got a country."

   Which of the following would most likely accept the ideas in this passage?

   A. Giuseppe Mazzini

   B. Camillo Cavour

   C. Victor Emmanuel

   D. Pope Pius IX

   E. Vincenzo Gioberti

GO ON TO THE NEXT PAGE

4. Which of the following statements best describes France in the early eighteenth century?

   A. France was the cultural and intellectual center of Europe.

   B. Other European nations considered France a weak and ineffective nation.

   C. France had been successful in asserting its superiority over England, its chief rival.

   D. The French system of government was among the most innovative in Europe.

   E. The French government was becoming more democratic.

5. Which statement constitutes a major decision reached at the Casablanca Conference?

   A. The United States and England agreed to invade Germany through the soft belly of Europe (Italy).

   B. Germany was demanded to surrender unconditionally.

   C. Meetings were scheduled for the development of the atomic bomb.

   D. Decisions were made as to how to divide Germany at the end of the war.

   E. A program on how to rebuild Europe was discussed.

6. Martin Luther believed salvation comes to an individual

   A. with the help of the clergy

   B. by living a monastic life

   C. with the intervention of a priest

   D. by faith alone

   E. by performing good works

7. The main characteristic of the Enlightenment was

   A. a rejection of traditional authority and a belief that all faith should reside in God

   B. an emphasis that reason and logical thinking could discover the laws that govern the universe

   C. the belief that man is born evil and there is little hope for future progress

   D. the best government is based on the Divine Right Theory of government

   E. a belief that traditional values combined with progress would improve society

8. The fall of Communism in countries such as Poland, Hungary, Czechoslovakia, Bulgaria, and Albania was characterized by

   A. a series of long wars with many casualties

   B. a peaceful transition

   C. treaties signed by each of these countries

   D. intervention by the United States

   E. civil war in these countries

9. All of the following factors contributed to the rise of Absolute rulers in Europe in the fifteenth century EXCEPT

   A. the need for a direct trade route to East Asia

   B. a series of wars between the Italian city-states

   C. the need for capital to finance explorations

   D. Asian and Italian monopolies on existing trade routes

   E. awakening spirit of nationalism

10. Which of the following is not associated with Lenin and the Communist Revolution?

   A. Land, Peace, and Bread

   B. The execution of Nicholas II

   C. The Treaty of Brest Litovsk

   D. War Communism

   E. October Manifesto

11. "Take up the White Man's burden — Send forth the best ye breed — Go bind your sons to exile — To serve your captives' need . . ."

   Which idea does the author of this passage support?

   A. Imperialism

   B. Nationalism

   C. Socialism

   D. Fascism

   E. Totalitarianism

12. Which was a key demand of the Chartists?

   A. compulsory workmen's compensation

   B. nationalizing key industries

   C. Protective Tariff against imported goods

   D. universal manhood suffrage

   E. granting women the right to vote

13. Which of the following was a consequence of the Russo-Japanese War?

   A. Communists became part of the government.

   B. Nicholas II reformed the military.

   C. Nicholas II shared power with the Duma.

   D. Nicholas II signed the October Manifesto establishing a Duma.

   E. Nicholas II granted the Duma greater control of the financial and foreign affairs.

14. Churchill's "Iron Curtain" speech was

   A. Britain's detailed military plan of attack against the Soviet Union

   B. an attempt to persuade the Eastern European nations to join the Western Bloc

   C. a symbol of the growing fear of Communism and the division between the Soviet-dominated states and the Western Bloc

   D. a rebuke of the United States for its leniency towards Communism

   E. a plea to Russia and the United States to attempt compromise

GO ON TO THE NEXT PAGE

15. Which of the following men did not support the unification of Italy?

   A. Bismarck

   B. Pope Pius IX

   C. Victor Emmanuel

   D. Napoleon III

   E. Duke of Parma

16. What was the main goal of Operation Barbarossa?

   A. punishing Stalin for providing help against Great Britain

   B. preventing an attack by the Soviet Union

   C. gaining control of the wheat fields of the Ukraine and the oil fields of the Caucasus

   D. establishing a Nazi Puppet State in Leningrad

   E. securing a water outlet to the east

17. What role did the Duke of Sully play in the rise of absolutism in France?

   A. As minister to Henry IV, he was instrumental in helping the monarch consolidate his power.

   B. He led the people of France in a revolution that, by suppressing the monarch, was able to demonstrate its strength.

   C. He was largely responsible for improving relations between the monarch and the Catholic Church.

   D. He advised Henry IV as to whom he should choose as an heir.

   E. He was a diplomat who maintained positive relations with other European nations.

18. The group of workers in the nineteenth century who opposed industrialization and smashed the machines were

   A. Chartists

   B. Utopian Socialists

   C. Marxists

   D. Capitalists

   E. Luddites

19. All of the following were Renaissance humanists EXCEPT

   A. Francesco Petrarcha

   B. Giovanni Boccaccio

   C. Johannes Gutenberg

   D. Baldassare Castiglione

   E. Pico della Mirandola

20. "I think therefore I am" expresses the philosophy of

   A. Voltaire

   B. Rousseau

   C. Francis Bacon

   D. Rene Descartes

   E. John Locke

21. Which was NOT part of Hitler's platform?

   A. Aryan supremacy

   B. exaggerated nationalism

   C. establishing an alliance with Communism

   D. public works program to reduce unemployment

   E. remilitarizing the German army and navy

22. The major result of the Balkan Crisis of 1912–1913 was

A. An alliance formed between Bulgaria and the Ottoman Empire.

B. France gained control of the Balkan region.

C. Hostility was created towards Austria-Hungary in Serbia and Russia.

D. Those living in Serbia and Austria-Hungary were granted political freedom.

E. A peace agreement was reached between the Balkan League and the Ottoman Empire.

23. (1) Reign of Terror

(2) The *Declaration of the Rights of Man and Citizen*

(3) The Meeting of the Estates General

(4) Tennis Court Oath

(5) Storming of the Bastille

What is the correct order of the above events?

A. 1, 5, 4, 3, 2

B. 3, 2, 5, 4, 1

C. 5, 1, 2, 3, 4

D. 3, 4, 5, 2, 1

E. 2, 3, 4, 4, 1

24. Which of the following statements would Ulrich Zwingli believe but Martin Luther reject?

A. Priests should not have to remain celibate.

B. People should not worship saints.

C. The Bible is the true Christian authority.

D. People should deny all sacraments.

E. The abuses committed by the Roman Catholic Church are intolerable.

25. All of the following contributed to the New Imperialism of the late nineteenth century EXCEPT

A. Western European nations viewed colonies as a market for manufactured goods.

B. Colonies provided raw materials for western European nations.

C. Some Europeans viewed colonies as an area in which to spread Christianity.

D. There was a desire to spread democracy.

E. Owning colonies was a sign of military power.

26. All are symbols of the Age of Metternich EXCEPT

A. Concert of Europe

B. Carlsbad Decree

C. The Six Acts

D. July Ordinances

E. The Boulanger Affair

GO ON TO THE NEXT PAGE

27. Which of the following men outlined guidelines for how a ruler could govern successfully?

   A. Thomas More

   B. Desiderius Erasmus

   C. Niccolo Machiavelli

   D. Montaigne

   E. Lorenza Valla

28. Which of the following was not a part of the *Declaration of the Rights of Man and Citizen?*

   A. Men are born free and equal before the law.

   B. Men are guaranteed freedom of speech, religion, and due process before the law.

   C. Taxes had to be paid according to the ability to pay.

   D. The right to rule rested not only on the king, but also on the general rule of the people.

   E. Feudalism is officially abolished.

29. Which of the following events helped to strengthen the supremacy of the Catholic Church?

   A. the Great Schism

   B. the Babylonian captivity

   C. the sale of indulgences

   D. the Council of Trent

   E. the Peace of Augsburg

30. Which of the following men was NOT an inventor during the early days of the Industrial Revolution?

   A. Thomas Malthus

   B. Eli Whitney

   C. Richard Arkwright

   D. Edmund Cartwright

   E. James Watt

31. The Yalta Conference has been a source of controversy because

   A. It was the first meeting between Stalin and Truman.

   B. Stalin refused to support the United States' war effort against Japan.

   C. Stalin disagreed over where the UN should be located.

   D. The status of free elections in the countries of Eastern Europe was liberated by the Soviet Union.

   E. The British received territory in Africa and the Middle East.

32. The *Massacre of Chios* by Eugene Delacroix glorified which of the following?

   A. the Revolution of 1848

   B. the Greek struggle for independence against the Ottoman Turks

   C. revolutions in Spain and Sardenia in 1830

   D. the election of Louis Napoleon in 1848

   E. the success of the revolutions of Latin America in the 1830s

33. The Schlieffen Plan was

    A. Germany's strategy on how to avoid a prolonged two-front war

    B. Russia's plan to attack Germany's partner, Austria-Hungary

    C. Germany's response to the Balkan crisis

    D. Serbia's declaration of war against Austria

    E. Russia's preparation for war against Serbia

34. The rule of James I created hostility in England because

    A. James refused to reform the Church of England.

    B. The people of England wanted James to be more involved in foreign affairs so that England could assert her superiority over Europe.

    C. The people of England believed that James was not a strong enough leader.

    D. James unfairly taxed the peasants.

    E. James agreed to an alliance with France without consulting with Parliament.

35. In the Crimean War, Cavour's major goal was

    A. to become an ally of Russia

    B. to secure trading rights from Russia

    C. to bring the question of Italian unification to the Peace Conference

    D. to acquire territories from England

    E. to convince Austria that Italian unification was a just cause

36. Which of the following countries was the first to establish a Fascist government in Europe?

    A. Germany

    B. Italy

    C. Spain

    D. Russia

    E. France

37. Which of the following individuals would not be considered part of the Scientific Revolution?

    A. Francis Bacon

    B. Baron de Montesquieu

    C. Rene Descartes

    D. Galileo Galilei

    E. Nicholas Copernicus

38. All of the following countries were involved in the "Scramble for Africa" in the late nineteenth century, EXCEPT

    A. Italy

    B. France

    C. Britain

    D. Austria-Hungary

    E. Portugal

GO ON TO THE NEXT PAGE

39. All of the following are associated with the June Days in Paris in 1848 EXCEPT

    A. class warfare among middle class peasants and the workers

    B. the selection of Louis Napoleon as president in 1848

    C. establishment of national workshops

    D. abdication of King Louis Philippe

    E. intervention by the Concert of Europe to prevent the spread of the revolution

40. Which of the following countries did not acquire territory from China in the late nineteenth century?

    A. Britain

    B. Japan

    C. Russia

    D. Germany

    E. United States

41. Which of the following groups became the spiritual soldiers of the Counter Reformation?

    A. Lutherans

    B. Jesuits

    C. Calvinists

    D. Baptists

    E. Anglicans

42. Olympe de Gouges is best known for

    A. leading the National Assembly

    B. writing the Civil Constitution of the Clergy

    C. writing the *Declaration of the Rights of Woman and Citizen*

    D. writing a series of pamphlets that spread the ideas of the revolution to the lower classes

    E. leading the royal family back to Paris when they had tried to flee the city

43. Which of the following countries was excluded from the conference at Versailles?

    A. Great Britain

    B. France

    C. United States

    D. Russia

    E. Italy

44. "Socialism in One Country" was a slogan coined by

    A. Stalin

    B. Trotsky

    C. Lenin

    D. Marx

    E. Bukharin

45. "Off with the beard!" A Russian cartoon from the late 1700s–early 1800s shows a barber cutting off a Russian nobleman's beard with a pair of scissors. This cartoon symbolizes what?

    A. Catherine the Great's efforts to control the nobles

    B. Europe's efforts to become sanitary

    C. Efforts of the Russian Orthodox Church to enforce a strict way for nobles to appear in public

    D. Peter the Great's efforts to Westernize Russia by making nobles adapt to Western style of dress

    E. a rite of passage of the Russian Orthodox religion

46. The city most influential in introducing intellectual and cultural ideas of the Renaissance was

    A. Paris

    B. Florence

    C. Venice

    D. London

    E. Rome

47. Karl Marx and Friedrich Engels in the *Communist Manifesto* claim that

    A. a Communist revolution would first come to an agricultural country

    B. there would be a worldwide revolution to end the abuses of capitalism

    C. workers of Communism would share in running the state economy

    D. capitalism could be reformed

    E. the proletariat would be the only class to survive the Communist revolution

48. "Kings are God's lieutenants on earth."

    The above quotation represents which type of government?

    A. direct democracy

    B. totalitarianism

    C. republic

    D. rule by Divine Right

    E. limited monarchy

49. What are the correct chronological war moves in the process of Bismarck's drive to unify Germany?

    A. Denmark, Austria, France

    B. France, Austria, Denmark

    C. Austria, Denmark, France

    D. Austria, France, Denmark

    E. France, Denmark, Austria

50. What enabled Great Britain to dominate India from 1763 to 1947?

    A. British respect for Hindu customs

    B. closer cooperation between Muslims and Hindus living in India

    C. British support of home rule

    D. differences in languages and religion created divisions within the population of India

    E. British social reforms

GO ON TO THE NEXT PAGE

51. "Each of us puts his person and all his power in common under the supreme direction of the general will, and . . . whoever refused to obey the general will shall be compelled to do so."

The ideas contained in this passage best represent the views of

A. Thomas Hobbes

B. Jean Jacques Rousseau

C. John Locke

D. Voltaire

E. Montesquieu

52. A major problem of the Weimar Republic was

A. it was primarily a two-party system

B. there was no provision for women suffrage

C. the right of workers to unionize was prohibited by law

D. the inability to effectively solve Germany's economic problems

E. government nationalized all the industries

53. A major result of Bismarck's Kulturkampf in Germany was

A. The Catholic Church was allowed to establish a separate school without government supervision.

B. The state discontinued the requirement that everyone be married before a civil authority.

C. The Jesuits began to open up more schools in Germany.

D. The Catholic Center Party gained strength.

E. The State provided educational funds for Catholic education.

54. Which of the following was NOT a result of England's Glorious Revolution?

A. The Divine Right Theory ended in England.

B. Parliament asserted its supremacy over the monarchy.

C. England adopted both Catholicism and Anglicanism as its official religions.

D. Parliament passed the Bill of Rights.

E. It was the first step towards a constitutional monarchy.

55. Article 231 of the Versailles Treaty resulted in

A. Germany taking sole responsibility for the war

B. establishing the League of Nations

C. creating the new nation of Poland

D. denouncing all secret treaties

E. demilitarizing Germany

56. "I will not accept the crown from the gutter," was a statement uttered in 1848 by

A. Frederich Wilhelm, King of Prussia

B. Louis Philippe, King of France

C. Ferdinand I, King of Austria

D. Alexander I, Tsar of Russia

E. Victor Emmanuel, King of Sardinia

57. "Labour, like all other things which are purchased and sold, . . . has its natural market price. That price which is necessary to enable the labourers . . . to subsist and to perpetuate their race."

This passage is associated with

A. David Ricardo, *The Principles of Political Economy and Taxation*

B. Thomas Malthus, *The Principles of Population*

C. Herbert Spencer, *Principles of Sociology*

D. Adam Smith, *Wealth of Nations*

E. John Stuart Mills, *On Liberty*

58. The Civil Constitution of the Clergy resulted in

A. the end of absolute monarchy in France

B. the church's subjection to state control

C. strengthening the power of the papacy

D. the beheading of Marie Antoinette

E. the restoration of the French absolute monarchy

59. Henry Tudor's (Henry VII) most famous accomplishment was

A. constructing the Versailles Palace in France

B. helping to give rise to the bourgeoisie class

C. establishing the Star Chamber in England

D. helping the House of York in the War of the Roses

E. becoming a patron of the arts

60. The Conservative Party in Great Britain during the 1920s was led by

A. Winston Churchill

B. Stanley Baldwin

C. Arthur Balfour

D. Neville Chamberlain

E. Lloyd George

61. Nicholas I (b. 1796, ruled 1825–1855), Czar of Russia, supported

A. modernization of Russia

B. a liberal constitution for the government

C. emancipation of the serfs

D. orthodoxy, autocracy, and nationalism

E. a policy of tolerance towards non-Russians living in the empire

62. The Meiji Restoration in Japan was characterized by

A. a return to isolation

B. the adaptation of democracy

C. a return to feudalism

D. the abolition of the position of the emperor

E. the modernization and reform of Japan in order for it to compete with Western Powers

GO ON TO THE NEXT PAGE

63. The Romantic poetry of William Wordsworth and William Blake were a reaction against

   A. nationalism

   B. the horrors of the Industrial Revolution and the scientific rationalism of the Enlightenment

   C. democracy

   D. the growing influence of the Catholic Church

   E. growth of labor unions

64. Under Joseph Stalin, the Soviet Union emphasized a Command Economy and a Five Year Plan to primarily

   A. make consumer goods more affordable

   B. encourage farmers to sell more goods on the retail markets

   C. increase its industrial output by developing heavy industry

   D. expand exports to the Western countries

   E. create demands for more imported goods

65. Which was NOT a major characteristic of the Scientific Revolution of the seventeenth century?

   A. growth of a learned society, such as the Royal Society of London

   B. challenged medieval superstition and general acceptance of Aristotle's theories

   C. a widespread growth of knowledge among the general population

   D. a modern scientific method developed that stressed reason over tradition

   E. uncovering much knowledge about the physical world

66. *The Painting of Guernica* by Pablo Picasso was inspired by

   A. the Spanish Civil War (1936–1939)

   B. Hitler's rise to power

   C. Mussolini's rise to power

   D. Italy's invasion of Ethiopia

   E. Nazi-Soviet Non-Aggression Pact

67. All of the following states came into existence after World War I EXCEPT

   A. Albania

   B. Finland

   C. Czechoslovakia

   D. Yugoslavia

   E. Estonia

68. As a result of the Napoleonic Code, women in France

   A. were able to play an active role in the government

   B. were unfairly held in prisons

   C. were able to vote

   D. were able to own property

   E. were given little or no rights

69. All of the following are results of the Franco-Prussian War EXCEPT

   A. Bismarck's policy of Blood and Iron had been successful.

   B. The Second German Empire was created.

   C. France's influence in Europe dating from Louis XIV had ended.

   D. England's fear that Germany would upset the balance of power in Europe.

   E. Bismarck's policy became more lenient toward France.

70. What is the correct chronological order?

   1) The Glorious Revolution in England

   2) James I becomes king of England

   3) Oliver Cromwell becomes Lord Protector of England

   4) Charles I is beheaded

   5) Charles I is restored to power

   A. 5, 3, 4, 2, 1

   B. 2, 4, 3, 5, 1

   C. 4, 3, 2, 1, 5

   D. 1, 5, 4, 3, 2

   E. 3, 4, 2, 1, 5

71. The Tanzit reforms of the nineteenth century in the Ottoman Empire sought to achieve all of the following EXCEPT

   A. equality before the law for Jews, Christians, and Muslims

   B. modernization of the economy

   C. reform the military

   D. establish democracy

   E. halt the growth of nationalism in the empire

72. During the fifteenth century, Ferdinand and Isabella made Spain

   A. a place where people of all religions could reside

   B. a strong royal monarchy by using the church and consolidating royal authority

   C. more isolated from the rest of Europe

   D. less unified than it had been in the medieval ages

   E. a place where aristocratic power was most powerful

73. In his book, *Wealth of Nations,* Adam Smith promoted a belief in

   A. Capitalism

   B. Imperialism

   C. Mercantilism

   D. Communism

   E. Socialism

74. Napoleon's Continental System was

   A. a successful means of defeating Great Britain

   B. a series of military attacks against Austria

   C. economic warfare against Great Britain

   D. a jobs program for France

   E. an improved system of public schools

GO ON TO THE NEXT PAGE

75. All of the following were members of the Quadruple Alliance EXCEPT

A. Prussia

B. Russia

C. Great Britain

D. Spain

E. Austria

76. All of the following were characteristics of Gorbachev's perestroika EXCEPT

A. There was less government planning.

B. Local factory managers received more power.

C. Soviet citizens could operate small retail businesses.

D. Nuclear weapons were disarmed.

E. Farmers were able to sell some of their goods on the free market.

77. All of the following were a major result of the Industrial Revolution EXCEPT

A. establishment of Royal Society of London to spur research

B. growth of capitalism

C. increase in the standard of living

D. rise of the middle class and working class

E. growth of cities

78. The July Revolution of 1830 led to the downfall of the regime of

A. Charles X

B. Louis XVII

C. Louis Napoleon

D. Talleyrand

E. Alphonse La Martine

79. The Dual Monarchy referred to

A. the Kingdom of Two Sicilies

B. Austria-Hungary

C. the United Kingdom of Great Britain and Ireland

D. Piedmont-Sardinia

E. the Papal States

80. Which of the following statements was the result of World War I?

A. Russia became a dominant power replacing Germany.

B. Germany became a democratic republic.

C. The Ottoman Empire expanded its territories.

D. Germany underwent an economic revival.

E. The United States recognized the Soviet Union as the legitimate Government of the country.

EUROPEAN HISTORY

SECTION II

Part A

(Suggested writing time — 45 minutes)

Percent of Section II score — 45

Directions: The following question is based on the accompanying Documents 1–10. (Some of the documents have been edited for the purpose of this exercise.) This question is designed to test your ability to work with historical documents. As you analyze the documents, take into account both the sources of the documents and the authors' points of view. Write an essay on the following topic that integrates your analysis of the documents. **Do not simply summarize the documents individually.** You may refer to relevant historical facts and developments not mentioned in the documents.

1. Discuss and analyze the causes of the New Imperialism.

Historical Background: By the early part of the nineteenth century it appeared that the countries of Europe had lost interest in building overseas empires. However, the last third of the nineteenth century saw a new scramble for colonies. Britain, France, Germany, Belgium, Italy, and Portugal engaged in a race to annex the undeveloped areas of the world. By 1914, one-third of the world's people were under colonial control with the countries of Europe holding the lion's share.

Document 1

All great nations in the fullness of their strength have desired to set their mark upon barbarian lands. All over the globe today we see the peoples of Europe creating a mighty aristocracy of the white races. Those who take no share in this great rivalry will play a pitiable part in time to come. . . . It is a sound and normal trait in a civilized nation to avert the existing dangers of over-population by colonization on a large scale. This puts no check upon nature, and . . . augments the national strength of the mother country at the same time.

Source: Heinrich von Treitschke, *Politics* (1897)

GO ON TO THE NEXT PAGE

Document 2

No one in France . . . doubts the benefits of colonization and the advantages which it offers both to the country which undertakes it and to that which receives it. Everyone agrees that colonies offer markets for raw materials, the means of production, the products lacking to the mother-country; that they open markets to all the commerce and all the industries of an old country, by the wants, by the new needs of the people with whom they are in relation. . . .

Source: The French Society of Colonial and Maritime Studies, 1876. A. Murphy, *The Ideology of French Imperialism*, Catholic University, 1948.

Document 3

Take up the White Man's burden —
    Send forth the best ye breed —
Go bind your sons to exile
    To serve your captives' need;
To wait in heavy harness
    On fluttered folk and wild —
Your new-caught, sullen peoples,
    Half devil and half child.

Source: Rudyard Kipling, British poet, *The White Man's Burden* (1899).

Document 4

In the area of economics, I am placing before you . . . the need for outlets. Why? Because next door Germany is setting up trade barriers; because across the ocean the United States of America have become protectionists . . .; because not only are those great markets shrinking . . . but these great states are beginning to pour into our own markets products not seen there before. . . . We must say openly that indeed the higher races have a right over the lower races. . . . They have the duty to civilize the inferior races . . . I say that French colonial policy, the policy of colonial expansion . . . was inspired by the fact that a navy such as ours cannot do without safe harbors, defenses, supply centers on the high seas . . . At present, as you know, a warship . . . cannot carry more than two weeks' supply of coal. . . . Hence the need to have places of supply, shelters, ports for defense and provisioning . . . .

Source: Jules Ferry, "Speech Before the French Chamber of Deputies," March 28, 1884.

Document 5

We . . . must recognize that in order that we may have more employment to give we must create more demand. Give me the demand for more goods and then I will undertake to give plenty of employment in making the goods; and the only thing, in my opinion, that the government can do in order to meet this great difficulty . . . , is so to arrange its policy that . . . new markets shall be created, and that old markets shall be effectually developed. . . . For these reasons, . . . I would never lose the hold which we now have over our great Indian dependency, by far the greatest and most valuable of all the customers we have or ever shall have in this country. For the same reasons I approve of the continued occupation of Egypt, and for the same reasons I have urged upon this government, and upon previous governments, the necessity for using every legitimate opportunity to extend our influence and control in that great African continent which is now being opened up to civilization and to commerce.

Source: Joseph Chamberlain, British Secretary of State for the colonies, 1893. *The Imperialism Reader,* edited by Richard M. Brace, D. Von Nostrand Company, Inc., 1962.

Document 6

In spite of the fact that we have no such fleet as we should have, we have conquered for ourselves a place in the sun. It will now be my task to see to it that this place in the sun shall remain our undisputed possession, in order that the sun's rays may fall fruitfully upon our activity and trade in foreign parts, that our industry and agriculture may develop within the state and our sailing sports upon the water for our future lies upon the water. The more Germans go out upon the water, whether it be in races or regattas, whether it be in journeys across the ocean, or in the service of the battle flag, so much the better it will be for us.

Source: Kaiser Wilhelm II of Germany: Speech to the North German Regatta Association, 1901.

Document 7

It seems to me that God, with infinite wisdom and skill, is training the Anglo-Saxon race for an hour sure to come in the world's future . . . The unoccupied arable lands of the earth are limited, and will soon be taken . . .Then will the world center upon a new stage of its history — *the final competition of races, for which the Anglo-Saxon is being schooled.* . . . Then this race of unequalled energy . . . the representative, let us hope, of the largest liberty, the purest Christianity, the highest civilization . . . will spread itself over the earth. . . . And can any one doubt that the result of this competition of races will be the "survival of the fittest"?

Source: Josiah Strong, American Protestant Minister, *Our Country: Its Possible Future and Its Present Crisis* (1885).

Document 8

I contend that we (Britons) are the finest race in the world, and the more of the world we inhabit, the better it is for the human race. . . . It is our duty to seize every opportunity of acquiring more territory and we should keep this one idea steadily before our eyes that more territory simply means more of the Anglo-Saxon race, more of the best, the most human, most honourable race the world possesses.

Source: Cecil Rhodes, a British Imperialist, *Confessions of Faith,* 1877.

GO ON TO THE NEXT PAGE

Section ▮ Free-Response Essays

Document 9

. . . In order to keep your forty millions here from eating each other for lack of other victuals, we beyond the seas must keep open as much of the surface of this planet as we can for the overflow of your population to inhabit and . . . create markets where you can dispose of the produce of your factories and of your mines. The Empire, I am always telling you, is a bread-and-butter question. If you have not to be cannibals, you have got to be Imperialists."

Source: W. T. Stead, an English journalist, *A History of Mystery,* 1897.

Document 10

. . . Imperialism is often confused with commerce or with the opening of commercial markets. . . . Imperialism means something quite different from the sale of purchase of commodities. It entails a profound action on a people and a territory, providing the inhabitants with some education and regular justice, teaching them the division of labour and the uses of capital when they are ignorant of these things. It opens an area not only to the merchandise of the mother country, but to its capital and its savings, to its engineers, to its overseers, to its emigrants. . . . Such a transformation of a barbarian country cannot be accomplished by simple commercial relations.

Source: Paul Leroy Beaulieu, a French imperialist (1891) Ref.: S. Pollard et al, *Documents of European Economic History,* Vol. 2, Edward Arnold, 1968.

EUROPEAN HISTORY

SECTION II

Part B

(Suggested planning and writing time — 70 minutes)

Percent of Section II score — 55

Directions: You are to answer TWO questions, one from each group of three questions below. Make your selections carefully, choosing the questions that you are best prepared to answer thoroughly in the time permitted. You should spend 5 minutes organizing or outlining each essay. In writing your essays, use specific examples to support your answer. If time permits when you finish writing, check your work. Be certain to number your answers as the questions are numbered below.

Group 1

Choose ONE question from this group. The suggested writing time for this question is 30 minutes. You are advised to spend 5 minutes planning your answer in the area below.

1. Compare and contrast the religious ideas of Martin Luther and John Calvin.

2. Discuss and analyze the ideas of John Locke and Jean Jacques Rousseau.

3. Discuss and assess Peter the Great's (1682–1725) success in trying to modernize Russia.

Group 2

Choose ONE question from this group. The suggested writing time for this question is 30 minutes. You are advised to spend 5 minutes planning your answer in the area below.

1. Historians have claimed that the Versailles Treaty laid the seeds of distrust that caused World War II. Evaluate to what extent this statement is accurate.

2. Discuss and analyze the causes of the Cold War.

3. Karl Marx wrote that all of history was a class struggle. Discuss and analyze Marx's view of historical development.

273

Answer Key for Practice Test I

Section I: Multiple-Choice Questions

1. D	21. C	41. B	61. D
2. C	22. C	42. C	62. E
3. A	23. D	43. D	63. B
4. A	24. D	44. A	64. C
5. B	25. D	45. D	65. C
6. D	26. E	46. B	66. A
7. B	27. C	47. B	67. A
8. B	28. E	48. D	68. E
9. B	29. D	49. A	69. E
10. E	30. A	50. D	70. B
11. A	31. D	51. B	71. D
12. D	32. B	52. D	72. B
13. D	33. A	53. D	73. A
14. C	34. A	54. C	74. C
15. B	35. C	55. A	75. D
16. C	36. B	56. A	76. D
17. A	37. B	57. A	77. A
18. E	38. D	58. B	78. A
19. C	39. E	59. C	79. B
20. D	40. E	60. B	80. B

Section II: Free-Response Essays

Student essays and analysis appear beginning on page 288.

Answers and Explanations for Practice Test I

Section I: Multiple-Choice Questions

1. **D.** The desire of certain countries to spread democracy was not an underlying cause of World War I. The Alliance System dividing Europe into armed camps between the Triple Alliance and the Triple Entente raised tensions. The excessive nationalism of minority groups in the Balkans divided the Austrian-Hungarian Empire and Russia. The buildup of the armed forces in Germany and England as well as the rivalry in Africa over colonies created the causes that led to World War I. The European countries wanted to protect the balance of power and not spread political ideology.

2. **C.** Humanism focused on worldly and secular themes and the importance of the individual. Humanism was a literary movement that began in Italy during the fourteenth century and stressed that secular subjects were just as important as religious themes. Humanists believed that man had unlimited potential and glorified his abilities; they idealized the importance of God and the afterlife but that was not their main focus. Many Humanists stressed the use of the vernacular, not Latin, and made little effort to focus on the status of women in society.

3. **A.** Giuseppe Mazzini supported the idea stated in this passage. Mazzini was the founder of Young Italy, a nationalist organization that wanted to unite Italy by expelling Austria from Italy. He favored a democratic republican government for Italy. Cavour, prime minister of Piedmont-Sardinia, favored a constitutional monarchy with Victor Emmanuel as king. Pope Pius IX opposed unification of Italy. Vincenzo Gioberti wanted a united Italy with a confederation type of government.

4. **A.** In the early eighteenth century, France was the cultural center of Europe and it was the home of the Enlightenment. French was the international language, and France was the most populous nation with a population of 25.5 million people. French exports were greater than those of Great Britain. Although France was not considered a weak nation, it had never been successful in defeating Great Britain during the long reign of Louis XIV. The French government was not innovative, and still functioned as a Medieval Society referred to as the Old Regime. The French government was an absolute monarchy and little effort was made to become more democratic until the French Revolution in 1789.

5. **B.** In January 1943, Roosevelt and Churchill met at Casablanca where they agreed to demand the unconditional surrender of the Axis countries. They made this public announcement because Stalin was fearful that the Allies would sign a separate treaty with Germany. Roosevelt and Churchill also agreed to launch an invasion of Italy through Sicily. They knew that Stalin wanted a second front in Europe against France to take the pressure off Russia, which Churchill felt was carrying the brunt of the war. The other answer choices are wrong for the following reasons: Roosevelt and Churchill did not agree to invade Germany; Russia was never informed at any of the conferences about the United States' development of the atomic bomb; Churchill, Stalin, and Roosevelt discussed the division of Germany at the Teheran and Yalta Conferences, not in Casablanca; and there was never any discussion on a rebuilding program at any of these conferences.

6. D. Martin Luther believed that salvation was achieved by faith alone. He considered the Bible the final authority and he urged each individual to read and interpret it. Luther rejected the intervention of saints, priests, the monastic life, and good works. He believed that each person should serve God in his or her own way.

7. B. A major characteristic of the Enlightenment was an emphasis that man — through reason and logical thinking — could discover the laws that govern the universe and that all laws of society and human nature could be explained by using rationality. Enlightenment thinkers rejected authority, and put faith in reason, not in God. They were optimists and rejected divine theory. They justified absolute rule by asserting that the king ruled because he ruled in the people's interest. The Enlightenment also valued progress over traditional values.

8. B. The fall of Communism in Poland, Hungary, Czechoslovakia, Bulgaria, and Albania was characterized by a peaceful transition and peaceful free elections, which took place between 1989 and 1991. These countries did not sign treaties with each other nor did the United States intervene. Civil war did not break out in any of these countries with the exception of Romania where there was political violence and casualties.

9. B. A series of wars between the Italian city-states did not contribute to the rise of absolute rulers in Europe in the fifteenth century. Divided into many different republics such as Florence, Venice, and Genoa, Italy was subjected to invasion throughout the fifteenth and sixteenth centuries. The need for direct trade routes to Asia and the need for capital in order to break the monopoly of the Italian/Asian states forced countries to centralize power in a king or queen, leading to national states or absolute monarchies. The awakening spirit of nationalism also helped increase the power of the rulers as a rallying point.

10. E. Lenin is not associated with the October Manifesto. In 1905, Czar Nicholas II issued the October Manifesto after the events known as Bloody Sunday. On Sunday, January 22, 1905, workers organized by Father Gapon, marched to present a petition to the czar at his winter palace in St. Petersburg. Nicholas II ordered his soldiers to fire on the crowd resulting in the death of hundreds. Bloody Sunday led to scattered uprisings across the nation, and eventually forced Nicholas II to make changes. In the October Manifesto, Nicholas II promised to create a lawmaking body, the Duma, and guarantee civil liberties. Lenin was not in Russia at the time of the October Manifesto. He was in Switzerland. In 1917, Lenin used the slogan, "Land, Peace, and Bread," to attract the support of the people and signed the Treaty of Brest Litovsk in 1918 to end Russia's participation in World War I. He also introduced the policy of War Communism in 1918 and ordered the execution of the czar in that same year.

11. A. Imperialism is the idea supported by Rudyard Kipling, the author of the passage. Kipling, like other Europeans, believed that it was the obligation of the Europeans to spread civilization to the uncivilized. The belief in the superiority of European civilization led to Imperialism, and missionaries believed that European control would help spread religion. Nationalism is a belief that each group of people is entitled to its own nation or government. Socialism is a system in which the government owns and operates all essential means of production, distribution, and exchange of goods. Fascism is a totalitarian system of government that glorifies the nation over the individual.

12. **D.** A key demand of the Chartists in Great Britain was universal manhood suffrage. In the People's Charter of 1838, from which the movement derived its name, city workers wanted to extend the franchise (voting rights); the 1838 Charter failed to achieve the Chartists' goals but eventually all of their demands, such as secret ballots, were passed by the beginning of the twentieth century. The Chartists were opposed to giving women the right to vote and their platform focused upon political reform not social changes such as workmen's compensation, nationalizing key industries, and protective tariffs.

13. **D.** One consequence of the Russo-Japanese War was that Nicholas II signed the October Manifesto establishing a Duma. Russia's defeat in the Russo-Japanese War led to widespread demand for reforms. When the czar's army fired on the crowds that demonstrated at the winter palace in St. Petersburg for shorter working hours and more representatives in government, (an event that became known as Bloody Sunday), the czar was forced to sign the October Manifesto providing for the creation of a lawmaking body, the Duma, elected by universal male suffrage as well as a guarantee of civil liberties. However, the Duma had little control over finances and foreign affairs. In 1906, Nicholas II dissolved the Duma and by the beginning of World War I, the Duma was like a debating society with little power. Nicholas II did not reform the military because he depended upon it for support. The Communists were not a major political influence in 1905 and would not gain many followers until World War I. Nicholas II did not really believe in sharing power with the Duma. The Duma could debate and pass laws, but the czar had the final power of veto.

14. **C.** Churchill's "Iron Curtain" speech, given in Fulton, Missouri, in 1946, was a symbol of the growing fear and division between the Soviet dominated states and the Western Bloc. It proclaimed that an Iron Curtain had descended over Eastern Europe and that Europe was divided between those who were controlled by the Soviet Union and those who followed the West led by the United States. This symbolic Iron Curtain divided Europe for 43 years until Communism collapsed in 1989. Churchill's speech was designed to create an awareness about the dangers of Communism; it was not a military plan, nor was it intended to persuade Eastern European countries to join the Western Bloc; furthermore, it was not a rebuke to the United States or a plea for compromise.

15. **B.** Pope Pius IX did not support Italian unification; he opposed the unification of Italy because he was afraid that it would end his temporal, or civil rule, over the Papal States. Bismarck supported Italian unification as a way to weaken Austrian influence and gain an ally in Prussia in the struggle for independence. Victor Emmanuel II was king of Piedmont-Sardinia who would become the first king of a United Italy in 1861. Napoleon III supported Italian unification because by fighting reactionary Austrians he would pacify the French liberals, whom he was suppressing. The Duchy of Parma voted for annexation to Sardinia after the people of Parma drove out the Austrians in 1860.

16. **C.** The main goal of Operation Barbarossa was to gain control of the wheat fields of the Ukraine and the oil fields of the Caucasus. By 1941, Hitler realized that he would be unable to defeat Great Britain and needed the wheat from the Ukraine and the oil from the Caucasus to enable him to carry on the war in the future. Stalin had no obligation to assist Hitler in the Battle of Britain and had no intention of attacking Germany, nor did Hitler want to establish a Puppet State in Leningrad. Hitler needed the resources of Russia; however, conquering Russia provided Germany with a land empire not a water outlet.

17. A. The Duke of Sully was instrumental in helping Henry IV in consolidating his power. Sully was a financial genius who reduced the debt by reforming the tax system. He constructed roads that improved transportation and promoted economic prosperity; he also strengthened the power of the monarchs by limiting the power of the nobles over the parliament. Sully did not lead a revolution in France nor did he have any control over who would be the heir to Henry IV. Henry IV and Sully's relationship with other European nations did not contribute to absolutism in France, and Henry IV and Sully had established peace with the Church when the king converted to Catholicism.

18. E. The Luddites were a group of nineteenth-century handicraft workers in northern England who opposed industrialization and smashed machinery, believing that the new machines were putting them out of work. Chartists were reformers in Great Britain who wanted to extend the franchise to city workers. Utopian Socialists and Marxists wanted to destroy the capitalist system by creating an ideal society or establishing Communism. Capitalists were the factory owners.

19. C. Johannes Gutenberg was a German who invented the movable print type in 1450, which increased the output of books. Francesco Petrarch, Giovanni Boccaccio, Baldassare Castiglione, and Pico della Mirandola were all Italian humanist writers of the Renaissance.

20. D. Rene Descartes expressed the view "I think therefore I am." Descartes was a French mathematician and philosopher who stressed inductive reasoning. His famous quote proved his belief in his own existence. Descartes' ideas promoted the Scientific Revolution. Voltaire and Rousseau were philosophers who attacked the abuses of society in order to change unjust conditions; Francis Bacon was an Englishman who promoted the scientific method, and John Locke was an English philosopher who wrote *Two Treatises on Government*, defending the Glorious Revolution in England.

21. C. Hitler's platform did not include establishing an alliance with Communism. By 1930, the Communists polled over six million votes and German Conservatives feared a Communist revolution. Hitler blamed the Communists for the Reichstag fire in February 1933, and he and the Nazi Party promised to fight Communism. Hitler's platform appealed to Aryan supremacy and his National Socialist Party provided for an extensive public works program to help the country out of the depression. Hitler also promised to remilitarize the army and navy as a way to show the Nazi Party's disdain for the Versailles Treaty.

22. C. The Balkan Crisis of 1912–13 created hostility in Serbia and Russia towards Austria-Hungary. In 1912, Serbia's dispute with Bulgaria over the spoils of war after they had joined together to defeat the Ottoman Empire led to Russia backing Serbia but Austria (supported by Germany), denying Serbia's goal of getting an outlet on the Adriatic Sea. Austria's approach reflected her fear of Russian influence in the Balkans and the greater fear that it would cause unrest among Serbians and other Slavic people in the Austria-Hungarian Empire. The Balkan Crisis did not result in political freedom for Serbians living in the Austria-Hungarian Empire: Austria continued to exercise control of the Serbians in order to dominate the many other ethnic groups living in its multinational empire. There was no alliance between Bulgaria and the Ottoman Empire; Bulgaria had defeated the Ottoman Empire in 1912. France was not involved in the Balkan Crisis of 1912–13.

23. D. The correct chronological order is: Meeting of the Estates General — May 1789; the Tennis Court Oath — June 1789; the Storming of the Bastille — July 14, 1789; the Declaration of the Rights of Man and Citizen — August 26, 1789; and the Reign of Terror — for 1793–94.

24. D. Martin Luther would reject Ulrich Zwingli's statement denying all sacraments. Luther, unlike Zwingli, believed in the sacraments of Baptism, Communion, and Penance. Zwingli denied all seven sacraments. Both accepted no celibacy for the priests, opposed the worshipping of saints, and regarded the Bible as the final authority.

25. D. The desire to spread democracy was not a factor that contributed to the New Imperialism. Instead, the New Imperialism was promoted by the Industrial Revolution. Colonies were considered a market for the manufacture of goods and a source of raw materials. Missionaries saw colonies as a way to spread Christianity to those who they believed had no religion. Many nations saw colonies as a symbol that their country had achieved a "place in the sun" as a military power.

26. E. The Boulanger Affair occurred in 1886–1889, 38 years after the Age of Metternich (1848). Boulanger was a general, favoring the monarchy, who tried to seize control of the Third Republic but failed. The Concert of Europe, the Carlsbad Decree in Austria, the Six Acts in England, and the July Ordinances in France were efforts to control the spread of democracy and nationalism. These terms are associated with the Age of Metternich.

27. C. Niccolo Machiavelli wrote *The Prince* in 1513 to provide guidelines for rulers who wanted to be successful. The book focused on how a ruler could maintain power by adapting the slogan "the end justifies the means." Machiavelli's ideal ruler had to be both a fox and a lion. Erasmus was a Dutch humanist who criticized the abuses of the church. Thomas More was an Englishman who wrote *Utopia*. Montaigne was a French writer and Lorenza Valla was an Italian humanist.

28. E. The *Declaration of the Rights of Man and Citizen* in France did not abolish feudalism. It was based on the principles of Enlightenment and the American Declaration of Independence. The National Assembly formed on August 4, 1789 ended feudalism by abolishing all special privileges of the nobles, such as their exemption from taxes. The *Declaration of the Rights of Man and Citizen* established equality before the law, civil liberties, and equitable distribution of taxation. It also limited the power of the monarchy.

29. D. The Council of Trent (1545–1563) strengthened the supremacy of the Catholic Church, reaffirming the dogma of the Church and contributing to the Catholic Church's effort to combat Protestants. It re-established the power of the Church by eliminating abuses such as simony and the sale of indulgences, which many people, including Luther, thought were corrupting the Church. The Jesuits became the spiritual leaders of the Council of Trent or Counter Reformation. The Great Schism and the Babylonian Captivity undermined the power of the papacy by quarreling over who should be pope. The Peace of Augsburg allowed the king to decide the religion of his people.

30. A. Thomas Malthus was not an inventor. He was an economist who believed that the population growth was increasing faster than the food supply. All of the other men were inventors: Eli Whitney — cotton gin; Richard Arkwright — water frame; Edmund Cartwright — power loom; James Watt — steam engine.

31. **D.** The Yalta Conference, held in February 1945, has been a source of controversy during the Cold War because of the status of free elections in the countries of Eastern Europe liberated by the Soviet Union. Roosevelt made concessions to Stalin by agreeing to allow him to hold free elections in the areas he controlled. Stalin gave a verbal agreement to allow elections but he rejected the suggestion of international supervision of these elections. Stalin's violation of the promise of self-determination for these countries became a source of friction between the United States and Russia, which contributed to the Cold War. The Teheran Conference was the first meeting of the Big Three. At Yalta, Stalin did agree to support the United States' declaration of war against Japan and there was no disagreement about the location of the United Nations. The status of British territory in Africa and the Middle East was not an issue at Yalta.

32. **B.** The *Massacre of Chios* by Eugene Delacroix glorified the Greek struggle for independence against the Ottoman Empire. The Greek struggle for freedom won the enthusiastic support of liberal nationalists and romantics such as Delacroix. He was the founder of the Romantic School of Painting. His painting illustrates the idealistic conception of the revolutionaries who are being oppressed by the Turks. Delacroix never painted any works of any revolutions in Spain, Sardenia, and Latin America. He also never painted the election of Louis Napoleon in 1848.

33. **A.** The Schlieffen Plan was Germany's strategy on how to avoid a prolonged two-front war. Under the Schlieffen Plan, German forces would sweep through France through Belgium and then turn to defeat Russia in the East. The plan was to knock off France within six weeks and then to transport troops to the eastern front to help the Austrians against the Russians. The plan did not consider any Russian action against Austria-Hungary nor was Serbia or the Balkans part of the strategy. The Schlieffen Plan was based on the premise that the Russian army would be slow to mobilize and thus give Germany enough time to defeat France quickly.

34. **A.** The rule of James I created hostility in England because he refused to reform the Church of England. James I antagonized the Puritans, a powerful Calvinist sect that considered the Church of England or Anglicanism too close to Catholicism and tried to change Anglican practices. The criticism of James I's foreign policy was that it was too pro-Catholic, not about England's involvement. James I angered people because he tried to rule by divine right. He created resentment because he tried to raise taxes without the consent of Parliament, which was mainly middle class, not peasants. James I did not have an alliance with Spain, but was friendly towards Spain.

35. **C.** Cavour's major goal in the Crimean War was to raise the issue of Italian unification at the Peace Conference. Cavour took Piedmont into the war against Russia with the hope of winning a place at the peace table in order to address the issue of Italian unification. Cavour did not become an ally of Russia nor did he receive trading rights and territories from England. He entered the war on the side of England and France and his goal was to unify Italy. Cavour realized that Austria would never agree to unification unless Piedmont-Sardinia received the support from other European powers such as France, Prussia, and England.

36. **B.** Italy was the first country to establish a Fascist dictator in 1922. Fascism (Nazism) was established in Germany in 1933 and Spain's Fascist regime was established in 1939. Russia set up a Communist regime in 1917. Fascism was never established as the main government in France.

37. **B.** Baron de Montesquieu should not be considered as part of the Scientific Revolution because he was a philosopher who wrote *The Spirit of the Law,* which describes how power of the government should be limited. Francis Bacon, Rene Descartes, Galileo Galilei, and Nicholas Copernicus all made important contributions to the Scientific Revolution.

38. **D.** Austria-Hungary never became involved in the partition of Africa during the period from 1870 to 1914. Italy, France, Portugal, and Great Britain all had colonies in Africa.

39. **E.** The Concert of Europe never intervened to prevent the spread of revolution in Paris in June of 1848; it had disbanded by that time. By 1820, England had withdrawn and Metternich was forced to flee Austria during its 1848 revolution. The June Days led to the abdication of Louis Philippe and the establishment of the Second French Republic with Louis Napoleon elected president. During the June Days in Paris, class warfare broke out among the workers, the peasants, and the middle class, who feared the radical Socialist demands and thought the national workshops were a waste of money.

40. **E.** The United States never acquired any territory in China in the nineteenth century. The United States was interested in China for trade. The United States believed that the European division of China would threaten the ability of the country to openly trade with China. In 1900, the United States issued the Open Door Policy which proposed that all nations be allowed to trade freely with China. Great Britain gained control of Hong Kong and areas near the Yangtze River. Japan gained control of Southern Manchuria after the Russo-Japanese War. Russia extended influence over Manchuria. Germany acquired a sphere of influence in Northeastern China over the Shantung Peninsula.

41. **B.** The Jesuits were the spiritual soldiers of the Counter Reformation. Founded by Ignatius Loyola, a former Spanish soldier and nobleman, the Jesuits were organized along military lines and were trained in education and philosophy. They revived the Inquisition to suppress heresy and reassert the dominance of Catholicism. Lutherans, Calvinists, Baptists, and Anglicans were Protestant sects that broke away form the Catholic Church.

42. **C.** Olympe de Gouges is best known for writing the *Declaration of the Rights of Woman and Citizen.* Women, she argued, suffered from double deprivation by the state and by their husbands and fathers. She criticized the male dominance of the French National Assembly for not doing anything about it, insisting that women should have the same rights as men. Olympe de Gouges was guillotined in 1793 as a victim of the Reign of Terror. She was never involved with the National Assembly nor did she write the Civil Constitution of the Clergy. She wrote primarily for the upper classes and was not associated with the royal family's march to Paris.

43. **D.** Russia was excluded from the Peace Conference at Versailles. In 1917, the Bolsheviks had established a Communist government in Russia and withdrew from the war in 1918. The Big Four — Great Britain, France, the United States, and Italy — attended the Versailles Conference. Italy walked out when the other countries refused to honor its agreement about its demands for territories from Austria-Hungary.

44. **A.** "Socialism in One Country" was a slogan coined by Stalin. Joseph Stalin believed that the Bolsheviks should build up Communism in Russia by making it stronger and improving conditions in the country before exporting worldwide revolutions. Trotsky believed that for Communism to be successful there had to be permanent revolutions

around the world. Lenin is associated with the slogan "Land, Peace, and Bread" and used this appeal to gain power in 1917. Marx believed that Communist revolutions had to be worldwide to ensure success. Bukharin was a conservative and wanted to extend the New Economic Policy and restore more private enterprise.

45. D. This cartoon represents Peter the Great's efforts to Westernize Russia by making nobles adapt to western style of dress. He was determined to introduce new techniques and ideas from Western Europe to make Russia stronger. Peter wanted to replace the old-fashioned robes of the Russian noblemen and also insisted that they shave their beards. During his reign from 1682–1725, Peter brought technical experts, teachers, and soldiers to help Russia achieve his goal of modernization. The cartoon doesn't symbolize any of the other choices.

46. B. Florence was the intellectual and cultural center of the Renaissance. Florence's Medici family, who had become wealthy from trading and banking, became patrons of the arts and were instrumental in luring people of talent to the city. Although Venice was a major trading center, it never became a cultural center in Italy; likewise, Rome was the center of the Catholic Church but not an intellectual and cultural center. Paris and London did not become cultural and intellectual centers until the seventeenth and eighteenth centuries.

47. B. Karl Marx and Friedrich Engels in the *Communist Manifesto* claimed that there would be a worldwide revolution to end the abuses of capitalism. They believed that history was a class struggle between the have's and have-not's, and that in the last stage of this struggle, the proletariat will rise and overthrow capitalism. They also believed that Communism would only come to industrial nations like Great Britain or the United States, not agricultural countries. Under pure Communism, the *Communist Manifesto* states, there would be no state, and society would be classless. Revolution against capitalism was inevitable because the workers were too oppressed and capitalism was doomed to extinction, not reform.

48. D. This quotation represents a government ruled by Divine Right. Divine Right is a belief that kings or queens receive all power from God to rule directly. Direct democracy, totalitarianism, republics, and limited monarchies do not claim that God is their source of political power.

49. A. The correct chronological order in Bismarck's drive to unify Germany is the Danish War — 1864; Austro Prussian War — 1866; and the Franco Prussian War — 1870–1871. Denmark must be first in any correct chronological sequence.

50. D. The people of India were divided linguistically among more than a dozen main languages and over 200 dialects. These differences between Hindus and Muslims also divided the population. In addition, India was divided into many independent states, each headed by its own prince. Britain used the principle of divide and conquer. The British did not respect Hindu customs. They outlawed the practice of suttee and other customs which they considered barbaric. There was little cooperation between Muslims and Hindus living in India. Mohammed Ali Jinnah founded the Muslim League in order to protect the rights of Muslims living in India. The British did not support home rule and British social reforms were not enough for India's needs.

51. **B.** The ideas contained in this passage best represent the views of Jean Jacques Rousseau. Rousseau wrote the *Social Contract* in which he stated that people create a government to protect each other from the inequalities that arise in society. The people submit to the general will, or the will of the majority, and this general will is supreme. Government enforces the general will as an absolute power or unlimited power. Rousseau believed that if a government failed, the people had the right to overthrow it. However, dictatorships used Rousseau's concept of general will to justify their governments. Thomas Hobbes, who wrote *The Leviathan,* defended royal absolutism and claimed that the people do not have the right to change the government. John Locke, Voltaire, and Montesquieu admired the British system of government. John Locke's *Two Treatises* provided for a government based on a social contract, but Locke was more concerned with individual rights and limits on the power of the government.

52. **D.** A major problem of the Weimar Republic was its inability to effectively solve Germany's economic problems. Until 1923, the Weimar Republic, instead of raising taxes, printed excessive quantities of paper money. This policy led to spiraling inflation where a loaf of bread cost 10,000 marks. The inflation hurt the middle class as savings and pensions became worthless. The Great Depression of 1929 created more havoc, putting over six million Germans out of work, adding to the perception that the Weimar Republic could not solve the nation's economic problems. The Weimar Republic had many different parties such as Communist, Socialist, Democratic, National-Socialist (Nazis), and a variety of minor parties. The Nazis gained a strong following by promising to improve the economy. In the Weimar Republic, women were allowed to vote and workers could unionize, but no industries were nationalized.

53. **D.** A major result of Bismarck's Kulturkampf in Germany was that the Catholic Center Party gained strength. In 1872, Bismarck launched his Kulturkampf, or battle for civilization, in which he required Catholics to put their allegiance to the state before the church. His attack on the church rallied its members, enabling the Catholic Center Party to gain strength in the Reichstag. A realist, Bismarck saw his mistake and made peace with the Church. Bismarck's Kulturkampf required that the state had the right to supervise Catholic education and they could not set up separate schools. The state required, and did not discontinue, the practice that everyone be married before a civil authority. Bismarck expelled the Jesuits from Germany.

54. **C.** As a result of the Glorious Revolution, England did not adopt both Catholicism and Anglicanism as her official religions. The Glorious Revolution, however, resulted in the passage of the Bill of Rights, which required all English rulers to be Anglicans. Catholicism and other religions were granted freedom of worship by the Toleration Act of 1689. The Bill of Rights of 1689 ensured the supremacy of Parliament over the monarchy, ended the Divine Right Theory, and laid the foundation for a constitutional monarchy in England.

55. **A.** Article 231 of the Versailles Treaty resulted in Germany taking sole responsibility for the war. Germany was also required to pay all war costs including civilian damages, pensions to widows, and others in the Allied countries. The establishment of the League of Nations, the creation of Poland, and the demilitarization of Germany are all contained in the Versailles Treaty but not in Article 231. The Versailles Treaty did not have a provision for denouncing all secret treaties.

56. A. Frederick William IV, King of Prussia, made this statement in 1849 when the Frankfurt Assembly offered him the crown of a united Germany. William was fearful that acceptance of the crown might lead to war with Austria. The King's refusal ended the Frankfurt Assembly, which had prepared a liberal constitution for a united Germany. None of the other monarchs were associated with the events of the Frankfurt Assembly.

57. A. This passage is associated with David Ricardo's *The Principles of Economy and Taxation*. Ricardo's main point was that labor was guided by the Iron Hand of wages, which included the belief that large families led to an increased supply of labor that lowers wages and raises unemployment. Malthus wrote about the fear of overpopulation. Herbert Spencer, a nineteenth-century English philosopher, wrote *The Principles of Sociology*. In this work, Spencer points out that the role of the state was to maintain a balance between freedom and justice. Smith wrote about the invisible hand of capitalism and Mills supported freedom for the individual but feared unrestrained freedom.

58. B. The Civil Constitution of the Clergy resulted in the Church's subjection to state control, declaring that the Catholic Church was independent from the pope and that the Catholic clergy was to be paid by the people. All members of the clergy had to swear allegiance to the government. The Civil Constitution was a religious measure to control the Catholic clergy and to reduce the influence of the papacy in France; it did not address the issue of restoring the French absolute monarch. The National Convention ended absolute monarchy in France in 1793 and was responsible for the beheading of Marie Antoinette.

59. C. Henry Tudor's (Henry VII) most famous accomplishment was establishing the Star Chamber in England. Henry VII used the Star Chamber to prevent aristocratic interference in the administration of justice. This procedure helped to promote stability and halted the period of anarchy that existed during the Hundred Years War. Louis XIV constructed the Versailles Palace. There was no rising bourgeoisie class in England nor was Henry VII a strong supporter of the arts. Henry VII opposed the House of York.

60. B. Stanley Baldwin was the leader of the Conservative Party in Great Britain during the 1920s, holding power from 1924–1929. Neville Chamberlain was the Conservative prime minister in 1937 and was replaced by Winston Churchill, another Conservative leader, at the beginning of World War II. Lloyd George was a liberal who led Britain to victory in World War I. Arthur Balfour was a British government official who gave support to the Zionist movement for the establishment of a homeland for the Jewish people in Palestine.

61. D. Nicholas I (b.1796, reigned 1825–1855), czar of Russia, supported orthodoxy (the strong connection between church and government), autocracy (absolute power of the czar), and nationalism (evidenced by suppressing non-Russians within the empire). Russia was the only country not affected by the revolutions of 1848. Nicholas I was a conservative who opposed modernization for fear it would undermine the state and had little use for a liberal constitution. Alexander II, not Nicholas I, emancipated the serfs.

62. E. The Meiji Restoration in Japan (1868–1912) was characterized by the modernization and reform of Japan in order for it to compete with Western powers. It revised Japan's policy of isolation, ended feudalism, and developed its military and industrial power. Japanese leaders sent students abroad to western countries to learn about their form of government, economics, technology, and customs. The Japanese adapted a constitution based on the model of Prussia with the emperor as its head. The Meiji government also established a banking system and modern shipyards and built up a modern army based on a draft. The Meiji Restoration did not introduce democracy and did not abolish the position of the emperor.

63. **B.** The Romantic poetry of William Wordsworth and William Blake was a reaction against the horrors of the Industrial Revolution and the scientific rationalism of the Enlightenment. Wordsworth and Blake criticized the Industrial Revolution. Blake called the early factories satanic mills and protested the hard life of the London poor. Wordsworth lamented the destruction of the rural villages and attacked the factories for the pollution of land and water. The Romantic poets did not reject nationalism or democracy, nor did they write in reaction to the growth of labor unions in England or the growing influence of the Catholic Church, which was not a dominant force in England in the nineteenth century.

64. **C.** The goal of Joseph Stalin's Command Economy and Five Year Plan was to increase the Soviet Union's industrial output by developing heavy industry, such as iron, steel, aluminum, and machinery to produce weapons to strengthen the country militarily. The Five Year Plan gave low priority to consumer goods and provided for collectivization of farms. It was not concerned with expanding exports to the West nor the importing of goods.

65. **C.** The Scientific Revolution did not result in the widespread growth of knowledge among the general population. Instead, it was primarily an intellectual revolution that did not affect the daily life of the people until the nineteenth century with the growth of the Industrial Revolution. Through scientific method, the Scientific Revolution challenged and rejected Aristotle's theories. The Scientific Revolution helped to uncover knowledge about the physical world as the Royal Society of England and other learned societies promoted scientific research.

66. **A.** *The Painting of Guernica* by Pablo Picasso was inspired by the Spanish Civil War (1936–1939). The Spanish Civil War involved a struggle between the Loyalists (Communists, democrats, and republicans) and the Spanish Fascists led by General Francisco Franco and aided by Hitler and Mussolini. The Soviet Union supported the Loyalists. In 1937, German bombers attacked the market square in the city of Guernica killing over 1,600 people. Picasso's painting, which is over 11 feet tall and 25 feet wide, became the symbol of the brutality of the war. Picasso's painting was not inspired by any of the other events such as Hitler's nor Mussolini's rise to power nor the invasion of Ethiopia or the Nazi-Soviet Non-Aggression Pact.

67. **A.** Albania was created as a result of the Balkan Crisis of 1912–1913. Austria, with the backing of Germany, created Albania out of the former Ottoman Empire lands to block Serbia's ambition to gain an outlet to the Adriatic Sea. Finland, Czechoslovakia, Yugoslavia, and Estonia were all new nations created at the Versailles Conference and carved out of the Austro-Hungarian and Russian Empires.

68. **E.** The Napoleonic Code established a uniform legal system to replace an outdated medieval system, but women lost rights. Although the Napoleonic Code reversed the Revolution Code of sharing inheritances among all heirs and even declared equal

inheritance rights for illegitimate offspring, it reaffirmed the traditional rights of male householders. A wife could not buy or sell property without her husband's approval. Napoleon saw the role of women as chiefly bearing and rearing children. Women were not unfairly imprisoned and the Napoleonic Code never provided for their political or economical equality.

69. E. Bismarck's policy did not become more lenient towards France as a result of the Franco-Prussian War. In fact, in his drive to defeat France during the Franco-Prussian War, Bismarck had brought Paris to submission by starving the city for over five months. In the Treaty of Frankfurt in 1871, he demanded that France pay a war indemnity of five billion gold francs and forced France to cede the border regions of Alsace and Lorraine. The French never reconciled themselves to the loss of these two border provinces. Bismarck's policy of Blood and Iron was successful in uniting Germany by defeating two major powers, Austria and France. The Second German Empire was created in 1871 when Wilhelm I was crowned German emperor. France had been the most dominant power on the continent since the early 1700s, but the new German Empire replaced France in that regard. Germany's victory frightened Great Britain who had followed a policy of isolation by trying to prevent any one country from dominating the continent. The fear of German dominance influenced Britain's foreign policy as well as that of France and Russia.

70. B. The correct chronological order is: James I becomes King of England in 1601; Charles I is beheaded in 1649; Oliver Cromwell becomes Lord Protector in 1653; Charles II is restored to power in 1660; the Glorious Revolution takes place in 1689.

71. D. The Tanzit reformers wanted to reform the crumbling empire on the European model but they did not support a democratic form of government. They wanted to create equality before the law for all religions but still wanted Islam to be the dominant religion. Tanzit reformers also realized that the sultan had to modernize his army and economy in order to survive. Finally, their multinational empire would only survive if they stemmed the growth of nationalism, which would prove difficult to achieve.

72. B. Ferdinand and Isabella made Spain a strong royal monarchy by using the Church and consolidating royal authority. They strengthened royal authority by using the hermandades or local police to enforce royal justice; they also revived the Inquisition to help consolidate their power. Ferdinand and Isabella expelled the Jews and drove the Moors from Spain. These rulers did not isolate themselves from Europe. They unified Spain and controlled the power of the aristocracy.

73. A. Adam Smith's *Wealth of Nations* focused on the invisible hand of supply and demand, which outlined the nucleus of a system known as capitalism. Smith's book criticized the mercantile system and argued that a laissez-faire approach to business would benefit the system. The ideas of Socialism and Communism (government control of the economy) were in direct opposition to Smith's belief in private enterprise. Imperialism was an attempt by European nations to extend their control over undeveloped areas of the world.

74. C. Napoleon's Continental System was economic warfare against Great Britain. Napoleon was unable to invade Great Britain and in 1812, Great Britain was the only country he did not control in Europe. The purpose of the Continental System was to prevent European nations from trading with the British. He hoped that by boycotting British goods, he would be able to bring Great Britain to its knees. The Continental System was not a jobs program, nor was it an educational program. Napoleon had defeated Austria when he implemented the Continental System.

75. **D.** Spain was never a member of the Quadruple Alliance. The Quadruple Alliance, or Concert of Europe, consisted of Austria, Prussia, Russia, and Great Britain. The purpose of the Alliance was to maintain the balance of power in Europe after the Congress of Vienna.

76. **D.** Perestroika was not designed to lead to nuclear disarmament. It was an economic program that involved less government planning by allowing some business and some farmers to operate on the free market system. Perestroika also allowed individuals greater power on the local economic level.

77. **A.** The Royal Society of London was established in the seventeenth century to provoke scientific research; it was not a result of the Industrial Revolution. The growth of capitalism, the increase in the standard of living, the rise of the middle and working class, and the growth of cities were a direct consequence of the Industrial Revolution.

78. **A.** The July Revolution of 1830 led to the downfall of the regime of Charles X. In 1830, the French drove out Charles X because he attempted to restore the conditions similar to the Old Regime, limited the right to vote, and suspended the legislature. After three days of the French rioting, Charles X abdicated and fled to England. Louis XVIII was king of France until 1824. Louis Napoleon, nephew of Napoleon Bonaparte, was elected president of the Second Republic in 1848. Talleyrand was a French government leader and Alphonse Le Martine was a moderate liberal who led the government in 1848.

79. **B.** The Dual Monarchy referred to Austria-Hungary. In 1867, the Augsleich, or Compromise of 1867, established the Dual Monarchy under which Austria and Hungary were separate states under the leadership of Franz Joseph who became emperor of Austria and king of Hungary. The Kingdom of Two Sicilies and Piedmont-Sardinia were part of the united Italy. The Papal States were the territories controlled by the Vatican. Great Britain and Ireland were never part of the Dual Monarchy.

80. **B.** A result of World War I was that Germany became a democratic republic from 1919–1933. At the war's end, the German people revolted against Kaiser Wilhelm II and overthrew his autocratic regime. The republic's constitution was drawn up at the town of Weimar. The Weimar Republic provided for a president who was elected by the people. The president was in charge of the army and could dissolve the Reichstag. In case of an emergency, he could suspend civil rights. The legislature was composed of the Reichstag, which was elected by the people and the Reichsrat, which represented the German states. Russia, which became known as the Soviet Union under Communism, suffered from famine and civil war after World War I and did not become a dominant power until the end of World War II. As a result of World War I, the Ottoman Empire was broken up, and some of the land was split between England and France, while Germany suffered from runaway inflation. The United States did not recognize the Soviet Union until 1933.

Section II: Free-Response Essays

Part A: First Sample Student DBQ Essay

By 1815, most European countries had very little need for colonies. Adam Smith argued that the burdens of colonialism outweighed its alleged benefits. As late as 1868, Bismarck, chancellor of Germany, thought that there were no advantages to colonies and Benjamin Disraeli, prime minister of Great Britain, called colonies a "millstone around our necks." These attitudes would come to an abrupt end by the 1880s and Europe would enter the age of the "New Imperialism." Economic, political, and social factors were behind the birth of this "New Imperialism." In the years between the Congress of Vienna in 1815 and the New Imperialism of the 1880s, strong, centrally governed nation-states had emerged in Europe. The Industrial Revolution had sparked tremendous economic growth in Europe and Westerners had a renewed pride that they were a unique and gifted people. Inspired by this growth and renewed confidence, Europeans embarked on a path of aggressive nationalism that led to the New Imperialism. Economic motives were important factors in the extensions of the political empires of European countries. The Industrial Revolution created needs that spurred overseas expansion. Many manufacturers wanted access to natural resources and also wanted to expand their markets. W. T. Stead, an English journalist, saw colonies as a "bread and butter issue" that could serve to create markets and could also be a market for their goods that they produced (Doc. 9). Joseph Chamberlain, the British Secretary of State for the colonies, insisted that the only way the government could create more employment and demand was to open up new markets. He argued that Britain should not only continue its occupation of Egypt and India but should extend its influence over Africa (Doc. 5). The French Society of Colonial and Maritime Studies also agreed with Chamberlain's views. They believed that colonies not only provided raw materials but also provided benefits for the mother country (Doc. 2). The quest of new markets, however, was also influenced by the rapid industrialization of Germany, Belgium, and other nations, which were able to satisfy their own home markets and were beginning to protect their markets from imports by establishing tariff barriers. Jules Ferry, twice prime minister of France (1880–81; 1883–85), alluded to that fear when he pointed out that Germany and the United States were setting up trade barriers, creating a shrinking market for French goods (Doc. 4). Thus, government became responsive enough to undertake the conquest of undeveloped territories. Asia and Africa became a special attraction because these areas offered the raw material needed for the industrial factories of Europe including cotton, silk, vegetable oils, and rare minerals. The products of the tropics were also welcomed in Europe.

Other Europeans argued that colonies also benefited the mother country because they would relieve the problem of overpopulation. W. T. Stead believed that the only way to keep people in England from cannibalism was to relocate many of them in these overseas areas (Doc. 9). The German Nationalist historian, Heinrich von Treitschke, argued that only by colonization on a large scale could a civilized country avoid the dangers of overpopulation (Doc. 1). However, Grover Clark, a historian in the 1930s, in a work entitled *The Balance Sheet of Imperialism*, claimed that most of the European population migrated to the traditional areas in North America and Australia rather than Asia and Africa because they did not offer the climatic or economic conditions necessary to attract large migrations of European settlers to these areas.

Closely connected to the economic motives were political and military issues. Many Europeans were convinced that colonies were essential to a great nation. Treitschke asserted that all great nations must extend their control over "barbarian land" or they would no longer be a great power in the future (Doc. 1). In a speech before the North German Regatta Association, Kaiser Wilhelm II reinforced Treitschke's view that Germany must expand overseas if she wants to continue to have her "place in the sun" (Doc. 6). In 1884–1885, Bismarck and Ferry called the Berlin Conference to lay down the basic rules for colonizing Africa so that no one European power would dominate the entire continent.

The belief in a "place in the sun" also was connected to military needs. Steam-powered merchant ships and naval vessels required bases around the world to take on coal and supplies. Ferry asserted that the French navy, which could not do without safe harbors and supply centers, inspired the policy of colonial expansion, (Doc. 4). Many Westerners during the time were influenced by the ideas of the American naval historian, Alfred T. Mahan, who believed that a strong nation could only survive by expanding its naval power. Of course, a strong navy required that a country acquire coaling and fueling bases around the world.

Humanitarian and religious goals influenced many westerners. Rudyard Kipling, perhaps the most influential of the British writers, encouraged Europeans to "take up the White Man's Burden." The goal was to civilize these people and spread Western civilization (Doc. 3). The nineteenth century French author, Paul Beaulieu, believed that imperialism "provides the inhabitants with some regular education and regular justice." He also claimed that the overall objective was to transform the barbarian countries (Doc. 10).

Behind the idea of a civilizing mission was the belief in the superiority of the West. Cecil Rhodes, the successful British Imperialist, argued that the more territory the British controlled, the better it was for the world since the Anglo-Saxon race was the most "honourable race" (Doc. 8). Ferry also believed that the superior races had a right over the lower races to spread civilization. Many Westerners had embraced the scientific ideas of Social Darwinism. In 1859, Charles Darwin had published *On The Origins of the Species* about the survival of the fittest and applied it to the European race. Some people, such as Josiah Strong, an American Protestant missionary, argued "the Anglo-Saxons were superior and that in the competition for unoccupied land the fittest would survive (Doc. 7). This meant that imperial conquests and destruction of the weaker races in Asia and Africa were nature's way of making society better by removing the weakest elements in society.

The emergence of the New Imperialism in Europe in the late 1800s was an outgrowth of the economic, political, and social development that had influenced the continent since the Congress of Vienna in 1814–1815. The economic thrust of robust industrial capitalism, the competitive pressure between the European nations, and the belief that Europeans were the superior race with an obligation to spread their civilization resulted in the transformation of the map in areas of the world such as Africa and Asia.

Reader's Comments on Part A: First Sample Student DBQ Essay

- The student has a clear, well-developed thesis.

- The essay is well organized and the student makes use of all of the documents.

- The authorship and point of view of each document is identified, such as Chamberlain, Ferry, and so on.

- The outside information is relevant (Grover Clark) and clarifies and assesses the ideas in the document.

- The student effectively discusses and analyzes the causes of the New Imperialism.

Possible student score: 8–9

Part A: Second Sample Student DBQ Essay

The New Imperialism had several causes behind its development. During the nineteenth century, many changes were occurring in Europe. These changes spurred many countries to seek colonies. The reasons for Europeans' taking aggressive steps towards colonizing new lands were many. From these new attitudes about imperialism came a new era in Europe — the age of New Imperialism.

Colonies were seen as a major source of profit to the mother country (Doc. 5). If a country possessed a colony, many profitable consequences resulted. They allowed the country to reap benefits such as an increase in revenue or more access to natural resources to expand markets.

Some countries chose to colonize because they felt it was their natural right to do so. Countries felt that it was their duty to take over lands because they were much more civilized. Europeans saw colonization as a way to spread civilization. Because Europe was much more advanced in technology and the arts, they took colonization as an opportunity to bring their novel ideas to foreign countries, which they saw as less progressive (Doc. 3). Britain especially saw their race as superior (Doc. 8). Because of this superiority, they felt as if they had to spread their race.

Countries also got involved in imperialism for the simple fact of prestige and honor. Those countries that had a lot of colonies were seen as a major world power. A lot of benefits came with having colonies. A country looked better to the outside world if it controlled a great number of colonies. European leaders used their new colonies to enhance their status and give off a better impression.

New Imperialism was a profitable time for Europe. Taking over new colonies was the result of many reasons, such as wanting more natural resources and more prestige. Europe changed dramatically during this time.

Reader's Comments on Part A: Second Sample Student DBQ Essay

- The thesis statement is never stated.

- Insufficient amount of documents listed.

- No supporting data when listing documents.

- Little or no outside relevant information.

- Conclusion is weak.

Possible student score: 1–3

Part B: First Sample Student Thematic Essay, Group 1-1

Martin Luther (1483–1564) and John Calvin (1509–1564) were in agreement that religious authority rested with the Bible and not the pope. The Bible was the final authority because each individual could read it and determine church practices and doctrine. There was no need for the pope or any higher authority. However, Luther and Calvin disagreed on how to interpret and apply the Scriptures to the community of believers. One of Luther's major doctrines was "justification by faith alone." From reading and pondering St. Paul's letter to the Romans (1:17) found in the New Testament, Luther concluded that what justifies a good man is not what the church knows as works (prayers, the sacraments, and indulgences) but faith alone. Luther rejected the church doctrine that good deeds were necessary for salvation. The Catholic Church, however, never really taught that indulgences or good works could compensate for the evils of sin. Luther believed that a man did not earn grace by good living; he did good because he possessed the grace of God.

Luther's faith in the Bible and the power of the individual to read and reflect on scriptures led to the conclusion that the church consisted of the entire community of Christian believers. Luther believed that every person should serve God in his or her individual calling. Medieval church-men, however, had tended to identify the church with their clergy. Luther, like most Protestants, agreed that the clergy was unnecessary except to serve as pastors of a congregation.

There were two main differences between Calvin and Luther. Calvin had his own ideas about the power of God, the nature of human beings, and the power of the state. Luther had rejected St. Augustine's idea of predestination. Calvin in *The Institutes of Christian Religion* made predestination the cornerstone of his religious beliefs. Calvin believed that human beings did not have free will because that would take away from the power of God. Man could not actively work to achieve salvation. God decides (predetermines) at the beginning of time who would be saved and who would be damned. Those predestined for salvation could be identified by their virtuous lives. In time, the elect could be determined by their economic and material success.

Unlike Luther, Calvin did not believe that the church should be ruled by the state. Calvinists did not recognize the subordination of the church to the state or the right of any government, king, or parliament to lay down laws for religion. Calvin believed in setting up a theocratic government run by church leaders.

Luther and Calvin agreed on the basic issues of the authority of the pope and the role of the individual in the church. However, they disagreed on how to interpret the role of God and the individual in society.

Reader's Comments on Part B: First Sample Student Thematic Essay, Group 1-1

- Specifically accounts for the differences between Luther and Calvin.
- Thesis is stated clearly and developed throughout the essay.
- Supports thesis with specific information, references to St. Paul, St. Augustine.
- Conclusion could be stronger.

Possible student score: 7–9 (more toward the lower end of the scale)

Part B: Second Sample Student Thematic Essay, Group 1-1

Martin Luther and John Calvin both brought new ideas about religion to their countries. They both definitely saw flaws in the Roman Catholic Church as it was. While they did agree on some major concepts, they did not see eye to eye on some issues.

Luther and Calvin both acknowledged that there was really no need for a pope in the church. They believed that real authority came from the Bible and not from what a priest said or did.

Luther, unlike Calvin, felt that the church should be run by the state. He also believed that an individual could interpret and reflect on the Bible in his/her own way. Luther also claimed that faith alone was good enough to achieve salvation.

Calvin did not believe in the church and state being separate. He hoped for a government ruled by the leaders of the church. The main idea behind Calvinism was the concept of predestination. Calvin did not feel that a person could do anything during his/her life to help achieve salvation. Luther did not believe in predestination.

Luther and Calvin were both pioneers in bringing about changes in how people practiced and viewed religion. They both were committed to correcting the flaws in the Roman Catholic Church. However, they failed to agree on certain ideas, which led to the creation of two different religions—Lutheranism and Calvinism.

Reader's Comments on Part B: Second Sample Student Thematic Essay, Group 1-1

- Thesis statement is poorly stated.

- Organization is weak.

- No elaboration of differences, such as Luther's views on the state.

- Fails to analyze the importance of predestination.

Possible student score: 1–3 (very weak)

Part B: First Sample Student Thematic Essay, Group 1-2

John Locke and Jean Jacques Rousseau agreed about man and the state of nature and the meaning of the social contract but drew different conclusions from these basic areas of agreement. John Locke was a political thinker and Jean Jacques Rousseau was a social philosopher. Locke's *Two Treatises on Government* and Rousseau's *Social Contract* would influence political thinkers for many years. John Locke, who was born into an Anglican family with Puritan leanings, was forced to flee England during the reign of Charles II (1660–1685) for his liberal views. In 1689, after James II was overthrown, Locke returned to England. In 1690, he published the *Two Treatises on Government* to justify the English Parliament in the Glorious Revolution. Locke argued that James II had violated nature's law and deserved to be deposed. Locke asserted that men are born free in the state of nature where they are happy, free, and entitled to the natural right of life, liberty, and property. To protect these rights, men formed societies by a social contract and transferred to the government the obligation of safeguarding these rights. If the government, which was party to the compact, failed to live up to this contract, the people have a right to overthrow it. This is what happened in England in 1688 and James II deserved to be deposed.

Jean Jacques Rousseau (1712–1778) was born into a poor family and led a disorganized life and felt uncomfortable in the social world of the Enlightenment. His book *The Social Contract* was published in France in 1762. Rousseau begins with Locke's ideas of the state of nature but he arrived at a different conclusion. He believed like Locke that man in the state of nature had certain rights. However, they disagreed after this. After people enter into a social contract to form a government, they give up all their rights to the control of the community and must submit to the general will. The general will is a kind of ideal representing what was best for the whole state, a will for the general good. If someone disagreed with the general will, it became necessary to "force a man to be free." The general will controls everything.

Locke and Rousseau began with the belief in the natural law and the state of nature but they reached different conclusions. Locke's ideas would influence the right of people to overthrow the government and the right of revolution would echo throughout Europe and in the British colonies in America. Rousseau's ideas fanned the flame of revolution, but dictators have used his focus on the right of the community over the individual in order to justify their undemocratic governments.

Reader's Comments on Part B: First Sample Student Thematic Essay, Group 1-2

- The thesis is clearly stated but simplistic.

- Student specifically points out the areas of agreement but also differences between Locke and Rousseau (general will; rights of individual versus community).

- The student fails to evaluate the full implication of the general will.

- The conclusion is good.

Possible student score: 4–5

Part B: Second Sample Student Thematic Essay, Group 1-2

John Locke and Jean Jacques Rousseau were two political thinkers who promoted the belief in the social contract and the state of nature. Locke wrote at the time of the Glorious Revolution and Rousseau wrote during the French Revolution. Locke and Rousseau believed in a social contract in which people entered to establish a government. Locke believed that this social contract or compact insured that Great Britain's government would protect the rights of the people.

Rousseau believed that government was a contract but the community was more important than the person. This idea led to problems for future years. The question of what was the general will lead to problems about the meaning of the social contract. Locke's social contract led to democracy.

Both Locke and Rousseau agreed on a social contract but disagreed on how society should interpret it.

Reader's Comments on Part B: Second Sample Student Thematic Essay, Group 1-2

- There is no thesis statement.

- The student does no real analysis of how Locke and Rousseau differ on the Social Contract.

- There are factual errors, such as Rousseau did not write during the French Revolution. He died in 1778.

- The essay does not refer to body of works of Locke and Rousseau.

- The essay is very superficial.

Possible student score: 1–3 (Very weak essay)

Part B: First Sample Student Thematic Essay, Group 1-3

Peter the Great was one of Russia's most influential leaders. Throughout his 36-year rule, he strove to constantly ensure that Russia became more modern — thus, more Western. He also ceaselessly built up and reformed the Russian army. While many of Peter the Great's reforms had positive effects on Russia, when his reign ended in 1725, the state of Russia was still very uncertain, and was not fully modernized.

Although Peter the Great came to the Russian throne in 1682 at the age of ten, he did not take control of the government until seven years later. Peter was not well educated, but his immense curiosity played a role in how he ruled. In the late seventeenth century, Peter traveled to European cities to observe their political, social, and economical practices. He took back to Russia not only his observations on life in Western Europe, but also a group of scholars, soldiers, and noblemen whom he had recruited and gathered throughout his travels. He would use these people and his observations to modernize Russia.

One of Peter the Great's most sweeping reforms was that of the Russian army. Before Peter's reign, the army was feeble, with part-time soldiers who were unskilled in modern military techniques. To improve Russia's military, Peter required that all noblemen serve in the army, or in civil service. In recognition of the skilled nature of many Western armies, Peter set up schools and universities to teach his noble soldiers the correct military techniques. Peter established a standing, regular army of 200,000 men, mainly commoners, who were required to serve in the military.

In addition to changes to Russia's military, Peter the Great felt it necessary to centralize his power, and he did so by bringing all Russians — including the Orthodox Church — under his control. He insisted that all of Russia would follow the European calendar, with the New Year's starting on January 1, rather than on September 1. In response to the practices he had observed while in Western Europe, Peter insisted that nobles shave their beards and dress in modern, Western-style clothing, in place of their old-fashioned robes and beards. Women were no longer required to veil their faces in public and were not required to seclude themselves in their houses. He invited women to his lavish parties, much to the disapproval of many citizens. In addition, Peter put an end to arranged marriages.

By the end of Peter the Great's reign, Russia had made great strides in many other areas. He increased the number of factories in Russia, and encouraged the exportation of Russian goods. Peter was responsible for making potatoes the staple crop of Russia. He simplified the Russian alphabet and developed Russia's system of education by forming academies to study mathematics, engineering, and science.

The greatest symbol of Peter's reign was the capital city of St. Petersburg. Located near the Baltic coast, St. Petersburg was a lavish city that was built mainly because Peter forced thousands of serfs to drain the swamps near the city. Many of these serfs died in the process, but after their work was done, Peter brought Italian architects and artisans to design a "Western" city.

Despite these numerous reforms and advances, Peter the Great was not entirely successful in modernizing Russia—for example, he failed to gain a warm water port that could remain open year round. During his 36-year rule, Peter and his army were constantly engaged in battle, yet Peter's territorial gains were minimal, at best. In general, Peter the Great did not leave a lasting legacy upon his death in 1725. Because he ruled primarily by fear tactics, many of his policies did not last after his death.

Peter the Great's biggest failure was his reliance on serfdom. The serfs who had helped to build his "window to the West" were actually holding Russia back from true modernization. As Peter continued to bring Western ideas into Russia, the divide between the poor and the educated elite widened. There was great hatred of Peter among those who were forced to work the land as serfs, as they saw no benefits to Peter's modernization. By clinging to a system of serfdom that had long been abolished in the rest of Europe, Peter the Great failed to fully modernize and Westernize Russia.

Reader's Comments on Part B: First Sample Student Thematic Essay, Group 1-3

- Good factual information about Peter's efforts to improve the military life at the court. However, there is an error in the number of years that he ruled. It should be 43 not 36.

- Information is organized and fully supports the thesis.

- Conclusion is detailed and analytical.

Possible student score: 8–9 (Very good essay)

Part B: Second Sample Student Thematic Essay, Group 1-3

Peter the Great ruled Russia from the late seventeenth century until the early eighteenth century. He tried to Westernize Russia through various economic and social reforms. He also built up the Russian military. His reforms were very successful and Russia became more like the other Western European nations due to Peter's reign.

Peter the Great wanted to make Russia as modern as other Western European nations. He studied other countries' political, economic, and social systems and used what he had learned in ruling Russia. His ultimate goal was to make Russia the most powerful and modern nation in Europe.

Peter improved Russia's economy by building more factories and trading with other countries. He also improved Russia's system of education. He treated women better, and invited them to parties at his castles. Peter forced men to shave their beards and made them dress the way people in the West were dressing. He tried to control all aspects of Russia, including religion. He did not let Russian Orthodox citizens practice their religion freely.

Peter greatly improved Russia's military. He made it more similar to armies in Western European countries, and he forced Russian noblemen to serve in the army. He also forced the peasants to serve in the army, so that Russia would have a full-time military. This was one way that he saw he could be more like Western European nations. He also taught the noblemen in his army how to fight properly.

Peter was a harsh leader. He relied on serfs to make many of his reforms. Serfs built Peter's capital city of St. Petersburg, and many of them died in the process. St. Petersburg was Peter the Great's vision of Westernization, and he achieved his goal at any cost, even if it meant the death of his citizens.

Peter's reforms were both good and bad for Russia. He did help to modernize Russia, although he treated the Russian peasants very poorly. This prevented Russia from being as modern a nation as possible.

Reader's Comments on Part B: Second Sample Student Thematic Essay, Group 1-3

- Factual information weak, too general. Peter the Great did allow the Russians to practice their religion.
- Thesis statement weak.
- Very superficial treatment.
- Conclusion weak.

Possible student score: 2–3 (Weak essay)

Part B: First Sample Student Thematic Essay, Group 2-1

The Versailles Treaty that ended World War I provided a temporary truce between England and France for dominance on the European continent. On November 11, 1918, Germany had signed the Armistice with the Western powers based on the belief that President Woodrow Wilson's ideals of the Fourteen Points would be the basis of the negotiated peace treaty. When the new German government, the Weimar Republic, refused to sign the treaty because of its harshness, the Western leaders informed Germany that they had to sign it or be prepared to resume hostilities. The severe restriction of the Versailles Treaty led to the belief in Germany that the country had been "Stabbed in the Back." This slogan would provide the rallying cry for the Nazis' rise to power whose main goal was to readdress the injustices of the Versailles Treaty.

The Versailles Treaty created bitterness among the German people. Germany resented Article 231, the War Guilt Clause, which required them to accept full responsibility for the war and pay the reparation costs that amounted to over $132 billion. The Germans also were angry that their military force was limited to 100,000 men, and Germany was stripped of its overseas colonies.

Adolf Hitler and the Nazis exploited this bitterness and focused on nationalists who refused to accept their defeat in World War I. Although Hitler and his National Socialist Party never received a majority of the votes, he was to portray the Weimar Republic as the government that had betrayed Germany. The economic condition of runaway inflation caused by the reparations debt imposed by the Versailles Treaty added to the discontent towards the Weimar Republic.

Hitler was also able to appeal to the extreme nationalists because he pointed out that the Versailles Treaty had removed valuable lands from the German Empire. Hitler struck a responsive chord with the German people when he demanded the Sudetenland, a region of Czechoslovakia where German-speaking people lived, be returned. Germans were also angry that they had lost Danzig to Poland in the Versailles Treaty. Danzig, which had been an old German town, was given to Poland so that Poland could have an outlet to the sea but it cut off the bulk of Germany from East Prussia.

Other countries also resented the Versailles Treaty. Italy had walked out of the conference because it did not get all the land it wanted. The United States rejected the treaty and the League of Nations' effectiveness was diminished. Japan was angry that the West refused to recognize its claims in China. Russia was angry because it had been excluded from the conference and lost the Baltic States. By the 1930s, England and France began to believe that the Versailles Treaty was unfair and that Hitler was correct in seeking to address the injustices. The Versailles Treaty did lay the seeds of distrust that led to World War II. The treaty was a factor that led to World War II, but the economic crisis created by the Great Depression and Adolf Hitler's ideas, leadership, and his ability to exploit these conditions also led to World War II.

Reader's Comments on Part B: First Sample Student Thematic Essay, Group 2-1

- The thesis is clearly stated.

- The essay addresses the specific criticisms of the Versailles Treaty.

- Student uses good detail and linkage with Versailles and the German people.

- The section on Hitler is well developed.

- Student could have developed the conclusion more.

Possible student score: 7–9 (Good essay)

Part B: Second Sample Student Thematic Essay, Group 2-1

Many people believe that the Treaty of Versailles was one of the biggest reasons for World War II. The Treaty of Versailles ended World War I. It placed blame for the war on Germany, and made Germany pay other countries many billions of dollars. The people of Germany were very angry because of this, and they began to resent that the rest of Europe made them take all the blame for World War I. Germany felt that they had been unfairly blamed for the first World War.

The Treaty of Versailles also required that the Germans have a much smaller army than they did at the start of World War I. This part of the treaty was an attempt to try to stop something like World War I from happening again. Germany resented this clause of the treaty, and their resentment eventually led to World War II.

While the Treaty of Versailles did not start World War II, it played a big role because the Germans felt angry because of what they had been forced to accept. Adolf Hitler, the man behind the start of World War II, used the anger of the German people to rise to power. After World War I, Germany's economy was bad and it was hard for people to find jobs. People became more and more angry, and blamed their bad situation on the Treaty of Versailles, which had forced Germany to pay billions of dollars to other European nations.

The Treaty of Versailles, which ended World War I, played a major role in the cause of World War II. The German people were angry at having to accept complete blame for the war, and Adolf Hitler capitalized on this anger. His rule eventually led to World War II.

Reader's Comments on Part B: Second Sample Student Thematic Essay, Group 2-1

- Factual information weak.
- No details about Hitler or the Great Depression.
- Very superficial.

Possible student score: 1–3 (Weak essay)

Part B: First Sample Student Thematic Essay, Group 2-2

At the end of World War II, most of Europe was in shambles and devastated from the war. However, out of this turmoil two super powers managed to emerge — the United States and the Soviet Union. These two countries were able to acquire enough economic resources and military might to dominate the world. Yet, with this new power came tense rivalry and a world becoming more and more divided. These tensions ultimately led to the Cold War.

The Cold War began some time after the end of World War II. It was a period of severe tension and hostility between the West and the Soviet Union without actual armed conflicts between the nations. The cause of this tension rested in the fact that Stalin in Eastern Europe had very different goals as compared to the Western powers.

As a result of seeing the horrors of the Nazi regime, the United States became an even bigger supporter of democracy. The Unites States believed that strengthening democracy would ensure tolerance and peace. Most Western Allies built new governments that focused on democratic constitutions to protect the rights of all citizens. The teaching of democratic principles was emphasized throughout the West.

Stalin, the leader of Russia at this time, had a different view about how to govern a country. He wanted Communism to spread throughout his country. Stalin also wished to protect Russia from any further invasions by the Germans. Stalin had his Red Army occupy lands in Eastern Europe. Stalin hoped that the West would accept this occupation.

However, Western leaders, such as Roosevelt and Churchill, did not agree to such a thing. They both rejected Stalin's view. Stalin chose to ignore the West's arguments and managed to install pro-Soviet Communist governments throughout Eastern Europe. This was done by destroying all rival political parties and even assassinating democratic leaders.

These acts committed by Stalin further increased the tension between Eastern Europe and the West. Churchill claimed that an "Iron Curtain" had descended across the continent. This term expressed the growing fear of Communism, which led to greater tensions. The United States took a bigger stand on democracy. In 1947, President Truman wrote a policy that stated that the United States would support any people who were trying to resist outside pressures. This policy came to be known as the Truman Doctrine. He made it clear to Stalin and all of Eastern Europe that the U.S. would resist any sort of expansion of Communism no matter where or at what cost. This policy instilled more fear in the East and helped to further increase tensions. The Marshall Plan, which assisted democratic countries who were in economic need further angered Stalin. Tensions over Germany led to the Berlin Blockade, which was resolved by a dramatic airlift that only added to the tensions between the West and the Soviet Union. In 1949, the creation of NATO, a defensive alliance against the spread of Communism, resulted in the formation of the Warsaw Pact by the Soviet bloc of nations. The tension between the United States and Russia was also escalated by the nuclear race. The arms race created the fear that nuclear warfare was a possibility and could destroy the world.

Both sides made many efforts to support their cause. The West led by the United States stood firm in its belief that democracy was the best government and that the spread of Communism had to be contained. The Soviet Union under Stalin was determined to ensure the supremacy of the Soviet Empire. These two opposing views led to the intense rivalry of the Cold War, which lasted for over 40 years.

Reader's Comments on Part B: First Sample Student Thematic Essay, Group 2-2

- The thesis statement is good.

- The essay is rich in detail but lacks analysis.

- Superficial treatment of the Iron Curtain, Truman Doctrine, and Marshall Plan.

- Conclusion weak.

Possible student score: 5–7 (Mixed essay)

Part B: Second Sample Student Thematic Essay, Group 2-2

There were many reasons why a Cold War existed between the West and the East after 1945. This war, which was called a Cold War because it did not involve any armed conflict between nations, led to over 40 years of severe tension between those countries that were democratic and those which were Communist.

The West, most especially the United States, believed that democracy was the best form of government. They did all that they could to spread democracy throughout the West. Stalin did not agree with the Western ideas. He felt that the best government was Communism. He spread this form of government through the East. Soon Europe was divided into the Eastern Soviet dominated region and the Western region.

Increasing tension forced both the East and the West to use all of their resources to further strengthen their side. The United States did not stay isolated but became a major world power in its support of democracy. Stalin grew more suspicious of the West, which caused the tension to mount even more. Stalin did all that he could to ensure that the East remains a strong Communist force.

The main reason behind the Cold War was the two opposing views held in the East and the West. The West supported democracy while the East claimed Communism was superior. This conflict led to severe tensions, which would last for more than 40 years and result in ongoing conflicts between the West and the East.

Reader's Comments on Part B: Second Sample Student Thematic Essay, Group 2-2

- Thesis statement is not clear.
- Little or no basic facts.
- Redundant sentence structure.
- Conclusion poor.

Possible student score: 1–2 (Very weak essay)

Part B: First Sample Student Thematic Essay, Group 2-3

Karl Marx (1818–1883) was a German writer and economist who is considered the Father of Communism. Marx wrote *The Communist Manifesto* in which he outlined his main political philosophy. Marx based his ideas in part on the teachings of the German philosopher William Hegel, who taught that history was a dialectic that was constantly changing as new ideas came into conflict with one another.

Like Hegel, Marx believed that history was a constant conflict. However, Marx believed that economic conditions, not ideas, determined the course of history. The class that possessed the economic power controlled the government and institutions. Laws and social systems are all developed in accord with society's economic base. No ruling class has ever been willing to give up power. The only way to achieve change was through revolution. Thus, conflict between classes was inevitable. Marx asserts that history was a struggle between the "haves and have-nots." Marx pointed out that in ancient times, the conflict was between the patrician and the plebeians. In the Middle Ages the struggle was between the lord and the serf. In the present day of the industrial society, the struggle is between the capitalist and the proletariat. Marx believed that the industrial society of capitalism was only a temporary phase. As the backbone of capitalism, the proletariat was the true productive class. Marx predicted that workers (proletariat) would seize control of the government from the capitalists and build a society in which the people owned everything. Without private property there would be a classless society and the government would wither away. The last stage of history for Marx would be pure Communism in which the goal would be "from each according to his ability to each according to his needs." The Marx view of history leaves out the importance of nationalism and religion. In his appeal that "working men of all countries unite," Marx did not realize that nationalism was a major part of history. The destruction of the Berlin Wall in 1989 demonstrated that Germans were German first and then Communists. Furthermore, Marx was writing at a time when the gap between the working poor contrasted sharply with the wealthy industrialists. Marx's prediction about the workers was erroneous. By 1900, conditions in Western Europe had changed. Workers, through unions, began to improve their standards of living. Rather than overthrow the government, workers gained rights to vote and used it to correct some of the injustices. Finally, Marx's prediction about Communist revolutions occurring in an industrial country was also misguided. The Communist Revolution took place in an agricultural country which according to Marx was not ripe for revolution. The State did not wither away but became more powerful.

Although Marx's view of history as a class struggle was erroneous, his philosophy had powerful appeal to the people. Marx's belief that economics determine history was a scientific analysis of human events which guaranteed the rise of Communism and its conclusion. Like religion, which guaranteed paradise in the afterlife, Marx promised happiness on earth. Marx's appeal was that he made Communism into a material religion.

Reader's Comments on Part B: First Sample Student Thematic Essay, Group 2-3

- Thesis statement not specifically clear.

- Rich in facts, but misplaced information. Marx's economic ideas are contained in *Das Kapital* and reference to Hegel should be Wilhelm Friedrich Hegel.

- Good analysis of errors of Marx's ideas.

- Conclusion is creative but needs greater analysis.

Possible student score: 7–8 (Strong essay)

Part B: Second Sample Student Thematic Essay, Group 2-3

Marx's view that all history was a class struggle helped to explain why society developed as it did in the past. In 1848, Karl Marx wrote *The Communist Manifesto* in response to the problems created by the Industrial Revolution. Marx believed that the difficult conditions that existed under capitalism made it inevitable that Communism would be successful. The problems of society were so bad that the worker thought he had no hope for the future. He worked

10–12 hours per day and there was no protection against accidents. Marx predicted that when the Communists gained control of society there would not be a division between workers and owners. A classless society would develop and the lack of goods would no longer create conflict.

In history, Marx predicted that there has always been a class struggle because the rich always seem to be getting richer by exploiting the poor. Under Communism, this exploitation would stop because there would no longer be any private property. Marx also predicted that there would be worldwide revolutions that would affect every country. Marx's prediction, however, never came true because Communism only came to Russia and China.

Reader's Comments on Part B: Second Sample Student Thematic Essay, Group 2-3

- Thesis statement not clear.
- No analysis of facts such as the difficult conditions under the Industrial Revolution.
- Very general, no details.

Possible student score: 1-3 (Weak essay)

Answer Sheet for Sample Practice Test II

Remove this sheet and use it to mark your answer for the multiple-choice section of Sample Practice Test II.

1 Ⓐ Ⓑ Ⓒ Ⓓ Ⓔ	21 Ⓐ Ⓑ Ⓒ Ⓓ Ⓔ	41 Ⓐ Ⓑ Ⓒ Ⓓ Ⓔ	61 Ⓐ Ⓑ Ⓒ Ⓓ Ⓔ
2 Ⓐ Ⓑ Ⓒ Ⓓ Ⓔ	22 Ⓐ Ⓑ Ⓒ Ⓓ Ⓔ	42 Ⓐ Ⓑ Ⓒ Ⓓ Ⓔ	62 Ⓐ Ⓑ Ⓒ Ⓓ Ⓔ
3 Ⓐ Ⓑ Ⓒ Ⓓ Ⓔ	23 Ⓐ Ⓑ Ⓒ Ⓓ Ⓔ	43 Ⓐ Ⓑ Ⓒ Ⓓ Ⓔ	63 Ⓐ Ⓑ Ⓒ Ⓓ Ⓔ
4 Ⓐ Ⓑ Ⓒ Ⓓ Ⓔ	24 Ⓐ Ⓑ Ⓒ Ⓓ Ⓔ	44 Ⓐ Ⓑ Ⓒ Ⓓ Ⓔ	64 Ⓐ Ⓑ Ⓒ Ⓓ Ⓔ
5 Ⓐ Ⓑ Ⓒ Ⓓ Ⓔ	25 Ⓐ Ⓑ Ⓒ Ⓓ Ⓔ	45 Ⓐ Ⓑ Ⓒ Ⓓ Ⓔ	65 Ⓐ Ⓑ Ⓒ Ⓓ Ⓔ
6 Ⓐ Ⓑ Ⓒ Ⓓ Ⓔ	26 Ⓐ Ⓑ Ⓒ Ⓓ Ⓔ	46 Ⓐ Ⓑ Ⓒ Ⓓ Ⓔ	66 Ⓐ Ⓑ Ⓒ Ⓓ Ⓒ
7 Ⓐ Ⓑ Ⓒ Ⓓ Ⓔ	27 Ⓐ Ⓑ Ⓒ Ⓓ Ⓔ	47 Ⓐ Ⓑ Ⓒ Ⓓ Ⓔ	67 Ⓐ Ⓑ Ⓒ Ⓓ Ⓔ
8 Ⓐ Ⓑ Ⓒ Ⓓ Ⓔ	28 Ⓐ Ⓑ Ⓒ Ⓓ Ⓔ	48 Ⓐ Ⓑ Ⓒ Ⓓ Ⓔ	68 Ⓐ Ⓑ Ⓒ Ⓓ Ⓔ
9 Ⓐ Ⓑ Ⓒ Ⓓ Ⓔ	29 Ⓐ Ⓑ Ⓒ Ⓓ Ⓔ	49 Ⓐ Ⓑ Ⓒ Ⓓ Ⓔ	69 Ⓐ Ⓑ Ⓒ Ⓓ Ⓔ
10 Ⓐ Ⓑ Ⓒ Ⓓ Ⓔ	30 Ⓐ Ⓑ Ⓒ Ⓓ Ⓔ	50 Ⓐ Ⓑ Ⓒ Ⓓ Ⓔ	70 Ⓐ Ⓑ Ⓒ Ⓓ Ⓔ
11 Ⓐ Ⓑ Ⓒ Ⓓ Ⓔ	31 Ⓐ Ⓑ Ⓒ Ⓓ Ⓔ	51 Ⓐ Ⓑ Ⓒ Ⓓ Ⓔ	71 Ⓐ Ⓑ Ⓒ Ⓓ Ⓔ
12 Ⓐ Ⓑ Ⓒ Ⓓ Ⓔ	32 Ⓐ Ⓑ Ⓒ Ⓓ Ⓔ	52 Ⓐ Ⓑ Ⓒ Ⓓ Ⓔ	72 Ⓐ Ⓑ Ⓒ Ⓓ Ⓔ
13 Ⓐ Ⓑ Ⓒ Ⓓ Ⓔ	33 Ⓐ Ⓑ Ⓒ Ⓓ Ⓔ	53 Ⓐ Ⓑ Ⓒ Ⓓ Ⓔ	73 Ⓐ Ⓑ Ⓒ Ⓓ Ⓔ
14 Ⓐ Ⓑ Ⓒ Ⓓ Ⓔ	34 Ⓐ Ⓑ Ⓒ Ⓓ Ⓔ	54 Ⓐ Ⓑ Ⓒ Ⓓ Ⓔ	74 Ⓐ Ⓑ Ⓒ Ⓓ Ⓔ
15 Ⓐ Ⓑ Ⓒ Ⓓ Ⓔ	35 Ⓐ Ⓑ Ⓒ Ⓓ Ⓔ	55 Ⓐ Ⓑ Ⓒ Ⓓ Ⓔ	75 Ⓐ Ⓑ Ⓒ Ⓓ Ⓔ
16 Ⓐ Ⓑ Ⓒ Ⓓ Ⓔ	36 Ⓐ Ⓑ Ⓒ Ⓓ Ⓔ	56 Ⓐ Ⓑ Ⓒ Ⓓ Ⓔ	76 Ⓐ Ⓑ Ⓒ Ⓓ Ⓔ
17 Ⓐ Ⓑ Ⓒ Ⓓ Ⓔ	37 Ⓐ Ⓑ Ⓒ Ⓓ Ⓔ	57 Ⓐ Ⓑ Ⓒ Ⓓ Ⓔ	77 Ⓐ Ⓑ Ⓒ Ⓓ Ⓔ
18 Ⓐ Ⓑ Ⓒ Ⓓ Ⓔ	38 Ⓐ Ⓑ Ⓒ Ⓓ Ⓔ	58 Ⓐ Ⓑ Ⓒ Ⓓ Ⓔ	78 Ⓐ Ⓑ Ⓒ Ⓓ Ⓔ
19 Ⓐ Ⓑ Ⓒ Ⓓ Ⓔ	39 Ⓐ Ⓑ Ⓒ Ⓓ Ⓔ	59 Ⓐ Ⓑ Ⓒ Ⓓ Ⓔ	79 Ⓐ Ⓑ Ⓒ Ⓓ Ⓔ
20 Ⓐ Ⓑ Ⓒ Ⓓ Ⓔ	40 Ⓐ Ⓑ Ⓒ Ⓓ Ⓔ	60 Ⓐ Ⓑ Ⓒ Ⓓ Ⓔ	80 Ⓐ Ⓑ Ⓒ Ⓓ Ⓔ

CUT HERE

Sample Practice Test II

Section I: Multiple-Choice Questions

Time: 55 minutes

80 Questions

Percent of total grade = 50%

Directions: Each of the questions or incomplete statements below is followed by five suggested answers or completions. Select the one that is best in each case and then fill in the corresponding oval on the answer sheet.

1. **Détente** resulted in all of the following EXCEPT

   A. the signing of the SALT Accords

   B. the Helsinki Pact

   C. President Nixon's visit to Moscow

   D. the revocation of the Brezhnev Doctrine

   E. the Soviet invasion of Afghanistan

2. The beginning of World War I was sparked by the assassination of

   A. Tsar Nicholas II

   B. Bismarck

   C. Archduke Francis Ferdinand

   D. Emperor Franz Joseph

   E. Kaiser Wilhelm II

3. The Renaissance was different from the Middle Ages in all of the following ways EXCEPT

   A. studying of civilizations of Greece and Rome was stressed

   B. kings became the major source of power

   C. the secular world was emphasized

   D. the individual was glorified

   E. churches were the dominant institutions in society

4. Which of the following statesmen insisted that Italy be only "a geographic expression"?

   A. Metternich

   B. Cavour

   C. Bismarck

   D. Louis Napoleon

   E. Napoleon I

GO ON TO THE NEXT PAGE

5. *Lettres de cachet* were symbols of:

A. French toleration of differences

B. the absolutism of the French monarchy

C. France's economic supremacy

D. the bourgeoisie's attempts at revolting against the monarchy

E. a series of reforms that tried to improve peasant life in France

6. The Final Solution refers to

A. Hitler's plan to attack the Soviet Union

B. the Allied Plan to begin the Second Front against Germany

C. the plan to exterminate Europe's Jewish population

D. the Allied plan to bomb Germany's cities

E. Hitler's decision to attack Poland

7. The Protestant Reformation was similar to the Renaissance because

A. It emphasized the importance of the individual and faith in the ability of human reason.

B. The influence of the church increased.

C. Political rulers became less important.

D. Education focused on the classical texts of Greece and Rome.

E. Florence flourished as the major intellectual and cultural center.

8. A common similarity between the Renaissance and the Enlightenment is that both

A. promoted traditional values

B. supported democracy

C. encouraged a belief in the futility of life

D. produced major cultural changes

E. encouraged the importance of religion as a stabilizing force in society

9. Which of the following nations was NOT a member of the original European Common Market?

A. West Germany

B. France

C. Great Britain

D. Italy

E. Belgium

10. What was one of the main characteristics of English absolutism in the seventeenth century?

A. English kings were successful in ruling without Parliament.

B. Absolutism in England stressed the role of the church.

C. England's constitutional absolutism limited the power of the king.

D. The English monarchy had the support of the Puritans.

E. The Tudor and Stuart monarchs were popular with the people.

11. Louis Blanc promoted a program that included

   A. national workshops supported by the government

   B. unions for workers

   C. that government should seize all the property of the individuals

   D. a worldwide revolution

   E. that government should support unemployment insurance

12. Which of the following countries never became a victim of imperialism?

   A. China

   B. India

   C. Japan

   D. Egypt

   E. Morocco

13. "When France sneezes, Europe catches a cold."

   What event would have caused Metternich to make this statement?

   A. The July Revolution of 1830 in France

   B. the election of Louis Philippe as king of France

   C. the election of Louis Napoleon as president of the Second French Republic in 1848

   D. the forming of the Quadruple Alliance

   E. The Peterloo Massacre

14. The most important officials in the Provisional government of Russia in 1917 were the

   A. Bolsheviks and Socialists

   B. Socialists and Czarist

   C. Mensheviks and Socialists

   D. Bolsheviks and Liberals

   E. Liberals and Socialists

15. What factor contributed to Yugoslavia's success in not falling under Soviet control?

   A. Marshal Tito's aggressive military campaign

   B. Yugoslavia does not border the Soviet Union

   C. a treaty between the Soviet Union and Yugoslavia

   D. military aid from the United States

   E. protection from Britain

16. Place the following events in the correct chronological order.

   1) Birth of the Commonwealth of Independent States

   2) Gorbachev's policy of glasnost

   3) Signing of the Paris Treaty

   4) Fall of the Berlin Wall

   A. 1, 3, 2, 4

   B. 4, 3, 2, 1

   C. 2, 4, 3, 1

   D. 1, 2, 3, 4

   E. 3, 4, 2, 1

GO ON TO THE NEXT PAGE

17. "The Sicilians are fighting against the enemies of Italy. It is the duty of every Italian to succor them . . . to arms. Let me put an end . . . to the miseries of so many centuries."

The author of this passage was

A. Giuseppe Garibaldi

B. Giuseppe Mazzini

C. Camillo Cavour

D. Victor Emmanuel

E. Napoleon III

18. The terms "White Man's Burden" and "Scramble for Africa" refer to a time period in history known as the

A. Age of Discovery

B. Age of Imperialism

C. Age of Nationalism

D. Cold War Era

E. Industrial Revolution

19. Which of the following was a factor in the success of the Tudor monarchy in England?

A. They had no real authority and let Parliament make all government decisions.

B. Parliament was never consulted.

C. They acquired many colonies overseas in lands such as Asia and Africa.

D. They maintained peaceful relations with the Catholic Church.

E. The Tudors ruled absolutely by consulting with Parliament.

20. Which one of the following inventors is correctly associated with his invention from the Agricultural Revolution?

A. Jethro Tull — scientific breeding of animals

B. Robert Blackwell — self-cleaning steel plow

C. Charles Newbold — the reaper

D. Charles Trump Townshend — crop rotation

E. John Deere — the seed drill

21. The Edict of Nantes in France granted religious freedom to the

A. Catholics

B. Jews

C. Huguenots

D. Baptists

E. Anglicans

22. The greatest influence in spreading the ideas of the Renaissance from Italy to other parts of the world was

A. the wealth of the Medici family

B. humanists traveling to other parts of Europe, preaching their ideas

C. the invention of the movable metal type and the printing press

D. the patronization of painters in Italy

E. the opening of new schools to teach Renaissance ideals

23. Newton is considered the greatest figure of the Scientific Revolution because he

   A. introduced the Scientific Method

   B. established a school of astronomy

   C. established the existence of God as a daily presence in life

   D. developed mathematical laws to explain the orderly manner in which planets revolved around the sun

   E. introduced the laws of universal gravitation which supported the medieval view of the universe

24. After World War II, Soviet domination of Eastern Europe was most directly the result of

   A. the United States' policy of isolationism

   B. growing democratic movements

   C. peace agreements supported by the United Nations

   D. Soviet military occupation of the region

   E. secret treaties between the Soviet Union and other Eastern European nations

25. The correct chronological order of the following events is

   1) Russo-Japanese War

   2) Mussolini seizes power in Italy

   3) Lenin introduces New Economic Policy

   4) Stalin begins party purges

   A. 2, 3, 4, 1

   B. 3, 4, 1, 2

   C. 1, 3, 2, 4

   D. 1, 2, 4, 3

   E. 2, 1, 3, 4

26. All of the following were results of World War I EXCEPT

   A. The Ottoman Empire was destroyed.

   B. Communism was established in Russia.

   C. The economies of Europe were weakened.

   D. Russia emerged as the leading world power.

   E. The Hapsburgs of Austria-Hungary and the Romanov Dynasty of Russia collapsed.

27. Hitler's first violation of the Treaty of Versailles was his

   A. occupation of the Rhineland

   B. remilitarization of Germany

   C. invasion of Russia

   D. signing of the agreement with Fascist Italy

   E. annexation of Austria

GO ON TO THE NEXT PAGE

28. An immediate effect of the Declaration of Pillnitz was

    A. The French received military support from other European nations.

    B. The French received financial support from other European nations.

    C. The people of Prussia and Austria began their own revolutions.

    D. France declared war on Austria.

    E. Austria and Prussia declared war on each other.

29. Which of the following problems did NOT contribute to the Protestant Reformation?

    A. sales of indulgences by priests

    B. simony

    C. the Great Schism

    D. nepotism

    E. the rise of reform leaders John Wycliffe and Jan Hus

30. The Peace of Westphalia

    A. denied Lutherans religious freedom

    B. increased the strength of the papacy

    C. marked the end of the Thirty Years War

    D. revoked the Peace of Augsburg

    E. weakened the strength of German princes

31. In the past, European nations have conquered other lands, made them into colonies, and controlled their economies.

Which of the following terms does the statement describe?

    A. Socialism

    B. Isolationism

    C. Imperialism

    D. Communism

    E. Militarism

32. A major issue dividing the delegates at the Frankfurt Assembly of 1848 was

    A. a disagreement over whether the Zollverein should be continued

    B. the need to address United German relations with France

    C. how to establish closer ties with Russia

    D. the status of Protestantism in Northern Germany and Catholicism in Southern Germany

    E. the struggle between those who wanted to include the German-speaking province of Austria under German rule and those delegates who wanted to exclude them

33. Mikhail Gorbachev's reforms included *perestroika*, which refers to

    A. the introduction of a police state in certain violent regions

    B. lowered price caps on agricultural goods

    C. economic restructuring that allowed some capitalist ventures

    D. rations for food, clothes, and other necessities

    E. free elections

34. Northern Humanists interpreted the ideas of the Italian Renaissance by

A. emphasizing Italian art

B. paying more attention to Biblical and early Christian themes

C. stressing more of a secular view

D. using vernacular language

E. supporting the study of poetry, history, astronomy, and music

35. The Thermidorian Reaction resulted in

A. the end of the Reign of Terror in France

B. Robespierre's rise to power

C. the death of nearly 40,000 people in France

D. the de-Christianization of France

E. the restoration of the French monarchy

36. A major component of Calvinism was John Calvin's belief that

A. man was born a sinner and God had already determined who was going to be saved and who was damned

B. priests were needed to interpret the Bible

C. saints were a symbol of worship

D. doing good deeds would help one's status in the afterlife

E. sacraments were essential

37. The Industrial Revolution began in England because

A. the country was rich in natural resources such as coal and iron ore

B. the English government encouraged migration from its colonies as a way to gain workers for the factories

C. France supplied the English government with technological information

D. the English government controlled production

E. the English government's social policy created a positive work ethic among the workers

38. Which was one of the effects of the Great Depression in Europe during the 1930s?

A. It led to the rise of Fascism in Italy.

B. It contributed to widespread dissatisfaction with Communism in Russia.

C. It created the situation that attracted supporters for the Nazi Party.

D. It renewed support in Great Britain and France for democracy.

E. It led to large-scale migration to the United States.

39. The riots in Manchester, England, after the Napoleonic War in 1819 led to

A. the Peterloo Massacre

B. the Government Works Program for the poor

C. the abolition of property qualifications for voting

D. the corn laws

E. limiting the power of the House of Lords

GO ON TO THE NEXT PAGE

40. In the early 1990s, Czechoslovakia

A. expanded its territory south into Bosnia-Herzegovina

B. peacefully divided into two independent nations

C. began stockpiling nuclear weapons

D. became the first nation to rejoin the Warsaw Pact

E. resisted a United Nations invasion of Slovakia

41. As Louis XIV's finance minister, Jean Baptiste Colbert, helped to

A. overthrow the French throne

B. ensure that every class received equal treatment under Louis XIV's rule

C. form a strong and peaceful relationship between the monarchy and the church

D. advance France's prosperity by his economic policies

E. promote peace in Europe

42. All of the following are associated with Bismarck and the unification of Germany EXCEPT

A. Helmuth Von Moltke

B. Franco-Prussian War

C. Austro-Prussian War

D. Berlin Conference of 1884

E. Danish War

43. In which country was the Carbonari first organized?

A. Italy

B. Portugal

C. Britain

D. Russia

E. Prussia

44. Who of the following is considered an Enlightenment Despot ruler?

A. Frederick the Great

B. Louis XIV

C. Alexander I

D. James I

E. Charles V

45. All of the following countries underwent a revolution or civil unrest between 1820 and 1830 EXCEPT

A. Portugal

B. Switzerland

C. Sardinia

D. Spain

E. Greece

46. In the early 1800s, English Parliament represented primarily the interests of the

A. middle class

B. urban workers

C. landed aristocracy

D. Anglican Church

E. emerging capitalist owners

47. Critics of the New Imperialism condemned it for all of the following reasons EXCEPT

    A. Imperialism benefited only the special interest groups, such as the Capitalists, rather than the nations.

    B. They rejected the Social Darwinism of Imperialism.

    C. Imperialism was benefiting the colonies at the expense of the economy of the mother country.

    D. Imperialists disregarded the culture of the colonial people.

    E. Imperialists had a double standard of liberty at home but dictatorship in the colonies.

48. How did Henry VIII make the Anglican Church different from the Roman Catholic Church?

    A. The king was the head of the church, not the pope.

    B. The sacraments were abolished.

    C. The Bible was no longer used in services.

    D. Priests did not perform worship services.

    E. Worship services were no longer held on Sundays.

49. All of the following were achievements of Napoleon EXCEPT:

    A. the Napoleonic Code

    B. peace with the Catholic Church

    C. annexed areas of Netherlands and Belgium to France

    D. strengthened the role and status of women in France

    E. modernized finance

50. The Lateran Treaty (1929) between Mussolini and Pope Pius XII resulted in

    A. an agreement to fight Communism

    B. recognition of the pope as the sovereign of Vatican City and Fascism as the legitimate government of Italy

    C. the abdication of the Italian king

    D. the return of papal lands to the different local governments in Italy

    E. a schedule for democratic elections for a parliamentary government

51. Which of the following events was NOT associated with Nikita Khrushchev?

    A. de-Stalinization

    B. a period of liberalization in Russia

    C. Russia's presence at the Geneva Summit

    D. revolutions in Poland and Hungary

    E. formation of the North Atlantic Treaty Alliance (NATO)

52. Voltaire's statement *ecrasez l'infame* (crush the horrible things) refers to

    A. the government of Louis XIV

    B. the Catholic Church

    C. the military

    D. the middle class

    E. the poor

GO ON TO THE NEXT PAGE

53. Which of the following statements summarizes one of the major themes of Machiavelli's *The Prince*?

    A. Loyalty to a city is a foolish diversion of human devotion.

    B. The end justifies the means.

    C. In diplomacy honesty is the best policy.

    D. Only through prayer can a man achieve his full measure of virtue.

    E. Civilization reached its lowest point during the Roman Republic.

54. One of the results of the Sadler Committee of 1832 was that it led to

    A. the formation of minimum wage laws for workers

    B. government recognition of unions

    C. passage of legislation regulating the employment of children in factories

    D. a demand for social legislation

    E. nationalization of the iron and steel industry

55. Which of the following did NOT happen after Charles I signed the Petition of Rights?

    A. Charles ruled for 11 years without Parliament.

    B. Calvinists in Scotland revolted against Charles' attempts to impose the Anglican religion on them.

    C. Charles was unable to levy taxes without Parliament's consent.

    D. The Long Parliament ruled for 20 years and passed laws that limited the power of the king.

    E. Charles requested money from Parliament for his military expedition against Spain.

56. Which of the following countries was never a member of the Warsaw Pact?

    A. Austria

    B. Poland

    C. Czechoslovakia

    D. Hungary

    E. Romania

57. Which of the following led to Britain's declaration of war on Germany in 1914?

    A. Austria's ultimatum to Serbia

    B. Germany's invasion of Belgium

    C. Germany's invasion of Russia

    D. Russia's support of Serbia

    E. Italy's decision to remain neutral

58. In which of the following ways did the Sepoy Mutiny affect India?

    A. Great Britain relinquished government control to the British East India Company.

    B. The British government assumed direct control of India.

    C. Islam and Hinduism became recognized as state religions.

    D. Parliamentary democracy was introduced in India.

    E. India gained its independence.

59. Which was NOT a major characteristic of the Scientific Revolution of the seventeenth century?

    A. growth of a learned society, such as the Royal Society of London

    B. challenged medieval superstition and general acceptance of Aristotle's theories

    C. a widespread growth of knowledge among the general population

    D. a modern scientific method developed that stressed reason over tradition

    E. much knowledge was uncovered about the physical world

60. The painting of *Guernica* by Pablo Picasso was inspired by

    A. the Spanish Civil War (1936–1939)

    B. Hitler's rise to power

    C. Mussolini's support of the Spanish Fascists

    D. Italy's invasion of Ethiopia

    E. The Nazi-Soviet Non-Aggression Pact

61. The Ausgleich or Compromise of 1867 established all of the following EXCEPT

    A. Dual monarchy of Austria-Hungary

    B. Franz Joseph became emperor

    C. each state had its own Parliament

    D. each half of the empire had control of its own nationalities

    E. a uniform educational and monetary system was set up

62. What impact did the reign of Louis XIV have on the Huguenots?

    A. They enjoyed a long period of religious freedom.

    B. They eventually left France because Louis XIV destroyed their property and took away their civil rights.

    C. They were sent to France's colonies to work the land.

    D. They were forced to live in poor conditions and many died due to disease.

    E. They became trusted advisers and provided wise counsel to Louis XIV.

63. The Allied . . . governments . . . affirm and Germany accepts responsibility for causing all the loss and damages to which the Allied . . . governments have been subjected . . . on them by the aggression of Germany.

In which of the following documents would this passage be found?

    A. The Atlantic Charter

    B. The Treaty of Versailles

    C. The Charter of the League of Nations

    D. The Treaty of Frankfurt

    E. The Treaty of Westphalia

GO ON TO THE NEXT PAGE

64. A major effect of the Revolution of 1848 in France was

    A. the return of the Bourbon Dynasty

    B. the establishment of National Workshops as a permanent government policy

    C. the intervention by Austria to uphold peace

    D. the return of Charles X from England

    E. the election of Louis Napoleon

65. Which of the following historians coined the term "Industrial Revolution?"

    A. Arnold Toynbee

    B. Saint-Simon

    C. Leopold Von Ranke

    D. Max Weber

    E. Jacob Burkhardt

66. All of the following were a result of the Catholic or Counter Reformation EXCEPT

    A. the creation of the Index of Prohibited Books in Catholic countries

    B. the medieval inquisition was revived, resulting in the deaths of heretics

    C. the abuses within the church, such as nepotism, and simony, were condemned

    D. the resurgence of more religious art

    E. the official abolishment of the sacraments

67. By 1807, Napoleon's Grand Empire included all of the following countries EXCEPT:

    A. Great Britain

    B. Italy

    C. Germany

    D. Netherlands

    E. Spain

68. Which was a major theme of Humanist writers?

    A. glorifying the individual and worldly subjects

    B. the role of religion in one's life

    C. the importance of feudalism

    D. the damaging effects of educating people through poetry and astronomy

    E. breaking away from the ideas of the classical writers of ancient Greece

69. What area was known as the Powder Keg of Europe at the beginning of the twentieth century?

    A. The Balkans

    B. The Russian Empire

    C. The German Empire

    D. The Ottoman Empire

    E. The Unified Italian States

70. During the Cold War, the United States and the Soviet Union were reluctant to become involved in direct conflict because

  A. Neither country wanted to fight a war on their soil.

  B. There was potential for global nuclear destruction.

  C. Both countries received pressure from nonaligned nations.

  D. The United Nations played a role in peacekeeping.

  E. There were increased tensions in the Middle East.

WONDER HOW LONG THE HONEYMOON WILL LAST?

©CORBIS

71. This cartoon symbolizes

  A. the Nazi-Soviet Non-Aggression Pact of 1939

  B. the formation of the Pact of Steel

  C. the Soviet Union's support of Hitler's occupation of the Rhineland

  D. the Soviet Union's and Germany's cooperation at the Munich Conference

  E. Germany's and the Soviet Union's support for General Franco in 1939

72. Which of the following has been one reason for opposition towards a common currency or the Euro?

  A. Nationalists believe that unity may destroy their countries' unique identities and their ability to control their economies.

  B. fear of backlash from hostile nations

  C. the United States' negative reaction to European Unity

  D. an unstable economy

  E. unwillingness of formerly communist nations to agree to the terms necessary to achieve European Unity

73. Which of the following men did NOT attend the Munich Conference?

  A. Neville Chamberlain

  B. Benito Mussolini

  C. Adolph Hitler

  D. Edmund Daladier

  E. Edward Benes

74. "Population, when unchecked, increases in a geometrical rate. Subsistence only increased in an arithmetical ratio."

The ideas in this passage are most associated with

  A. David Ricardo

  B. Thomas Malthus

  C. Louis Blanc

  D. John Locke

  E. Karl Marx

GO ON TO THE NEXT PAGE

75. The Reform Bills of 1832, 1867, 1884, 1918, and 1928 in Britain resulted in

   A. the expansion of voting rights among men and women

   B. limiting the power of the House of Commons

   C. increasing the power of the House of Lords

   D. establishing guidelines on the role of the monarchy in Great Britain

   E. establishing guidelines on the role of government in the economy

76. Which best describes the philosophers of the Enlightenment?

   A. They were mainly from England and Italy.

   B. They were enthusiastic supporters of the Catholic Church.

   C. They supported absolutism.

   D. They wished to reform society and used satire to spread their message.

   E. They rejected reason and stressed emotion.

77. Which was a major goal of the Jesuits?

   A. combating heresy and spreading the Catholic faith

   B. stopping the sale of indulgences

   C. stressing the Bible as the source of salvation

   D. demonstrating that good works were not necessary for salvation

   E. getting rid of the seven sacraments

78. Which of the following contributed to the outbreak of the nationalist movement in the Hapsburg Empire?

   A. a common language

   B. active support by Emperor Franz Joseph

   C. the role of German nationalists in organizing a secret national organization

   D. several national groups, such as the Serbs, Czechs, and Slovenes, occupying the same region

   E. support of England and France

79. The fifteenth century gave rise to the following powerful leaders EXCEPT

   A. Louis XI of France

   B. Henry VII of England

   C. Medicis in Florence

   D. Ferdinand and Isabella of Spain

   E. Charles I of England

80. The Hungarian Nationalist who led the fight for independence against Austria in the nineteenth century was

   A. Lajos Kossuth

   B. Ferdinand I

   C. Janos Kadar

   D. Eduard Benes

   E. Imre Nagy

EUROPEAN HISTORY

SECTION II

Part A

(Suggested writing time — 45 minutes)

Percent of Section II score — 45

Directions: The following question is based on the accompanying Documents 1–10. (Some of the documents have been edited for the purpose of this exercise.) This question is designed to test your ability to work with historical documents. As you analyze the documents, take into account both the sources of the documents and the authors' points of view. Write an essay on the following topic that integrates your analysis of the documents. **Do not simply summarize the documents individually.** You may refer to relevant historical facts and developments not mentioned in the documents.

1. Assess the following statement:

   The Industrial Revolution in the 1700s and 1800s caused immense suffering for the workers in English society.

   Historical Background: Arnold Toynbee coined the phrase "Industrial Revolution" to explain the economic development in England during the eighteenth and nineteenth centuries. To many, industrialization became synonymous with progress but for others, it created many problems. Critics attacked the Industrial Revolution for altering the nature of the workplace, the workforce, and the living conditions of the people.

Document 1

What time did you begin to work at a factory? — When I was six years old. . . .

What kind of mill is it? — Flax-mill. . . .

What were your hours of labour in that mill? — From 5 in the morning till 9 at night, when they were thronged.

For how long a time together have you worked that excessive length of time? — for about half a year.

GO ON TO THE NEXT PAGE

What were your usual hours of labour when you were not so thronged? — From 6 in the morning till 7 at night.

What time was allowed for your meals? — Forty minutes at noon.

Had you any time to get your breakfast or drinking? — No, we got it as we could.

And when your work was bad, you hardly had anytime to eat at all? — No; we were obliged to leave it or take it home, and when we did not take it, the overlooker took it, and gave it to his pigs.

Were the children beat up to their labour there? — Yes.

With what? — A strap; I have seen the overlooker go to the top end of the room, where the little girls hug the can to the backminders; he has taken a strap, and a whistle in his mouth, and sometimes he has got a chain and chained them, and strapped them all down the room. . . .

What was his reason for that? — He was angry.

Had the children committed any fault? — They were too slow.

Were the children excessively fatigued at that time? — Yes, it was in the afternoon.

Were the girls so struck as to leave marks upon their skin? — Yes . . . they were afraid of losing their work.

If the parents were to complain of this excessive ill-usage, the probable consequence would be the loss of the situation of the child? — Yes. . . .

Source: Testimony before the Sadler Committee (1831–1832).

Document 2

They come forth: the mine delivers its gang . . . Infants of four and five years of age, many of them girls, pretty and still soft and timid; entrusted with the fulfillment of responsible duties. . . . Their labour indeed is not severe, for that would be impossible, but it is passed in darkness and in solitude. . . . Hour after hour elapses, and all that reminds the infant trappers of the world they have quitted, and that which they have joined, is the passage of the coal-wagons for which they open the air-doors of the galleries, and on keeping which doors constantly closed, except at this moment of passage, the safety of the mine and the lives of the persons employed in it entirely depend.

Source: Benjamin Disraeli, *Sybil* (1865).

Document 3

Nothing shows in a clearer point of view the credulity of mankind . . . than the ready faith which was given to the tales of cruelty exercised by proprietors of cotton-mills towards young children. . . .

I have visited many factories . . . and I never saw a single instance of corporal chastisement inflicted on a child, or indeed did I ever see children in ill-humor. They seemed to be always cheerful and alert, taking pleasure in the light play of their muscles . . . the work of these lively elves seemed to resemble a sport, in which habit gave them a pleasing dexterity. Conscious of their skill, they were delighted to show it off to any stranger. As to exhaustion by the day's work, they evinced no trace of it on emerging from the mill in the evening; for they immediately began to skip about any neighboring playground, and to commence their little amusements with the same alacrity as boys issuing from a school. It is moreover my firm convictions that . . . children . . . would thrive better when employed in our modern factories than if left at home in apartments too often ill aired, damp, and cold. . . .

Source: Andrew Ure, *The Philosophy of Manufacturers* (1835).

Document 4

The little town of Hyde was at the beginning of the century a little hamlet of only 800 people, on the summit of a barren hill, the soil of which did not yield sufficient food for the inhabitants. The brothers Ashton have peopled and enriched this desert. . . . Mr. T. Ashton employs 1500 work people (in his factories). The young women are well and decently clothed. . . The houses inhabited by the work people form long and large streets. Mr. Aston has built 300 of them, which he lets (rents) for . . . 75 cents per week. . . . Everywhere is to be observed a cleanliness, which indicates order and comfort.

Source: Leon Faucher, *Manchester in 1844*.

Document 5

The employment of women at once breaks up the family; for when the wife spends twelve or thirteen hours every day in the mill, and the husband works the same length of time there or elsewhere, what becomes of the children? They grow up like wild weeds; they are put out to nurse for a shilling or eighteen pence a week, and how they are treated may be imagined. . . . That the general mortality among young children must be increased by the employment of the mothers is self-evident, and is placed beyond all doubt by notorious facts.

Women often return to the mill three or four days after confinement (for childbirth), leaving the baby, of course; in the dinner hour they must hurry home to feed the child and eat something. . . .

Source: Friedrich Engels, *The Impact of the Factory System on Women and the Family* (1892).

GO ON TO THE NEXT PAGE

Document 6

The village contains about 1500 inhabitants, of whom all who are capable of work are employed in and about the mills. Of these there are 500 children who are entirely fed, clothed, and educated by Mr. Dale. The others live with their parents in the village and have a weekly allowance for their work. The healthy appearance of these children has frequently attracted the attention of the traveler. Special regulations, adopted by Mr. Dale, have made this factory very different from the others in this kingdom. Out of the nearly 3,000 children employed in the mill from 1785–1797, only fourteen have died.

Source: Society for Bettering the Conditions and Increasing the Good Comforts of the Poor (1797).

Document 7

I am forced to admit that instead of being exaggerated, it is far from black enough to convey a true impression of the filth, ruin, and uninhabitableness, the defiance of all considerations of cleanliness, ventilation, and health which characterizes the construction of this single district, containing at least twenty to thirty thousand inhabitants. And such a district exists in the heart of the second city of England, the first manufacturing city of the world. If any one wishes to see in how little space a human being can move, how little air — and *such* air! — he can breathe, how little of civilization he may share and yet live, it is only necessary to travel hither. True, this is the *Old* Town, and the people of Manchester emphasize the fact whenever any one mentions to them the frightful condition of this Hell upon Earth; but what does that prove? Everything which here arouses horror and indignation is of recent origin, belongs to the *industrial epoch.*

Source: Friedrich Engels, *The Condition of the Working Class in England* (1844).

Document 8

. . . In most parts of England poor children are a burthen to their parents and to the parish; here the parish, which would else have to support them, is rid of all expense; they get their bread almost as soon as they can run about, and by the time they are seven or eight years old bring in money. . . . I was looking, while he spoke, at the unnatural dexterity with which the fingers of these little creatures were playing in the machinery, half giddy myself with the noise and the endless motion; and when he told me there was no rest in these walls, day or night, I thought that if Dante had peopled one of his hells with children, here was a scene worthy to have supplied him with new images of torment. . . . These children then said, 'have no time to receive instruction.' 'That, sir, he replied 'is the evil . . . you see them till they marry, and then they know nothing about domestic work, not even how to mend a stocking or boil a potato. But we are remedying this now, and send the children to school for an hour after they have done work.' . . . 'manufacturers are favourable to population, the poor are not afraid of having a family here, the parishes therefore have always plenty to apprentice, and we take them as fast as they can supply us.' . . .

Source: Robert Southey, *Letters From England* (1807).

Document 9

Cause of Death	Under 13 Years of age	13 and not exceeding 18 years of age	Over 18 Years of age
Fell down the shafts	13	12	31
Fell down the shaft from the rope breaking	1	-	2
Fell out when ascending	-	-	3
Drawn over the pulley	3	-	3
Fall of stone out of a skip down the shaft	1	-	3
Drowned in the mines	3	4	15
Fall of stones, coal, and rubbish in the mines	14	14	69
Injuries in coal pits, the nature of which is not specified	6	3	32
Crushed in coal pits	-	1	1
Explosion of gas	13	18	49
Suffocation of choke-damp	-	2	6
Explosion of gunpowder	-	1	3
By tram-wagons	4	5	12
Total	**58**	**60**	**229**

Source: John Saville, "Child Labor," *Working conditions In the Victorian Age: Common Cause of Death in Coal Mines.*

Document 10

As to the conclusions I have come to from the working of my mill for 11 instead of 12 hours each day, as previously, I am quite satisfied that both as much yarn and cloth may be produced at quite as low a cost in 11 as in 12 hours. It is my intention to make a further reduction to 10 1/2 hours, without the slightest fear of suffering loss. I find the hands work with greater energy and spirit; they are more cheerful, and happy. . . .

Source: Parliamentary Papers, 1845, XXV, pp. 456–7. A factory owner's view of industrialization.

STOP

EUROPEAN HISTORY

SECTION II

Part B

(Suggested planning and writing time — 70 minutes)

Percent of Section II score — 55

Directions: You are to answer TWO questions, one from each group of three questions below. Make your selections carefully, choosing the questions that you are best prepared to answer thoroughly in the time permitted. You should spend 5 minutes organizing or outlining each essay. In writing your essays, use specific examples to support your answer. If time permits when you finish writing, check your work. Be certain to number your answers as the questions are numbered below.

Group 1

Choose ONE question from this group. The suggested writing time for this question is 30 minutes. You are advised to spend 5 minutes planning your answer in the area below.

1. Discuss the role of women in the Renaissance.

2. Crane Brinton's book, *The Anatomy of Revolution,* asserts that revolutions follow a certain pattern: moderate, radical, and reactionary, ending with the emergence of a powerful leader. Assess this thesis in regard to the French Revolution.

3. Compare and contrast mercantilism with laissez faire.

Group 2

Choose ONE question from this group. The suggested writing time for this question is 30 minutes. You are advised to spend 5 minutes planning your answer in the area below.

1. Discuss the factors that contributed to the economic recovery of Western Europe after World War II.

2. Discuss the conditions that led to the rise of Fascism in Italy and Nazism in Germany.

3. Compare and contrast the unification of Germany with the unification of Italy.

STOP

Answer Key for Practice Test II

Section I: Multiple-Choice Questions

1. D	21. C	41. D	61. E
2. C	22. C	42. D	62. B
3. E	23. D	43. A	63. B
4. A	24. D	44. A	64. E
5. B	25. C	45. B	65. A
6. C	26. D	46. C	66. E
7. A	27. B	47. C	67. A
8. D	28. D	48. A	68. A
9. C	29. E	49. D	69. A
10. C	30. C	50. B	70. B
11. A	31. C	51. E	71. A
12. C	32. E	52. B	72. A
13. A	33. C	53. B	73. E
14. E	34. B	54. C	74. B
15. B	35. A	55. E	75. A
16. C	36. A	56. A	76. D
17. A	37. A	57. B	77. A
18. B	38. C	58. B	78. D
19. E	39. A	59. C	79. E
20. D	40. B	60. A	80. A

Section II: Free-Response Essays

Student essays and analysis appear beginning on page 345.

Answers and Explanations for Practice Test II

Section I: Multiple-Choice Questions

1. **D.** *Détente* did not result in the revocation of the Brezhnev Doctrine; rather it refers to a period of relaxation in tension between the United States and the Soviet Union during the 1970s when Leonid Brezhnev was leader. The Brezhnev Doctrine claimed that the Soviet Union had the right to intervene in any socialist country that needed it to do so. Brezhnev had intervened in Czechoslovakia in 1968 to end reform efforts by Alexander Dubcek to change Communism; likewise, in 1979, the Soviet Union invaded Afghanistan in order to keep the Communists in power. During the *détente* era, the SALT Accords limited the spread of nuclear weapons. President Nixon's visit to Moscow and Brezhnev's visit to the United States were both tense. The Helsinki Pact signed in 1975 was an agreement among the United States, Canada, the Soviet Union, and 33 European nations formally recognizing the division of Europe in the Cold War era.

2. **C.** The beginning of World War I was sparked by the assassination of Archduke Francis Ferdinand of Austria-Hungary. On June 28, 1914, Archduke Ferdinand and his wife were assassinated by a Serbian nationalist named Gavrilo Princip. When Serbia refused to agree to all of Austria's demands, the chain reaction that developed plunged Europe into World War I. Nicholas II was czar of Russia. Bismarck was chancellor of Prussia who had helped to unify Germany. Emperor Franz Joseph II was the leader of Austria-Hungary and Kaiser Wilhelm II was the leader of the German Empire.

3. **E.** During the Renaissance, the church was not the dominant institution in society. During the Middle Ages, the church played a major role in society because it provided religious, economic, and political leadership. By the time of the Renaissance, the influence of the church began to decline as kings in France and England began to centralize more power and tried to control the influence of the church. The Renaissance, which glorified the individual and insisted that the secular world was just as important as the religious world, also challenged the position of the church. Society began to study the civilizations of Greece and Rome, which seemed to provide a better understanding of the fifteenth-century world rather than the philosophy of the Middle Ages. The church in the Renaissance was important but was not the single focus of everything in the lives of the people.

4. **A.** At the Congress of Vienna in 1814–1815, Prince Klemens von Metternich insisted that Italy was only a "geographic expression." After the congress, Italy was divided into separate states with Austria annexing the rich industrialized provinces of Lombardy and Venetia. In the South, the Spanish Bourbon family ruled the Kingdom of the Two Sicilies. Cavour was the prime minister of Piedmont Sardinia who used war and diplomacy to unite Italy. Bismarck was the chancellor of Prussia whose policy led to the unification of Germany. Louis Napoleon and Napoleon I were both supporters of Italian unification.

5. B. The *lettres of cachet* were symbols of the absolutism of the French monarchy during the Old Regime. They were letters signed by the king and countersigned by the Secretary of State in France authorizing someone's imprisonment or exile without a recourse to a court of law. The Constituent Assembly in the French Revolution abolished it. *Lettres of cachet* were methods to insure absolute control of the French monarch; they were not concerned with toleration, or economic or political attempts to overthrow the monarchy.

6. C. The Final Solution refers to Hitler's plan to exterminate Europe's Jewish population. Hitler's National Socialist Program called for the disenfranchising of all Jews, the systematic organizing of the persecution of the Jews, the boycotting of Jews, expelling them from public life, and finally annihilating them. Beginning in November 1935, the Nazis implemented laws that stripped Jews of their civil rights and shipped them to concentration camps. In July 1941, Heinrich Himmler and Nazi leaders implemented plans (the Final Solution) to exterminate all the Jews in Europe and Hitler's empire. In the next four years, the Nazis rounded up Jews by the thousands and sent them to concentration camps such as Dachau in Germany and Auschwitz in Poland. Operation Barbarossa refers to Hitler's plan to invade Russia, and D-Day refers to the Allied plan to invade Germany through France. There are no specific terms to describe the Allied plan to attack German cities nor for Hitler's invasion of Poland.

7. A. The Protestant Reformation was similar to the Renaissance because it emphasized the importance of the individual and faith in the ability of human reason. Humanist writers believed in the ability of individuals to bring about change and stressed the use of reason rather than the acceptance of dogma as the basis of life. Erasmus' *Praise of Folly* was critical of many Church practices because they were based on superstition and ignorance. Luther and Calvin, leaders of the Protestant Reformation, believed in the power of the individual to read the Bible and determine church doctrine and practices. As in the Renaissance, Reformation leaders believed in glorifying the individual and his rationality. The influence of the church declined during the Protestant Reformation, which ended the religious unity of Europe. The role of political rulers, however, expanded during the Reformation as they gained control of Church land. The Reformation did not focus on classics nor was Florence the intellectual and cultural center. Catholics in Southern Europe and Protestants in Northern Europe developed their own distinct cultural centers.

8. D. The Renaissance (fifteenth century) and the Enlightenment (eighteenth century) were similar in that both produced cultural changes, or altered the way people looked at the world. The Renaissance encouraged a secular worldview of the world while the Enlightenment promoted the belief that human reason could uncover the plan that governed the universe. Belief in the power of the individual led to the rise of Humanism during the Renaissance and the rise of philosophers during the Enlightenment. The ideals of the Renaissance and the Enlightenment also affected the arts and sciences of the era. Neither of these periods promoted traditional values or democracy, nor did they encourage religion as a force in society. Both attacked traditional abuses that underlined society. Both were optimistic about the importance of life.

9. C. Great Britain was not a member of the original European Common Market. Britain ended its traditional policy of aloofness from European affairs and began to seek membership in the late 1960s. President Charles De Gaulle of France vetoed British entrance in 1967. However, in 1973, Britain became a member.

10. C. A characteristic of English absolutism in the seventeenth century was that it limited the power of the king. English absolutism developed along constitutional lines, by means of the Bill of Rights (1689), which meant that the power resided in the state (Parliament). and that the elections were to be free from the Crown's control. The English monarchs were not successful in ruling without Parliament (Charles I was beheaded and James II was expelled for trying to rule absolutely), nor did they depend upon the Anglican Church for absolute control. The Tudors were popular rulers but the Stuarts were unpopular because they tried to rule absolutely and pursued a foreign policy of friendship with Spain. In 1642, the Puritans led the revolt against Charles I because they opposed his efforts to rule absolutely.

11. A. Louis Blanc promoted a program that included national government-supported workshops. Blanc was a socialist who looked for solutions to problems created by the Industrial Revolution by reorganizing the economy. Blanc believed that the full power of the state should be directed towards setting up national workshops and factories to guarantee full employment. Blanc did not call for the formation of a workers union nor did he approve of the government seizure of property through worldwide revolution. He did not promote unemployment insurance, but he did endorse state-supported manufacturing centers in which workers would labor for themselves without the intervention of private capitalists.

12. C. Japan never became a victim of imperialism. Japan's government realized that after Commodore Perry's visit to Japan in 1853, Japan had to modernize or, like China, it would fall prey to Western imperialism. In 1868, the Meiji Restoration helped to make Japan strong enough to compete with the Western European powers. The Japanese leaders adopted Western technology, built up a modern army based on the Prussian model, constructed a large navy, and promoted manufacturing. The Japanese demonstrated their power in defeating Russia in the Russo-Japanese War of 1904–1905. Japan's victory shattered the myth of supremacy of the European race. India and Egypt came under British rule in the eighteenth and nineteenth centuries, and Morocco came under French power in the nineteenth century. China began to be divided up by European nations after its defeat in the Opium War of 1839–1842.

13. A. France's July Revolution of 1830 — in response to King Charles X's suspension of the legislature, limitations on the right to vote, and restrictions of the press — caused Prince Klemens von Metternich to make this statement. He believed that this uprising would have a horrible influence on the rest of Europe and devastating effects not only in France but in the rest of the continent. Metternich would not have seen the election of Louis Philipe as king or Napoleon as president of France as a threat to Europe because they did not start a tide of other revolutions outside of France. The Peterloo Massacre took place in Manchester, England, in 1819 and involved the deaths and numerous injuries of innocent people peacefully gathered for petitioning Parliament. This massacre did not spark revolts outside of England.

14. E. The most important officials in Russia's Provisional government in 1917 were the Liberals and Socialists. On March 15, 1917, Czar Nicholas II abdicated and a Provisional government headed by Liberal Democrat Prince George Lvov, and later in July by the Moderate Socialist Alexander Kerensky, was established. Dominated by the middle class Liberals, the Provisional government quickly guaranteed civil liberties such as freedom of the press and speech and sought to establish a Western European style of democracy. Both the Liberals and Socialists rejected social revolution, considering the continuation of the war to be the most important objective. However, the failure of the Provisional government to implement social reform resulted in the loss of support among workers and peasants. The Bolsheviks, Mensheviks, and Czarists did not have a major role in the Provisional government. Lenin, who was the leader of the Bolsheviks (Communists), was in Switzerland and did not arrive in Russia until April 1917, when the Germans provided him with safe passage into Russia.

15. **B.** Yugoslavia's success in not falling under Soviet control was that Yugoslavia did not border on the Soviet Union. Although Josip Broz Tito (1892–1980) was as much a nationalist as a Communist and insisted on developing his own national policies, which angered Stalin and resulted in Yugoslavia's expulsion from the international Communist movement, Yugoslavia did not border the Soviet Union like Poland, Hungary, and Czechoslovakia, making it difficult for Stalin to control Yugoslavia. In addition, Tito had the support of the people and was able to resist Soviet pressure while developing his own form of Communism that held together Yugoslavia's different ethnic groups and also won aid from the West. Tito did not pursue an aggressive military campaign against the Soviet Union nor was there a treaty between the two countries. Tito also did not receive protection from England or military aid from the United States. He was successful in holding the country together by not allowing each state to develop its own separate state. After Tito's death in 1980, Yugoslavia broke up into different nation states which led to civil war and chaos in the region.

16. **C.** The correct chronological order of events is Gorbachev's policy of *glasnost* (1985), Fall of the Berlin Wall (1989), Signing of the Paris Accords (1990), and Birth of the Commonwealth of Independent States (1991).

17. **A.** Giuseppe Garibaldi was the author of this passage. Garibaldi was a military leader who invaded Sicily with his army of 1,000 Red Shirts and, once joined by rebels in Southern Italy, conquered Sicily. Garibaldi then crossed to the Italian mainland and gave permission to unite the Two Sicilies with the Kingdom of Piedmont-Sardinia.

18. **B.** The terms "White Man's Burden" and "Scramble for Africa" refers to the time period known as the Age of Imperialism. The Age of Imperialism covers the time span between 1870 and 1914 when European states established vast empires, mainly in Africa, but also in Asia and the Middle East. The "White Man's Burden" was a term used by the nineteenth-century British poet Rudyard Kipling, expressing the belief that Europeans had an obligation to civilize the uncivilized people in Africa. "Scramble for Africa" described how Europe divided up the continent of Africa during this time period. None of the time periods describe these terms.

19. **E.** A factor in the success of the Tudor monarchy in England was that the Tudors ruled absolutely by consulting Parliament. When Henry broke with the Roman Catholic Church, he asked Parliament's support to legalize his actions; he also met with Parliament regularly to confirm laws and to seek its approval on levying taxes. Elizabeth I, like her father, also consulted Parliament but controlled with a firm hand. The Tudors' skillful handling of Parliament made them poplar and successful leaders. The Tudors were not actively involved in acquiring colonies, nor were they friendly with Catholic Spain considering Henry VIII's divorce from his Spanish wife, Catherine of Aragon.

20. D. Charles Trump Townshend is correctly associated with crop rotation. This process improved upon the older methods of crop rotation such as the medieval three-field system. In the 1750s, Townshend won the nickname "Turnip Townshend" for urging farmers to grow turnips, which restored exhausted soil. By encouraging farmers to drain extensively, manure heavily, and sow crops in regular rotation without fallowing, the farmers were able to produce larger crops. Crop rotation helped to conserve soil fertility and made more land available for production. Jethro Tull invented the seed drill. Robert Blackwell developed the scientific breeding of animals. Charles Newbold invented the cast iron plow, and John Deere invented the self-cleaning plow.

21. C. The Edict of Nantes granted religious freedom to the Huguenots, a Calvinist minority living in France. From 1562–1589, frequent religious strifes existed between the Catholic majority and the Huguenots, which culminated in the St. Bartholomew Day Massacre in which more than 20,000 Huguenots were killed. In 1589, Henry IV of Navarre, a Calvinist leader, issued the Edict of Nantes to end the religious wars in France and allow for religious and civil freedom to the Protestant minority. There were no Baptists or Anglicans in France; Jews were denied religious freedom and were not affected by the edict.

22. C. The invention of the movable metal type and the printing press were instrumental in spreading the ideas of the Renaissance from Italy to other parts of the world. In 1450, Johannes Gutenberg, a German printer, invented the movable metal type and the printing press. As compared to the medieval hand-copying of books, the printing press increased output and was much cheaper. The printing press sprang up in Italy, Germany, England, and the Netherlands. As books became more readily available, more people learned to read and write. The increased circulation of books by Italian writers helped to spread the ideas of the Renaissance to other parts of Europe. By 1500, the printing press had turned out more than 20 million volumes. The Medici family promoted art in Italy but not outside of the Italian Peninsula. Students traveled to Italy to learn about the Renaissance but Humanists did not travel outside of Italy. Patronization of painters in Italy and the Opening of new schools to teach Renaissance ideals had a limited influence.

23. D. Newton is considered the greatest figure of the Scientific Revolution because he developed the mathematical laws to explain the orderly manner in which the planets revolved around the sun. In 1687, Isaac Newton published his work, *Mathematical Principles of Natural Philosophy,* in which he described the universe as a giant clock that worked in ways that could be expressed mathematically. Newton viewed God as a clockmaker who was not involved in the daily existences of life. Newton's laws of universal gravitation rejected the medieval view of the universe which was God-centered, instead showing that man could understand the universe around him by using his reason and that theology was not needed to understand the forces of nature. Sir Francis Bacon introduced the scientific method.

24. D. Soviet domination of Eastern Europe following World War II was most directly the result of the USSR's military occupation of the region. As the Red Army marched towards Berlin and pushed German troops out of Eastern Europe, Soviet troops remained in the region. Wanting to create a buffer zone to protect Russia from future invasions, Stalin insisted at the wartime conferences of Teheran, Yalta, and Potsdam that whoever occupied the territory would control the area. Communists in Poland and elsewhere in Eastern Europe, backed by the Red Army, destroyed the opposition and openly established pro-Stalin Communist governments in Eastern Europe. Fearing future conflict, the Western powers were unwilling to interfere. The United States followed a policy of containment not isolationism. A democratic movement would not develop in Eastern Europe until the 1980s, nor was the United Nations involved in the problems in Eastern Europe.

25. C. The correct chronological order for these events is the Russo-Japanese War (1904–1905), Lenin introduces the New Economic Policy (1921), Mussolini Seized power in Italy (1922), Stalin begins party purges (1934–1938).

26. D. Russia's emergence as leading world power was not a result of World War I, but instead occurred after World War II. In 1917, the Communists overthrew Czar Nicholas II and established the first Communist government on the European continent, after which Lenin and his Communist followers faced a number of obstacles, including a three-year civil war, famine, and the disbandment of the Russian Empire. The Communists did not establish firm control in Russia until 1921.

27. B. Hitler's first violation of the Treaty of Versailles was his remilitarization of Germany. In March 1935, Hitler dramatically repudiated the provisions of the Versailles Treaty that intended to keep Germany disarmed and openly built up the German armed forces. France, Great Britain, and later Italy protested the violation of an international treaty but did nothing specifically about it. Soon after, England entered into a naval agreement with Germany. Hitler occupied the Rhineland in 1936 and annexed Austria in 1938 — again violations against the Versailles Treaty that the world chose to ignore. The signing of the Rome-Berlin Axis and the invasion of Russia were not connected to the Versailles Treaty.

28. D. The immediate effect of the Declaration of Pillnitz was that France declared war on Austria. The Declaration of Pillnitz was issued by the king of Prussia and the emperor of Austria in 1791 and stated that Prussia and Austria would intervene in order to preserve the French monarchy from the rebels. The revolutionaries in France took this threat of intervention very seriously; the Legislative Assembly of France declared war first on Austria, then on Prussia, Britain, and other countries. The declaration did not allocate military support and financial support from other European nations, nor did it declare that the people of Prussia and Austria should begin revolutions of their own or declare war on one another.

29. E. John Wycliffe and Jan Hus were not successful in trying to reform the Catholic Church. Wycliffe, an English priest, and Hus, a Bohemian religious leader, condemned the wealth of the Church, the pope's religious authority, and the Bible as supreme authority. Both of these men were harshly persecuted and denounced by the pope; Hus was burned at the stake for his beliefs, but his followers, known as the Hussites, fought the Church for many years before they were defeated. These two unsuccessful reformers paved the way for the success of Martin Luther. Selling indulgences (accepting money for Church pardons), simony (selling of Church positions), the Great Schism of 1378 to 1417 (rival popes), and nepotism (appointing relatives to Church positions) all contributed to the Protestant Reformation.

30. C. The Peace of Westphalia ended the Thirty Years War (1618–1648), a religious war in Central Europe between Protestant and Catholic rulers. The Peace of Westphalia did not deny religious freedom for Lutherans, nor did it revoke The Peace of Augsburg — rather, it reaffirmed it, giving Lutheran as well as Catholic rulers the right to determine the religion of their people. The German princes remained strong; at the end of the war, there were over 300 states with no central government. Germany, in fact, was divided for the next 200 years. The power of the papacy actually declined because the states gained power as they assumed greater control of both the Protestant and Catholic churches.

31. **C.** Imperialism, a policy whereby one country extends authority over a weaker area or region through direct military conquest or through economic control, is the term described in this statement. Imperialism also results in control of the social life of the area. Socialism is a system in which the government owns and operates the factors of production. Communism is a form of Socialism proposed by Karl Marx and Friedrich Engels, that involved a classless society after the working men overthrow capitalism. Isolationism is a foreign policy option that supports avoiding permanent alliances. Militarism is a policy that encourages the building of large standing armies to ensure the strength of the nation.

32. **E.** A major issue dividing the delegates at the Frankfurt Assembly of 1848 was the struggle between the Grossdeutsche delegates who wanted to include the German-speaking province of Austria under German rule and the Kleindeutsche delegates who wanted to exclude it and include only Prussia with the small German states. When the Austrians opposed any division of their territory, the delegates decided on a united Germany that excluded Austria, a crisis that further weakened the Frankfurt Assembly. The assembly had no conflict about whether or not to address relations with France or how to establish closer ties with Russia because its focus was on Germany alone. Neither the status of religion, nor the Zollverein, were causes of conflict.

33. **C.** Perestroika refers to economic restructuring. Gorbachev's program included less government planning, more power to local factory managers to make production decisions, the ability of some citizens to operate small retail businesses, and permission to farmers to grow some food that could be sold on the free market. Perestroika does not refer to the introduction of a police state in certain violent regions; lowered price caps on agricultural goods; rations for necessities; or free elections.

34. **B.** Northern Humanists interpreted the ideas of the Italian Renaissance by paying more attention to Biblical and early Christian themes. Like the Italian Humanists, Northern Humanists stressed the classics but believed that the revival of learning should be used to bring about religious and moral change by combining the ideas of the ancient world with Christian culture. Writers such as Desiderius Erasmus and Sir Thomas Moore promoted broad reforms based on Christian ideals.

35. **A.** The Thermidorian Reaction was the name given to the time period after the execution of Robespierre in 1794 that marked the end of the Reign of Terror — a period of mass executions of those presumed to be enemies of the state. Robespierre rose to power during the Reign of Terror. After he was killed and the terror ended, moderates took control of the Convention. The death of nearly 40,000 French people, the de-Christianization of France, and the restoration of the French monarchy all occurred during the Reign of Terror.

36. **A.** John Calvin believed in the doctrine of predestination, the essence of which is that man is born a sinner and that God has already determined who is going to be saved and who is damned. Those who were predestined for salvation could be identified by their

virtuous life, even by their material success. Calvin, like Luther, thought that people should read and interpret the Bible for themselves with no need for priests and saints. Calvin rejected the idea that doing good deeds would influence one's afterlife, since God had predestined who would be saved; Calvin also rejected the importance of the sacraments.

37. **A.** The Industrial Revolution began in England because the country was rich in natural resources, including water power and coal to fuel steam power; iron ore to make machines, tools, and buildings; rivers for domestic transport of goods, and good harbors to facilitate trade with the rest of the continent and the world. England's available supply of workers came not from the migration from the colonies but due to the Agricultural Revolution, which provided workers who were no longer needed on the farms. The English government encouraged businesses to invest but never assumed control of productive resources. Adam Smith's philosophy of *laissez faire* of limited government interference influenced the government. Until the mid-nineteenth century, the British government did not adopt a social policy of helping the workers.

38. **C.** The Great Depression created the situation that attracted supporters for the Nazi Party (more rightly known as the National Socialist Workers Party, or NSDAP), one of the many political parties under the Weimar Republic. After listening to Hitler blame the depression on the Jews and the injustices of the Versailles Treaty, many Germans began to support the Nazi Party.

In 1932, with six million Germans unemployed, the Nazi Party pooled over 12 million votes or 37% of the vote and became the largest party in the Reichstag (the German Parliament). On January 30, 1933, German President Paul von Hindenburg asked Hitler to become chancellor. The other options are wrong for the following reasons: Fascism had gained control of Italy in 1922 before the Great Depression occurred, the Depression did not affect Russia in the way it did other European countries, many people in England and France were attracted to Communism because they lost faith in the ability of democracy to solve the Depression's economic problems, and the Great Depression did not lead to large-scale migration to the United States because of the U.S.'s poor economic conditions.

39. **A.** The food riots in Manchester, England, caused by a temporary depression after the Napoleonic War, led to the Peterloo Massacre, also called the Manchester Massacre, which took place on August 16, 1819. The Peterloo Massacre led to repressive measures. Parliament passed the Six Acts, which banned demonstrations and imposed censorship. Eventually, beginning in 1832, Parliament began to make changes such as lowering qualifications for voting, repealing the corn laws, limiting the power of the House of Lords, and instituting programs to help the poor. These changes would take place throughout the nineteenth and early twentieth century.

40. **B.** In the early 1990s, Czechoslovakia peacefully divided into two independent nations. After the downfall of Communism, ethnic tensions in some of the former satellites emerged; however Vaclav Havel, a dissident playwright, and others were able to control ethnic and national tensions that might have destroyed the post-Communist government. Havel was elected president of Czechoslovakia and was famous for his bloodless "Velvet Revolution" — "a peaceful divorce" that split Czechoslovakia into the Czech Republic and

Slovakia. The goal of rejoining the West, especially the European Union and NATO, was a powerful force towards this peaceful transition. The Czech Republic joined NATO in 1999.

In the 1990s, Bosnia and Herzegovina were involved in a civil war and the Czech Republic was not involved. The Warsaw Pact ended in 1991 and Czechoslovakia never had nuclear weapons.

41. D. Louis XIV's finance minister, Jean Baptiste Colbert (1619–1683), helped to advance France's prosperity by his economic policies. Colbert's goal was to make France self-sufficient by achieving a favorable balance of trade and to centralize the economy through government control of trade and industry. He also encouraged French industry by enacting high foreign tariffs and a strong merchant marine. France's strong economic position enabled Louis XIV to pursue an aggressive foreign policy and make France the center of culture in the seventeenth century. Colbert supported the monarch and did not promote equality for all classes; in fact, under Colbert, the peasant class was hit hard by the government's heavy taxation. Colbert's main focus was on the economy rather than government's relationship with the church; moreover, he did not have an impact on peace in Europe. During Louis XIV's long reign, France was involved in four major wars.

42. D. All of the following are associated with Bismarck and the unification of Germany EXCEPT Berlin Conference of 1884. Bismarck and Jules Ferry, prime minister of France, convened the Congress of Berlin in 1884–1885 to lay the basic rules for colonizing Africa. The Berlin Conference led to the scramble for Africa. Helmuth Von Moltke was a Prussian general chief of staff who strengthened the armed forces that enabled Bismarck to achieve military success. The Danish War, the Austro-Prussian War, and the Franco-Prussian War were all steps in the unification of Germany.

43. A. The Carbonari was a secret society that was first organized in Italy in the early nineteenth century and also flourished in Spain and France. Carbonari in Italian means charcoal burners. The society originated in the Kingdom of Naples in the 1800s and drew its members from all stations in life, particularly, the army. The Carbonari was a closely organized society that advocated political freedom for the Italians against Austrian control of Italy. The Carbonari was partially responsible for uprisings in Naples in 1820, Spain in 1820, and Piedmonte in 1821. After 1830, the Carbonari disappeared and most of its members joined the Young Italy Society. The Carbonari did not exist in Britain, Portugal, Russia, or Prussia.

44. A. Frederick the Great of Prussia is considered an Enlightened Despot, an absolute monarch who adopted the ideals of the Enlightenment to bring about social and political changes. Frederick the Great was an absolute ruler who supported literature, music, and science, tolerated religious differences, reduced censorship, improved education, and ordered equal treatment for all persons. He also drained swamps and introduced new agricultural methods that helped peasants grow new crops such as potatoes. He was motivated by the desire to make his country stronger and his own government more effective. He was not a believer in democracy, however. Louis XIV of France and James I of England were absolute monarchs, Emanuel Kant was a philosopher, and Charles V was a Holy Roman Emperor who believed in absolutism.

45. B. Switzerland was the only country that did not experience a revolution or civil unrest in the years between 1820 and 1830. The Congress of Vienna had guaranteed Switzerland's neutrality as well as its independence. In 1847, the Catholic Cantons succeeded and organized a separate union called the Sonderbund, but they were defeated and rejoined the Federation of Swiss States. In the 1820s, revolutions broke out in Portugal, Sardinia, Greece, and Spain. The revolutions in Spain and Sardinia were crushed, but they were successful in Greece and Portugal.

46. C. In the 1800s, the English Parliament represented primarily the interest of the landed aristocracy. England was not a true democracy in the nineteenth century; only about 5% of the population had the right to elect the members of the House of Commons. Voting was limited to men who owned a substantial amount of property. Women could not vote and as a result, the upper landed aristocracy ran the government. In addition, the House of Lords, which was made up of hereditary nobles and high-ranking clergy of the Anglican Church, had the right to veto any laws passed by the House of Commons. The middle class, urban workers, and capitalist owners would gradually gain the right to vote through the passage of the Reform Bills of 1832, 1867, and 1884. The Anglican clergy was part of the House of Lords but the landed aristocracy ran the government, not the clergy.

47. C. Critics of the New Imperialism never asserted that imperialism was benefiting the colonies at the expense of the economy of the mother country. Rather, the critics claimed that imperialism only benefited the capitalists, not the entire nation. Lenin, for instance, called imperialism the last stage of capitalism. Other critics insisted that imperialism was undemocratic because it violated the principles of self-government as well as the culture of the people. These critics also rejected the idea of Social Darwinism and insisted that profits were the main motive behind the exploitation of these areas.

48. A. Henry VIII (b.1491, ruled 1509–1547) led the Protestant Reformation in England by making the king, not the pope, the head of the church. Henry VIII broke with the Catholic Church in 1527, when the pope refused to grant him a divorce from his Spanish wife, Catherine of Aragon. In 1534, Henry VIII, working through Parliament, passed the Act of Supremacy, which took control of the English church. He shut down the monasteries and took over church lands, thus strengthening the monarchy. Henry VIII retained most Catholic forms of worship: Sacraments were not abolished, and priests were allowed to perform services on Sunday.

49. D. Napoleon accomplished many things as emperor, except strengthening the role and status of the women in France. The Napoleonic Code, although embodying principles of the Enlightenment—such as equality for all citizens before the law, religious toleration, and advancement based upon merit—lost women many of the rights that they had gained during the French Revolution. The code considered women as minors who could not exercise the rights of citizenship.

50. B. The Lateran Treaty between Mussolini and Pius XII resulted in the recognition of the pope as the sovereign of the Vatican States and Fascism as the legitimate government of Italy. The purpose of the treaty was to end the dispute between the Italians and the government over the seizure of church land during the unification of Italy. The pact established Catholicism as the state religion and acknowledged the existence of the Vatican, which is about a square mile, as an independent state not legally within Italy at all. The papacy gained independence from national or secular authority. The Lateran Pact strengthened Mussolini's influence over the Catholics, who were 99% of the population.

51. **E.** The formation of NATO was not an event associated with Nikita Khrushchev. Khrushchev was the leader of the Soviet Union from 1956 to 1964; NATO, on the other hand, was formed in 1949 during the Stalin Era. Khrushchev attacked Stalin's cult of personality and supported a "thaw" in the Cold War by allowing greater intellectual freedom. Although his anti-Stalin campaign led to failed uprisings in Hungary and Poland, his policy of peaceful coexistence also led to a number of Summit meetings at Geneva and Vienna to discuss East/West relations.

52. **B.** Voltaire's statement *ecrasez l'infame* refers to the Catholic Church. Born Francois Marie Arouet (1649–1778), Voltaire challenged the authority of the Catholic Church, attacking its beliefs and practices. He hated all forms of religious intolerance and promoted simply the idea of "love God and your neighbor as yourself." In *Candide,* Voltaire wrote against the evils of organized religion and was subsequently imprisoned for his views. Voltaire was not a believer in social and economic equality in human affairs. Like most writers of the Enlightenment, he was suspicious of the middle class, the military, or the poor. Voltaire believed in the importance of laws to protect the freedom of the weak against the ambitions of the stronger.

53. **B.** A major theme of Machiavelli's 1513 work, *The Prince,* is that the end justifies the means. *The Prince* functions as an instruction guide on how a ruler should rule, stating that a ruler should not be moral but should do what is best for the state, and use any means necessary to maintain power, and assure the success of the government. Machiavelli did not dismiss loyalty as long as it was used to help a ruler rule effectively. He believed, however, that human beings are selfish and out to advance only their own interests. For this reason, Machiavelli dismissed honesty and prayers as a way to promote diplomacy or full virtue. He admired the Roman Republic and dreamed of a united Italy.

54. **C.** One result of the Sadler Committee was that it led to the passage of legislation regulating the employment of children in factories. In 1832, Michael Sadler, a British Legislative Leader, secured a parliamentary investigation of conditions in the textile factories. The Sadler Committee discovered that children worked 12–14 hours per day and were regularly abused by factory owners. The immediate effects of the investigation was the passage of the Factory Act of 1833, which prohibited the employers from hiring children under the age of nine, and children under the age of 13 could work no longer than nine hours per day and those 13–18 could work no more than 12 hours per day in the textile industry. The Sadler Committee only investigated the textile industry and did not address the issue of unions, minimum wage, social legislation, and the nationalization of iron and steel.

55. **E.** Charles I did not request money from Parliament for his military expedition against Spain. The Stuarts had established a friendly relationship with Spain. In 1637 Charles I tried to impose Anglicanism on Calvinists living in Scotland. They revolted and Charles was forced to call Parliament to raise money for the war. Parliament refused after three weeks of open debate. During his reign, Charles I (1625–1640) disregarded the Petition of Rights for 11 years but was unable to levy taxes. However, the Long Parliament (1640–1660) did eventually pass laws that limited the power of the king.

However, when he needed additional money for his military expedition against Spain, he requested a forced loan from his wealthier subjects. Several members of the gentry refused to vote for the loans and Charles threw them into jail. In 1628, Parliament again declined to give Charles additional resources unless he signed the Petition of Rights.

56. **A.** Austria was never a member of the Warsaw Pact. On December 19, 1945, the federal parliament of Austria declared the country's permanent neutrality. All of the other countries were members of the Warsaw Pact, which was a defensive alliance created in 1955. The treaty was dissolved in 1991 with the collapse of the Soviet Union.

57. **B.** England declared war on Germany when Germany invaded Belgium. Belgium was a neutral country whose neutrality had been recognized by all the major powers of Europe since 1839. England felt committed to protect Belgium, fearing that a powerful Germany would threaten British national interests on the European continent. Britain's decision was not based on Austria's ultimatum to Serbia, Italy's declaration of neutrality, or Russia's support of Serbia.

58. **B.** As a result of the Sepoy Mutiny in 1857, the British assumed direct control of India in 1858, ending the rule of the British East India Company. The British introduced social educational and technological reforms that helped India become the "Brightest Jewel of the Crown." However, the British policy was always motivated by how the colony would benefit the mother country. The Sepoy Mutiny did not result in recognizing either Hinduism or Islam as the state religion. Neither democracy nor independence was introduced into India.

59. **C.** The Scientific Revolution did not lead to a widespread growth of knowledge among the general population; it actually had little impact on the economic life and living standards of the masses until the late eighteenth century. The Scientific Revolution of the seventeenth century was primarily an intellectual revolution, which led to the formation of societies such as the Royal Society of England, the purpose of which was to promote the growth of scientific ideas among different countries. The Scientific Revolution led to the scientific method of observation, which opened up a greater knowledge of the physical world in which the sun and not the earth was the center of the universe. The heliocentric theory of the universe destroyed the belief in the Aristotelian medieval view of the earth as the center of the universe.

60. **A.** The painting of *Guernica* by Pablo Picasso was inspired by the Spanish Civil War (1936–1939). Hitler and Mussolini supported General Francisco Franco in his struggle for power against the Spanish Loyalists, who included democrats, republicans, and communists. In 1937, the bombing of a Spanish town, Guernica, by German bombers led to the death of 1,600 people. Picasso's work of art captured the brutality of the day. Picasso never painted a work of art about Mussolini's support of the Spanish Fascists, Hitler's rise to power, Italy's invasion of Ethiopia, or the Nazi-Soviet Non-Aggression Pact.

61. **E.** The Ausgleich Compromise of 1867 did not provide for a uniform educational and monetary system. It did, however, establish the Dual Monarchy under which Austria and Hungary became separate states. Under the Ausgleich Compromise, each country had its own government and independence in local matters such as education, but was joined together on common issues such as foreign affairs, military defense, and finance. The

delegates of the two parliaments met together alternatively in Vienna and Budapest, and both Austrians and Hungarians were appointed to this common ministry; also Franz Joseph became both emperor of Austria and king of Hungary.

62. **B.** Louis XIV's reign eventually forced the Huguenots to leave France because he destroyed their property and took away their civil rights. Seeing the Protestants' minority as a threat to religious unity, in 1685 Louis XIV canceled the Edict of Nantes, which in 1598 had granted religious toleration to the Huguenots. In response, thousands of artisans and business people fled the country. This loss of some of the most prosperous of Louis' subjects was a blow to the economy. The Huguenots were not sent to French colonies but fled to the New World, many of them settling in New York. They never became trusted advisors of Louis XIV nor were they forced to live in poverty.

63. **B.** This passage is part of Article 231 of the Versailles Treaty. In Article 231, Germany accepted responsibility for the war by signing the "War Guilt" clause, and as a result was obligated to pay reparations to the Allies for the cost of the war. The final reparations bill came to $132 billion, which Germany had to pay over 30 years. The Atlantic Charter was a joint statement of principle issued by Franklin D. Roosevelt of the United States and Winston Churchill in 1941. The charter contained many of the ideas of Wilson's Fourteen Points. The charter of the League of Nations (1919) described the function of the League and how it was to be organized. The Treaty of Frankfurt (1871) ended the Franco-Prussian War and the Treaty of Westphalia (1648) concluded the Thirty Years War.

64. **E.** A major effect of the Revolution of 1848 in France was the election of Louis Napoleon, also known as Napoleon II, as president of the Republic. In February of 1848, revolutions broke out in Paris, which led to the abdication of King Louis Philippe. A group of liberals, radicals, and socialists proclaimed the Second Republic with a strong president and a one-house legislature elected by universal male suffrage. The division among the different groups and the bitter legacy of the class warfare of June 1948 influenced the presidential election in December. The overwhelming winner was Louis Napoleon, the nephew of Napoleon I. Louis Napoleon attracted the working class by presenting himself as a man who cared about social issues such as poverty. Weary of instability, the French welcomed a strong personality who would bring peace to France. The Revolution of 1848 did not result in the return of the Bourbons or the return of Charles X from England. In June, the National Assembly shut down the National Workshops that had contributed to the class warfare. Austria, which experienced its own series of revolutions, did not intervene in France.

65. **A.** Arnold Toynbee coined the term the "Industrial Revolution" in 1880. Toynbee used this term to describe the rapid growth of the use of machinery that dramatically affected agriculture, industry, and transportation. Historians tend to refer to the economic development in England during the eighteenth and nineteenth centuries as stages of economic growth in which total productivity was increasing and productivity per man was also increasing. Saint Simon was a French reformer who promoted the end of private property. Max Weber was a German writer who attributed the rise of the middle class in Europe to the Protestant work ethic promoted by Calvinism. Jacob Burkhardt was a historian who wrote about the Renaissance. Leopold Von Ranke was a famous historian who introduced the seminar method of teaching.

66. **E.** The official abolishment of the sacraments was not a result of the Catholic or Counter Reformation. The Council of Trent (1545–1563), the central piece of the Counter Reformation, reaffirmed the dogma of the Church. The council, which met intermittently for about twenty years, reasserted the validity of the seven sacraments, ended the abuses within the Church, called for more religious art, and created an Index of Prohibited books, such as the writings of Erasmus and Galileo. It also revived the Inquisition and attacked heretics.

67. **A.** Great Britain was the only country that remained outside of Napoleon's European empire by 1807. Napoleon's conquests redrew the map of Europe; he annexed some areas to France, including the Netherlands and Belgium, and even included parts of Italy and Germany into his empire. Napoleon cut Prussian territory in half and forced alliances on European powers from Madrid to Moscow. In 1805, he tried to invade England, but the French fleet was defeated at the Battle of Trafalgar. Napoleon even tried to reduce Britain's commerce by closing European ports to British goods. However, Napoleon was ultimately unsuccessful in making Great Britain a part of his empire.

68. **A.** Humanist writers focused on glorifying the individual and worldly subjects. Humanist writers believed that man was the measure of all things and they had faith in man's unlimited potential to achieve success; they also believed in the creative powers of man and were concerned mostly with secular subjects rather than strictly religious themes. Writers such as Petrarch and Castiglione wrote about love and courtly behavior; others like Mirandola and Bruni stressed the importance of man's role in a secular society. Humanist writers focused on how the classical societies of ancient Greece and Rome were models for them rather than the system of feudalism. Humanist writers encouraged positive effects of education and used the classics as a way to understand their society.

69. **A.** The Balkans were known as the Powder Keg of Europe at the beginning of the twentieth century. Home to many different ethnic groups and having a long history of ethnic uprisings and ethnic clashes, the Balkan Peninsula in the southeastern corner of Europe was an explosion waiting to happen. Nationalism was a powerful force in the Balkans as each group wanted to extend its borders. These nationalist sentiments became wrapped up with ambitions of the European powers to divide up the Ottoman Empire, which included the Balkan region. Thus, England and France sometimes supported Russia against the Ottomans. Germany supported Austrian authority over national groups but encouraged the Ottomans because of their strategic location at the eastern end of the Mediterranean. This intrigue — combined with the demand of the subject nationalities of the Serbians, Croatians, and Bulgarians — made the situation more intense.

70. **B.** During the Cold War (1947–1989), the United States and the Soviet Union were reluctant to become involved in direct conflict because of the potential for global nuclear destruction. Recognizing that mutual interests necessitated avoiding nuclear war, the United States and the Soviet Union even established a hotline that enabled their two leaders to speak directly with each other to avoid any misunderstandings. During the Cold War the United States and the Soviet Union never directly confronted each other but used their influence to support groups that promoted their own interests. During the Korean War, the United States supported South Korea, and the Soviet Union with China supported North Korea. In the Middle East and in the Third World, the two countries supported individuals that were pro-West or pro-Communist, respectively. The Cuban Missile Crisis

of 1962 between the United States and the Soviet Union was the closest the two nations came to a direct conflict with each other. The U.N.'s effectiveness as a world policeman depended upon the support of the United States and the Soviet Union.

71. **A.** The cartoon of a wedding picture representing Hitler as the groom and Stalin as the bride symbolizes the Nazi-Soviet Non-Aggression Pact. In August 1939, the world was shocked to learn that Hitler had signed a Ten Year Non-Aggression Pact with Stalin. This pact protected Germany from a two-front war, which had been an issue in World War I. The cartoon also suggests that the honeymoon between these two people would be short-lived. The formation of the Pact of Steel, the Soviet Union's support of Hitler's occupation of the Rhineland, the Soviet Union's and Germany's cooperation at the Munich Conference, and Germany's and the Soviet Union's support for General Franco in 1939 are not depicted in this cartoon.

72. **A.** Nationalists are opposed to European unity because they believe it will destroy their countries' unique identities. In 1991, the European Union signed the Treaty of Maastricht, agreeing to introduce a common currency (Euro) by 2002. The treaty, however, allowed member nations to choose if and when to join the single currency. Great Britain, Denmark, and Sweden were the only nations to agree not to adapt the Euro, believing that their currency reflects their national identity. William Hague, a member of the British Conservative Party, also believes that Britain should be in Europe but not run by Europe. He is critical of a common currency because he fears that bankers and financial leaders of Europe will make decision that can have a negative effect on his country. Hague and others believe that a single currency should be opposed until there are federal structures in place to manage it more democratically. There have been vigorous debates within the countries of Sweden, Denmark, and Britain about the Euro but not hostility. The United States understands the economic threat of the European Union but has not been opposed to the concept. The members of the European Union believe that by coordinating their economic polices they can improve their economy which has been in a slump for the past few years. Former Communist nations, such as Poland, Hungary, and other Eastern European countries, are trying to enter the European Union.

73. **E.** Edward Benes of Czechoslovakia did not attend the Munich Conference. Benes became president of Czechoslovakia in 1935. He resigned after the Munich Conference. At the Munich Conference of September 1938, attended by Chamberlain, Mussolini, Hitler, and Daladier, these leaders agreed to Hitler's demand for the Sudentenland, a German-speaking region of Czechoslovakia. Chamberlain and Daladier claimed that they gave in to Hitler's demand because that would be his last request for land in Europe. In March 1939, Hitler took over all of Czechoslovakia.

74. **B.** Thomas Malthus would agree with the ideas expressed in this passage. In an *Essay on the Principles of Population* (1798), Malthus asserted that the population tended to increase more rapidly than the food supply. Without wars and epidemics to destroy the surplus population, the poor would suffer. Malthus encouraged people to have small families in order to stop the population growth. David Ricardo was associated with the "iron laws of wages" that forced workers to accept lower wages. Louis Blanc was a French reformer who advocated National Workshops during the French Revolution of 1848. John Locke was a seventeenth-century philosopher who wrote *Two Treatises of*

Government to demonstrate his support for the Glorious Revolution of 1690. Locke believed in the social contract theory of government. Karl Marx wrote *The Communist Manifesto.*

75. **A.** The Reform Bills of 1832, 1867, 1884, 1918, and 1928 resulted in the expansion of voting rights among men and women. The Reform Bill of 1832 was the first step towards evolutionary democracy in England; reducing property qualifications for voters increased the number of voters from 500,000 to 800,000. The Reform Bill of 1867 further reduced property qualifications for voting to enfranchise the city workers. By 1884, agricultural workers received the right to vote. In 1918, all men over the age of 21 and women over the age of 30 were able to vote, and in 1928, all women over the age of 21 were granted the franchise. These reform bills did not specifically address the issues of the power of the House of Commons or the House of Lords or the role of the monarchy or the government in Great Britain.

76. **D.** The philosophers of the Enlightenment tried to apply the ideas of science and the Enlightenment to reform society and used satire to spread their message. Writers such as Voltaire and Montesquieu wrote satire because they were fearful that direct attacks would lead to their imprisonment. The philosophers were primarily from France and attacked the organized structure of the church. They did not support democracy over absolutism but supported the idea that human institutions should conform to logic and reason. The philosophers thought that reason, and not emotion, would provide an understanding of the meaning of the world.

77. **A.** A major goal of the Jesuits was to combat heresy and spread the Catholic faith. Ignatius Loyola, the founder of the Jesuits in 1534, believed that he was a soldier of God. The Jesuits received vigorous training in education, philosophy, and were expected to have absolute obedience to the church. Led by Loyola, the Jesuits became advisers to Catholic kings and spread their message to Asia, Africa, the Americas, and parts of southern Germany. They also used the Inquisition, especially in Spain and Italy, to combat heresy. The Council of Trent had prohibited the sale of indulgences, rejected the belief of the Bible as the source of salvation, and reaffirmed the importance of good works and the seven sacraments.

78. **D.** The outbreak of the nationalist movement in the Hapsburg Empire occurred because several national groups such as Serbs, Czechs, and Slovenes occupied the same region. The chief problem for Austria and Hungary was the question of governing many different nationalities and different minorities within the two countries. The Ausgleich Compromise of 1867, which made Austria and Hungary separate states, treated Austria as a German nation state and Hungary as a Magyar nation state. However, Germans formed less than one-half of the people of Austria, as did the Magyars of Hungary. Austria also included the Slovenes and Czechs, as did the Magyars of Hungary who also included Czechs and Poles.

79. **E.** Charles I of England was the Stuart king who ruled during the seventeenth century. He tried to govern without Parliament, which led to a civil war in England from 1642 to 1649. In 1649, Charles I was beheaded. Louis XI of France, Henry VII of England, the Medici family of Florence, and Ferdinand and Isabella of Spain were all powerful leaders during the Renaissance in Europe. All of these leaders consolidated power, which promoted a sense of authority and leadership. They established dominance by curbing the power of the nobles and centralizing their control.

80. **A.** Lajos Kossuth (1802–1894) was the Hungarian nationalist and fiery orator who led the fight for independence against Austria in the nineteenth century. Kossuth's liberal and nationalist program against Austria led to his arrest in 1837, but popular pressure forced Metternich to release him in 1840. Kossuth was one of the principle figures of the Hungarian Revolt in 1848 against the Austrian government. When the Austrian government prepared to move against Hungary, Kossuth became head of the Hungarian government of national defense. In April 1849, the Hungarian government declared its independence and Kossuth became president. The Hungarians won several victories but when Russian troops intervened in 1849, Kossuth was forced to resign and fled to Turkey and later to England. Ferdinand I was the emperor of Austria who agreed to the Hungarian demands for independence but abdicated in March 1848. Janos Kadar was a Hungarian political leader who was placed into power by Joseph Stalin in 1956 after the Soviets had crushed the revolt led by Imre Nagy. Eduard Benes was the leader of Czechoslovakia before World War II.

Section II: Free-Response Essays

Part A: First Sample Student DBQ Essay

The Industrial Revolution was a turning point in history. Until the mid-1750s, most people in Great Britain had worked the land using simple basic tools and had lived in rural towns. By 1850, many country villages had grown into industrial towns and these cities swelled with workers who labored in factories. Work in the factories affected families as well as the quality of life in these industrial towns. The Industrial Revolution in Great Britain would cause immense problems for the working class people.

In the 1750s, the market town of Manchester, England, had a population of about 45,000 people. Within a few years, it exploded into a center of textile industry and by 1850, had swelled to about 300,000. Visitors to the town were horrified at the living conditions. In 1845, Friedrich Engels noted that Manchester was like "Hell on Earth" (Doc. 7). Others found exactly the opposite. In the town of Hyde, the houses were pleasant and everything seemed clean and orderly (Doc. 4). Although Engels was a Socialist and blamed these poor conditions on industrialization (Doc. 8), he was accurate in pointing out the inhumane conditions in the city. There were no plants and no sanitary and building codes to control the growth of cities. Cholera and other diseases spread rapidly. Alex de Tocqueville, the French aristocrat who visited Manchester in 1835, described the black smoke that blanketed the city and how the homes of the poor were scattered in random order around the factories. He believed that in Manchester, "civilized man turned almost into a savage."

At the heart of the industrial city was the factory. The factory work, unlike the farm work which changed with the seasons, was very structured and the same week after week. Hours were long. Shifts lasted from 12 to 16 hours (Doc. 1). Women made up much of the new industrial work force. Many employers preferred women who were often paid less than men, even for the same work. Factory work created special problems for women. The new jobs forced them out of the homes for 12 hours a day and many of them had to return to work a few days after giving birth. Women also had to run home to feed their children during dinner. Engels asserted that "the employment of women at once breaks up the family" (Doc. 5).

The Industrial Revolution greatly affected children. Factories and mines hired many boys and girls. Benjamin Disraeli, a novelist and prime minister of Great Britain (1868; 1874–80), described the horrible conditions of young girls of four and five who were forced to work in the coal mines (Doc. 2). Disraeli was a reformer who was hoping to gain the working class support for a group of reforming aristocrats in the Conservative Party.

In 1832, Michael Sadler, a British legislator, began a parliamentary investigation into the conditions in the textile industry in order to expose the abuses of child labor. He found many children began work at six years old and usually worked from five in the morning until nine in the evening (Doc. 1). They worked six days a week, with only a half hour for lunch and an hour for dinner. Children were often beaten simply because factory owners thought they did not work hard enough and wanted to keep them awake. Other factory owners were just angry at them. Many children were afraid to report these instances because their parents might lose their jobs.

Factory owners scoffed at reports of poor working conditions and cruelty to children. One British manufacturer indicated that he was going to reduce work hours to 10½ because he wanted his workers to be happy and cheerful and that it was more productive (Doc. 10). The Society for Bettering the Conditions and Increasing the Comfort of the Poor pointed out that there were factories where children were well treated and not abused (Doc. 6). Furthermore, wealthy manufacturers insisted that the children were not beaten and that working in a factory was better than being home in a cold and damp apartment (Doc. 3). The question of child labor was difficult because parents had come to depend upon the children's extra income to survive. Some factory owners thought that children working in the factories took the burden off the parents because children provided money for the family and removed the problem of how they would be fed (Doc. 8). These business men, of course, glossed over the fact that children needed to be educated, insisting that one hour a day was enough (Doc. 8).

Industry also posed a question of safety. Factories were seldom well lit or clean. Machines caused injuries in numerous ways. The most dangerous conditions were found in the mines. Frequent accidents and damp conditions affected the workers. In 1838, over 347 workers died in work-related accidents in coal mines (Doc. 9). The Ashley Mines Commisison Report would highlight these problems and lead to laws regulating employment of children in mines and factories.

Tocqueville's comments about Manchester that "from this filthy sewer pure gold flows" shows the best and worst of the city influenced by the Industrial Revolution. The Industrial Revolution caused immense suffering for the working class of the city. However, the gold that flowed from the factories led to the rise of a middle class who changed the social structure of Great Britain which in turn raised the living standards of the workers.

Reader's Comments on Part A: First Sample Student DBQ Essay

- The thesis is clear and well developed.

- The student uses all the documents and analyzes them rather than just describes them.

- The student effectively uses outside information such as the Sadler Report, Ashley Commission, and Toqueville.

- The conclusion is good.

Possible student score: 8–9

Part A: Second Sample Student DBQ Essay

The Industrial Revolution had a profound effect on Great Britain. In the 1700s and 1800s, economic development would lead to changes in the lives of workers and children as well as life in the cities.

The growth of cities led to the rise of factories around these towns. Workers in these factories usually toiled 12 to 16 hours per day and were given very little time for lunch and dinner (Doc. 1). The factories also employed many children. Children were forced to work long hours and were often beaten if they did not work hard enough (Doc. 1).

Women were also employed in these factories. Employers found women easier to manage and thought that women could more easily adapt to machines than men. Women working in the factories caused disruption within the family. Many women had to leave their children who were taken care of by others. Some women had to run home in between the dinner hour to feed their children (Doc. 5).

Working in factories was difficult and many children and workers were hurt. Factories were poorly ventilated, workers were exposed to constant danger of injuries, and there were no laws to protect them. Children working in mines suffered many accidents (Doc. 9).

Many factory owners believed that children working in factories helped society because it made sure that the children were able to earn money and they did not become a burden to society (Doc. 8). Others claimed that children were not mistreated and working in the factories was better than living in damp apartments (Doc. 3).

The Industrial Revolution also led to the growth of cities. In Manchester, England, the quality of life was uneven. The city grew to over 70,000 people by the beginning of the nineteenth century. Visitors to the city had mixed emotions. Some criticized the poor conditions (Doc. 7), while others praised how good the city appeared (Doc. 4).

The Industrial Revolution would initially cause suffering and pain. However, reformers would bring about changes in the social structure that would help to bring positive benefits to the working people of Great Britain.

Reader's Comments on Part A: Second Sample Student DBQ Essay

- The thesis is superficial.
- The student doesn't analyze any of the documents.
- There is no use of information.
- Organization of the argument is poor.

Possible student score: 4–5

Part B: First Sample Student Thematic Essay, Group 1-1

According to Baldassare Castiglione's book, *The Courtier* (1528), upper-class women were expected to know the classics and be charming but were not expected to seek fame. Their role was to inspire art but rarely create it. Upper-class Renaissance women were better educated than the women of the Middle Ages. However, they had less influence than medieval women. In terms of the kind of work that they performed, access to property, and their role in shaping their society, women in the Renaissance ruling class generally had less power than comparable women in the feudal age.

During the Middle Ages, few women could read or write outside of the convent. In the cities of the Renaissance, upper-class girls received an education similar to boys. Young ladies studied the writings of ancient Greece and Rome. Some women could even speak one or two modern languages, such as French or Spanish.

Laurea Cereta (1469–1499) illustrated the success and failure of Renaissance women. She was well educated and knew languages, philosophy, and mathematics. However, like all women of the Renaissance, she had to choose between marriage and full social participation or else study and withdraw from the world. She chose marriage. Cereta and other women of the urban upper middle class, in addition to the classical education, received training in painting, music, and dance. However, it was expected that their education would prepare them for the social function of running a household. An educated woman was supposed to know how to attract a husband and run a good household, whereas an educated man was supposed to know how to rule and participate in public affairs. Thus, Renaissance women were supposed to be decorative, affable, and charming.

A few women, such as Isabella d'Este, did exercise some power. Born into the ruling class of Ferrara, she married the ruler of another city state, Mantua. She brought many Renaissance artists to her court and created an art collection that was famous throughout Europe. She was also skilled in politics. When her husband was taken captive, she defended Mantua and won his freedom.

Women's status also declined in regard to love and sex. In the medieval books, manners shaped the man to please the woman. According to Castiglione, the women were supposed to make themselves pleasing to men. Renaissance Humanists laid the foundation for the bourgeoisie double standard, men were supposed to act in the public sector and women belonged in the home.

The Renaissance had very little impact on the lives of ordinary women. Women continued to perform economic functions, such as working on the farms or helping their husbands run businesses. Women continued to work as housekeepers and midwives. Since educational opportunities were limited, very few women as well as men received an education. This educational divide would create a distinct class difference between the "educated elite" who promoted the arts and the mass of people who supported "popular culture."

The Renaissance is the golden age of art and literature but for women it was an era of mixed blessings. Upper-class women were better educated but their role in society became well defined and their influence declined in comparison to the medieval period.

Reader's Comments on Part B: First Sample Student Thematic Essay, Group 1-1

- The student uses good details to support the thesis statement.
- The response is well organized.
- The essay gives a good comparison between the Middle Ages and the Renaissance.
- The student's analysis of the role of ordinary women is good.
- The essay's discussion of relationship between men and women reinforces the thesis statement.

Possible student score: 8–9

Part B: Second Sample Student Thematic Essay, Group 1-1

The role of women in the Renaissance declined. Upper-class women were well educated and learned the classics of ancient Greece and Rome. Women received the same education as young men. Some young women even learned how to speak modern languages such as Spanish or French.

The purpose of Renaissance education was to prepare women for the function of running a household. Women were not expected to participate in the power structure but were expected to support men in their public function. Thus Renaissance women received better educational opportunities than women in the Middle Ages, but their role in society was limited. A woman's fulfillment was in getting married and being a good house organizer. The role of Renaissance women was to enhance the position of their husband.

There were some women such as Artemisia Gentileschi, who achieved international renown for her painting, but she was the exception, not the rule. Women were not expected to seek fame. Furthermore, the job of women was to make themselves pleasing to men since the women's role was to manage the home. The life of ordinary women was not greatly affected by the Renaissance. Ordinary women continued to work in agriculture and industry. They received very little education and their role in society was not altered.

Reader's Comments on Part B: Second Sample Student Thematic Essay, Group 1-1

- The thesis is superficial.

- The essay never goes into depth regarding role of women in comparison to men.

- The essay gives good facts to support women who achieved fame.

- The student gives little analysis of the role of ordinary women.

- The essay needs more in-depth analysis, such as how women were expected to support their men, the importance of Castiglione's book, *The Courtier,* and how women were expected to be charming but not seek fame.

Possible student score: 3–4

Part B: First Sample Student Thematic Essay, Group 1-2

The French Revolution follows Crane Brinton's thesis that all revolutions go through three stages: Moderate, Radical, and Reactionary, which ultimately lead to the rise of dictatorships and a period of stability.

In May 1789, Louis XVI called the Estates General (the French Parliament), which had not met since 1614 to help him solve the nation's financial crisis. A six week deadlock over voting ended when the Third Estate (middle class) declared itself the National Assembly and took the "Tennis Court Oath" not to disband until they had written a constitution. The French Revolution had begun and had entered its Moderate Stage. The king consented to the formation of the National Assembly where voting would be per capita, not by unit. During this Moderate Stage, the National Assembly would take steps to end the abuses of the Old Regime. The National Assembly abolished feudalism and passed the Declaration of the Rights of Man and Citizen, which guaranteed freedom of speech, religion, and due process to all men. The principles of the declaration were captured by the slogan of "Liberty, Equality, and Fraternity." The National Assembly also passed the Civil Constitution of the Clergy, which ended papal authority over the French church and dissolved monasteries and convents. This attack on the Church turned many people against the revolution and made the Church a bitter enemy of the revolution. In 1791, the National Assembly wrote a constitution that provided for a limited monarchy and a legislative assembly whose members had to be property owners and elected by taxpaying citizens. By 1791, the middle class and many peasants were satisfied with the revolution. However, there were many groups in France that were dissatisfied and were opposed to a limited constitutional monarchy.

In 1792, the French Revolution entered its Radical Stage when the National Convention, which had replaced the National Assembly, abolished the monarchy and proclaimed a French Republic. There was a split in the convention. The Jacobins, led by Maximilien Robespierre, wanted a centralized government with the power to help the poor and control the economy. The Girondists (a more moderate group) wanted a middle class republic. In 1793, Louis XVI and Marie Antoinette were beheaded. This act sent shock waves through all of Europe and a coalition of European nations was formed to stop the spread of the revolution. Faced with economic difficulties at home (rising prices and unemployment) and the fear of foreign invasion, the Jacobins created the Committee of Public Safety which had dictatorial powers. The goal of this Twelve Man Committee of Public Safety was to save the revolution from foreign invasion and domestic enemies. Military service became mandatory and over 1.1 million men rallied to their country. In the meantime, the Committee of Public Safety instituted a Reign of Terror (July 1793–1794). All persons suspected of treason were put to death. Over 40,000 people were killed. Food rationing was introduced, monetary controls were set up to stop inflation, and all material was censored. Robespierre, known as Mr. Incorruptible, was the architect of the Reign of Terror and proclaimed a republic of virtue. He wanted to de-Christianize France and turn the Cathedral of Notre Dame into the Temple of Reason. By 1794, the Reign of Terror was out of control and the people turned against the government. In March 1794, Robespierre executed Danton, one of the Jacobin Committee leaders, for urging an end to the Reign of Terror. Fearful of what would happen next, the National Convention arrested Robespierre. He was put to death, thus ending the Radical Stage of the Revolution.

In 1795, France entered the Reactionary Stage. The National Convention drew up the Constitution of 1795. This constitution set up a five-man Directory with a two-house legislature that was elected by male citizens who owned property. The Directory held power from 1795–1799. It was a weak, dictatorial, and corrupt government that faced serious problems. The sans-culottes and the aristocracy were critical of the government's policies. When rising bread prices stirred riots in October 1795, the Directory ordered Napoleon, who was a strong leader and happened to be in Paris, to crush the riots. He saved the government but ultimately he would end up destroying the government. In 1799, Napoleon, who considered himself to be a "Son of the Revolution," took control of France as First Consul and later became emperor for life. Many people in France, especially the middle class, supported Napoleon because he restored stability after years of chaos.

The French Revolution, which began with moderate efforts to reform the French government, progressed to the Radical Stage of terror and concluded with a return to stability in the person of Napoleon. The emergence of Napoleon would lend stability at the expense of political freedom.

Reader's Comments on Part B: First Sample Student Thematic Essay, Group 1-2

- The thesis statement is clear and well developed.

- The student effectively assesses each stage of the revolution.

- The student makes excellent use of specific facts (Declaration of Rights of Man and Citizen, Reign of Terror, and Directory).

- The essay lacks depth on the appeal of Napoleon.

- The student's showing the loss of freedom makes both the summary and conclusion effective.

Possible student score: 7–8

Part B: Second Sample Student Thematic Essay, Group 1-2

The French Revolution, like all revolutions, followed a moderate, radical, and reactionary stage. After the reactionary stage, a strong ruler emerged.

France in 1789 was in chaos. Louis XVI called the Estates General. There were immediate problems which led to a new government called the National Assembly. The National Assembly ended the Old Regime and passed laws granting civil rights to people. The National Assembly also limited the power of the Catholic Church and created a limited monarchy. The National Convention in 1792 abolished the monarchy and set up a republic which began the Radical Stage. The Radical Stage included the Reign of Terror. Robespierre, a Jacobin, led the Reign of Terror, which resulted in the loss of over 40,000 people. Robespierre also wanted to create a Republic of Virtue. He was beheaded in 1794 and thus ended the Radical Stage.

The Reactionary Stage began with the selection of the Directory to lead France. The Directory was a weak government because voting was restricted to male property owners. The Directory was corrupt and was unable to deal with the economic problems facing the nation. In the midst of this chaos, Napoleon, a victorious general, promised the people a return to order and stability. In 1799, Napoleon seized power and by 1804, became emperor. Napoleon's one-man rule had established order at the expense of freedom.

Reader's Comments on Part B: Second Sample Student Thematic Essay, Group 1-2

- The thesis statement is weak.

- The student's use of facts is extremely limited. The student gives a cursory mention of Declaration of Rights and the end of feudalism.

- The content of the essay is too general.

Possible student score: 3-4

Part B: First Sample Student Thematic Essay, Group 1-3

Mercantilism was an economic policy that influenced Europe from the sixteenth to the eighteenth century during the era of colonization and the rise of absolutism. Laissez faire was an outgrowth of the philosophy of the Enlightenment and became the economic theory associated with the Industrial Revolution and laid the foundation for the system of capitalism.

During the 1500s and 1600s, European nations adapted the economic policy of mercantilism. The theory of mercantilism was based on the fact that a country's power depended primarily on how much wealth a nation accumulated. The accumulation of wealth would strengthen the national economy. The core of mercantilism included a belief that a nation's wealth was measured in its supply of gold and silver. The supply of gold and silver depended upon a favorable balance of trade, which required that a country had to export more than it imported. Mercantilism went hand in hand with colonization; colonies were central to the mercantile system. In addition to providing gold and silver, colonies also served as a source of raw materials and markets for manufactured goods from the mother country. Colonies existed for the benefit of the mother country. Governments passed strict navigation laws regulating trade and forbidding the colonies to set up industries to manufacture goods or trade with other countries. Thus, political absolutism that had extended over the country was extended into the economic area. The government also adapted a single national currency, standard weights and measures, and sold monopolies to larger producers in certain industries as well overseas trading empires. As the wealth of a nation increased, the power and prestige of the nation or monarch would be enhanced.

In the eighteenth century, physiocrats (Enlightenment thinkers who searched for a natural law to explain economics) rejected the ideas associated with mercantilism. They insisted that the government end its restriction of trade and ease its regulation of the economy. They also wanted industry and businesses to manufacture and sell goods free from government interference. These physiocrats supported a free market unregulated by the government, hence the term laissez faire (leave business alone). The Enlightenment thinkers criticized the mercantile idea that nations grow wealthy by placing heavy tariffs on foreign goods. They argued that government regulations only interfere with the production of wealth.

Adam Smith (1723–1790), a professor at the University of Glasgow, Scotland, skillfully presented the ideas of laissez faire in the book *Wealth of Nations* (1776). Smith attacked mercantilism for providing unjust privileges for private monopolies and government favorites. He argued that economic liberty guaranteed economic progress. Smith claimed that the government should not interfere with the economy. He urged that individuals pursuing their own economic interests would benefit the entire nation and lead to expanded resources for the nation. The rising bourgeoisie, or middle class, supported these ideas because it allowed them to increase their economic power at the expense of the aristocracy. Smith's idea that a natural law governed economics would become the foundation of laissez-faire capitalism. The concept of the market place and the importance of the laws of supply and demand would greatly influence Britain and other industrial economies.

Like Smith, economists Thomas Malthus and David Ricardo supported the notion of a natural law for economics. Malthus, in *An Essay on the Principle of Population,* argued that the population tended to increase more rapidly than the food supply. The only check on population growth was war, disease, and famine. Ricardo, in his Iron Laws of wages, noted that when wages were high, families have more children. But more children increase the supply of labor which leads to lower wages. Like Malthus, Ricardo saw no hope for the poor. Smith, Malthus, and Ricardo opposed any government help for the poor. The supporters of laissez-faire economics believed that only through hard work and effort could individuals improve their position in life.

Mercantilism and laissez faire represent two different types of economic policies. Mercantilism outlines a detailed government policy regulating the economy whose objective is to increase the wealth of the state as well as the power of the ruler. Laissez faire focuses on the importance of individual economic freedom, which benefits the productive resources of the country. Both of these philosophies were never taken to their fullest extent. Mercantile countries, such as England, found it difficult to carry out the navigation laws and followed a policy of benign neglect towards the colonies. Laissez-faire economics was sharply modified by the efforts of social reformers throughout the late nineteenth and twentieth centuries.

Reader's Comments on Part B: First Sample Student Thematic Essay, Group 1–3

- The thesis is well developed in contrasting mercantilism and laissez faire.

- The connection with absolutism and the Enlightenment is very good.

- Inclusion of Malthus and Ricardo demonstrates a good understanding of laissez faire.

- The essay is very analytical.

Possible student score: 8–9

Part B: Second Sample Student Thematic Essay, Group 1–3

Mercantilism and laissez faire were two economic policies reflecting the political and social philosophy of a particular era.

Mercantilism was an economic system that existed in Europe from the sixteenth to the eighteenth century. Mercantilists believed that the wealth of a nation was measured by the supply of gold and silver and that nations must maintain a favorable balance of trade by exporting more goods than they import. Colonies existed for the benefit of the mother country. Colonies provided the raw materials not available in Europe and enriched the mother country by serving as markets for manufactured goods. European nations passed strict navigation laws to ensure that colonies traded only with the mother country.

In 1776, Adam Smith wrote *The Wealth of Nations*. In this book, Smith presented the idea of laissez faire. Smith argued that laissez faire (leave business alone) would benefit the rising bourgeoisie. The rising middle class wanted the government to discard the policy of mercantilism with its restriction of trade and industry. These capitalists wanted the government to manufacture and sell their goods free from government interference. Smith believed that economic liberty guaranteed economic progress. Unlike mercantilism, which prompted strict government control, laissez faire promoted the idea that each individual would benefit by being able to pursue his own interest. While laissez faire supported the absolute monarchs of Europe from the sixteenth to the eighteenth century, laissez faire provided the foundation for the industrial development of Western society.

Reader's Comments on Part B: Second Sample Student Thematic Essay, Group 1-3

- Thesis statement is superficial — reference to the social and political era is not explained, and issues addressed, but in a weak way.

- Description of mercantilism is good but not analytical.

- Description of laissez faire is weak — lack of connection to the idea of natural law and Enlightenment.

- The essay fails to connect to the ideas of Malthus and Ricardo.

- The student gives little effort in comparing and contrasting the two systems.

Possible student score: 4–5

Part B: First Sample Student Thematic Essay, Group 2-1

World War II left Europe physically devastated and in a state of economic chaos. Economic conditions in Western Europe were terrible. Simply finding enough food to eat was a constant problem. Runaway inflation and black markets testified to severe shortages and hardships. The economic aid provided by the United States via the Marshall Plan and the close cooperation of the European nations through the Common Market promoted growth and revived the economies of these Western European countries.

Much of Western Europe lay in ruins in 1947. Europe's problems included large-scale unemployment, lack of food, and economic turmoil. The United States was fearful that these conditions could lead to the rise of Communism. In June 1947, Secretary of State John Marshall proposed the European Economic Recovery Program (Marshall Plan). The United States promised to provide food, machines, and other materials to any European country that needed it. The United States also offered aid to the Soviet Union and its satellite nations, but Stalin rejected the offer. He claimed that the Marshall Plan was a way for the United States to extend its economic control over Eastern Europe. In March 1948, Congress approved the Marshall Plan providing $12.5 billion economic assistance to Europe. As the Marshall Plan aid poured into the battered economies of Western Europe, the United States helped the economic recovery get off to a quick start. Furthermore, economic growth became a basic objective of all the Western governments who were determined to avoid the economic chaos of the 1930s. In addition, many workers were willing to work hard for low wages in the hope for a better future.

The spirit of cooperation also helped Europe's recovery from World War II. The close support among European nations required by the Marshall Plan contributed to economic growth. In 1950, French Foreign Minister Robert Schuman proposed an economic union of Western Europe to integrate all European steel production. In 1952, France, West Germany, Belgium, Italy, the Netherlands, and Luxembourg set up the European Coal and Steel Community. This independent agency set up prices and otherwise regulated the coal and steel industries of member nations. This close cooperation spurred economic growth and also did much to reduce the old rivalries, particularly between France and Germany. In 1957, these same six nations signed the Treaty of Rome to form the Common Market to expand free trade. The goal of the organization was the reduction of all tariffs among the six and also to include the free movement of capital and economic policies and institutions. The Common Market was a great success and added to the economic miracle of Western Europe.

The Marshall Plan and the formation of the Common Market, which abandoned the protectionism of many Western European nations, led to a push towards a united Europe, and contributed to the revival of Europe until the 1960s. By 1963, Western Europe was producing more than 2½ times as much as it had produced before the war. Never before had the European economy grown so fast. Europe had truly undergone an economic miracle.

Reader's Comments on Part B: First Sample Student Thematic Essay, Group 2-1

- The thesis statement is very clear.

- The student makes good use of concrete facts (Marshall Plan, Common Market).

- The overall organization of the essay is good.

- The conclusion is good.

Possible student score: 8–9

Part B: Second Sample Student Thematic Essay, Group 2-1

After World War II, the economic conditions of Western Europe deteriorated. The people of Europe were left with little money and shortages of food. To the rest of the world, it appeared as if Western Europe was in complete chaos with no relief in sight.

New leaders who came to power after the war tried to improve conditions in Western Europe. Christian Democrats played an important role in leadership. They provided effective leadership and authority which helped improve the economy. Socialists and Communists also provided effective leadership and made changes for the better in certain countries. But even with new leaders, Western Europe was still struggling. Outside help finally came from the United States. The United States promised food, economic aid, and military protection for those countries who required it. This support eventually allowed Western Europe to rebuild and rejuvenate itself. Conditions in Europe were not as bad as they had been. The help of the United States made a considerable difference in Europe's economic status.

Even though the aid of the United States had a huge impact on the economy, the governments of Western Europe made a real effort to make economic growth their main priority and to avoid the dangerous times of the 1930s. The economies of Western Europe were further helped by the fact that these countries began to come together to try and improve Europe's economy as a whole rather than focus on individual countries. This sense of unity had a significant impact on their economic recovery.

Reader's Comments on Part B: Second Sample Student Thematic Essay, Group 2-1

- The thesis statement is unclear.
- The essay is too general — there is no specific reference to the Marshall Plan nor the European Common Market.
- The student gives very little analysis.

Possible student score: 3–4

Part B: First Sample Student DBQ Essay, Group 2-2

As Europe recovered from World War I, two dictators rose to power in Italy and Germany. Italy's Benito Mussolini attempted to impose a Fascist government on his country, and Germany's Adolf Hitler ruled his country with Nazism.

Before World War I began, Italy appeared ready to move towards a democratic system of government. The existing parliamentary regime had granted universal male suffrage, and the state had a constitution that granted its citizens civil rights. However, several factors weakened Italy's strides towards democracy. The poverty of Italy's many peasants made it hard for them to be truly interested in the growth of Italian nationalism; they were more concerned with the affairs of their smaller villages. There were conflicts between the Catholic Church and Italy — the Church opposed Italy's growing liberalism. As World War I began, so did Italy's socialist movement. Socialists opposed Italy's entry into World War I.

After World War I, Italy was an embittered state. Although they had fought on the side of the Allies with the hopes of expanding Italy's territory, the Treaty of Versailles failed to provide the anticipated territorial gains. Workers and peasants, who had been promised social and land re-forms in exchange for their support in the war, did not receive what the government had promised them. The Russian Revolution inspired the growing numbers of Italian Socialists. These Socialists worked with Russian Bolsheviks to seize land and businesses, which in turn scared Italian landowners. At the conclusion of World War I, the pope lifted the ban on Catholics in government. As more and more conservative Catholics became involved in the government, the political scene in Italy grew more and more confused.

It seemed the perfect time for a charismatic, dominating leader to rise to power in Italy. Benito Mussolini had been a Socialist until he supported Italy's entry into World War I, and fought in World War I. After he returned home, he organized other veterans into a "union of forces" — or Fascists. He began his rise to power by combining nationalism and socialism, and by promising territorial expansion, worker benefits, and land reform for peasants. When his movement — which was similar to the already-established Socialist movement — failed to gain momentum, Mussolini used anti-Socialist propaganda to persuade conservative and middle class Italians to join his cause.

357

Mussolini began to repress the Socialist movement with increasing violence. He presented himself as the disciplinarian who was necessary to bring stability to Italy. By capitalizing on the fears of the middle class and conservative Italians, Mussolini was able to gain power. In 1922, Mussolini and the Fascists announced a march on Rome to demand that the government make changes. As thousands of Fascists chanted "On to Rome" and swarmed into the city, King Victor Emmanuel II bowed to pressure. Fearing a civil war, he asked Mussolini to form a government as prime minister. Without firing a shot, Mussolini received the legal authority from the king to become the leader of Italy. He received dictatorial powers to rule for one year, but by 1925 had eliminated all opposition through violence and terror.

Adolf Hitler also used the post–World War I climate to rise to power in Germany. Hitler was personally shattered by Germany's defeat in the First World War. A devout nationalist, Hitler was convinced that Germany's defeat was the fault of Jews and Marxists. Like many of the German people, Hitler was particularly bitter that Germany had been forced to accept full blame for the war. At the end of World War I, Hitler joined the German Workers' Party, which also denounced Jews and Marxists and promised an orderly, united German community.

When it appeared that the post–World War I government of the Weimar Republic was on the brink of collapse, Hitler and the German Workers' Party attempted to take control of the government. Although Hitler was put in jail, this revolt planted the first seeds of Nazism. Upon his release from jail, Hitler built his National Socialist German Workers' — or Nazi — Party. By 1928, the Nazi Party grew to include 100,000 members. However, they were still a small movement and in the 1928 election, they received less than 3 percent of the votes in the general election.

Ultimately, the economic crisis in Germany played the greatest role in Hitler's rise to power. In addition to the $132 billion in reparations that Germany was forced to pay the Allied nations, the Great Depression of 1929 hit an already-deprived Germany very hard. Unemployment rose to record numbers, and Hitler realized it would greatly help his cause to pay attention to Germany's economic climate. As unemployment rose, the Germans began to panic and turned to the Nazis to solve their problems. Year by year, as the existing German government became less and less effective, the Nazis became more and more prominent. The Weimar Republic was unable to stabilize Germany's plummeting economy, and their attempts at recovery — including slashing prices and wages — were very unpopular.

Hitler also benefited from the inability of Germany's Social Democrats and Communists to compromise. Although both parties together outnumbered the Nazis in the Reichstag, the two groups were unable to see past their differing ideologies. Socialists pleaded for a temporary alliance to block Hitler's rise, but they were unsuccessful — which paved the way for Hitler to reign in Germany.

Although their paths to power were quite different, both Mussolini and Hitler rose to power on the heels of the instability resulting from the First World War. They were able to capitalize on growing anxiety and political infighting — the results of which led to the Second World War.

Reader's Comments on Part B: First Sample Student Thematic Essay, Group 2-2

- The thesis statement is very clear.

- The student gives a good comparison of the two leaders.

- The essay has an excellent analysis of conditions within the two countries.

- The conclusion is good.

Possible student score: 8–9

Part B: Second Sample Student Thematic Essay, Group 2-2

Fascism and Nazism were two systems of government that happened in Italy and Germany after World War I. Fascism was in Italy, and Mussolini led the movement. Mussolini wanted to completely control Italy — he was a dictator. The Italian people listened to him because the country was poor. Italy needed a strong leader, and Mussolini was the right man for the job. He used his charisma to convince the people of Italy that he should rule their country, and after World War I, the king of Italy handed over power to Mussolini. After he got power, Mussolini used violence and intimidation to crush his enemies — the socialists in Italy. Little by little, Mussolini gained complete control of Italy due to his brutal tactics. By the time World War II began, Italy was a dictatorship with Mussolini as the dictator. He had successfully brought fascism to Italy.

In Germany, Adolf Hitler was the reason why Nazism existed. He was also a powerful leader who took total control of his country. The German people were very bitter about what had happened to them after World War I. They had to take all the blame for the war, and they thought this was very unfair. They also had to pay billions of dollars to other countries in Europe, and because of this, their economy was bad and many people lost their jobs. Hitler promised them that all of this would change. He held rallies and riots and made them even angrier about what had happened in World War I. He used this anger to motivate the people of Germany to vote for his Nazi party and to spread Nazi ideas throughout Germany.

Hitler blamed Jews and Communists for what happened in World War I, and he eventually convinced the other German people that Jews and Communists were to blame for World War I. Using these tactics, Hitler was able to spread Nazism throughout Germany and eventually throughout other countries in Europe. Hitler promised the German people that Nazism would solve the economic problems in Germany. He promised the Germans more jobs and better wages. This was a major reason why the German people were so receptive to Hitler's ideas — they were so bitter about what World War I had done to their economy that they were willing to listen to any leader who promised that things would improve. Hitler's dynamic personality was a driving and motivating force for the spread of Nazism.

Fascism rose in Italy because of Mussolini and Nazism rose in Germany because of Hitler. These two men were responsible for the rise of these dictatorial governments, which eventually led to World War II.

Reader's Comments on Part B: Second Sample Student Thematic Essay, Group 2-2

- The thesis statement is superficial.

- The content of the essay is too general.

- The student doesn't analyze the conditions within the two countries.

- The essay is weak overall.

Possible student score: 1-3

Part B: First Sample Student Thematic Essay, Group 2-3

The unification of Germany and the unification of Italy were indicative of the growing spirit of nationalism throughout Europe.

Before 1860, Italy was not a nation. As Metternich, the leader of Austria, expressed, Italy was merely "a geographical expression." Under Metternich, Austria took control of the northern provinces of Lombardy and Venetia. An Italian monarch ruled Sardinia and Piedmont, and Tuscany shared northern and central Italy with several smaller states. The papacy ruled Central Italy and Rome, and a branch of the Bourbons ruled Naples and Sicily, as they had for the past 100 years.

From the beginning to the middle of the nineteenth century, many Italians favored unification, and leaders such as Mazzini and Gioberti attempted to unify Italy through a democratic centralized republic and a federation of states under the power of a pope, respectively. Another consideration was for the independent kingdom of Sardinia-Piedmont to lead Italy. This third alternative appeared to be the most feasible, as a democratic republic seemed too radical an idea and a federation of states ruled by the pope seemed unlikely, especially since the pope had been forced — for a brief span — out of Italy.

From 1850-1861, Camillo di Cavour was Sardinia's dominant figure in government. Cavour came from a noble family and began as a manager of his father's large estates in Piedmont. Before entering politics, Cavour met with much success through various economic ventures including sugar mills, banks, and railroads. When he entered politics after 1848, Cavour only wanted to unify the northern and central Italian states, and did not want to include the Papal States or the Two Sicilies. Cavour realized that because Austria controlled Lombardy and Venetia, he would not be able to unify northern Italy without a powerful ally to force Austria out of these areas. To accomplish this, Cavour forged a secret alliance against Austria with Napoleon III of France.

Armed with this alliance, Cavour enticed Austria into attacking Sardinia and, with France's aid, successfully crushed Austria. However, Napoleon III was disgusted by the nature of war and was criticized by French Catholics for supporting Cavour, the pope's enemy. To appease all sides, Napoleon III signed a compromise peace with Austria that gave Sardinia only Lombardy. An angry Cavour resigned, only to be brought back to Italy by the growing spirit of nationalism throughout the Italian states. Italy ignored Napoleon III's compromise peace and demanded they be joined with Sardinia — eventually, the Italians got their way and Cavour returned to power in 1860.

However, intense patriots such as Giuseppe Garibaldi, believed the Italian unification had further to go. Born into a peasant family, Garibaldi personified romantic nationalism. After a 12-year exile in South America, Garibaldi returned to Italy to fight against Austria. By the end of the war, Garibaldi was a powerful figure in Italian politics. In 1860, Garibaldi's guerrilla band of "Red Shirts" was able to defeat a 20,000-man army and take Palermo. He and his men marched towards Naples and were ready to attack Rome and the pope. As he realized that an attack on Rome would antagonize France, Cavour smartly intercepted Garibaldi before he and his troops got to Rome. Garibaldi did not oppose Cavour and the people of the South voted to join Sardinia. Italy was at last united — at least politically.

As these events occurred in Italy, Germany also struggled with its own process of unification. The unification of Germany spanned several decades. Much like Italy had been, after 1815, the German Confederation was a conglomerate of 39 different sovereign states. Frederick Wilhelm IV of Prussia attempted to unify Germany but Austria — with support from Russia — blocked Wilhelm's attempt. As the nineteenth century progressed, and as economic growth spread throughout the rest of Europe, Prussia was instrumental in helping to form a customs union. The Zollverein, as this union was called, stimulated trade and improved the economies of its member-states. Because it was not economically beneficial or feasible for Austria to join the Zollverein, Austria tried to get the southern German states to leave Zollverein to no avail. As the members of Zollverein grew stronger and stronger, Prussia gained more and more of an advantage in its struggle with Austria.

As the German states witnessed the unification of Italy, Prussia changed greatly. The middle-class Prussians wanted to assert parliamentary power over the king. William I — who had replaced Wilhelm — wanted to double the size of Prussia's army. This did not appeal to middle-class Prussians who wanted to not only demilitarize but also wanted to make sure that the army remained under the control of Parliament and did not become its own governing body. By 1862, these middle-class Prussians had successfully won a majority of seats in Parliament and had defeated William I's proposed military budget. Ready to abdicate his throne, William turned to Otto von Bismarck.

The appointment of Bismarck was not met with satisfaction, as Bismarck soon showed that he would rule despite Parliament's disapproval. In order to draw attention away from domestic dissent, Bismarck maneuvered Prussia into a war with Austria. In the span of seven weeks, Prussia defeated Austria. The German Confederation was dissolved and Austria agreed to withdraw from German affairs. An expanded Prussia ruled the new North German Confederation while the mainly Catholic southern states remained independent but formed alliances with Prussia.

After the war, Bismarck restructured the government and chartered a federal constitution for the North German confederation. Each state had local government, but the king of Prussia — William I — became president of the confederation, and the chancellor — Bismarck — reported only to William I. Bismarck also formed a two-house legislature, with each house sharing equally in the making of laws. In a radical move, lower house members were elected by universal male suffrage. This enabled the king and chancellor to bypass the middle class but to also retain power. Realizing that Bismarck had yet to appease the middle class, he made a peace offering by asking Parliament to retroactively approve Prussia's spending from 1862 to 1866. The Parliament readily accepted Bismarck's offer. In 1867, Bismarck brought the four southern German states into a customs parliament and although these states were initially unwilling to go further, Germany was but a few steps away from unity.

The Franco-Prussian war from 1870–1871 was the last piece in the puzzle of German unification. Bismarck was astute enough to realize that war with France was the answer he needed to fully unify Germany. France was becoming alarmed by Prussia's growing power and decided that a war would be a way to assert its power over Prussia. From the very start of the war, the southern German states completely supported Bismarck. Because Bismarck had been so lenient with Austria after Prussia defeated them a few years earlier, Germany was able to easily defeat France's troops. After five months, Bismarck's campaign was successful and Germany was at last united under a two-house legislature, much like the one Bismarck set up in 1867.

Unlike Italy, Germany emerged from its process of unification feeling powerful, cohesive, and very proud. Whereas Cavour had been hesitant and unenthusiastic about bringing the southern Italian states into his new nation, Bismarck forged a war for the very purpose of bringing southern German states into his new empire. Prussia, which had been one of Europe's weaker nations, emerged from the unification of Germany as Europe's powerhouse.

Reader's Comments on Part B: First Sample Student Thematic Essay, Group 2-3

- The thesis is well stated and fully developed.

- The content of the essay is very specific regarding the role of Cavour and Bismarck.

- The student's analysis of the data is excellent, especially regarding Cavour in Italy and Bismarck's relationship with the German states.

- The essay is insightful.

Possible student score: 8–9

Part B: Second Sample Student Thematic Essay, Group 2-3

In the middle of the nineteenth century, two major European nations were unified — Italy and Germany, because of growing nationalism throughout Europe.

Italy was unified because of a man named Cavour. He was the leader of Piedmont and wanted to unite Italy so that he could have more power in Europe. Before Cavour, other leaders had tried to unify Italy but it did not work. One plan was for Italy to be unified and ruled by the pope — but not everyone supported that idea. Another plan was for Italy to be a federation — but many people objected to that idea and thought it was too radical. However, because of the nationalism that was spreading through Europe, many Italians wanted a unified nation.

Cavour helped with this goal of unification. However, he did not want to include all of Italy in this new nation. Cavour thought that only the northern Italian states should be included in a united Italy. However, a patriot from the South — Garibaldi — wanted the South to be a part of Italy. He was ready to fight Cavour and his troops, but Cavour realized it would be better to compromise with Garibaldi. Eventually, Cavour agreed to join the northern and the southern parts of Italy, mostly due to the political influence and public support of Garibaldi. However, even though Italy was unified in name, many people considered the North and the South to be two separate parts — Cavour had only unified Italy to appease Garibaldi's army, and Italy was not truly unified.

German unification was a much longer process than the unification process of Italy. Germany was unified due to the efforts of Bismarck. Bismarck was an aristocratic Prussian who wanted to expand Prussia, and he also wanted to make sure that Austria did not have power over Germany. Before it was unified, Germany was a collection of many independent states, each with their own government. Bismarck set up an economic alliance between Prussia and many of the German states, and Austria was left out of the alliance. Then, Austria and Prussia went to war — and Prussia won in less than two months. Bismarck did not make the Austrians sign a very harsh treaty, but he was able to ensure that Austria did not hold any power over Germany.

Bismarck was a powerful man, and after the war with Austria, he set up a system of government that made him second in command to only the Prussian king. After the war, Bismarck succeeded in bringing together most of Germany. Only the southern German states were not a part of the newly expanded Prussia. Soon after the war between Prussia and Austria was another war — this time between Prussia and France. Bismarck needed this war so that the southern German states would join his newly expanded empire. After a very short war, France was defeated and the southern German states joined Bismarck's empire. Germany was finally unified.

Nationalism and strong leadership were two things that the Italian and German unification had in common. However, Germany's process of unification took much longer and Italy's was much less cohesive than Germany's.

Reader's Comments on Part B: Second Sample Student Thematic Essay, Group 2-3

- The thesis statement is not well defined.
- The content of the essay is very superficial.
- The student gives little discussion of important facts, such as Franco-Prussian War and the role of Garibaldi.
- The essay is weak overall.

Possible student score: 1–3

Answer Sheet for Sample Practice Test III

Remove this sheet and use it to mark your answer for the multiple-choice section of Sample Practice Test III.

1 Ⓐ Ⓑ Ⓒ Ⓓ Ⓔ	21 Ⓐ Ⓑ Ⓒ Ⓓ Ⓔ	41 Ⓐ Ⓑ Ⓒ Ⓓ Ⓔ	61 Ⓐ Ⓑ Ⓒ Ⓓ Ⓔ
2 Ⓐ Ⓑ Ⓒ Ⓓ Ⓔ	22 Ⓐ Ⓑ Ⓒ Ⓓ Ⓔ	42 Ⓐ Ⓑ Ⓒ Ⓓ Ⓔ	62 Ⓐ Ⓑ Ⓒ Ⓓ Ⓔ
3 Ⓐ Ⓑ Ⓒ Ⓓ Ⓔ	23 Ⓐ Ⓑ Ⓒ Ⓓ Ⓔ	43 Ⓐ Ⓑ Ⓒ Ⓓ Ⓔ	63 Ⓐ Ⓑ Ⓒ Ⓓ Ⓔ
4 Ⓐ Ⓑ Ⓒ Ⓓ Ⓔ	24 Ⓐ Ⓑ Ⓒ Ⓓ Ⓔ	44 Ⓐ Ⓑ Ⓒ Ⓓ Ⓔ	64 Ⓐ Ⓑ Ⓒ Ⓓ Ⓔ
5 Ⓐ Ⓑ Ⓒ Ⓓ Ⓔ	25 Ⓐ Ⓑ Ⓒ Ⓓ Ⓔ	45 Ⓐ Ⓑ Ⓒ Ⓓ Ⓔ	65 Ⓐ Ⓑ Ⓒ Ⓓ Ⓔ
6 Ⓐ Ⓑ Ⓒ Ⓓ Ⓔ	26 Ⓐ Ⓑ Ⓒ Ⓓ Ⓔ	46 Ⓐ Ⓑ Ⓒ Ⓓ Ⓔ	66 Ⓐ Ⓑ Ⓒ Ⓓ Ⓔ
7 Ⓐ Ⓑ Ⓒ Ⓓ Ⓔ	27 Ⓐ Ⓑ Ⓒ Ⓓ Ⓔ	47 Ⓐ Ⓑ Ⓒ Ⓓ Ⓔ	67 Ⓐ Ⓑ Ⓒ Ⓓ Ⓔ
8 Ⓐ Ⓑ Ⓒ Ⓓ Ⓔ	28 Ⓐ Ⓑ Ⓒ Ⓓ Ⓔ	48 Ⓐ Ⓑ Ⓒ Ⓓ Ⓔ	68 Ⓐ Ⓑ Ⓒ Ⓓ Ⓔ
9 Ⓐ Ⓑ Ⓒ Ⓓ Ⓔ	29 Ⓐ Ⓑ Ⓒ Ⓓ Ⓔ	49 Ⓐ Ⓑ Ⓒ Ⓓ Ⓔ	69 Ⓐ Ⓑ Ⓒ Ⓓ Ⓔ
10 Ⓐ Ⓑ Ⓒ Ⓓ Ⓔ	30 Ⓐ Ⓑ Ⓒ Ⓓ Ⓔ	50 Ⓐ Ⓑ Ⓒ Ⓓ Ⓔ	70 Ⓐ Ⓑ Ⓒ Ⓓ Ⓔ
11 Ⓐ Ⓑ Ⓒ Ⓓ Ⓔ	31 Ⓐ Ⓑ Ⓒ Ⓓ Ⓔ	51 Ⓐ Ⓑ Ⓒ Ⓓ Ⓔ	71 Ⓐ Ⓑ Ⓒ Ⓓ Ⓔ
12 Ⓐ Ⓑ Ⓒ Ⓓ Ⓔ	32 Ⓐ Ⓑ Ⓒ Ⓓ Ⓔ	52 Ⓐ Ⓑ Ⓒ Ⓓ Ⓔ	72 Ⓐ Ⓑ Ⓒ Ⓓ Ⓔ
13 Ⓐ Ⓑ Ⓒ Ⓓ Ⓔ	33 Ⓐ Ⓑ Ⓒ Ⓓ Ⓔ	53 Ⓐ Ⓑ Ⓒ Ⓓ Ⓔ	73 Ⓐ Ⓑ Ⓒ Ⓓ Ⓔ
14 Ⓐ Ⓑ Ⓒ Ⓓ Ⓔ	34 Ⓐ Ⓑ Ⓒ Ⓓ Ⓔ	54 Ⓐ Ⓑ Ⓒ Ⓓ Ⓔ	74 Ⓐ Ⓑ Ⓒ Ⓓ Ⓔ
15 Ⓐ Ⓑ Ⓒ Ⓓ Ⓔ	35 Ⓐ Ⓑ Ⓒ Ⓓ Ⓔ	55 Ⓐ Ⓑ Ⓒ Ⓓ Ⓔ	75 Ⓐ Ⓑ Ⓒ Ⓓ Ⓔ
16 Ⓐ Ⓑ Ⓒ Ⓓ Ⓔ	36 Ⓐ Ⓑ Ⓒ Ⓓ Ⓔ	56 Ⓐ Ⓑ Ⓒ Ⓓ Ⓔ	76 Ⓐ Ⓑ Ⓒ Ⓓ Ⓔ
17 Ⓐ Ⓑ Ⓒ Ⓓ Ⓔ	37 Ⓐ Ⓑ Ⓒ Ⓓ Ⓔ	57 Ⓐ Ⓑ Ⓒ Ⓓ Ⓔ	77 Ⓐ Ⓑ Ⓒ Ⓓ Ⓔ
18 Ⓐ Ⓑ Ⓒ Ⓓ Ⓔ	38 Ⓐ Ⓑ Ⓒ Ⓓ Ⓔ	58 Ⓐ Ⓑ Ⓒ Ⓓ Ⓔ	78 Ⓐ Ⓑ Ⓒ Ⓓ Ⓔ
19 Ⓐ Ⓑ Ⓒ Ⓓ Ⓔ	39 Ⓐ Ⓑ Ⓒ Ⓓ Ⓔ	59 Ⓐ Ⓑ Ⓒ Ⓓ Ⓔ	79 Ⓐ Ⓑ Ⓒ Ⓓ Ⓔ
20 Ⓐ Ⓑ Ⓒ Ⓓ Ⓔ	40 Ⓐ Ⓑ Ⓒ Ⓓ Ⓔ	60 Ⓐ Ⓑ Ⓒ Ⓓ Ⓔ	80 Ⓐ Ⓑ Ⓒ Ⓓ Ⓔ

CUT HERE

Section I: Multiple-Choice Questions

Time: 55 minutes

80 Questions

Percent of total grade = 50%

Directions: Each of the questions or incomplete statements below is followed by five suggested answers or completions. Select the one that is best in each case and then fill in the corresponding oval on the answer sheet.

1. Which of the following was NOT part of the fighting in World War I?

   A. trench warfare

   B. poison gas

   C. submarines

   D. tanks

   E. radar

2. The Medici family helped with the prosperity of Florence by doing all of the following EXCEPT

   A. donating their money to the church

   B. sponsoring the arts

   C. providing political and artistic leadership

   D. supporting popular causes

   E. becoming patrons of artists and writers such as Michelangelo and Botticelli

3. In 1868, which area in Italy was not part of the United Kingdom of Italy?

   A. Kingdom of Two Sicilies

   B. Lombardy

   C. Venetia

   D. Papal States

   E. Tuscany

4. Maximilien Robespierre was

   A. the leader of the *sans-culottes*

   B. a Girondist leader

   C. a spokesperson for the Catholic Church

   D. one of the king's biggest supporters

   E. a middle-class lawyer who represented Paris' working class radicals

GO ON TO THE NEXT PAGE

5. Which British invention helped turn the tide in the Battle of Britain against Germany?

A. V-2 missile

B. rapid-fire anti-aircraft gun

C. radar

D. the tank

E. the RAF spit fire plan

6. As a result of the Congress of Vienna, Belgium

A. was returned to Spain

B. was given to France

C. was granted independence

D. became neutral

E. was given to the Netherlands

7. Johannes Kepler's work on the first three laws of planetary motion that were based on mathematical relations helped to

A. support Newton's law of gravity

B. uphold the Aristotelian view of the universe

C. reinforce Galileo's theory of the universe

D. prove that Ptolemy's view of the earth as the center of the universe was correct

E. support Tycho Brahe's data about the planets moving in an elliptical orbit

8. The death of Marshall Tito resulted in

A. a period of peace among the many different ethnic groups of Yugoslavia

B. disarmament of Yugoslavia's nuclear weapons

C. the unification of Yugoslavia

D. a period of chaos in Yugoslavia due to ethnic conflicts

E. economic prosperity

9. Portugal's role in the Age of Discovery included all of the following EXCEPT

A. exploring overseas lands in the Middle East and Africa

B. bringing Christianity to Arab and African lands

C. inspiring Spain and other European nations to join the Age of Discovery

D. discovering the first water route to India

E. developing a unique system of diplomacy to forge relationships with its colonized lands

10. Mercantilism was an economic policy in which

A. laws of supply and demand determined the price of goods

B. government owned the factors of production

C. the workers shared in the profits

D. a nation's wealth was measured by its gold and silver

E. individuals could follow their own interests for the good of the country

11. The main reason for the Berlin Conference of 1884/1885 was

    A. to prevent Belgium from taking over all of Africa

    B. to work with African nations to develop an economic program

    C. to limit trading practices on the Congo River

    D. to establish guidelines for dividing up Africa in order to avoid conflicts among European nations

    E. to allow Italy an opportunity to establish colonies for its surplus population

12. Which of the following men called for national workshops to guarantee full employment for the workers?

    A. Louis Blanc

    B. Robert Owens

    C. Pierre Proudhon

    D. Charles Fourier

    E. Georg Friedrich Wilhelm Hegel

13. Which is the most accurate statement about the Soviet Union under Lenin?

    A. It was a classless society.

    B. Capitalism was abolished.

    C. The government allowed limited democratic reforms.

    D. The Communist Party had absolute control.

    E. Lenin had selected Stalin as his successor before he died.

14. The 38th parallel refers to

    A. a condition of the Treaty of Versailles

    B. the Soviet area of Germany

    C. officially neutral land

    D. the point of division between North Korea and South Korea

    E. safe airspace for Western Bloc air crafts

15. Milosevic's policy of "ethnic cleansing" was:

    A. the forced removal of non-Serbian groups from Serbian-controlled areas

    B. a way to ensure peace throughout Yugoslavia

    C. a plan of attack against his neighboring countries

    D. a treaty with the former Soviet Union

    E. a way to unite all Serbs and non-Serbs into a greater Yugoslavia

16. The Seven Weeks War in 1866 between Austria and Prussia led to

    A. annexation of Schleswig/Holstein by Prussia

    B. Austria paying a huge indemnity to Prussia

    C. Austria recognizing Prussian dominance of the German states

    D. Napoleon III's decision to support unification of northern and southern Germany

    E. a quick victory by Austria

GO ON TO THE NEXT PAGE

17. The Balfour Declaration of 1917:

    A. ended Austria-Hungary's participation in the war

    B. laid the foundation for the League of Nations

    C. guaranteed the re-establishment of Belgian neutrality

    D. declared the right of Jews to a homeland in Palestine

    E. supported American entrance into World War I

18. During the Stuart Restoration, what was one accomplishment of Parliament?

    A. They passed the Habeas Corpus act, prohibiting imprisonment without due cause.

    B. They successfully prevented Charles II's Catholic brother from inheriting the throne.

    C. They revoked Charles II's secret treaty with France.

    D. They limited the power of the monarchy.

    E. They negotiated lucrative treaties with other European nations.

19. Which was considered to be the leading example of the new textile industrial city of the Industrial Revolution during the late eighteenth and nineteenth centuries in England?

    A. Manchester

    B. Liverpool

    C. London

    D. Birmingham

    E. Sheffield

20. Machiavelli would most likely support a politician who would:

    A. manipulate people and use any means to gain power

    B. govern his actions by moral considerations

    C. take actions to weaken the government and let the people govern

    D. govern with the help of the church

    E. take a passive approach when dealing with problems

21. Enlightened Despots believed in all of the following EXCEPT:

    A. reform of the educational system

    B. use of reason to examine the world

    C. democracy

    D. religious toleration

    E. support of art, literature, and science

22. Place the following events in the proper chronological order:

    (1) Khrushchev forced to retire

    (2) U-2 incident

    (3) Cuban Missile Crisis

    (4) Berlin Wall built

    A. 2, 4, 3, 1

    B. 1, 2, 3, 4

    C. 4, 1, 2, 3

    D. 3, 4, 2, 1

    E. 4, 1, 3, 2

23. In Night of the Long Knives in June 1934, Hitler ordered the Black Shirts to

    A. arrest all Jews

    B. destroy the Weimar Republic

    C. put to death Ernst Röhm, his friend and leader of the Brown Shirts, and 1,000 of his troops

    D. arrest all members of the Communist Party

    E. begin occupying the Rhineland

24. All of the following are included in the Fourteen Points of Woodrow Wilson EXCEPT:

    A. the end of secret diplomacy

    B. freedom of the seas

    C. reduction of arms

    D. free trade

    E. preventing countries from having to pay war reparations

25. Napoleon's *coup d'etat* resulted in

    A. the restoration of the French monarchy

    B. the restoration of the Directory as the governing body of France

    C. his defeat and exile

    D. the formation of the Consulate

    E. a period of peace in France

26. A major difference between Calvinists and Lutherans was that John Calvin, unlike Martin Luther, believed:

    A. salvation came through faith alone

    B. the church was higher than the state and should have a role in the government

    C. the Bible was not the final authority

    D. people have free will to do what they think is right

    E. one's faith has nothing to do with economic status

27. A major reason for British interest in controlling the Suez Canal was:

    A. Egypt's valuable mineral resources

    B. the strategic location of the Suez Canal

    C. to spread Christianity to Egypt

    D. Egypt's value as a market place for British goods

    E. Egypt's control of the spice trade

28. A major result of the Reform Act of 1832 was:

    A. abolishing rotten boroughs

    B. outlawing the secret ballots

    C. abolishing the House of Lords veto power

    D. government funding for public housing

    E. extending suffrage to women

GO ON TO THE NEXT PAGE

29. The Marshall Plan was:

    A. a recovery program that gave over $17 billion in economic aid to European nations

    B. the United States build up of nuclear weapons

    C. a treaty between the nations of NATO and the nations of the Warsaw Pact

    D. a military invasion of West Germany

    E. a way for Russia to further increase their control over Eastern European nations

30. During the Renaissance after the Hundred Years War, the monarchy in France:

    A. was consolidated most effectively by Louis XI

    B. overturned by the rise of the bourgeoisie

    C. weakened because of the rise of feudal anarchy

    D. joined with the church to fix the damages caused by the war

    E. completely crumbled due to the devastation of the war

31. All of the following were a result of Napoleon's Russian invasion EXCEPT:

    A. Napoleon gained further control over France and other parts of Europe.

    B. Napoleon lost three-fourths of his army.

    C. Napoleon abdicated his throne.

    D. Napoleon was forced into exile.

    E. Louis XVIII was restored to the throne.

32. The Council of Trent supported all of the following statements EXCEPT:

    A. Salvation was obtained by good works and faith.

    B. The Bible was the source of religious authority and faith.

    C. An individual does not need the guidance of the church for understanding their faith.

    D. Seminary education of the clergy is a must in each diocese.

    E. Certain books, such as those of Galileo and Erasmus, should not be read.

33. Reformers such as Robert Owen who tried to establish model communities, were known as:

    A. Luddites

    B. Communists

    C. Utopian Socialists

    D. Fascists

    E. Anarchists

34. The Spirit of Locarno in 1925 referred to

A. the agreement to end German reparations payment

B. the United States joining the League of Nations

C. the symbol of a new era of cooperation between France and Germany

D. the removal of the War Guilt Clause from the Versailles Treaty

E. the agreement of European nations to denounce war as an instrument of foreign policy

35. The beautification of Paris during the presidency of Louis Napoleon was under the supervision of:

A. George Haussmann

B. Edwin Chadwick

C. Louis Pasteur

D. Joseph Lester

E. Gustavus Vasa

36. In the late 1980s, Mikhail Gorbachev's decision to stop interfering in the internal affairs of Eastern European nations led directly to:

A. the collapse of the free-market economies in the region

B. an increase in Cold War tensions

C. a renewal of religious violence between Orthodox Christians and Russian Jews

D. the collapse of NATO

E. the collapse of the Communist governments in the region

37. All of the following states came into existence after World War I EXCEPT:

A. Albania

B. Finland

C. Czechoslovakia

D. Yugoslavia

E. Estonia

38. Don Quixote was:

A. a political manifesto

B. a painting that depicted the glory of Spanish colonialism

C. a series of maps that depicted Spain's African colonies

D. a work of fiction that described Spain in the sixteenth century

E. a handbook on protocol in the Spanish court

39. All of the following statements are true about United Italy in 1871 EXCEPT:

A. a division between the industrial North and agricultural South

B. the Catholic Church's support of the newly united government

C. the government adapted a policy of ambitious nationalism and imperialism

D. a strong lack of a democratic tradition

E. a large population growth led to migration as people were unable to earn a living

GO ON TO THE NEXT PAGE

40. One result of Stalin's policy of collectivization was:

    A. surplus agricultural crops

    B. a widespread food shortage

    C. an increase of exports of agricultural products to Western Europe

    D. the establishment of a strong agricultural base to support the expansion of the Soviet Union's heavy industry

    E. a renewed cooperation between Kulaks and the Soviet government

41. What was a major goal of Peter the Great's foreign policy?

    A. to establish complete control of Poland from Prussia

    B. to join an alliance with France against England

    C. to limit the expansion of Austria's influence in the Balkans

    D. to acquire a window on the West along the Baltic Sea

    E. to gain a port on the Black Sea

42. "The Scramble for Africa was due to the growing commercial rivalry which brought home . . . the vital necessity of securing the only remaining fields for industrial enterprises and expansion."

The author of this passage would support the belief that the motive for imperialism was

    A. religious

    B. economic

    C. political

    D. military

    E. humanitarian

43. Which group gained suffrage as a result of the Reform Bill of 1832?

    A. middle class

    B. women

    C. landed aristocracy

    D. urban working class

    E. peasants

44. The Sepoy Rebellion and the Boxer Rebellion were similar in that they both were:

    A. attempts to improve relations with Western powers

    B. victories against the imperialistic countries

    C. reactions to Western imperialism

    D. efforts to develop democratic governments

    E. revolutions against traditional monarchs

45. All of the following were results of the Protestant Reformation EXCEPT:

    A. a series of religious wars in the sixteen and seventeenth centuries between Catholics and Protestants

    B. the religious unity of Europe grew stronger out of the conflict

    C. the state was seen as superior to the church

    D. education and reading increased throughout Europe

    E. northern Europe became predominantly Protestant and southern Europe was mostly Catholic

46. "Whenever the legislators endeavor to take away and destroy the property of the people or to reduce them to slavery . . . they put themselves into a state of war with the people who are thereupon absolved from any further obedience."

Which one of the following men would support the ideas in this passage?

A. Thomas Hobbes

B. Louis XIV

C. Charles V

D. John Locke

E. Jacques Bousset

47. Which of the following countries did not attend the Versailles Conference?

A. Russia and Germany

B. Germany and Japan

C. Russia and Japan

D. Italy and Germany

E. Russia and Italy

48. The term "Peace in Our Time" refers to:

A. the signing of the Locarno Pact

B. the Versailles Treaty

C. the Kellogg-Briand Peace Pact

D. the agreement at the Munich Conference of 1938

E. the Lateran Pact

49. Konrad Adenauer was instrumental in:

A. furthering the Communist cause

B. negotiating an alliance between the Soviet Union and the Western Bloc

C. the disarmament of the Soviet Union

D. the economic recovery of Western Germany

E. the unification of Germany

50. The goal of the Royal Society of London, founded in 1660, was to:

A. support the restoration of the British king

B. encourage scientific research

C. promote overseas exploration

D. establish a closer tie between government and scientific research

E. use political powers to restrict scientific research

51. The Renaissance had the following effects on women EXCEPT:

A. the status of upper-class women declined

B. the life of the ordinary woman was directly affected

C. women's status declined regarding sex and love

D. women studied the classics

E. women were forbidden from becoming involved in public affairs

GO ON TO THE NEXT PAGE

52. "Population, when unchecked, increases in a geometrical rate. Subsistence only increases in an arithmetical ratio."

The ideas in this passage are most associated with

A. David Ricardo

B. Thomas Malthus

C. Louis Blanc

D. John Locke

E. Karl Marx

53. Which of the following groups was involved in the St. Bartholomew Day Massacres of 1572?

A. Roundheads

B. Puritans

C. French Calvinists

D. French Jews

E. Lutherans

54. The purpose of the Maginot Line in France was

A. to prevent another German invasion by building massive fortifications along the border

B. a series of alliances with Eastern European countries to encircle Germany

C. to provide work for the unemployed created by the Great Depression

D. to prevent the spread of revolutions in the newly formed national governments of Eastern Europe

E. to stop the spread of Bolshevism in the newly formed Soviet Union

55. The Ottoman Empire and the Austrian Empire were most similar in that:

A. both contained multinational ethnic groups

B. both were constitutional monarchies

C. both were not affected by the growth of nationalism in the 1870s

D. both tried to promote some economic modernization

E. neither of them had a strong effective military organization

56. The initial reaction of the Russian government to the fighting that broke out in Chechnya in the 1990s demonstrated that Russia:

A. needs the United States' resources to ensure stability in the region

B. has little control over its arsenal of nuclear weapons

C. will defend its remaining republics against foreign invasion

D. favors re-establishing communism

E. is unwilling to grant independence to dissenting ethnic groups

57. "If anyone wishes to see in how little space a human being can move, how little air and such air . . . he can breathe, how little civilization he may share . . . it is only necessary to travel hither."
—Friedrich Engels

This quotation describes the negative effects of

A. the Industrial Revolution

B. Imperialism

C. the Glorious Revolution

D. the Black Death

E. the French Revolution

58. The political thinkers of the Enlightenment, such as Locke and Rousseau, supported the idea that:

A. Government is a social contract designed to protect the rights of the people.

B. Absolute Monarchy is the best form of government.

C. All individuals exist for the benefit of the state.

D. The power of the king and nobles should be strengthened to ensure stability.

E. The military is the backbone of society.

59. Which of the following Russian leaders believed in the idea of "permanent revolutions" to insure the success of Communism?

A. Joseph Stalin

B. Vladimir Lenin

C. Leon Trotsky

D. Alexander Kerensky

E. Nikolai Bukharin

60. Which event contributed to the formation of the Dual Monarchy?

A. Franco-Prussian War

B. Danish War

C. Austro-Prussian War

D. Crimean War

E. Russo-Turkish War

61. Martin Luther's statement before the Diet of Worms that "my conscience is captive to the Word of God," was referring to his belief in:

A. the need for indulgences

B. good works

C. the supremacy of the pope

D. the supremacy of the Bible over the authority of the pope and the church

E. the seven sacraments

GO ON TO THE NEXT PAGE

62. "No man's land is an eerie sight. At early dawn in the pale gray light. Never a house and never a hedge."
— J. Knight-Adkin, *No Man's Land*

The above quotation describes the situation created by

A. World War I

B. World War II

C. the French Revolution

D. the Franco-Prussian War

E. the Spanish Civil War

63. Lithuania's declaration of independence in 1990 and the election of Lech Walesa as leader of Poland demonstrated

A. the continued growth of Communism

B. increased cooperation among Russia and their allies

C. the spirit of self-determination and nationalism

D. the influence of the Russian military

E. the collapse of NATO

64. Which of the following wrote *The Social Contract*?

A. Jean Jacques Rousseau

B. Baron de Montesquieu

C. John Locke

D. Denis Diderot

E. Thomas Hobbes

65. What was contained in the Atlantic Charter of 1941?

A. demands for the unconditional surrender of Germany

B. a statement about the evils of Communism

C. a plea for the world to open up negotiations to end the war

D. a statement of British and United States principles about their goals in World War II

E. a statement providing economic aid to the Soviet Union to fight Germany

66. "The Jacobin Revolution is carried on by men of no rank, of no consideration, of wild, savage minds, full of levity, arrogance, and presumption, without morals."

The ideas in this passage would most likely be associated with

A. Edmund Burke

B. Louis XVI

C. Maximilien Robespierre

D. Jacques Necker

E. Louis XVIII

67. All of the following were results of the Thirty Years War EXCEPT:

 A. The Edict of Restitution was revoked.

 B. Protestantism was established in Europe.

 C. Calvinism was recognized.

 D. The role of the church in politics increased.

 E. The concept of the balance of power between nations emerged.

68. Jean Auguste Dominique Ingres' portrait of Napoleon in splendid robes entitled *Napoleon on His Imperial Throne* conveys the image of Napoleon as:

 A. the Son of the Revolution

 B. a democratic ruler

 C. a God-like figure

 D. a lover of liberty

 E. a military leader

69. Which is a common characteristic of the *Divine Comedy*, *Canterbury Tales*, and *The Decameron*?

 A. They were written by Italian Humanists.

 B. They were written in Latin.

 C. They were written in the vernacular.

 D. They were stories about the need to rid Italy of foreign invaders.

 E. They were stories glorifying the heritage of Greece and Rome.

70. The Triple Entente and the Triple Alliance were formed prior to:

 A. World War I

 B. World War II

 C. the formation of the United Nations

 D. the formation of the League of Nations

 E. the signing of the Versailles Treaty

71. Willy Brandt, leader of the Social Democratic Party in Western Germany, was associated with:

 A. containment of Communism

 B. the economic miracle of West Germany

 C. tough policies towards the Soviet Union

 D. Ostpolitik

 E. destruction of the Berlin Wall

GO ON TO THE NEXT PAGE

© Massimo Listri/CORBIS

72. Which event in Italian unification is represented in the picture?

A. the meeting of Cavour and Garibaldi over the invasion of the Kingdom of Two Sicilies

B. the meeting of Garibaldi with the representatives of the Papal States

C. Garibaldi's decision to return to Italy

D. Garibaldi's handing over the conquests of Southern Italy to Victor Emmanuel to help unite Italy

E. Victor Emmanuel's decision to allow Garibaldi to form a government in the Kingdom of the Two Sicilies

73. The Great Exposition of 1851 held in the Crystal Palace in Britain showed:

A. the success of imperialism

B. the achievements of the government's immigration policy

C. the success of British socialism

D. the growth of industry and population of Great Britain

E. the success of the British military establishment

74. Which was NOT a result of the Peace of Augsburg?

   A. Northern Germany became Lutheran.

   B. Southern Germany became Catholic.

   C. The prince of each area determined the religion of the subjects.

   D. Freedom of religion was not tolerated.

   E. Calvinism was recognized as a religion in the German states.

75. The issue of Home Rule in British politics during the nineteenth century referred to:

   A. using Irish taxes to support the Anglican Church

   B. political freedom for the Catholics living in England

   C. independence for India

   D. self-government for Ireland

   E. extension of civil rights for women in England

76. Which was NOT a belief of Voltaire?

   A. admired the British system of government

   B. supported religious tolerance and urged religious freedom

   C. attacked the evils of organized religion

   D. felt that God was a constant influence in the life of each individual

   E. praised Enlightened Despotism

77. Which of the following allowed the Allies to establish a Second Front in Europe?

   A. Battle of the Bulge

   B. Invasion of Normandy

   C. Allied Bombing of Dresden

   D. Invasion of Italy

   E. Battle of Stalingrad

78. In which of the following areas was Bismarck considered a pioneer?

   A. social and economic reform

   B. social reform

   C. military reform

   D. judicial reform

   E. political reform

79. The Father of Humanism was

   A. Picco della Mirandola

   B. Francesco Petrarch

   C. Baldassare Castiglione

   D. Dante

   E. Giovanni Boccaccio

80. Which of the following leaders is associated with the formation of the Fifth Republic in France?

   A. Leon Blum

   B. Charles DeGaulle

   C. Francois Mitterand

   D. Georges Pompidou

   E. Edmund Daladier

STOP

EUROPEAN HISTORY

SECTION II

Part A

(Suggested writing time — 45 minutes)

Percent of Section II score — 45

Directions: The following question is based on the accompanying Documents 1–10. (Some of the documents have been edited for the purpose of this exercise.) This question is designed to test your ability to work with historical documents. As you analyze the documents, take into account both the sources of the documents and the authors' points of view. Write an essay on the following topic that integrates your analysis of the documents. **Do not simply summarize the documents individually.** You may refer to relevant historical facts and developments not mentioned in the documents.

---

1. Assess the following statement: The Cold War was an inevitable outgrowth of the ideological and political differences between the United States and the Soviet Union.

Historical Background: The wartime alliance from 1941 to 1945 among the United States, Soviet Union, and Great Britain against Hitler had been an expedient relationship, whose goal was to destroy Nazism. With the victory over Hitler assured in 1945, Europe became the battleground again for a new war, the Cold War. Between 1945 and 1950, wartime alliances would break down and result in the division of Europe into two hostile camps. The Cold War would determine relations for the next forty years.

Document 1

The USSR still lives in antagonistic 'capitalist encirclement' from which in the long run there can be no permanent peaceful co-existence as stated by Stalin in 1927. . . . at the bottom of the Kremlin's neurotic view of world affairs is traditional and instinctive Russian sense of insecurity. . . . We must see that our public is educated in the realities of Russian situation . . . it must be done by government . . . there would be less hysterical anti-Sovietism in our country if the realities were better understood by the people . . . We must formulate and put forward for other nations a much more positive and constructive picture of the sort of world we would like to see than we have put forward in the past. It is not enough to urge the people to develop political processes similar to our own. Many foreign peoples, in Europe at least, are tired and frightened by experiences of the past, and are less interested in abstract freedom than in security. They are seeking guidance rather than responsibilities. We should be better able than the Russians to give them this. And unless we do, the Russians certainly will.

Source: George Kennan, excerpts from *A Long Telegram from Moscow,* February 26, 1946.

Document 2

It would be wrong to believe that the Second World War broke out accidentally or was a result of the mistakes of some or other statesmen, though mistakes certainly were made. In reality, the war broke out as an inevitable result of the development of world economic and political forces on the basis of modern monopoly capitalism. . . . Marxists have stated more than once that the capitalist system of world economy conceals in itself the elements of general crisis and military clashes . . . Our victory means, in the first place, that our Soviet social system has won, that the Soviet social system successfully withstood the trial in the flames of war and proved its perfect viability. . . . The war has shown that the Soviet social system is a truly popular system, which has grown from the people and enjoys its powerful support, that the Soviet social system is a perfectly viable and stable form of organization of society. . . . The point now is that the Soviet social system has proved more viable and stable than a non-Soviet social system, that the Soviet social system is a better form of organization of society than any non-Soviet social system.

Source: Joseph Stalin, *The Soviet Victory: Capitalism Versus Communism,* February, 1946.

Document 3

I now come to the . . . danger, which threatens the cottage home and ordinary people, namely tyranny. We cannot be blind to the fact that the liberties enjoyed by individual citizens throughout the United States and British Empire are not valid in a considerable number of countries, some of which are very powerful. . . . A shadow has fallen upon the scenes so lately lighted by the Allied victory. Nobody knows what Soviet Russia and its Communist international organization intends to do in the immediate future, or what are the limits . . . From Stettin in the Baltic to Trieste in the Adriatics, an iron curtain has descended across the continent. Behind that line lie all the capitals of the ancient states of central and eastern Europe. . . . all these famous cities and the populations around them lie in the Soviet sphere and all are subject, in one form or another, not only to Soviet influence but to a very high and increasing measure of control from Moscow. . . .

Source: Winston Churchill, "Iron Curtain Speech," March 5, 1946.

Document 4

In substance, Mr. Churchill now stands in the position of a firebrand of war. And Mr. Churchill is not alone here. He has friends not only in England but also in the United States of America. . . . As a result of the German invasion, the Soviet Union has irrevocably lost . . . 7,000,000 people. . . . the Soviet Union cannot forget them. One can ask therefore, what can be surprising in the fact that the Soviet Union, in a desire to ensure its security for the future, tries to achieve that these countries

GO ON TO THE NEXT PAGE

Section II Free Response Essays

should have governments whose relations to the Soviet Union are loyal? How can one, without having lost one's reason, qualify these peaceful aspirations of the Soviet Union as 'expansionist tendencies' of our Government? . . .

Source: Joseph Stalin, "Reply to Churchill," *New York Times*, March 14, 1946.

Document 5

. . . The Government of the United States has made frequent protests against coercion and intimidation, in violation of the Yalta agreement, in Poland, Rumania, and Bulgaria. . . . One way of life is based upon the will of the majority, and is distinguished by free institutions, representative governments, . . . The second way of life is based upon the will of a minority forcibly imposed upon the majority. It relies upon terror and oppression, . . . I believe that it must be the policy of the United States to support free peoples who are resisting attempted subjugation by armed minorities or by outside pressures. I believe that we must assist free peoples to work out their own destinies in their own way. . . . The seeds of totalitarian regimes are nurtured by misery and want. They spread and grow in the evil soil of poverty and strife. They reach their full growth when the hope of a people for a better life has died. We must keep that hope alive. . . . I propose giving Greece and Turkey $400 million in aid.

Source: President Harry Truman's Speech to Congress, March, 12, 1947, *Public Papers of the President*, Harry S. Truman, 1947.

Document 6

The truth of the matter is that Europe for the next three or four years . . . must have substantial additional help or face economic social and political deterioration of a very grave character. . . . It is logical that the United States should do whatever it is able to do to assist in the return of normal economic health in the world, without which there can be no political stability and no assured peace. Our policy is directed not against any country or doctrine but against hunger, poverty, desperation, and chaos. Its purpose should be the revival of a working economy in which free institutions can exist. Such assistance, I am convinced, must not be on a piecement basis as various crises develop. Any assistance that this Government may render in the future should provide a cure rather than a mere palliative. Any government that is willing to assist in the task of recovery will find full cooperation, I am sure, on the part of the United States Government. Any government which maneuvers to block the recovery of other countries, or groups which seek to perpetuate human misery in order to profit there from politically or otherwise will encounter the opposition of the United States. . . .

Source: The Marshall Plan: Department of State Bulletin, June 15, 1947, pp. 1159-1160.

Document 7

. . . the death of Stalin, by shaking the superstructure of discipline, by admitting for a brief moment the clash of several opinions and the consequent opportunity for a slightly larger area of discussion at the summit, has given the communist machinery of politics a momentary opportunity to review some of its errors. But, unless communism ceases to be communism, the process of discipline calls for a new tightening of control, a new struggle to apply the logic of a single man to a world of dark and uncertain phenomena.

Source: Theodore White, *An Assessment of Communism,* 1953.

Document 8

We must assert that in regard to those persons who in their time had opposed the party line, there were often no sufficient reasons for their physical annihilation. . . . Thus, Stalin had sanctioned . . . the most brutal violation of Socialist legality, torture, and oppression.

Source: Self Renewal: The Attack on Stalin (June 1956), Congressional Record, 84th Congress, 2nd Session, June 4, 1956, pp. 9390-9402.

Document 9

The 'Communist Logic' . . . is diametrically opposed to our own. Thus, the Communist refers to the iron curtain police states as 'democracies,' and any defensive move on the part of the Western powers is condemned as 'aggression.' The Communist thus builds for himself a topsy-turvy world with a completely distorted set of values. For this reason, it is practically impossible to win an argument with a hard-core Communist. . . . The Communist mind cannot and will not engage in a detached examination of ideas. Talking to a Communist about his own ideas, then, is like listening to a phonograph record. His answers will invariably follow a definite pattern because he can never admit . . . that the basis for his ideas may not be sound.

Source: "How to Spot a Communist," *U.S.A.,* an American magazine of fact and opinion, 1955.

Document 10

. . . We believe that in the competition with capitalism socialism will win. . . . We believe that this victory will be won in peaceful competition and not by way of unleashing a war. We have stood, we stand and we will stand by the positions of peaceful competition of states with different social systems. . . . The victory of communism is inevitable! . . . Long live the heroic party of the communists of the Soviet Union, created and tempered in struggle by the great Lenin! Long live the indestructible unity of the international Communist and workers' movement and the fraternal solidarity of the proletarians of all countries! . . . Under the all conquering banner of Marxism-Leninism, under the leadership of the Communist party, forward to the victory of communism!

Source: Nikita Khrushchev's Speech to 22nd Communist Part Congress, *Current Soviet Policies,* IV.

EUROPEAN HISTORY

SECTION II

Part B

(Suggested planning and writing time — 70 minutes)

Percent of Section II score — 55

Directions: You are to answer TWO questions, one from each group of three questions below. Make your selections carefully, choosing the questions that you are best prepared to answer thoroughly in the time permitted. You should spend 5 minutes organizing or outlining each essay. In writing your essays, use specific examples to support your answer. If time permits when you finish writing, check your work. Be certain to number your answers as the questions are numbered below.

Group 1

Choose ONE question from this group. The suggested writing time for this question is 30 minutes. You are advised to spend 5 minutes planning your answer in the area below.

1. Discuss the reasons for the beginning of the Industrial Revolution in England.

2. Discuss the factors that contributed to the birth of the Renaissance in Italy.

3. Assess and analyze the central concepts of the Enlightenment.

Group 2

Choose ONE question from this group. The suggested writing time for this question is 30 minutes. You are advised to spend 5 minutes planning your answer in the area below.

1. Assess the validity of the following: Democracy in Great Britain was achieved through evolution rather than revolution.

2. Discuss the effectiveness of the Congress of Vienna (1814/1815) and the Versailles Treaty in building a lasting peace.

3. The 1920s has been refered to as the "era of disillusionment." Show how the literature of the 1920s reflected this approach.

Section ▮▮ Free Response Essays

Answer Key for Practice Test III

Section I: Multiple-Choice Questions

1. E	21. C	41. D	61. D
2. A	22. A	42. B	62. A
3. D	23. C	43. A	63. C
4. E	24. E	44. C	64. A
5. C	25. D	45. B	65. D
6. E	26. B	46. D	66. A
7. E	27. B	47. A	67. D
8. D	28. A	48. D	68. C
9. E	29. A	49. D	69. C
10. D	30. A	50. B	70. A
11. D	31. A	51. B	71. D
12. A	32. C	52. B	72. D
13. D	33. C	53. C	73. D
14. D	34. C	54. A	74. E
15. A	35. A	55. A	75. D
16. C	36. E	56. E	76. D
17. D	37. A	57. A	77. B
18. A	38. D	58. A	78. B
19. A	39. B	59. C	79. B
20. A	40. B	60. C	80. B

Section II: Free-Response Essays

Student essays and analysis appear beginning on page 405.

Answers and Explanations to Practice Test III

Section I: Multiple-Choice Questions

1. **E.** Radar was first used in combat in World War II. Radar was developed in the late 1930s and could tell the number, speed, and direction of incoming warplanes. World War I was called the "Great War" and the "War to End all Wars" because of the brutality of its trench warfare, poison gas attacks, and the advent of armored tanks. The Germans, who called them U-boats, also used submarines extensively.

2. **A.** While quite often the Medici family commissioned and paid various artists to decorate or design churches, they did not give their money directly to the church. The Medicis were a wealthy family who derived much of their fortune from international banking. They came to power in Florence around 1434 at a time when the city's political system was undergoing frequent changes of leadership. Consequently, they were politically shrewd and maintained power by supporting many popular causes. They also were strong supporters of the arts, which was often simply another political decision on their part, as the arts were a way of influencing opinion. Nevertheless, without financial support of the Medicis, such great artists as Michelangelo and Botticelli might not have become household names.

3. **D.** In 1866, the Papal States was not part of the United Kingdom of Italy. After the collapse of Rome, Italy had been ruled by a succession of foreign powers: Ostrogoths, Lombards, Franks, Arabs, Normans, Germans, Spanish, Byzantines, and French. By 1815, the country was roughly divided into several spheres: the Sardinian kingdom, which ruled the island of Sardinia and northwestern Italy; the Lombardo-Venetian Kingdom, which was ruled by Austria, in the North; the Papal States, which controlled the central portion of the peninsula; and the Kingdom of the Two Sicilies in the South. During the nineteenth century, Italian nationalism grew in strength, and there was increasing sentiment for unification. During 1859–61, nationalist uprisings deposed local rulers and united most of Italy with Sardinia. On March 17, 1861, the united Kingdom of Italy was proclaimed under the House of Savoy, with the exception of the Papal States and Venice. The latter was finally added in 1866.

4. **E.** Maximilien Robespierre was a middle-class lawyer who represented Paris' working-class radicals. As a Jacobin, he vigorously opposed the Girondist leaders. While the *sans-culottes* were a working class faction, the popular George Jacques Danton led them. The revolution had abolished Catholicism and executed the king, thus Robespierre was neither a spokesman for the church nor a supporter of the king.

5. **C.** The Battle of Britain (August 1940–June 1941) was the air war between German bombers and British fighter planes, and the invention of radar helped turn the tide in Britain's favor. With radar, England could detect German bombers as they approached and send fighter planes to meet them directly. The V-2 missile was one of Hitler's

weapons, an unmanned bomb sent to fly straight into English cities. The Spit Fire was one type of British plane involved in the battle, but Germany had planes of comparable quality. Antiaircraft guns were not as effective as fighters in defending against bomber attacks. The tank was not involved in the Battle of Britain because it was strictly an air battle.

6. **E.** After the Congress of Vienna in 1815, Belgium was given to the Netherlands. In 1830, a rebellion broke out in Brussels against King William I and Belgium declared her independence. In 1839, Belgium's neutrality was granted by the major powers including Prussia. Belgium was not returned nor given to either France or Spain after the Congress of Vienna.

7. **E.** Johannes Kepler's work on the first three laws of planetary motion based on mathematical relationships supported Tycho Brahe's data about the planets moving in elliptical orbits. Before Tycho Brahe, astronomers used to observe the planets and Moon at certain points of their orbits. Brahe however carefully measured their full course of movement through the sky. In doing so he uncovered certain orbital anomalies, which his young assistant at the time, Kepler, was able to incorporate mathematically to demonstrate that the planets moved in elliptical orbits. Brahe still believed the Ptolemaic and Aristotelian view, however, that the earth was the center of the universe, which was shown to be wrong by Copernicus and Galileo.

8. **D.** The death of Marshall Tito in 1980 resulted in a period of chaos in Yugoslavia due to ethnic conflicts. Tito had been viewed as a benevolent father by the multiple ethnic groups and republics that made up the united Yugoslavia. Upon his death, this unity began to disintegrate. An outbreak of ethnic violence among Croats, Muslims, Bosnians, and others soon led to demands for autonomy by the republics. After Tito's death, Yugoslavia suffered economic hardship.

9. **E.** The Portuguese system of exploration did not rely on diplomacy to build relationships with colonized lands, but rather relied on heavily fortified outposts and regarded the non-Christian natives warily, believing that they need not keep any promises to such "infidels," thus earning a reputation for cruelty. Portuguese explorer Henry the Navigator initiated the search for a sea route to India, which was accomplished by Vasco da Gama. Other Portuguese expeditions also explored parts of Africa and Arabia, bringing Christianity with them. This success inspired neighboring Spain and other European powers to join in search of their own colonies.

10. **D.** Mercantilism was an economic policy in which a nation's wealth was measured by its gold and silver. This policy prevailed in the major trading and exploring nations of the sixteenth through eighteenth centuries. These countries believed that by maximizing exports and minimizing imports, they could build vast stores of precious metals from the payments received. This would increase their wealth and power by allowing them to build stronger armies and navies for further overseas conquest. While this implies a high degree of government involvement in trade policy and protection of trade routes, it did not require that governments own the factors of production. As a theory of international trade, mercantilism also says nothing about individual interests or whether workers should share in profits. Mercantilism also artificially distorts supply and demand by limiting imports while encouraging exports.

11. **D.** The main reason for the Berlin Conference of 1884/1885 was to establish guidelines for dividing up Africa in order to avoid conflicts among European nations. After the mid-nineteenth century, the great imperialist powers of Europe began to have a strong interest in further African exploration. This was mainly due to the belief that the African continent might hold vast supplies of raw materials to fuel Europe's greater industrialization. The conference met in Berlin from 1884 to 1885 and established "spheres of influence" in Africa for England, Austria-Hungary, France, Germany, Russia, America, Portugal, Denmark, the Netherlands, Sweden, Turkey, Spain, Italy, and Belgium. Rather than limit trade, the conference opened trade widely by eliminating most tariffs on African goods and opening the coast to all nations. The Belgians under Leopold II had control of a large portion of the Congo prior to the conference, but there was no fear they would take over all of Africa. African nations did not participate in the conference.

12. **A.** Louis Blanc, the "reformist" socialist, called for national workshops to guarantee full employment for workers in 1848. Robert Owens and Charles Fourier were the pioneering utopian socialists who hoped to build model communities. Hegel was a German philosopher whose ideas of history as a product of conflict between new and old ideas were applied by Karl Marx and Friedrich Engels to social classes to argue for the overthrow of capitalism. Proudhon was a French social theorist who more closely espoused anarchy. Blanc organized a Workers Party and played a major role in the French Revolution of 1848. The government allowed his national workshops for the unemployed but shut them down in June 1848. The government's decision led to workers' revolts that were eventually suppressed.

13. **D.** The Communist Party had absolute control of the Soviet Union under Lenin, and did not permit even limited democratic reforms. The Soviet Union did not do away with classes under Lenin. Tensions between the rural peasant class and the urban working class were high during his rule. And the leaders of the Communist Party constituted their own elite class. Capitalism was not abolished entirely either. Lenin allowed the peasantry to dispose of their surplus goods within the limits of "local trade" and instituted the quasi-capitalist New Economic Policy, which he justified as necessary given the devastation of the recent civil war. Lenin distrusted Stalin towards the end of his life and hoped that Trotsky would succeed him. He hoped to remove Stalin from high Party office but fell ill and died before he could accomplish this. After a power struggle, Stalin consolidated his power. Stalin had Trotsky assassinated in Mexico in 1940.

14. **D.** The 38th parallel refers to the point of division between North Korea and South Korea. This became the divider of the two Koreas in 1945 with the surrender of Japan in World War II. The U.S. and Russia, allied against Japan in the Pacific, agreed that north of the 38th parallel, Japanese forces would surrender to the Soviets. South of it they would surrender to the Americans. In 1950, the Korean War would begin when North Korean troops crossed this line, and the armistice that ended it re-established the parallel as the border of the two Koreas.

15. **A.** Slobodan Milosevic's policy of "ethnic cleansing" describes the forced removal of non-Serbian groups from Serbian controlled areas. Milosevic was a former Communist who turned Nationalist and became a national hero to many Serbians within Yugoslavia. He was indicted and tried for war crimes for his policy of forcibly relocating, imprisoning, or killing non-Serbian Muslims and Croats during the Yugoslav civil wars. He did not attack neighboring countries, but focused on creating a pure Serbian state out of the remains of the old Yugoslavia.

16. C. The Seven Weeks War in 1866 between Austria and Prussia led to Austria's recognition of Prussian dominance over the German states. The war came about shortly after the capture of Schleswig/Holstein from Denmark by a united Prussian and Austrian force. The future of this territory was to have been decided by the Treaty of Gastein in 1865, but both Austria and Prussia accused each other of breaking it, and led them to fight for dominance of the German states. The Treaty of Prague ended the war. Napoleon III was following the feud in Germany closely and had his own designs on the territory, but had to shelve these plans in light of the German nationalist movement. He was forced to settle for Luxembourg and a possible French annexation of Belgium.

17. D. The Balfour Declaration of 1917 declared the right of Jews to a homeland in Palestine. During the First World War, British policy became gradually committed to the idea of establishing a Jewish home in Palestine. After discussions in the British Cabinet, and consultation with Zionist leaders, the decision was made known in the form of a letter by Arthur James Lord Balfour to Lord Rothschild. The letter represents the first political recognition of Zionist aims by a great power. Woodrow Wilson's Fourteen Points laid the foundation for the League of Nations after World War I.

18. A. During the Stuart Restoration, Parliament passed the Habeas Corpus act in 1679. The act held judges responsible for the well being of prisoners in their custody, guaranteed speedy trials, and prohibited a person from being tried twice for the same crime. Parliament was not able to prevent Charles II's Catholic brother James II from inheriting the throne in 1685, nor did they revoke Charles II's secret Treaty of Dover, which he struck with the French in 1670. Parliament did not further limit the powers of the monarchy during the Restoration, and did not negotiate lucrative treaties with other European nations.

19. A. Manchester was a leading example of the new industrial city. Manchester had a ready access to waterpower. It also had available labor from the nearby countryside and an outlet to the sea at Liverpool. Manchester formed the center of Britain's bustling cotton industry. During the 1800s, Manchester's rapid and unplanned population growth (25,000 in 1772 but 360,000 by 1850) made its living conditions intolerable for many poor people who worked there. Liverpool was a seaport city. Birmingham and Sheffield were iron-smelting centers. London was the country's capital and Europe's largest city with a population of about one million by 1800.

20. A. Machiavelli would most likely support a politician who would manipulate people and use any means to gain power. Though Machiavelli wrote his book *The Prince* as advice for Lorenzo di Medici, its philosophy can be extended to any political leader. Machiavelli suggests that the leader of a state should disregard any moral considerations when acting on behalf of the state, which would include religious considerations on behalf of the church. Machiavelli would not support taking action to weaken the government, as he saw the sole duty of a leader to be strengthening and preserving the state. He would also not support taking a passive approach to problems. Rather, any approach that solved the problem would be justifiable to Machiavelli, whose theory has often been summarized in the phrase "the ends justify the means."

21. C. The Enlightened Despot, a type of ruler first described by the French philosopher Voltaire, had absolute power and thus would not support democracy. Enlightened Despots theoretically governed in the best interests of their subjects and thus would support art, literature, and science, religious toleration, use of reason to examine the world, and education.

22. A. The correct chronological order is U2 Incident (1960), Berlin Wall built (1961), Cuban Missile Crisis (1962), Khrushchev forced to retire (1964).

23. C. On the Night of the Long Knives in June 1934, Hitler ordered his Black Shirts to put to death Ernst Roehm, his friend and leader of the Brown Shirts, and 1,000 of his troops. The Brown Shirts had been Hitler's trusted storm troopers, but they included many members who wanted to become a revolutionary army to replace the regular German army. The regular army officer corps was very conservative, and the Brown Shirts represented a threat to their tradition and privileges. To gain the support of the regular army officers, whom he needed to hold power, Hitler had Roehm and 1,000 Brown Shirts killed. The Versailles Treaty had prohibited German troops from entering the Rhineland, but Hitler repudiated this provision and began occupying the region in March 1936. In November 1938, Hitler initiated the harsher phase of Jewish persecution by arresting thousands of Jews in what was known as Kristalnacht or "Night of the Broken Glass." The Weimar Republic, the name for Germany's post-Versailles government, was eroded gradually by the rise of Hitler's Nazi Party on the right and the Communist Party on the left. Once installed as chancellor, Hitler finished consolidating his power by blaming Communists for a fire in the Reichstag and arresting many members of the Communist Party in February 1933.

24. E. Woodrow Wilson's Fourteen Points did not prevent countries from having to pay war reparations. The Treaty of Versailles, which ended World War I, in fact called for Germany to pay reparations to the victors. Wilson composed his Fourteen Points as a foundation on which a just peace could be achieved after World War I. The central idea was to establish a degree of self determination for the successor states that would make up postwar Europe. Thus the points called for freedom of the seas, the end of secret diplomacy, free trade, and a reduction in arms.

25. D. Napoleon's *coup d'etat* in 1799 overthrew the government of the Directory and resulted in the formation of the Consulate. In imitation of the ancient Roman system, the Consulate was composed of three elected consuls. Napoleon was named First Consul and thus wielded all of the power. He was exiled in 1814 and then returned for 100 days until the Battle of Waterloo forced him out of office.

26. B. John Calvin, unlike Martin Luther, believed the church was higher than the state and should have a role in the government. Calvin believed that societies should be politically structured according to biblical principles. Luther, however, believed that the church had the power to preach the Gospel and to perform sacraments, but that it should not participate in affairs of the state. Both men believed in free will, salvation by faith alone, that the Bible was the final religious authority, and that economic status did not a have a relation to how faithful one was.

27. B. A major reason for British interest in controlling the Suez Canal was its strategic location. The Suez was the critical link between the British Empire's territories in India and the British mainland via the Mediterranean. Control by any other nation threatened to divide the British Empire in half and force the British navy and trading ships to have to navigate all the way around Africa to reach India and back. Britain was not interested in Egypt for any other reason, such as minerals, Christianity, spices, or as a marketplace.

28. A. A major result of the Reform Act of 1832 was the abolishment of rotten boroughs, which were parliamentary constituencies that had declined significantly in population but still could elect members of Parliament. In addition to this redistricting of Parliament, the Reform Act laid out the property ownership criteria for which men could vote in Parliamentary elections, but did not extend suffrage to women. The act did not address secret ballots, the House of Lords' veto power, or government funding for public housing.

29. A. The Marshall Plan was a recovery program that gave over $17 billion in economic aid to European nations. It was so named because it originated in a commencement speech at Harvard in 1947 by Secretary of State George Catlett Marshall. Under what became known as "The Marshall Plan," the United States provided the aid while the countries themselves organized their reconstruction plans. The ultimate goal of the plan was to prevent the spread of Communism in Western Europe and to stabilize the continent to make it fertile for the development of democracy and free markets. There was never a treaty between NATO and the Warsaw Pact, the umbrella enemies of the Cold War. West Germany was never militarily invaded.

30. A. During the Renaissance after the Hundred Years War, the monarchy of France was consolidated most effectively by Louis XI. The monarchy had been weakened already by the years of war, and the great French nobles held much of the power in the country. Rather than let it crumble or be overturned, Louis XI laid the foundation for absolute monarchy in France, and by promoting industry and commerce he increased the country's wealth. The rise of the bourgeoisie class actually aided Louis XI in his efforts, as he relied on its support to counterbalance the most powerful of the French nobles.

31. A. Napoleon did not gain further control over France and other parts of Europe as a result of his Russian invasion of 1812. Rather, he overextended his armies and lost three-fourths of his troops in both combat and in the harsh Russian winter. With his armies and supplies severely weakened by the Russian campaign, Napoleon lost the Battle of Nations at Leipzig in 1813 to a combined Russian, Austrian, and Prussian army. He was thus forced to abdicate his throne as emperor, the title he had taken in 1804, and flee into exile, whereupon Louis XVIII was restored to the throne.

32. C. The Council of Trent, convened in 1545 to definitively state the doctrines of the Roman Catholic Church in response to the "heresies" of the Protestant movements, did not support the idea that individuals could understand faith without church guidance. In its final decrees issued in 1563 the council did, however, support the belief that salvation was obtained by both good works and faith, that the Bible was the source of religious authority as well as faith, and that seminaries in each diocese must educate the clergy. The council also formulated a list of forbidden books, including works by Galileo and Erasmus.

33. C. Reformers such as Robert Owen, who tried to establish model communities, were known as Utopian Socialists. These thinkers hoped to establish a world of cooperative communes that would be dedicated to the fair treatment of all individuals. This was in response to the industrial revolution and its perceived mistreatment of industrial workers at the hands of wealthy industrialists and factory owners. Luddites were also opponents of the Industrial Revolution who expressed their views by attacking and destroying factories and mills. Communists were a group who believed that all property and means of production should be owned by the state and shared by all. Anarchists believe in the complete overthrow of all systems of government. Fascists believe in consolidating power in a single dictator, with a strong emphasis on nationalism, militarism, and often racism.

34. C. The Spirit of Locarno in 1925 referred to a symbol of a new era of cooperation between France and Germany. In 1925, several European nations signed a series of treaties at Locarno, Switzerland. Germany and France as well as Britain, Italy, and Belgium agreed to guarantee Germany's western boundaries and they accepted the Versailles settlement's demilitarized zones. The treaties also agreed to settle common border disputes with Poland and Czechoslovakia by peaceful means. The effect of the treaties of Locarno was far reaching and gave Europeans a sense of growing security and stability in international affairs. Efforts were never made to end German reparation payments. The Dawes and Young Plans were designed to reduce but not abolish German reparations. The United States never joined the League of Nations. Article 231 (the War Guilt Clause) was never removed from the Versailles Treaty. The Kellogg-Briand Pact (1928) outlawed war as an instrument of foreign policy.

35. A. George Haussmann supervised the beautification of Paris during the presidency of Louis Napoleon. Under Haussmann, Paris endured a rapid, total, and violent transformation, during which much was demolished and rebuilt and many people forcibly relocated. Edwin Chadwick was an English reformer who campaigned for changes in sanitation, education, and transportation during the nineteenth century. Pasteur was a medical scientist most noted for inventing the vaccine. Gustavus Vasa was the king who united Sweden in the sixteenth century.

36. E. In the late 1980s, Mikhail Gorbachev's decision to stop interfering in the internal affairs of Eastern European nations led directly to the collapse of the communist governments in the region. The satellite states of the Soviet Union depended heavily on financial, military, and diplomatic support from the Soviet Union. When Gorbachev began to hold some of this support back to preserve the Soviet Union's own resources under his policy of *glasnost,* the smaller states could not maintain communism alone in the face of popular sentiment in favor of free markets and democracy.

37. A. Albania did not come into existence after World War I. Albania became an independent state prior to World War I, after a three-year armed struggle by Albanian nationalists against the Ottoman Empire. Its independence was formalized by a conference of the great European powers in London in 1912, which decided its borders. It was not until 1929 that the kingdom of the Serbs, Croats, and Slovenes became known as Yugoslavia. Finland declared and was granted its independence from Russia in December of 1917 following the Russian Revolution, but it would take another year of civil war between Bolshevik-inspired Red forces and so-called White government forces. Estonia's independence from Russia was made official in February of 1920. The creation of Czechoslovakia followed a prolonged struggle by the Czechs against their Austrian rulers. The Treaty of St. Germain in September of 1919 formally recognized the new republic.

38. D. *Don Quixote* is a work of fiction, written by Miguel de Cervantes, that describes Spain in the sixteenth century by mocking the type of romantic and chivalrous novels that were so popular at the time. It was not meant to be a political manifesto, nor was it connected to colonialism or Spanish court protocol.

39. B. The United Kingdom of Italy in 1871 did not enjoy the support of the Catholic Church. The Church, via the pope, had ruled large parts of Italy for over 1,000 years, until the United kingdom of Italy seized most of the Papal States between 1869 and 1870. In 1870, the Kingdom, seriously infringing on the Church's sovereignty, annexed Rome itself. Disputes between Italy and what became known as the "prisoner popes" would last until Vatican City was established in 1929.

40. B. One result of Stalin's policy of collectivization was a widespread food shortage. Stalin believed collectivization of individual farms would improve productivity and produce more food for the growing industrial labor force; he also hoped that a surplus of crops could be exported to fund industrialization as well. Collectivization was further expected to free many peasants for industrial work in the cities. To this end, Stalin focused particular hostility on the wealthier peasants, or kulaks, resulting in the deportation or disappearance of about one million kulak households. Forced collectivization of the remaining peasants, which was often fiercely resisted, did not have the results Stalin expected; instead, they effected a disastrous disruption of agricultural productivity and a catastrophic famine in 1932–33. The plan backfired and did not achieve its surplus or export goals, and did not help the Soviet Union's industrial expansion.

41. D. One of the Peter the Great's major goals in foreign policy was to acquire a window on the West along the Baltic Sea. Thus, in 1700 he started the Northern War with Sweden, in the course of which, St. Petersburg was founded and Russia conquered the vast lands on the Baltic coast. Peter gained access to the Black Sea, though not a port, very early in his reign by defeating the Turks who controlled the mouth of the Don River at the Sea of Azov, which is connected to the Black Sea. Peter was infatuated with the West and traveled extensively in Poland, England, and Austria. He hoped to make Russia more "European" based on these visits and tried to enlist the aid of these countries in fighting the Turks to his south.

42. B. The author of this passage would support the belief that the motive for imperialism was economic. The view that nations expand and conquer new territories in order to gain access to raw materials for industrial expansion back home is a purely economic viewpoint. The author of the passage does not attribute the "Scramble for Africa" to religious, political, military, or humanitarian desires but to "industrial enterprise."

43. A. As a result of the Reform Bill of 1832, the middle class gained suffrage. The bill set the minimum property requirement for voting. The aristocracy already had the vote, but this requirement enfranchised a larger section of the middle class. Women, peasants, and the urban working class who could not meet this figure did not attain suffrage under the bill.

44. C. The Sepoy Rebellion and the Boxer Rebellion were similar in that both were reactions to Western imperialism. The Sepoy Mutiny, or Rebellion, in 1857 was an Indian revolt against the British. It was led by native soldiers called Sepoys, who were protesting the policy of the British East India Company. In 1857, the Sepoy soldiers refused to accept cartridges for their rifles that were sealed with beef and pork fat. To use the cartridges, soldiers had to bite off the seal. Both Hindus, who considered the cow sacred, and Muslims, who did not eat pork, were angry. The Sepoy Mutiny (Rebellion) lasted more than a year. The British government sent troops to help the British East India Company. The mutiny was a turning point in Indian history. After 1858, the British government took direct control of India. The Boxers in China were a secret society formed in 1899. Their goal was to drive out foreigners who were destroying their land with their Western technology. In 1900, the Boxers attacked foreign communities across China. They also attacked foreign embassies in Beijing. Western powers sent 25,000 troops to crush the Boxers and rescue foreigners who were in Beijing. The Sepoys and Boxers did not want to improve relations with Western powers. They rejected Western values. Neither of these rebellions were victorious, nor were they democratic movements or revolts against traditional monarchs. These rebellions were attacks against Western influence.

45. **B.** The Protestant Reformation led to more religious division in Europe, which caused a series of religious wars in both the sixteenth and seventeenth centuries between predominately Catholic Southern Europe and predominately Protestant Northern Europe. Following on Luther's belief that the church did not have a role in state government, the state came to be seen as superior to the church in many parts of Europe. Education and reading increased throughout Europe also, driven by a renewed focus on religious debate at the same time as the invention of the printing press.

46. **D.** John Locke would support the ideas in this passage. In 1690, John Locke wrote *Two Treatises of Government* to justify the Glorious Revolution, in which he asserted that people entered into a social contract to create a government to protect their basic rights of life, liberty, and property. The power of the government is limited and if the government, which was party to the compact, fails to live up to its purpose, or exceeds its authority, the people have the right to alter or abolish it. Thomas Hobbes, a seventeenth-century English philosopher, wrote *The Leviathan* to emphasize his belief that government must be all-powerful and absolute. Louis XIV was the absolute king of France who ruled from 1643–1715. Charles V was an absolute Hapsburg monarch of Spain who became the Holy Roman Emperor in 1519. Jacques Bousset was a seventeenth-century French bishop who wrote *Discourse on Universal History* in which he summed up the theory of Divine Right rule.

47. **A.** Neither Russia nor Germany attended the Versailles Conference. In November 1917, the Bolsheviks overthrew the provisional government of Kerensky and set up the first Communist regime in Russia. In March 1918, the Communist government signed the Treaty of Brest-Litovsk that ended Russian participation in World War I. Germany, who had signed an armistice on November 11, 1918, to stop the fighting, was not invited to attend the peace conference. Japan attended the Versailles Conference but was not an integral member of the Big Four meeting among France, England, United States, and Italy. Italy walked out of the conference because she was upset at the refusal of England and France to give her additional territory in Europe and Africa.

48. **D.** The phrase "peace in our time" referred to the agreement at the Munich Conference of 1938. At the conference, Britain and France had agreed to allow Hitler to gain the Sudetenland, a region of Czechoslovakia that he had claimed on the pretext that there was a large German population living there. When British Prime Minister Neville Chamberlain returned to London, he proclaimed he had achieved "peace in our time." Those words would later be used mockingly when it became clear that Britain and France had merely appeased Hitler and failed to stop his expansionist designs. The Versailles Treaty had ended World War I, and the Locarno Pact was a follow up to the Versailles Treaty in 1925 under which England, France, Germany, Italy, Poland, and Belgium made mutual assurances as to borders and demilitarization of the Rhine. This treaty would be known by the phrase "Spirit of Locarno" and symbolized hopes for a new era of peace and goodwill. The Kellogg-Briand Pact was a treaty between the United States and other powers providing for the renunciation of war as an instrument of national policy. The Lateran Pact of 1929, signed by Benito Mussolini, resolved the "prisoner pope" dilemma and granted the Roman church its own city-state in the Vatican at Rome.

49. **D.** Konrad Adenauer was instrumental in the economic recovery of Western Germany. Adenauer was the chancellor of West Germany from 1949–1963. He had been mayor of Cologne and president of the Prussian State Council but was dismissed by the Nazis

in1933. During his term of office as chancellor, the Federal Republic of Germany, as West Germany was known, developed into a stable democracy and into one of the leading industrial and social states. The achievement of national sovereignty, close ties with the free West, reconciliation with France, and the consolidation of the social market economy were all achieved under Adenauer. He did not preside over the reunification of East and West Germany much later in 1990 and did not negotiate any treaties between the Soviet Union and the West.

50. B. The goal of the Royal Society of London, founded in 1660, was to encourage scientific research. Its founding fellows included many of the most of the important scientists of the day, including Christopher Wren, who wrote the preamble to its charter. The restoration of Charles II had already happened prior to its founding, and the society was not involved in overseas expansion nor in politics.

51. B. During the Renaissance, the life of the ordinary woman was not directly affected. Women continued to perform economic functions, such as working on the farms or helping their husbands run businesses. Women also continued to work as housekeepers and midwives. Educational opportunities were limited for ordinary women. Renaissance women studied the classics and received an education similar to boys. However, as Castiglione pointed out in *The Courtier,* upper-class women were expected to know the classics but not to seek fame. It was expected that education would prepare them for the social functions of how to attract a husband and run a good household. An educated man was supposed to know how to rule and participate in public affairs. Renaissance women were supposed to be decorative, affable, and charming. Upper-class roles declined as they had less power than comparable women in the Middle Ages. Women's status declined in regard to sex and love since their main role was to be pleasing as objects to men.

52. B. The ideas in this passage are most associated with Thomas Malthus. Malthus believed that humans are capable of reproducing faster than the earth's resources can be expanded to support this growth. Malthus' conclusion was that unless reproduction was regulated, famine would naturally spread globally. His ideas were not popular with social reformers such as the Utopian Socialists who believed that under the ideal social system, all of mankind's ills could be solved. David Ricardo was one of the founders of classical economics. John Locke was a philosopher who wrote on both government and economics. Karl Marx was a socialist who formulated the principles of Marxism, and Louis Blanc was a "reformist" socialist who believed that the class problems of capitalism could be solved and a compromise reached with the "bourgeoisie." He advocated National Workshops to help the unemployed.

53. C. French Calvinists, also called Huguenots, were the victims of the St. Bartholomew Day massacre, in which over 20,000 of them were killed by Catholic factions. The massacres were part of the Religious Wars in France between different Christian faiths, and did not involve the French Jews. The Puritans were a group of Protestants that arose in the sixteenth century within the Church of England, and the Roundheads were a subset of Puritans who supported Parliament over Charles I in the British civil war, hence neither was involved in St. Bartholomew Day massacres in France. Lutheranism had its following primarily in German territories, whereas Calvinism flourished in France.

54. A. The purpose of the Maginot Line was to prevent another German invasion. The Maginot Line was a mighty system of fortifications extending along the eastern frontier of France from the Swiss border to the Belgian border. It was named for Andre Maginot, the

French Minister of War. Construction was begun in 1929 but was not complete at the outbreak of World War II. The Maginot Line offered a sense of security, but it proved of little value to France in the face of German mobile warfare in 1940. The Maginot Line was not a series of alliances nor was it designed to prevent the spread of revolutions. The Maginot Line was not intended to solve an unemployment problem caused by the Great Depression. The sole purpose of this fortification was military.

55. **A.** The Ottoman Empire and the Austrian Empire were most similar in that they both contained multiple national ethnic groups. The Ottoman Empire was a blend of many different tribal groups from across Anatolia and modern Turkey, including Turks, Arabs, Slavs, Copts, Persians, Mongols, and Greeks. The Austrian Empire contained Austrian Germans, Hungarians, Slovenes, Poles, Czechs, Slovaks, Ruthenians, Romanians, Serbs, and Croats. In both Austria and the Ottoman Empire the people practiced the Roman Catholic, Protestant, Eastern Orthodox, and Muslim religions. Both empires were severely weakened by the growth of nationalism in the 1870s. Both empires followed the principle of centralized absolute authority in the monarch and thus were not constitutional monarchies. Finally, both empires failed to promote economic modernization and fell behind relative to western Europe, while their militaries were ineffective, as evidenced by Austria's resounding loss to Prussia in the Seven Weeks War.

56. **E.** The initial reaction of the Russian government to the fighting that broke out in Chechnya in the 1990s demonstrated that Russia is unwilling to grant independence to dissenting ethnic groups. When the largely Muslim population of Chechnya attempted to form their own Muslim republic apart from Russia, it set off a violent guerilla war between federal Russian troops and Chechen fighters. The response to Chechnya was a clear sign to other ethnic groups left in the Russian republic that the Russian government is unwilling to allow further secessions following the initial breakup up the Soviet Union and its republic. Thus far, Russia has maintained control of its nuclear arsenal, though it is a source of concern to the United States. The Russian government does not favor re-establishing communism. The Chechen fighters were not a foreign invader, and thus the Russian reaction did not address how Russia might react to a foreign invasion.

57. **A.** This statement by Friedrich Engels in *The Conditions of the Working Class in England* describes the negative effects of the Industrial Revolution in regard to the horrible living conditions in the new industrial city of Manchester. Manchester, along with the port of Liverpool, formed the center of Britain's bustling cotton industry. In 1750, the town of Manchester numbered 17,000 people, but by 1850, it had swelled to 300,000 people. The rapid, unplanned growth made it a filthy sewer for the poor people who worked there. Imperialism describes how a strong country exerts control over a weaker one. The Glorious Revolution of 1688 ended absolute rule in England and led to the creation of a constitutional monarchy. The Black Death or Bubonic Plague (1347–1350) was a contagious deadly disease whose death toll is estimated to have exceeded 100 million people in Europe, Asia, and Africa.

58. **A.** The political thinkers of the Enlightenment such as Locke and Rousseau supported the ideal that government was a social contract designed to protect the rights of the people. Locke's *Two Treatises of Government* and Rousseau's *Social Contract* claimed that governments were formed to protect the rights of the people and when the government violated the rights of the people, the people have the right to overthrow the government. Rousseau, unlike Locke, was not concerned with individual rights. He emphasized the

concept of the general will, the rule of the majority. To enforce the general will the government has unlimited powers. Absolute monarchy, further strengthening the power of kings and nobles, or putting the state ahead of individuals, are all in contradiction of this principle. While important, they did not see a military as the backbone of society.

59. C. Leon Trotsky (Lev Bronstein), one of the principal leaders in the founding of the Soviet Union, developed the theory of permanent revolution. He declared that in Russia, a bourgeosie and socialist revolution would be combined and that a proletarian revolution in one country would spread throughout the world. He believed that only by encouraging revolution worldwide would Communism be successful in Russia. Stalin coined the phrase "socialism in one country," asserting that the Soviet Union should build up Communism within the country before it can successfully promote revolution worldwide. Vladimir Lenin, the Father of Russian Communism and the first leader of the Soviet Union, was a pragmatic leader whose main concern was to seize power and avoid ideological debates. Lenin's statement "promises are like the crust of pie, they are made to be broken," summarizes his views. Alexander Kerensky was a Socialist who was the leader of the Provisional Government that the Bolsheviks overthrew in 1917. Nikolai Bukarin was a leading economic theorist who supported Stalin's idea of building Socialism in one country.

60. C. The Austro-Prussian, or Seven Weeks War, left Austria in a weakened position, having ceded Venice to Italy and dominance of Germany to Prussia. In order to shore up her strength, Austria revised its constitution and made the state of Hungary an equal partner in its empire in 1867. This became known as the Dual Monarchy of Austria-Hungary. The Franco-Prussian War of 1870–1871 asserted the newly unified Germany's dominance over France and forced the overthrow of Napoleon III. The other wars occurred before the establishment of the Dual Monarchy: The Danish War was a phase of the Thirty Year's War lasting from 1625–1629, the Crimean War of 1853–1856 was a contest between Russia and an alliance of France England and Turkey, and the Russo-Turkish War took place between Russia and Turkey in 1877/78.

61. D. Martin Luther's statement before the Diet of Worms reflects his belief in the supremacy of the Bible over the authority of the pope. Luther believed that religious authority rested with the Bible, not the pope. For Luther the Bible was the final authority because each individual could determine for himself church doctrines and practices. There was no need for a higher authority. Luther rejected indulgences and good works as a way to achieve salvation. He stressed justification by faith alone. Luther only accepted the sacraments of baptism, communion, and penance.

62. A. The quotation refers to situations created by World War I. On the western front, the military stalemate led to trench warfare. The Allies (England, France, and Russia) and the Central Powers (Germany and Austria-Hungary) created a vast system of trenches from the Swiss frontier to the English Channel. The space between the two trenches gained the name "no man's land" and troops occasionally were sent over the top to attack the enemy trenches. When the officers ordered an attack, their men went over the top of the trenches into this bombed out landscape of "no man's land." Casualties were staggering. At Verdun, both sides lost over 700,000 men. This poem written by J. Knight-Adkin describes the horrors of World War I in 1917 and does not relate to the French Revolution of 1789, the Franco-Prussian War (1870–71), or the Spanish Civil War (1936–39). Germany's use of blitzkrieg (lightning war) in World War II (1939) rendered trench warfare obsolete.

63. C. These events demonstrate the spirit of self-determination and nationalism. Lithuania had been an independent state between World War I and World War II until annexed by the Soviet Union in 1940. In March 1990, Lithuania declared its independence. The election of Lech Walesa as leader of Poland also demonstrated the spirit of self-determination. After World War II, Poland was a Soviet satellite and denied the right of self-government. In 1980, Lech Walesa formed Solidarity in Poland to protest economic hardships. The Polish Communist leadership declared martial law and arrested Walesa and other leaders. In 1989, the Communist government legalized Solidarity and held free democratic elections for the first time in 50 years. On July 4, Solidarity candidates had outpolled Communists. Party members became the first freely elected opposition in a Communist country. In 1990, Lech Walesa was elected president of Poland. All of these events showed the decline of Communism and a lack of cooperation among Russia and their satellites as well as Russia's reluctance to use military power to meet these issues. Gorbachev was criticized for using military force against Lithuania. NATO is still operational and has not collapsed since the demise of the Soviet Union.

64. A. Jean Jacques Rousseau wrote *The Social Contract* in 1762 in which he explained his political philosophy. Montesquieu wrote *The Spirit of the Law* (1748); Locke wrote *Two Treatises on Government* (1690); Diderot was the editor of the *Encyclopedia* (1747); Hobbes wrote *The Leviathan* (1651).

65. D. The Atlantic Charter of 1941 contained statements of British and United States goals and principles which would serve as the basis of the Allied peace plan at the end of World War II. Fashioned along the ideals of Wilson's Fourteen Points, British Prime Minister Winston Churchill and United States President Franklin D. Roosevelt called for peace without territorial expansion and pledged to support the rights of all people for free elections and self determination for all liberated nations. They called for the final destruction of Nazi tyranny and called for a permanent system of general security (United Nations). The Casablanca Conference in January 1943 called for the unconditional surrender of Germany. The United States, Great Britain, and Russia had become Allies after Germany's invasion of Russia in June 1941. The Atlantic Charter was not a plea to end the war but a commitment to destroy Nazi tyranny. The Land Lease Act, not the Atlantic Charter, provided economic aid to Great Britain.

66. A. Edmund Burke, a conservative Englishman who wrote *Reflections on the Revolution in France,* would support the ideas in this passage. Burke's book illustrates the French Revolution's destruction of the fabric of French society, and defends inherited privileges in a general and glorified unrepresentative Parliament. Louis XVI was king of France who was beheaded in January 1793. Maximilien Robespierre was a Jacobin leader who began the Reign of Terror. Jacques Necker was Financial Minister to Louis XVI who advocated reforming the tax system in 1789 in order for the government to solve its financial crisis. Louis XVIII was the brother of Louis XVI who was selected by the Congress of Vienna to be king of France in 1815.

67. D. The role of the church in politics did not increase as a result of the Thirty Years War. The Treaty of Westphalia that ended the war marked the end of the idea of the Holy Roman Empire in Europe that was ruled spiritually by a pope and temporally by an emperor. What emerged was a modern Europe composed of a community of many sovereign states. Protestantism became firmly established in many of them, including official recognition of Calvinism alongside Lutheranism. The Edict of Restitution was revoked, and the concept of a balance of power was born between the large states of Spain and France.

401

68. C. Jean Auguste Dominique's portrait entitled *Napoleon on His Imperial Throne* conveys the image of Napoleon as a god-like figure. On December 2, 1804, Napoleon dressed in a splendid robe of purple velvet, walked down the aisle of the Cathedral of Notre Dame. The pope had a crown to place on his head but Napoleon took it from him and placed it on his own head. This defiant gesture showed that Napoleon thought he was more powerful than the pope who traditionally crowned the rulers of France. This portrait reinforces the majestic and god-like qualities of Napoleon. The portrait does not convey the message that Napoleon was the Son of the Revolution or a democratic ruler or a lover of liberty or a military leader. This painting projects Napoleon in a regal manner.

69. C. Dante's *Divine Comedy,* Boccaccio's *The Decameron,* and Chaucer's *The Canterbury Tales* were all written in the vernacular: Dante and Boccaccio in Italian and Chaucer in English. Chaucer was an English writer, not an Italian Humanist. None of these stories glorify ancient civilizations or call for getting rid of Italy's foreign invaders. Dante's *Divine Comedy* describes his imaginary trip through hell, purgatory, and heaven. Boccaccios's *The Decameron* relates the stories of young men and women who had fled Florence to escape the Black Death. Chaucer's *The Canterbury Tales* are stories related by pilgrims' journeying to the religious shrines at Canterbury.

70. A. The Triple Entente and Triple Alliance were formed prior to World War I in 1914. The Triple Entente was formed in 1907 in response to the growing fear about the rising power of Germany; it did not bind Britain to fight with France and Russia, but it certainly guaranteed that Britain would not fight against them. The Triple Alliance was formed in 1882 when Italy, Austria, and Hungary agreed to a defensive military alliance. By 1907, two rival camps existed in Europe, the Triple Alliance versus the Triple Entente. A dispute between two rival powers could draw the continent into war. The signing of the Versailles Treaty (1919), the formation of the League of Nations, World War II (1939), and the formation of the U.N. (1945) are not related to the Triple Entente and Triple Alliance.

71. D. Willy Brandt, leader of the Social Democratic Party in Western Germany, was associated with Ostpolitik. In 1969, Willy Brandt became the chancellor of Germany. Brandt tried to ease tensions with Communist neighbors to the east. His policy of Ostpolitik, or Eastern policy, was designed to improve relations with Communist Eastern Europe. He opened economic doors to Eastern Europe and led West Germany to reach agreement to normalize relations with the Soviet Union and Poland in 1972. Brandt's initiative eventually led to the establishment of diplomatic ties between West Germany and East Germany a year later. Brandt's ultimate goal of a unified Germany would not be attainable until 1990. Brandt was not a hardliner towards the Soviet Union nor did he fear the expansion of Communism. He never called for the destruction of the Berlin Wall but referred to the structure as a barrier to unification. Konrad Adenauer, German chancellor from 1949–1963, is associated with the economic miracle of West Germany.

72. D. This picture represents Garibaldi handing over the conquest of Southern Italy to Victor Emmanuel to help unite all of Italy. Giuseppe Garibaldi, as an Italian nationalist who, with his band of 1,000 Red Shirts, landed in Sicily in May 1860. Cavour, prime minster of Sardinia, had united Northern Italy but had reservations about the area south of Rome. Garibaldi joined by rebels in Southern Italy, soon gained control of the Two Sicilies. Garibaldi's success alarmed Cavour, who feared that Garibaldi might set up a republic in the South. Cavour sent troops to deal with Garibaldi and linked up with him in Naples.

Garibaldi, as represented in this picture, in a patriotic move, turned over Naples and Sicily to Victor Emmanuel. For the sake of national interest, he put aside his republican sentiments and accepted the plebiscite that united southern and northern Italy. In 1861, Victor Emmanuel was crowned king of Italy. Neither Cavour nor the Papal States are represented in this picture. Garibaldi was already in Italy in 1860 and Cavour and Victor Emmanuel were not in support of a separate government for Southern Italy.

73. D. The Great Exposition of 1851 held in the Crystal Palace showed the growth of industry and population in Britain. The Great Exposition attracted more than six million visitors, many of whom journeyed to London on the newly-built railroad. Companies and countries displayed their products, and prizes were awarded. The variety of British products reinforced the belief that Britain was the workshop of the world. The Great Exposition of 1851 was intended to show the achievements of the Industrial Revolution and was not organized to highlight its imperialistic policies, British socialism, military establishment, or its immigration policy.

74. E. The Peace of Augsburg did not recognize Calvinism as a major religion in the German states. The Peace of Augsburg (1555) officially recognized Lutheranism, which resulted in Northern Germany becoming Lutheran and Southern Germany predominantly Catholic. Freedom of religion was not tolerated. Rulers established state churches in which all subjects of the area had to belong. Dissidents, whether Lutherans or Catholics, had to convert or leave. The Treaty of Westphalia would recognize Calvinism as a major religion on the European continent.

75. D. The issue of Home Rule in British politics during the nineteenth century referred to self-government for Ireland. England conquered Ireland during the Middle Ages and, for several hundred years, ruled the country harshly. During the nineteenth century, the Irish continued to press for self-government and independence. The discussion over self-government or home rule disrupted English politics. Many were opposed to home rule because of their concern for Ireland's Protestants who made up a small minority of the population. Most Protestants lived in Northern Ireland, known as Ulster. Irish Protestants were fearful about their rights in a country dominated by Catholics. Twice in the late nineteenth century, Parliament defeated William Gladstone's proposals for Irish home rule. In the 1870s, Charles Parnell, an Irish nationalist, rallied Irish members of Parliament to press for home rule. Finally in 1914, Parliament passed a Home Rule Bill but it was delayed when World War I broke out in Europe. In 1922, the British granted independence to the Irish Free State, later called Eire. The largely Protestant Northern country (Ulster) remained under British rule. In 1809, the Disestablishment Act ended taxation of Irish Catholics for the support of the Anglican Church. In 1829, the Catholic Emancipation Act declared Catholics eligible for public office. Women would not be granted civil rights until the beginning of the twentieth century. Home rule or independence for India did not dominate British politics until the twentieth century.

76. D. Voltaire believed in a distant deistic God who did not constantly influence the life of each individual. Voltaire thought that God was a clockmaker who built an orderly universe and then let it operate under the laws of science. While in exile in England, Voltaire came to admire the British system of government and that country's policy of religious tolerance. He believed that organized religion only led people to fight wars and commit crimes in the name of their faith. He invented the idea of the Enlightened Despot.

77. B. The Invasion of Normandy in France (D-Day) on June 6, 1944, established the Second Front in Europe. The invasion was the largest amphibious assault of the war. The invasion of France meant that Germany was under attack on the eastern and western fronts. The Battle of the Bulge (December 1944) was Germany's last-gasp counterattack in Belgium. The Allied bombing of Dresden (February 1945) in Germany resulted in the death of 135,000 people. The Invasion of Italy (July 1943) resulted in the fall of Mussolini but not a Second Front. The Battle of Stalingrad (1943) was a turning point in the war against Germany in Russia but was not the beginning of the Second Front.

78. B. German Chancellor Otto von Bismarck played a pioneering role in European social reform. Bismarck actually disliked Socialism and in 1875 passed a series of anti-socialist laws to prevent socialist parties from meeting. However, Bismarck was aware that the popular demand for social reform was impossible to oppress fully. Thus Bismarck began a program of welfare programs to improve conditions for German workers, such as medical insurance, sick pay, and old-age pensions. These reforms pleased the working class and took the pressure off Bismarck for more radical reforms. Bismarck made some attempts to reform the German military and political system, but it was his social reforms that were pioneering, in that Europe had seen nothing like them previously.

79. B. Francesco Petrarca (1304–1374) was considered the "Father of Humanism." He assembled a library of Greek and Roman manuscripts. Through his efforts, the ancient classics of Homer, Cicero, and Virgil became known to Western Europe. Petrarca wrote sonnets in Italian as well as epics in Latin. He was a new kind of writer who used language to convey moods of discouragement and satisfaction. Dante is known as the "Father of Modern Italian." He was the first to write an important work in the vernacular. Pico della Mirandola was an early Humanist who was a scholar of law and philosophy. Giovanni Boccaccio wrote *The Decameron* in the vernacular. Baldassare Castiglione wrote *The Courtier,* which set the criteria on how to be the ideal Renaissance man.

80. B. Charles DeGaulle is associated with the rise of the Fifth Republic in France in 1958. The Fourth Republic, which had ruled from 1946, was weak because its multi-party system failed to provide stable and effective government. The government also was unable to solve the Algerian issue. Colonial war in Vietnam and in Algeria had demoralized France. Longtime settlers of Algeria and the French military opposed Algerian nationalists who wanted independence. Fearing civil war, the National Assembly confirmed Charles DeGaulle, who had led the Free French during World War II, as president with unlimited power for six months. He also agreed to submit his constitutional reforms directly to the people. In 1958, DeGaulle's constitution for the Fifth Republic received overwhelming popular approval. The constitution gave DeGaulle strong presidential power. The people, instead of the legislature, directly elected a president to a seven-year majority vote of the people. In 1962, DeGaulle settled the Algerian crisis by granting Algeria its independence. Throughout the 1960s, DeGaulle worked hard to restore French prestige and power. In 1969, DeGaulle resigned after his demands for a new constitution to reduce the power of the Senate was rejected. Leon Blum was the leader of the Popular Front in France during the 1930s. Francois Mitterand was leader of France from 1981–1995. George Pompidou became president of France from 1969–1974. Edmund Daladier was the French prime minister who attended the Munich Conference in 1938.

Section II: Free-Response Essays

Part A: First Sample Student DBQ Essay

During World War II, the United States and the Soviet Union had joined forces to fight against Germany. The triumphant embrace of American and Russian soldiers on the banks of the Elbe River in defeated Germany, in April 1945, was not representative of the feelings of the leaders of these two countries. The leaders of the United States and the Soviet Union regarded each other in a less than friendly attitude. By 1947, the United States and the Soviet Union would be involved in a contest that became known as the Cold War.

The roots of the Cold War (1947–1990) were an outgrowth of long-standing political and ideological differences between the United States and the Soviet Union. The uneasy relationship between the United States and the Soviet Union was not created at the end of World War II. The roots were primarily philosophical. The United States, founded on democratic principles of the will of the majority and by freedom of individual liberties, was in direct contrast to the totalitarian system created by Communists in Russia under the leadership of Lenin and Stalin.

Although Lenin and Stalin had to make adjustments to Marx's philosophy, they never completely abandoned the belief of a worldwide revolution of workers. The United States, which cherished the principle of individualism and capitalism, felt threatened by Communism and it became a great evil in the American mind. Thus, when the United States and others decided to sleep with the enemy and join Stalin in the crusade against Hitler, Russia became the lesser of two evils.

During World War II, this alliance of expediency began to crack. Stalin was very critical of the Allies for delaying their invasion of German-occupied Europe until 1944 and the Allies (United States and Great Britain) were angry at the Soviet Union for its reluctance to grant free elections in Eastern Europe. Stalin ignored the agreement at Yalta and soon Communist governments gained control in Albania, Bulgaria, Hungary, Czechoslovakia, Romania, Poland, and Yugoslavia. The United States' response to Stalin's actions was to get tough. Harry S. Truman, Roosevelt's successor, decided to cut off all aid to Russia by early 1947. WWII was still going on in the East and the Potsdam Conference had not yet happened. In October 1945, he declared that the United States would never recognize any government established by force against the free will of the people.

In February, George Kennan, charge d'affaires in Moscow from 1944 to 1946, drafted "The Long Telegram" in which he underscored the centuries-old Russian sense of insecurity and their belief that there was no possibility of peace and coexistence between the United States and Russia (Doc. 1). The "Long Telegram" sounded the alarm over Soviet expansionism and became a warning about the coming Cold War. Kennan, who had been asked by Washington to explain the Soviet's behavior in Eastern Europe, also insisted that the United States assume a leadership role.

Stalin, whose goal was to create a buffer zone in Eastern Europe and spread Communism, became obsessive in the face of a perceived Western encroachment. Stalin believed that World

War II was an inevitable result of the development of world economic and political forces on the basis of capitalism (Doc. 2). He insisted that Russia's victory in World War II had proven "that the Soviet system was not doomed to failure" and that it was a better system of government than any other form. These statements reflect Stalin's apprehension and distrust about the United States and Western European countries.

In March 1946, former British Minister Winston Churchill, who had long distrusted Stalin, spoke of the dangers to basic liberties posed by the Soviet system of government. He declared that an "Iron Curtain" (Doc. 3) had descended over Eastern Europe trapping Hungary, Czechoslovakia, Bulgaria, Romania, Poland, and East Germany. Churchill's "Iron Curtain Speech" expressed the growing fear of Communism. The speech also came to represent Europe's division between a democratic Western Europe and a Communist Eastern Europe. Stalin responded by calling Churchill "a firebrand of war" who had friends in the United States. Once again, Stalin also reminded Churchill that the Soviet Union had lost seven million men in World War II, much more than the United States and Britain combined (Doc. 4). Stalin claimed that the Soviet Union was interested in establishing security in the countries of Eastern Europe and posed the question, "How can one, without having lost one's reason, qualify these peaceful aspirations of the Soviet Union as expansionist tendencies?"

Like Churchill, Truman saw Communism as an evil force creeping across Europe and threatening countries around the world. When Stalin began to put pressure on Greece and Turkey, the Greek government requested economic assistance from the United States. In a speech before Congress, President Truman contrasted democracy and Communism and asked for economic aid for Greece and Turkey (Doc. 5). Truman asserted that "it must be the policy of the United States to support free peoples who are resisting attempted subjugation by armed minorities or by outside pressures" (Doc. 5). The policy, known as the Truman Doctrine, was rooted in the idea of containment, limiting Communism to the areas under Soviet control, and resisting its expansion in Europe or elsewhere in the world. George Kennan proposed this approach, believing that Communism would eventually destroy itself. The Truman Doctrine committed the United States to an active policy of promoting ideological divisions between it and the Soviet Union.

By the spring of 1947, many Americans believed that Stalin was ready to export Communism throughout Europe. In June 1947, George Marshall proposed the Marshall Plan, which provided economic aid to any European country that requested it (Doc. 6). Marshall noted that the policy was directed not against any doctrine but against hunger and poverty (Doc. 6). However, he pointed out that any country that tried to block the recovery of other countries would not get help from the United States. This was an obvious reference to the Soviet Union.

The Marshall Plan, which also advocated the rebuilding of West Germany, was an example of the policy of Soviet containment. Truman offered aid to the Soviet Union and its satellites. Stalin rejected the Marshall Plan and saw containment as encirclement by the capitalist world, which wanted to isolate the Soviet Union. Distrust and tensions between the United States and the Soviet Union continued in 1948 as the Berlin Airlift removed the fear of war. By 1950, people began to assess what the second half of the century might bring. When Joseph Stalin died in 1953, many wondered how this might affect the Cold War. Theodore White, an American journalist, noted, "nothing would really change unless Communism ceases to be Communism" (Doc. 7). The brutal struggle for power in the Soviet Union reinforced this view. The knowledge that the Soviet Union had developed the H-Bomb, several hundred times more lethal than the A-Bomb, added to the fears about the future. The Cold War paranoia was revealed in a United States army publication on "How to Spot a Communist" in 1955 that claimed that "the Communist logic was opposed to our own. There is little hope in talking to them."

Although there was a "thaw" in the Cold War after 1957, when Nikita Khrushchev became the leader of the Soviet Union and began to dismantle the legacy of Joseph Stalin (Doc. 8). However, the basic antagonism was still beneath the surface. In 1956, Khrushchev claimed that he would bury us. It was during this time that the Berlin Wall was built (1961) and the United States and the Soviet Union almost went to war over Cuba. In 1962, Khrushchev's speech before the 22nd Congress of the Communist Party still contained the arguments outlining the belief that "Communism will destroy capitalism" (Doc. 10). Unlike Stalin, he did not foresee a violent struggle but one in which Communism and capitalism can peacefully coexist with Communism as the winner (Doc. 10).

The Cold War would continue until the 1990s. This 45-year struggle became an ideological struggle between the two systems of government and which one was better. The political problems and conflicts between the United States and the Soviet Union stemmed from the philosophical differences that divided a democracy, a capitalist system versus a Communist totalitarian system, as practiced by the leaders of the Soviet Union.

Reader's Comments on Part A: First Sample Student DBQ Essay

- The thesis is stated very clearly.

- The student makes excellent use of documents.

- Plenty of factual information is included in the essay.

- The student gives an accurate analysis of information—Kennans' ideas and containment.

- The essay is very good.

- The essay is well detailed.

Possible student score: 8–9

Part A: Second Sample Student DBQ Essay

The Cold War was an ideological struggle between the United States and Russia. In 1947, the wartime alliance between the United States and the Soviet Union broke down over how to reconstruct war-torn Europe. The roots of this conflict were inevitable.

In 1946, Stalin claimed that rivalry was inevitable between capitalism and Communism (Doc. 2). He claimed that the Soviet system was better and destined for victory. George Kennan, in a telegram to Washington, pointed out that the behavior of the Soviet Union was based on insecurities and that the United States needed to exert leadership (Doc. 1).

Winston Churchill reinforced the fear of Communism in March 1946 when he aroused the fear of an "Iron Curtain" that had spread over Eastern Europe (Doc. 3). Churchill's Iron Curtain Speech struck a responsive chord in the United States.

Truman, who feared the spread of Communism, was determined to stop its spread. In 1947, Truman, in an address before Congress, asked for economic aid and military aid to fight Communism in Greece and Turkey (Doc. 5). His policy led to containment, which was designed to stop the spread of Communism. In 1947, the Marshall Plan extended Truman's ideas to all of Europe (Doc. 6).

The Cold War was identified with Joseph Stalin, and his death in 1953 led to speculation about the future of this ideological conflict. Theodore White believed that nothing would change unless Communism changed (Doc. 7). Tensions became relaxed during the late 1950s, when Nikita Khrushchev became leader of the Soviet Union in 1956. He promoted a peaceful coexistence between the United States and the Soviet Union (Doc. 10). However, he like Stalin, believed in the ultimate victory of Communism. The method had changed but not the message.

The Cold War that lasted over 45 years was unavoidable

Reader's Comments on Part A: Second Sample Student DBQ Essay

- The thesis statement is very weak.

- The student does not analyze the documents/facts.

- The student does not use all the documents.

- Gaps in development of facts and organization of the essay.

- The student gives the topic superficial treatment.

Possible student score: 4–5

Part B: First Sample Student Thematic Essay, Group 1-1

The Industrial Revolution refers to the greatly increased output of machine-made goods that began in England during the eighteenth century. The Industrial Revolution started in England and spread to continental Europe and North America. The roots of industrialization that took place in England grew out of a number of developments.

The Commercial Revolution that spurred the economic expansion of the eighteenth century helped to serve mercantilist England very well. The colonial empire that England built in Asia and in the African slave trade provided a growing market for English manufactured goods. England's colonial empire also provided her with a ready access to the raw materials needed for the development of many industries. For example, England's control of India after 1763 provided the cotton necessary for the textile industry.

England had an abundance of its own natural resources. These included waterpower, coal to fuel the new machines, and iron ore to construct machines, tools, and buildings. England was blessed with an abundance of rivers for inland transportation. In an age when it was cheaper to ship goods by water rather than by land, no part of England was more than twenty miles from navigable water. These rivers and the building of the canals provided easy movement of England's enormous deposits of natural resources. Furthermore, there were no tariffs within the country to hamper trade as there were in France before 1789 and in the divided German states.

Agriculture also helped to bring about the Industrial Revolution in England. The Enclosure Movement released a supply of cheap labor for the growing industrial factories. In the 1700s, English farmers were second only to the Dutch in productivity. As English farmers adopted new methods of farming, such as crop rotation and other scientific methods of agriculture, food production increased and food prices declined. This meant that many British families had more income to spend on manufactured goods. Thus, the demand for goods within the country complemented the demand from the colonies.

Britain also had an expanding economy to support industrialization. Industry had grown at less than 1% between 1700 and 1760, but it grew by 3% annually between 1801 and 1831. Business people invested in the manufacture of new inventions. Britain's highly-developed banking system also contributed to the country's industrialization. People were encouraged to invest in new industries and expand their operations.

England's political stability also led to industrial leadership. Unlike eighteenth-century France, the monarchy and aristocracy, which had ruled the country since 1689, provided stable and predictable government. Parliament also passed laws protecting business and helping expansion.

All of these factors contributed to the beginning of the Industrial Revolution in England. Other countries had some advantages. However, Britain had all the factors of production (land, labor, capital/wealth) to produce the goods and services that the Industrial Revolution required.

Reader's Comments on Part B: First Sample Student Thematic Essay, Group 1-1

- The thesis statement clear and well developed.

- The student analyzes and discusses basic reasons.

- The supporting information of the essay is good (use of river transportation/investment rate/political stability).

- The essay has a good conclusion.

Possible student score: 8–9

Part B: Second Sample Student Thematic Essay, Group 1-1

The Industrial Revolution was an important turning point in our history. The changes that began in Western Europe managed to spread throughout the globe and change the lives of people forever. This Industrial Revolution started in Britain around 1750 and lasted for almost 100 years.

Britain's access to many natural resources contributed to the birth of the Industrial Revolution in this country. Even though it was a small nation, it had large supplies of coal and iron. With the invention and arrival of new machinery came the factor of needing people to actually run the machines. Britain's population had many who were unemployed, ready and willing to mine the coal and iron, build the factories, and run the machines.

Britain had a stable government. This helped to support large economic growth which was imperative for the Industrial Revolution. The well-organized government was able to accommodate the changes that resulted from new technology and not let things get out of control. Britain's government was properly equipped to meet the changes that were occurring.

During the 1700s, Britain's economy prospered immensely. Trade from a growing empire overseas brought in large sums of money. The business class accumulated wealth to invest in things, such as mines, railroads, and factories.

All of these factors helped Britain become the birthplace of the Industrial Revolution. Natural resources, a growing population, good economic conditions, and a stable government allowed Britain to take an early lead in industry. People began to take a real interest in coal, iron, and machinery. Britain paved the way for other countries to follow in their path and bring about immense changes in their own countries.

Reader's Comments on Part B: Second Sample Student Thematic Essay, Group 1-1

- The essay has a superficial thesis statement.
- The student needs to give a more in-depth analysis.
- The essay needs more supporting information.
- The conclusion is weak.

Possible student score: 3–4

Part B: First Sample Student Thematic Essay, Group 1-2

The foundation of the Renaissance was economic growth in Italy from the early eleventh century to the fourteenth century. This growth included population expansion, commerce, and financial development, and increasing political power of self-governing cities. As this economic prosperity continued, artistic endeavors flourished, particularly from the late thirteenth century until the late sixteenth century. Scholars refer to this artistic growth as the Renaissance, and it would not have occurred without the economic growth in Italy.

Northern Italian cities were the leaders in the economic growth in the early eleventh century. By the middle of the twelfth century, Venice — bolstered by its powerful merchant marine —

met with much wealth through overseas trade. Venice also benefited greatly from the Fourth Crusade to Constantinople. In 1204, the Venetians and the Crusaders stormed Constantinople and, before sacking the city, were able to bring back thousands of valuable relics that they later sold throughout Europe.

Other northern cities such as Genoa and Milan grew prosperous because of their successful trading with the Middle East and other northern European cities and nations. Because of their geographical position, northern cities were the natural crossroads for trade between the East and the West. Like Venice, Genoa became wealthy due to overseas trade, and in the early fourteenth century, both Genoa and Venice built ships that were able to sail year-round. With these improvements, ships could transport more goods and could travel much quicker. Italian merchants were able to directly buy goods from such lands as England, and then sail to places such as North Africa and sell those goods.

Despite the geographical advantages of such cities as Venice and Genoa, the Renaissance first appeared in the city of Florence. Although it was an inland city without convenient access to naval transportation, by the end of the thirteenth century, Florentine merchants and bankers gained control of papal banking. As papal tax collectors, Florentine mercantile families dominated European banking and had offices in cities from North Africa to London. The profits from these endeavors were funneled back into the city's industries.

The most profitable business venture for Florence was its wool industry. Florentines purchased the finest-quality wool from England and Spain and because they had developed efficient manufacturing techniques for such wool, they were able to produce the highest-quality products. This manufacturing technique brought employment opportunities to thousands of Florentines. The products of these workers' labor brought the highest prices in European, Asian, and African bazaars.

Florence was so strong that it was able to maintain its economic superiority even after King Edward II of England refused to pay his debt to Florence and after the Black Death claimed the lives of almost half of Florence's population. Because their economic foundation was so strong, Florence was able to withstand such setbacks. Their ever-increasing wealth planted the first seeds of the Italian Renaissance, during which painters, philosophers, and all artists were able to flourish.

Reader's Comments on Part B: First Sample Student Thematic Essay, Group 1-2

- The thesis statement is clear and well developed.
- The student gives good supporting data on the role of each Italian city-state, and the importance of Genoa and Venice.
- The student provides good insight about the culture of the period.
- The student's analysis of Florence is good, but lacks mention of the Medici family.
- The essay has an effective summary and conclusion.

Possible student score: 6–7

Part B: Second Sample Student Thematic Essay, Group 1–2

The Renaissance began in Italy in the early fourteenth century. Before the Renaissance began, Italy was the wealthiest nation in Europe. They had many bankers who made money and then they were able to use this money to pay for artists and writers to paint and write.

At the time that the Renaissance began, Italy was organized into small city-states, and each of the city-states had its own form of government. Venice was the richest of Italy's many city-states. Venice is located in Northern Italy and it was able to be rich because it was located near the water. Being by the water meant that Venice could have large fleets of ships. These ships were then able to sail to many different countries and bring goods to many people. People paid high prices for these goods, and Venice made a lot of money. It was only natural that the Renaissance happened in the richest of Italy's city-states. Venice had a plentiful economy and was able to support artists.

Geography was a big factor in the Italian Renaissance. The cities in Northern Italy were the gateway to distant lands in the Middle East and Asia. In order to trade with these nations, other city-states had to pass through the city-states in Northern Italy, and these city-states were able to capitalize and make many profits, which increased their economic prosperity.

Another important northern city was Florence — the birthplace of the Renaissance. Florence was extremely wealthy due to successful overseas trading. The bankers of Florence were Europe's most successful businessmen. They insured that Florence's wealth would be maintained — such wealth would eventually pave the way for the Renaissance to begin.

The Renaissance began in Italy because Italy was the wealthiest nation in Europe. Italians were able to use this wealth to support and encourage the growth of artistic endeavors. Without the wealthy Italian city-states, the Renaissance would not have occurred.

Reader's Comments on Part B: Second Sample Student Thematic Essay, Group 1–2

- The student's thesis statement is weak.
- The student does not explore the role of bankers.
- The role of Venice in the essay is weak.
- The essay gives an adequate analysis of geography.
- The content of the essay is too general.

Possible student score: 3–4

Part B: First Sample Student Thematic Essay, Group 1–3

As the Renaissance blossomed throughout Europe, it gave rise to many important movements, one of which was the Scientific Revolution. Scholars of the Renaissance sought to unearth knowledge in all spheres of life. They discovered the modern scientific method — a theoretical, experimental, and critical way of obtaining knowledge. As these scholars delved deeper into the mysteries of mathematics and science, they began to form communities whose members desired to fully understand life. Although this revolution did not immediately directly affect the everyday lives of Europeans, it did lay the foundation for one of Europe's most important intellectual movements — the Enlightenment. Influenced by the consequences of the Scientific Revolution, the Enlightenment was an innovative worldview that spread through Europe in the eighteenth century and was centered upon several main concepts that all related to methods.

The most fundamental principle of the Enlightenment was that the methods and techniques of modern science could be used to explore and comprehend all aspects of life. Intellectuals of the Enlightenment called this "reason." Reason dictated that nothing was to be accepted on faith alone; people should subject everything in life to rational, critical, and scientific thinking. Reason went hand-in-hand with the scientific method. This rejection of faith-based acceptance often put Enlightenment scholars into direct conflict with churches, whose very beliefs were based on the word of the Bible and Christian theology.

Another important concept of the Enlightenment was that the scientific method could be used to reveal not only the laws of nature but also the laws of human society. The Enlightenment gave birth to the social sciences, which in turn gave birth to the third concept of the Enlightenment: progress. The scholars of the Enlightenment believed that the scientific method, along with their insatiable curiosity and their commitment to reason, held the potential to create better societies and better people. This belief was validated by several economic and social improvements throughout the eighteenth century.

The concepts of the Enlightenment had varying effects on the people of Europe. The secular notions of reason, scientific exploration, and the rejection of blind acceptance based on faith held little merit to the peasants and urban poor. These groups were consumed by their daily struggles to sustain themselves and their families. In fact, many of these people resented the thinkers of the Enlightenment for attacking their traditional beliefs. However, for the urban middle class and the aristocracy, the secular nature of the Enlightenment had profound effects on their lives. In addition to renewing the Renaissance's spirit of worldly explanations, the Enlightenment greatly impacted the culture and way of thinking of the middle class and aristocracy. In years to come, the Enlightenment would continue to shape the concept of the modern mind.

Reader's Comments on Part B: First Sample Student Thematic Essay, Group 1-3

- The thesis statement gives a good background and the connection to Renaissance is excellent.

- The ideas of Enlightenment in the essay are very clear.

- The student's inclusion of a few Enlightenment thinkers, such as Locke and Rousseau, would have been helpful.

- The essay is very analytical.

Possible student score: 8–9

Part B: Second Sample Student Thematic Essay, Group 1-3

The Enlightenment was a period that came after the Renaissance in Europe. It was very similar to the Renaissance, except that it did not focus as much on art as the Renaissance did. During the Enlightenment, people were encouraged to explore all aspects of life, and were encouraged to gain as much knowledge as possible. This is like the Renaissance, where people wanted to be as learned as possible. The thinkers of the Enlightenment discovered new philosophies and ways of thinking that were very different from what people in Europe thought and believed.

People in the Enlightenment were very scientific and logical in their way of thinking. They were interested in knowledge and facts, and they wanted to get as much knowledge and as many facts as possible. They believed that people were able to become very knowledgeable only through the constant examination of everything. A true Enlightenment thinker would not just accept anything—he would have to discover it for himself. This was a conflict because the church told people to accept things based on faith alone. This was the opposite of what people in the Enlightenment thought. Enlightened people wanted to use facts to discover everything, and they did not believe that faith was a good enough reason to believe in something. They were skeptical of any conclusion that they did not arrive at themselves.

People in the Enlightenment analyzed things using the scientific method, which was a very specific way to analyze. It was very logical and rational, which was another reason why the enlightened thinkers clashed with the church, which did not follow the scientific method.

The Enlightenment greatly affected all of Europe, except for people who continued to follow the church's teachings of faith. Despite conflicts with the church, the people who followed the Enlightenment were inspired by the curiosity of the time. Everyone wanted to gain new knowledge, and the Enlightenment encouraged the intellectual growth of everyone. Europe was never the same after the Enlightenment. It affected people for generations to follow.

Reader's Comments on Part B: Second Sample Student Thematic Essay, Group 1-3

- The thesis statement is not clear—what does scientific mean?
- The student needs to develop on the relationship with the church.
- The essay doesn't give specific effects of Enlightenment on Europe.
- Overall, the essay is weak.

Possible student score: 3–4

Part B: First Sample Student Thematic Essay, Group 2-1

In the early 1800s, England was a constitutional monarchy, but the British government was not democratic. The British Parliament was made up of the House of Lords and the House of

Commons. The House of Lords was hereditary nobles and the House of Commons was elected by less than 5% of the people. Voting was limited to men who owned large amounts of property and women could not vote. During the 1800s, democracy gradually expanded so that by the 1900s political democracy would be extended to all groups within Great Britain. In the struggle for democracy, reformers accomplished their purpose by a gradual approach and the art of compromise. In Britain, each opposing side gave in a little to avoid violence. Unlike the French, the British achieved reforms without the bitter bloodshed of revolution. In the 1830s, as revolution flared on the continent, the Whigs, who represented the middle class, and the Tories, who represented nobles and landowners, battled over a reform bill. Parliament leaders in England feared that the revolution of 1830 in France would spread to Britain. The struggle was over extending the suffrage (right to vote) to the emerging middle class. Parliament passed the Great Reform Bill of 1832 and reduced the qualification for voters in order to enfranchise the middle class, thus increasing the number of voters from 500,000 to over 800,000 (still only about 5% of the British adult male population). The Bill also abolished the rotten boroughs, or empty districts, which gave thriving new industrial cities more representation.

The Reform Bill did not bring about full democracy but it was a moderate step forward and gave a greater political voice to the middle class. However, the Reform Bill of 1832 did not enfranchise city workers. In the 1830s, workers organized the Chartist Movement to fight for their rights. The Chartists presented their demands called "The People's Charter of 1838." The Chartists demanded universal male suffrage, a secret ballot, annual parliamentary elections, the end of property qualifications for serving in Parliament, and pay for members of Parliament. The Chartists did not call for women's rights. However, women in the Chartist Movement organized the first British Association to work for women's suffrage. The Chartists presented petitions twice to Parliament with over a million signatures. In 1848, as revolutions swept across Europe, the Chartists organized a third march on Parliament. Fearing violence, Parliament suppressed the march. However, the Chartist protests convinced many people that the workers had sound complaints. The Chartist movement died after 1848, but in time Parliament would pass most of the Chartist demands.

Throughout the nineteenth century, workers continued to press for political reform, and Parliament eventually responded. New political parties emerged to support reform efforts. Benjamin Disraeli forged the old Tory Party into the modern Conservative Party and the Whigs, led by William Gladstone, were transformed into the Liberal Party. Both of these men fought for political reform. In 1867, Disraeli supported a bill to extend voting rights to city workers. The Reform Bill of 1867 doubled the size of the electorate. Disraeli had hoped that endorsing this bill would get the working class to support the Conservative Party. Disraeli's hopes never materialized. In the Reform Bill of 1884, Gladstone and the Liberals supported the right to vote for the agricultural workers. By the century's end, almost all of the demands of the now defunct Chartists were achieved except for annual parliamentary elections.

Women in Great Britain, as elsewhere, struggled to gain the right of suffrage against strong opposition. After decades of peaceful efforts, Emmeline Pankhurst in 1903 formed the Women's Social and Political Union. The WSPU became the militant organization for women's rights. Their members led hunger strikes and were imprisoned many times. They cut telegraph wires and committed arson. One WSPU member, Emily Davison, lost her life when she threw herself in front of a horse at the English Derby. Women did not win the right to vote in national elections in Great Britain until after World War I.

The fight for democracy in Great Britain was a long struggle that evolved throughout the nineteenth and early twentieth century. The struggle for democracy was a gradual process in Great Britain but proved more permanent and had a permanent affect on English society. Each of the Reform Bills extended the voting franchise so that all sectors of society became part of the political process.

Reader's Comments on Part B: First Sample Student Thematic Essay, Group 2-1

- The thesis statement is very specific.
- The thesis is well developed — use of facts such as Reform Bills, Chartist Movement.
- The connection with England and revolutions in Europe is good.
- The student gives a detailed analysis of facts.
- The essay is weak on the topic of the women's movement.
- The student needs to develop the conclusion more.

Possible student score: 7–8

Part B: Second Sample Student Thematic Essay, Group 2-1

The development of democracy in Great Britain was an evolutionary one that took 100 years to achieve. Great Britain in the 1800s would evolve from a limited democracy to a full democracy by the 1900s.

In the 1800s, Great Britain was not a true democracy and limited to those who owned property. In 1832, Parliament passed the Reform Bill. This bill extended the franchise to factory owners, bankers, and merchants. The Reform Bill also abolished the rotten boroughs in Great Britain.

In the 1830s, workers formed the Chartist Movement. The Chartist Movement called for suffrage for all men, especially city workers. The Chartists also called for secret ballots and an end to the property qualifications for serving in Parliament. The Chartists did not achieve their goals but throughout the nineteenth century their goals would be implemented.

The Reform Bill of 1867 reduced property qualifications for voting so as to enfranchise city workers. The Conservatives (formerly Tory) Party supported this bill. The Reform Bill of 1884 extended the right to agricultural workers. The Liberal Party led by Prime Minister William Gladstone supported this bill.

By the 1890s, most of England's adult males had the right to vote but women were denied the suffrage. Throughout the 1880s, the fight for women's suffrage became a dominant issue. Led by Emmeline Pankhurst of the Women's Social and Political Union, they became very militant. They committed arson, heckled members of Parliament, and conducted hunger strikes. By 1918, women over the age of 30 gained the right to vote. It was not until 1928 that all women over 21 could vote.

The growth of democracy in Great Britain was a long struggle that led to an extension of democracy for different groups in British society. The process was evolutionary rather than revolutionary.

Reader's Comments on Part B: Second Sample Student Thematic Essay, Group 2-1

- The thesis statement needs development — What made Great Britain undemocratic?
- The student needs to give more detail on the Reform Bills — Why were they passed?
- The emphasis on women in the essay is weak.
- The conclusion is weak.

Possible student score: 3–4

Part B: First Sample Student Thematic Essay, Group 2-2

The Congress of Vienna of 1814–1815 was a peace conference to reconstruct war-torn Europe following Napoleon's defeat. The Versailles Treaty (1919) was a meeting to reconstruct Europe after Germany's defeat in World War I. The Congress of Vienna would create a framework of peace for Europe that lasted 100 years. The Versailles Treaty did little to build a lasting peace and by 1939, the world was plunged into another major war.

England, Russia, Prussia, Austria, and France attended the Congress of Vienna. Their goal was to turn back the clock to pre-1789 in order to insure order and stability. Although the leaders at the congress had different goals, they agreed to establish a balance of power so that France would be contained and never become strong enough to dominate the continent. The diplomats wanted to restore the power of the monarchs based on the principle of legitimacy. Former rulers deposed by the French Revolution or Napoleon were returned to power. Thus, Louis XVIII, brother of executed Louis XVI, regained the throne. Hereditary rulers were returned to Spain, Holland, the Italian states of Sardinia-Piedmont, and the Two Sicilies. The congress denied many national groups independence and unity. Belgians, Poles, and Finns were handed over to foreign governments. Russia was given part of Poland and Finland, and Holland was forced to give up Ceylon and South Africa to Great Britain but gained Belgium. Austria obtained the Italian provinces of Lombardy and Venetia. All of these steps represented contempt for democracy and a denial of nationalism.

The Congress or Peace of Vienna was a political triumph in many ways. The Peace of Vienna was the most far-reaching diplomatic agreement between the Treaty of Westphalia of 1648 and the Versailles Treaty, which ended World War I. It had many strong points. It was fair enough so that no one country could hold a grudge. It created a minimum of resentment in France. The Treaty ended two centuries of colonial rivalry and stabilized the international system until the twentieth century. The European Balance of Power would stabilize the international system until the unification of Germany in 1871, and not until World War I (1914) did Europe have another general war. However, the statesmen of Vienna underestimated the growing force of nationalism and failed to see how the Industrial Revolution would change the social and political structure of society. Despite these shortcomings, the Peace of Vienna created a time of peace in Europe for close to 100 years. Only during the Pax Romana did society enjoy such relative harmony.

At the end of World War I in 1918, the Allied countries (England, France, United States, Italy) met at the Palace of Versailles, outside Paris, to draw up a peace treaty to deal with the defeat of the Central Powers (Germany, Austria-Hungary, Turkey, and Bulgaria). The Versailles Treaty dealt with Germany. The Allied countries or Big Four had different objectives at the conference. England and France did not agree with Wilson's vision of peace based on the Fourteen Points. Some of these Fourteen Points included reduced national armies and navies, self-determination, and the formation of a League of Nations. France and England wanted a peace that protected national security. The French were determined to punish Germany. Georges Clemenceau, the French Premier, wanted revenge for all that France had lost. The French had lost more than a million soldiers.

The differences among the United States, Britain, and France led to a heated debate. Finally, on June 28, 1919, the Treaty of Versailles was signed. The treaty was far from the ideals requested by Wilson. A League of Nations was created; Germany accepted sole responsibility for the war and had to pay reparation to the Allied countries. Germany also lost substantial territory and was forced to reduce its armed forces to 100,000 volunteers and was forbidden from having an air force.

The Versailles Treaty that was designed to put an end to the German menace was a failure. Germany was angry and bitter. They resented the War Guilt Clause and felt betrayed by the peace treaty. The treaty transferred German-inhabited territory, such as the Saar to France and Danzig to Poland. Germany lost all of her colonies. While Germany disarmed, the other nations remained armed. The treaty, however, was too severe to conciliate but not severe enough to destroy. From the very beginning, Germany showed no real intention to live up to the treaty and Allied countries believed that parts of the treaty were unenforceable. Other countries were also unhappy with the Versailles Treaty. The United States rejected the treaty and was forced to sign a separate treaty with Germany. Italy was angry because she would not get all the land she was promised. Japan was upset that the West refused to recognize its claims in China. Russia, under the control of Communism, was also annoyed that they were excluded from the Versailles Conference and that Poland and the Baltic states were carved out of their empire. France was disappointed with England for backing out of a defensive alliance with her. England, by 1919, was beginning to express more fear about the Communists in Russia than the Germans.

The Congress of Vienna created a lasting peace that enabled Europe to grow and prosper throughout the nineteenth century. On the other hand, the Versailles Treaty did not establish a lasting peace but created resentment that sponsored the international climate for two decades and helped spark World War II. Wilson's dream of a lasting peace was never achieved.

Reader's Comments on Part B: First Sample Student Thematic Essay, Group 2-2

- The thesis is very well organized and developed.
- The student's analysis of data is excellent — purpose of Congress of Vienna, Versailles Treaty.
- The student's comparisons of two treaties is very analytical.
- The overall organization of the essay is good.

Possible student score: 8–9

Part B: Second Sample Student Thematic Essay, Group 2-2

The Congress of Vienna and the Treaty of Versailles were alike in trying to reconstruct Europe, but only the Congress of Vienna achieved its objective.

The Congress of Vienna met to reconstruct Europe after the Napoleonic War. The purpose of the congress was to turn the clock back to the pre-1789 era and to ensure that France never became a powerful force in Europe. To achieve these objectives, the leaders at Vienna restored the former kings to the throne of Spain and the Kingdom of Two Sicilies, and Louis XVIII, brother of Louis XVI to the throne of France. The congress also created nations such as Belgium and the Netherlands to contain French power. The Congress of Vienna ignored the principles of the French Revolution and denied the principle of nationalism and democracy. Nevertheless, the settlement of Vienna created a balance of power that established peace in Europe for almost 100 years.

The Versailles Conference met at the end of World War I to decide how to deal with a defeated Germany. The Allied countries of England, France, the United States, and Italy had different objectives. Italy wanted territory that had been promised to her. England and France wanted to punish Germany and ensure that German power would never threaten Europe again. The United States' main goal was the League of Nations.

The Allies disagreed vigorously during the conference but on June 28, 1919, they signed the Versailles Treaty with Germany. Germany was treated harshly. She had to disarm, give up her colonies, admit war guilt, and also pay reparations for all damages caused by the war. In addition, Germany was forced to transfer German-inhabited territory to France and Poland. The treaty angered the German people who claimed, "they had been stabbed in the back."

The Versailles Treaty, unlike the Congress of Vienna, did not establish a lasting peace. Germany was angry about the harshness of the treaty. The United States rejected the Treaty of Versailles and England and France were unwilling to enforce it. The Versailles Treaty was a temporary truce that created conditions that led to World War II in 1939.

Reader's Comments on Part B: Second Sample Student Thematic Essay, Group 2-2

- The student gives superficial treatment to facts.
- The essay ignores basic facts, such as nationalism and democracy.
- The essay never discusses the role of the Fourteen Points.
- The essay includes little or no analysis.
- Overall, the essay is weak.

Possible student score: 1–3

Part B: First Sample Student Thematic Essay, Group 2-3

The brutality of World War I led to disillusionment in the 1920s about the values of Western civilization, which had been built on the belief in reason and progress. For many people, World War I symbolized a moral breakdown of Western civilization. A general climate of pessimism developed as well as an alienation and fear about the future. Writers expressed their anxieties by creating unsettling visions of the present and the future.

In 1918, Oswald Spengler, a German high school teacher, published *The Decline of the West*. Spengler believed that every culture experiences a life cycle of growth. For Spengler, Western society was in its old age and was near the end of its life. In 1922, T. S. Eliot, an American living in England, wrote in his famous poem, *The Waste Land,* that Western society had lost its spiritual value. The American novelist, Ernest Hemingway, in *The Sun Also Rises*, describes the emptiness of young people whose lives had been destroyed by war as they struggled to live in a world they did not understand. Austrian-born author Franz Kafka's novels also showed how World War I had affected many writers. His books, *The Trial* (1925) and *The Castle* (1926), portray helpless individuals crushed in threatening situations they cannot understand nor escape. Kafka had been writing before World War I but much of his work was published after his death in 1924. His novels struck a responsive chord among many whom Gertrude Stein referred to as "the lost generation."

Some novelists also began to use the stream of consciousness technique to explore the human psyche. Influenced by Sigmund Freud's ideas, writers began to probe a character's thoughts and feelings without imposing logic or order. One famous stream of consciousness novel was *Ulysses,* which was written by James Joyce and published in 1922. This book focuses on a single day in the life of three men living in Dublin. Joyce broke with conventional grammar and sentence structure and blends words together to mirror the workings of the human mind. The language of *Ulysses* was intended to reflect the chaos of modern life, which was unintelligible.

World War I created uncertainty about Western society. Before 1914, most people in the West still believed in progress, reason, and the rights of the individual. World War I destroyed this faith and optimism and led to uncertainty and pessimism. The French poet and critic Paul Valery in the early 1920s expressed this feeling best when he wrote, "The storm has died away and still we are restless, uneasy as if the storm was about to break. . . . We fear the future, not without reason."

Reader's Comments on Part B: First Sample Student Thematic Essay, Group 2-3

- The thesis is well developed.
- The essay is well organized
- The student gives good factual references to Spengler, T. S. Eliot, and other authors.
- The conclusion is excellent.

Possible student score: 8–9

Part B: Second Sample Student Thematic Essay, Group 2-3

The literature of the 1920s expressed the disillusionment of the era. Prior to World War I, people had hope in the future. World War I destroyed this optimism.

In 1922, T. S. Eliot wrote in a poem, *The Wasteland,* about this pessimism and lack of hope for the future. In 1924, the Irish poet William Butler Yeats also conveyed a sense of dark times ahead in the poem, *The Second Coming*.

Novelists also projected this feeling of uneasiness. Ernest Hemingway wrote about the futility of the young who had lost their innocence and hope because of the horrors of World War I. Throughout the 1920s, there seemed little hope for the future. F. Scott Fitzgerald wrote about the lost generation in his famous book, *The Great Gatsby*. For him and others of his generation, life was empty as you move from one meaningless experience to another without direction or hope.

Other novelists began to incorporate the ideas of Freud into their writings. Rejecting the emphasis of reason, they used a stream of consciousness to explore the psyche of the individual. Novelists such as Virginia Woolf and James Joyce tried to show that the emotion of the mind, like the modern world, was not intelligent and could not be understood. This uncertainty led to anxiety and fear for the future.

World War I left an indelible mark on society. For the writers of the 1920s, it was reflected in literature that reinforced pessimism, uncertainty, and a loss of hope. Gertrude Stein remarked that the young people who served in World War I were "the lost generation."

Reader's Comments on Part B: Second Sample Student Thematic Essay, Group 2-3

- Thesis is weak and needs development.

- The essay has many redundant phrases.

- The student's analysis of Fitzgerald is brief, but informative.

- The essay gives insufficient elaboration of other authors and their works.

- Overall, the essay is weak.

Possible student score: 3–4